# Visual Basic Controls

# Desk Reference

Mark Pruett

Gregg Irwin

C. Woody Butler

Waite Group Press™
Corte Madera, CA

Publisher ▲ Mitchell Waite
Editor-in-Chief ▲ Scott Calamar
Editorial Director ▲ Joel Fugazzotto
Managing Editor ▲ John Crudo
Content Editor ▲ Heidi Brumbaugh
Copy Editor ▲ Deborah Craig
Technical Reviewer ▲ Frank Sommers
Design ▲ Kristin Peterson
Production ▲ Deborah Anker, Karen Johnston, Sestina Quarequio
Cover Design ▲ Cecile Kaufman
Production Manager ▲ Cecile Kaufman

© 1995 by The Waite Group, Inc.

Published by Waite Group Press™, 200 Tamal Plaza, Corte Madera, CA 94925.

Waite Group Press is distributed to bookstores and book wholesalers by Publishers Group West, Box 8843, Emeryville, CA 94662, 1-800-788-3123 (in California 1-510-658-3453).

Printed in the United States of America
95 96 97 98 • 10 9 8 7 6 5 4 3 2 1

Pruett, Mark.

　　Visual basic controls desk reference CD / Pruett, Mark. C. Woody Butler. Gregg Irwin.
　　Includes index.
　　ISBN: 1-878739-87-5: $44.95
　　1. BASIC (Computer program language) 2. Microsoft Visual BASIC.

I. Butler, C. Woody. II. Irwin, Gregg. III. Title.
QA76.73.B3P78
005.265--dc20                                                    94-43492
　　　　　　　　　　　　　　　　　　　　　　　　　　　　　　　CIP

## DEDICATIONS

To Maggie, for everything.

▲ Mark Pruett

To my wife Stacy for all her love and support, and to my son James for always reminding me of what's really important in life.

▲ Gregg Irwin

To my Mom for the brains,
To my Dad for the heart,
and to Theresa for letting me -
Honey, I'll get the plants in NEXT year!

▲ Woody Butler

## ACKNOWLEDGMENTS  MARK PRUETT

A book this big requires the work and dedication of a lot of people. I owe much thanks to Mitch Waite for his support and guidance, and for his constant enthusiasm for this project. Thanks also to John Crudo, for his guidance and friendship, and for his many thoughtful insights on the finer points of the Power Rangers (there are none). Thanks to Heidi Brumbaugh for her suggestions and direction; the book is much better for it, though I now run in Pavlovian terror at the sight of a red pen. And thanks to Frank Sommer for the monumental task of reviewing, putting together, and testing the CD that accompanies this book.

 GREGG IRWIN

First, thanks to Mitch Waite for giving me this wonderful opportunity. Thanks also to John Crudo and Mark Pruett for guiding me throughout the project. A big round of applause to everyone at The Waite Group who, somehow, coordinated and assembled a project of this magnitude and made it fun in the process. Finally, thanks to Rich Marston who allowed me the time to work on this book even when seemingly insurmountable deadlines loomed before us. Thanks everybody.

## C. WOODY BUTLER

I'd like to thank the people from Microhelp, BennetTec, Farpoint, Weimar, Crescent, BitsPerSecond/Pinnacle, and Crystal for all their help and their wonderful controls. I'd also like to thank all the people on CompuServe that have helped me directly or indirectly over the years solve many of the problems I've had writing applications in Visual Basic. Finally I'd like to thank Mitch Waite, all the people from The Waite Group, and Mark and Gregg, for the opportunity to work on this book and the wonderful time I had (really!) doing it!

## ABOUT THE AUTHORS

Mark Pruett is a programmer and writer living in rustic central Virginia. He has worked on a variety of computers and with a variety of languages over the past 12 years. He received a B.S. in Mathematics from Virginia Commonwealth University in 1985.

Gregg Irwin is an independent developer who specializes in Visual Basic. He has developed software for some of the largest financial institutions in the nation. Gregg has also been a Microsoft PSS MVP for Visual Basic for the past three years.

C. Woody Butler, a Senior Information Analyst for a major defense contractor, develops client servers in Visual Basic and Powerbuilder. He has been programming for over ten years, having started as a mainframe Cobol programmer.

# TABLE OF CONTENTS

# CONTENTS

## CHAPTER 1 ▲ WIDGETS

# CHAPTER 2 ▲ SPREADSHEETS AND GRIDS

# CHAPTER 3 ▲ WORD PROCESSORS AND TEXT EDITORS

## CHAPTER 4 ▲ CONTROL LIBRARIES

## CHAPTER 5 ▲ COMMUNICATIONS

## CHAPTER 6 ▲ CHARTING AND GRAPHING CONTROLS

## CHAPTER 7 ▲ MULTIMEDIA

## CHAPTER 9 ▲ SYSTEM TOOLS

## CHAPTER 10 ▲ TEXT AND DATA MANIPULATION

# INTRODUCTION

Visual Basic has revolutionized programming in two distinct ways. The first, and most obvious revolution was in user interface design. With its visual approach to design, Visual Basic takes a task that had previously been time-consuming, tedious, and complex, and makes it intuitive and simple. The user interface, which previously may have accounted for as much as 75 percent of program code, can now be accomplished with little or no code at all.

The second revolution, which is the reason for this book, may not be quite as obvious, but its effect on productivity is at least as profound. Visual Basic is a component-based programming language. Reuseable software components, in the form of Visual Basic controls, or VBXs, let the programmer seemlessly extend Visual Basic's native toolsets. It didn't take third-party developers long to realize this. The market for third-party controls is a huge and growing business.

Some people argue that Visual Basic is flawed because it's not object-oriented. The basic principles of OOP are encapsulation, inheritance, and polymorphism. One of the major advantages of object-oriented programming is that it affords a higher degree of reuse than conventional languages. Why is that? Because it allows the code and data of a logical object to be encapsulated into a neat package, one that has clearly defined interfaces. This is also an excellent description of a Visual Basic control. Visual Basic controls excel at encapsulation.

In practice, what this means for you, the programmer, is that you have a lot less code to write. Need spreadsheet capabilities in your app? Drop in a control. A word processor? There are several to choose from.

## What's In This Book

The pool of Visual Basic controls is huge, and there was no way we could cover every control on the market. What we tried to do was pick a wide and representative sample, and then show you what could be done with each of them. We broke the book into chapters, each of which cover a general function performed by a set of controls. So you'll find chapters on spreadsheets, multimedia, widgets, word processors, and image processing, as well as many other categories. Within each chapter, you'll find a section on each control. We provide an overview of the control, but we don't try to replace the control's documentation. Instead this book gives you concise information on the important aspects of each control to help you quickly assess its usefulness to you. We then provide an example program that shows the strengths of the control. Whenever possible, we tried to build examples that showed a real-world use for the control. Several of the examples stand as useful and complete programs in their own right. You'll find a full-featured Autodesk Animator flic viewer, a generic spell-checking utility, a Visual Basic source code "pretty printer," a generic xBase file viewer, and an arcade-style video game, to mention a few.

To avoid confusion, we made a general rule: we would use only the featured control and standard Visual Basic controls in the example programs. In this way, there would be no confusion as to what functionality was being provided by the control itself. The intent of the examples is to showcase the strengths of a particular control, and we didn't want to muddy the waters by including multiple controls in a single project.

## What We Left Out

In any project of this size, you've got to draw the line somewhere. We made a few simple rules to help us decide what to include in this book, then we bent those rules slightly. One rule was that we would include only Visual Basic controls, which are files with a .VBX extension: no DLLs or code libraries. We broke this rule slightly when a DLL or control library could add balance or counterpoint to the controls in a chapter. But these exceptions are very much in the minority. Almost everything in this book is a .VBX.

Another rule we made wass to exclude any control that required special hardware. This means that controls that handle input from scanners, or communicate with terminal emulation boards, or talk to analog-to-digital converters were not included. We bent this rule slightly to include communications and multimedia controls, as we felt that a majority of programmers probably owned or had access to the requisite hardware.

In the interest of saving space in the book, we didn't include the source code to the example programs in Chapter 4, which covers control libraries. Because control libraries required larger example programs, we felt this was a reasonable trade-off. Be assured that all the source code to the Chapter 4 example programs is available on the accompanying CD.

## How This Book Is Organized

There are 12 chapters in this book, each containing several sections describing individual controls. Each section contains an explanation of a control, followed by an example program that showcases that control.

**Chapter 1 ▲ Widgets**   Widgets are controls that serve some specific, well-defined, user interface purpose. A widget can be any relatively small user interface element: a check box, label, knob, slider, or text box, to name a few. A well-defined widget can save a programmer huge amounts of time, and help make a user interface much easier to use.

**Chapter 2 ▲ Spreadsheets and Grids**   Spreadsheets are one of the most popular categories of commercial applications, so it should not be surprising that they are a

popular class of controls as well. Spreadsheets are one of the best ways to present, view, and manipulate large quantities of related information.

**Chapter 3 ▲ Word Processors and Text Editors**  Many applications have to deal with large amounts of text. Unfortunately, the Visual Basic multi-line text control is not well-suited for this task. The controls in this section fill the void, providing a wide range of text processing capabilities, from high-powered text editors that can handle large volumes of ASCII text easily, to full-blown word processors that sport Rich Text Format (.RTF), hypertext, and advanced formatting and printing features.

**Chapter 4 ▲ Control Libraries**  More and more control vendors are packaging their products as libraries: collections of controls available as a set. The control libraries in this chapter are collections of widgets that are bundled together. This is an eclectic and diverse group; you'll find everything from 3D check boxes to playing cards.

**Chapter 5 ▲ Communications**  Now that the Information Superhighway is garnering so much interest, you may have an urgent need to include communications capabilities into applications. These controls provide the means to add serial communications to your Visual Basic apps.

**Chapter 6 ▲ Charting and Graphing Controls**  Sometimes the only way to make your point is to draw a picture. The controls in this chapter help you do that. Some are designed to plot and display data, while others are designed to generate presentation graphics.

**Chapter 7 ▲ Multimedia**  Multimedia is the buzzword of the '90s. These controls can make it work for you. You'll learn how to include interesting fade effects in bitmaps, play sounds and music, and display animations and even full-motion video in your Visual Basic applications. You can even control audio CDs and Video Laser Discs!

**Chapter 8 ▲ Bitmap and Image Processing**Windows displays pictures as bitmaps, and Visual Basic includes two native controls that do this quite well. But if you want to go further than mere display, you'll need to look at these controls. The controls in this chapter will let you scroll, rotate, draw, alter, manipulate, print, color reduce, and compress images.

**Chapter 9 ▲ System Tools**  Visual Basic hides many of the complexities of the Windows environment from the programmer. This is one of the reasons VB is so easy to learn and use. But there are times when you need to access the power of Windows, and that's where these tools come in. You'll learn how to intercept and process Windows messages, accept files from File Manager, read and write Initialization (.INI) files, manipulate timers, and, in general, harness the hidden powers of Windows.

**Chapter 10 ▲ Text and Data Manipulation**   Many programming problems boil down to the manipulation of chunks of data. The controls in this section, in one way or another, accomplish this task. You'll find spell-checkers, special purpose text processors, and .ZIP-compatible compression libraries.

**Chapter 11 ▲ Database Controls and Libraries**   At the heart of many applications is some type of database. The database is a computer's "long term memory" and there are myriad standards for database storage. The controls and libraries in this section either provide access to, or simplify and enhance access to, several database formats.

**Chapter 12 ▲ Other Interesting Controls**   These are the controls that didn't fit neatly into any of the other categories. They include everything from controls that implement new data structures, to controls that deterine version control conflicts, to controls that implement complete expert systems languages.

# About the Example Programs and the CD

Controls must be distributed with an application, and this poses a potential dilemma for the creators of the control. How do they allow distribution of the control but prevent unlicensed developers from building new applications with it? Control vendors have several options when distributing their controls.

The most common method, and the one used by most of the larger commercial control vendors, is to provide the licensed developer with a special license file. This file is detected by the control (.VBX) and allows the developer to load the control from within the Visual Basic environment at design time. Without the license file, the control's .VBX will only work with a compiled (.EXE) Visual Basic program. The programmer can distribute the .VBX file with his or her finished application, but must not distribute the license file.

Another method, used more commonly by shareware control developers, is to provide an unregistered control with a "nag" screen, a window that pops up when the control is loaded and announces to the user that the control is not registered. The developer can acquire a registered version of the control, without the nag screen, directly from the vendor. The advantage of this approach is that it permits the programmer to fully evaluate a control before purchasing it, but effectively discourages unauthorized use of the control.

There are other variations as well. Some vendors provide "design-time only" controls that work fine from within the Visual Basic environment, but which cannot be used to create an executable file.

On our CD, you'll find several variations, depending upon the vendor. Table I-1 at the end of this Introduction identifies the type of sample control we've included for each evaluation. Many of the controls are run-time only; you'll have to run the example program using the included executable (.EXE) file. In these cases, the source code for the example program is still included, so that if you choose to purchase the control from the vendor, you can run and modify the example program however you wish.

We've tried to include as many design-time controls as possible. These controls allow you to experiment and tinker with the example programs, and even create your own programs, to determine if a control meets you needs. Some vendors even created design-time versions of their controls especially for this book.

You should be able to re-create all the programs in this book using only the text as a guide (with the exception of Chapter 4; see the section, What We Left Out, above). You'll need Visual Basic 3.0, of course, and for some of the examples you'll need the Professional Edition.

The CD is organized very simply, with subdirectories for each chapter. Within each of these subdirectories are sections for each individual control or library that we covered. Generally, we recommend that you copy a directory from the CD and run it from your hard disk, though in most cases this is not absolutely necessary.

# Who This Book Is For

This book was designed for the intermediate to advanced Visual Basic programmer. You should already have a good idea what controls are, and how they are used in a Visual Basic project. This book is oriented toward the reader who wants to know how to exploit the incredible wealth of controls available today.

Control developers may find this book useful as well, as this book provides a wide survey of the designs of existing controls. By studying the different methods used to encapsulate behavior into properties and events, developers can gain insight on what works well and what doesn't. The best controls are so well thought out that their use is almost transparent. These controls have well-designed default behaviors, and often require a minimum of programming.

We hope you enjoy the book. We had a lot of fun writing the example programs, and were always amazed at the power Visual Basic controls can bring to a project.

**Table I-1**   A Profile of the Evaluation Demos in Visual Basic Controls Desk Reference

| CHAPTER | CONTROL | DEMO TYPE |
|---|---|---|
| 4 | 3D Controls (THREED.VBX)† | Run-Time |
| 4 | 3D Widgets† | Run-Time |
| 9 | Alarm (ALARM.VBX) | Design-Time |
| 3 | ALLText HT/Pro (ATX30H.VBX) | Run-Time |
| 1 | Animated Button (ANIBUTON.VBX) | Run-Time* |
| 9 | App-Link (APPLINK.VBX) | Run-Time |
| 12 | Assoc (ASSOC.VBX) | Freeware |
| 4 | Aware/VBX† | Run-Time |

*(continued on next page)*

*(continued from previous page)*

| CHAPTER | CONTROL | DEMO TYPE |
|---------|---------|-----------|
| 1 | BmpLst (BMPLST.VBX) | Design-Time |
| 4 | CCF-Cursors† | Run-Time |
| 6 | Chartbuilder (GRAPH.VBX) | Run-Time* |
| 10 | Compression Plus (COMPRESS.DLL) | Run-Time‡ |
| 4 | Custom Control Factory† (CCBUTTON.VBX) | Run-Time |
| 5 | Crescent PDQComm (PDQCOMM2.VBX) | Run-Time |
| 11 | Crystal Reports (CRYSTAL.VBX) | Run-Time |
| 11 | Data Control | Run-Time* |
| 11 | Data Widgets† | Run-Time |
| 4 | Designer Widgets† | Run-Time |
| 3 | Early Morning Editor (EMEDIT.VBX) | Shareware |
| 9 | FMDrop (FMDROP1.VBX) | Design-Time |
| 2 | Formula One/VBX (VTSS.VBX) | Run-Time |
| 7 | FXTools/VB† | Run-Time |
| 2 | Gantt/VBX (GANTTVBX.VBX) | Run-Time |
| 1 | Gauge (GAUGE.VBX) | Run-Time |
| 6 | Graph (GRAPH.VBX) | Run-Time |
| 2 | Grid (GRID.VBX) | Run-Time* |
| 2 | Grid/VBX (FPGRID10.VBX) | Run-Time |
| 1 | iList (ILIST.VBX) | Shareware |
| 8 | ImageKnife (KNIFE.VBX) | Run-Time |
| 8 | ImageMan/VB† | Run-Time |
| 8 | ImageStream - VB (ISVB.VBX) | Run-Time |
| 9 | IniCon (INICON3.VBX) | Design-Time |
| 12 | JoyStk (JOYSTK1.VBX) | Design-Time |
| 8 | JPEG Image Compressor VBX (VSIMAGE.VBX) | Run-Time |
| 9 | Key Status (KEYSTAT.VBX) | Run-Time* |
| 12 | M.4 (M4CTRL.VBX) | Run-Time |
| 1 | Masked Edit (MSMASKED.VBX) | Run-Time* |
| 7 | MediaKnife/VBX | Run-Time |
| 9 | MenuEv (MENUEV3.VBX) | Design-Time |
| 9 | Message Hook (MSGHOOK.VBX) | Complete◊ |
| 1 | Microsoft Outline (MSOUTLIN.VBX) | Run-Time* |
| 5 | Microsoft MSCOMM (MSCOMM.VBX) | Run-Time |
| 7 | Multimedia MCI (MCI.VBX) | Run-Time* |
| 9 | OLE 2.0 Control (MSOLE2.VBX) | Run-Time* |
| 1 | OxButton (OXBUTTON.VBX) | Shareware |
| 8 | PicScroll (PICSCRLL.VBX) | Run-Time |
| 8 | Picture Clip (PICCLIP.VBX) | Run-TIme* |
| 1 | Prompt (PROMPT.VBX) | Shareware |

| CHAPTER | CONTROL | DEMO TYPE |
|---------|---------|-----------|
| 4 | QuickPak Professional for Windows† | Run-Time |
| 3 | Raven Write (RAVENW.VBX) | Run-Time |
| 1 | Slider (SLIDER.VBX) | Shareware |
| 10 | SpellPro (MHSPELL.VBX) | Run-Time |
| 1 | Spin Button (SPIN.VBX) | Run-Time* |
| 2 | Spread/VBX (SPREAD20.VBX) | Run-Time |
| 9 | SpyWorks-VB† | Run-Time |
| 1 | Tab/VBX (TABVBX10.VBX) | Run-Time |
| 1 | TList (TLIST.VBX) | Run-Time |
| 2 | TrueGrid (TRUEGRID.VBX) | Run-Time |
| 4 | VB Tools 4.0† | Run-Time |
| 9 | VB Messenger (VBMSG.VBX) | Run-Time |
| 1 | VBCTL3D (VBCTL3D.VBX) | Run-Time |
| 7 | VBPlay Animation (VBPLAY.VBX) | Shareware |
| 3 | VBViewer (MHVIEW.VBX) | Run-Time |
| 8 | VBX Artist (ARTIST.VBX) | Run-Time |
| 11 | VB/ISAM (VBIS23DM.DLL) | Run-Time‡ |
| 12 | Version Stamper-VB (DWVSTAMP.VBX) | Run-Time |
| 1 | VS Elastic (VSVBX.VBX) | Run-Time |
| 1 | Videosoft Index Tab (VSVBX.VBX) | Run-Time |
| 11 | Visual/db† | Run-Time∞ |
| 10 | VSAwk (VSVBX.VBX) | Run-Time |
| 10 | VT-Speller (VTSPELL.VBX) | Run-Time |
| 4 | WsHelp† (WSHELP.VBX) | Run-Time |
| 1 | XLabel (XLABEL.VBX) | Shareware |
| 12 | ZipInf (ZIPINF1.VBX) | Design-Time |

*A version of this control ships with VB Professional Edition
†This is a set of multiple controls
‡This control is a DLL
◊Message Hook is a full functioning control originally developed by Waite Group Press for *Visual Basic How-To, Second Edition* and provided in this book for readers of *Visual Basic Controls Desk Reference*
∞Visual/db is a VB library of VB code

# INSTALLATION

A shell program on the CD provided with *Visual Basic Controls Desk Reference CD* makes it easy for you to run the example programs and sample the featured controls and control libraries.

## Using the Visual Basic Controls Desk Reference CD

To start the program, place the Visual Basic Controls Desk Reference CD in the CD drive, and follow these steps:

1. Click on the File option in Windows Program Manager to open the File menu.

2. Click on the Run... option in the File menu.

3. Type:

```
d:\vbcdr.exe (ENTER)
```

as shown in Figure I-1. Of course, this command line assumes that your CD-ROM drive is the D: drive. If the configuration of your computer is different, replace d: the appropriate drive letter.

4. Once the program loads, your screen should look like Figure I-2.

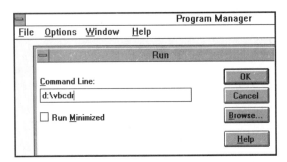

**Figure I-1** VBCDR.EXE starts the *Visual Basic Control Desk CD* Reference program

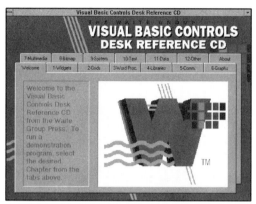

Figure I-2 The main screen

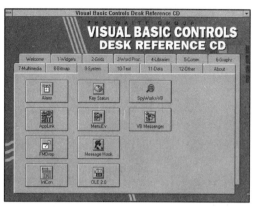

Figure I-3 Once a chapter is opened, you can click on a button to run the corresponding example

## Using the Shell

A shell program lets you navigate easily through the examples. When running, the shell, you need only to click on a tab to view the controls covered in a particular chapter and run the corresponding examples. For example, to examine the controls covered in Chapter 9, *System Tools*, click on the tab labeled "9-System." The screen will look like Figure I-3; click on a button to start a demo program for any of the featured controls.

## Copying the Files

You may any of the material on the CD to your hard disk using either the DOS COPY command or the Windows File Manager. The controls and their related files are organized on the CD as they are in the book; each chapter has its own directory. Table I-2 matches the directories on the CD with the chapters of the book.

The Chapters and Their Corresponding Directories

| BOOK CHAPTER NUMBER AND NAME | DOS DIRECTORY NAME |
| --- | --- |
| 1-Widgets | 01WIDGET |
| 2-Grids and Spreadsheets | 02GRIDS |
| 3-Word Processing and Text Editors | 03WORDPR |
| 4-Libraries | 04CNTLIB |
| 5-Communications | 05COMMUN |
| 6-Charting and Graphing Controls | 06GRAPHS |
| 7-Multimedia | 07MULTIM |
| 8-Bitmap and Image Processing | 08BITMAP |
| 9-System Tools | 09SYSTEM |

(continued on next page)

*(continued from previous page)*

| BOOK CHAPTER NUMBER AND NAME | DOS DIRECTORY NAME |
| --- | --- |
| 10-Text and Data Manipulation | 10TEXT |
| 11-Database Controls and Libraries | 11DATA |
| 12-Other Interesting Controls | 12OTHER |

Within each chapter directory is a subdirectory for each control covered in that chapter. For example, in the book, VideoSoft's Elastic control is examined in Chapter 1, so you would find those files in a subdirectory of 01WIDGET (in this case, the subdirectory is named VSELASTI).

## Bonus Subdirectories

Within some of the control subdirectories, you'll find further subdirectories, called BONUS subdirectories. These subdirectories contain extra goodies related to the control but not required for the demonstration of it. These may include additional information, files, example programs, demos, and so on.

# WIDGETS

**W**idgets can be defined loosely as controls that provide a specific, well-defined, user interface element. Many of the standard Visual Basic controls fall into this category: text controls, list boxes, command buttons, and the like, are all widgets. We tend to think of widgets as controls that are not overly complex. A word processing or spreadsheet control is probably too large to be considered a widget. So you can refine the definition by adding that most widgets provide a single, relatively simple function.

This is not to imply that widgets are trivial. A well-designed widget used in just the right place can profoundly affect an application's ease-of-use. Similarly, the misguided use of a widget can confuse and discourage your users. Widgets are by far the largest single category of controls on the market today.

This chapter includes a little bit of everything: outlines, tabs, buttons, sliders, labels, gauges, and lists. Here is a list of the controls discussed in this chapter:

**Animated Button**  This control lets you build all kinds of interesting buttons using bitmaps as the "frames" of animation sequences. We'll use this versatile control to build a car radio simulator with realistic-looking push buttons.

**BmpLst**  You can combine text and bitmaps in a multicolumn list box with this control. We'll use it to create a flexible icon viewing program.

**Gauge**  You can use this control to create visually impressive meters and gauges. Design your own bitmapped gauge backgrounds, or use one of the four designs from our sample application.

**iList**  This control adds built-in search capabilities to the traditional list box. Our sample application uses a text control to perform character-by-character searches through the items in an iList control.

**Masked Edit**  Control data entry with this variation of the text control. Use the Masked Edit control to validate numeric and date fields as the data is entered.

**Microsoft Outline**  Use this control to build hierarchical lists, and add a bitmapped picture to list items for increased emphasis. We use this control to display information about the planets in our solar system.

**OxButton**  The OxButton control is a replacement for the standard command button, with the added ability to display a bitmap and text in virtually any location on the button face.

**Prompt**  Build terminal-style applications with the Prompt control. We build a DOS-prompt simulation as an example. You can use Prompt to create anything from text adventure games to command interpreters.

**Slider**  Create your own analog-style slider controls with this variation on the traditional horizontal and vertical scroll bars. We'll build a graphic equalizer simulator to show you the realistic appearance and ease-of-use that Slider provides.

**Spin Button**  You can use this simple control in tandem with a label or text control to easily increment or decrement values. We'll use it to build a simple RGB color-mixing program.

**Tab/VBX**  FarPoint's Tab/VBX lets you add the appearance of tabbed folders to your applications. It provides a comprehensive array of properties that allow you to meet your user interface requirements with very few limitations.

**TList**  This versatile outline control gives you greater control over the text and graphics than does the Microsoft Outline control that comes with Visual Basic. You can specify separate bitmaps and fonts for each item, and can have individual lines word wrapped.

▲ **VBCtl3D** This deceptively simple control can give a 3D look to your existing standard controls, including list boxes and option buttons. One instance of this control on a VB form is all you need to completely change the appearance of menus, common dialogs, and controls.

▲ **VSElastic** Use the VSElastic control to automatically resize other controls, add 3D effects, create splitter bars, or even act as a progress meter.

▲ **VSIndexTab** This tab-style control can be curtomized in a variety of ways. You can create vertical or horizontal tabs, and choose from numerous 3D styles and tab shapes.

▲ **XLabel** XLabel permits you to rotate your TrueType fonts at any angle, letting you place labels vertically or diagonally. You can even spin labels at run time to create interesting visual effects.

# Animated Button (ANIBUTON.VBX)

| USAGE: | Custom Button Animation |
| MANUFACTURER: | Desaware |
| COST: | Provided with Visual Basic 3.0 Professional Edition |

There are accepted standards for the appearance of graphical user interfaces. These standards create uniform and recognizable interface elements for programs. The familiar Windows menus, gray buttons, scrolling list boxes, and text boxes are a comfort to users who don't want to have to learn Yet Another Graphical Interface.

But sometimes you need to chuck all that out the window. Sometimes, to make an application easier to use or more intuitive, you need to make things look *nonstandard*. The Animated Button control, or AniButton, is designed for just this purpose. If you need the function of a button or check box, but need a radically different appearance, this may be the tool for you.

## Syntax

Controls that seem to move usually show a series of animation *frames*, and AniButton is no exception. To create these frames you need to use another tool, such as an icon or bitmap editor. Windows Paintbrush is a serviceable bitmap editor; you may also want to consider a resource editor such as Borland's Resource Workshop, which supports both bitmaps and icons. An icon editor such as IconWorks, one of the sample programs that comes with Visual Basic 3.0, works nicely for creating small (32-by-32 pixel) button animations.

For a list of the nonstandard properties and event of the AniButton control see Table 1-1.

**Table 1-1** The AniButton control also has the nonstandard event click

### PROPERTIES

| | | |
|---|---|---|
| CCBfileLoad | CCBfileSave | ClearFirst |
| ClickFilter | Cycle | Frame |

*(continued on next page)*

**PROPERTIES**

*(continued from previous page)*

| | | |
|---|---|---|
| HideFocusBox | PictDrawMode | Picture |
| PictureXPos | PictureYPos | SpecialOp |
| Speed | TextPosition | TextXpos |
| TextYpos | Value | |

**EVENT**

Click

**Building the Frames** The quality of any AniButton is a direct result of the creativity devoted to designing the frame bitmaps. For most programs, your goal will be to create a button whose purpose is immediately obvious from its appearance. This usually means you'll design a button that mimics the form and function of some type of real-world object. For example, everybody knows what a wall-mounted light switch is. If you faithfully re-create a light switch using the AniButton, your user will already know how the control works.

Once you have designed the frame bitmaps, you need to tell the AniButton control how to use them. AniButton provides three methods for animating your frames. You set the method via the *Cycle* property, whose settings are explained in Table 1-2.

**Table 1-2** Settings for the Cycle property

| VALUE | MEANING |
|---|---|
| 0 | Push Button: Display the first half of the frames when the button is pressed. Display the second half of the frames when the button is released, and then return to the first frame. This is the default setting. |
| 1 | Multi-State Button: Move to the next frame when the button is released. This setting increments through the animation one frame per click, looping back to the first frame when the last frame is clicked. The Value property is set to the new frame number on each click. |
| 2 | Two-State Button: Display the first half of the frames when the button is clicked the first time, and display the second half of the frames when the button is clicked again, returning to the first frame. |

Once you've decided what type of animation cycling to use, and drawn your frame bitmaps, you need to build your AniButton. The first step is to drag an AniButton from the Visual Basic Toolbox to a form. Once the control is on the form, you can use the Properties Window and select the *Frame* property. Double-clicking on this property opens the Select Frame dialog, as shown in Figure 1-1. This little tool lets you build your animation sequence. From this dialog you can load your bitmaps from disk, or paste them in from the Windows Clipboard, for each frame of your animation.

You don't want your button to move too slowly or too fast. The *Speed* property, an integer between 0 and 32,767, sets the millisecond delay between frames. The documentation recommends that you use a value of less than 100, since large values may degrade system performance.

**Reusing Buttons** The bitmaps and frame information about the AniButton are saved with your project. If you want to save a button definition—perhaps so you can easily use the button in other projects—use the *CCBfileSave* property. When you assign a file name to this property, the button information is saved to a special file with a .CCB extension. To use one of these button definitions in another project, just assign the *CCBfileLoad* property the name of a valid CCB file.

**Fine-Tuning Button Appearance** The AniButton has a *Caption* property, as do many other controls, but the *TextPosition* property allows you to control where the caption appears relative to the bitmap animation. Table 1-3 lists the possible *TextPosition* values.

**Table 1-3** Settings for the TextPosition property

| VALUE | MEANING |
| --- | --- |
| 0 | The caption is displayed inside the bitmap (this is the default). |
| 1 | The caption is displayed to the right of the bitmap. |
| 2 | The caption is displayed to the left of the bitmap. |
| 3 | The caption is displayed above the bitmap. |
| 4 | The caption is displayed below the bitmap. |

While the *TextPosition* property sets the general orientation of the bitmap and the caption, the *PictureXpos*, *PictureYpos*, *TextXpos,* and *TextYpos* properties let you fine-tune the placement of these two elements. These integer properties represent the percentage (0 to 100) placement from the top-left corner of the bitmap area or the caption area. By default, these properties are set to 50, which centers them in their respective areas.

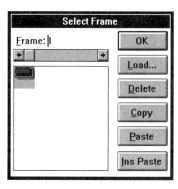

**Figure 1-1** The AniButton
Select Frame dialog

For example, Figure 1-2 shows our example program at design time. It uses five identical AniButtons. The *TextPosition* is set to display the text above the picture, with *TextXpos* and *TextYpos* both set to 50. This centers the numbers 1, 2, 3, 4, and 5 in the area above the picture.

The *PictDrawMode* property determines how the bitmaps are drawn within the control. By default this property is set to 0, which means that the AniButton control will use the values of the *PictureXpos*, *PictureYpos*, *TextXpos*, and *TextYpos* properties to display the control. If *PictDrawMode* is set to 1, the control is automatically sized to fit the largest frame of animation. If the property is set to 2, the bitmaps are stretched or contracted to fit the size of the control.

Visual Basic indicates that a control with a *Caption* property has the focus by drawing a dotted-line border around the caption. The AniButton control is no exception, but there are times when a custom button would look better if it did not display this focus box. Set the AniButton *HideFocusBox* property to *True* to prevent display of the focus box.

Since the AniButton control consists of both a caption and a bitmap area, by default a *Click* event is triggered any time you click anywhere in either area. But since this isn't appropriate for every bitmap/caption combination, the *ClickFilter* property lets you specify what part of the control will cause a *Click* event to fire. Table 1-4 lists the different settings for the *ClickFilter* property.

**Table 1-4** Settings for the ClickFilter property

| VALUE | MEANING |
| --- | --- |
| 0 | Mouse clicks are detected for entire control (this is the default). |
| 1 | Mouse clicks are detected over the caption text or the bitmap. |
| 2 | Mouse clicks are detected on the bitmap only. |
| 3 | Mouse clicks are detected on the caption text only. |

# Example

The example program uses AniButtons and a few other standard controls to create a car radio simulator, as shown in Figure 1-3. The row of five "radio" buttons, as well as the Off/On and Exit buttons, are all AniButton controls. When one of the radio buttons is pushed, an audio wave (WAV) file associated with that "station" is played. (Assuming

**Figure 1-2** Example program at design time, showing text and picture positions

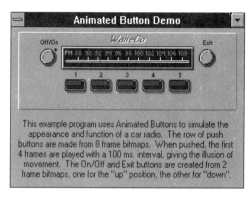

**Figure 1-3** The AniButton example program

that you've remembered to turn the radio on!) The names of the WAV files are loaded from a text file called RADIO.TXT, which should be in the same directory as the AniButton example program. By changing this text file, you can customize the program to play any WAV files you want.

## Steps

1. Create a new project called ANIBTN.MAK. Create a new form that includes the objects and properties shown in Tables 1-5. Save this form as ANIBTN.FRM.

**Table 1-5** Objects and properties for ANIBTN.FRM

| OBJECT | PROPERTY | SETTING |
|--------|----------|---------|
| Form | FormName | Form1 |
| | BackColor | &H00C0C0C0& |
| | BorderStyle | 1 'Fixed Single |
| | Caption | "Animated Button Demo" |
| | MaxButton | 0 'False |
| Line | Name | Line2 |
| | BorderColor | &H00FFFFFF& |
| | X1 | 150 |
| | X2 | 4680 |
| | Y1 | 90 |
| | Y2 | 90 |
| Line | Name | Line3 |
| | BorderColor | &H00808080& |
| | X1 | 180 |
| | X2 | 4680 |
| | Y1 | 1590 |
| | Y2 | 1590 |

*(continued on next page)*

| OBJECT | PROPERTY | SETTING |
|---|---|---|
| *(continued from previous page)* | | |
| Line | Name | Line4 |
| | BorderColor | &H00808080& |
| | X1 | 4680 |
| | X2 | 4680 |
| | Y1 | 90 |
| | Y2 | 1590 |
| Label | Name | Label1 |
| | Alignment | 2 'Center |
| | BackStyle | 0 'Transparent |
| | Caption | "This example program uses Animated Buttons to simulate the appearance and function of a car radio. The row of push buttons is made from eight frame bitmaps. When pushed, the first four frames are played with a 100 ms. interval, giving the illusion of movement. The On/Off and Exit buttons are created from two frame bitmaps, one for the "up" position, the other for "down" |
| | FontBold | 0 'False |
| | ForeColor | &H00800000& |
| Image | Name | Image1 |
| | Picture | (set at design time in Properties window) |
| PictureBox | Name | picStations |
| | AutoSize | -1 'True |
| | BorderStyle | 0 'None |
| | Index | 0 |
| | Picture | (set at design time in Properties window) |
| AniPushButton | Name | aniOnOff |
| | BackColor | &H00C0C0C0& |
| | Caption | "Off/On" |
| | ClickFilter | 2 'Picture only |
| | Cycle | 1 'By frame |
| | FontBold | 0 'False |
| | FontName | "Small Fonts" |
| | FontSize | 6 |
| | HideFocusBox | -1 'True |
| | Picture | (set at design time in Properties window) |
| | TextPosition | 3 'Above |

| OBJECT | PROPERTY | SETTING |
| --- | --- | --- |
| | TextYpos | 0 |
| AniPushButton | Name | AniRadio |
| | BackColor | &H00C0C0C0& |
| | Caption | "1" |
| | ClickFilter | 2 'Picture only |
| | Cycle | 2 '2-state 1/2 & 1/2 |
| | FontBold | 0 'False |
| | FontName | "Small Fonts" |
| | FontSize | 6 |
| | ForeColor | &H00000000& |
| | HideFocusBox | -1 'True |
| | Index | 0 |
| | PictDrawMode | 1 'Autosize control |
| | Picture | (set at design time in Properties window) |
| | PictureYpos | 20 |
| | Speed | 80 |
| | TextPosition | 3 'Above |
| AniPushButton | Name | AniRadio |
| | Index | 1 |
| | Caption | "2" |
| AniPushButton | Name | AniRadio |
| | Index | 2 |
| | Caption | "3" |
| AniPushButton | Name | AniRadio |
| | Index | 3 |
| | Caption | "4" |
| AniPushButton | Name | AniRadio |
| | Index | 4 |
| | Caption | "5" |
| AniPushButton | Name | aniExit |
| | BackColor | &H00C0C0C0& |
| | Caption | "Exit" |
| | ClickFilter | 2 'Picture only |
| | Cycle | 1 'By frame |
| | FontBold | 0 'False |
| | FontName | "Small Fonts" |
| | FontSize | 6 |
| | HideFocusBox | -1 'True |
| | Picture | (set at design time in Properties window) |

*(continued on next page)*

| OBJECT | PROPERTY | SETTING |
|---|---|---|
| *(continued from previous page)* | | |
| | TextPosition | 3 'Above |
| | TextYpos | 0 |
| PictureBox | Name | picStations |
| | AutoSize | -1 'True |
| | BorderStyle | 0 'None |
| | Index | 1 |
| | Picture | (set at design time in Properties window) |
| | Visible | 0 'False |
| PictureBox | Name | picStations |
| | AutoSize | -1 'True |
| | BorderStyle | 0 'None |
| | Index | 2 |
| | Picture | (set at design time in Properties window) |
| | Visible | 0 'False |

2. Place the following control in Table 1-6 within the picStations PictureBox control. Make sure to select the picStations control before placing the line object inside it.

**Table 1-6** The linPointer line control contained in the picStations picture control

| OBJECT | PROPERTY | SETTING |
|---|---|---|
| Line | Name | linPointer |
| | BorderColor | &H000000FF& |
| | X1 | 810 |
| | X2 | 810 |
| | Y1 | 90 |
| | Y2 | 390 |

3. After creating the form, put the following code in the declarations section of ANIBTN.FRM:

```
Option Explicit
'-----------------------------------------------
' Variables, Constants and function declarations
' used by the AniButton example program.
'-----------------------------------------------

' Stores the number of radio buttons.
Dim MaxRadioBtns As Integer

' Boolean that tracks whether or not radio is currently on.
Dim RadioOn As Integer

' Array of sound file names.
```

```
Dim RadioFiles() As String

' Functions and constants used to play sounds.
Declare Function sndPlaySound Lib "MMSystem" (lpsound As Any, ByVal flag As Integer) As Integer
Declare Function sndKillSound Lib "MMSystem" Alias "sndPlaySound" (ByVal lpszNull As Long,
ByVal flags)

Const SND_SYNC = &H0        ' Return when sound ends (the default)
Const SND_ASYNC = &H1       ' Return as soon as sound starts
Const SND_NODEFAULT = &H2   ' Don't play default sound if not found
Const SND_MEMORY = &H4      ' lpszSoundName -> memory image of file
Const SND_LOOP = &H8        ' Loop continuously; needs SND_ASYNC
Const SND_NOSTOP = &H10     ' Don't interrupt sound to play new one

' Global string used for by NoiseGet() and PlayStatic() to play WAV files in memory
Dim SoundBuffer As String
```

4. Add the following functions and subroutines to ANIBTN.FRM. This code does all the processing for the AniButton example program. When the Off/On button is clicked we set a Boolean in the *AniOnOff_Click* event, *RadioOn*, to track whether the radio has been turned on. If the radio is being turned on, we check if any of the five "radio" buttons are in the down position; if so, we begin playing the associated WAV file. WAV files are played using the Windows *sndPlaySound API* call—a call to the MMSYSTEM dynamic link library. Music is played asynchronously, which allows other Windows events (such as our pushing of buttons) to be processed while the music continues to play.

```
Sub aniExit_Click ()
'-----------------------------------------------------
' Exit the program.
'-----------------------------------------------------
    Unload Me
End Sub

Sub aniOnOff_Click ()
'-----------------------------------------------------
' Clicking this AniButton turns the radio on and
' off.
'-----------------------------------------------------
Dim i As Integer

    picStations(0).Picture = picStations(aniOnOff.Value).Picture

    ' Turn radio on.
    If aniOnOff.Value = 2 Then
        PlayStatic
        RadioOn = True
        For i = 0 To MaxRadioBtns - 1
            If AniRadio(i).Value = 2 Then
                PlayRadio i
            End If
        Next
    ' Turn radio off
    Else
        RadioOn = False
        PlayStatic  'Playing static here stops any current music.
    End If
End Sub
```

*(continued on next page)*

*(continued from previous page)*

```
Sub AniRadio_Click (Index As Integer)
'----------------------------------------------------
' If the radio is on, pushing one of these buttons
' forces any currently down button back up, moves
' the station needle, and plays the new selection.
'----------------------------------------------------
Dim i As Integer

    If RadioOn Then PlayStatic

    ' If Value is 1, then the current selection
    ' has been 'popped up', so we exit.
    If AniRadio(Index).Value = 1 Then Exit Sub

    ' Look for the currently 'down' button and
    ' pop it up.
    For i = 0 To MaxRadioBtns - 1
        If (AniRadio(i).Value = 2) And (i  Index) Then
            AniRadio(i).Value = 1
            Exit For
        End If
    Next

    ' Move the station needle
    linPointer.Visible = False
    linPointer.X1 = AniRadio(Index).Left + (AniRadio(Index).Width \ 2) - picStations(0).Left
    linPointer.X2 = linPointer.X1
    linPointer.Visible = True

    ' Play the new selection.
    If RadioOn Then PlayRadio Index
End Sub

Sub Form_Load ()
'----------------------------------------------------
' Center the form, load the 'static' sound into
' memory, and load the music file names into an array.
'----------------------------------------------------
Dim result As Integer

    ' Center the form on the screen.
    Me.Move (Screen.Width - Me.Width) \ 2, (Screen.Height - Me.Height) \ 2

    ' Set the number of 'radio' buttons at bottom of window
    MaxRadioBtns = 5

    ' Load the 'radio static' sound into memory.
    result = NoiseGet(App.Path & "\STATIC.WAV")

    ' Get all the music WAV file names from RADIO.TXT.
    GetRadioFileNames
End Sub

Sub Form_Unload (Cancel As Integer)
'----------------------------------------------------
' Playing Static will cut off any music that's
' currently playing before we exit.
'----------------------------------------------------
```

```
    PlayStatic
End Sub

Sub GetRadioFileNames ()
'--------------------------------------------------
' RADIO.TXT is a text file that contains the names
' of 5 WAV files.  This routine loads the names
' into the array RadioFiles().
'--------------------------------------------------
Dim fnum As Integer
Dim i As Integer

    On Error GoTo GetRadioFileNames_Error

    i = 0
    fnum = FreeFile
    Open App.Path & "\RADIO.TXT" For Input As fnum

    While Not EOF(fnum)
        ReDim Preserve RadioFiles(i + 1)
        Line Input #fnum, RadioFiles(i)
        i = i + 1
    Wend

    Close fnum

Exit Sub
GetRadioFileNames_Error:
    RadioFiles(i) = ""
    Resume Next
End Sub

Function NoiseGet (ByVal FileName) As Integer
'------------------------------------------------------------
' Load a sound file into the global string variable
' SoundBuffer.  This must be called before PlayStatic
'------------------------------------------------------------
Dim buffer As String
Dim fnum As Integer

    On Error GoTo NoiseGet_Error

    buffer = Space$(1024)
    SoundBuffer = ""
    fnum = FreeFile
    Open FileName For Binary As fnum
    Do While Not EOF(fnum)
        Get #fnum, , buffer      ' Load in 1K chunks
        SoundBuffer = SoundBuffer & buffer
    Loop
    Close fnum
    SoundBuffer = Trim$(SoundBuffer)

Exit Function

NoiseGet_Error:
    NoiseGet = False
    SoundBuffer = ""
    Exit Function
End Function
```

*(continued on next page)*

*(continued from previous page)*

```
Sub PlayRadio (ByVal Index As Integer)
'----------------------------------------------------
' Play the WAV file whose name is stored in
' RadioFiles(Index).
'----------------------------------------------------
Dim SoundFile As String
Dim result As Integer

    If InStr(RadioFiles(Index), ":\") = 2 Then
        SoundFile = Trim$(RadioFiles(Index))
    Else
        SoundFile = App.Path & "\" & Trim$(RadioFiles(Index))
    End If
    result = sndPlaySound(ByVal SoundFile, SND_ASYNC Or SND_LOOP Or SND_NODEFAULT)
End Sub

Sub PlayStatic ()
'------------------------------------------------------------
' Plays a sound previously loaded into memory with function
' NoiseGet().
'------------------------------------------------------------
Dim r As Integer   ' synchronously

    If SoundBuffer = "" Then Exit Sub
    r = sndPlaySound(ByVal SoundBuffer, SND_SYNC Or SND_MEMORY)

End Sub
```

## Tips and Comments

When creating bitmaps to use as frames for your button animation, it's helpful to be aware of some existing conventions, particularly if you're creating 3D effects. The Visual Design Guide, an application that comes with Visual Basic, is a useful resource for designing controls whose appearance is consistent with the rest of Windows. Of primary importance is the convention that the "light source" in Windows always originates from the upper-left side. If you vary from this, your objects will appear "wrong" to users, even if they can't tell you exactly why.

When drawing your series of individual bitmap frames, start with the frame in which the object is in the "at rest" or starting position. This is usually the first frame. Once you complete and save the first frame, create a second frame using the first bitmap, but save it under a different name. (It's useful to include a number in the file name to help distinguish the sequence: FRAME1.BMP, FRAME2.BMP, and so on.) Change the bitmap to create the next frame in the sequence. The radio button bitmaps in the example program were created in this way. Using a bitmap editor, you can "slice out" and then slightly reposition just the part of the frame that is moving. With the radio buttons, the rectangle that represented the "moving" section of the button was selected and then moved 1 pixel to the right and 1 pixel down over the bitmap. The 1-pixel wide gap left behind by the move was then filled in by hand. This process was repeated to create four frames used in the animation sequence.

# BmpLst (BmpLst.VBX)

| | |
|---|---|
| USAGE: | Combining Text and Graphics in a List Box |
| MANUFACTURER: | Mabry Software |
| COST: | $20 ($15 via CompuServe) |

BmpLst lets you combine a bitmap and text in a scrolling, multicolumn list box. Positioning options let you place the bitmap above, below, or on either side of the text.

## Syntax

In many ways, the BmpLst control works the same as a standard Visual Basic list box control. The differences are related to the positioning and assigning of bitmaps. Here are the nonstandard properties of BmpLst shown in Table 1-7.

**Table 1-7** Nonstandard properties of the BmpLst control

| |
|---|
| BorderEffect |
| ScreenUpdate |
| BottomMargin |
| TopMargin |
| Picture |
| VertGap |

Assigning bitmaps is easy. Once you've added a list item, by using the *AddItem* method just as you would for a normal list box, you can assign a bitmap to that item's *Picture* property. This snippet of code shows how:

```
BmpLst1.AddItem "An image from another control"
BmpLst1.Picture(BMPLst1.NewIndex) = Picture1.Image

Bmpst1.AddItem "An image from a file"
BmpLst.Picture(BmpLst.NewIndex) = LoadPicture("mypic.bmp")
```

The preceding example adds two items to the list. Both are assigned bitmaps; the first item copies an image from an existing Picture control, while the second uses the Visual Basic *LoadPicture* function to load a bitmap file from disk.

You control the position of the bitmap through the *ItemPlacement* property, which indicates the position of the bitmap relative to the list text. Table 1-8 shows the valid values for the *Item Placement* property.

**Table 1-8** Values for the ItemPlacement property

| VALUE | MEANING |
|---|---|
| 0 | Bitmap above text |
| 1 | Bitmap below text |
| 2 | Bitmap to left of text |
| 3 | Bitmap to right of text |

The *ItemWidth* and *ItemHeight* properties set the dimensions for the bitmap in the list. These properties, along with the *TopMargin, BottomMargin,* and *VertGap* properties, allow you to fine-tune the orientation of the bitmap and text.

You can set a 3D border effect with the *BorderEffect* property, whose valid values are given in Table 1-9.

**Table 1-9** BorderEffect property values

| VALUE | MEANING |
|---|---|
| 0 | No border effect |
| 1 | Raised border effect |
| 2 | Lowered border effect |
| 3 | Inset border effect |

Since drawing bitmaps to the screen can be a time-consuming process, and the sight of the BmpLst control updating itself can be distracting, the control provides a Boolean ScreenUpdate property. By default, this property is set to True, which means that the BmpLst will update itself automatically. When set to False, BmpLst does not repaint itself on the screen, even when its contents change. This is especially useful when you are loading a large number of bitmaps into the BmpLst control.

# Example

The example program is a fully functional browser that uses the BmpLst control to display a scrolling list of all the icons found in a particular directory. The program is shown in Figure 1-4. A radio button lets you choose between viewing icon (ICO) files and viewing the icons inside executable (EXE, DLL, and VBX) files. Loading the icon files is trivial; we just use the *LoadPicture* function and assign the image directly to the

**Figure 1-4** The BmpLst demo, an Icon Navigator

item's *Picture* property. Extracting the icons from executable files requires a bit more work; we use the Windows API calls *ExtractIcon* and *DrawIcon* to load the icon image into an invisible Picture control, and then assign the image from there into the BmpLst *Picture* property.

Another invisible control, this time a File List control, easily searches directories for the files we want. By changing the File List's *Pattern* property, we can look for either icons or executables.

If you click on an icon in the BmpLst box, an enlarged picture of the icon is displayed in a zoom window that allows you to see an icon in better detail.

## Steps

1. Create a new project called BMPLST.MAK. Add the BmpLst control, BMPLST1.VBX, to the project. Create a new form with the objects and properties described in Tables 1-10 and 1-11. Save this form as BMPLST.FRM.

**Table 1-10** Objects and properties of BMPLST.FRM

| OBJECT | PROPERTY | SETTING |
|---|---|---|
| Form | FormName | frmBmpLst |
| | BackColor | &H00C0C0C0& |
| | Caption | "BmpLst Demo - Icon Navigator" |
| | FillStyle | 0 'Solid |
| Label | Name | Label2 |
| | BackStyle | 0 'Transparent |
| | Caption | "Drives" |
| | ForeColor | &H00800000& |
| Label | Name | Label3 |
| | BackStyle | 0 'Transparent |
| | Caption | "Icon Files" |
| | ForeColor | &H00800000& |
| Label | Name | lblIconInfo |
| | BackStyle | 0 'Transparent |
| | FontBold | 0 'False |
| | ForeColor | &H00800000& |
| | Tag | "3d" |
| Label | Name | Label4 |
| | BackStyle | 0 'Transparent |
| | Caption | "Zoom View" |
| | ForeColor | &H00800000& |
| Label | Name | Label5 |
| | BackStyle | 0 'Transparent |
| | Tag | "3d" |

*(continued on next page)*

| OBJECT | PROPERTY | SETTING |
| --- | --- | --- |
| *(continued from previous page)* | | |
| DirListBox | Name | Dir1 |
| | Tag | "3D" |
| BmpList | Name | bmpIcons |
| | BackColor | &H00FFFFFF& |
| | BorderEffect | 0 'None |
| | BorderStyle | 1 'Fixed Single |
| | BottomMargin | 10 |
| | ColDelim | "        " |
| | FontBold | 0 'False |
| | ForeColor | &H00000000& |
| | ItemHeight | 900 |
| | ItemPlacement | 0 'Top |
| | ItemWidth | 1200 |
| | LeftMargin | 120 |
| | MultiColumn | 1 'True |
| | MultiSelect | 0 'None |
| | NumColumns | 2 |
| | Sorted | -1 'True |
| | Tag | "3d" |
| | TopMargin | 100 |
| | VertGap | 10 |
| FileListBox | Name | File1 |
| | Pattern | "*.ico" |
| | Visible | 0 'False |
| DriveListBox | Name | Drive1 |
| | Tag | "3d" |
| PictureBox | Name | Picture1 |
| | BackColor | &H00FFFFFF& |
| | DrawMode | 15 'Merge Pen |
| | Tag | "3d" |
| VScrollBar | Name | VScroll1 |
| | LargeChange | 20 |
| | Max | 1875 |
| | Min | 490 |
| | SmallChange | 5 |
| | Tag | "3d" |
| | Value | 1875 |
| OptionButton | Name | optGetIco |

| OBJECT | PROPERTY | SETTING |
|---|---|---|
| | BackColor | &H00C0C0C0& |
| | Caption | "View Icon Files" |
| | ForeColor | &H00000000& |
| | Value | -1 'True |
| OptionButton | Name | optGetExe |
| | BackColor | &H00C0C0C0& |
| | Caption | "View icons in EXE/DLL" |
| | ForeColor | &H00000000& |
| PictureBox | Name | picFromExe |
| | AutoRedraw | -1 'True |
| | Visible | 0 'False |

2. Place the following image control inside the Picture1 picture box control. Make sure to select the Picture1 control before placing imgIcon inside it.

**Table 1-11** The imgIcon image control contained within the Picture1 control

| OBJECT | PROPERTY | SETTING |
|---|---|---|
| Image | Name | imgIcon |
| | Stretch | -1 'True |

3. After creating BMPLST.FRM, add the following code in the form's declaration section.

```
Option Explicit
'-------------------------------------------------
' Constants used in the BmpLst Demo.
'-------------------------------------------------

Const MINIMIZED = 1

' Color Constants
Const DARK_GRAY = &H808080
Const WHITE = &HFFFFFF
Const BLACK = &H0

' Cursor shape constants
Const CSR_NORMAL = 0
Const CSR_HOURGLASS = 11

Declare Function ExtractIcon Lib "shell.dll" (ByVal hinst As Integer, ByVal lpszExeName As
String, ByVal iIcon As Integer) As Integer
Declare Function DrawIcon Lib "User" (ByVal hDC As Integer, ByVal x As Integer, ByVal y As
Integer, ByVal hIcon As Integer) As Integer
```

4. Add the following subroutines to BMPLST.FRM. The *Make3D* subroutine provides a 3D appearance to some of the controls without the added overhead of special controls.

This subroutine is called in the form's *Paint* event, which checks each control's *Tag* property for the string "3D", which in turn triggers a call to *Make3D* for that control.

```
Sub bmpIcons_Click ()
'---------------------------------------------------
' Update the zoom box and file info label.
'---------------------------------------------------
Dim FullFileName As String

    If bmpIcons.ListIndex < 0 Then Exit Sub

    FullFileName = Dir1.Path
    If Right$(FullFileName, 1)  "\" Then FullFileName = FullFileName & "\"
    FullFileName = FullFileName & bmpIcons.List(bmpIcons.ListIndex)

    lblIconInfo = FullFileName & " - Modified: " & FileDateTime(FullFileName)
    imgIcon.Picture = bmpIcons.Picture(bmpIcons.ListIndex)
End Sub

Sub Dir1_Change ()
'---------------------------------------------------
' Scan the invisible FileList control for icon
' files and put them in the BmpLst box.
'---------------------------------------------------
    GetAllIcons
End Sub

Sub Drive1_Change ()
'---------------------------------------------------
' When the drive changes, change the Directory.
'---------------------------------------------------
    Dir1.Path = Drive1.Drive
End Sub

Sub Form_Load ()
'---------------------------------------------------
' Center the form on the screen.
'---------------------------------------------------

    Me.Move (Screen.Width - Me.Width) \ 2, (Screen.Height - Me.Height) \ 2

    picFromEXE.Width = 36 * Screen.TwipsPerPixelX
    picFromEXE.Height = 36 * Screen.TwipsPerPixelY
End Sub

Sub Form_Paint ()
'---------------------------------------------------
' Put a 3D border around any control tagged "3D".
'---------------------------------------------------
Dim i As Integer

    For i = 0 To Me.Controls.Count - 1
        If UCase$(Me.Controls(i).Tag) = "3D" Then
            Make3D Me, Me.Controls(i)
        End If
    Next
End Sub

Sub Form_Resize ()
```

```
'--------------------------------------------------
' Resize the bmpIcons and lblIconInfo controls
' when the window is resized.
'--------------------------------------------------
Dim NumCols As Integer

    If WindowState = MINIMIZED Then Exit Sub

    lblIconInfo.Width = (Me.ScaleWidth - lblIconInfo.Left - Dir1.Left)

    bmpIcons.Height = (Me.ScaleHeight - bmpIcons.Top - Dir1.Left)
    bmpIcons.Width = (Me.ScaleWidth - bmpIcons.Left - Dir1.Left)
    NumCols = (bmpIcons.Width \ bmpIcons.ItemWidth)
    If NumCols >= 1 Then
        bmpIcons.NumColumns = NumCols
    End If
    Me.Refresh
End Sub

Sub GetAllIcons ()
'--------------------------------------------------
' Scan the invisible FileList control for icon
' files and put them in the BmpLst box.
'--------------------------------------------------
Dim i As Integer

    If optGetICO Then
        File1.Pattern = "*.ico"
    Else
        File1.Pattern = "*.exe;*.dll;*.vbx"
    End If
    File1.Path = Dir1.Path

    lblIconInfo = ""
    imgIcon.Picture = LoadPicture()

    Screen.MousePointer = CSR_HOURGLASS
    bmpIcons.ScreenUpdate = False

    ' Get rid of current list contents.
    bmpIcons.Clear

    If optGetICO Then
        For i = 0 To File1.ListCount - 1
            File1.ListIndex = i
            bmpIcons.AddItem File1.List(i)
            bmpIcons.Picture(bmpIcons.NewIndex) = LoadPicture(File1.Path & "\" &
File1.FileName)
        Next
    Else
        For i = 0 To File1.ListCount - 1
            File1.ListIndex = i
            ShowIcons File1.List(i)
        Next
    End If

    bmpIcons.ScreenUpdate = True
    Screen.MousePointer = CSR_NORMAL

End Sub
```

*(continued on next page)*

*(continued from previous page)*

```vb
Sub Make3D (pic As Form, ctl As Control)
'-----------------------------------------------------
' Wrap a 3D effect around a control on a form.
'-----------------------------------------------------
Dim AdjustX As Integer, AdjustY As Integer
Dim RightSide As Single

    AdjustX = Screen.TwipsPerPixelX
    AdjustY = Screen.TwipsPerPixelY

    ' Set the top shading line.
    pic.Line (ctl.Left - AdjustX, ctl.Top - AdjustY)-(ctl.Left + ctl.Width, ctl.Top - AdjustY), DARK_GRAY
    pic.Line -(ctl.Left + ctl.Width, ctl.Top + ctl.Height), WHITE
    pic.Line -(ctl.Left - AdjustX, ctl.Top + ctl.Height), WHITE
    pic.Line -(ctl.Left - AdjustX, ctl.Top - AdjustY), DARK_GRAY
End Sub

Sub optGetExe_Click ()
    GetAllIcons
End Sub

Sub optGetIco_Click ()
    GetAllIcons
End Sub

Sub ShowIcons (ByVal AFile As String)
'-----------------------------------------------------
' Extract all the icons from AFile and add them
' to the Bitmap List Box.
'-----------------------------------------------------
Dim result As Integer
Dim hinst As Integer
Dim iIcon As Integer
Dim i As Integer

    hinst = 0
    iIcon = 0
    result = 2
    result = ExtractIcon(hinst, AFile, iIcon)
    Do While result > 1
        picFromEXE.Cls
        result = DrawIcon(picFromEXE.hDC, 0, 0, result)

        bmpIcons.AddItem AFile
        bmpIcons.Picture(bmpIcons.NewIndex) = picFromEXE.Image

        iIcon = iIcon + 1
        result = ExtractIcon(hinst, AFile, iIcon)
    Loop

End Sub

Sub VScroll1_Change ()
'-----------------------------------------------------
' Adjust the size of the image when scroller moves.
'-----------------------------------------------------
    imgIcon.Width = Vscroll1.Value
    imgIcon.Height = Vscroll1.Value
End Sub
```

## Tips and Comments

The BmpLst control combines the best elements of icons and list boxes, allowing you to provide specific text with the extra visual cue of a picture. You can use this control for applications such as menuing systems or icon viewers (as in our example).

One note on the 3D effects around some of the controls in the example program. These were done without the use of third-party controls, using only the Visual Basic *Line* command. The subroutine *Make3D* encloses any control within a 3D border around it. This technique is hardly new, but there is one spin on it in this program: the way we decided which controls to make 3D. Look at the form's *Paint* event and you'll see a for loop that cycles through the Visual Basic *Controls* collection. Each control in the collection is checked, and if its *Tag* property has been set to the string "3D", the *Make3D* routine is called for that control. This provides an easy way to determine at design time which controls will be given a 3D effect.

# Gauge (GAUGE.VBX)

| USAGE: | Graphical Display of Numeric Data |
|---|---|
| MANUFACTURER: | MicroHelp, Inc. |
| COST: | Provided with Visual Basic 3.0 Professional Edition |

The Gauge control lets you display graphically a specified range of numeric data. A user-defined background bitmap allows you to customize the control's appearance to mimic actual gauges and other analog devices.

## Syntax

The Gauge control supports four basic gauge styles: vertical or horizontal "bar-style" gauges, and half-circle or full-circle "needle-style" gauges. The bar-style gauges are useful for simulating thermometers or displaying "percent complete" status bars. The needle-style gauges can depict components such as pressure gauges or decibel meters. The nonstandard properties and event of the Gauge control are listed in Table 1-12.

**Table 1-12** Nonstandard properties and event for the Gauge control

**PROPERTIES**

| | | | |
|---|---|---|---|
| BackColor | ForeColor | Height | InnerBottom |
| InnerLeft | InnerRight | InnerTop | Max |
| Min | NeedleWidth | Picture | Style |
| Value | Visible | | |

**EVENT**

Change

The *Style* property selects the general appearance of the gauge, but the real character of the control is determined by the bitmap you select as the control's background. You set this with the *Picture* property. Based on the style chosen for the control (see Table 1-13), either a bar or needle is drawn over the bitmap background.

**Table 1-13** Values for the Style property

| VALUE | MEANING |
| --- | --- |
| 0 | Horizontal bar |
| 1 | Vertical bar |
| 2 | Full-circle needle |
| 3 | Semi-circle needle |

The *Value* property determines the current position of the indicator (bar or needle) on the gauge face. *Min* and *Max* properties set the range of values that can be displayed on the gauge. If a value greater than the *Max* is set the control automatically sets the *Value* property equal to *Max*. Likewise, the control's value is automatically reset to *Min* if it is set below that value.

Four properties—*InnerBottom, InnerLeft, InnerRight,* and *InnerTop*—are used to restrict the area inside the bitmap on which the bar or needle indicator is displayed. You can think of these four properties as margins from the edge of the background bitmap. They determine how many pixels from the edges the bar or needle will appear. This area set by the four *Inner* properties is filled with the color determined by the *ForeColor* property.

The background bitmaps do not need to be set at design time. You can use the Visual Basic *LoadPicture* function to load a bitmap from disk at run time.

The Gauge control supports most of the standard Visual Basic events, including drag, mouse, and key events. The control also supports the *GotFocus* and *LostFocus* events, although there are no visual cues when a gauge has received the focus. (You could provide such a cue by changing the background bitmap when the control receives and loses the focus.)

One special event is provided with the Gauge control: The *Change* event is triggered every time the *Value* property changes.

# Example

This example displays four gauge controls, one of each type. The background bitmaps, shown in Figure 1-5, give you a feel for the radically different appearance these controls can have.

### Steps

1. Create a new project called GAUGDEMO.MAK. Add the Gauge control, GAUGE.VBX, to the project. Create a new form with the objects and properties described in Table 1-14. Save this form as GAUGDEMO.FRM. You will need to design background bitmaps for each of the four gauge controls, using a bitmap editor such as

**Figure 1-5** The Gauge demo at run time

Windows Paintbrush. Then you assign this bitmap to the control's *Picture* property at design time.

**Table 1-14** Objects and properties of GAUGDEMO.FRM

| OBJECT | PROPERTY | SETTING |
|---|---|---|
| Form | FormName | frmGauge |
| | BackColor | &H00C0C0C0& |
| | BorderStyle | 3 'Fixed Double |
| | Caption | "Gauge Demo" |
| | ForeColor | &H008080FF& |
| | MaxButton | 0 'False |
| Label | Name | Label1 |
| | Alignment | 2 'Center |
| | BackStyle | 0 'Transparent |
| | Caption | "Value" |
| | FontBold | 0 'False |
| | ForeColor | &H00000080& |
| Label | Name | Label2 |
| | Alignment | 2 'Center |
| | BackStyle | 0 'Transparent |
| | Caption | "Move the Slider Control or Press the Random Button to move Gauges" |
| | ForeColor | &H00800000& |
| Gauge | Name | Gauge1 |
| | Autosize | -1 'True |
| | BackColor | &H00C0C0C0& |
| | ForeColor | &H00000000& |
| | InnerBottom | 6 |

*(continued on next page)*

| OBJECT | PROPERTY | SETTING |
|---|---|---|
| *(continued from previous page)* | | |
| | InnerLeft | 5 |
| | InnerRight | 6 |
| | InnerTop | 5 |
| | Max | 100 |
| | NeedleWidth | 1 |
| | Picture | (set at design time in Properties window) |
| | Style | 3 ''Full' Needle |
| | Value | 50 |
| HScrollBar | Name | hscrGaugeValue |
| | LargeChange | 4 |
| | Max | 100 |
| | SmallChange | 2 |
| Gauge | Name | Gauge2 |
| | Autosize | -1 'True |
| | BackColor | &H00FFFF80& |
| | ForeColor | &H008080FF& |
| | InnerBottom | 9 |
| | InnerLeft | 25 |
| | InnerRight | 27 |
| | InnerTop | 7 |
| | Max | 100 |
| | NeedleWidth | 1 |
| | Picture | (set at design time in Properties window) |
| Gauge | Name | Gauge3 |
| | Autosize | -1 'True |
| | InnerBottom | 24 |
| | InnerLeft | 10 |
| | InnerRight | 10 |
| | InnerTop | 5 |
| | Max | 100 |
| | NeedleWidth | 3 |
| | Picture | (set at design time in Properties window) |
| | Style | 2 ''Semi' Needle |
| Gauge | Name | Gauge4 |
| | Autosize | -1 'True |
| | BackColor | &H00FFFFC0& |
| | ForeColor | &H00800000& |
| | InnerBottom | 37 |

| OBJECT | PROPERTY | SETTING |
|---|---|---|
| | InnerLeft | 22 |
| | InnerRight | 10 |
| | InnerTop | 28 |
| | Max | 100 |
| | NeedleWidth | 1 |
| | Picture | (set at design time in Properties window) |
| | Style | 1 'Vertical Bar |
| | Value | 23 |
| CommandButton | Name | btnExit |
| | Caption | "E&xit" |
| CommandButton | Name | btnRandom |
| | Caption | "Random" |
| CommandButton | Name | btnStop |
| | Caption | "&Stop!" |
| | Visible | 0 'False |

2. After creating the form, add the following code to the declarations section.

```
Option Explicit
'------------------------------------------------
' Variables global to this form
'------------------------------------------------
Dim StopRandom As Integer
```

3. Add the following subroutines to GAUGDEMO.FRM. The horizontal scroller's *Change* event does most of the little work there is to do, changing the value of each gauge whenever the scroller is moved. The Random button just sets up a loop that randomly changes the scroller value.

```
Sub btnExit_Click ()
'------------------------------------------------
' Unload the form when the Exit button is pushed.
'------------------------------------------------
    Unload Me
End Sub
Sub btnRandom_Click ()
'------------------------------------------------
' When the Random button is pushed, begin to
' randomly change the gauge values by resetting the
' value of the horizontal scroller.
'------------------------------------------------
Dim Target As Integer, OldTarget As Integer
Dim i As Integer
Dim direction As Integer
    StopRandom = False
    btnRandom.Visible = False
    btnStop.Top = btnRandom.Top
    btnStop.Visible = True
    btnExit.Enabled = False
```

*(continued on next page)*

*(continued from previous page)*

```
    Randomize
    While Not StopRandom
        Target = (Rnd * 100)
        If Target > OldTarget Then
            direction = 1
        Else
            direction = -1
        End If
        For i = OldTarget To Target Step (direction * 7)
            hscrGaugeValue.Value = i
            DoEvents
        Next
        OldTarget = Target
    Wend
    hscrGaugeValue.Value = Target
End Sub
Sub btnStop_Click ()
'-------------------------------------------------------
' Reset the values of the form's buttons and set
' the StopRandom boolean.  This will cause the loop
' in the btnRandom. Click event to terminate.
'-------------------------------------------------------
    btnRandom.Visible = True
    btnStop.Visible = False
    btnExit.Enabled = True

    StopRandom = True
End Sub

Sub Form_Load ()
'-------------------------------------------------------
' Center the window on the screen.
'-------------------------------------------------------
    Me.Move (Screen.Width - Me.Width) \ 2, (Screen.Height - Me.Height) \ 2
End Sub

Sub Form_Unload (Cancel As Integer)
'-------------------------------------------------------
' When unloading the form, first make sure that the
' Random loop has terminated.  Just for fun, roll
' the scroller back down to zero before terminating
' the program.
'-------------------------------------------------------
Dim i As Integer

    StopRandom = False
    DoEvents
    For i = hscrGaugeValue.Value To 0 Step -5
        hscrGaugeValue.Value = i
    Next
End Sub

Sub hscrGaugeValue_Change ()
'-------------------------------------------------------
' Set the values of all the gauges to the new value
' of the scroller.
'-------------------------------------------------------
    Gauge1.Value = hscrGaugeValue.Value
```

```
    Gauge2.Value = hscrGaugeValue.Value
    Gauge3.Value = hscrGaugeValue.Value
    Gauge4.Value = hscrGaugeValue.Value

    lblValue.Caption = Format$(hscrGaugeValue.Value)
    lblValue.Refresh
End Sub
```

## Tips and Comments

If you use a little imagination in your choice of a bitmap, this control can provide some truly stunning effects. The best way to approach this control is to first design the background bitmap. After placing the control on the form, set the *Picture* property to display the bitmap you've designed. Set the *AutoSize* property to *True* so that the control is automatically set to the size of your bitmap.

Next, set the *Min* and *Max* properties of the gauge, and temporarily set the *Value* property to the same value as *Max*. For horizontal and vertical bar gauges this allows you to more easily set the *Inner* properties. Finally, adjust *InnerLeft, InnerRight, InnerTop,* and *InnerBottom* so that the bar or needle appears correctly over the bitmap. You may need to experiment to get a perfect fit.

##  iList (ILIST.VBX)

| USAGE: | Extended List Box |
|---|---|
| MANUFACTURER: | Ian Taylor (Freeware) |
| COST: | N/A |

The iList control serves as an extended replacement to the standard Visual Basic list box control, providing functions for quickly handling multiple item selections, and for searching for an item in a list.

## Syntax

In most respects, the iList control acts much like a standard Visual Basic list box. The most immediately obvious difference is that this control *always* allows selection of multiple items. (The standard list box uses the *MultiSelect* property to determine what type of multiple selection, if any, is provided.) The iList control uses either the left mouse button or the keyboard spacebar to select list items. This behavior is the same as that of the standard list box when *MultiSelect* is set to Simple Multiple Selection (a value of 1). The nonstandard properties of the iList control are listed in Table 1-15.

**Table 1-15** Nonstandard properties of the iList control

| FindItem | FoundItem | ItemData |
|---|---|---|
| ListSelCount | Selected | TopIndex |

The iList control provides functions for quickly retrieving and setting the indexes of selected items. These are not set by control methods, but by calls to functions within the control's VBX file. The two functions *GetSelected()* and *SetSelected()* must be declared in your Visual Basic program:

```
Declare Function GetSelected Lib "ILIST.VBX" (Ctrl As Control, ByVal ArrSize As Integer,
TargetArray As Integer) As Integer

Declare Function SetSelected Lib "ILIST.VBX" (Ctrl As Control, ByVal ArrSize As Integer,
TargetArray As Integer) As Integer
```

You pass both of these functions an array of integers. This array contains the indexes of the list items that have been selected or will be selected.

*GetSelected()* is passed three parameters. The first is the iList control that is being examined. The second parameter is an integer indicating the size (number of elements) of the array. You can determine this value by using the *SelCount* property of the iList control. The array, or actually the first element of the array, is passed as the last parameter. On successful completion, *GetSelected()* returns the indexes of all selected elements in the iList control. This function returns a value of *True* if sucessful, or *False* otherwise.

*SetSelected()* works in a similar manner. You set an array of integers with the values of list box items to be selected. Pass the iList control and the number of array elements as the first two parameters. As in *GetSelected()*, the last parameter is the first element of the array.

Several properties of the iList control differ from the standard list box. Where the standard list box uses the *Clear* method to remove all items from a list, the iList control uses the *Reset* property. This property, when set to any value, removes all items from the list box.

The *TopIndex* property is useful for finding and setting the first visible item at the top of a list box. When assigned a value, *TopIndex* causes the list box to be scrolled to that index. For example, the statement

```
iList1.TopIndex = 3
```

causes the iList control to scroll down so that its fourth element is positioned at the top of the list box.

As mentioned, the *SelCount* property returns the number of items currently selected. A value of 0 in *SelCount* indicates that no items are selected.

The iList control provides a simple method for searching the items in the list box. When the property *FindItem* is set to a string value, the iList control searches for the first matching item in the list. Partial matches are considered hits, so if *FindItem* were assigned "all", it would match "allow", but not "aloud". The index of the matched list item is placed in the *FoundItem* property. If no matches are found, *FoundItem* is assigned a value of -1.

# Example

This example program, shown in Figure 1-6, illustrates the built-in function for retrieving multiple list selections, as well as the intrinsic search capabilities of the iList control.

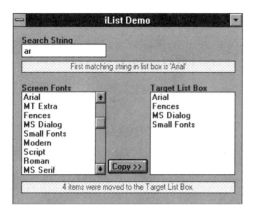

**Figure 1-6** The iList demo program

Two iList controls have been placed on the form. The first list is filled with the names of available screen fonts when the form is loaded. The second list is a target list box into which selected items from the font list can be copied. To test this feature, select one or more items from the font list, and then press the Copy button. The program uses the *GetSelected()* function to copy all the selected items to the Target list box. Event routine *btnCopyItems_Click* first checks whether any items have been selected. If they have, the *SelectArr* array is redimensioned to hold the number of indexes currently selected, and the *GetSelected()* function is called. If the function is successful, the current contents of the target list box (iList2) are cleared, and all the newly selected items are copied. Lastly, we redimension the *SelectArr* array to zero to free up the memory used by it.

This example also demonstrates the search capabilities of iList. When text is typed into the edit control in the upper-left corner of the form, the edit control's *Change* event is triggered, allowing us to search the list box on each keystroke. In the *Change* event, we first ensure that any selected items are deselected, and then search for the new string using the *FindItem* property. If a match is found (based on the value of the *FoundItem* property), that list item is scrolled into view using the *TopIndex* property and the item is selected.

## Steps

1. Create a new form called ILIST.MAK. Add the iList control, ILIST.VBX, to the project. Create a new form with the objects and properties described in Table 1-16. Save this form as ILIST.FRM.

**Table 1-16** Objects and properties of ILIST.FRM

| OBJECT | PROPERTY | SETTING |
|--------|----------|---------|
| Form | FormName | frmIList |
| | BackColor | &H00C0C0C0& |
| | BorderStyle | 1 'Fixed Single |
| | Caption | "iList Demo" |

*(continued on next page)*

| OBJECT | PROPERTY | SETTING |
|---|---|---|
| *(continued from previous page)* | | |
| | MaxButton | 0 'False |
| Label | Name | Label2 |
| | BackStyle | 0 'Transparent |
| | Caption | "Screen Fonts" |
| | ForeColor | &H00FF0000& |
| Label | Name | Label3 |
| | BackStyle | 0 'Transparent |
| | Caption | "Target List Box" |
| | ForeColor | &H00FF0000& |
| Label | Name | lblFontsCopied |
| | Alignment | 2 'Center |
| | BackColor | &H0080FFFF& |
| | BorderStyle | 1 'Fixed Single |
| | Caption | "Select several screen fonts, then press the Copy button." |
| | FontBold | 0 'False |
| | ForeColor | &H000000FF& |
| Label | Name | lblSearchMatch |
| | Alignment | 2 'Center |
| | BackColor | &H0080FFFF& |
| | BorderStyle | 1 'Fixed Single |
| | FontBold | 0 'False |
| | ForeColor | &H000000FF& |
| iList | Name | iList1 |
| | Caption | "iList1" |
| | ForeColor | &H00000080& |
| iList | Name | iList2 |
| | Caption | "iList2" |
| | ForeColor | &H00000080& |
| CommandButton | Name | btnCopyItems |
| | Caption | "&Copy >>" |
| TextBox | Name | txtSearchStr |

2. After creating ILIST.FRM, add the following code to the form's declarations section.

```
Option Explicit

Dim SelectArr() As Integer
Dim DefCopyLabel As String

Declare Function GetSelected Lib "ILIST.VBX" (Ctrl As Control, ByVal ArrSize As Integer,
TargetArray As Integer) As Integer
```

3. Next, add the following subroutines to ILIST.FRM. The *btnCopyItems_Click* event subroutine shows how to use the *GetSelected()* function to extract selected items from an iList control.

```
Sub btnCopyItems_Click ()
'----------------------------------------------------
' Use the GetSelected() function to quickly copy
' selected items from one iList box to another.
'----------------------------------------------------
Dim OK As Integer
Dim i As Integer
Dim NumSelected As Integer

    If iList1.SelCount > 0 Then
        ReDim SelectArr(iList1.SelCount)
        NumSelected = iList1.SelCount
        OK = GetSelected(iList1, NumSelected, SelectArr(0))
        If OK Then
            iList2.Reset = True
            For i = NumSelected - 1 To 0 Step -1
                iList2.AddItem iList1.List(SelectArr(i)), 0
                iList1.Selected(SelectArr(i)) = False
            Next
            lblFontsCopied.Caption = Format$(NumSelected) & " items were moved to the Target
List Box."
        End If
        ReDim SelectArr(0) 'release the array memory
    End If
End Sub

Sub Form_Load ()
'----------------------------------------------------
' Center the form on the screen.
'----------------------------------------------------
Dim i As Integer

    Me.Move (Screen.Width - Me.Width) \ 2, (Screen.Height - Me.Height) \ 2

    ' Initialize the first list box with the names of screen fonts.
    For i = 0 To Screen.FontCount - 1
        iList1.AddItem Screen.Fonts(i), 0
    Next
    DefCopyLabel = lblFontsCopied.Caption
End Sub

Sub iList1_GotFocus ()
'----------------------------------------------------
' Reset the default caption when the list box gets
' the focus.
'----------------------------------------------------
    If lblFontsCopied.Caption  DefCopyLabel Then
        lblFontsCopied.Caption = DefCopyLabel
    End If
End Sub

Sub txtSearchStr_Change ()
'----------------------------------------------------
' Search the list box for a string that matches
' what is currently in the edit control.
'----------------------------------------------------
```

*(continued on next page)*

*(continued from previous page)*

```
Dim i As Integer

    ' Deselect anything currently selected.
    For i = 0 To iList1.ListCount - 1
        If iList1.Selected(i) Then
            iList1.Selected(i) = False
        End If
    Next
    ' Try to find a match to what's in the edit field.
    iList1.FindItem = txtSearchStr.Text
    ' If we've found something, move down to it and
    ' select it.
    If iList1.FoundItem >= 0 Then
        iList1.TopIndex = iList1.FoundItem
        lblSearchMatch.Caption = "First matching string in list box is '" & ⇒
iList1.List(iList1.FoundItem) & "'"
        If Not iList1.Selected(iList1.FoundItem) Then
            iList1.Selected(iList1.FoundItem) = True
        End If
    Else
        lblSearchMatch.Caption = "No match was found for the search string."
    End If
End Sub
```

## Tips and Comments

Unlike the standard list box, iList does not provide a *Sorted* property, so you must perform any sorting of list items before placing them in the control. This can easily be accomplished by first placing the items in a standard list box whose visible property has been set to false. Visual Basic will automatically sort them, and you can then move them one by one into the iList list. This technique is very useful for quick and easy sorts on lists of reasonable length. This control provides a faster and easier method for selecting multiple items, and provides a simple and quick built-in mechanism for list box searching.

 # Masked Edit (MSMASKED.VBX)

| USAGE: | Formatted and Validated Data Entry |
|---|---|
| MANUFACTURER: | Microsoft |
| COST: | Provided with Visual Basic 3.0 Professional Edition |

The Masked Edit control is a text entry control with built-in formatting and validation features. This control can automatically embed formatting characters into a text string as it is entered by the user.

## Syntax

The Masked Edit control is essentially a superset of the standard text entry control. It provides much greater control over what text can be entered and how it is displayed. Table 1-17 lists the Masked Edit control's nonstandard properties and event.

**Table 1-17** Nonstandard properties and event of the Masked Edit control

**PROPERTIES**

| | | |
|---|---|---|
| AutoTab | ClipMode | ClipText |
| FontUnderline | Format | FormattedText |
| Mask | MaxLength | SelText |
| Text | | |

**EVENT**

ValidationError

To better understand this control, it's helpful to consider two aspects of text entry separately. First, there is the question of how we allow text to be accepted into the control. Second, we consider how the data is displayed after text entry is complete.

When looking at the process of text entry, the first property to examine is the *Mask*. This property defines the input mask that the control uses to determine what characters can be typed into the control, and at what positions they can be typed. The *Mask* property can be set at either design time or run time. The *Mask* is a string that can contain special purpose placeholder characters. For example,

```
MaskedEdit1.Mask = "?###-XYZ"
```

defines a mask that will allow any letter "A" through "Z" in the first position ("?" is a placeholder for any letter, upper or lowercase), any digit "0" through "9" in the second through fourth position ("#" is a placeholder for any digit), followed by the character string "-XYZ". Any character that is not a special placeholder is displayed as itself. When a Masked Edit field with this mask defined has the focus, the input line looks like this:

```
____-XYZ
```

The control displays an underscore character at any position where data can legally be entered. In this example, the last four characters, "-XYZ", cannot be overtyped.

Table 1-18 lists the special validation characters recognized by *Mask*.

**Table 1-18** Special characters used in the Mask property

| CHARACTER | MEANING |
|---|---|
| # | Digit placeholder |
| . | Decimal placeholder |
| , | Thousands separator |
| : | Time separator |
| / | Date separator |
| \ | Literal character indicator; tells the control not to treat the following character as a special mask character |
| & | Character placeholder |
| A | Alphanumeric placeholder |
| ? | Letter placeholder |

The Masked Edit control validates the input data for every keystroke entered by the user. Whenever a typed character doesn't match the input mask, the *ValidationError* event is triggered. This event is passed the entire invalid string and an integer that indicates at what position in the string the invalid characters begin.

The *PromptChar* property defines what character indicates that a position in the control accepts user input. By default, the underscore character is used, but you can set this value to any other character at design time or run time. If no mask is specified, no prompt character is displayed, even if one has been set.

Related to *PromptChar* is the *PromptInclude* property, a Boolean value that determines whether any mask characters (including literals) are included in the *Text* property. For example, if a mask of "##-##-##" has been defined and the user types the date "09-12-94" into the Masked Edit field, the value of the *Text* property differs depending on the value of the *PromptInclude* property. By default, *PromptInclude* is *True*, and the text field will contain the string "09-12-94"; if *PromptInclude* is set to *False, Text* will be set to "091294".

The *Format* property determines how the data appears in the control when the control no longer has the input focus. This property uses the same formatting conventions as the Visual Basic *Format$* function, but does not support named formats. If the input data can be properly formatted using this property, the formatted value is displayed in the Masked Edit control when this control loses the input focus. This formatted text can be inspected within the program using the *FormattedText* property.

You can use the *AutoTab* property to speed up the data entry process on forms with multiple data entry fields. When this property is set to *True*, the input focus is automatically shifted to the next control in tab order when the current Masked Edit field has been filled with valid data.

# Example

The example program (Figure 1-7) allows you to interactively set the *Mask, Format, PromptChar,* and *PromptInclude* properties for a Masked Edit control and see the results of these changes.

For the program, we've set the input mask to "##/##/##", which would be a common input mask for a date entry field. We have also set the *Format* property to "dddddd", which is defined as a long date format. To try out this format, just type a valid date into the Masked Edit field. Notice that for this mask, the slash characters are skipped automatically. Any literal characters in a mask are skipped in this way. Also note that entering any nondigit character into the field causes a validation error. These errors are displayed in the error field at the bottom of the form.

Try changing the *Mask, Format,* and *Prompt* properties, and watch how these changes affect the *Text* and *FormattedText* properties.

Since the *Mask* and *Format* properties are independent of one another, it is quite possible to define an input mask that cannot be formatted properly for output. This doesn't cause any error; the formatting is simply not used when displaying the value of the field.

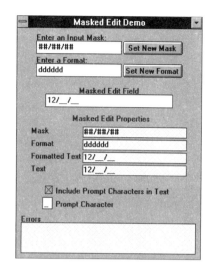

**Figure 1-7** The Masked Edit program

## Steps

1. Create a new project called MASKED.MAK. Add the Masked Edit control, MSMASKED.VBX, to the project. Create a new form with the objects and properties described in Table 1-19. Save this form as MASKED.FRM.

**Table 1-19** Objects and properties of MASKED.FRM

| OBJECT | PROPERTY | SETTING |
|--------|----------|---------|
| Form | FormName | frmMaskEdit |
| | BackColor | &H00C0C0C0& |
| | BorderStyle | 1 'Fixed Single |
| | Caption | "Masked Edit Demo" |
| | MaxButton | 0 'False |
| Label | Name | Label2 |
| | Alignment | 2 'Center |
| | BackStyle | 0 'Transparent |
| | Caption | "Masked Edit Field" |
| | ForeColor | &H00FF0000& |
| Label | Name | Label3 |
| | BackStyle | 0 'Transparent |
| | Caption | "Mask" |
| | ForeColor | &H00FF0000& |
| Label | Name | Label4 |
| | BackStyle | 0 'Transparent |
| | Caption | "Format" |

*(continued on next page)*

| OBJECT | PROPERTY | SETTING |
|---|---|---|
| *(continued from previous page)* | | |
| | ForeColor | &H00FF0000& |
| Label | Name | Label5 |
| | BackStyle | 0 'Transparent |
| | Caption | "Formatted Text" |
| | ForeColor | &H00FF0000& |
| Label | Name | lblFormat |
| | BackColor | &H00E0FFFF& |
| | BorderStyle | 1 'Fixed Single |
| Label | Name | lblFormattedText |
| | BackColor | &H00E0FFFF& |
| | BorderStyle | 1 'Fixed Single |
| Label | Name | lblCurrentMask |
| | BackColor | &H00E0FFFF& |
| | BorderStyle | 1 'Fixed Single |
| Label | Name | lblError |
| | BackColor | &H00E0FFFF& |
| | BorderStyle | 1 'Fixed Single |
| | FontBold | 0 'False |
| | ForeColor | &H00000080& |
| Label | Name | Label6 |
| | BackStyle | 0 'Transparent |
| | Caption | "Errors" |
| | ForeColor | &H00FF0000& |
| Label | Name | Label7 |
| | BackStyle | 0 'Transparent |
| | Caption | "Text" |
| | ForeColor | &H00FF0000& |
| Label | Name | lblText |
| | BackColor | &H00E0FFFF& |
| | BorderStyle | 1 'Fixed Single |
| Label | Name | Label8 |
| | BackStyle | 0 'Transparent |
| | Caption | "Enter a Format:" |
| | ForeColor | &H00FF0000& |
| Label | Name | Label9 |
| | Alignment | 2 'Center |
| | BackStyle | 0 'Transparent |
| | Caption | "Masked Edit Properties" |
| | ForeColor | &H00000080& |

| OBJECT | PROPERTY | SETTING |
|--------|----------|---------|
| Label | Name | Label10 |
|  | BackStyle | 0 'Transparent |
|  | Caption | "Prompt Character" |
|  | ForeColor | &H00FF0000& |
| MaskEdBox | Name | MaskedEdit1 |
|  | PromptChar | "_" |
| TextBox | Name | txtNewMask |
|  | MaxLength | 20 |
| CommandButton | Name | btnNewMask |
|  | Caption | "Set New Mask" |
| TextBox | Name | txtNewFormat |
|  | MaxLength | 20 |
| CommandButton | Name | btnNewFormat |
|  | Caption | "Set New Format" |
| CheckBox | Name | chkPromptInclude |
|  | BackColor | &H00C0C0C0& |
|  | Caption | "Include Prompt Characters in Text" |
|  | ForeColor | &H00FF0000& |
|  | Value | 1 'Checked |
| TextBox | Name | txtPromptChar |
|  | MaxLength | 1 |
|  | Text | "_" |

2. After creating the form, add the following code to the declarations section:

```
Option Explicit
'----------------------------------------------------
' Variables global to this form
'----------------------------------------------------

Dim StopRandom As Integer
```

3. Next, add the following subroutines to MASKED.FRM. This code handles changing the mask and text values, as well as displaying any validation error messages that occur.

```
Sub btnNewFormat_Click ()
'----------------------------------------------------
' Set the new Masked Edit format.
'----------------------------------------------------
    MaskedEdit1.Format = txtNewFormat.Text
    UpdateLabels
End Sub

Sub btnNewMask_Click ()
'----------------------------------------------------
' Set the new Masked Edit input mask.
'----------------------------------------------------
```

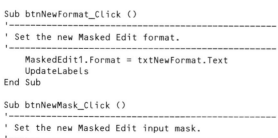

(continued on next page)

*(continued from previous page)*

```vb
      MaskedEdit1.Mask = txtNewMask.Text
      UpdateLabels
End Sub

Sub chkPromptInclude_Click ()
'----------------------------------------------------
' Set the Masked Edit control's PromptInclude
' property.
'----------------------------------------------------
    If chkPromptInclude.Value = 1 Then
        MaskedEdit1.PromptInclude = True
    Else
        MaskedEdit1.PromptInclude = False
    End If
    UpdateLabels
End Sub

Sub Form_Load ()
'----------------------------------------------------
' Center the form on the screen, and set the initial
' values for the Masked Edit field's Mask and Format
' properties.
'----------------------------------------------------

    Me.Move (Screen.Width - Me.Width) \ 2, (Screen.Height - Me.Height) \ 2

    txtNewMask.Text = "##/##/##"
    txtNewFormat = "dddddd"

    btnNewMask.Value = 1
    btnNewFormat.Value = 1
End Sub

Sub MaskedEdit1_GotFocus ()
'----------------------------------------------------
' Update labels when Masked Edit control gets focus.
'----------------------------------------------------
    UpdateLabels
End Sub

Sub MaskedEdit1_KeyDown (KeyCode As Integer, Shift As Integer)
'----------------------------------------------------
' Update labels and reset the Error label whenever
' a key is down.
'----------------------------------------------------
    UpdateLabels
    lblError.Caption = ""
End Sub

Sub MaskedEdit1_KeyPress (KeyAscii As Integer)
'----------------------------------------------------
' Update labels with current Masked Edit values
' whenever a key is pressed.
'----------------------------------------------------
    UpdateLabels
End Sub

Sub MaskedEdit1_LostFocus ()
```

```
'---------------------------------------------------------
' Update all labels when leaving the Masked Edit
' control.
'---------------------------------------------------------
    UpdateLabels
End Sub

Sub MaskedEdit1_ValidationError (InvalidText As String, StartPosition As Integer)
'---------------------------------------------------------
' Tell the user whenever a validation error is
' triggered.
'---------------------------------------------------------
    lblError.Caption = "The text entered, '" & InvalidText & "', is invalid starting at
position " & Format$(StartPosition) & "."
End Sub

Sub txtPromptChar_Change ()
'---------------------------------------------------------
' Change the Masked Edit control's Prompt Character.
'---------------------------------------------------------

    If Len(txtPromptChar) = 1 Then
        MaskedEdit1.PromptChar = txtPromptChar.Text
        UpdateLabels
    End If
End Sub

Sub UpdateLabels ()
'---------------------------------------------------------
' Update the property labels with the current state
' of the Masked Edit control.
'---------------------------------------------------------
    lblCurrentMask.Caption = MaskedEdit1.Mask
    lblFormat.Caption = MaskedEdit1.Format
    lblFormattedText.Caption = MaskedEdit1.FormattedText
    lblText.Caption = MaskedEdit1.Text
End Sub
```

## Tips and Comments

Because the Masked Edit control doesn't truly understand data values such as dates, what was entered into the control still may be not valid. In our example program, using the initial mask of "##/##/##", it is possible to enter "valid" dates such as "99/99/99" or "01/00/94". So even when you use this control, some additional data validation will almost certainly be necessary.

# Microsoft Outline (MSOUTLIN.VBX)

| USAGE: | Display of Tree-Structured Data |
|---|---|
| MANUFACTURER: | Microsoft |
| COST: | Provided with Visual Basic 3.0 Professional Edition |

The MS Outline control provides a flexible mechanism for displaying hierarchical or tree-structured data. Data is displayed in a list box that allows subordinate branches to be expanded and contracted through either user input or program control.

# Syntax

The closest relative to the MS Outline control is the standard list box, and in fact they share some common properties such as *List, ListIndex,* and *ListIndex.* The processing of the Outline control can be considerably more complex, however, and several properties, events, and methods, listed in Table 1-20, are unique to it.

**Table 1-20** Nonstandard properties and events of the MS Outline control

| PROPERTIES | | |
|---|---|---|
| Expand | FullPath | HasSubItems |
| Indent | IsItemVisible | List |
| PathSeparator | PictureClosed | PictureLeaf |
| PictureMinus | PictureOpen | PicturePlus |
| PictureType | Style | TopIndex |
| **EVENTS** | | |
| Collapse | Expand | PictureClick |
| **METHODS** | | |
| AddItem | RemoveItem | |

The MS Outline control differs from a conventional list box because items not only have an index value, which specifies their location relative to the top of the list, but also have an indentation level, which indicates their hierarchical relationship to other items in the list. This indentation is specified by the *Indent(index)* property. The indentation level must never increase by more than one between parent and child items, otherwise a run time error (32001) occurs.

To illustrate this indentation, consider the following code fragment, which adds three items to an empty Outline control:

```
Outline1.Indent(1) = 1
Outline1.AddItem "First", 1
Outline1.AddItem "Second", 2
Outline1.AddItem "Third", 3
```

The first line sets the indentation level for the first item to one. If this line were omitted, the indentation level would have been set to zero by default—with the undesirable effect of making the items invisible. The second and third items will also be set to an indentation level of one by default. At this point, the Outline control will appear much the same as that of a standard list box. However, if we execute this line of code:

```
Outline1.Indent(3) = 2
```

the third item of the list is now nested one level deeper than its predecessor. Item 2 is now the parent of item 3, and item 3 does not initially appear when the list is displayed. If you click on item 2, item 3 will appear indented below it.

Item 3 is now called a *subordinate item* or *subitem*. Within a program, you can use the *HasSubItems(index)* property to determine whether a particular list item has any subordinate items. This property returns an integer Boolean value.

The *Style* property determines the appearance of the Outline control, and what pictures, if any, are used within the control. A list of possible styles is provided in Table 1-21.

**Table 1-21** Values of the Style property

| VALUE | MEANING |
| --- | --- |
| 0 | Only text is displayed. |
| 1 | Both text and picture are displayed. |
| 2 | Plus/minus and text are displayed (default). |
| 3 | Plus/minus, picture, and text are displayed. |
| 4 | Tree lines and text are displayed. |
| 5 | Tree lines, picture, and text are displayed. |

The pictures that can be displayed to the left of text items are determined by five *Picture* properties. The first three—*PictureClosed, PictureOpen, and PictureLeaf*—determine what bitmap is displayed when styles 1, 3, or 5 are used. The other two properties—*PicturePlus and PictureMinus*—determine what picture is used when styles 2 or 3 are chosen. These pictures can be either BMP or ICO format bitmaps. Unlike many controls that provide picture properties, the Outline control has default bitmaps that are used if none are specified at design time or run time.

The *FullPath(index)* property is useful for quickly returning a string containing the entire path of an item. When you use the Outline control to display data such as file directories, you can easily employ this property to derive a fully qualified file or directory name. Given an item index, *FullPath* returns a string concatenating the indexed item with all of its parent items. Individual items in the string are separated by a special character determined by the *PathSeparator* property. By default, *PathSeparator* is set to the backslash character ("\"), but it can be set to any character at design time or run time.

The Outline control handles three events. The *Expand* event is triggered whenever an item is expanded, making its subordinate items visible. This event receives one parameter, the index of the item being expanded. The complement to this event is *Collapse,* which is triggered whenever an item's subordinates are made invisible. Like *Expand, Collapse* receives a parameter indicating the index of the item being collapsed. Finally, the *PictureClick* event is triggered whenever the picture on an item is clicked, and it also receives as a parameter the index of the item affected.

The Outline control uses the familiar *AddItem* and *RemoveItem* methods to add and remove outline items. *AddItem* works much like its conventional list box counterpart. However, the *RemoveItem* method removes not only the item specified in its index parameter, but any subordinate items as well. Although you can't do this with the standard list box, you can add items to the Outline control by specifying a new index number in the *List* property. For example, the statement

```
Outline1.List (5) = "This is a new entry"
```

adds the new item if *Outline1.List(5)* doesn't already exist.

# Example

This example, shown in Figure 1-8, displays a list of the planets in the solar system, with additional information available by expanding items in the outline list.

You can expand or contract items in the outline by clicking on the picture that appears to the left of the text. The Expand All and Collapse All buttons demonstrate the use of the *Expand(index)* property, which you can use to expand or collapse items under program control.

The label at the bottom of the form displays the value in the *FullPath* property for the currently selected item. Notice that the individual items displayed in this label are separated by a colon; this character was set by changing the value of the *PathSeparator* property.

## Steps

1. Create a new project called OUTLINE.MAK. Add the MS Outline control, MSOUTLIN.VBX, to the project. Create a new form with the objects and properties described in Table 1-22. Save this form as OUTLINE.FRM. The picture bitmaps used by the Outline control can be created with a bitmap editor such as Windows PaintBrush, and set in the Visual Basic Properties window at design time.

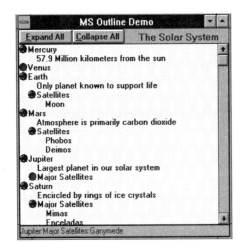

**Figure 1-8** The Outline control demo program

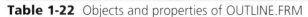
**Table 1-22** Objects and properties of OUTLINE.FRM

| OBJECT | PROPERTY | SETTING |
|---|---|---|
| Form | FormName | frmOutline |
| | BackColor | &H00C0C0C0& |
| | Caption | "MS Outline Demo" |
| Label | Name | Label1 |
| | Alignment | 2 'Center |
| | BackStyle | 0 'Transparent |
| | Caption | "The Solar System" |
| | FontSize | 9.75 |
| | ForeColor | &H00FF0000& |
| Outline | Name | Outline1 |
| | BackColor | &H00E0FFFF& |
| | PathSeparator | ":" |
| | PictureClosed | (set at design time in Properties window) |
| | PictureLeaf | (set at design time in Properties window) |
| | PictureMinus | (set at design time in Properties window) |
| | PictureOpen | (set at design time in Properties window) |
| | PicturePlus | (set at design time in Properties window) |
| | Style | 2 'Plus/Minus and Text |
| CommandButton | Name | btnExpand |
| | Caption | "&Expand All" |
| CommandButton | Name | btnCollapse |
| | Caption | "&Collapse All" |

2. This program reads the data displayed in the Outline control from a text file called OUTLINE.DAT. Create this file using a standard text editor (such as Notepad) that can embed tab characters into a text file. In the text file, indicate the desired level of indentation by the number of tab characters found at the beginning of a line. The function *LoadOutline* fills an Outline control based on the contents of a text file formatted in this way. The file listing that follows can be used as a guide. Make sure you create the indentations at the beginning of subordinate lines by using the Tab key.

```
Mercury
        57.9 Million kilometers from the sun
Venus
        Covered by a dense layer of gaseous sulfuric acid
Earth
        Only planet known to support life
        Satellites
                Moon
Mars
        Atmosphere is primarily carbon dioxide
        Satellites
```

*(continued on next page)*

*(continued from previous page)*

```
                Phobos
                Deimos
Jupiter
        Largest planet in our solar system
        Major Satellites
                Callisto
                Ganymede
                Europa
                Io
Saturn
        Encircled by rings of ice crystals
        Major Satellites
                Mimas
                Enceladas
                Tethys
                Dion
                Rhea
                Iapetus
Uranus
        Discovered on March 13, 1781 by Sir William Herschel
        Major Satellites
                Titania
                Oberon
                Ariel
                Umbriel
                Miranda
Neptune
        First planet discovered from calculations based on movement of other planets
        Major Satellites
                Triton
                Nereid
Pluto
        Discovered in 1930 by Clyde Tombaugh
```

3. Add the following code to the declarations section of form OUTLINE.FRM, created in step 1.

```
Option Explicit
'----------------------------------------------------
' Declare constants used in this form.
'----------------------------------------------------


Const MB_ICONSTOP = 10
```

4. Next, add the following subroutines and functions to OUTLINE.FRM.

```
Sub btnCollapse_Click ()
'----------------------------------------------------
' Traverse the entire outline list, collapsing any
' open branches.
'----------------------------------------------------
Dim i As Integer

    For i = 0 To Outline1.ListCount - 1
            Outline1.Expand(i) = False
    Next
End Sub
```

```
Sub btnExpand_Click ()
'----------------------------------------------------
' Traverse the entire outline list, expanding any
' closed branches.
'----------------------------------------------------
Dim i As Integer

    For i = 0 To Outline1.ListCount - 1
        Outline1.Expand(i) = True
    Next
End Sub

Sub Form_Load ()
'----------------------------------------------------
' Center the form on the screen, and load outline
' data from a text file.
'----------------------------------------------------
Dim idx As Integer
Dim success As Integer

    Me.Move (Screen.Width - Me.Width) \ 2, (Screen.Height - Me.Height) \ 2

    success = LoadOutline(Outline1, App.Path & "\OUTLINE.DAT")
    If Not success Then
      MsgBox "Unable to load outline data from text file.", MB_ICONSTOP, "Error"
      End
    End If
End Sub

Sub Form_Resize ()
'----------------------------------------------------
' Size the outline and label controls to fit the
' current size of the form.
'----------------------------------------------------

    Outline1.Move 0, btnExpand.Height, Me.ScaleWidth, Me.ScaleHeight - btnExpand.Height -
lblFullPath.Height
    lblFullPath.Move 0, btnExpand.Height + Outline1.Height, Me.ScaleWidth, lblFullPath.Height
End Sub

Function LoadOutline (OutCntl As Outline, AFile As String) As Integer
'----------------------------------------------------
' This function will load an Outline control based
' on the contents of a text file.  The text file
' contains one outline entry per line, with the
' indentation level determined by the number of
' leading tab characters.
'----------------------------------------------------
Dim Fnum As Integer
Dim ALine As String
Dim ATAB As String
Dim Indent As Integer
Dim index As Integer

    ATAB = Chr$(9)

    LoadOutline = False
    On Error GoTo LoadOutline_Error
    Fnum = FreeFile
    Open AFile For Input As Fnum
```

*(continued on next page)*

*(continued from previous page)*

```
    index = 0
    Do While Not EOF(Fnum)
        Line Input #Fnum, ALine
        Indent = 1
        Do While (Indent <= Len(ALine)) And (Mid$(ALine, Indent, 1) = ATAB)
            Indent = Indent + 1
        Loop
        ALine = Mid$(ALine, Indent)
        index = index + 1
        ' Add a new outline item
        OutCntl.AddItem ALine, index
        ' Set the new items indentation level based
        ' on the number of tab characters.
        OutCntl.Indent(index) = Indent
    Loop
    Close Fnum
    LoadOutline = True
Exit Function

LoadOutline_Error:
    Exit Function
End Function

Sub Outline1_Click ()
'-------------------------------------------------
' Display the full path of the currently selected
' item.
'-------------------------------------------------

    lblFullPath.Caption = Outline1.FullPath(Outline1.ListIndex)
End Sub
```

## Tips and Comments

When dealing with this control, make sure to build and maintain the proper hierarchy. A good way to conceptualize this control is as a list box whose items are sometimes hidden. The index of an item always refers to its position relative to the top of the list, regardless of its indentation level; the fifth item in the list is always the fifth item in the list. Indentation, on the other hand, always refers to an item's relation to its predecessors. If item *n* is indented with a value of 3 and item *n-1* also has an indentation level of 3, these items are siblings; if *n-1* has a value of 2, it is item *n*'s parent.

# OxButton (OXBUTTON.VBX)

| USAGE: | Graphical Replacement for a Command Button |
|---|---|
| MANUFACTURER: | Opaque Software |
| COST: | $15 |

The OxButton control, a replacement for a standard Visual Basic command button, can display a bitmap, and display text with either an inset or raised 3D effect.  OxButton gives you complete control over the placement and orientation of both the picture and the text. This control also provides some unique features to help you design buttons. Several standard, built-in bitmaps let you quickly make use of custom buttons.

## Syntax

OxButton works much like a conventional command button. You select the button from the Visual Basic toolbox, placing and sizing it as you would any other button. However, if you click the right mouse button while the mouse pointer is over an OxButton, you'll notice an immediate difference: a floating pop-up menu appears next to the control. This menu gives you quick access to the Visual Basic Properties menu, and also lets you call up the *ControlWiz,* a little application with which you can visually design the appearance of text and graphics on your button. The ControlWiz is shown in Figure 1-9.

The ControlWiz is divided into four sections, each accessible by a tab: Styles, Bitmaps, Position, and Font. All of the properties that are set by the ControlWiz can also be set directly in the Visual Basic Properties window, but the ControlWiz saves you a great deal of time when you're initially designing a button.

OxButton comes with 16 built-in bitmaps that you can use to quickly add a picture to a button. Figure 1-9 shows the ControlWiz screen that displays these built-in pictures. If you use Borland Windows development tools, these bitmaps should be recognizable since they are based on the custom buttons that you can design with those products.

Another attribute these buttons share with the Borland buttons is the moving drop shadow that appears beneath each bitmap. This shadow is displayed automatically by the control; it is not part of the original bitmap picture. When the button is pressed, the original picture doesn't move, but its shadow shifts in sync with the depressed button. Table 1-23 lists properties that are unique to the OxButton control or that require special consideration.

**Figure 1-9** The OxButton ControlWiz

**Table 1-23** Special properties of the OxButton control

| (DesignNames) | (SetDefault) | (ControlWiz) |
|---|---|---|
| BackColor | Font3D | PictureDown |
| Pictures | PictureUp | PictureX |
| PictureY | ShadowColor | TextX |
| TextY | | |

Several of these properties let you specify and fine-tune the placement of the bitmap picture on the button. *PictureX* and *PictureY* provide the coordinates for the bitmap. If the value is a positive integer, it indicates the number of twips from the left or top of the button. If the number is negative, it indicates how far from the right or bottom to place the bitmap. This gives you an easy, flexible way to orient the picture from either side of the button. A value of 0 tells OxButton to center the picture on the button.

If you want to use one of the standard bitmaps that OxButton provides, just select a bitmap by specifying its number in the *Pictures* property.

To specify your own custom bitmap, set the *Pictures* property to 0 and set the *PictureUp* and *PictureDown* properties to the names of two bitmap files. Bitmaps can be in the BMP, ICO, WMF, or DIB format. *PictureUp* designates the picture that will be displayed when the button is at rest. *PictureDown* is a second bitmap that is displayed when the button is pressed. The *PictureDown* bitmap is optional; if none is specified, the *PictureUp* bitmap is used instead. You can, however, use the *PictureDown* bitmap to create some very interesting animation effects.

The drop shadow that appears beneath the bitmap is usually displayed as dark gray. You can change this color using the *ShadowColor* property. You can change the background color of the button itself using the *BackColor* property, which is not available for standard Visual Basic command buttons.

You specify the placement of text much as you specify the placement of the picture. Use the *TextX* and *TextY* properties to position the text within the button. As with the *PictureX* and *PictureY* properties, orientation from the edge of the button is determined by whether the property value is positive (top and left orientation), negative (bottom and right orientation), or 0 (centered).

By default the text has an inset 3D appearance. You can alter this look by changing the *Font3D* property. Table 1-24 lists the different settings for this property.

**Table 1-24** Values for the Font3D property

| VALUE | MEANING |
|---|---|
| 0 | No font is displayed (the text is invisible) |
| 1 | Normal (no 3D effect is used) |
| 2 | A raised 3D effect is used |
| 3 | An inset 3D effect is used |

In addition to the ControlWiz, the OxButton control provides some design time features to helps you work with these buttons. The *DesignNames* property, when set to *True,* displays the *Name* property of each control as a label inside the button during design time. This convenience makes it easy to keep track of buttons that have similar appearances, and is a good visual cue.

The *SetDefault* property, when double-clicked in the Visual Basic Properties window, sets the default property values to those of the currently selected OxButton. Any subsequent OxButton that is created will use those defaults. The properties whose defaults are set are listed in Table 1-25.

**Table 1-25** Properties affected by SetDefault

| | | |
|---|---|---|
| BackColor | PictureX | TextX |
| Font3D | PictureY | TextY |
| ForeColor | ShadowColor | Visible |

## Example

This example program in Figure 1-10 shows off some of the features of OxButton. Modify the first OxButton (Button 1) by changing its settings using the controls to its right. At run time, you can modify the placement of the picture and text, the color of the drop shadow, and the appearance of the text. This button uses the standard pictures accessible through the *Pictures* property. Click the button to cycle through all the standard pictures that are available.

The second OxButton (Button 2) shows the use of two custom bitmaps to create an animated effect of an exploding firecracker. Hold down the button to see the second bitmap. Just for fun, we play a little wave audio file to make a popping noise when this button is pressed. Also, we've changed the background color of this button to show that not all buttons have to be gray.

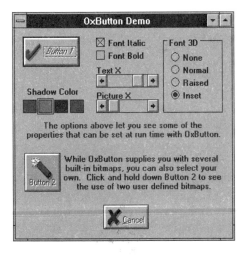

**Figure 1-10** The OxButton example program

## Steps

1. Create a new project called OXBTN.MAK. Create a new form with the objects and properties shown in Table 1-26. Save this form as OXBUTN.FRM.

**Table 1-26** OxButton main form's objects and properties

| OBJECT | PROPERTY | SETTING |
|--------|----------|---------|
| Label | Name | Label2 |
| | Alignment | 2 'Center |
| | BackStyle | 0 'Transparent |
| | Caption | "The options above let you see some of the properties that you can set at run time with OxButton." |
| | ForeColor | &H00000080& |
| Label | Name | Label3 |
| | Alignment | 2 'Center |
| | BackStyle | 0 'Transparent |
| | Caption | "While OxButton supplies you with several built-in bitmaps, you can also select your own. Click and hold down Button 2 to see the use of two user-defined bitmaps." |
| | ForeColor | &H00000080& |
| Label | Name | Label4 |
| | BackStyle | 0 'Transparent |
| | Caption | "Shadow Color" |
| Label | Name | Label5 |
| | BackStyle | 0 'Transparent |
| | Caption | "Text X" |
| Shape | Name | shpBorder |
| | Index | 0 |
| | Visible | 0 'False |
| Shape | Name | shpBorder |
| | Index | 1 |
| Shape | Name | shpBorder |
| | Index | 2 |
| | Visible | 0 'False |
| Shape | Name | shpBorder |
| | Index | 3 |
| | Visible | 0 'False |
| OXButton | Name | OXButton1 |

| OBJECT | PROPERTY | SETTING |
|---|---|---|
| | BackColor | &H00C0C0C0& |
| | Caption | "Button 1" |
| | Font3D | 3 'Inset |
| | FontBold | 0 'False |
| | FontItalic | -1 'True |
| | ForeColor | &H00000000& |
| | Pictures | 1 'Okay |
| | PictureX | 40 |
| | ShadowColor | &H00808080& |
| | TextX | -90 |
| OXButton | Name | OXButton2 |
| | BackColor | &H00FFFF00& |
| | Caption | "Button 2" |
| | Font3D | 3 'Inset |
| | FontBold | 0 'False |
| | ForeColor | &H00800000& |
| | PictureDown | (set at design time in Properties window) |
| | Pictures | 1 'Okay |
| | PictureUp | (set at design time in Properties window) |
| | PictureY | 70 |
| | ShadowColor | &H00808080& |
| | TextY | -70 |
| CheckBox | Name | chkItalics |
| | BackColor | &H00C0C0C0& |
| | Caption | "Font Italic" |
| | Value | 1 'Checked |
| CheckBox | Name | chkBold |
| | BackColor | &H00C0C0C0& |
| | Caption | "Font Bold" |
| Frame | Name | fraFont3D |
| | BackColor | &H00C0C0C0& |
| | Caption | "Font 3D" |
| HScrollBar | Name | hscrPictureX |
| | LargeChange | 10 |
| | Max | 1000 |
| | Min | 1 |
| | SmallChange | 5 |
| | Value | 40 |

*(continued on next page)*

| OBJECT | PROPERTY | SETTING |
|---|---|---|
| *(continued from previous page)* | | |
| PictureBox | Name | picColorBox |
| | BackColor | &H00008000& |
| | Index | 0 |
| PictureBox | Name | picColorBox |
| | BackColor | &H00808080& |
| | Index | 1 |
| PictureBox | Name | picColorBox |
| | BackColor | &H00FF0000& |
| | Index | 2 |
| PictureBox | Name | picColorBox |
| | BackColor | &H000000FF& |
| | Index | 3 |
| HScrollBar | Name | hscrTextX |
| | LargeChange | 10 |
| | Max | -1 |
| | Min | -600 |
| | SmallChange | 5 |
| | Value | -90 |
| OXButton | Name | oxbtnCancel |
| | BackColor | &H00C0C0C0& |
| | Caption | "&Cancel" |
| | Font3D | 3 'Inset |
| | FontBold | 0 'False |
| | ForeColor | &H00000000& |
| | Pictures | 2 'Cancel |
| | PictureX | 70 |
| | PictureY | -70 |
| | ShadowColor | &H00808080& |
| | TextX | -90 |
| | TextY | -70 |
| Form | FormName | frmOxButton |
| | BackColor | &H00C0C0C0& |
| | Caption | "OxButton Demo" |

2. Place the controls shown in Table 1-27 within the fraFont3D Frame control. Make sure to select the fraFont3D control before adding these controls.

**Table 1-27** Controls contained inside the fraFont3D control

| OBJECT | PROPERTY | SETTING |
|---|---|---|
| OptionButton | Name | optFont3D |
| | BackColor | &H00C0C0C0& |
| | Caption | "None" |
| | Index | 0 |
| OptionButton | Name | optFont3D |
| | BackColor | &H00C0C0C0& |
| | Caption | "Normal" |
| | Index | 1 |
| OptionButton | Name | optFont3D |
| | BackColor | &H00C0C0C0& |
| | Caption | "Raised" |
| | Index | 2 |
| OptionButton | Name | optFont3D |
| | BackColor | &H00C0C0C0& |
| | Caption | "Inset" |
| | Index | 3 |
| | Value | -1 'True |

3. Add the following code to the declarations section of the OXBTN1 form.

```
Option Explicit
'---------------------------------------------------
' Constants, variables and declarations used in
' the OxButton example program.
'---------------------------------------------------

' Functions and constants used to play sounds.
Declare Function sndPlaySound Lib "MMSystem" (lpsound As Any, ByVal flag As Integer) As Integer
Declare Function sndKillSound Lib "MMSystem" Alias "sndPlaySound" (ByVal lpszNull As Long,
ByVal flags)

Const SND_SYNC = &H0        ' Return when sound ends (the default)
Const SND_ASYNC = &H1       ' Return as soon as sound starts
Const SND_NODEFAULT = &H2   ' Don't play default sound if not found
Const SND_MEMORY = &H4      ' lpszSoundName -> memory image of file
Const SND_LOOP = &H8        ' Loop continuously; needs SND_ASYNC
Const SND_NOSTOP = &H10     ' Don't interrupt sound to play new one

' Global string used for by NoiseGet() and NoisePlay() to play .WAV files in memory
Dim SoundBuffer As String
```

4. Add the following subroutines to the OXBTN1 form. These subroutines change the properties of the OxButton controls, and process events from the OXButtons themselves.

```
Sub chkBold_Click ()
'---------------------------------------------------
' Set the FontBold property based on new check box value.
'---------------------------------------------------
```

*(continued on next page)*

*(continued from previous page)*

```
    OxButton1.FontBold = (chkBold = 1)
End Sub

Sub chkItalics_Click ()
'-------------------------------------------------------
' Set the FontItalic property based on new check box value.
'-------------------------------------------------------
    OxButton1.FontItalic = (chkItalics = 1)
End Sub

Sub Form_Load ()
'-------------------------------------------------------
' Center the form on the screen, and retrieve the
' "pop" sound into memory.
'-------------------------------------------------------
Dim result As Integer

    Me.Move (Screen.Width - Me.Width) \ 2, (Screen.Height - Me.Height) \ 2

    result = NoiseGet(App.Path & "\pop.wav")
End Sub

Sub hscrPictureX_Change ()
'-------------------------------------------------------
' Change the PictureX property based on the new
' value of the scroller.
'-------------------------------------------------------
    OxButton1.PictureX = hscrPictureX
End Sub

Sub hscrTextX_Change ()
'-------------------------------------------------------
' Change the value of the TextX property based on
' the new position of the scroller.
'-------------------------------------------------------
    OxButton1.TextX = hscrTextX
End Sub

Function NoiseGet (ByVal FileName) As Integer
'----------------------------------------------------------------
' Load a sound file into the global string variable
' SoundBuffer.  This must be called before NoisePlay.
'----------------------------------------------------------------
Dim buffer As String
Dim f As Integer

    On Error GoTo NoiseGet_Error

    buffer = Space$(1024)
    SoundBuffer = ""
    f = FreeFile
    Open FileName For Binary As f
    Do While Not EOF(f)
        Get #f, , buffer       ' Load in 1K chunks
        SoundBuffer = SoundBuffer & buffer
    Loop
    Close f
    SoundBuffer = Trim$(SoundBuffer)
```

```
Exit Function

NoiseGet_Error:
    NoiseGet = False
    SoundBuffer = ""
    Exit Function
End Function

Sub NoisePlay ()
'-------------------------------------------------------------
' Plays a sound previously loaded into memory with function
' NoiseGet().
'-------------------------------------------------------------
Dim r As Integer   ' asynchronously

    If SoundBuffer = "" Then Exit Sub
    r = sndPlaySound(ByVal SoundBuffer, SND_ASYNC Or SND_MEMORY)

End Sub

Sub optFont3D_Click (index As Integer)
'---------------------------------------------------
' Set the Font3D property according to the value
' of the index of the option button control array.
'---------------------------------------------------
    OxButton1.Font3D = index
End Sub

Sub oxbtnCancel_Click ()
'---------------------------------------------------
' Exit the program.
'---------------------------------------------------
    Unload Me
End Sub

Sub OXButton1_Click ()
'---------------------------------------------------
' Cycle through the available pictures.
'---------------------------------------------------
    OxButton1.Pictures = ((OxButton1.Pictures + 1) Mod 17)
End Sub

Sub OXButton2_MouseDown (Button As Integer, Shift As Integer, X As Single, Y As Single)
'---------------------------------------------------
' Play the previously loaded sound when the button
' is pushed.
'---------------------------------------------------
    NoisePlay
End Sub

Sub picColorBox_Click (index As Integer)
'---------------------------------------------------
' Change the ShadowColor property when the user
' clicks on one of the members of the Picture Box
' control array.
'---------------------------------------------------
Dim i As Integer

    For i = 0 To 3
        If i = index Then
```

*(continued on next page)*

*(continued from previous page)*

```
                shpBorder(i).Visible = True
        Else
                shpBorder(i).Visible = False
        End If
    Next
    OxButton1.ShadowColor = picColorBox(index).BackColor
End Sub
```

## Tips and Comments

You can use the OxButton control as a more flexible replacement for the 3D Command Button that comes with Visual Basic Professional Edition. It's also not a bad way to fool other programmers into thinking that your program was written with a Borland compiler, if you're inclined toward subterfuge.

# Prompt (PROMPT.VBX)

| USAGE: | Interactive Command-Line Processing |
|---|---|
| MANUFACTURER: | Andrew S. Dean |
| COST: | $15 |

The Prompt control is an extended text editing control with special features to allow command-line input. You can use this control to create a variety of teletype or dumb-terminal-style interfaces. It is useful for creating applications such as text adventure games and command interpreters.

## Syntax

The Prompt control is almost identical to the standard Visual Basic multiline text box, but several properties and an additional event, listed in Table 1-28, have been provided to facilitate command-line parsing and input.

**Table 1-28** Nonstandard properties and event for Prompt control

| PROPERTIES | | |
|---|---|---|
| AppendText | Command | NumWords |
| ScrollBars | Words | |
| EVENT | | |
| Enter | | |

The Prompt control's *Enter* event is the heart of this control. This event is triggered whenever the (ENTER) key is pressed. Within the *Enter* event, several properties can be inspected to determine what command was last typed. The most basic of these properties is *Command*, which returns as a string the last text line of the control. The *Command* property is read-only.

Since command lines often consist of multiple words (often referred to as tokens), the Prompt control provides properties for processing the individual tokens on a command line. The *Words* property array contains each token of the last command line as a separate string. The *NumWords* property determines how many tokens are in the *Words* array. The range of the *Words* array indexes is from 0 to *NumWords*-1.

By default, the tokens on the command line are delimited by one or more spaces. You can change the character that separates individual tokens on a command line by setting the *WordDelimiters* property. Consecutive delimiters are treated as a single separator.

Setting the *AppendText* property with a text string appends that string to the end of the current text in the Prompt control. For example,

```
Prompt1.AppendText = "ABCDEF"
```

would be equivalent to the statement

```
Prompt1.Text = Prompt1.Text & "ABCDEF"
```

If a new line is required when formatting text output, it must be included in the text using the carriage return/line feed characters (ASCII characters 13 and 10, respectively).

The *ScrollBars* property determines what type of scroll bars are displayed on the control. The possible values are shown in Table 1-29.

**Table 1-29** Values of the ScrollBars property

| VALUE | MEANING |
| --- | --- |
| 0 | No scroll bars |
| 1 | Horizontal scroll bars only |
| 2 | Vertical scroll bars only |
| 3 | Both horizontal and vertical scroll bars |

# Example

This example, shown in Figure 1-11, uses the Prompt control to implement a simple DOS command interpreter. Only a few commands are implemented, but the program is structured such that it can be easily expanded.

The Prompt control's *Enter* event, *Prompt1_Enter,* is little more than a *Select Case* statement that dispatches commands to separate functions for processing. Commands are identified as the first token (after the pseudo-DOS prompt) on the command line. Each of the command subroutines returns a text string that the *Enter* event appends to the Prompt control's text using the *AppendText* property. For example, the DIR command causes the *Command_dir()* function to be called. This function retrieves the current directory information, formats it, and stores it in a string that is passed back to the *Enter* event. The *Enter* event then displays the directory information by appending the text to the Prompt control.

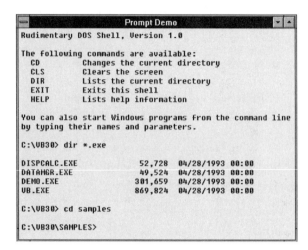

**Figure 1-11** The
Prompt demo program

The example program supports five internal commands: DIR, CD, CLS, HELP, and EXIT. In addition, the program considers anything not recognized as an internal command as a program command line, and attempts to run it through a call to the Windows *WinExec* API call. To test this out, try typing the name of a Windows program. For example, typing Notepad runs the Windows Notepad program.

Note that the pseudo-DOS prompt displayed at the start of each command line is always interpreted as the first token, *Words(0),* and so the first keyword that we actually need to consider is *Words(1).*

## Steps

1. Create a new project called PROMPT.MAK. Add the Prompt control, PROMPT.VBX, to the project. Create a new form with the objects and properties described in Table 1-30. Save this form as PROMPT.FRM.

**Table 1-30** Objects and properties for PROMPT.FRM

| OBJECT | PROPERTY | SETTING |
|--------|----------|---------|
| Form | FormName | frmPrompt |
| | Caption | "Prompt Demo" |
| | FontBold | 0 'False |
| Prompt | Name | Prompt1 |
| | WordDelimiters | " " |

2. After creating PROMPT.FRM, add the following code to the form's declarations section.

```
Option Explicit
'-------------------------------------------------
' Declare all variables, constants and external
' functions used in this form.
'-------------------------------------------------
```

```
Dim CRLF As String

' Directory attribute constants
Const ATTR_NORMAL = 0
Const ATTR_DIRECTORY = 16

' Constant used by WinExec
Const SW_SHOWNORMAL = 1

' Windows API call declarations
Declare Function Winexec Lib "Kernel" (ByVal lpCmdLine As String, ByVal nCmdShow As Integer) As
Integer
```

3. Next, add the following functions and subroutines to PROMPT.FRM.

```
Function Command_cd () As String
'---------------------------------------------------
' Process the Change Directory (CD) command.
'---------------------------------------------------
Dim TextOut As String

    On Error GoTo Command_cd_Error

    If Prompt1.NumWords = 3 Then
        ChDir Prompt1.Words(2)
        TextOut = TextOut & CRLF
    ' If no path was given, provide some help.
    Else
        TextOut = CRLF & "Usage: CD new-path"
    End If
    Command_cd = TextOut
Exit Function

Command_cd_Error:
    TextOut = CRLF & "Path not found"
    Resume Next
End Function

Function Command_Cls () As String
'---------------------------------------------------
' Process the Clear Screen (CLS) command.
'---------------------------------------------------

    ' Remove any text currently in Prompt1 control.
    Prompt1.Text = ""
    Command_Cls = ""
End Function

Function Command_dir () As String
'---------------------------------------------------
' Process the List Directory (DIR) command.
'---------------------------------------------------
Dim FileName As String
Dim DirName As String
Dim FileSpec As String
Dim TextOut As String
Dim TimeStamp As String
```

*(continued on next page)*

*(continued from previous page)*

```vb
    On Error GoTo Command_dir_Error

    ' Set the default file spec.
    FileSpec = "*.*"
    If Prompt1.NumWords = 3 Then
        FileSpec = Prompt1.Words(2)
    End If

    ' Build the directory listing.
    TextOut = CRLF
    FileName = Dir$(FileSpec, ATTR_NORMAL Or ATTR_DIRECTORY)
    While FileName <> ""
        If Left$(FileName, 1) <> "." Then
        DirName = CurDir$
        If Right$(DirName, 1) <> "\" Then DirName = DirName & "\"

        ' File name
        TextOut = TextOut & CRLF & Left$(FileName & Space$(16), 16)

        ' File size (unless it's a directory)
        If (GetAttr(DirName & FileName) And ATTR_DIRECTORY) <> 0 Then
            TextOut = TextOut & Right$(Space$(15) & "<DIR>", 15) & "  "
        Else
            TextOut = TextOut & Right$(Space$(15) & Format$(FileLen(DirName & FileName),⇒
"#,###,###,###"), 15) & "  "
        End If

        ' File date and time
        TimeStamp = FileDateTime(DirName & FileName)
        TextOut = TextOut & Format$(TimeStamp, "MM/DD/YYYY") & " "
        TextOut = TextOut & Format$(TimeStamp, "HH:MM") & " "
    End If

    ' Get next file name from directory
    FileName = Dir
    Wend
    Command_dir = TextOut & CRLF
Exit Function

Command_dir_Error:
    Resume Next
End Function

Function Command_help () As String
'------------------------------------------------
' Process the Help (HELP) command.
'------------------------------------------------
Dim TextOut As String

    TextOut = CRLF & "The following commands are available:" & CRLF
    TextOut = TextOut & "  CD        Changes the current directory" & CRLF
    TextOut = TextOut & "  CLS       Clears the screen" & CRLF
    TextOut = TextOut & "  DIR       Lists the current directory" & CRLF
    TextOut = TextOut & "  EXIT      Exits this shell" & CRLF
    TextOut = TextOut & "  HELP      Lists help information" & CRLF & CRLF
    TextOut = TextOut & "Windows programs can also be started from the command line" & CRLF
    TextOut = TextOut & "by typing their names and parameters." & CRLF

    Command_help = TextOut
```

```
End Function

Function Command_run () As String
'----------------------------------------------------
' Process the Run command.  This is called if no
' internal command is recognized.
'----------------------------------------------------
Dim retcode As Integer
Dim TextOut As String
Dim cmdline As String

    ' Remove our "prompt" (the "C:\>"), which is always the
    ' first token on the command line.  What's left is the
    ' actual command line.
    cmdline = Mid$(Prompt1.Command, InStr(Prompt1.Command, " ") + 1)

    retcode = Winexec(cmdline, SW_SHOWNORMAL)
    If retcode < 32 Then
            TextOut = CRLF & "Bad command or file name" & CRLF
    Else
            TextOut = CRLF
    End If
    Command_run = TextOut
End Function

Sub Form_Load ()
'----------------------------------------------------
' Center the form on the screen, and set initial
' text for the DOS shell.
'----------------------------------------------------

    Me.Move (Screen.Width - Me.Width) \ 2, (Screen.Height - Me.Height) \ 2

    ' Initialize Carriage Return / Line Feed variable
    CRLF = Chr$(13) & Chr$(10)

    Prompt1.AppendText = "Rudimentary DOS Shell, Version 1.0" & CRLF
    Prompt1.AppendText = Command_help()
    Prompt1.AppendText = CRLF & CurDir$ & "> "

End Sub

Sub Form_Resize ()
'----------------------------------------------------
' Size the Prompt control to fit the form.
'----------------------------------------------------
    Prompt1.Move 0, 0, Me.ScaleWidth, Me.ScaleHeight
End Sub

Sub Prompt1_Enter (InputLine As String)
'----------------------------------------------------
' Process commands
'----------------------------------------------------
Dim TextOut As String

    If Prompt1.NumWords > 1 Then
      Select Case LCase$(Prompt1.Words(1))
          Case "dir"
                TextOut = Command_dir()
```

*(continued on next page)*

*(continued from previous page)*

```
        Case "cd"
               TextOut = Command_cd()
        Case "cls"
               TextOut = Command_Cls()
        Case "help"
               TextOut = Command_help()
        Case "exit"
          End
        Case Else
          TextOut = Command_run()
    End Select
  End If

  TextOut = TextOut & CRLF & CurDir$ & "> "
  Prompt1.AppendText = TextOut

End Sub

Sub Prompt1_KeyPress (KeyAscii As Integer)
'------------------------------------------------
' It's necessary to "eat" the Enter key, so that
' we can keep the command cursor on the same line
' as our "C:\>" DOS prompt.
'------------------------------------------------
    If KeyAscii = 13 Then
         KeyAscii = 0
    End If
End Sub
```

## Tips and Comments

By default, the Prompt control processes the (ENTER) key by first calling the *Enter* event, followed by the standard *KeyPress* event. *Keypress* processes the (ENTER) key in the same way that a normal multiline text box would, by moving the cursor down to the beginning of a new line for input.

This created a problem for programs like our example DOS shell. In that program, we wanted to display the equivalent of the DOS C:\> prompt *on the same line as the input cursor.* Normally, we redisplay the DOS prompt after processing each command, at the end of the *Event* routine. Unfortunately, after we display the DOS prompt the *KeyPress* event is triggered for the (ENTER) key that was pressed, moving the cursor down to the line below our DOS prompt.

The solution to this problem turns out to be simple: In the *KeyPress* event, check for and discard the (ENTER) key. This keeps the input cursor where we want it, on the same line as the DOS prompt.

# Slider (SLIDER.VBX)

| USAGE: | Graphical Replacement for Scroll Bar |
| --- | --- |
| MANUFACTURER: | Northeast Data Corp. |
| COST: | $50 |

VSlider and HSlider are simple-to-use vertical and horizontal controls that are easy on Windows resources. They represent analog controls, like the slider control on a graphic equalizer. Slider allows you to use a bitmap picture for both the background and the thumb of the slider control. This gives you additional flexibility in presenting your interface, since you're not stuck with the "same old" slider. Slider allows both keyboard and mouse input. You can press the appropriate arrow keys to move the thumb, or the user can drag the thumb with the mouse. You can also click on the control above or below the thumb to move the thumb in the direction of the mouse cursor, or double-click on the bar to move the thumb directly to the mouse cursor.

## Syntax

Slider gives you several ways to receive input from the user. The *ThumbPos* event lets you have instant response, and the *ThumbUp* event lets you have a response only when the thumb is released. You should also use the *Click*, *DoubleClick*, and *KeyDown* events to track any keyboard or mouse events. See Table 1-31 for a list of custom properties and events for SLIDER.VBX.

**Table 1-31** Slider custom properties and events

**PROPERTIES**

| | | |
| --- | --- | --- |
| BevelInner | BevelOuter | BevelInnerWidth |
| BevelOuterWidth | BorderWidth | FocusPict |
| Max | Min | Pos |
| Range | ThumbPict | TickMarks |
| TickStyle | | |

**EVENTS**

| | |
| --- | --- |
| ThumbPos | ThumbUp |

You can control the background color of the slider, but you can only control the appearance of the thumb by giving it a custom bitmap. You can also give the slider itself a custom bitmap for its background. Thumb allows for both a *ThumbPict* and *FocusPict* property. The *FocusPict* property governs the appearance of the thumb when the slider has the focus, and *ThumbPict* determines what the thumb looks like at all other times. The thumb takes its size from the size of the bitmap. In contrast, you have to size the slider to the size of any bitmap to be used for its background. You can control the appearance of the tickmarks on the slider using the *TickMark* and *TickStyle* properties.

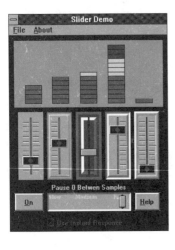

**Figure 1-12** The Slider example program

*TickMark* governs where ticks appear on the slider, while *TickStyle* controls their optional 3D appearance. You can also give the slider itself a 3D appearance using the *BevelInner* and *BevelOuter* properties.

Slider has three properties for governing position of the thumb: *Max, Min,* and *Pos. Max* and *Min* are the top and bottom of the range of inputs returned by *Pos.* You can also control whether *Max* is the top or bottom of the slider using the *Range* property.

# Example

The sample program shown in Figure 1-12 simulates a five-band graphic equalizer controlled by five slider controls. The five vertical sliders demonstrate different appearances of VSlider, while the horizontal slider has a custom bitmap for a background. Four of the five vertical sliders also have custom thumb bitmaps to give the appearance of a red LED light in the button. The fifth vertical slider and the horizontal slider both have standard thumbs.

### Steps

1. Create a new project called SLIDER.MAK and add SLIDER.VBX. Create a new form with the objects and properties shown in Table 1-32. Save this form as SLIDER.FRM.

**Table 1-32** Slider main form's objects and properties

| OBJECT | PROPERTY | SETTING |
|--------|----------|---------|
| Form | FormName | slider |
| | BackColor | &H00000000& |
| | BorderStyle | 3 'Fixed Doubl |
| | Caption | "Slider Demo" |

| OBJECT | PROPERTY | SETTING |
|---|---|---|
| | MaxButton | 0 'False |
| | MinButton | 0 'False |
| Label | Name | lblSampleRate |
| | Alignment | 2 'Center |
| | BackStyle | 0 'Transparent |
| | Caption | "Pause 0 Betwen Samples" |
| | ForeColor | &H0000FFFF& |
| VSlider | Name | VSlider1 |
| | BackColor | &H00C0C0C0& |
| | BevelInner | 0 'None |
| | BevelInnerWidth | 1 |
| | BevelOuter | 0 'None |
| | BevelOuterWidth | 1 |
| | BorderWidth | 3 |
| | FocusPict | (set at design time in Properties window) |
| | Index | 0 |
| | Max | 11 |
| | Min | 0 |
| | Pos | 11 |
| | Range | 1 'Invert |
| | ThumbPict | (set at design time in Properties window) |
| | TickMarks | 3 'Both |
| | TickStyle | 1 'Inset |
| VSlider | Name | VSlider1 |
| | BackColor | &H00C0C0C0& |
| | BevelInner | 2 'Raised |
| | BevelInnerWidth | 1 |
| | BevelOuter | 3 'Frame |
| | BevelOuterWidth | 2 |
| | BorderWidth | 3 |
| | FocusPict | (set at design time in Properties window) |
| | Index | 1 |
| | Max | 11 |
| | Min | 0 |
| | Pos | 11 |
| | Range | 1 'Invert |
| | ThumbPict | (set at design time in Properties window) |
| | TickMarks | 1 'Left |
| | TickStyle | 1 'Inset |

*(continued on next page)*

| OBJECT | PROPERTY | SETTING |
|---|---|---|
| *(continued from previous page)* | | |
| VSlider | Name | VSlider1 |
| | BackColor | &H00C0C0C0& |
| | BevelInner | 2 'Raised |
| | BevelInnerWidth | 3 |
| | BevelOuter | 1 'Inset |
| | BevelOuterWidth | 3 |
| | BorderWidth | 1 |
| | FocusPict | (set at design time in Properties window) |
| | Index | 3 |
| | Max | 11 |
| | Min | 0 |
| | Pos | 11 |
| | Range | 1 'Invert |
| | ThumbPict | (set at design time in Properties window) |
| | TickMarks | 2 'Right |
| | TickStyle | 1 'Inset |
| VSlider | Name | VSlider1 |
| | BackColor | &H00C0C0C0& |
| | BevelInner | 1 'Inset |
| | BevelInnerWidth | 1 |
| | BevelOuter | 2 'Raised |
| | BevelOuterWidth | 3 |
| | BorderWidth | 3 |
| | FocusPict | (set at design time in Properties window) |
| | Index | 4 |
| | Max | 11 |
| | Min | 0 |
| | Pos | 11 |
| | Range | 1 'Invert |
| | ThumbPict | (set at design time in Properties window) |
| | TickMarks | 3 'Both |
| | TickStyle | 1 'Inset |
| PictureBox | Name | picEqualizerWindow |
| | BackColor | &H00FFFF00& |
| | FillColor | &H00FFFF00& |
| | FillStyle | 0 'Solid |
| | ScaleMode | 0 'User |

| OBJECT | PROPERTY | SETTING |
|--------|----------|---------|
| CommandButton | Name | btnSwitch |
| | Caption | "&On" |
| HSlider | Name | HSlider1 |
| | BackColor | &H00C0C0C0& |
| | BevelInner | 0 'None |
| | BevelInnerWidth | 1 |
| | BevelOuter | 1 'Inset |
| | BevelOuterWidth | 3 |
| | BorderWidth | 3 |
| | Max | 100 |
| | Min | 0 |
| | Picture | (set at design time in Properties window) |
| | Pos | 0 |
| | Range | 1 'Invert |
| | TickMarks | 3 'Both |
| | TickStyle | 0 'Normal |
| CheckBox | Name | chkThumbUp |
| | BackColor | &H00000000& |
| | Caption | "&Use Instant Response" |
| | ForeColor | &H000000FF& |
| | Value | 1 'Checked |
| CommandButton | Name | Command1 |
| | Caption | "&Help" |
| VSlider | Name | VSlider1 |
| | BackColor | &H000000FF& |
| | BevelInner | 2 'Raised |
| | BevelInnerWidth | 5 |
| | BevelOuter | 3 'Frame |
| | BevelOuterWidth | 5 |
| | BorderWidth | 5 |
| | FocusPict | (set at design time in Properties window) |
| | Index | 2 |
| | Max | 11 |
| | Min | 0 |
| | Pos | 11 |
| | Range | 1 'Invert |
| | TickMarks | 0 'None |
| | TickStyle | 1 'Inset |

2. Add the menu items shown in Table 1-33 to the slider form.

**Table 1-33** Slider main form's menu

| CAPTION | NAME |
|---------|------|
| &File | mnuFile |
| ----E&xit | mnuExit |
| &About | mnuAbout |

3. Add the following code to the declarations section of the slider form. These constants are used for bounds for arrays and drawing, and colors for drawing.

```
Option Explicit
'-------------------------------------------------------
' Constants, variables and declarations used in
' the Slider example program.
'-------------------------------------------------------

Const BLACK = 0
Const GREEN = 2
Const YELLOW = 14
Const RED = 12

Const MAXROWS = 4 ' 0 to 5
Const BARWIDTH = 3
Const BARHEIGHT = 1
Const LEFTOFFSET = 2
Const BARBOTTOM = 13
Const DRAWROWS = 5
```

4. Add the following subroutines to the slider form. These subroutines control the drawing of the simulated graphic equalizer using data input from the slider controls.

Most of the work happens in a While loop contained in the MoveBars sub. The While loop draws the equalizer bars while the btnSwitch command button caption equals &On. When the user clicks btnSwitch, the *btnSwitch_click* event runs concurrently with the *MoveBars* sub to change the *btnSwitch.caption* property to &Off, signaling the drawing loop in *MoveBars* to terminate. This only works if there's a DoEvents somewhere in the drawing loop allowing VB to process the click message.

```
Sub Form_Load ()
    Randomize

    ' Center "me" in the desktop.
    Me.Move (Screen.Width - Me.Width) \ 2, (Screen.Height - Me.Height) \ 2

    Me.Show

    ' This code is to prevent a possible problem
    ' with the "nag window" from slider.vbx.
    If Me.WindowState <> 0 Then Me.WindowState = 0

    MoveBars
End Sub

Sub Form_Unload (Cancel As Integer)
```

```
        End
End Sub

Sub HSlider1_DblClick ()
    lblSampleRate.Caption = "Pause " & Str(hslider1.Pos) & " Between Samples"
End Sub

Sub HSlider1_ThumbPos (i As Integer)
    If chkThumbUp = 1 Then   ' checked
        lblSampleRate.Caption = "Pause " & Str(hslider1.Pos) & " Between Samples"
    End If
End Sub

Sub HSlider1_ThumbUp (i As Integer)
    lblSampleRate.Caption = "Pause " & Str(hslider1.Pos) & " Between Samples"
End Sub

Sub mnuAbout_Click ()
    frmabout.Show 1
End Sub

Sub mnuExit_Click ()
Unload frmabout
Unload Me
End Sub

Sub MoveBars ()

    Dim i As Integer
    Dim moveto As Integer
    Dim nexttimer As Single
    ReDim barloc(0 To MAXROWS) As Integer

    While btnSwitch.Caption = "&On"
        For i = 0 To MAXROWS
            moveto = (Int((4 + 0 + 1) * Rnd + 0) - 2) + VSlider1(i).Pos
            If moveto > picEqualizerWindow.ScaleHeight Then
                moveto = picEqualizerWindow.ScaleHeight
            End If
            If moveto < 0 Then
                moveto = 0
            End If
            While moveto <> barloc(i)
                ' Be polite and let windows process messages.
                DoEvents
                'if it's less, draw it.
                If moveto < barloc(i) Then
                    If (picEqualizerWindow.ScaleHeight / 2) < barloc(i) Then
                        picEqualizerWindow.FillColor = QBColor(GREEN) ' Color me green.
                    Else
                        If (picEqualizerWindow.ScaleHeight / 4) < barloc(i) Then
                            picEqualizerWindow.FillColor = QBColor(YELLOW) ' Warning, warning!
                        Else
                            picEqualizerWindow.FillColor = QBColor(RED) ' Overload!
                        End If
                    End If
                    picEqualizerWindow.Line (DRAWROWS * i + LEFTOFFSET, barloc(i))-(DRAWROWS *
i + LEFTOFFSET + BARWIDTH, barloc(i) + BARHEIGHT), QBColor(BLACK), B
                    barloc(i) = barloc(i) - 1
                Else
                    ' If it's more, erase it.
```

*(continued on next page)*

*(continued from previous page)*

```
                barloc(i) = barloc(i) + 1
                picEqualizerWindow.Line (DRAWROWS * i + LEFTOFFSET, barloc(i))-(DRAWROWS *
i + LEFTOFFSET + BARWIDTH, barloc(i) + BARHEIGHT), picEqualizerWindow.BackColor, B
            End If
                picEqualizerWindow.FillColor = picEqualizerWindow.BackColor
        Wend
    Next i
    nexttimer = Timer + hslider1.Pos / 100
    While Timer < nexttimer
        DoEvents
    Wend
    Wend

    picEqualizerWindow.Refresh

    For i = 0 To 4
        VSlider1(i).Pos = VSlider1(i).Max
        barloc(i) = BARBOTTOM
        picEqualizerWindow.FillColor = QBColor(GREEN)
        picEqualizerWindow.Line (DRAWROWS * i + LEFTOFFSET, BARBOTTOM)-(DRAWROWS * i +
LEFTOFFSET + BARWIDTH, BARBOTTOM + BARHEIGHT), QBColor(BLACK), B
    Next i

    picEqualizerWindow.FillColor = picEqualizerWindow.BackColor

End Sub

Sub picEqualizerWindow_Paint ()
    ' Redraw the EQ bars if some rude window wiped them out.
    Dim i As Integer, j  As Integer
    Static firsttime As Integer

    If firsttime = 0 Then
        firsttime = 1
        Exit Sub
    End If

    picEqualizerWindow.Cls

    If btnSwitch.Caption = "&Off" Then Exit Sub

    For i = 0 To MAXROWS
        For j = barloc(i) + 1 To BARBOTTOM
            If (picEqualizerWindow.ScaleHeight / 2) < j Then
                picEqualizerWindow.FillColor = QBColor(GREEN) ' color me green
            Else
                If (picEqualizerWindow.ScaleHeight / 4) < j Then
                    picEqualizerWindow.FillColor = QBColor(YELLOW) ' warning, warning!
                Else
                    picEqualizerWindow.FillColor = QBColor(RED) ' Overload!
                End If
            End If
            picEqualizerWindow.Line (DRAWROWS * i + LEFTOFFSET, j)-(DRAWROWS * i + LEFTOFFSET +
BARWIDTH, j + BARHEIGHT), QBColor(BLACK), B
        Next j
    Next i

    ' Restore the fillcolor to the backcolor.
    picEqualizerWindow.FillColor = picEqualizerWindow.BackColor

End Sub
```

## Tips and Comments

You might want to try commenting out the code in the *picEqualizerWindow.Paint* event and turning the *picEqualizerWindow.AutoRedraw* .property on to see the effect *AutoRedraw* has on "high-speed" graphics.

Slider makes a more intuitive replacement for a scroll bar because it resembles something most people have seen in a nonelectronic context, unlike the standard Windows scroll bar. There are some limitations in your control over Slider's appearance, but not so much as to make it unusable. Slider's very efficient use of Windows resources makes it a good tool for your VB toolbox.

# Spin Button (SPIN.VBX)

| USAGE: | Incrementing and Decrementing Values |
|---|---|
| MANUFACTURER: | Microsoft/Outrider Systems, Inc. |
| COST: | Provided with Visual Basic 3.0 Professional Edition |

The Spin Button control is designed to work in tandem with another control, usually a label or text control, to increment and decrement numeric values. The Spin Button controls the speed at which these values change.

## Syntax

A Spin Button is similar in concept to a scroll bar. Its nonstandard properties and events are listed in Table 1-34. It consists of two arrow buttons pointing away from each other. The Spin Button control has only two events, *SpinUp* and *SpinDown,* which are fired whenever the left mouse button is held down over one of the arrow buttons. As the mouse button is held down, multiple *SpinUp* or *SpinDown* events are fired, with the frequency based on a *Delay* property. This integer property establishes the millisecond delay between the firing of the spin events, and has a range from 0 to 32,767. The default is a 250 millisecond delay between events.

**Table 1-34** Nonstandard properties and events for the Spin Button control

### PROPERTIES

| | | | |
|---|---|---|---|
| BorderColor | BorderThickness | Delay | LightColor |
| ShadeColor | ShadowBackcolor | ShadowForecolor | ShadowThickness |
| SpinOrientation | TdThickness | | |

### EVENTS

| | |
|---|---|
| SpinDown | SpinUp |

Usually, you use the Spin Button with another control to provide an easy method for setting numeric values. For instance, you might place a label control displaying a number next to the Spin Button, and have the number value incremented and decremented in the spin events.

```
Sub Spin1_SpinUp ()
    Label1 = Val(Label1) + 1
    if Label1 > MAX_VALUE then Label1 = MAX_VALUE
End Sub

Sub Spin1 SpinDown ()
    Label1 = Val(Label1) - 1
    if Label1 < MIN_VALUE then Label1 = MIN_VALUE
End Sub
```

Most of the other properties of the Spin Button are used for changing its appearance. The most important of these is *SpinOrientation,* which when set to 0 displays a vertical Spin Button, and when set to 1 displays a horizontal Spin Button. Several properties let you optionally display a shadow behind the button. If *ShadowThickness* is set to a value greater than 0, a shadow with that pixel width is displayed. The *ShadowForecolor* and *ShadowBackcolor* properties set the colors of the shadow and the background, respectively.

Other properties let you give the button a beveled 3D appearance. If the *TdThickness* property is set to a value greater than 0, the borders of the button appear beveled by the specified number of pixels. The shading of the beveled area is determined by the *LightColor* property, which sets the color of the top and left bevels, and the *ShadeColor* property, which sets the color of the right and bottom bevels.

# Example

The example program uses three spin buttons to create a color mixing palette. Each button modifies the value in an associated label control. These numeric label values then update the color mixing picture box control's *BackColor* property using Visual Basic's *RGB()* function. In addition, each button has its own smaller picture box that's updated to show how much of that particular color has been added. The program is shown in Figure 1-13.

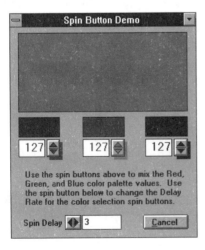

**Figure 1-13** The Spin Button example program

By using control arrays, we managed to reduce the amount of code in this example considerably. The spin buttons, and their associated picture boxes and labels, are all control arrays. This allows us to use the same code to increment all three spin buttons.

## Steps

1. Create a new project called SPIN.MAK. Add the Spin Button control, SPIN.VBX, to the project. Create a new form called SPIN.FRM, with the objects and properties described in Table 1-35. Save this form as SPIN.FRM.

**Table 1-35** Objects and properties of SPIN.FRM

| OBJECT | PROPERTY | SETTING |
|--------|----------|---------|
| Form | FormName | frmSpin |
| | BackColor | &H00C0C0C0& |
| | BorderStyle | 1 'Fixed Single |
| | Caption | "Spin Button Demo" |
| | MaxButton | 0 'False |
| Label | Name | Label2 |
| | BackStyle | 0 'Transparent |
| | Caption | "Use the spin buttons above to mix the Red,Green, and Blue color palette values. Use the spin button below to change the Delay Rate for the color selection spin buttons." |
| | ForeColor | &H00000080& |
| Label | Name | lblColorVal |
| | Alignment | 1 'Right Justify |
| | BackColor | &H00FFFFFF& |
| | BorderStyle | 1 'Fixed Single |
| | Caption | "127" |
| | FontSize | 12 |
| | ForeColor | &H00FF0000& |
| | Index | 2 |
| Label | Name | lblColorVal |
| | Alignment | 1 'Right Justify |
| | BackColor | &H00FFFFFF& |
| | BorderStyle | 1 'Fixed Single |
| | Caption | "127" |
| | FontSize | 12 |
| | ForeColor | &H00008000& |
| | Index | 1 |
| Label | Name | lblColorVal |
| | Alignment | 1 'Right Justify |

(continued on next page)

| OBJECT | PROPERTY | SETTING |
|---|---|---|
| *(continued from previous page)* | | |
| | BackColor | &H00FFFFFF& |
| | BorderStyle | 1 'Fixed Single |
| | Caption | "127" |
| | FontSize | 12 |
| | ForeColor | &H000000FF& |
| | Index | 0 |
| PictureBox | Name | picColor |
| | BackColor | &H00000000& |
| PictureBox | Name | picAColor |
| | BackColor | &H00000000& |
| | Index | 0 |
| PictureBox | Name | picAColor |
| | BackColor | &H00000000& |
| | Index | 1 |
| PictureBox | Name | picAColor |
| | BackColor | &H00000000& |
| | Index | 2 |
| SpinButton | Name | spinSpeed |
| | Delay | 3 |
| | ShadowBackColor | &H00C0C0C0& |
| | SpinOrientation | 1 'Horizontal |
| | TdThickness | 2 |
| TextBox | Name | txtSpeed |
| | Text | "3" |
| CommandButton | | Name    btnCancel |
| | Caption | "&Cancel" |
| SpinButton | Name | spinSetColor |
| | ForeColor | &H00800000& |
| | Index | 2 |
| | ShadowBackColor | &H00C0C0C0& |
| | ShadowForeColor | &H00FF0000& |
| | ShadowThickness | 4 |
| | SpinForeColor | &H00FF0000& |
| | TdThickness | 2 |
| SpinButton | Name | spinSetColor |
| | ForeColor | &H00008000& |
| | Index | 1 |
| | ShadowBackColor | &H00C0C0C0& |
| | ShadowForeColor | &H0000FF00& |

| OBJECT | PROPERTY | SETTING |
|---|---|---|
| | ShadowThickness | 4 |
| | SpinForeColor | &H0000FF00& |
| | TdThickness | 2 |
| SpinButton | Name | spinSetColor |
| | ForeColor | &H00000080& |
| | Index | 0 |
| | ShadowBackColor | &H00C0C0C0& |
| | ShadowForeColor | &H000000FF& |
| | ShadowThickness | 4 |
| | SpinForeColor | &H000000FF& |
| | TdThickness | 2 |

2. After creating SPIN.FRM, add the following code to the form's declarations section.

```
Option Explicit
'--------------------------------------------------
' Set up constants used for Spin Button demo.
'--------------------------------------------------

' This is the highest allowable Spin Delay value.
Const MAX_SPEED = 32767

' Used to finesse the text box.
Const KEY_BACK = &H8
Const KEY_LEFT = &H25
Const KEY_RIGHT = &H27
```

3. Next, add the following subroutines to SPIN.FRM.

```
Sub btnCancel_Click ()
'--------------------------------------------------
' Exit the program.
'--------------------------------------------------
    Unload Me
End Sub

Sub Form_Load ()
'--------------------------------------------------
' Set initial color values and center the form.
'--------------------------------------------------
Dim i As Integer

    Me.Move (Screen.Width - Me.Width) \ 2, (Screen.Height - Me.Height) \ 2

    picAColor(0).BackColor = RGB(lblColorVal(0), 0, 0)
    picAColor(1).BackColor = RGB(0, lblColorVal(1), 0)
    picAColor(2).BackColor = RGB(0, 0, lblColorVal(2))

    picColor.BackColor = RGB(lblColorVal(0), lblColorVal(1), lblColorVal(2))
End Sub
```

(continued on next page)

*(continued from previous page)*

```vb
Sub spinSetColor_SpinDown (Index As Integer)
'----------------------------------------------------
' Lower the amount of this color.
'----------------------------------------------------
    spinSetColor(Index).Delay = Val(txtSpeed)

    lblColorVal(Index) = lblColorVal(Index) - 1
    If lblColorVal(Index) < 0 Then lblColorVal(Index) = 0

    UpdateColors Index
End Sub

Sub spinSetColor_SpinUp (Index As Integer)
'----------------------------------------------------
' Raise the amount of this color.
'----------------------------------------------------
    spinSetColor(Index).Delay = Val(txtSpeed)

    lblColorVal(Index) = lblColorVal(Index) + 1
    If lblColorVal(Index) > 255 Then lblColorVal(Index) = 255

    UpdateColors Index
End Sub

Sub spinSpeed_SpinDown ()
'----------------------------------------------------
' Lower the value used for delay rate.
'----------------------------------------------------

    txtSpeed = Val(txtSpeed) - 1
    If txtSpeed < 0 Then txtSpeed = 0
End Sub

Sub spinSpeed_SpinUp ()
'----------------------------------------------------
' Increase the value used for delay rate.
'----------------------------------------------------
    txtSpeed = Val(txtSpeed) + 1
    If txtSpeed > MAX_SPEED Then txtSpeed = MAX_SPEED
End Sub

Sub txtSpeed_KeyPress (KeyAscii As Integer)
'----------------------------------------------------
' Make sure we don't get an invalid delay number.
'----------------------------------------------------
Dim NewVal As Integer

    If (KeyAscii = KEY_BACK) Or (KeyAscii = KEY_LEFT) Or (KeyAscii = KEY_RIGHT) Then
        Exit Sub
    ElseIf (Chr$(KeyAscii) < "0") Or (Chr$(KeyAscii) > "9") Then
        KeyAscii = 0
        Exit Sub
    Else
        NewVal = Val(txtSpeed & Chr$(KeyAscii))
        If (NewVal < 0) Or (NewVal > MAX_SPEED) Then
            KeyAscii = 0
        End If
    End If
End Sub

Sub UpdateColors (ByVal Index As Integer)
```

```
'------------------------------------------------------
' Update the colors in the picture boxes.
'------------------------------------------------------
    picColor.BackColor = RGB(lblColorVal(0), lblColorVal(1), lblColorVal(2))
    Select Case Index
        Case 0: picAColor(Index).BackColor = RGB(lblColorVal(Index), 0, 0)
        Case 1: picAColor(Index).BackColor = RGB(0, lblColorVal(Index), 0)
        Case 2: picAColor(Index).BackColor = RGB(0, 0, lblColorVal(Index))
    End Select
    lblColorVal(Index).Refresh
End Sub
```

## Tips and Comments

In the example program, you might notice a fair amount of code in the Spin Delay text box *KeyPress* events. One of the challenges of using the Spin Button in tandem with a text control is the quirky way text boxes and the spin button handle *LostFocus* events. If you were typing in the text box and then clicked on one of the spin buttons, you might expect that the text box would fire a *LostFocus* event and the focus would shift to that spin button. This is what happens when you click on a normal command button, but not the spin button. No text box *LostFocus* event is fired, so *LostFocus* is useless for data validation, hence the slightly circuitous resort to checking data in the *KeyPress* event. You'll need to be careful of this when coding spin button/text box combinations in your programs.

# Tab/VBX (TABVBX10.VBX)

| | |
|---|---|
| USAGE: | Folder Tab Control |
| MANUFACTURER: | FarPoint Technologies |
| COST: | $49.00 |

FarPoint's Tab/VBX control allows you to add the appearance of tabbed folders to your applications. While some Tab controls offer limited flexibility in the appearance of the tabs, Tab/VBX provides a comprehensive array of properties that allow you to match your user interface requirements with very few limitations.

## Syntax

You can use a single Tab/VBX control for each group of tabs that is to appear on a form. Table 1-36 lists the nonstandard properties, events, and functions for Tab/VBX.

**Table 1-36** Tab/VBX nonstandard properties, events, and functions

### PROPERTIES

| | | |
|---|---|---|
| ActiveTab | ActiveTabBold | AlignPictureH |
| AlignPictureV | AlignTextH | AlignTextV |
| ApplyTo | BackColor | BorderAlignTextH |

*(continued on next page)*

## PROPERTIES

*(continued from previous page)*

| | | |
|---|---|---|
| BorderText | BorderTextOrientation | BorderTextFlip |
| ClientHeight | ClientLeft | ClientTop |
| ClientWidth | FlipText | ForeColor |
| FrameColor | FrameThreeDHighlightColor | FrameThreeDShadowColor |
| FrameThreeDStyle | FrameThreeDWidth | FrameWidth |
| GrayAreaColor | LineHCount | LineHWidth |
| LineVCount | LineVWidth | MarginLeft |
| MarginRight | NoPrefix | Orientation |
| OutlineColor | OutlineInside | OutlineInsideColor |
| OutlineOutside | OutlineOutsideColor | ShowFocusRect |
| Tab | TabCaption | TabCount |
| TabHeight | TabMaxWidth | TabPicture |
| TabSeparator | TabShape | TabsPerRow |
| TabState | TextRotation | ThreeD |
| ThreeDHighlightColor | ThreeDShadowColor | ThreeDStyle |
| ThreeDText | ThreeDTextHighlightColor | ThreeDTextOffset |
| ThreeDTextShadowColor | ThreeDWidth | WordWrap |

## EVENTS

| | | |
|---|---|---|
| ClientClick | DblClick | TabAcitvate |
| TabShown | | |

## FUNCTIONS

| | |
|---|---|
| TabAssignChild | TabRemoveChild |

The *TabCount* property controls how many tabs appear. The *TabsPerRow* property tells Tab/VBX how many tabs should appear on each row so multiple rows of tabs can be handled by a single Tab/VBX control. If *TabCount* is greater than *TabsPerRow,* Tab/VBX automatically displays as many rows as necessary to accommodate all the tabs. If *TabsPerRow* is set to 0, the tabs will be of varying widths, based on the amount of text in the tab. If *TabsPerRow* is greater than 0, the tabs will all be the same size and they fill the width of the control entirely (Figure 1-14).

You can limit the size of the tabs with the *TabMaxWidth* property, and you can also force Tab/VBX to leave space on either end of the row of tabs with the *MarginLeft* and *MarginRight* properties. The *TabSeparator* property lets you to leave a gap between tabs, and *TabShape* allows you to choose Cornered, Rounded, or Slanted tabs. *TabHeight* controls the height of the tabs, this property is very useful if pictures are used in tabs or if the *WordWrap* property is used for multiline captions in tabs. If *WordWrap* is set to *True,* text in a tab will automatically wrap to a new line if it is too long to fit on the tab or if a new line character (Chr$(10)) is embedded in the text. The *Orientation* property controls where the tabs appear (Table 1-37).

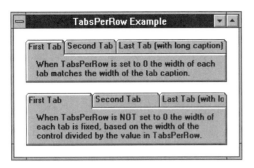

**Figure 1-14** Tab/VBX TabsPerRow example

**Table 1-37** Tab/VBX Orientation property values

| VALUE | MEANING |
|---|---|
| 0 | Tabs are on the top of the control. |
| 1 | Tabs are on the right side of the control. |
| 2 | Tabs are on the bottom of the control. |
| 3 | Tabs are on the left side of the control. |

**Words and Pictures** If you orient the tabs anywhere but on the top you will appreciate the *FlipText* property, which allows you to change the orientation of the text on the tabs. For instance, if you orient the tabs on the bottom of the control, the text will appear upside-down. You can set the *FlipText* property to *True* to make the text appear right-side up again. You can position text in a tab (Left, Center, or Right) with *AlignTextH* and *AlignTextV*. If you place pictures in the tabs, you can position the pictures with *AlignPictureH* and *AlignPictureV*. *AlignPictureH* also controls whether the picture appears to the left or right of any text in the tab.

Some properties of a Tab/VBX control affect all the tabs within the control and some properties affect individual tabs. The *ApplyTo* property tells Tab/VBX how to apply certain properties such as colors and fonts (Table 1-38).

**Table 1-38** Tab/VBX ApplyTo property values

| VALUE | MEANING |
|---|---|
| 0 | Specified color or font applies to all tabs |
| 1 | Specified color or font applies to active tab only |
| 2 | Specified color or font applies to a specific tab (determined by the Tab property) |

The *Tab* property specifies which tab is affected by the *ApplyTo*, *BackColor*, *ForeColor*, *TabCaption*, *TabPicture*, and *TabState* properties. You can set *Tab* -1 at design time, which indicates that all controls placed on the Tab/VBX control (while *Tab* is -1) will appear on all tabs within that control, rather than on a single, specific tab.

*TabCaption* specifies the text that will appear on a tab and *TabPicture* assigns a picture to a tab. You can only set *TabPicture* at run time which means you'll need to distribute graphics files with your app or store pictures in the app using Image or Picture controls. *TabState* enables, disables, or hides individual tabs within the Tab/VBX control. You can suppress the small focus rectangle that appears around the caption by setting the *ShowFocusRect* property to *False*. *ForeColor* and *BackColor* can affect all tabs, or individual tabs, based on the setting of the *ApplyTo* property. By default the tabs are drawn with 3D borders, but you can turn off the 3D effect by setting the *ThreeD* property to *False*. If you use 3D borders, you can use the *ThreeDHighlight* and *ThreeDShadow* color properties to change the color of the 3D bevels. If you use a standard gray background (&HC0C0C0), the defaults are fine. You can also drawn the caption text with a 3D effect by setting the *ThreeDText* property to one of the available 3D options. The text can appear raised or lowered, with light or heavy shading. You can also fine-tune the appearance of the 3D text with the *ThreeDTextHighlight*, *ThreeDTextShadow*, and *ThreeDTextOffset* properties. The *GrayAreaColor* property controls the color between the tabs so the Tab/VBX control can blend in with the *BackColor* of the form it's placed on.

**Working with Tabs**   If for some reason you need to know the size or position of the client area of a Tab/VBX control, you can use the *ClientLeft*, *ClientTop*, *ClientHeight*, and *ClientWidth* properties. The client area of a Tab/VBX control is the area in which you can place child controls.

You can use the *ActiveTab* property to set or retrieve the currently active tab on a Tab/VBX control so you can switch between tabs programmatically. *ActiveTabBold* controls whether the caption for the active tab is drawn with a bold font to make it stand out from the other tabs.

There are only four events for the Tab/VBX control. *ClientClick* and *DblClick* both provide the X and Y coordinates where the mouse was clicked. *TabActivated* fires when a tab becomes the active tab, but before any of its controls are drawn. *TabShown* fires after the controls are shown on the new active tab.

Tab/VBX also provides two functions for moving controls from one tab to another. *TabAssignChild* moves a control from one tab to another and *TabRemoveChild* removes a control from a tab.

# Example

The sample program (Figure 1-15) is simple but demonstrates many of the capabilities of the Tab/VBX control. When the user selects a tab, the *TabShown* event fires. We use the *TabShown* event as our trigger to search the list for an item that starts with the letter of the selected tab. If no matching item is found, that tab will be disabled using the *TabState* property. Tabs C and D have Tab/VBX controls nested inside them that show how pictures and colors can be applied to individual tabs and how the color of the active tab can be changed. The position of the tabs can also be changed at run time, although any repositioning of child controls must be done manually. The color scheme was chosen to demonstrate the flexibility of Tab/VBX.

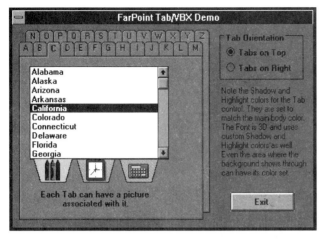

1 ◄

**Figure 1-15** FarPoint Tab/VBX sample program

## Steps

1. Create a new project called FPTAB.MAK. Create a new form with the objects and properties shown in Table 1-39. Save this form as FPTAB.FRM.

**Table 1-39** Tab/VBX main form's objects and properties

| OBJECT | PROPERTY | SETTING |
|---|---|---|
| Form | FormName | frmMain |
| | BackColor | &H00808000& |
| | BorderStyle | 3 'Fixed Double |
| | Caption | "FarPoint Tab/VBX Demo" |
| | MaxButton | 0 'False |
| | MinButton | 0 'False |
| | ScaleMode | 3 'Pixel |
| Frame | Name | fraTabOrientation |
| | BackColor | &H00808000& |
| | Caption | "Tab Orientation" |
| CommandButton | Name | btnExit |
| | Caption | "Exit" |
| ListBox | Name | lstMain |
| | Sorted | -1 'True |
| TabCtl | Name | fpTabMain |
| | AlignTextH | 1 'Center |
| | BackColor | &H00C0C000& |
| | FontBold | 0 'False |

*(continued on next page)*

| OBJECT | PROPERTY | SETTING |
|---|---|---|
| *(continued from previous page)* | | |
| | GrayAreaColor | &H00808000& |
| | ShowFocusRect | 0 'False |
| | TabCaption | (set at design time in Properties window) |
| | TabCount | 26 |
| | TabHeight | 20 |
| | TabsPerRow | 13 |
| | ThreeDHighlightColor= | |
| | ThreeDShadowColor= | |
| | ThreeDText | 4 'Lowered w/ heavy shading |
| | ThreeDTextHighlightColor= | |
| | ThreeDTextShadowColor= | |

2. Place the controls inside the fpTabMain Tab control as shown in Table 1-40.

**Table 1-40** Controls placed inside the fpTabMain Tab control

| OBJECT | PROPERTY | SETTING |
|---|---|---|
| TabCtl | Name | fpTabColorDemo |
| | AlignPictureH | 1 'Center |
| | AlignPictureV | 1 'Center |
| | AlignTextH | 1 'Center |
| | AlignTextV | 2 'Bottom |
| | GrayAreaColor | &H00C0C000& |
| | Orientation | 3 'Left |
| | ShowFocusRect | 0 'False |
| | TabCaption | (set at design time in Properties window) |
| | TabCount | 3 |
| | TabHeight | 210 |
| | TabShape | 2 'Rounded |
| | TabsPerRow | 3 |
| TabCtl | Name | fpTabPicDemo |
| | AlignPictureH | 1 'Center |
| | AlignPictureV | 1 'Center |
| | BackColor | &H0000C0C0& |
| | Enabled | 0 'False |
| | GrayAreaColor | &H00C0C000& |
| | MarginLeft | 90 |
| | MarginRight | 240 |

| OBJECT | PROPERTY | SETTING |
|--------|----------|---------|
| | Orientation | 2 'Bottom |
| | ShowFocusRect | 0 'False |
| | TabCaption | (set at design time in Properties window) |
| | TabCount | 3 |
| | TabHeight | 500 |
| | TabSeparator | 8 |
| | TabShape | 1 'Slanted |
| | TabsPerRow | 3 |
| | ThreeD | 0 'False |

3. Place the controls shown in Table 1-41 within the fpTabColorDemo TabCtl control.

**Table 1-41** Controls placed within the fpTabColorDemo TabCtl control

| OBJECT | PROPERTY | SETTING |
|--------|----------|---------|
| Label | Name | lblTabColorDemo |
| | Alignment | 2 'Center |
| | BackStyle | 0 'Transparent |
| | Caption | "These Tabs show that each Tab can have a different color scheme." |

4. Place the following controls within the fraTabOrientation Frame control shown in Table 1-42.

**Table 1-42** Controls placed within the fraTabOrientation Frame control

| OBJECT | PROPERTY | SETTING |
|--------|----------|---------|
| OptionButton | Name | optTabOrientation |
| | BackColor | &H00808000& |
| | Caption | "Tabs on Top" |
| | Index | 0 |
| | Value | -1 'True |
| OptionButton | Name | optTabOrientation |
| | BackColor | &H00808000& |
| | Caption | "Tabs on Right" |
| | Index | 1 |

5. Add the following code to the FPTAB form.

```
Option Explicit
DefInt A-Z

' Orientation
```

*(continued on next page)*

*(continued from previous page)*

```
Const TABVBX_ORIENTATION_TOP = 0
Const TABVBX_ORIENTATION_RIGHT = 1

' TabState
Const TABVBX_STATE_DISABLED_TEXT = 2

' ApplyTo
Const TABVBX_APPLYTO_DEFAULT = 0
Const TABVBX_APPLYTO_ACTIVE = 1
Const TABVBX_APPLYTO_TAB = 2


Declare Function SendMessage Lib "User" (ByVal hWnd As Integer, ByVal wMsg As Integer, ByVal
wParam As Integer, lParam As Any) As Long
Const WM_USER = &H400
Const LB_FINDSTRING = (WM_USER + 16)

Sub btnExit_Click ()

    Unload Me

End Sub

Sub Form_Load ()

    Me.Move (Screen.Width - Width) \ 2, (Screen.Height - Height) \ 2

    Call LoadList
    Call LoadTabPictures
    Call SetTabColors

End Sub

Sub fpTabColorDemo_TabActivate (TabToActivate As Integer)
'------------------------------------------------
'-- Change the ForeColor of the active Tab to
'   make it stand out from the background.
'------------------------------------------------

    Select Case TabToActivate%
        Case 0
            lblTabColorDemo.ForeColor = &HFFFFFF
        Case 1
            lblTabColorDemo.ForeColor = &H0&
        Case 2
            lblTabColorDemo.ForeColor = &HFFFF&
    End Select

End Sub

Sub fpTabMain_TabShown (ActiveTab As Integer)
'------------------------------------------------
'-- Search the list of States for the first item
'   that starts with the letter of the selected
'   Tab.
'------------------------------------------------
    Dim ItemFound%
    Dim LookupKey$
```

```
    '-- Get the letter of the selected tab
    LookupKey$ = Chr$(ActiveTab% + 65)

    '-- Search the list for an item that starts with that letter.
    ItemFound% = SendMessage((lstMain.hWnd), LB_FINDSTRING, -1, ByVal LookupKey$)
    If ItemFound% <> -1 Then
        lstMain.ListIndex = ItemFound%
    Else
        '-- If no match was found then disable the Tab.
        fpTabMain.Tab = ActiveTab%
        fpTabMain.TabState = TABVBX_STATE_DISABLED_TEXT
    End If

End Sub

Sub fpTabPicDemo_TabActivate (TabToActivate As Integer)
'-------------------------------------------------------
'-- Change the BackColor of the active Tab to
'   bright yellow to make it stand out.
'-------------------------------------------------------

    fpTabPicDemo.ApplyTo = TABVBX_APPLYTO_ACTIVE
    fpTabPicDemo.BackColor = &HFFFF&

End Sub

Sub LoadList ()

    lstMain.AddItem "Alabama"
    lstMain.AddItem "Alaska"
    lstMain.AddItem "Arizona"
    lstMain.AddItem "Arkansas"
    lstMain.AddItem "California"
    lstMain.AddItem "Colorado"
    lstMain.AddItem "Connecticut"
    lstMain.AddItem "Delaware"
    lstMain.AddItem "Florida"
    lstMain.AddItem "Georgia"
    lstMain.AddItem "Hawaii"
    lstMain.AddItem "Idaho"
    lstMain.AddItem "Illinois"
    lstMain.AddItem "Indiana"
    lstMain.AddItem "Iowa"
    lstMain.AddItem "Kansas"
    lstMain.AddItem "Kentucky"
    lstMain.AddItem "Louisiana"
    lstMain.AddItem "Maine"
    lstMain.AddItem "Maryland"
    lstMain.AddItem "Massachusets"
    lstMain.AddItem "Michigan"
    lstMain.AddItem "Minnesota"
    lstMain.AddItem "Mississippi"
    lstMain.AddItem "Missouri"
    lstMain.AddItem "Montana"
    lstMain.AddItem "Nebraska"
    lstMain.AddItem "Nevada"
    lstMain.AddItem "New Hampshire"
    lstMain.AddItem "New Jersey"
    lstMain.AddItem "New Mexico"
    lstMain.AddItem "New York"
```

*(continued on next page)*

*(continued from previous page)*

```
        lstMain.AddItem "North Carolina"
        lstMain.AddItem "North Dakota"
        lstMain.AddItem "Ohio"
        lstMain.AddItem "Oklahoma"
        lstMain.AddItem "Oregon"
        lstMain.AddItem "Pennsylvania"
        lstMain.AddItem "Rhode Island"
        lstMain.AddItem "South Carolina"
        lstMain.AddItem "South Dakota"
        lstMain.AddItem "Tennesee"
        lstMain.AddItem "Texas"
        lstMain.AddItem "Utah"
        lstMain.AddItem "Vermont"
        lstMain.AddItem "Virginia"
        lstMain.AddItem "Washington"
        lstMain.AddItem "West Virginia"
        lstMain.AddItem "Wisconson"
        lstMain.AddItem "Wyoming"

End Sub

Sub LoadTabPictures ()
    Dim i%

    For i% = 0 To 2
        fpTabPicDemo.Tab = i%
        fpTabPicDemo.TabPicture = imgTabPicture(i%).Picture
    Next i%

End Sub

Sub optTabOrientation_Click (Index As Integer)

    Select Case Index%
        Case 0 '-- Tabs on Top
            fpTabMain.Orientation = TABVBX_ORIENTATION_TOP
        Case 1 '-- Tabs on Right
            fpTabMain.Orientation = TABVBX_ORIENTATION_RIGHT
    End Select

End Sub

Sub SetTabColors ()

    fptabColorDemo.ApplyTo = TABVBX_APPLYTO_TAB

    fptabColorDemo.Tab = 0
    fptabColorDemo.BackColor = &HFF&
    fptabColorDemo.ForeColor = &HFFFFFF

    fptabColorDemo.Tab = 1
    fptabColorDemo.BackColor = &HFF00&
    fptabColorDemo.ForeColor = &H0&

    fptabColorDemo.Tab = 2
    fptabColorDemo.BackColor = &HFF0000
    fptabColorDemo.ForeColor = &HFFFF&

End Sub
```

## Tips and Comments

There is much to like about Tab/VBX. A nice feature that you shouldn't overlook is the ability to create controls that appear no matter which tab is active. Certain run-time only properties (such as *TabPicture*) would be much easier to use if they were available at design time. It would also be nice to be able to specify individual tab colors at design time rather than having to use *ApplyTo* to set them at run time. In the world of Tab controls, FarPoint's is one of the most powerful. Perhaps its strongest feature is that it allows almost complete customization of the appearance of the tabs so they can be made to blend in with any user interface scheme.

# TList (TLIST.VBX)

| USAGE: | Display of Tree-Structured Data |
| --- | --- |
| MANUFACTURER: | Bennet-Tec Information Systems |
| COST: | $125 |

TList is an outline control similar in general function to the Microsoft Outline control that comes with the Professional Edition of Visual Basic 3.0. TList gives you much more control over graphic and text settings than the Outline control, allowing separate bitmap and font attributes for each item, the ability to store different types of data for each item (an enhancement to the standard *ItemData* property), multiple lines of text for each item, three different list indexing schemes, and drag and drop support.

## Syntax

A TList control displays data in a hierarchical list format. It's special properties, events, and methods are listed in Table 1-43. Each item in the list has four basic visual elements: text, a picture, tree lines, and an indentation level. All these items should be familiar to users of the Microsoft Outline control, but while there are visual similarities between these controls, TList has significant differences. Outline controls such as TList are basically just extended list controls whose items sport the additional property of *indentation*—that is, items can be subordinate to their predecessors. Outline controls usually let you hide subordinate levels, in effect "collapsing" or hiding subordinate items.

**Table 1-43** Nonstandard properties, events, methods, and functions for TList

**PROPERTIES**

| | | |
| --- | --- | --- |
| About | Add | Align |
| BackColor | BorderStyle | ClearItem |
| CoerceIndex | CopyItem | CopyItemSub |
| CopySelected | CurrentIndexMethod | CurrentItem |
| DisableNoScroll | DragHighlight | DropTarget |

*(continued on next page)*

## PROPERTIES

*(continued from previous page)*

| | | |
|---|---|---|
| Expand | FixedSize | FullPath |
| HasSubItems | Image | ImageStretch |
| Insert | InsertItem | InvImage |
| InvStyle | IsItemVisible | ItemBackColor |
| ItemFontBold | ItemFontItalic | ItemFontName |
| ItemFontSize | ItemFontStrike | ItemFontUnder |
| ItemForeColor | ItemImageDefHeight | ItemImageDefWidth |
| ItemIntValue | ItemLngValue | ItemMultiLine |
| ItemSngValue | ItemStrValue | ItemType |
| List | ListCount | ListIndex |
| MultiSelect | NoIntegralHeight | PathSeparator |
| PictureClosed | PictureInverted | PictureLeaf |
| PictureOpen | PictureRoot | PictureType |
| Redraw | SelBackColor | Selected |
| SelForeColor | Shift | ShiftStep |
| ShowChildren | TopIndex | ViewStyle |
| WidthOfText | | |

## EVENTS

| | | |
|---|---|---|
| Collapse | Expand | PictureClick |
| PictureDblClick | | |

## METHODS

| | | |
|---|---|---|
| AddItem | Clear | Refresh |
| RemoveItem | | |

## FUNCTIONS

| | |
|---|---|
| TListFreeBuffer | TListIsValidBuffer |

There are three different ways to view the index of a TList, and you can change the current method at both design time and run time via the *CurrentIndexMethod* property. The default indexing method is similar to that used by the Microsoft Outline control. This method simply numbers all list items, with the first item indexed as 0 and the last item indexed as *ListCount* - 1, where *ListCount* is the total number of items in the outline.

The second indexing method is similar to the first, except collapsed items are excluded from the indexing scheme. Under this index scheme, collapsed items cannot be accessed, as they have no index value. This scheme is useful when you need to process only those items that are visible to the user.

The last indexing scheme is analogous to the DOS directory structure. In this scheme, each item that has subordinate items is like a DOS directory, and each "leaf" item (an item with no subordinates) is like a DOS file. This indexing structure uses the concept of a *current item*, which is similar in concept to the current directory in DOS. Only those items that are immediately subordinate to the current item are given index values, and so only those items are accessible. *CurrentItem* is a string property that is set to a value similar to a directory path in DOS; *CurrentItem* contains the path to the currently selected item. Each item that makes up a part of the path is separated by a separator string, specified by the *PathSeparator* property, which is analogous to the backslash character used in DOS paths.

For clarity, all examples in this section use the default indexing scheme, in which all items are accessible by index.

### Building and Maintaining a List

You can build TList outlines using the standard *AddItem* method, which adds items to the end of a list. This property has been extended to allow an index parameter. In this example

```
TList1.AddItem SomeText, Index
```

the *Index* parameter indicates that the text, *SomeText,* should be inserted as the last subordinate item for the item *Index.*

TList's *InsertItem()* property array allows you to insert items into the middle of a list. For example, the following example

```
TList1.InsertItem(3) = SomeText
```

inserts a new line containing the string *SomeText* at the same indentation level before item 3. All items below the new item are reindexed when the new item is added.

The *RemoveItem* method removes items from the list. It takes a single parameter, *Index,* which indicates the index of the item to remove. When an item is removed from the list, any of its subordinate items are removed as well, so this method can have the effect of removing several items.

### Adding Pictures to Lists

You can assign pictures to individual list items using the *Image()* and *InvImage()* property arrays. The *Image()* property defines the picture displayed when an item is not selected, while *InvImage()* defines the picture shown when an item is highlighted. You can load images using the same methods you use to load a standard *Picture* property, including loading bitmaps or icons from disk using the *LoadPicture* function. Setting an *Image()* property array element to 0 causes TList to use the picture defined by the *Picture...* properties instead.

You can use the *Picture...*properties—*PictureRoot, PictureOpen, PictureClosed, PictureLeaf,* and *PictureInverted*—to set the image that is displayed when an item is in a particular state. You can think of these properties as global picture defaults; they are used if no *Image()* value is set for a particular item.

Two events, *PictureClick* and *PictureDblClick,* are fired when the picture portion of an item is clicked or double-clicked. Note that clicking on the picture also fires the TList control's standard *Click* and *DblClick* events, so two events are fired when a TList picture is clicked.

### Expanding and Collapsing Branches

Subordinate branches do not automatically expand or collapse when their parent item is clicked, which may come as a surprise to users of the Microsoft Outline control. Rather, expanding and collapsing is controlled by the *Expand* property. When this Boolean property is set to *True,* any direct subordinates of the current item become visible. Likewise, when this property is set to *False,* subordinate items are hidden. With this property, you can select what event will trigger expansion or contraction of branches. The following subroutine shows a simple way to expand and collapse branches in reaction to a single click on an item's picture.

```
Sub TList1_PictureClick ()
    TList1.Expand(TList1.ListIndex) = Not TList1.Expand(TList1.ListIndex)
End Sub
```

When a branch is expanded or collapsed with the *Expand* property, either an *Expand* or *Collapse* event is fired. Both of these events pass as a parameter the index of the item that was expanded. To determine if an item is visible, use the *IsItemVisible()* Boolean property array. This property returns *True* if the item referenced by its index is currently visible.

### Changing an Item's Appearance

The TList control provides numerous *Item...* property arrays for setting the appearance of individual items. You can use the *ItemForeColor()* and *ItemBackColor()* properties to set an item's text or background colors. The *ItemFont...* properties let you change all the standard font properties for any item. For example, you can set subordinate items in a smaller or different font size (or both) to help the user distinguish them from their parents. The *ItemMultiLine* property array lets you wrap the text of an item so that it appears on multiple lines. These properties, in conjunction with the *Image()* property array discussed earlier, give you complete control over the appearance of an item.

### Storing Additional Information for an Item

Ordinary list boxes have an *ItemData* property, a long integer value that lets you store some additional information for each item in a list. While this feature is quite useful, the restriction to only integer data is a limitation.

TList expands this concept with the *Item...Value* properties, a set of property arrays that let you store integer, long integer, single-precision real numbers, or strings of user-defined data for each item in a list. Only one value may be stored per list item, but each item can store data in any of the four data formats. An *ItemType* property array also makes it easier to determine what data type was assigned during run time.

### Moving Branches

TList provides a special memory area, called a *TreeBuffer,* into which you can copy entire branches of a TList, and later graft them back onto the same or another TList. This TreeBuffer is analogous to the Window's Clipboard, which you can use to transfer data from one application to another.

You can use several properties to copy selected sections of a TList into a TreeBuffer. The *CopyItem()* property copies an item and any of its subordinate branches to a

TreeBuffer. TreeBuffers are initially declared as string variables, with the caveat that the memory they allocate should be released with a call to the *TListFreeBuffer* function when the TreeBuffer is no longer needed. The following example shows how you can use *CopyItem* to copy the currently selected item to a TreeBuffer, and then later free the buffer using *TListFreeBuffer*.

```
Dim TreeBuffer as String

TreeBuffer = TList1.CopyItem(TList1.ListIndex)
...
TListFreeBuffer (TreeBuffer)
```

Two similar properties, *CopyItemSub* and *CopySelected*, let you copy just an item's subordinates or all selected items to a TreeBuffer. Once items are in a TreeBuffer, you can add or insert them into the same or another TList control. The *Add* property adds buffered items to the end of a specified item's subordinate list, as shown here:

```
TList1.Add(TList1.ListIndex) = TreeBuffer
```

In the example, a TList branch was previously copied into *TreeBuffer;* now it is placed after any subordinate items of the currently selected item. You can insert items into a TList from a TreeBuffer using the *Insert* property, which inserts the contents of a TreeBuffer above the specified index.

# Example

The example program, shown in Figure 1-16, reads a text file called COUNTRY.TXT, and uses the comma-delimited information in it to build an outline containing information about different countries. The example illustrates how different font styles and pictures can be used for each item in a TList.

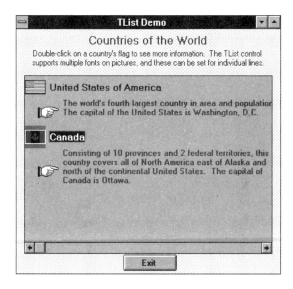

**Figure 1-16** The TList example program

## Steps

1. Create a new project called TLIST.MAK.  Add the TLIST.VBX control to the project. Create a new form with the objects and properties described in Table 1-44. Save this form as TLIST.FRM.

**Table 1-44** Objects and properties for TLIST.FRM

| OBJECT | PROPERTY | SETTING |
|---|---|---|
| Form | FormName | frmTlist |
| | BackColor | &H0080FFFF& |
| | BorderStyle | 1 'Fixed Single |
| | Caption | "TList Demo" |
| Label | Name | Label2 |
| | Alignment | 2 'Center |
| | BackStyle | 0 'Transparent |
| | Caption | "Double-click on a country's flag to see more information. The TList control supports multiple fonts on pictures, and these can be set for individual lines." |
| | FontBold | 0 'False |
| TList | Name | TList1 |
| | BackColor | &H00C0C0C0& |
| | FontSize | 9.75 |
| | ForeColor | &H00FF0000& |
| | PictureLeaf | (set at design time in Properties window) |
| | SelBackColor | &H00800000& |
| | SelForeColor | &H00FFFFFF& |
| | ViewStyle | 1 'Picture, Text |
| CommandButton | Name | btnExit |
| | Caption | "Exit" |

2. After creating TLIST.FRM, add the following code to the form's declarations section.

```
Option Explicit
'----------------------------------------------------
' Constants used in the TList demo program.
'----------------------------------------------------

' MsgBox constants
Const MB_OK = &H0
Const MB_ICONSTOP = &H10
Const MB_ICONQUESTION = &H20
Const MB_ICONEXCLAMATION = &H30
Const MB_ICONINFORMATION = &H40

' Color constant for subordinate TList items
Const DARK_RED = &HC0&
```

3. Add the following code to TLIST.FRM, making sure to put event code into the proper subroutines. The *LoadCountryFile* subroutine is called from the *Form_Load* event, and interprets the comma-delimited text file, which was created using the Windows Notepad with the Word Wrap feature turned on.

```
Sub btnExit_Click ()
'-----------------------------------------------------
' Exit program.
'-----------------------------------------------------
    Unload Me
End Sub

Sub Form_Load ()
'-----------------------------------------------------
' Center the form and load outline file.
'-----------------------------------------------------
    Me.Move (Screen.Width - Me.Width) \ 2, (Screen.Height - Me.Height) \ 2

    LoadCountryFile
End Sub

Sub LoadCountryFile ()
'-----------------------------------------------------
' Use information in the COUNTRY.TXT text file to
' build the TList outline.
'-----------------------------------------------------
Dim fnum As Integer
Dim APath As String
Dim AFile As String
Dim Parent As Integer
Dim APicture As String
Dim ALine As String
Dim LineNum As Integer

    On Error GoTo LoadCountryFile_Error

    fnum = FreeFile
    APath = App.Path
    If Right$(APath, 1) <> "\" Then APath = APath & "\"

    AFile = APath & "COUNTRY.TXT"
    Open AFile For Input As fnum

    ' Process the COUNTRY.TXT file.
    Do While Not EOF(fnum)
        Input #fnum, LineNum, Parent, APicture, ALine

        ' Add a new Tlist item.
        TList1.AddItem ALine, Parent

        ' If the item is subordinate, then make these special settings.
        If Parent <> -1 Then
            TList1.ItemMultiLine(TList1.ListCount - 1) = True
            TList1.ItemFontSize(TList1.ListCount - 1) = 8.25
            TList1.ItemForeColor(TList1.ListCount - 1) = DARK_RED
            TList1.ItemMultiLine(TList1.ListCount - 1) = True
        End If
```

*(continued on next page)*

*(continued from previous page)*

```
        ' If no picture specified in text file, use the default one.
        If APicture <> "" Then
            TList1.Image(TList1.ListCount - 1) = LoadPicture(APath & APicture)
        End If
    Loop
    Close fnum
Exit Sub

LoadCountryFile_Error:
    MsgBox "Error loading outline file.", MB_OK & MB_ICONSTOP, "Error"
    End
End Sub

Sub TList1_DblClick ()
'----------------------------------------------------
' Toggle any subordinate items on or off.
'----------------------------------------------------
    TList1.Expand(TList1.ListIndex) = Not TList1.Expand(TList1.ListIndex)
End Sub
```

4. Create a file in the same directory as your application, using Windows Notepad with the Word Wrap feature turned on. The text should be formatted like the following example—as a comma-delimited file with individual records separated by carriage returns. The first field corresponds to the list index for the entry, the second field is the index of this item's parent (or -1 if the item is at the root level), the third field is the file name of an icon or bitmap that will be displayed with the item (or an empty string, "", if the default icon is to be used), and the final field is the text to be displayed with this item.

```
0,-1,"FLGUSA02.ICO","United States of America"
1,0,"","The world's fourth largest country in area and population.  The capital ...."
2,-1,"FLGCAN.ICO","Canada"
3,2,"","Consisting of 10 provinces and 2 federal territories, this country covers all ..."
```

## Tips and Comments

TList is a versatile outline control that is powerful enough to use virtually anywhere that you need to display hierarchical data. Its ability to control the attributes of individual list items makes it a good replacement for standard nonhierarchical list boxes as well. You can also use this control by assigning only pictures (no text) to items as a scrollable button bar.

# VBCtl3D (VBCTL3D.VBX)

| | |
|---|---|
| USAGE: | Adding 3D Effects to Standard Controls |
| MANUFACTURER: | Haas Service GmbH and Simplex Software |
| COST: | $29 |

When added to a Visual Basic form, the VBCtl3D control gives a 3D look to existing standard controls such as text boxes, option buttons, and list boxes. This 3D effect extends to menus, message boxes, and common dialogs as well. You need only one instance of the control to give an entire application a 3D effect.

## Syntax

VBCtl3D is remarkably easy to use, but its effect on the appearance of an application is profound. To use this control, you simply add it to your project, and then place an instance of the control on a form, preferably the first form being displayed. Table 1-45 lists VBCtl3D's few nonstandard properties.

**Table 1-45** Nonstandard properties of the VBCtl3D control

| |
|---|
| (Add Classes) |
| IgnoreColors |
| No3DMenus |

In design mode, as soon as the control is placed on any form, you will see an immediate change. The Visual Basic design time environment takes on a 3D appearance. Visual Basic's menus and dialogs all look different. This is an instant notification that the VBCtl3D control is working behind the scenes.

VBCtl3D changes the appearance of standard Visual Basic controls such as the text control and option buttons. The forms themselves acquire a light gray background, and controls placed on the form take on an inset or raised appearance. The controls that VBCtl3D recognizes are listed in Table 1-46.

**Table 1-46** Standard controls recognized by VBCtl3D

| | | |
|---|---|---|
| Check Box | Combo Box | Directory List Box |
| Drive List Box | File List Box | Form |
| Frame | Image | Label |
| List Box | Menu | Option Button |
| Picture Box | | |

For new applications, that's about all there is to it. Just start by placing the VBCtl3D control on an empty form, and then watch other controls magically transform themselves. This control does provide a few customization features, as well as ways to disable the 3D effect.

VBCtl3D uses a control's *BackColor* property as its cue to alter a control's appearance. If the control's BackColor property is set to hexidecimal 80000005, which is the window background color, VBCtl3D attempts to change the look of that control. If the control has any other *BackColor* value, VBCtl3D does nothing to its appearance. This provides a simple way to avoid the 3D appearance in selected controls.

You can short-circuit the use of *BackColor* as a cue to prevent display of the 3D effect by using the *IgnoreColors* property. When this property is set to *True*, VBCtl3D will attempt to draw controls with a 3D appearance regardless of their *BackColor* setting.

By default, menus are affected by this 3D look as well. Since this style is not usual, even in applications that otherwise have a 3D appearance, VBCtl3D provides a way to disable this feature. The *No3DMenus* property, when set to *True,* prevents VBCtl3D from changing the appearance of menus. You can only change this property at design time; attempting to change the value at run time results in an error.

You can extend the 3D appearance provided by VBCtl3D to other controls as well, if they tend to look like standard controls. The Visual Basic Masked Edit control is a good example of this. The Masked Edit control looks like a standard text box, even though it doesn't behave like one. You can tell VBCtl3D to treat such controls like their standard cousins by using the *Add Classes* dialog that is available in the Visual Basic Properties window at design time. This dialog, shown in Figure 1-17, lets you add controls to those standard ones that it automatically supports. By entering the class name of a control into one of the category fields and pressing the Add To List button, you can tell VBCtl3D to change the control's appearance as well. Generally, you add a new control to the category that it most resembles, so, for example, you would add a Masked Edit control to the Text Box list. (As it happens, the Masked Edit control has already been included in the list of custom controls recognized by VBCtl3D, but it serves as the best practical example.)

While the *Add Classes* dialog gives you a way to customize a single application at design time, VBCtl3D also lets you set global defaults for any application. The optional VBCTL3D INI file is a standard Windows INI file that, if present, is used by any instance of VBCtl3D to determine the default behavior of controls.

VBCTL3D.INI (if you use this file, place in the Windows directory), has a General section and sections for identifying nonstandard custom controls that VBCtl3D should convert to the 3D look. The General section includes three keywords: *Disabled, No3DMenus,* and *IgnoreColors.* You can assign these three keywords a true or false value, indicated in the INI file by a 1 or a 0. All are set to 0, or *False,* by default. You can use *Disabled* to globally turn off the 3D effect created by VBCtl3D. This keyword is useful if the user prefers the standard appearance of the controls. *No3DMenus* serves the same

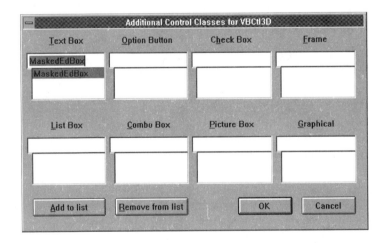

**Figure 1-17** The Add Classes dialog box

purpose as the property of the same name, but its effect is global and, if set to *True*, it overrides a *False* value in the *No3DMenus* property. Similarly, *IgnoreColors* works like the *IgnoreColors* property.

You can use other sections of the INI file to register nonstandard custom controls that should be drawn in the 3D style. Each section is named for standard control such as a Text control or a Frame. Keywords under these sections are the names of custom controls that should be drawn in the same 3D style. For example, you could register the Masked Edit control discussed earlier by assigning a *True* value of 1 to the keyword, as shown here.

```
[TextBoxControls]
MaskedEdBox = 1
```

You can disable the 3D appearance of the Masked Edit control by assigning a value of 0 to its entry in VBCTL3D.INI. This INI file is entirely optional, and is not required to use the VBCtl3D control.

# Example

The example program is quite simple, but shows how to selectively control the 3D appearance of controls. The program is shown in its initial, two-dimensional state in Figure 1-18.

The form contains several standard controls, including option buttons, check boxes, text controls, and frames. The appearance is flat and unappealing. Press the Toggle 3D button and the form's appearance changes dramatically, as shown in Figure 1-19.

Pressing the Show Message Box button makes a simple call to the Visual Basic *MsgBox* function, but the appearance of the message box has become 3D as well. VBCtl3D automatically changes the appearance of common dialog windows, including the standard message box.

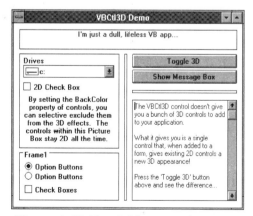

**Figure 1-18** The VBCtl3D example program in two dimensions

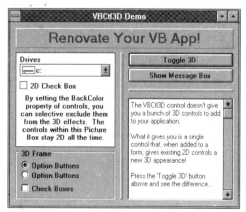

**Figure 1-19** The VBCtl3D example after toggling to 3D

Notice that the controls in the upper-left corner did not change their appearance when we toggled to 3D mode. Here the *BackColor* property was used to supress the 3D effect. These controls had their *BackColor* property set to a value other than hexadecimal &H80000005, which VBCtl3D uses as a signal to convert a control to 3D appearance.

## Steps

1. Create a new project called VBCTL3D.MAK. Add the 3D Control, VBCTL3D.VBX, to the project. Create a new form with the objects and properties described in Table 1-47. Save this form as VBCTL3D1.FRM.

**Table 1-47** Objects and properties of the VBCTL3D1.FRM

| OBJECT | PROPERTY | SETTING |
| --- | --- | --- |
| Form | FormName | frmVBCtl3D |
| | BackColor | &H00FFFFFF& |
| | Caption | "VBCtl3D Demo" |
| Label | Name | Label4 |
| | BackColor | &H00FFFFFF& |
| | BorderStyle | 1 'Fixed Single |
| Label | Name | Label5 |
| | BackColor | &H00FFFFFF& |
| | BorderStyle | 1 'Fixed Single |
| Ctl3D | Name | Ctl3D1 |
| | ClassList | (set at design time in Properties window) |
| TextBox | Name | txtDesc |
| | BackColor | &H00FFFFFF& |
| | FontBold | 0 'False |
| | ForeColor | &H00800000& |
| | MultiLine | -1 'True |
| | ScrollBars | 2 'Vertical |
| CommandButton | Name | btnToggle3D |
| | Caption | "Toggle 3D" |
| PictureBox | Name | Picture1 |
| | BackColor | &H00FFFFFF& |
| | Tag | "/ignore/" |
| CommandButton | Name | btnMsgBox |
| | Caption | "Show Message Box" |
| Frame | Name | Frame1 |
| | BackColor | &H00FFFFFF& |
| | Caption | "Frame1" |

2. Place the controls shown in Table 1-48 within the Picture1 PictureBox control. Make sure you select the Picture1 control before adding these controls.

**Table 1-48** Controls contained inside the Picture1 control

| OBJECT | PROPERTY | SETTING |
|---|---|---|
| Label | Name | Label1 |
| | BackColor | &H00FFFFFF& |
| | BackStyle | 0 'Transparent |
| | Caption | "Drives" |
| | ForeColor | &H00800000& |
| | Tag | "/ignore/" |
| Label | Name | Label2 |
| | Alignment | 2 'Center |
| | BackColor | &H00FFFFFF& |
| | BackStyle | 0 'Transparent |
| | Caption | "By setting the BackColor property of controls, you can selectively exclude them from the 3D effects. The controls within this Picture Box stay 2D all the time." |
| | ForeColor | &H00800000& |
| | Tag | "/ignore/" |
| CheckBox | Name | Check2 |
| | BackColor | &H00FFFFFF& |
| | Caption | "2D Check Box" |
| | ForeColor | &H00800000& |
| | Tag | "/ignore/" |
| DriveListBox | Name | Drive1 |
| | BackColor | &H00FFFFFF& |
| | ForeColor | &H00800000& |
| | Tag | "/ignore/" |

3. Place the controls shown in Table 1-49 within the Frame1 frame control. Again, make sure you select the Frame1 control before adding these controls.

**Table 1-49** Controls contained inside the Frame1 control

| OBJECT | PROPERTY | SETTING |
|---|---|---|
| OptionButton | Name | Option1 |
| | BackColor | &H00FFFFFF& |
| | Caption | "Option Buttons" |
| | Value | -1 'True |
| CheckBox | Name | Check1 |
| | BackColor | &H00FFFFFF& |
| | Caption | "Check Boxes" |

*(continued on next page)*

| OBJECT | PROPERTY | SETTING |
|---|---|---|
| *(continued from previous page)* | | |
| OptionButton | Name | Option2 |
| | BackColor | &H00FFFFFF& |
| | Caption | "Option Buttons" |

4. After creating VBCTL3D1.FRM, add the following code to the form's declaration section.

```
Option Explicit
'-------------------------------------------------
' Constants used in the VBCtl3D example program.
'-------------------------------------------------

Const WIN_BACKCOLOR = &H80000005
Const LIGHT_GRAY = &HC0C0C0
Const WHITE = &HFFFFFF

'  MessageBox() Flags
Const MB_OK = &H0
Const MB_ICONEXCLAMATION = &H30
Const MB_ICONAsterisk = &H40
```

5. Next, add the following event subroutines to VBCTL3D1.FRM.

```
Sub btnMsgBox_Click ()
'-------------------------------------------------
' Display a message box to illustrate the 3D effect.
'-------------------------------------------------
    MsgBox "The 3D Effect is also used when displaying Message Boxes and Common Dialogs, so
your application has a consistent 3D appearance.", MB_OK Or MB_ICONAsterisk, "3D Message Box"
End Sub

Sub btnToggle3D_Click ()
'-------------------------------------------------
' Toggle between 3D and 2D appearance by setting
' the BackColor property.
'-------------------------------------------------
Dim i As Integer

    On Error Resume Next

    ' Use the form's background color as a cue for the current mode (2D or 3D).
    If Me.BackColor <> LIGHT_GRAY Then
        Me.BackColor = LIGHT_GRAY
        For i = 0 To controls.Count - 1
            If InStr(controls(i).Tag, "/ignore/") = 0 Then
                controls(i).BackColor = WIN_BACKCOLOR
            End If
        Next
        Frame1.Caption = "3D Frame"
        lblBanner.FontSize = 18
        lblBanner = "Renovate Your VB App!"

    Else
        Me.BackColor = WHITE
```

```
        For i = 0 To controls.Count - 1
            If InStr(controls(i).Tag, "/ignore/") = 0 Then
                controls(i).BackColor = WHITE
            End If
        Next
        Frame1.Caption = "2D Frame"
        lblBanner.FontSize = 8.25
        lblBanner = "Admit it. You liked me better the other way didn't you?"
    End If
End Sub

Sub Form_Load ()
'---------------------------------------------------
' Center the form on the screen, and initialize the
' description text box.
'---------------------------------------------------
Dim CRLF As String

    CRLF = Chr$(13) & Chr$(10)

    Me.Move (Screen.Width - Me.Width) \ 2, (Screen.Height - Me.Height) \ 2

    txtDesc = txtDesc & "The VBCtl3D control doesn't give you a "
    txtDesc = txtDesc & "bunch of 3D controls to add to your application." & CRLF & CRLF
    txtDesc = txtDesc & "What it gives you is a single control that, when added to "
    txtDesc = txtDesc & "a form, gives existing 2D controls a new 3D appearance!" & CRLF & CRLF
    txtDesc = txtDesc & "Press the 'Toggle 3D' button above and see the difference..."

End Sub
```

## Tips and Comments

When using the VBCtl3D control, be aware that when you set a form's *BorderStyle* to 3 - Fixed Double, VBCtl3D will apply a 3D effect to the fixed, double border as well. There is no option for turning this feature off, so even if you disable the 3D effect of controls in the form (using the *BackColor* property, as discussed earlier), the form's border will remain 3D.

The same holds true for message boxes, common dialogs, and menus. While you can control when the 3D effect is applied to controls, you cannot turn off the effect for these other objects as well. But you can still globally disable them using the *Disabled* keyword in the VBCTL3D.INI file.

# VSElastic (VSVBX.VBX)

| USAGE: | Resolution Independence, Automatic Labels, Autosizing Controls |
| --- | --- |
| MANUFACTURER: | Videosoft |
| COST: | $45 |

Videosoft's VSElastic control addresses the fact that VB apps are not, by nature, resolution independent. This control can automatically resize child controls placed inside it to help improve the situation. It can also add 3D effects to its children, create splitter bar effects, and act as a progress meter.

## Syntax

When you add a VSElastic control to a VB form, you can position it manually or you can use the *Align* property to have it position and size itself automatically when the form is resized. VSElastic's *Align* property isn't the standard *Align* property found in Picture Boxes. Picture Boxes, and controls that support the standard *Align* property, can be placed directly on MDI forms, VSElastic controls cannot. The standard *Align* property supports *Top* and *Bottom* alignment; VSElastic also supports *Left* and *Right* alignment as well as a setting that causes the control to expand to completely fill its parent container. Table 1-50 lists the nonstandard properties and events for the VSElastic control.

**Table 1-50** VSElastic nonstandard properties and events

### PROPERTIES

| | | |
|---|---|---|
| About | AccessKey | Align |
| AutoSizeChildren | BevelChildren | BevelInner |
| BevelInnerWidth | BevelOuter | BevelOuterWidth |
| BorderWidth | CaptionPos | ChildSpacing |
| FloodColor | FloodDirection | FloodPercent |
| MaxChildSize | MinChildSize | ShadowColor |
| Splitter | Style | TagPosition |
| TagWidth | WordWrap | |

### EVENTS

| | |
|---|---|
| RealignFrame | ResizeChildren |

You control how a VSElastic resizes its children with the *AutosizeChildren* property. The control can keep the children all the same size horizontally or vertically; it can resize only a single control, keeping the rest at their original size; and it can be told to resize only other VSElastic controls inside it. VSElastics can be nested which allows you to create complex autosizing schemes to suit your needs. As of version 4.0 each VSElastic can contain a maximum of 255 child controls so nesting may become a requirement in some cases just to overcome that limit. The *ChildSpacing* property tells the VSElastic how much space to leave between child controls when it resizes them. The VSElastic control isn't human so it can't tell what looks good. In order to enforce some limits on it you can use the *MinChildSize* and *MaxChildSize* properties so controls that are resized never get too small or too large.

In addition to resizing its children, a VSElastic can add 3D effects to them. It offers both *BevelInner* and *BevelOuter* properties, which you can mix and match as the sample program demonstrates. There are ten possible settings for *BevelInner* and *BevelOuter*: *Raised, Raised Outlined, Inset, Inset Outlined, Fillet, Groove,* and for *BevelInner, Shadow, Raised New Look* and *Inset New Look* (Table 1-51).

**Table 1-51** VSElastic BevelInner and BevelOuter values

| VALUE | MEANING |
| --- | --- |
| 0 | None |
| 1 | Raised |
| 2 | Raised outlined |
| 3 | Inset |
| 4 | Inset outlined |
| 5 | Fillet |
| 6 | Groove |
| 7 | Shadow (BevelInner only) |
| 8 | Raised New Look |
| 9 | Inset New Look |

You can also set the width of each bevel independently via the *BevelInnerWidth* and *BevelOuterWidth* properties. If the bevel is set to *Shadow*, you can also set its *ShadowColor*. You can tell the VS Elastic whether to add the effects to its children with the *BevelChildren* property.

If you want to use the VSElastic as a progress meter, use the *FloodColor, FloodDirection,* and *FloodPercent* properties. The VSElastic can flood in four directions (Left, Right, Up, Down) whereas some meter controls can only flood in two (Left and Right).

VSElastics can also simulate labels for each child control. It's common to have a label in front of a text box so this is a very useful feature. The *TagWidth* property determines how wide the labels will be; they're all the same width. *TagPosition* can be set to draw the labels to the *Left, Right, Below,* or *Above* the controls. The text for each label is taken from the *Tag* property of the child control and, if the label contains an ampersand (&), you can turn on the *AccessKey* property to enable hot key access to controls.

# Example

The sample program (Figure 1-20) uses 3 main VSElastic controls. The first is used as the toolbar and its *Align* property is set to *Top*. The second is the status bar and its *Align* property is set to *Bottom*. The last covers the center portion of the Form; its *Align* property is set to *Fill Container*. *Uneven* sizing is used by both the toolbar and the status bar. The toolbar resizes a nested VSElastic control and the status bar resizes a standard VB Label.

The main VSElastic also has the *Splitter* property turned on, which allows us to resize its child controls at run time (Figure 1-21). The fourth VSElastic is used as a progress meter and is nested inside the toolbar VSElastic. The buttons with the chevrons (>> and <<) cause the fourth Elastic to flood in opposite directions. The New Look button will cycle through seven different 3D styles that are easily achieved using the Bevel related properties (*BevelInner, BevelOuter, BorderWidth,* and *ShadowColor*).

The status bar contains only standard VB Label controls. The 3D effects are all provided by their parent VS Elastic.

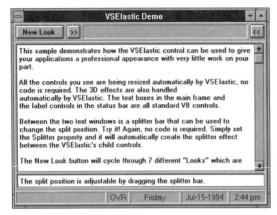

**Figure 1-20** Autosizing and 3D effects courtesy of VSElastic

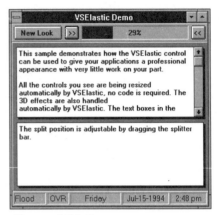

**Figure 1-21** Progress meter, resized window, and a new look

## Steps

1. Create a new project called VSELSTIC.MAK. Create a new form with the objects and properties shown in Table 1-52. Save this form as VSELSTIC.FRM.

**Table 1-52** VSELSTIC main form's objects and properties

| OBJECT | PROPERTY | SETTING |
|---|---|---|
| Form | FormName | frmMain |
| | BackColor | &H00C0C0C0& |
| | Caption | "VSElastic Demo" |
| VideoSoftElastic | Name | vseToolbar |
| | Align | 1 'Align Top |
| | AutoSizeChildren | 5 'Elastics Only Horizontal |
| | BackColor | &H00C0C0C0& |
| | BevelInnerWidth | 0 |
| | BevelOuter | 1 'Raised |
| | BevelOuterWidth | 1 |
| | BorderWidth | 4 |
| | ChildSpacing | 5 |
| VideoSoftElastic | Name | vseStatusBar |
| | Align | 2 'Align Bottom |
| | AutoSizeChildren | 2 'Uneven Horizontal |
| | BackColor | &H00C0C0C0& |
| | BevelOuter | 1 'Raised |
| | BevelOuterWidth | 1 |
| | BorderWidth | 4 |
| | ChildSpacing | 5 |

| OBJECT | PROPERTY | SETTING |
|--------|----------|---------|
| VideoSoftElastic | Name | vseMain |
| | Align | 5 'Fill Container |
| | AutoSizeChildren | 3 'Uneven Vertical |
| | BackColor | &H00C0C0C0& |
| | BevelOuter | 1 'Raised |
| | BevelOuterWidth | 1 |
| | BorderWidth | 5 |
| | ChildSpacing | 5 |
| | FloodDirection | 3 'Up |
| | Splitter | 1 'Yes (with uneven spacing) |

2. Place the objects shown in Table 1-53 in the the vseStatusBar VSElastic control.

**Table 1-53** VSELSTIC vseStatusBar objects and properties

| OBJECT | PROPERTY | SETTING |
|--------|----------|---------|
| Label | Name | lblCurTime |
| | Alignment | 2 'Center |
| | BackStyle | 0 'Transparent |
| | FontBold | 0 'False |
| | FontSize | 9.75 |
| Label | Name | lblCurDate |
| | Alignment | 2 'Center |
| | BackStyle | 0 'Transparent |
| | FontBold | 0 'False |
| | FontSize | 9.75 |
| Label | Name | lblWeekday |
| | Alignment | 2 'Center |
| | BackStyle | 0 'Transparent |
| | FontBold | 0 'False |
| | FontSize | 9.75 |
| Label | Name | lblInsertMode |
| | Alignment | 2 'Center |
| | BackStyle | 0 'Transparent |
| | Caption | "OVR" |
| | FontBold | 0 'False |
| | FontSize | 9.75 |
| Label | Name | lblStatusBar |
| | BackStyle | 0 'Transparent |
| | Caption | "Status Bar" |
| | FontBold | 0 'False |
| | FontSize | 9.75 |

3.  Place the objects shown in Table 1-54 in the the vseToolbar VSElastic control.

**Table 1-54** VSELSTIC vseToolbar objects and properties

| OBJECT | PROPERTY | SETTING |
|---|---|---|
| CommandButton | Name | cmdNewLook |
| | Caption | "New Look" |
| CommandButton | Name | cmdStartFlood |
| | Caption | " >>" |
| | Index | 0 |
| CommandButton | Name | cmdStartFlood |
| | Caption | "<<" |
| | Index | 1 |
| VideoSoftElastic | Name | vseMeter |
| | AutoSizeChildren | 2 'Uneven Horizontal |
| | BackColor | &H00C0C0C0& |
| | BevelInner | 0 'None |
| | BevelInnerWidth | 0 |
| | BevelOuter | 3 'Inset |
| | BevelOuterWidth | 1 |
| | BorderWidth | 1 |
| | Caption | "An Elastic control can be a meter too ! Press >> or << to test." |
| | CaptionPos | 4 'Center Center |
| | FloodColor | &H00FF0000& |
| | FloodDirection | 1 'Right |
| | FontBold | 0 'False |

4.  Place the objects shown in Table 1-55 in the the vseMain VSElastic control.

**Table 1-55** VSELSTIC vseMain objects and properties

| OBJECT | PROPERTY | SETTING |
|---|---|---|
| TextBox | Name | txtEditor |
| | Index | 1 |
| | MultiLine | -1 'True |
| | Text | "You can adust split position by dragging the splitter bar. " |
| TextBox | Name | txtEditor |
| | Index | 0 |
| | MultiLine | -1 'True |
| | ScrollBars | 2 'Vertical |

5. Add the following code to VSELSTIC form.

```
Sub ChangeLook ()
    Static LookIndex As Integer

    LookIndex% = LookIndex% + 1
    Select Case LookIndex% Mod 7
        Case 0
            vseMain.BackColor = LIGHTGRAY
            vseMain.BevelInner = VSE_BEVEL_INSET
            vseMain.BevelOuter = VSE_BEVEL_RAISED
            vseMain.BevelInnerWidth = 1
            vseMain.BevelOuterWidth = 1
            vseMain.BorderWidth = 5
            vseMain.ChildSpacing = 5
            vseMain.ShadowColor = DARKGRAY
        Case 1
            vseMain.BackColor = GREEN
            vseMain.BorderWidth = 0
            vseMain.ChildSpacing = 3
        Case 2
            vseMain.BackColor = LIGHTGRAY
            vseMain.BevelInner = VSE_BEVEL_SHADOW
            vseMain.BevelInnerWidth = 3
            vseMain.BorderWidth = 8
            vseMain.ChildSpacing = 8
        Case 3
            vseMain.BackColor = GREEN
            vseMain.ShadowColor = DARKGREEN
        Case 4
            vseMain.ShadowColor = DARKGRAY
        Case 5
            vseMain.ShadowColor = BLACK
        Case 6
            vseMain.BackColor = LIGHTGRAY
            vseMain.BevelInner = VSE_BEVEL_RAISED
            vseMain.BevelOuter = VSE_BEVEL_INSET
            vseMain.BevelInnerWidth = 1
            vseMain.BevelOuterWidth = 1
            vseMain.BorderWidth = 5
            vseMain.ChildSpacing = 5
    End Select

End Sub

Sub cmdNewLook_Click ()

    Call ChangeLook

End Sub

Sub cmdNewLook_MouseMove (Button As Integer, Shift As Integer, X As Single, Y As Single)

    Call UpdateStatus("Change Look of main panel area")

End Sub

Sub cmdStartFlood_Click (Index As Integer)
    Dim i As Integer
```

(continued on next page)

*(continued from previous page)*

```vb
    Select Case Index%
        Case 0
            vseMeter.FloodDirection = VSE_FLOOD_RIGHT
        Case 1
            vseMeter.FloodDirection = VSE_FLOOD_LEFT
    End Select

    For i% = 0 To 100
        vseMeter.FloodPercent = i%
        vseMeter.Caption = CStr(i%) & "%"
        DoEvents
    Next i%
    vseMeter.FloodPercent = 0
    vseMeter.Caption = "An Elastic control can be a meter too! Press >> or << to test."

End Sub

Sub cmdStartFlood_MouseMove (Index As Integer, Button As Integer, Shift As Integer, X As
Single, Y As Single)

    Select Case Index%
        Case 0
            Call UpdateStatus("Flood left-to-right")
        Case 1
            Call UpdateStatus("Flood right-to-left")
    End Select

End Sub

Sub Form_Load ()

    Me.Move (Screen.Width - Width) \ 2, (Screen.Height - height) \ 2

End Sub

Sub tmrMain_Timer ()

    lblCurTime.Caption = Format$(Now, "h:nn am/pm")

End Sub

Sub UpdateStatus (NewStatus As String)

    lblStatusBar.Caption = NewStatus$

End Sub

Sub vseToolbar_MouseMove (Button As Integer, Shift As Integer, X As Single, Y As Single)

    Call UpdateStatus("")

End Sub
```

6. Create a new module named VSELSTIC.BAS and add the following code to the declarations section.

```vb
Option Explicit
DefInt A-Z
```

```
Global Const BLACK = &H0&
Global Const DARKGRAY = &H808080
Global Const LIGHTGRAY = &HC0C0C0
Global Const GREEN = &HFF00&
Global Const DARKGREEN = &H8000&

Global Const VSE_BEVEL_NONE = 0
Global Const VSE_BEVEL_RAISED = 1
Global Const VSE_BEVEL_RAISED_OUTLINED = 2
Global Const VSE_BEVEL_INSET = 3
Global Const VSE_BEVEL_INSET_OUTLINED = 4
Global Const VSE_BEVEL_FILLET = 5
Global Const VSE_BEVEL_GROOVED = 6
Global Const VSE_BEVEL_SHADOW = 7

Global Const VSE_FLOOD_NONE = 0
Global Const VSE_FLOOD_RIGHT = 1
Global Const VSE_FLOOD_LEFT = 2
Global Const VSE_FLOOD_UP = 3
Global Const VSE_FLOOD_DOWN = 4
```

7. Add the following code to VSELSTIC.BAS module.

```
Sub Main ()
    Dim Filename As String
    Dim Buffer   As String
    Dim hFile    As Integer

    frmMain!lblWeekday.Caption = Format$(Now, "dddd")
    frmMain!lblCurDate.Caption = Format$(Now, "mmm-dd-yyyy")
    frmMain!lblCurTime.Caption = Format$(Now, "h:nn am/pm")

    Filename$ = App.Path & "\VSELSTC1.TXT"
    On Error Resume Next
        Buffer$ = Space$(FileLen(Filename$))
        hFile% = FreeFile
        Open Filename$ For Binary As #hFile%
            Get #hFile%, , Buffer$
        Close #hFile%
    On Error GoTo 0
    frmMain!txtEditor(0).Text = Buffer$

    frmMain.Show

End Sub
```

## Tips and Comments

When you use *Uneven* sizing, the control that gets resized is the one that's highest in the *ZOrder*. This can trip you up if you add and delete controls and forget to bring the desired control to the top of the *ZOrder* again.

Nesting VSElastics inside one another gives you a great deal of flexibility in how autosizing is handled, and shouldn't be overlooked when designing an application with VSElastic.

# VSIndexTab (VSVBX.VBX)

| USAGE: | Folder Tab Control |
|---|---|
| MANUFACTURER: | Videosoft |
| COST: | $ 45 |

The folder tab, or index tab, metaphor is becoming increasingly popular and there are now a variety of controls that allow you to add these features to your applications very easily. No two are alike and each has its strengths and weaknesses. Videosoft's VSIndexTab offers a lot of power that's not obvious at first glance.

## Syntax

When you first add a Videosoft Index Tab (VSIndexTab) to a form you will see a single white tab at the bottom of the control. The position of the tab(s) is controlled by the *Position* property (Table 1-56).

**Table 1-56** VSIndexTab Position property values

| VALUE | MEANING |
|---|---|
| 0 | Top |
| 1 | Bottom |
| 2 | Left |
| 3 | Right |
| 4 | Right, face text in |

You don't need to create another VSIndexTab control to have more than one tab appear on the VSIndexTab control. You determine the number of tabs on the control by using the *Caption* property. To add another tab to a control, insert a pipe symbol (|) in the *Caption*. The *TabCaption* property sets or retrieves the caption for an individual tab. New tabs can be added and existing tabs deleted with the *TabCaption* property as well. If you want to insert an invisible tab on the VSIndexTab, use a dash (-) for its caption. To disable specific tabs within a VSIndexTab, use the *TabEnabled* property. Table 1-57 lists all nonstandard properties and events for the VSIndexTab control.

**Table 1-57** VSIndexTab nonstandard properties and events

| PROPERTIES | | |
|---|---|---|
| About | AutoScroll | AutoSwitch |
| BackSheets | BackTabColor | BoldCurrent |
| BorderWidth | Caption | ClientLeft |
| ClientHeight | ClientTop | ClientWidth |
| CurrTab | DogEars | FirstTab |
| FrontTabColor | FrontTabForeColor | MouseOver |

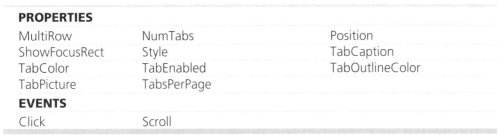

## PROPERTIES

| | | |
|---|---|---|
| MultiRow | NumTabs | Position |
| ShowFocusRect | Style | TabCaption |
| TabColor | TabEnabled | TabOutlineColor |
| TabPicture | TabsPerPage | |

## EVENTS

| | |
|---|---|
| Click | Scroll |

The size of each tab varies based on the width of the caption for that particular tab. If you want all your tabs to be the same size, set the *TabsPerPage* property to a nonzero value. The width of each tab will be equal to the width of the VSIndexTab divided by the value contained in *TabsPerPage*. If the number of tabs on a VSIndexTab control is greater than the value in the *TabsPerPage* property, the *AutoScroll, DogEars, FirstTab, MultiRow,* and *MultiRowOffset* properties come into play, determining how the tabs will be displayed.

If *AutoScroll* is *True,* the tabs' appearance will not be altered but the tabs that aren't visible are still accessible. We'll call these virtual tabs. In this case, the tabs will scroll automatically so that the current tab is always visible. The tabs can be navigated with the arrow keys; mnemonic keys can also be used to access virtual tabs. If the *DogEars* property is *True* and there are more tabs than can be displayed, then the upper corner of the tabs at the edge of the row will appear "dog eared" to indicate that there are more tabs in that direction. Clicking on the dog ears is another way to bring virtual tabs into view. One, final, way to navigate virtual tabs is to change the *FirstTab* property in code. *FirstTab* controls which tab appears first (leftmost) in the row. On a related note, the *CurrTab* property indicates which tab is currently active. If the *MultiRow* property is *True,* all the tabs will appear—new rows will be added automatically if necessary.

The *Style* property affects the shape and appearance of the tabs themselves. The possible options appear in Table 1-58. If you plan to use dog ears on your tabs, you should use a *Style* value of 6 or 7. The dog ears don't look quite right with the other styles.

**Table 1-58** VSIndexTab Style property values

| VALUE | MEANING |
|---|---|
| 0 | Slanted lines |
| 1 | Slanted lines plus 3D effect |
| 2 | Rounded corners |
| 3 | Rounded corners plus 3D effect |
| 4 | Chamfered corners |
| 5 | Chamfered corners plus 3D effect |
| 6 | Straight sides |
| 7 | Straight sides plus 3D effect |
| 8 | Cut corners |
| 9 | Cut corners plus 3D effect |

Four color-related properties provide a certain degree of control over the appearance of the tabs. *BackTabColor* affects all the inactive tabs; *FrontTabColor* affects the active tab; *FrontTabForeColor* is used for the caption of the active tab; and *TabColor*, like *TabCaption*, affects only the specified tab. *TabColor* is referenced like an array where each tab is an element. For example, to set the color of the third tab you would use *TabColor(2)*. Tab indexes are zero based. The *TabPicture* property is used in the same way to load pictures into individual tabs. Bitmaps (BMP), Icons (ICO), or MetaFiles may be loaded into the *TabPicture* property.

Because VSIndexTab is a container control, it may act as a parent to other controls, including other VSIndexTabs. Figure 1-22 shows how the controls can be nested, with different styles being used for each. The *AutoSwitch* property makes it easy to assign child controls. If *AutoSwitch* is *False*, the nested containers are assigned to tabs based on their location (the *Left* property to be specific), which can make design sessions a challenge. Using *AutoSwitch*, at design time, you simply right-double-click on the tab of your choice to activate it. The tab will then appear just as it will at run time, simplifying the whole process.

Only three events are fired by a VSIndexTab, but they're important ones. The *PreClick* event is fired before the user switches to a different tab. The *Click* event is fired when a new tab becomes the active tab. To find out which tab is active, use the *CurrTab* property. The *Scroll* event is fired when the *FirstTab* property changes. This can only happen if you have more tabs than can be displayed and *MultiRow* is *False*. The *MouseOver* property, indicating which tab the mouse is currently over, can be used to good effect with the standard VB *MouseMove* event to provide a dynamic status display.

# Example

The example program (Figure 1-23) makes use of the properties that affect the aesthetics of the VSIndexTab as well as the functionality (i.e., scolling tabs). There are

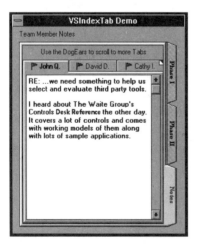

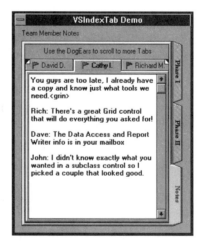

**Figure 1-22** VSIndexTab Example showing how tabs can be nested

**Figure 1-23** VSIndexTab sample program

two VSIndexTab controls on the form. One has tabs on the right and the other, nested inside the first one, has tabs on the top. The inner VSIndexTab also uses dog ears to make the most of the limited space available. Bitmaps (red flags) are loaded into the inner VSIndexTab control on startup and when a tab is activated the bitmap for that tab is changed to a green flag.

## Steps

1. Create a new project called VSTAB.MAK. Create a new form with the objects and properties shown in Table 1-59. Save this form as VSTAB.FRM. Before proceeding to Step 2, be sure the *AutoSize* property of VSTab is set to *False*.

**Table 1-59** VSIndexTab main form's objects and properties

| OBJECT | PROPERTY | SETTING |
|---|---|---|
| Form | FormName | frmMain |
| | BackColor | &H00C0C0C0& |
| | BorderStyle | 3 'Fixed Double |
| | Caption | "VSIndexTab Demo" |
| | MaxButton | 0 'False |
| | MinButton | 0 'False |
| | ScaleMode | 3 'Pixel |
| Image | Name | imgTabPicture |
| | Index | 0 |
| | Picture | (Red Flag bitmap set at design time in Properties window) |
| | Visible | 0 'False |
| Image | Name | imgTabPicture |
| | Index | 1 |
| | Picture | (Green Flag bitmap set at time in Properties window) |
| | Visible | 0 'False |
| VideoSoftIndexTab | Name | vstTab |
| | AutoSize | False |
| | BackTabColor | &H0000C0C0& |
| | BoldCurrent | 0 'False |
| | BorderWidth | 2 |
| | Caption | "Phase IIPhase IIINotes" |
| | DogEars | 0 'False |
| | FrontTabColor | &H0000FFFF& |
| | FrontTabForeColor | &H000000FF& |
| | Position | 4 'Right face in |
| | ShowFocusRect | 0 'False |
| | Style | 1 'Slanted 3D |
| | TabsPerPage | 3 |

2. Place the objects shown in Table 1-60 in the the vstTab control. Each tab in the VSIndexTab control has an associated container control that becomes visible when the tab becomes active. Picture Boxes are used in the sample program. Once you've placed the three Picture Box containers, set the vstTab *AutoSize* property back to *True*. When you do, PicTab(0) fills the first tab.

**Table 1-60** VSIndexTab vstTab objects and properties

| OBJECT | PROPERTY | SETTING |
|---|---|---|
| PictureBox | Name | picTab |
| | BackColor | &H00C0C0C0& |
| | Index | 0 |
| PictureBox | Name | picTab |
| | BackColor | &H00C0C0C0& |
| | Index | 1 |
| PictureBox | Name | picTab |
| | BackColor | &H00C0C0C0& |
| | Index | 2 |

3. Place the objects shown in Table 1-61 in the the picTab(0) Picture Box.

**Table 1-61** VSIndexTab picTab(0) objects and properties

| OBJECT | PROPERTY | SETTING |
|---|---|---|
| TextBox | Name | txtPage |
| | Index | 0 |
| | MultiLine | -1 'True |
| | ScrollBars | 2 'Vertical |

4. Place the objects shown in Table 1-62 in the the picTab(1) Picture Box. Make the container of the second tab visible by double-clicking on it with the right mouse button.

**Table 1-62** VSIndexTab picTab(1) objects and properties

| OBJECT | PROPERTY | SETTING |
|---|---|---|
| TextBox | Name | txtPage |
| | Index | 1 |
| | MultiLine | -1 'True |
| | ScrollBars | 2 'Vertical |

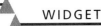

5. Double-click on the third tab. Place the objects shown in Table 1-63 in the picTab(2) Picture Box. Double-right-click on the first tab to make it the default tab.

**Table 1-63** VSIndexTab picTab(2) objects and properties

| OBJECT | PROPERTY | SETTING |
|---|---|---|
| Label | Name | lblDogEarNote |
| | Alignment | 2 'Center |
| | BackStyle | 0 'Transparent |
| | Caption | "Use the DogEars to scroll to more Tabs" |
| | FontBold | 0 'False |
| VideoSoftIndexTab | Name | vstNotes |
| | BackSheets | 0 'None |
| | BorderWidth | 3 |
| | Caption | "John Q.IDavid D.ICathy I.IRichard M.ISusan T." |
| | FontBold | 0 'False |
| | FrontTabColor | &H00C0C0C0& |
| | Position | 0 'Top |
| | Style | 7 'Straight 3D |
| | TabsPerPage | 3 |

6. Place the objects shown in Table 1-64 in the the vstNotes VSIndexTab control.

**Table 1-64** VSIndexTab vstNotes objects and properties

| OBJECT | PROPERTY | SETTING |
|---|---|---|
| TextBox | Name | txtNotes |
| | MultiLine | -1 'True |
| | ScrollBars | 2 'Vertical |

7. Add the following code to the declarations section of the VSTAB form.

```
Option Explicit
DefInt A-Z

Const MB_OK = 0
Const MB_ICONSTOP = 16
```

8. Add the following code to the VSTAB form.

```
Sub Form_Load ()

    Me.Move (Screen.Width - Width) \ 2, (Screen.Height - Height) \ 2
```

(continued on next page)

*(continued from previous page)*

```vb
    '-- Load text into First two pages
    Call LoadFiles

    '-- Force the first Notes Tab to
    '   load its associated text.
    Call vstNotes_Click

End Sub

Sub LoadFiles ()
'--------------------------------------------------
'-- This procedure loads sample text files into
'   the text boxes on the first two Tabs.
'--------------------------------------------------
    Dim Buffer   As String
    Dim Filename As String
    Dim hFile    As Integer

    On Error GoTo LoadFilesErr
        Filename$ = App.Path & "\PHASE1.TXT"
        Buffer$ = Space$(FileLen(Filename$))
        hFile% = FreeFile
        Open Filename For Binary As #hFile%
            Get #hFile%, , Buffer$
        Close #hFile%
        txtPage(0).Text = Buffer$

        Filename$ = App.Path & "\PHASE2.TXT"
        Buffer$ = Space$(FileLen(Filename$))
        hFile% = FreeFile
        Open Filename For Binary As #hFile%
            Get #hFile%, , Buffer$
        Close #hFile%
        txtPage(1).Text = Buffer$

On Error GoTo 0

LoadFilesExit:
    Exit Sub

LoadFilesErr:
    MsgBox "Error in LoadFiles", MB_OK + MB_ICONSTOP, "Error$(Err)"
    Resume Next

End Sub

Sub vstNotes_Click ()
    Dim CRLF As String
    Dim Note As String

    CRLF$ = Chr$(13) & Chr$(10)

    '-- Load the Green Flag bitmap over the Red Flag bitmap
    vstNotes.TabPicture(vstNotes.CurrTab) = imgTabPicture(1).Picture

    '-- Load sample text for the current tab into the text box
    Select Case vstNotes.CurrTab
        Case 0
```

```
            Note$ = "RE: ...we need something to help us select and evaluate third party
tools." & CRLF$ & CRLF$
            Note$ = Note$ & "I heard about The Waite Group's Controls Desk Reference the other
day."
            Note$ = Note$ & " It covers a lot of controls and comes with working models of them
along with lots of sample applications."
        Case 1
            Note$ = "I heard the same thing as John."
        Case 2
            Note$ = "You guys are too late. I already have a copy and know just what tools we
need.<grin>" & CRLF$ & CRLF$
            Note$ = Note$ & "Rich: There's a great Grid control that will do everything you
asked for!" & CRLF$ & CRLF$
            Note$ = Note$ & "Dave: The Data Access and Report Writer info is in your mailbox" &
CRLF$ & CRLF$
            Note$ = Note$ & "John: I didn't know exactly what you wanted in a subclass control
so I picked a couple that looked good."
        Case 3
            Note$ = "RE: Grid - Thanks Cath! I was thinking I might have to compromise the
design."
        Case 4
            Note$ = "Boy, I allocate 4 weeks for tool evaluation and you guys are done in 4
hours!"
    End Select

    txtNotes.Text = Note$

End Sub

Sub vstTab_Click ()
    Dim i%

    '-- Initialize all Tabs on vstTabNotes with
    '   the Red Flag bitmap.
    If vstTab.CurrTab = 2 Then
        For i% = 0 To vstNotes.NumTabs - 1
            vstNotes.TabPicture(i%) = imgTabPicture(0).Picture
        Next i%
    End If

End Sub

Sub vstTab_MouseMove (Button As Integer, Shift As Integer, X As Single, Y As Single)

    '-- Display a message to indicate which Tab the mouse is over.
    Select Case vstTab.MouseOver
        Case 0
            lblMouseOverTab.Caption = "Specs and Analysis"
        Case 1
            lblMouseOverTab.Caption = "Initial Development"
        Case 2
            lblMouseOverTab.Caption = "Team Member Notes"
    End Select

End Sub
```

9. Create a new text file called PHASE1.TXT using Notepad or something similar and add the following text to it. The existence of the file is critical to the operation of the sample program but the contents are not.

Phase I will entail the following:

1. Specification
2. Analysis
3. Initial input from prospective users

John's team will be responsible for Specification and Analysis, and Marketing will talk to existing customers to solicit their input.

10. Create a new text file called PHASE2.TXT using Notepad or something similar and add the following text to it. The existence of the file is critical to the operation of the sample program; the contents of the file are not.

Phase II will pick up where Phase I leaves off:

1. Filter input from users to determine initial feature set
2. Select development tools and environment
3. Initial coding

It looks like we'll be following Windows standards and we will try to keep up with the big boys as far as features go.

VB looks like a good development environment but we need something to help us select and evaluate third-party tools. Anybody know of anything?

—Susan

## Tips and Comments

Videosoft's VSIndexTab has a lot of power hidden in behind a concise interface. By default the tabs appear on the bottom, non-3D, slanted line style, and the active tab is white. If you want to emulate the Microsoft look (a common goal), you'll have to reset all those defaults when you create a new VSIndexTab. An alternative is to set the *Template* property to 1-Redmond.

There are other tricks that aren't obvious, or even documented, that may surprise you. If you set the *BorderWidth* to a negative value (approximately the height of the tabs), the tabs won't be visible but you can still activate them in code and create dynamic dialogs just like Microsoft can (for example the control set on a dialog changes based on what item is selected in a list). Videosoft's VSElastic control is contained in the same VBX file as VSIndexTab, as is VSAwk. VSElastic and VSIndexTab complement each other and provide a wide range of functionality in a solid package.

# XLabel (XLABEL.VBX)

| USAGE: | Display of Static Text at Any Angle |
| --- | --- |
| MANUFACTURER: | Mark Hanson |
| COST: | $12 |

The XLabel control can be used as a replacement for the standard Visual Basic label control; it has the additional ability to display text at any angle.

# Syntax

The XLabel control provides many of the properties and events of a standard label control, but adds support for angular display when TrueType fonts are selected. Table 1-65 lists XLabel's nonstandard properties.

**Table 1-65** Nonstandard properties of the XLabel control

| | | |
|---|---|---|
| AlignmentH | AlignmentV | Angle |
| ShadowColor | Shadowed | |

The XLabel control replaces the conventional label's *Alignment* property with the two properties *AlignmentH* and *AlignmentV*, which control horizontal and vertical text alignment. Values for these properties are given in Tables 1-66 and 1-67.

**Table 1-66** Values for the AlignmentH property

| VALUE | MEANING |
|---|---|
| 0 | Text is aligned to the left of the control. |
| 1 | Text is aligned to the center of the control. |
| 2 | Text is aligned to the right of the control. |

**Table 1-67** Values for the AlignmentV property

| VALUE | MEANING |
|---|---|
| 0 | Text is aligned to the top of the control. |
| 1 | Text is aligned to the middle of the control. |
| 2 | Text is aligned to the bottom of the control. |

The *Shadowed* property determines whether the font is displayed on a shadowed background. This property can be set to either *True* or *False*. The light source for the shadow effect comes from the upper-right corner, whereas most standard 3D effects fix the light source at the upper-left corner. The *ShadowColor* property sets the color of the shadow that appears to be projected on the background.

The *Angle* property determines the orientation of text within the control. You can position text at any angle from 0 to 359 degrees by setting the integer value of this property. This property is particularly useful when you are positioning text labels to the left or right of another control. If the *FontName* property is set to any non-TrueType font, the value of the *Angle* property is ignored and the text is displayed horizontally.

# Example

The example program (see Figure 1-24) shows how to set the angle and appearance of the XLabel control. There are two XLabel controls on the form. The first, *XLabel1*, is within the box at the center of the form. (The box was created by setting *XLabel1*'s standard *BorderStyle* property to *True,* just as you would with a standard label control.) The second, *XLabel2,* is used as a conventional multiline label at the top of the form.

The scroll bar on the right-side of the form can be used to increment the text in the box. To set the text spinning on its own, just press the spin button. The Shadowed Text check box will enable the *Shadowed* property of both XLabel controls.

## Steps

1. Create a new project called XLABEL.MAK. Add the Xlabel control, XLABEL.VBX, to the project. Create a new form with the objects and properties described in Table 1-68. Save this form as XLABEL.FRM.

**Table 1-68** Objects and properties for XLABEL.FRM

| OBJECT | PROPERTY | SETTING |
|---|---|---|
| Form | FormName | Form1 |
| | BackColor | &H00C0C0C0& |
| | BorderStyle | 1 'Fixed Single |
| | Caption | "XLabel Demo" |
| | MaxButton | 0 'False |
| XLabel | Name | XLabel2 |
| | AlignmentH | 1 'Center |
| | BackStyle | 0 'Transparent |
| | Caption | "Use the scroller to rotate the XLabel text within the window." |
| | FontName | "Arial" |
| | ForeColor | &H00800000& |
| | ShadowColor | &H00808080& |
| | WordWrap | -1 'True |
| VScrollBar | Name | vscrSetAngle |
| | LargeChange | 5 |
| | Max | 360 |
| CheckBox | Name | chkShadowed |
| | BackColor | &H00C0C0C0& |
| | Caption | "Shadowed Text" |
| | ForeColor | &H00800000& |
| CommandButton | Name | btnSpin |
| | Caption | "&Spin" |
| | Default | -1 'True |

**Figure 1-24** Using the XLabel demo to rotate text

2. After creating XLABEL.FRM, add the following code to the form's declarations section.

```
Option Explicit

' Used to continue, or turn off, spinning of the text.
Dim Spinning As Integer
```

3. Next, add the following event subroutines to XLABEL.FRM.

```
Sub btnSpin_Click ()
'-------------------------------------------------------
' Begins (and stops) "automatic" spinning of the
' text whenever the Spin button is pushed.
'-------------------------------------------------------
Dim delay As Integer

    ' If it's a spin button, start spinning.
    If btnSpin.Caption = "&Spin" Then
        btnSpin.Caption = "&Stop"
        vscrSetAngle.Enabled = False
        XLabel1.Caption = "Help Me! I'm getting DIZZY! Stop It!"
        Spinning = True
        While Spinning
            XLabel1.Angle = (XLabel1.Angle + 5) Mod 360
            For delay = 1 To 1000
            Next
            DoEvents
        Wend
        ' Reset everything to "pre-spin" condition.
        btnSpin.Caption = "&Spin"
        vscrSetAngle.Enabled = True
        vscrSetAngle.Value = XLabel1.Angle
    ' Otherwise, it's already spinning, so stop it.
    Else
        Spinning = False
    End If
End Sub

Sub chkShadowed_Click ()
'-------------------------------------------------------
' Turn on/off text shadowing of the XLabel control.
'-------------------------------------------------------
    If chkShadowed.Value = 1 Then
```

(continued on next page)

*(continued from previous page)*

```
        XLabel1.Shadowed = True
        XLabel2.Shadowed = True
    Else
        XLabel1.Shadowed = False
        XLabel2.Shadowed = False
    End If
End Sub

Sub Form_Load ()
'----------------------------------------------------
' Center the form on the screen.
'----------------------------------------------------

    Me.Move (Screen.Width - Me.Width) \ 2, (Screen.Height - Me.Height) \ 2
End Sub

Sub vscrSetAngle_Change ()
'----------------------------------------------------
' Set the angle of the XLabel control whenever the
' scroller's value changes.
'----------------------------------------------------
    XLabel1.Angle = vscrSetAngle.Value
    XLabel1.Caption = "XLabel1 at " & Format$(vscrSetAngle.Value) & " Degrees"
End Sub
```

## Tips and Comments

Several features of the XLabel control are mutually exclusive. The shadowed font effect is only active when the value of the *Angle* property is 0, so you can have the text shaded, or at an angle, but not both. Likewise, the *WordWrap* property is supported, but only at a 0 degree angle.

XLabel can be a very useful tool when Windows real estate is at a premium. You can place labels vertically to the left or right of a control to save space, or use interesting rotational effects to create eye-catching About boxes.

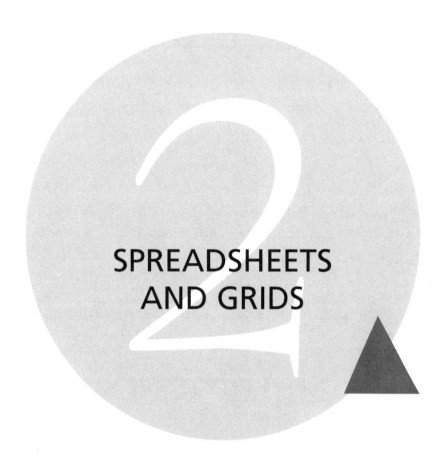

# SPREADSHEETS
# AND GRIDS

From the time the original VB professional toolkit shipped with the first Grid control for VB, developers have been clamoring for more capabilities: direct editing, control over individual cell formatting, pictures in cells, bound data access, virtual memory management, and more. There may still be a few unanswered prayers for features but, on the whole, third-party developers have risen to the challenge and produced some of the most complete and complex custom controls available. Among the six controls covered in this chapter there are, collectively, nearly 700 custom properties, more than 125 custom events, and almost 250 callable functions.

This chapter illustrates how you can use these grid controls to:

▲ Build tabular data browser/editors where columns may contain check boxes, combo boxes, or pictures

▲ Load and display tab-delimited files in table format

▲ Provide drag-and-drop support for data in the grid

▲ Cut and Paste data from the Clipboard

▲ Build fully functional spreadsheets with support for in-cell formulas and individual cell formatting

▲ Provide a customizable, interactive Gantt chart interface for task scheduling applications

With the breadth and depth of these controls the sky truly is the limit. By using the controls in this chapter alone, you could build powerful database, spreadsheet, and project scheduling applications. With a short side trip to Chapter 3, which covers word processing, you could put together your own suite of applications just like the big shots.

# Formula One/VBX (VTSS.VBX)

| USAGE: | Spreadsheet, Data Grid |
|---|---|
| MANUFACTURER: | Visual Tools |
| COST: | $249 |

Most grid controls on the market focus on acting as data grids for tabular entry and display of data. While Formula One can act as a bound data grid, its focus is on acting as a spreadsheet, which it does extremely well. In addition to 17 custom events and more than 100 custom properties, Formula One provides over 200 functions for manipulating the control and its associated data. As if that weren't enough, there are 125 built-in worksheet functions (for example, SUM, AVERAGE) that the user can enter directly in a worksheet.

## Syntax

Formula One actually consists of two VBX controls: the Worksheet and the Edit Bar. The Worksheet is the main control where you will do most of your work. The Edit Bar is a supporting control. You don't have to use this control but it can make it easier for users to enter and edit long formulas. You link an Edit Bar to a Worksheet by setting the Worksheet's *EditName* property to the name of the Edit Bar control. Multiple worksheets can share a single *Edit Bar*; Formula One handles focus tracking (that is, the active Worksheet uses the Edit Bar) automatically so you don't have to.

Once you place a Worksheet on a form, you can, of course, edit its properties in the Properties window. You can also double-click on the Worksheet with the right mouse button to open the Worksheet Designer (Figure 2-1).

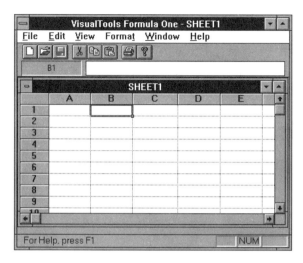

**Figure 2-1** Formula One Worksheet Designer

The Worksheet Designer looks like a basic spreadsheet application. You design the Worksheet just as if you were editing a worksheet in Excel, for example, formatting and all. This approach allows you to create formatted worksheets quickly and easily. The Worksheet Designer can also be launched at run time if the AllowAppLaunch property is set to *True*. Table 2-1 summarizes the nonstandard properties, events, and functions for the Formula One control.

**Table 2-1** Nonstandard properties, events, and functions for Formula One

**PROPERTIES**

| | | |
|---|---|---|
| AllowAppLaunch | AllowArrows | AllowDelete |
| AllowEditHeaders | AllowFillRange | AllowFormulas |
| AllowInCellEditing | AllowMoveRange | AllowResize |
| AllowSelections | AllowTabs | AutoRecalc |
| Col | DataAutoAddNew | DataChanged |
| DataConnected | DataFieldChanged | DataFieldCount |
| DataFieldNumber | DataFields | DataHdrField |
| DataRowBase | DataRowCount | DataRowsBuffered |
| DataSetColumnFormats | DataSetColumnNames | DataSetColumnWidths |
| DataSetMaxCol | DataSetMaxRow | DoCancelEdit |
| DoClick | DoDataNewRow | DoDataRowLoad |
| DoDblClick | DoEndEdit | DoEndRecalc |
| DoSelChange | DoStartEdit | DoStartRecalc |
| DoTopLeftChanged | EditName | EnableProtection |
| Entry | ExtraColor | FileName |

*(continued on next page)*

## PROPERTIES

*(continued from previous page)*

| | | |
|---|---|---|
| FixedCol | FixedCols | FixedRow |
| FixedRows | FormattedText | Formula |
| LeftCol | MaxCol | MaxRow |
| MinCol | MinRow | Number |
| PrintArea | PrintBottomMargin | PrintColHeading |
| PrintFooter | PrintGridLines | PrintHCenter |
| PrintHeader | PrintLeftMargin | PrintLeftToRight |
| PrintNoColor | PrintRightMargin | PrintRowHeading |
| PrintTitles | PrintTopMargin | PrintVCenter |
| ReadFile | Repaint | Row |
| RowMode | Selection | SelEndCol |
| SelEndRow | SelStartCol | SelStartRow |
| ShowColHeading | ShowGridLines | ShowHScrollBar |
| ShowRowHeading | ShowSelections | ShowVScrollBar |
| SS | TableName | Text |
| TopRow | WriteExcel4 | WriteFile |

## EVENTS

| | | |
|---|---|---|
| CancelEdit | DataNewRow | DataRowLoad |
| DblClick | EndEdit | EndRecalc |
| SelChange | StartEdit | StartRecalc |
| TopLeftChanged | | |

## FUNCTIONS

| | | |
|---|---|---|
| SSAddColPageBreak | SSGetLastCol | SSSetColWidthAuto |
| SSAddPageBreak | SSGetLastColForRow | SSSetDefinedName |
| SSAddRowPageBreak | SSGetLastRow | SSSetDefWindowProc |
| SSAddSelection | SSGetLeftCol | SSSetDoSetCursor |
| SSAttach | SSGetLogicalRC | SSSetEnableProtection |
| SSAttachToSS | SSGetMaxCol | SSSetEnterMovesDown |
| SSCalculationDlg | SSGetMaxRow | SSSetEntry |
| SSCallWindowProc | SSGetMinCol | SSSetEntryRC |
| SSCancelEdit | SSGetMinRow | SSSetExtraColor |
| SSCanEditPaste | SSGetNumber | SSSetFireEvent |
| SSCheckModified | SSGetNumberRC | SSSetFixedCols |
| SSCheckRecalc | SSGetPrintArea | SSSetFixedRows |
| SSClearClipboard | SSGetPrintBottomMargin | SSSetFont |
| SSClearRange | SSGetPrintColHeading | SSSetFormula |
| SSColorPaletteDlg | SSGetPrintFooter | SSSetFormulaRC |
| SSColWidthDlg | SSGetPrintGridLines | SSSetHdrHeight |

## FUNCTIONS

| | | |
|---|---|---|
| SSCopyAll | SSGetPrintHCenter | SSSetHdrSelection |
| SSCopyRange | SSGetPrintHeader | SSSetHdrWidth |
| SSDefinedNameDlg | SSGetPrintLeftMargin | SSSetIteration |
| SSDelete | SSGetPrintLeftToRight | SSSetLeftCol |
| SSDeleteDefinedName | SSGetPrintNoColor | SSSetLogicalRC |
| SSDeleteRange | SSGetPrintRightMargin | SSSetMaxCol |
| SSDeleteTable | SSGetPrintRowHeading | SSSetMaxRow |
| SSEditBarDelete | SSGetPrintTitles | SSSetMinCol |
| SSEditBarHeight | SSGetPrintTopMargin | SSSetMinRow |
| SSEditBarMove | SSGetPrintVCenter | SSSetNumber |
| SSEditBarNew | SSGetRepaint | SSSetNumberFormat |
| SSEditClear | SSGetRowHeight | SSSetNumberRC |
| SSEditCopy | SSGetRowMode | SSSetPattern |
| SSEditCopyDown | SSGetSelection | SSSetPrintArea |
| SSEditCopyRight | SSGetSelectionCount | SSSetPrintAreaFromSelection |
| SSEditCut | SSGetSelectionRef | SSSetPrintBottomMargin |
| SSEditDelete | SSGetShowColHeading | SSSetPrintColHeading |
| SSEditInsert | SSGetShowFormulas | SSSetPrintFooter |
| SSEditPaste | SSGetShowGridLines | SSSetPrintGridLines |
| SSEndEdit | SSGetShowHScrollBar | SSSetPrintHCenter |
| SSErrorNumberToText | SSGetShowRowHeading | SSSetPrintHeader |
| SSFilePageSetupDlg | SSGetShowSelections | SSSetPrintLeftMargin |
| SSFilePrint | SSGetShowVScrollBar | SSSetPrintLeftToRight |
| SSFilePrintSetupDlg | SSGetShowZeroValues | SSSetPrintNoColor |
| SSFormatAlignmentDlg | SSGetSSEdit | SSSetPrintRightMargin |
| SSFormatBorderDlg | SSGetText | SSSetPrintRowHeading |
| SSFormatCurrency0 | SSGetTextRC | SSSetPrintTitles |
| SSFormatCurrency2 | SSGetTitle | SSSetPrintTitlesFromSelection |
| SSFormatFixed | SSGetTopRow | SSSetPrintTopMargin |
| SSFormatFixed2 | SSGetTypeRC | SSSetPrintVCenter |
| SSFormatFontDlg | SSGotoDlg | SSSetProtection |
| SSFormatFraction | SSInitTable | SSSetRepaint |
| SSFormatGeneral | SSInsertRange | SSSetRowHeight |
| SSFormatHmmampm | SSMaxCol | SSSetRowHeightAuto |
| SSFormatMdyy | SSMaxRow | SSSetRowMode |
| SSFormatNumberDlg | SSMoveRange | SSSetRowText |
| SSFormatPatternDlg | SSNew | SSSetSelection |
| SSFormatPercent | SSNextColPageBreak | SSSetSelectionRef |
| SSFormatRCNr | SSNextRowPageBreak | SSSetShowColHeading |
| SSFormatScientific | SSOpenFileDlg | SSSetShowFormulas |

*(continued on next page)*

## FUNCTIONS

*(continued from previous page)*

| | | |
|---|---|---|
| SSGetActiveCell | SSProtectionDlg | SSSetShowGridLines |
| SSGetAllowArrows | SSRangeToTwips | SSSetShowHScrollBar |
| SSGetAllowDelete | SSRead | SSSetShowRowHeading |
| SSGetAllowEditHeaders | SSReadIO | SSSetShowSelections |
| SSGetAllowFillRange | SSRecalc | SSSetShowVScrollBar |
| SSGetAllowFormulas | SSRemoveColPageBreak | SSSetShowZeroValues |
| SSGetAllowInCellEditing | SSRemovePageBreak | SSSetSSEdit |
| SSGetAllowMoveRange | SSRemoveRowPageBreak | SSSetText |
| SSGetAllowResize | SSRowHeightDlg | SSSetTextRC |
| SSGetAllowSelections | SSSaveFileDlg | SSSetTitle |
| SSGetAllowTabs | SSSaveWindowInfo | SSSetTopLeftText |
| SSGetAutoRecalc | SSSetActiveCell | SSSetTopRow |
| SSGetBackColor | SSSetAlignment | SSShowActiveCell |
| SSGetColWidth | SSSetAllowArrows | SSSort |
| SSGetDefinedName | SSSetAllowDelete | SSSort3 |
| SSGetEnableProtection | SSSetAllowEditHeaders | SSSortDlg |
| SSGetEnterMovesDown | SSSetAllowFillRange | SSStartEdit |
| SSGetEntry | SSSetAllowFormulas | SSSwapTables |
| SSGetEntryRC | SSSetAllowInCellEditing | SSTransactCommit |
| SSGetExtraColor | SSSetAllowMoveRange | SSTransactRollback |
| SSGetFireEvent | SSSetAllowResize | SSTransactStart |
| SSGetFixedCols | SSSetAllowSelections | SSTwipsToRC |
| SSGetFixedRows | SSSetAllowTabs | SSUpdate |
| SSGetFormattedText | SSSetAppName | SSVBXCopyCellsFromDoubleArray |
| SSGetFormattedTextRC | SSSetAutoRecalc | SSVBXCopyCellsToDoubleArray |
| SSGetFormula | SSSetBackColor | SSVersion |
| SSGetFormulaRC | SSSetBorder | SSWrite |
| SSGetHdrSelection | SSSetColText | SSWriteIO |
| SSGetIteration | SSSetColWidth | |

**Built-In Dialogs** Formula One contains built-in dialogs to let the user alter the appearance of the worksheet, as commercial spreadsheet applications do. There are 17 dialogs available (Table 2-2), just a function call away.

**Table 2-2** Formula One built-in dialogs

| DIALOG BOX FUNCTION | PURPOSE |
|---|---|
| SSCalculationDlg | Enable/disable automatic recalculation |
| SSColorPaletteDlg | Edit colors in the color palette |

**2** ◄

| DIALOG BOX FUNCTION | PURPOSE |
|---|---|
| SSColWidthDlg | Set width of selected columns, set default column width, show/hide selected columns |
| SSDefinedNameDlg | Add/delete user-defined names |
| SSFilePageSetupDlg | Define header, footer, margins, page print order, page centering |
| SSFilePrintSetupDlg | Select printer, page orientation, paper size |
| SSFormatAlignmentDlg | Set horizontal and vertical alignment of data, enable/disable word wrapping |
| SSFormatBorderDlg | Specify border placement, line style, color |
| SSFormatFontDlg | Specify font, point size, font style, color |
| SSFormatNumberDlg | Define custom number formats |
| SSFormatPatternDlg | Specify fill pattern, foreground color, background color |
| SSGotoDlg | Select worksheet page to display |
| SSOpenFileDlg | Open worksheets from disk |
| SSProtectionDlg | Specify whether cells are locked and hidden |
| SSRowHeightDlg | Set height of selected rows, set default row height, show/hide selected rows |
| SSSaveFileDlg | Save current file in Formula One or Excel 4.0 format |
| SSSortDlg | Set sorting method and sort keys |

**Worksheet Functions**  Like all spreadsheets, Formula One supports formulas in cells and provides a number of built-in worksheet functions (Table 2-3). This alone makes Formula One a very capable spreadsheet. Visual Tools also has gone the extra mile by allowing you to use the *CALL* worksheet function to call custom functions that reside in DLLs. This capability allows you to extend Formula One in countless ways.

**Table 2-3**  Formula One built-in worksheet functions

**WORKSHEET FUNCTIONS**

| | | |
|---|---|---|
| ABS | INDEX | PROPER |
| ACOS | INDIRECT | PV |
| ACOSH | INT | RAND |
| ADDRESS | IPMT | RATE |
| AND | IRR | REPLACE |
| ASIN | ISBLANK | REPT |
| ASINH | ISERR | RIGHT |
| ATAN | ISERROR | ROUND |
| ATAN2 | ISLOGICAL | ROW |
| ATANH | ISNA | ROWS |

*(continued on next page)*

## WORKSHEET FUNCTIONS

*(continued from previous page)*

| | | |
|---|---|---|
| AVERAGE | ISNONTEXT | SEARCH |
| CALL | ISNUMBER | SECOND |
| CEILING | ISREF | SIGN |
| CHAR | ISTEXT | SIN |
| CHOOSE | LEFT | SINH |
| CLEAN | LEN | SLN |
| CODE | LN | SQRT |
| COLUMN | LOG | STDEV |
| COLUMNS | LOG10 | STDEVP |
| COS | LOOKUP | SUBSTITUTE |
| COSH | LOWER | SUM |
| COUNT | MATCH | SUMSQ |
| COUNTA | MAX | SYD |
| DATE | MID | T |
| DATEVALUE | MIN | TAN |
| DAY | MINUTE | TANH |
| DB | MIRR | TEXT |
| DDB | MOD | TIME |
| DOLLAR | MONTH | TIMEVALUE |
| ERROR.TYPE | N | TODAY |
| EVEN | NA | TRIM |
| EXACT | NOT | TRUE |
| EXP | NOW | TRUNC |
| FACT | NPER | TYPE |
| FALSE | NPV | UPPER |
| FIND | ODD | VALUE |
| FIXED | OFFSET | VAR |
| FLOOR | OR | VARP |
| FV | PI | VDB |
| HLOOKUP | PMT | VLOOKUP |
| HOUR | PPMT | WEEKDAY |
| IF | PRODUCT | YEAR |

# Example

The sample program (Figure 2-2) shows how easy it is to create a true spreadsheet application using Formula One. Very few properties or functions are used and yet a basic, functional spreadsheet has been implemented.

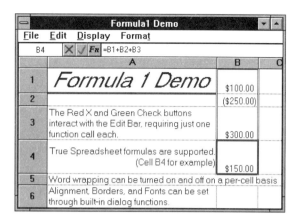

**Figure 2-2** Formula One sample program

A good portion of the work in this program is handled by the built-in dialogs. File input and output are handled by the *ReadFile*, *WriteFile*, and *WriteExcel4* properties. The Edit menu options (Cut, Copy, and Paste) use Formula One functions (*SSEditCut*, *SSEditCopy*, *SSEditPaste*) so the user can cut and paste ranges without any further intervention on your part. The buttons to the left of the Edit Bar (with the red X and the green check mark) make use of functions that interact with the Edit Bar (*SSCancelEdit*, *SSEndEdit*) to emulate the functionality (i.e., editing in a wider box above the spreadsheet) found in commercial spreadsheets. The text box directly above and to the left of the worksheet displays the currently selected cells, which take one line of code, and can also be used to set the current selection in the worksheet. Simply type the desired selection and press the (ENTER) key.

## Steps

1. Create a new project called Formula One.MAK. Create a new form with the objects and properties shown in Table 2-4. Save this form as FORMULA1.FRM.

**Table 2-4** Formula One main form's objects and properties

| OBJECT | PROPERTY | SETTING |
|---|---|---|
| Image | Name | imgEditButton |
| | Index | 0 |
| | Picture | (set at design time in Properties window) |
| Image | Name | imgEditButton |
| | Index | 1 |
| | Picture | (set at design time in Properties window) |
| Image | Name | imgEditButton |
| | Index | 2 |

*(continued on next page)*

| OBJECT | PROPERTY | SETTING |
|---|---|---|
| *(continued from previous page)* | | |
| | Picture | (set at design time in Properties window) |
| SSEdit | Name | SSEdit1 |
| | EditName | "SSEdit1" |
| SSView | Name | Sheet1 |
| | AllowAppLaunch | -1 'True |
| | DataAutoAddNew | -1 'True |
| | DataConnected | -1 'True |
| | DataFields | " " |
| | DataHdrField | " " |
| | DataSetColumnFormats= | 'True |
| | DataSetColumnNames= | 'True |
| | DataSetColumnWidths= | 'True |
| | DataSetMaxCol | -1 'True |
| | DataSetMaxRow | -1 'True |
| | DoCancelEdit | -1 'True |
| | DoClick | -1 'True |
| | DoDataNewRow | -1 'True |
| | DoDataRowLoad | -1 'True |
| | DoDblClick | -1 'True |
| | DoEndEdit | -1 'True |
| | DoEndRecalc | -1 'True |
| | DoSelChange | -1 'True |
| | DoStartEdit | -1 'True |
| | DoStartRecalc | -1 'True |
| | DoTopLeftChanged= | 'True |
| | EditName | "SSEdit1" |
| | FileName | (set at design time in Properties window) |
| | TableName | "Sheet1" |
| TextBox | Name | txtCurSelection |
| | Alignment | 2 'Center |
| | FontBold | 0 'False |
| | MultiLine | -1 'True |
| | Text | "A1" |
| Form | FormName | frmMain |
| | Caption | "Formula One Demo" |
| | ScaleMode | 3 'Pixel |

2. Add a menu to the FORMULA1.FRM form using the Visual Basic Menu Design window, setting the captions and names as shown in Table 2-5. Note that the menus are set up as control arrays.

**Table 2-5** Menu definition for FORMULA1.FRM

| CAPTION | NAME | INDEX | CHECKED |
|---|---|---|---|
| &File | mnuMain | 0 | |
|     &Open... | mnuFile | 0 | |
|     &Save | mnuFile | 1 | |
|     Save &As... | mnuFile | 2 | |
|      | mnuFile | 3 | |
|     Pa&ge Setup... | mnuFile | 4 | |
|     &Print... | mnuFile | 5 | |
|      | mnuFile | 6 | |
|     E&xit | mnuFile | 7 | |
| &Edit | mnuMain | 1 | |
|     Cu&t | mnuEdit | 0 | |
|     &Copy | mnuEdit | 1 | |
|     &Paste | mnuEdit | 2 | |
|      | mnuEdit | 3 | |
|     &Goto | mnuEdit | 4 | |
| &Display | mnuMain | 2 | |
|     &Grid Lines | mnuDisplay | 0 | True |
|     &Column Headers | mnuDisplay | 1 | True |
|     &Row Headers | mnuDisplay | 2 | True |
| Forma&t | mnuMain | 3 | |
|     &Alignment... | mnuFormat | 0 | |
|     &Font... | mnuFormat | 1 | |
|     &Border... | mnuFormat | 2 | |
|     &Pattern... | mnuFormat | 3 | |
|     Ce&ll Protection... | mnuFormat | 4 | |
|     Custom &Number... | mnuFormat | 5 | |
|      | mnuFormat | 6 | |
|     Column &Width... | mnuFormat | 7 | |
|     Row &Height... | mnuFormat | 8 | |
|      | mnuFormat | 9 | |
|     Color &Palette... | mnuFormat | 10 | |

3. Add the following code to the FORMULA1 form.

```
Sub Form_Resize ()

    If Me.WindowState  MINIMIZED Then
        Sheet1.Width = Me.ScaleWidth
        Sheet1.Height = Me.ScaleHeight - Sheet1.Top
    End If

End Sub

Sub Form_Unload (Cancel As Integer)

    Sheet1.FileName = "F1DEMO.VS"

End Sub

Sub imgEditButton_Click (Index As Integer)
'------------------------------------------
'-- These are the small Edit buttons next to
'   the Edit Bar.
'------------------------------------------
    Dim SSErr%

    Select Case Index%
        Case 0
            '-- Cancel any editing that occurred.
            SSErr% = SSCancelEdit(gSS&)
        Case 1
            '-- Commit any editing that occurred.
            SSErr% = SSEndEdit(gSS&)
        Case 2
            '-- Display the Calculations dialog.
            SSErr% = SSCalculationDlg(gSS&)
    End Select

End Sub

Sub mnuDisplay_Click (Index As Integer)

    mnuDisplay(Index%).Checked = Not (mnuDisplay(Index%).Checked)

    Select Case Index%
        Case MNU_DISPLAY_GRID_LINES
            Sheet1.ShowGridLines = Not (Sheet1.ShowGridLines)
        Case MNU_DISPLAY_COL_HEADERS
            Sheet1.ShowColHeading = Not (Sheet1.ShowColHeading)
        Case MNU_DISPLAY_ROW_HEADERS
            Sheet1.ShowRowHeading = Not (Sheet1.ShowRowHeading)
    End Select

End Sub

Sub mnuEdit_Click (Index As Integer)
    Dim SSErr%

    Select Case Index%
Case MNU_EDIT_CUT
            SSErr% = SSEditCut(gSS&)
        Case MNU_EDIT_COPY
```

```
                SSErr% = SSEditCopy(gSS&)
            Case MNU_EDIT_PASTE
                SSErr% = SSEditPaste(gSS&)
            Case MNU_EDIT_GOTO
                SSErr% = SSGotoDlg%(gSS&)
        End Select

End Sub

Sub mnuFile_Click (Index As Integer)
    Dim SSErr%
    Dim Title$
    Dim hWndParent%
    Dim FileName$
    Dim BufferSize%
    Dim FileType%
    Dim Msg$

    BufferSize% = 255
    FileName$ = Space$(BufferSize%)
    hWndParent% = Me.hWnd

    Select Case Index%
        Case MNU_FILE_OPEN
            '-- Note that when a file is opened we don't have to do anything different
            '    whether it's a Formula1(vts) file or an Excel(xls) file.
            Title$ = "Open File"
            SSErr% = SSOpenFileDlg%(Title$, hWndParent%, FileName$, BufferSize%)
            If SSErr% = SSERROR_NONE Then
                Sheet1.ReadFile = Trim$(FileName$)
                Sheet1.FileName = Trim$(FileName$)
            Else
                Msg$ = Space$(BufferSize%)
                SSErr% = SSErrorNumberToText(SSErr%, Msg$, Len(Msg$))
                MsgBox Trim$(Msg$), MB_OK + MB_ICONSTOP, "Error Loading File"
            End If
        Case MNU_FILE_SAVE
            If Len(Sheet1.FileName) Then
                Sheet1.WriteFile = Sheet1.FileName
            Else
                Sheet1.WriteFile = App.Path & "\F1DEMO.VTS"
                Sheet1.FileName = App.Path & "\F1DEMO.VTS"
            End If
        Case MNU_FILE_SAVE_AS
            Title$ = "Save File"
            SSErr% = SSSaveFileDlg%(gSS&, Title$, FileName$, BufferSize%, FileType%)
            If SSErr% = SSERROR_NONE Then
                If FileType% = kFileExcel4% Then
                    Sheet1.WriteExcel4 = FileName$
                Else
                    Sheet1.WriteFile = FileName$
                End If
            Else
                Msg$ = Space$(BufferSize%)
                SSErr% = SSErrorNumberToText(SSErr%, Msg$, Len(Msg$))
                MsgBox Trim$(Msg$), MB_OK + MB_ICONSTOP, "Error Saving File"
            End If
        Case MNU_FILE_PAGE_SETUP
            SSErr% = SSFilePageSetupDlg(gSS&)
```

*(continued on next page)*

*(continued from previous page)*

```
            Case MNU_FILE_PRINT
                SSErr% = SSFilePrintSetupDlg(gSS&)
            Case MNU_FILE_EXIT
                Unload Me
        End Select

End Sub

Sub mnuFormat_Click (Index As Integer)
'------------------------------------------------
'-- The Format menu simply launches the built-in
'   dialogs. Everything else is handled auto-
'   matically by FormulaOne.
'------------------------------------------------
    Dim SSErr%

    Select Case Index%
        Case MNU_FORMAT_ALIGNMENT
            SSErr% = SSFormatAlignmentDlg(gSS&)
        Case MNU_FORMAT_FONT
            SSErr% = SSFormatFontDlg(gSS&)
        Case MNU_FORMAT_BORDER
            SSErr% = SSFormatBorderDlg(gSS&)
        Case MNU_FORMAT_PATTERN
            SSErr% = SSFormatPatternDlg(gSS&)
        Case MNU_FORMAT_CELL_PROTECTION
            SSErr% = SSProtectionDlg(gSS&)
        Case MNU_FORMAT_CUSTOM_NUMBER
            SSErr% = SSFormatNumberDlg(gSS&)
        Case MNU_FORMAT_COLUMN_WIDTH
            SSErr% = SSColWidthDlg(gSS&)
        Case MNU_FORMAT_ROW_HEIGHT
            SSErr% = SSRowHeightDlg(gSS&)
        Case MNU_FORMAT_COLOR_PALETTE
            SSErr% = SSColorPaletteDlg(gSS&)
    End Select

End Sub

Sub Sheet1_SelChange ()

    txtCurSelection.Text = Sheet1.Selection

End Sub

Sub txtCurSelection_KeyPress (KeyAscii As Integer)

    If KeyAscii% = KEY_ENTER Then
        KeyAscii% = 0
        Sheet1.Selection = txtCurSelection.Text
        Sheet1.SetFocus
    End If

End Sub
```

4. Create a new module called FORMULA1.BAS and add the following code to the declarations section of the module.

```
Option Explicit
DefInt A-Z
```

```
Global Const MB_OK = 0
Global Const MB_ICONSTOP = 16

Global Const MINIMIZED = 1

Global Const KEY_ENTER = &HD

Global Const DARKGRAY = &H808080
Global Const WHITE = &HFFFFFF

Global Const MNU_FILE_OPEN = 0
Global Const MNU_FILE_SAVE = 1
Global Const MNU_FILE_SAVE_AS = 2
Global Const MNU_FILE_PAGE_SETUP = 4
Global Const MNU_FILE_PRINT = 5
Global Const MNU_FILE_EXIT = 7

Global Const MNU_EDIT_CUT = 0
Global Const MNU_EDIT_COPY = 1
Global Const MNU_EDIT_PASTE = 2
Global Const MNU_EDIT_GOTO = 4

Global Const MNU_DISPLAY_GRID_LINES = 0
Global Const MNU_DISPLAY_COL_HEADERS = 1
Global Const MNU_DISPLAY_ROW_HEADERS = 2

Global Const MNU_FORMAT_ALIGNMENT = 0
Global Const MNU_FORMAT_FONT = 1
Global Const MNU_FORMAT_BORDER = 2
Global Const MNU_FORMAT_PATTERN = 3
Global Const MNU_FORMAT_CELL_PROTECTION = 4
Global Const MNU_FORMAT_CUSTOM_NUMBER = 5
Global Const MNU_FORMAT_COLUMN_WIDTH = 7
Global Const MNU_FORMAT_ROW_HEIGHT = 8
Global Const MNU_FORMAT_COLOR_PALETTE = 10

Global gSS&        '-- SS property for main Formula1 Control

'----------------------------------------------------
' Formula1 Declarations
'----------------------------------------------------

Global Const kFileFormulaOne = 1
Global Const kFileExcel4 = 2

Global Const SSERROR_NONE = 0

Declare Function SSCalculationDlg% Lib "VTSSDLL.DLL" (ByVal hSS&)
Declare Function SSCancelEdit% Lib "VTSSDLL.DLL" (ByVal hSS&)
Declare Function SSColorPaletteDlg% Lib "VTSSDLL.DLL" (ByVal hSS&)
Declare Function SSColWidthDlg% Lib "VTSSDLL.DLL" (ByVal hSS&)
Declare Function SSEditClear% Lib "VTSSDLL.DLL" (ByVal hSS&, ByVal nClearType%)
Declare Function SSEditCopy% Lib "VTSSDLL.DLL" (ByVal hSS&)
Declare Function SSEditCopyDown% Lib "VTSSDLL.DLL" (ByVal hSS&)
Declare Function SSEditCopyRight% Lib "VTSSDLL.DLL" (ByVal hSS&)
Declare Function SSEditCut% Lib "VTSSDLL.DLL" (ByVal hSS&)
Declare Function SSEditPaste% Lib "VTSSDLL.DLL" (ByVal hSS&)
Declare Function SSEndEdit% Lib "VTSSDLL.DLL" (ByVal hSS&)
Declare Function SSErrorNumberToText% Lib "VTSSDLL.DLL" (ByVal nError%, ByVal pBuf$, ByVal
nBufSize%)
```

*(continued on next page)*

*(continued from previous page)*

```
Declare Function SSFilePageSetupDlg% Lib "VTSSDLL.DLL" (ByVal hSS&)
Declare Function SSFilePrintSetupDlg% Lib "VTSSDLL.DLL" (ByVal hSS&)
Declare Function SSFormatAlignmentDlg% Lib "VTSSDLL.DLL" (ByVal hSS&)
Declare Function SSFormatBorderDlg% Lib "VTSSDLL.DLL" (ByVal hSS&)
Declare Function SSFormatFontDlg% Lib "VTSSDLL.DLL" (ByVal hSS&)
Declare Function SSFormatNumberDlg% Lib "VTSSDLL.DLL" (ByVal hSS&)
Declare Function SSFormatPatternDlg% Lib "VTSSDLL.DLL" (ByVal hSS&)
Declare Function SSGotoDlg% Lib "VTSSDLL.DLL" (ByVal hSS&)
Declare Function SSOpenFileDlg% Lib "VTSSDLL.DLL" (ByVal pTitle$, ByVal hWndParent%, ByVal
pBuf$, ByVal nBufSize%)
Declare Function SSProtectionDlg% Lib "VTSSDLL.DLL" (ByVal hSS&)
Declare Function SSRead% Lib "VTSSDLL.DLL" (ByVal hSS&, ByVal pPathName$, pFileType%)
Declare Function SSRowHeightDlg% Lib "VTSSDLL.DLL" (ByVal hSS&)
Declare Function SSSaveFileDlg% Lib "VTSSDLL.DLL" (ByVal hSS&, ByVal pTitle$, ByVal pBuf$,
ByVal nBufSize%, pFileType%)
Declare Function SSWrite% Lib "VTSSDLL.DLL" (ByVal hSS&, ByVal pPathName$, ByVal nFileType%)
```

5. Add the following code to the FORMULA1.BAS module.

```
Sub Main ()
'------------------------------------------------
'-- Set Global SS property reference (gSS&) and
'   load the sample file.
'------------------------------------------------

    Load frmMain
        gSS& = frmMain!Sheet1.SS
        If Len(Dir$(App.Path & "\F1Demo.VTS")) Then
            frmMain!Sheet1.ReadFile = App.Path & "\F1Demo.VTS"
            frmMain!Sheet1.FileName = App.Path & "\F1Demo.VTS"
        End If
    frmMain.Show

End Sub
```

## Tips and Comments

While most grids target the database developer, Visual Tools has produced a solid, high-performance spreadsheet control, with database functionality, built in to boot. If your application requires spreadsheet functionality, such as in-cell formulas and individual cell formatting, particularly if Excel files are to be used, Formula One is an outstanding choice. Formula One does so much automatically that you can truly concentrate on the specifics of the application at hand. Formula One is a large, complex control and it will take some time before you know all its tricks and foibles. At the same time, it offers a nice, shallow learning curve so you can be extremely productive in the meantime.

# Gantt/VBX (GANTTVBX.VBX)

| USAGE: | Gantt Chart |
|---|---|
| MANUFACTURER: | AddSoft |
| COST: | $249 |

The Gantt/VBX control falls into the grid and spreadsheet category but, unlike any other grid represented here, Gantt/VBX is not a data grid or a spreadsheet but an honest-to-goodness Gantt control. (A Gantt control/chart displays a list of tasks and a bar chart showing task durations, start dates, and finish dates.) Its appearance is fully customizable at both design time and run time. At run time, it is also fully interactive, meaning that the user can use the mouse to move and resize bars in the Gantt area. Gantt/VBX fires a wide variety of events to keep you apprised of all changes made.

## Syntax

As with most custom controls, you can configure Gantt/VBX by setting properties in the VB Properties window. However, you can also use custom dialogs that are built into the control, which is much easier because of the large number of available properties. The dialogs each have an associated property (for example *TimescalesDialog*). When you double-click on the property in the Properties window, the dialog is displayed. Table 2-6 lists the nonstandard properties, events, and functions for Gantt/VBX. The nonstandard properties are grouped according to their functions. Many of Gantt/VBXs properties are property arrays as denoted by the trailing parentheses.

**Table 2-6** Gantt/VBX nonstandard properties, events, and functions

### GENERAL PROPERTIES

| | | |
|---|---|---|
| About | BarHeightPercent | BevelHighlightColor |
| BevelShadowColor | BevelWidth | BorderStyle |
| GeneralDialog | GridMajorColor | GridMajorThickness |
| HeaderHeight | ListItemHeight | ListWidth |
| MasterDialog | ProcessTab | ResizeHeader |
| ResizeListColumns | ResizeListItems | ResizeListWidth |
| ScrollBarWidth | ScrollBarColor | |

### DATA/TIME PROPERTIES

| | | |
|---|---|---|
| CurrentTimeColor | CurrentTimeLine | DateTimeBeg |
| DateTimeDialog | DateTimeEnd | DateTimeView |

### TIMESCALE PROPERTIES

| | | |
|---|---|---|
| TimescalesDialog | TSBackColor | TSBevel |
| TSGridColor | TSGridThickness | TSMajor |

*(continued on next page)*

## TIMESCALE PROPERTIES

*(continued from previous page)*

| | | |
|---|---|---|
| TSMajorCount | TSMajorFontColor | TSMajorFontName |
| TSMajorFontSize | TSMajorFontBold | TSMajorFontItalic |
| TSMajorFontStrike | TSMajorFontUnder | TSMajorFormat |
| TSMajorGrid | TSMinor | TSMinorCount |
| TSMinorFontBold | TSMinorFontItalic | TSMinorFontColor |
| TSMinorFontName | TSMinorFontSize | TSMinorFontStrike |
| TSMinorFontUnder | TSMinorFormat | TSMinorGrid |

## GANTT PROPERTIES

| | | |
|---|---|---|
| GanttBackColor | GanttBevel | GanttDialog |
| GanttFontBold | GanttFontColor | GanttFontItalic |
| GanttFontName | GanttFontSize | GanttFontStrike |
| GanttFontUnder | GanttGridLineCount | GanttGridThickness |
| GanttGridColor | | |

## LIST HEADER PROPERTIES

| | | |
|---|---|---|
| ListHdrBackColor | ListHdrBevel | ListHdrDialog |
| ListHdrFontBold | ListHdrFontColor | ListHdrFontItalic |
| ListHdrFontName | ListHdrFontSize | ListHdrFontStrike |
| ListHdrFontUnder | ListHdrGridThickness | ListHdrGridColor |

## LIST PROPERTIES

| | | |
|---|---|---|
| ListBackColor | ListBevel | ListDialog |
| ListFontBold | ListFontColor | ListFontItalic |
| ListFontName | ListFontSize | ListFontStrike |
| ListFontUnder | ListGridColor | ListGridLineCount |
| ListGridThickness | | |

## LIST COLUMN PROPERTIES

| | | |
|---|---|---|
| Caption | ColAlignment() | ColEditable() |
| ColField() | ColFormat() | ColFrozen() |
| ColLabel() | ColResizable() | ColumnsDialog |
| ColVisible() | ColWidth() | |

## LIST BAR PROPERTIES

| | | |
|---|---|---|
| BarAdjustable() | BarBegColor() | BarBegField() |
| BarBegSymbol() | BarBegType() | BarColor() |
| BarEndColor() | BarEndField() | BarEndSymbol() |
| BarEndType() | BarPattern() | BarsDialog |
| BarStyle() | BarTextField() | BarTextFormat() |
| BarTextLocation() | | |

## LIST DATA PROPERTIES

| | | |
|---|---|---|
| ListActBeg() | ListActDur() | ListActEnd() |
| ListAssigned() | ListClear | ListCurrentCol |
| ListCurrentRow | ListDelete() | ListDepends() |
| ListInsert() | ListIsEmpty() | ListItemView |
| ListLoad | ListMaxItems | ListName() |
| ListPerComp() | ListPlanBeg() | ListPlanDur() |
| ListPlanEnd() | ListSave | ListSlackDur() |
| ListSlackEnd() | ListSort | ListType() |
| ListUser1() | ListUser2() | ListUser3() |
| ListUser4() | | |

## EVENTS

| | | |
|---|---|---|
| ActualBegChanged | ActualDurChanged | ActualEndChanged |
| AssignedChanged | BarBegDoubleClick | BarBegSingleClick |
| BarDoubleClick | BarEndDoubleClick | BarEndSingleClick |
| BarSingleClick | CellDoubleClick | CellGotFocus |
| CellLostFocus | ColWidthChanged | ControlGotFocus |
| ControlLostFocus | DateTimeViewChanged | DependsChanged |
| GanttBackDoubleClick | GanttBackSingleClick | HeaderHeightChanged |
| InsertModeChanged | ListHdrDoubleClick | ListHdrSingleClick |
| ListItemHeightChanged | ListItemViewChanged | ListWidthChanged |
| NameChanged | PercentCompleteChanged | PlannedBegChanged |
| PlannedDurChanged | PlannedEndChanged | SlackDurChanged |
| SlackEndChanged | TaskChanged | TSMajorDoubleClick |
| TSMajorSingleClick | TSMinorDoubleClick | TSMinorSingleClick |
| TypeChanged | User1Changed | User2Changed |
| User3Changed | User4Changed | |

## FUNCTIONS

| | |
|---|---|
| GanttVBXConvertFromDateTime | GanttVBXConvertFromDuration |
| GanttVBXConvertToDateTime | GanttVBXConvertToDuration |
| GanttVBXGetDateTime | GanttVBXListAdd |
| GanttVBXListAddActual | GanttVBXListAddAssignedDepends |
| GanttVBXListAddPlanned | GanttVBXListAddSlack |
| GanttVBXListAddUser | |

**On the Whole** The Gantt/VBX control is visibly and logically divided into four quadrants (Figure 2-3): the list (lower-left), list header (upper-left), time scale (upper-right), and the actual Gantt area (lower-right). Each quadrant has certain properties associated with it and some properties also relate to the control in general and how each quadrant appears and behaves.

Dividers between the quadrants allow the quadrants to be resized at run time. You control the color and width of the dividers by using the *GridMajorColor* and *GridMajorThickness* properties. By setting the *ResizeHeaders* and/or *ResizeListWidth* properties to *False*, you can prevent users from resizing the quadrants. The list area (left quadrants) is composed of multiple columns that can also be individually resized, unless the *ResizeListColumns* property is *False*. Each quadrant has bevel (*GanttBevel*, *ListBevel*, *ListHdrBevel*, and *TSBevel*) properties to control their 3D appearance, and the Gantt/VBX has general properties (*BevelHighlightColor*, *BevelShadowColor*, *BevelWidth*) that affect all quadrants' bevels. You control the range of dates encompassed by the Gantt control with the *DateTimeBeg* and *DateTimeEnd* properties.

**List**   You can think of each row in the Gantt control as a record in a database. The *ListLoad* and *ListSave* properties allow Gantt/VBX to read and write CSV (comma separated value) files without any further intervention on your part. Gantt/VBX also provides callable functions for loading data into Gantt/VBX manually. Each record contains 18 fields (Table 2-7), which are displayed in columns in the list, one record per row. The field titles are displayed in the list header. Gantt/VBXs list data properties are property arrays, each element being equal to the corresponding row in the Gantt control. Data can be read and written via these properties. The *ListType()* property array determines the number and type of bars drawn for each list item. You aren't required to use all the available fields, of course, and the Columns dialog allows you to customize the list to suit your needs.

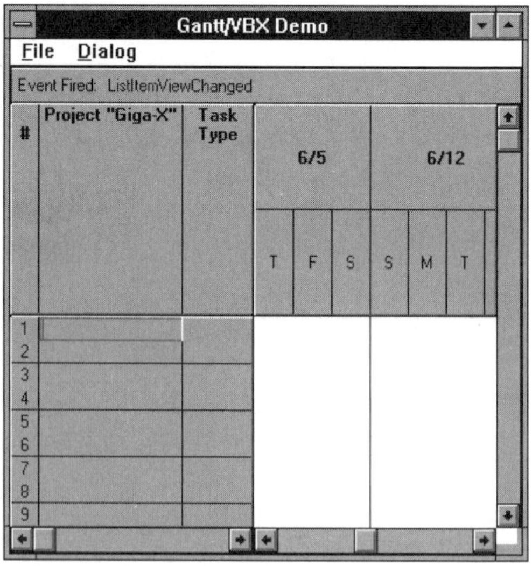

**Figure 2-3** Gantt/VBX with equal quadrant divisions

**Table 2-7** Gantt/VBX list data fields and related properties

| FIELD | RELATED PROPERTY |
| --- | --- |
| Task # | NA (Row number in list) |
| Name | ListName() |
| Task Type | ListType |
| Planned Begin | ListPlanBeg() |
| Planned End | ListPlanEnd() |
| Planned Duration | ListPlanDur() |
| Actual Begin | ListActBeg() |
| Actual End | ListActEnd() |
| Actual Duration | ListActDur() |
| % Complete | ListPerComp() |
| Slack End | ListSlackEnd() |
| Slack Duration | ListSlackDur() |
| Depends On | ListDepends() |
| Assigned To | ListAssigned() |
| User 1 | ListUser1() |
| User 2 | ListUser2() |
| User 3 | ListUser3() |
| User 4 | ListUser4() |

**Gantt**   The bars in the Gantt area are fully configurable at both design time and run time. There are 14 bar types available (Table 2-8). Each has a predefined meaning, but you can change the meaning to fit your application's needs.

**Table 2-8** Gantt/VBX bar types and related list data

| BAR | RELATED LIST DATA |
| --- | --- |
| 0-Critical Planned | "planned beg" and "planned end" dates |
| 1-Critical Actual | "actual beg" and "actual end" dates |
| 2-NonCritical Planned | "planned beg" and "planned end" dates |
| 3- NonCritical Actual | "actual beg" and "actual end" dates |
| 4-Summary Planned | "planned beg" and "planned end" dates |
| 5-Summary Actual | "actual beg" and "actual end" dates |
| 6-Milestone | "planned beg" date |
| 7-Completed Milestone | "actual beg" date |
| 8-Progress | "planned beg" and "planned end" dates and "PerComp" |
| 9-Slack | "planned end" and "slack end" dates |
| 10-User 1 | any two dates |
| 11-User 2 | any two dates |
| 12-User 3 | any two dates |
| 13-User 4 | any two dates |

By default the user can resize the list, header, list columns, and rows. You can disable these features by setting the *ResizeListWidth*, *ResizeHeader*, *ResizeListColumns*, and *ResizeListItems* properties to *False*, respectively. If you do, the user can drag the bars in the Gantt area but Gantt/VBX doesn't change the data in the list when this happens. You are responsible for updating all your data. Gantt/VBX simply fires events to indicate user actions. For instance, if the *TSMinorDoubleClick* event is fired you could "zoom" the time scale by increasing the *TSMinor* property.

# Example

The sample program (Figure 2-4) makes use of Gantt/VBX's built-in dialogs (Table 2-9) to allow customization of the controls' appearance. It also demonstrates how easily you can load and save files directly to/from the Gantt control using the *ListLoad* and *ListSave* properties. You can edit directly in the list area and use the File Save menu option to save the data. Use the File Open menu option to load the data you saved. The data will be stored in a file called GANTTDMO.CSV. You can also use the mouse to manipulate the bars in the Gantt area directly; GANTT/VBX is fully interactive.

**Table 2-9** Gantt/VBX built-in dialogs

| DIALOG | PURPOSE |
| --- | --- |
| MasterDialog | Provides access to all other dialogs |
| GeneralDialog | General Gantt/VBX properties |
| DateTimeDialog | Set beginning and ending date/time and current time line properties |
| TimescalesDialog | Set major and minor time scale properties |
| GanttDialog | Set Gantt font, backcolor, bevel, and grid properties |
| ListHdrDialog | Set list header font, backcolor, bevel, and grid properties |
| ListDialog | Set list font, backcolor, bevel, grid properties, and maximum number of listitems |
| ColumnsDialog | Change all column settings (field, format, label, width, alignment, and attributes) |
| BarsDialog | Change all bar settings (style, pattern, location, field, format, symbols, run time adjustability) |

Because the Gantt/VBX control is unique among grid controls, because it serves a specific purpose rather than being a general purpose grid, the events this control fires are also unique, and there are quite a few of them. For this reason, the sample program updates the status area (just below the menu) with information about what events are fired as you work with the control at run time. This should help you become familiar with the events and determine how each is triggered.

## Steps

1. Create a new project called GANTTDMO.MAK. Create a new form with the objects and properties shown in Table 2-10. Save this form as GANTTDMO.FRM.

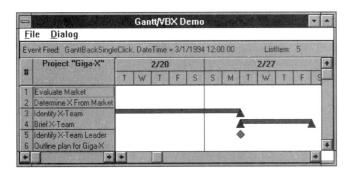

**Figure 2-4** Gantt/VBX demo main screen

**Table 2-10** Gantt/VBX main form's objects and properties

| OBJECT | PROPERTY | SETTING |
|---|---|---|
| Form | FormName | frmMain |
| | BackColor | &H00C0C0C0& |
| | Caption | "Gantt/VBX Demo" |
| | ClipControls | 0 'False |
| | ScaleMode | 3 'Pixel |
| PictureBox | Name | picToolbar |
| | Align | 1 'Align Top |
| | BackColor | &H00C0C0C0& |
| | ClipControls | 0 'False |
| | ScaleMode | 3 'Pixel |
| GanttVBX | Name | gntMain |
| | BevelWidth | 1 |
| | BorderStyle | 0 'None |
| | Caption | "Project ""DeskRef""" |
| | CurrentTimeLine | -1 'True |
| | DateTimeBeg | "1/1/1994 0:00.00" |
| | DateTimeEnd | "1/1/1995 0:00.00" |
| | DateTimeView | "6/9/1994 15:36.27" |
| | GanttBackColor | &H00FFFFFF& |
| | GanttBevel | 0 'None |
| | GanttGridColor | &H00000000& |
| | GridMajorColor | &H00000000& |
| | HeaderHeight | 40 |
| | ListBackColor | &H00C0C0C0& |
| | ListBevel | 2 'Raised |

*(continued on next page)*

147

| OBJECT | PROPERTY | SETTING |
|---|---|---|
| *(continued from previous page)* | | |
| | ListGridColor | &H00000000& |
| | ListGridLineCount | 2 |
| | ListGridThickness | 1 |
| | ListHdrBackColor | &H00C0C0C0& |
| | ListHdrBevel | 2 'Raised |
| | ListHdrGridColor | &H00000000& |
| | ListItemHeight | 16 |
| | ListItemView | 0 |
| | ListMaxItems | 100 |
| | ListWidth | 145 |
| | ProcessTab | -1 'True |
| | ResizeHeader | -1 'True |
| | ResizeListColumns | 'True |
| | ResizeListItems | -1 'True |
| | ResizeListWidth | -1 'True |
| | ScrollBarColor | &H00C0C0C0& |
| | ScrollBarWidth | 18 |
| | TSBackColor | &H00C0C0C0& |
| | TSBevel | 2 'Raised |
| | TSGridColor | &H00000000& |
| | TSGridThickness | 1 |
| | TSMajor | 3 'Week |
| | TSMajorCount | 1 |
| | TSMajorFormat | 0 '12/31 |
| | TSMajorGrid | -1 'True |
| | TSMinor | 4 'Day |
| | TSMinorCount | 1 |
| | TSMinorFormat | 9 'F |
| | TSMinorGrid | 0 'False |

2. Place the controls shown in Table 2-11 within the picToolbar PictureBox control.

**Table 2-11** Gantt/VBX picToolbar child objects and properties

| OBJECT | PROPERTY | SETTING |
|---|---|---|
| Label | Name | lblEventFired |
| | BackStyle | 0 'Transparent |
| | Caption | "Event Fired: " |
| | FontBold | 0 'False |

| OBJECT | PROPERTY | SETTING |
|--------|----------|---------|
|  | Index | 0 |
| Label | Name | lblListItem |
|  | BackStyle | 0 'Transparent |
|  | Caption | "ListItem:" |
|  | FontBold | 0 'False |
|  | Index | 0 |
| Label | Name | lblEventFired |
|  | BackStyle | 0 'Transparent |
|  | Caption | "Event Fired: " |
|  | FontBold | 0 'False |
|  | ForeColor | &H00FF0000& |
|  | Index | 1 |
| Label | Name | lblListItem |
|  | BackStyle | 0 'Transparent |
|  | Caption | "ListItem:" |
|  | FontBold | 0 'False |
|  | ForeColor | &H00FF0000& |
|  | Index | 1 |

3. Add a menu to the GANTTDMO.FRM form using the Visual Basic Menu Design window, setting the captions and names as shown in Table 2-12. Note that the menus are set up as control arrays.

**Table 2-12**  Menu definition for GANTTDMO.FRM

| CAPTION | NAME | INDEX |
|---------|------|-------|
| &File | mnuMain | 0 |
| − − − −&Open | mnuFile | 0 |
| − − − −&Save | mnuFile | 1 |
| − − − − | mnuFile | 2 |
| − − − −E&xit | mnuFile | 3 |
| &Dialog | mnuMain | 1 |
| − − − −&Bars... | mnuDialog | 0 |
| − − − −&Columns... | mnuDialog | 1 |
| − − − −&Gantt... | mnuDialog | 2 |
| − − − −&List... | mnuDialog | 3 |
| − − − −&Header... | mnuDialog | 4 |
| − − − −&Timescale... | mnuDialog | 5 |
| − − − −&Date/Time... | mnuDialog | 6 |
| − − − −Ge&neral... | mnuDialog | 7 |

4. Add the following code to the declarations section of the GANTTDMO form.

```
Option Explicit
DefInt A-Z

Const MNU_FILE_OPEN = 0
Const MNU_FILE_SAVE = 1
Const MNU_FILE_EXIT = 3

Const MNU_DLG_BARS = 0
Const MNU_DLG_COLS = 1
Const MNU_DLG_GANTT = 2
Const MNU_DLG_LIST = 3
Const MNU_DLG_LIST_HEADER = 4
Const MNU_DLG_TIMESCALES = 5
Const MNU_DLG_DATETIME = 6
Const MNU_DLG_GENERAL = 7
```

5. Add the following code to the GANTTDMO form.

```
Sub Form_Resize ()

    gntMain.Width = frmMain.ScaleWidth
    gntMain.Height = frmMain.ScaleHeight - gntMain.Top

End Sub

Sub Form_Unload (Cancel As Integer)

    End

End Sub

Sub gntMain_ActualBegChanged (ListItem As Integer, ActualBeg As String)

    Call UpdateEventStatus("ActualBegChanged " & ActualBeg$)
    Call UpdateListItem(ListItem%)

End Sub

Sub gntMain_ActualDurChanged (ListItem As Integer, ActualDur As String)

    Call UpdateEventStatus("ActualDurChanged " & ActualDur$)
    Call UpdateListItem(ListItem%)

End Sub

Sub gntMain_ActualEndChanged (ListItem As Integer, ActualEnd As String)

    Call UpdateEventStatus("ActualEndChanged " & ActualEnd$)
    Call UpdateListItem(ListItem%)

End Sub

Sub gntMain_AssignedChanged (ListItem As Integer, Assigned As String)

    Call UpdateEventStatus("AssignedChanged " & Assigned$)
    Call UpdateListItem(ListItem%)

End Sub

Sub gntMain_BarBegDoubleClick (ListItem As Integer, BarType As Integer)
```

```
    Call UpdateEventStatus("BarBegDoubleClick, BarType = " & CStr(BarType%))
    Call UpdateListItem(ListItem%)

End Sub

Sub gntMain_BarBegSingleClick (ListItem As Integer, BarType As Integer)

    Call UpdateEventStatus("BarBegSingleClick, BarType = " & CStr(BarType%))
    Call UpdateListItem(ListItem%)

End Sub

Sub gntMain_BarDoubleClick (ListItem As Integer, BarType As Integer)

    Call UpdateEventStatus("BarDoubleClick, BarType = " & CStr(BarType%))
    Call UpdateListItem(ListItem%)

End Sub

Sub gntMain_BarEndDoubleClick (ListItem As Integer, BarType As Integer)

    Call UpdateEventStatus("BarEndDoubleClick, BarType = " & CStr(BarType%))
    Call UpdateListItem(ListItem%)

End Sub

Sub gntMain_BarEndSingleClick (ListItem As Integer, BarType As Integer)

    Call UpdateEventStatus("BarEndSingleClick, BarType = " & CStr(BarType%))
    Call UpdateListItem(ListItem%)

End Sub

Sub gntMain_BarSingleClick (ListItem As Integer, BarType As Integer)

    Call UpdateEventStatus("BarSingleClick, BarType = " & CStr(BarType%))
    Call UpdateListItem(ListItem%)

End Sub

Sub gntMain_CellDoubleClick (ListItem As Integer, Column As Integer)

    Call UpdateEventStatus("CellDoubleClick, Column = " & CStr(Column%))
    Call UpdateListItem(ListItem%)

End Sub

Sub gntMain_CellGotFocus (ListItem As Integer, Column As Integer)

    Call UpdateEventStatus("CellGotFocus, Column = " & CStr(Column%))
    Call UpdateListItem(ListItem%)

End Sub

Sub gntMain_CellLostFocus (ListItem As Integer, Column As Integer)

    Call UpdateEventStatus("CellLostFocus, Column = " & CStr(Column%))
```

*(continued on next page)*

*(continued from previous page)*

```
    Call UpdateListItem(ListItem%)

End Sub

Sub gntMain_ColWidthChanged (Column As Integer, ColWidth As Integer)

    Call UpdateEventStatus("ColWidthChanged, Column = " & CStr(Column%) & ", ColWidth = " &
CStr(ColWidth%))

End Sub

Sub gntMain_ControlGotFocus (ListItem As Integer, Column As Integer)

    Call UpdateEventStatus("ControlGotFocus, Column = " & CStr(Column%))
    Call UpdateListItem(ListItem%)

End Sub

Sub gntMain_ControlLostFocus (ListItem As Integer, Column As Integer)

    Call UpdateEventStatus("ControlLostFocus, Column = " & CStr(Column%))
    Call UpdateListItem(ListItem%)

End Sub

Sub gntMain_DateTimeViewChanged (DateTime As String)

    Call UpdateEventStatus("DateTimeViewChanged, DateTime = " & DateTime$)

End Sub

Sub gntMain_DependsChanged (ListItem As Integer, Depends As String)

    Call UpdateEventStatus("DependsChanged, Depends = " & Depends$)
    Call UpdateListItem(ListItem%)

End Sub

Sub gntMain_GanttBackDoubleClick (ListItem As Integer, DateTime As String)

    Call UpdateEventStatus("GanttBackDoubleClick, DateTime = " & DateTime$)
    Call UpdateListItem(ListItem%)

End Sub

Sub gntMain_GanttBackSingleClick (ListItem As Integer, DateTime As String)

    Call UpdateEventStatus("GanttBackSingleClick, DateTime = " & DateTime$)
    Call UpdateListItem(ListItem%)

End Sub

Sub gntMain_HeaderHeightChanged (HeaderWidth As Integer)

    Call UpdateEventStatus("HeaderHeightChanged, HeaderWidth = " & CStr(HeaderWidth%))

End Sub

Sub gntMain_InsertModeChanged (InsMode As Integer)
```

```
        Call UpdateEventStatus("InsertModeChanged, InsMode = " & CStr(InsMode%))

End Sub

Sub gntMain_ListHdrDoubleClick (Column As Integer)

        Call UpdateEventStatus("ListHdrDoubleClick, Column = " & CStr(Column%))

End Sub

Sub gntMain_ListHdrSingleClick (Column As Integer)

        Call UpdateEventStatus("ListHdrSingleClick, Column = " & CStr(Column%))

End Sub

Sub gntMain_ListItemHeightChanged (ItemHeight As Integer)

        Call UpdateEventStatus("ListItemHeightChanged, ItemHeight = " & CStr(ItemHeight%))

End Sub

Sub gntMain_ListItemViewChanged (ListItem As Integer)

        Call UpdateEventStatus("ListItemViewChanged")
        Call UpdateListItem(ListItem%)

End Sub

Sub gntMain_ListWidthChanged (ListWidth As Integer)

        Call UpdateEventStatus("ListWidthChanged, ListWidth = " & CStr(ListWidth%))

End Sub

Sub gntMain_NameChanged (ListItem As Integer, TaskName As String)

        Call UpdateEventStatus("NameChanged, TaskName = " & TaskName$)
        Call UpdateListItem(ListItem%)

End Sub

Sub gntMain_PercentCompleteChanged (ListItem As Integer, PerComp As Integer)

        Call UpdateEventStatus("PercentCompleteChanged, PerComp = " & CStr(PerComp%))
        Call UpdateListItem(ListItem%)

End Sub

Sub gntMain_PlannedBegChanged (ListItem As Integer, PlannedBeg As String)

        Call UpdateEventStatus("PlannedBegChanged, PlannedBeg = " & PlannedBeg$)
        Call UpdateListItem(ListItem%)

End Sub

Sub gntMain_PlannedDurChanged (ListItem As Integer, PlannedDur As String)

        Call UpdateEventStatus("PlannedDurChanged, PlannedDur = " & PlannedDur$)
```

*(continued on next page)*

*(continued from previous page)*

```
    Call UpdateListItem(ListItem%)

End Sub

Sub gntMain_PlannedEndChanged (ListItem As Integer, PlannedEnd As String)

    Call UpdateEventStatus("PlannedEndChanged, PlannedEnd = " & PlannedEnd$)
    Call UpdateListItem(ListItem%)

End Sub

Sub gntMain_SlackDurChanged (ListItem As Integer, SlackDur As String)

    Call UpdateEventStatus("SlackDurChanged, SlackDur = " & SlackDur$)
    Call UpdateListItem(ListItem%)

End Sub

Sub gntMain_SlackEndChanged (ListItem As Integer, SlackEnd As String)

    Call UpdateEventStatus("SlackEndChanged, SlackEnd = " & SlackEnd$)
    Call UpdateListItem(ListItem%)

End Sub

Sub gntMain_TaskChanged (ListItem As Integer)

    Call UpdateEventStatus("TaskChanged")
    Call UpdateListItem(ListItem%)

End Sub

Sub gntMain_TSMajorDoubleClick (TSMajor As Integer)

    Call UpdateEventStatus("TSMajorDoubleClick, TSMajor = " & CStr(TSMajor%))

End Sub

Sub gntMain_TSMajorSingleClick (TSMajor As Integer)

    Call UpdateEventStatus("TSMajorSingleClick, TSMajor = " & CStr(TSMajor%))

End Sub

Sub gntMain_TSMinorDoubleClick (TSMinor As Integer)

    Call UpdateEventStatus("TSMinorDoubleClick, TSMinor = " & CStr(TSMinor%))

End Sub

Sub gntMain_TSMinorSingleClick (TSMinor As Integer)

    Call UpdateEventStatus("TSMinorSingleClick, TSMinor = " & CStr(TSMinor%))

End Sub

Sub gntMain_TypeChanged (ListItem As Integer, TaskType As Integer)

    Call UpdateEventStatus("TypeChanged, TaskType = " & CStr(TaskType%))
```

```
        Call UpdateListItem(ListItem%)

End Sub

Sub gntMain_User1Changed (ListItem As Integer, User1 As String)

        Call UpdateEventStatus("User1Changed, User1 = " & User1$)
        Call UpdateListItem(ListItem%)

End Sub

Sub gntMain_User2Changed (ListItem As Integer, User2 As String)

        Call UpdateEventStatus("User2Changed, User2 = " & User2$)
        Call UpdateListItem(ListItem%)

End Sub

Sub gntMain_User3Changed (ListItem As Integer, User3 As String)

        Call UpdateEventStatus("User3Changed, User3 = " & User3$)
        Call UpdateListItem(ListItem%)

End Sub

Sub gntMain_User4Changed (ListItem As Integer, User4 As String)

        Call UpdateEventStatus("User4Changed, User4 = " & User4$)
        Call UpdateListItem(ListItem%)

End Sub

Sub mnuDialog_Click (Index As Integer)
'------------------------------------------------
'-- The dialog menu options simply display the
'   built-in dialogs. They handle everything else.
'------------------------------------------------

        Select Case Index%
            Case MNU_DLG_BARS
                gntMain.BarsDialog = GANTT_DLG_OPEN
            Case MNU_DLG_COLS
                gntMain.ColumnsDialog = GANTT_DLG_OPEN
            Case MNU_DLG_GANTT
                gntMain.GanttDialog = GANTT_DLG_OPEN
            Case MNU_DLG_LIST
                gntMain.ListDialog = GANTT_DLG_OPEN
            Case MNU_DLG_LIST_HEADER
                gntMain.ListHdrDialog = GANTT_DLG_OPEN
            Case MNU_DLG_TIMESCALES
                gntMain.TimescalesDialog = GANTT_DLG_OPEN
            Case MNU_DLG_DATETIME
                gntMain.DateTimeDialog = GANTT_DLG_OPEN
            Case MNU_DLG_GENERAL
                gntMain.GeneralDialog = GANTT_DLG_OPEN
        End Select

End Sub

Sub mnuFile_Click (Index As Integer)
```

*(continued on next page)*

*(continued from previous page)*

```
    Select Case Index
        Case MNU_FILE_OPEN
            gntMain.ListLoad = App.Path & "\GANTTDMO.CSV"
        Case MNU_FILE_SAVE
            gntMain.ListSave = App.Path & "\GANTTDMO.CSV"
        '-----------------
        Case MNU_FILE_EXIT
            Unload Me
    End Select

End Sub

Sub picToolbar_Paint ()

    picToolbar.Line (0, 0)-(picToolbar.Width - 1, 0), WHITE

End Sub
```

6. Create a new module called GANTTDMO.BAS and add the following code to the declarations section.

```
Option Explicit
DefInt A-Z

Global Const DEBUG_MODE = False

Global Const GANTT_DLG_OPEN = 0

Global Const DARKGRAY = &H808080
Global Const WHITE = &HFFFFFF
```

7. Add the following code to the GANTTDMO.BAS module.

```
Sub UpdateEventStatus (Event$)

    frmMain!lblEventFired(1).Caption = Event$

    If DEBUG_MODE Then
        Debug.Print "Event Fired: " & Event$
    End If

End Sub

Sub UpdateListItem (ListItem%)

    frmMain!lblListItem(1).Caption = CStr(ListItem%)

    If DEBUG_MODE Then
        Debug.Print "ListItem: " & CStr(ListItem%)
    End If

End Sub
```

## Tips and Comments

The flexibility of Gantt/VBX should allow you to use it in any number of applications—not just the obvious ones like project management, but whenever time scheduling is called for. Due to its size and completeness, Gantt/VBX takes awhile to learn but features like the built-in dialogs can help make you productive while you get up to speed.

Here's a small note from the not-so-obvious bin. You can adjust the color and width of the scroll bars on Gantt/VBX via the *ScrollBarColor* and *ScrollBarWidth* properties. By setting *ScrollBarWidth* to 0, you can effectively remove the scroll bars.

# Grid (GRID.VBX)

| USAGE: | Unbound Grid |
|---|---|
| MANUFACTURER: | Microsoft |
| COST: | Included with VB Professional |

There are now a number of grid controls, but the one that started it all is GRID.VBX, which comes with VB. GRID.VBX is a good, basic grid control with some unique features not available in certain of the larger, more complex grid controls.

## Syntax

While some of the larger grid controls offer literally hundreds of properties and dozens of events, GRID.VBX provides a clear, concise interface with just 22 nonstandard properties and 2 custom events (Table 2-13).

**Table 2-13** GRID.VBX nonstandard properties and events

**PROPERTIES**

| | | |
|---|---|---|
| CellSelected | Clip | Col |
| ColAlignment | Cols | ColWidth |
| FillStyle | FixedAlignment | FixedCols |
| FixedRows | GridLines | HighLight |
| LeftCol | Row | RowHeight |
| Rows | Scrollbars | SelEndCol |
| SelEndRow | SelStartCol | SelStartRow |
| TopRow | | |

**EVENTS**

| | |
|---|---|
| RowColChange | SelChange |

With GRID.VBX, as with most grid controls, you use the *Rows* and *Cols* properties to set the number of rows and columns in the grid. A grid can have a maximum of 2,000 rows and 400 columns, which should be enough for most purposes. You can also use the *Rows* and *Cols* properties to read the number of rows or columns in a grid. This is useful because the grid control supports the *AddItem* method for adding new rows to a grid, just like a list box. *RowHeight* and *ColWidth* control the height and width of the rows and columns in the grid. Both *RowHeight* and *ColWidth* are specified in Twips and there is no straightforward way to adjust the scale to character height and width based on the font used in the grid. You can work around this problem by setting the font properties on the grid's parent form to match those of the grid, setting the form's *ScaleMode* to twips, and using the form's *TextWidth* and *TextHeight* properties to calculate values for *RowHeight* and *ColWidth*. If there are more rows and/or columns than can be displayed on the grid, scroll bars are added automatically. The number of fixed (nonscrollable) rows and columns is controlled by the *FixedRows* and *FixedCols* properties, which can be changed at run time. The *GridLines* property determines whether separating lines appear between rows and columns in the grid.

The current cell is determined by the *Row* and *Col* properties, which are both read/write so you can set the current cell from code. When the current cell changes, a *RowColChange* event fires to inform you of the change. Assigning a string to the *Text* property loads that string into the current cell. You can also load a picture into the current cell via the *Picture* property and *LoadPicture*. The *FillStyle* property (Table 2-14) acts differently for Grid than for most other controls. If *FillStyle* is set to *Single*, assigning a string to the *Text* property places the string only in the current cell. If *FillStyle* is set to *Repeat*, the string is assigned to all the currently selected cells.

**Table 2-14** Grid FillStyle property values

| VALUE | MEANING |
| --- | --- |
| 0 | Single |
| 1 | Repeat |

Since the grid can be scrolled, you may want to find out what part of the grid is currently displayed. The *TopRow* and *LeftCol* properties tell you which are the first visible row and column, not counting fixed rows and columns. It is also possible to scroll the grid programmatically by assigning values to *TopRow* and *LeftCol*.

The standard *ForeColor* and *BackColor* properties apply to the grid, but fixed rows and columns always have a gray background. Selected cells appear highlighted if the *Highlight* property is set to *True*, but you can't control the highlight color. If *Highlight* is *False*, there is no visual indication of what cells are selected. You can use the *CellSelected* property to determine whether the current cell lies within the range of selected cells, regardless of whether the *Highlight* is *True* or *False*. If multiple rows and columns are selected, you can determine the range of the current selection by reading four properties that track the starting row and column (*SelStartRow*, *SelStartCol*) and the ending row and column (*SelEndRow*, *SelEndCol*) for the selection. You can use those four properties to control what cells are selected programmatically. Whenever the range of selected cells changes, the grid fires a *SelChange* event. *Clip* determines the contents of the whole range of selected cells as opposed to just a single cell. By assigning a string to the *Clip* property, you can load text into some or all of the currently selected cells. The format of the *Clip* property defines each cell within a row as being separated by a tab character (Chr$(9)) and each row being separated by a carriage return (Chr$(13)). Being able to control the selection of cells with *SelStartRow*, *SelStartCol*, *SelEndRow*, and *SelEndCol* makes the *Clip* property far more valuable than it might be otherwise and provides a convenient mechanism for loading comma-delimited ASCII files into a grid control.

You can left-justify, center, or right-justify each column individually, by changing the setting of the *ColAlignment* property. You use the *FixedAlignment* property to align only the fixed cells in a column. In addition to the three standard alignments, this propery has a fourth option that tells the grid to use the *ColAlignment* property for that column. You can use *FixedAlignment* to align headings (fixed cells) differently than the rest of the cells in a column. For instance, you could left-align a column but center its heading(s).

# Example

The Grid sample program (Figure 2-5) shows how simple it is to work with GRID.VBX. The *Clip* property both sets data into cells and clears data from cells. The current cell is tracked and displayed via the *RowColChange* event, and both the number and alignment of fixed rows and columns are adjustable at run time.

## Steps

1. Create a new project called GRIDDMO.MAK. Create a new form with the objects and properties shown in Table 2-15. Save this form as GRIDDMO.FRM.

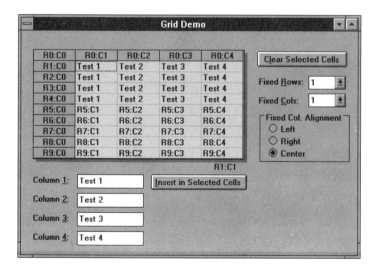

**Figure 2-5** Grid demo main form

**Table 2-15** Grid main form's objects and properties

| OBJECT | PROPERTY | SETTING |
|--------|----------|---------|
| Form | FormName | frmMain |
| | BackColor | &H00C0C0C0& |
| | Caption | "Grid Demo" |
| | ScaleMode | 3 'Pixel |
| Frame | Name | fraFixedColAlignment |
| | BackColor | &H00C0C0C0& |
| | Caption | "Fixed Col. Alignment" |
| Line | Name | linShadow |
| | BorderColor | &H00808080& |
| | BorderWidth | 4 |
| | Index | 0 |
| | X1 | 25 |
| | X2 | 343 |
| | Y1 | 192 |
| | Y2 | 192 |
| Line | Name | linShadow |
| | BorderColor | &H00808080& |
| | BorderWidth | 4 |
| | Index | 1 |
| | X1 | 343 |
| | X2 | 343 |
| | Y1 | 35 |
| | Y2 | 188 |
| Label | Name | lblColumnText |
| | BackStyle | 0 'Transparent |
| | Caption | "Column &1:" |
| | Index | 0 |
| Label | Name | lblColumnText |
| | BackStyle | 0 'Transparent |
| | Caption | "Column &2:" |
| | Index | 1 |
| Label | Name | lblColumnText |
| | BackStyle | 0 'Transparent |
| | Caption | "Column &3:" |
| | Index | 2 |
| Label | Name | lblColumnText |

| OBJECT | PROPERTY | SETTING |
|---|---|---|
| | BackStyle | 0 'Transparent |
| | Caption | "Column &4:" |
| | Index | 3 |
| Label | Name | lblFixedRows |
| | BackStyle | 0 'Transparent |
| | Caption | "Fixed &Rows:" |
| Label | Name | lblFixedCols |
| | BackStyle | 0 'Transparent |
| | Caption | "Fixed &Cols:" |
| Label | Name | lblCurCell |
| | BackStyle | 0 'Transparent |
| | ForeColor | &H00FF0000& |
| Grid | Name | grdMain |
| | BackColor | &H0000FFFF& |
| | Cols | 5 |
| | Rows | 10 |
| TextBox | Name | txtColumnText |
| | Index | 0 |
| | Text | "Test 1" |
| TextBox | Name | txtColumnText |
| | Index | 1 |
| | Text | "Test 2" |
| TextBox | Name | txtColumnText |
| | Index | 2 |
| | Text | "Test 3" |
| TextBox | Name | txtColumnText |
| | Index | 3 |
| | Text | "Test 4" |
| CommandButton | Name | btnInsert |
| | Caption | "&Insert in Selected Cells" |
| CommandButton | Name | btnClear |
| | Caption | "C&lear Selected Cells" |
| ComboBox | Name | cmbFixedRows |
| | Style | 2 'Dropdown List |
| ComboBox | Name | cmbFixedCols |
| | Style | 2 'Dropdown List |

2. Place the controls shown in Table 2-16 within the fraFixedColAlignment Frame control.

**Table 2-16** Grid fraFixedColAlignment child objects and properties

| OBJECT | PROPERTY | SETTING |
|--------|----------|---------|
| OptionButton | Name | optFixedColAlignment |
| | BackColor | &H00C0C0C0& |
| | Caption | "Left" |
| | Index | 0 |
| | Value | -1 'True |
| OptionButton | Name | optFixedColAlignment |
| | BackColor | &H00C0C0C0& |
| | Caption | "Right" |
| | Index | 1 |
| OptionButton | Name | optFixedColAlignment |
| | BackColor | &H00C0C0C0& |
| | Caption | "Center" |
| | Index | 2 |

3. Add the following code to the the GRIDDMO form.

```
Option Explicit
DefInt A-Z


Sub btnClear_Click ()

    '-- Clear out all text in selected cells.
    grdMain.Clip = ""

End Sub

Sub btnInsert_Click ()
    Dim RowText As String
    Dim NewText As String
    Dim i       As Integer

    '-- Build the text for one row.
    For i% = 0 To 3
        If RowText$  "" Then
            RowText$ = RowText$ & Chr$(9)
        End If
            RowText$ = RowText$ & txtColumnText(i%).Text
    Next i%
    '-- Add a carriage return for each row selected.
    For i% = grdMain.SelStartRow To grdMain.SelEndRow
        NewText$ = NewText$ & RowText$ & Chr$(13)
    Next i%

    grdMain.Clip = NewText$
```

```
End Sub

Sub cmbFixedCols_Click ()

    grdMain.FixedCols = cmbFixedCols.ListIndex

End Sub

Sub cmbFixedRows_Click ()

    grdMain.FixedRows = cmbFixedRows.ListIndex

End Sub

Sub Form_Load ()
    Dim Row%
    Dim RowHeight%
    Dim Col%
    Dim ColWidth%

    Me.Move (Screen.Width - Width) \ 2, (Screen.Height - Height) \ 2

    '-- Create evenly sized rows and columns
    '   that fill the grid. Note that the RowHeight
    '   and ColWidth properties are adjusted down
    '   slightly (-15, -30). If this isn't done then
    '   scroll bars will be forced on.
    RowHeight% = (grdMain.Height * Screen.TwipsPerPixelY) \ grdMain.Rows - 15
    For Row% = 0 To grdMain.Rows - 1
        grdMain.RowHeight(Row%) = RowHeight%
    Next Row%
    ColWidth% = (grdMain.Width * Screen.TwipsPerPixelX) \ grdMain.Cols - 30
    For Col% = 0 To grdMain.Cols - 1
        grdMain.ColWidth(Col%) = ColWidth%
    Next Col%

    Call LoadGrid

    '-- Load combo boxes.
    For Row% = 0 To grdMain.Rows - 1
        cmbFixedRows.AddItem CStr(Row%)
    Next Row%
    For Col% = 0 To grdMain.Cols - 1
        cmbFixedCols.AddItem CStr(Col%)
    Next Col%

    cmbFixedRows.ListIndex = 1
    cmbFixedCols.ListIndex = 1

End Sub

Sub grdMain_RowColChange ()
    Dim Row$
    Dim Col$

    Row$ = "R" & CStr(grdMain.Row)
    Col$ = "C" & CStr(grdMain.Col)
    lblCurCell.Caption = Row$ & ":" & Col$

End Sub
```

*(continued on next page)*

*(continued from previous page)*

```
Sub LoadGrid ()
    Dim Row%
    Dim Col%
    Dim RowID$
    Dim ColID$

    For Row% = 0 To grdMain.Rows - 1
        grdMain.Row = Row%
        RowID$ = "R" & CStr(Row%)
        For Col% = 0 To grdMain.Cols - 1
            grdMain.Col = Col%
            ColID$ = "C" & CStr(Col%)
            grdMain.Text = RowID$ & ":" & ColID$
        Next Col%
    Next Row%

End Sub

Sub optFixedColAlignment_Click (Index As Integer)
    Dim i%

    For i% = 0 To grdMain.Cols - 1
        grdMain.FixedAlignment(i%) = Index%
    Next i%

End Sub
```

## Tips and Comments

While GRID.VBX is not nearly as powerful as most other grid controls, and it can't act as a bound control, it has its advantages. First, it comes with VB so you can't beat the price. Second, it's very straightforward and easy to use when compared to the larger, more complex grid controls on the market. Third, while this is not usually a deciding factor, it is much smaller than other grid controls. It weighs in at around 50K, while other grid controls are between 300K and 500K in size.

If you don't need a bound grid, direct editing, or detailed control over individual cells' appearances GRID.VBX is a good, basic grid control that should serve you well.

# Grid/VBX (FPGRID 10.VBX)

| USAGE: | Bound/Unbound Grid |
| --- | --- |
| MANUFACTURER: | FarPoint Technologies |
| COST: | $99 |

The Grid/VBX control is a scaled-down version of FarPoint's Spread/VBX control and, as such, it has much in common with Spread/VBX. Grid/VBX can act as a bound grid much like other data aware controls. Unlike other bound controls, however, it can also be bound to the Q+E/Lib database. You can use Grid/VBX as an unbound grid very effectively, and the appearance of the grid is fully customizable both at design time and run time. At design time, you can use the Interface Designer provided by FarPoint to adjust the grid's properties in an interactive fashion.

# Syntax

The majority of Grid/VBX's properties are used to define the attributes (both appearance and operation) of individual cells or groups of cells. Table 2-17 lists all nonstandard properties, events, and functions for Grid/VBX.

**Table 2-17**  Grid/VBX nonstandard properties, events, and functions

**PROPERTIES**

| | | |
|---|---|---|
| Action | ActiveCol | ActiveRow |
| BackColor | BlockMode | CellType |
| ChangeMade | Clip | Col |
| Col2 | ColHidden | ColWidth |
| DataConnect | DataField | DataSelect |
| DAutoSave | DAutoSizeCols | DInformActiveRowChange |
| DisplayColHeaders | DisplayRowHeaders | EditMode |
| EditModePermanent | EditModeReplace | FontBold |
| FontItalic | FontName | FontSize |
| FontStrikethru | FontUnderline | ForeColor |
| GrayAreaBackColor | GridColor | GridShowHoriz |
| GridShowVert | GridSolid | InterfaceDesigner |
| IsBlockSelected | LeftCol | LoadPicture |
| LoadTabFile | Lock | MaxCols |
| MaxRows | MoveActiveOnFocus | ProcessTab |
| Redraw | Row | Row2 |
| RowHeight | RowHidden | ScrollBars |
| SelBlockCol | SelBlockCol2 | SelBlockRow |
| SelBlockRow2 | SelectBlockOptions | ShadowColor |
| ShadowDark | ShadowText | Text |
| TopRow | TypeButtonAlign | TypeButtonColor |
| TypeButtonPicture | TypeButtonPictureDown | TypeButtonText |
| TypeButtonTextColor | TypeButtonType | TypeCheckCenter |
| TypeCheckPicture | TypeCheckText | TypeComboBoxCurSel |
| TypeComboBoxList | TypeDateCentury | TypeDateFormat |
| TypeDateMax | TypeDateMin | TypeEditLen |
| TypeFloatDecimalPlaces | TypeFloatMax | TypeFloatMin |
| TypeFloatMoney | TypeFloatSeparator | TypeHAlign |
| TypePicDefaultText | TypePicMask | TypePictCenter |
| TypePictMaintainScale | TypePictPicture | TypePictStretch |

*(continued on next page)*

## PROPERTIES

*(continued from previous page)*

| | | |
|---|---|---|
| TypeTextAlignVert | TypeTextShadow | TypeTextWordWrap |
| TypeTime24Hour | TypeTimeMax | TypeTimeMin |
| TypeTimeSeconds | UnitType | UserResize |
| Value | VirtualMaxRows | VirtualMode |

## EVENTS

| | | |
|---|---|---|
| Advance | BlockSelected | ButtonClicked |
| Change | Click | DataAddNew |
| DataColConfig | DblClick | EditError |
| EditMode | LeaveCell | QueryData |
| SelChange | VirtualClearData | |

## FUNCTIONS

| | | |
|---|---|---|
| GetCellDirtyFlag | GetDataConnectHandle | GetDataSelectHandle |
| fpGetText | SaveTabFile | SetCellDirtyFlag |
| fpSetText | | |

Like most grid controls, Grid/VBX has *Row* and *Col* properties. However, *Row* and *Col* do not refer to the row and column of the currently active cell; for that you use the *ActiveRow* and *ActiveCol* properties. With Grid/VBX, you use *Row* and *Col* to specify a row or column on which an operation is to be performed. Operations include setting the *CellType* of cells (more on *CellType* later), locking cells to prevent editing, setting cell colors, and so forth. You can trigger any operations by setting the *Action* property of the control (Table 2-18). FarPoint provides a module (FPGRID.BAS) that includes symbolic constants for many nonstandard properties. The *BlockMode* property, if *True*, allows operations to be performed on a block, or range, of cells. For block operations, *Row* and *Col* define the beginning of the block and *Row2* and *Col2* define the end of the block.

**Table 2-18** Grid/VBX Action property values (values are not contiguous)

| SETTING | DESCRIPTION |
|---|---|
| 0 | Set the currently active cell. |
| 2 | Select a block of cells. |
| 3 | Clear grid, row, column, or cell. |
| 4 | Delete column. If BlockMode is True, Col2 is used to specify a range of columns. |
| 5 | Delete row. If BlockMode is True, Row2 is used to specify a range of rows. |
| 6 | Insert column. If BlockMode is True, Col2 is used to specify a range of columns. |
| 7 | Insert row. If BlockMode is True, Row2 is used to specify a range of rows. |

| SETTING | DESCRIPTION |
|---------|-------------|
| 12 | Remove data from cell, row, column or entire grid control. |
| 14 | Deselect a block of cells if one was previously selected. |
| 15 | Save all records in a bound grid that have been modified if DAutoSave is False. |
| 28 | Clear and reset all attributes of the grid back to the default settings. |
| 30 | Discard current data and rerequest the data currently in the buffer. This Action must be used with virtual Mode. |
| 31 | Force the data to be refreshed from the database. This Action is used when grid is bound to the Q+E /Lib database. |

Specifying the attributes for individual cells is easy both at design time and run time. At design time, double-clicking the *InterfaceDesigner* property launches the Interface Designer which allows you to specify the attributes of individual cells quickly and easily. Attributes include things like font information, editability, and *CellType*. The *CellType* determines the type of data displayed in a cell (Table 2-19). You can set the *CellType* for an entire row or column as easily as for a single cell, as the example program demonstrates.

**Table 2-19**  Grid/VBX CellType property values

| SETTING | DESCRIPTION | SYMBOLIC CONSTANT |
|---------|-------------|-------------------|
| 0 | Date | SS_CELL_TYPE_DATE |
| 1 | Edit | SS_CELL_TYPE_EDIT |
| 2 | Float | SS_CELL_TYPE_FLOAT |
| 4 | PIC | SS_CELL_TYPE_PIC |
| 5 | Static text | SS_CELL_TYPE_STATIC_TEXT |
| 6 | Time | SS_CELL_TYPE_TIME |
| 7 | Button | SS_CELL_TYPE_BUTTON |
| 8 | Combo box | SS_CELL_TYPE_COMBOBOX |
| 9 | Picture | SS_CELL_TYPE_PICTURE |
| 10 | Check box | SS_CELL_TYPE_CHECKBOX |

For each *CellType*, there are one or more properties that control the format of the cell. All of these properties begin with *Type* so they are easily recognizable. Table 2-20 summarizes the *Type* properties.

**Table 2-20**  Grid/VBX CellType related properties

| CELLTYPE | PROPERTIES |
|----------|------------|
| Date | TypeDateCentury |
| | TypeDateFormat |

*(continued on next page)*

| CELLTYPE | PROPERTIES |
|---|---|
| *(continued from previous page)* | |
| | TypeDateMax |
| | TypeDateMin |
| Edit | TypeEditLen |
| Float | TypeFloatDecimalPlaces |
| | TypeFloatMax |
| | TypeFloatMin |
| | TypeFloatMoney |
| | TypeFloatSeparator |
| PIC | TypePicDefText |
| | TypePicMask |
| Static Text | TypeHAlign |
| | TypeTextAlignVert |
| | TypeTextShadow |
| | WordWrap |
| Time | TypeTime24Hour |
| | TypeTimeMax |
| | TypeTimeMin |
| | TypeTimeSeconds |
| Button | TypeButtonAlign |
| | TypeButtonColor |
| | TypeButtonPicture |
| | TypeButtonPictureDown |
| | TypeButtonText |
| | TypeButtonTextColor |
| | TypeButtonType |
| Combo Box | TypeComboBoxList |
| | TypeComboBoxCurSel |
| Picture | TypePictCenter |
| | TypePictMaintainScale |
| | TypePictPicture |
| | TypePictStretch |
| Check Box | TypeCheckCenter |
| | TypeCheckPicture |
| | TypeCheckText |

If the large number of properties looks a bit intimidating, don't worry. The Grid/VBX Interface Designer has a Learn mode and an Event Monitor to help you become familiar with Grid/VBX. Using Learn mode is simple. While the Learn check box in the toolbar area of the Interface Designer is checked, all modifications to the grid are recorded in a buffer. While this check box is unchecked, the contents of the buffer are placed in the Clipboard and may be examined or pasted into the current project directly. The Event Monitor works in much the same way but it monitors grid events rather than modifications.

# Example

The sample program (Figure 2-6) is very simple, and demonstrates how much Grid/VBX can do even with very little code behind it. The grid is not operating in bound mode, but instead reads and writes tab-delimited files automatically using the *SaveTabFile* function and *LoadTabFile* property. The *Action* property is used to add, insert, and delete rows in the grid. The Category and Mail columns contain a combo box and a check box, respectively, and we simply set the *CellType* when the form was loaded; Grid/VBX does the rest. We could also have used the Interface Designer to specify the edit types at design time.

## Steps

1. Create a new project called GRIDVBX.MAK. Create a new form with the objects and properties shown in Table 2-21. Save this form as GRIDVBX.FRM.

**Table 2-21** Grid/VBX main form's objects and properties

| OBJECT | PROPERTY | SETTING |
|---|---|---|
| SpreadSheet | Name | grdMain |
| | BorderStyle | 0 'None |
| | DAutoSizeCols | 0 'Off |
| | GrayAreaBackColor | &H00808000& |
| | GridColor | &H00808000& |
| | MaxCols | 4 |
| | ProcessTab | -1 'True |
| | ShadowColor | &H00808000& |
| | ShadowDark | &H00000000& |
| Form | FormName | frmMain |
| | Caption | "Grid/VBX Demo" |
| | ScaleMode | 3 'Pixel |

2. Add a menu to the GRIDVBX.FRM form using the Visual Basic Menu Design window, setting the captions and names as shown in Table 2-22. Note that the menus are set up as control arrays.

**Figure 2-6** Grid/VBX sample program

**Table 2-22** Menu definition for GRIDVBX.FRM

| CAPTION | NAME | INDEX |
|---------|------|-------|
| &File | mnuMain | 0 |
| – – – – &Open | mnuFile | 0 |
| – – – – &Save | mnuFile | 1 |
| – – – – – | mnuFile | 2 |
| – – – – E&xit | mnuFile | 3 |
| &Edit | mnuMain | 1 |
| – – – – &Add Row | mnuEdit | 0 |
| – – – – &Insert Row | mnuEdit | 1 |
| – – – – &Delete Row | mnuEdit | 2 |

3. Add the following code to the GRIDVBX form.

```
Sub Form_Load ()

'-- Set the column headings.
    Call fpSetText(grdMain, 1, 0, "First")
    Call fpSetText(grdMain, 2, 0, "Last")
    Call fpSetText(grdMain, 3, 0, "Category")
    Call fpSetText(grdMain, 4, 0, "Mail")

'-- Create a combo box column and load the combo list.
    grdMain.Row = -1
    grdMain.Col = 3
    grdMain.CellType = SS_CELL_TYPE_COMBOBOX
    grdMain.TypeComboBoxList = "Friend" & Chr$(9) & "Relative" & Chr$(9) & "Client"

'-- Create a check box column and set the check box text.
    grdMain.Row = -1
    grdMain.Col = 4
    grdMain.BackColor = GRAY
    grdMain.ForeColor = GREEN
    grdMain.CellType = SS_CELL_TYPE_CHECKBOX
    grdMain.TypeCheckCenter = True
    grdMain.TypeCheckText = "Xmas List"
```

```
'-- Set the column widths.
    grdMain.ColWidth(1) = 10
    grdMain.ColWidth(2) = 10
    grdMain.ColWidth(3) = 10
    grdMain.ColWidth(4) = 11

End Sub

Sub Form_Resize ()

    grdMain.Width = frmMain.ScaleWidth
    grdMain.Height = frmMain.ScaleHeight

End Sub

Sub mnuEdit_Click (Index As Integer)

    Select Case Index%
        Case MNU_EDIT_ADD
            grdMain.MaxRows = grdMain.MaxRows + 1
            grdMain.Row = grdMain.MaxRows
            grdMain.Col = 1
            grdMain.Action = SS_ACTION_ACTIVE_CELL
        Case MNU_EDIT_INSERT
            grdMain.MaxRows = grdMain.MaxRows + 1
            grdMain.Row = grdMain.ActiveRow
            grdMain.Action = SS_ACTION_INSERT_ROW
        Case MNU_EDIT_DELETE
            grdMain.Row = grdMain.ActiveRow
            grdMain.Action = SS_ACTION_DELETE_ROW
            grdMain.MaxRows = grdMain.MaxRows - 1
    End Select

End Sub

Sub mnuFile_Click (Index As Integer)
    Dim SaveOK%

    Select Case Index%
        Case MNU_FILE_OPEN
            grdMain.LoadTabFile = App.Path & "\" & TAB_FILE
        Case MNU_FILE_SAVE
            SaveOK% = SaveTabFile(grdMain, App.Path & "\" & TAB_FILE)
            If Not SaveOK% Then
                MsgBox "Error Saving Tab File!"
            End If
        '-----------------
        Case MNU_FILE_EXIT
            Unload Me
    End Select

End Sub
```

4. Create a new module called GRIDVBX.BAS and add the following code to the declarations section.

```
Option Explicit
DefInt A-Z
```

*(continued on next page)*

*(continued from previous page)*

```
Declare Function SaveTabFile Lib "FPGRID10.VBX" (SS As Control, ByVal FileName As String) As
Integer
Declare Sub fpSetText Lib "FPGRID10.VBX" (SS As Control, ByVal Col As Long, ByVal Row As Long,
lpVar As Variant)

Global Const SS_ACTION_ACTIVE_CELL = 0
Global Const SS_ACTION_DELETE_ROW = 5
Global Const SS_ACTION_INSERT_COL = 6
Global Const SS_ACTION_INSERT_ROW = 7

Global Const SS_CELL_TYPE_COMBOBOX = 8
Global Const SS_CELL_TYPE_CHECKBOX = 10


Global Const GRAY = &HCOCOCO
Global Const GREEN = &HFF00&

Global Const MNU_FILE_OPEN = 0
Global Const MNU_FILE_SAVE = 1
Global Const MNU_FILE_EXIT = 3

Global Const MNU_EDIT_ADD = 0
Global Const MNU_EDIT_INSERT = 1
Global Const MNU_EDIT_DELETE = 2

Global Const TAB_FILE = "GRIDVBX.TSV"
```

## Tips and Comments

As you can see, Grid/VBX is very flexible when it comes to cell formatting and appearance. It is also fairly efficient and the manual gives optimization tips to help improve performance if necessary. Grid/VBX is the smaller of the FarPoint grid controls but it still weighs in at a healthy 380K. Grid/VBX's unique ability to bind to the Q+E/Lib database and the fact that it can be used with C/C++ environments that support VBXs make it very attractive in situations where data and tool portability is a concern.

# Spread/VBX (SPREAD20.VBX)

| USAGE: | Bound Grid, Spreadsheet |
| --- | --- |
| MANUFACTURER: | FarPoint Technologies |
| COST: | $245 |

Spread/VBX is the premier grid control from FarPoint Technologies. Its capabilities go far beyond those of FarPoint's Grid/VBX control, but the two share a common heritage and upgrading an application from Grid/VBX to Spread/VBX should be a painless process. Some grid controls focus on the data access aspect of development and others on emulating true spreadsheet functionality. Spread/VBX balances the two. Rather than using one grid control for spreadsheet functionality and another for data access you can use Spread/VBX and get both.

# Syntax

Spread/VBX has more than 200 properties, 27 custom events, and 34 callable functions. Most of Spread/VBX's properties are used to define the attributes (both appearance and operation) of individual cells or groups of cells. Table 2-23 lists all nonstandard properties, events, and functions for Spread/VBX.

**Table 2-23**  Spread/VBX nonstandard properties, events, and functions

## PROPERTIES

| | | |
|---|---|---|
| Action | ActiveCol | ActiveRow |
| AllowCellOverflow | AllowDragDrop | AllowMultiBlocks |
| AllowUserFormulas | ArrowsExitEditMode | AutoCalc |
| AutoClipboard | AutoSize | BackColor |
| BlockMode | BorderStyle | ButtonDrawMode |
| CalcDependencies | CellBorderColor | CellBorderStyle |
| CellBorderType | CellType | ChangeMade |
| Clip | ClipValue | Col |
| Col2 | ColHeaderDisplay | ColHidden |
| ColsFrozen | ColPageBreak | ColWidth |
| CursorStyle | CursorType | DataColCnt |
| DataConnect | DataField | DataFillEvent |
| DataRowCnt | DataSelect | DataSource |
| DAutoCellTypes | DAutoFill | DAutoHeadings |
| DAutoSave | DAutoSizeCols | DestCol |
| DestRow | DisplayColHeaders | DisplayRowHeaders |
| EditEnterAction | EditMode | EditModePermanent |
| EditModeReplace | FileNum | FloatDefCurrencyChar |
| FloatDefDecimalChar | FloatDefSepChar | FontBold |
| FontItalic | FontName | FontSize |
| FontStrikethru | FontUnderline | ForeColor |
| Formula | GrayAreaBackColor | GridColor |
| GridShowHoriz | GridShowVert | GridSolid |
| hDCPrinter | InterfaceDesigner | IsBlockSelected |
| Left | LeftCol | LoadTabFile |
| Lock | LockBackColor | LockForeColor |
| MaxCols | MaxRows | MaxTextCellHeight |
| MaxTextCellWidth | MaxTextColWidth | MaxTextRowHeight |
| MoveActiveOnFocus | MultiSelCount | MultiSelIndex |

*(continued on next page)*

## PROPERTIES

*(continued from previous page)*

| | | |
|---|---|---|
| NoBeep | NoBorder | OperationMode |
| Position | PrintAbortMsg | PrintBorder |
| PrintColHeaders | PrintColor | PrintFooter |
| PrintGrid | PrintHeader | PrintJobName |
| PrintMarginBottom | PrintMarginLeft | PrintMarginRight |
| PrintMarginTop | PrintPageEnd | PrintPageStart |
| PrintRowHeaders | PrintShadows | PrintType |
| PrintUseDataMax | ProcessTab | Protect |
| Redraw | RestrictCols | RestrictRows |
| RetainSelBlock | Row | Row2 |
| RowHeaderDisplay | RowHeight | RowHidden |
| RowPageBreak | RowsFrozen | ScrollBarExtMode |
| ScrollBarMaxAlign | ScrollBars | ScrollBarShowMax |
| SelBlockCol | SelBlockCol2 | SelBlockRow |
| SelBlockRow2 | SelectBlockOptions | SelLength |
| SelModeIndex | SelModeSelCount | SelModeSelected |
| SelStart | SelText | ShadowColor |
| ShadowDark | ShadowText | SortBy |
| SortKey | SortKeyOrder | StartingColNumber |
| StartingRowNumber | Text | TopRow |
| TypeButtonAlign | TypeButtonBorderColor | TypeButtonColor |
| TypeButtonDarkColor | TypeButtonLightColor | TypeButtonPicture |
| TypeButtonPictureDown | TypeButtonShadowSize | TypeButtonText |
| TypeButtonTextColor | TypeButtonType | TypeCheckCenter |
| TypeCheckPicture | TypeCheckText | TypeCheckTextAlign |
| TypeComboBoxCount | TypeComboBoxCurSel | TypeComboBoxEditable |
| TypeComboBoxIndex | TypeComboBoxList | TypeComboBoxString |
| TypeDateCentury | TypeDateFormat | TypeDateMax |
| TypeDateMin | TypeDateSeparator | TypeEditCharCase |
| TypeEditCharSet | TypeEditLen | TypeEditMultiLine |
| TypeEditPassword | TypeFloatCurrencyChar | TypeFloatDecimalChar |
| TypeFloatDecimalPlaces | TypeFloatMax | TypeFloatMin |
| TypeFloatMoney | TypeFloatSeparator | TypeFloatSepChar |
| TypeHAlign | TypeIntegerMax | TypeIntegerMin |
| TypeIntegerSpinInc | TypeIntegerSpinWrap | TypeOwnerDrawStyle |
| TypePicDefaultText | TypePicMask | TypePictCenter |
| TypePictMaintainScale | TypePictPicture | TypePictStretch |
| TypeSpin | TypeTextAlignVert | TypeTextPrefix |

## PROPERTIES

| | | |
|---|---|---|
| TypeTextShadow | TypeTextShadowIn | TypeTextWordWrap |
| TypeTime24Hour | TypeTimeMax | TypeTimeMin |
| TypeTimeSeconds | TypeTimeSeparator | UnitType |
| UserResize | UserResizeCol | UserResizeRow |
| Value | VirtualCurRowCount | VirtualCurTop |
| VirtualMaxRows | VirtualMode | VirtualOverlap |
| VirtualRows | VirtualScrollBuffer | VisibleCols |
| VisibleRows | VScrollSpecial | VScrollSpecialType |

## EVENTS

| | | |
|---|---|---|
| Advance | BlockSelected | ButtonClicked |
| Change | Click | ColWidthChange |
| CustomFunction | DataAddNew | DataColConfig |
| DataFill | DblClick | DragDropBlock |
| DrawItem | EditError | EditMode |
| EnterRow | LeaveCell | LeaveRow |
| PrintAbort | QueryData | RightClick |
| RowHeightChange | SelChange | TopLeftChange |
| UserFormulaEntered | VirtualClearData | |

## FUNCTIONS

| | |
|---|---|
| SpreadAddCustomFunction | SpreadCFGetDoubleParam |
| SpreadCFGetLongParam | SpreadCFGetParamInfo |
| SpreadCFGetStringParam | SpreadCFSetResult |
| SpreadColWidthToTwips | SpreadGetBottomRightCell |
| SpreadGetCellDirtyFlag | SpreadGetCellFromScreenCoord |
| SpreadGetCellPos | SpreadGetClientArea |
| SpreadGetColItemData | SpreadGetDataConnectHandle |
| SpreadGetDataFillData | SpreadGetDataSelectHandle |
| SpreadGetFirstValidCell | SpreadGetItemData |
| SpreadGetLastValidCell | SpreadGetMultiSelItem |
| SpreadGetRowItemData | SpreadGetText |
| SpreadIsCellSelected | SpreadIsFormulaValid |
| SpreadIsVisible | SpreadRowHeightToTwips |
| SpreadSetCellDirtyFlag | SpreadSetColItemData |
| SpreadSetDataFillData | SpreadSetItemData |
| SpreadSetRowItemData | SpreadSetText |
| SpreadTwipsToColWidth | SpreadTwipsToRowHeight |

Like most grid controls, Spread/VBX has *Row* and *Col* properties. However, *Row* and *Col* do not refer to the row and column of the currently active cell; for that you use the *ActiveRow* and *ActiveCol* properties. With Spread/VBX, you use *Row* and *Col* to specify a row or column on which an operation is to be performed. Operations include setting the

*CellType* of cells (more on *CellType* later), locking cells to prevent editing, setting cell colors, and so forth. You can trigger any operations by setting the *Action* property of the control (Table 2-24). FarPoint provides a file (VB_CONST.TXT) that includes symbolic constants for many nonstandard properties. The *BlockMode* property, if *True*, allows operations to be performed on a block, or range, of cells. For block operations, *Row* and *Col* define the beginning of the block and *Row2* and *Col2* define the end of the block.

**Table 2-24** Spread/VBX Action property values

| SETTING | DESCRIPTION |
| --- | --- |
| 0 | Set the currently active cell. |
| 1 | Go to specified cell without changing the active cell. |
| 2 | Select a block of cells. |
| 3 | Clear grid, row, column, or cell. |
| 4 | Delete column. If BlockMode is True, Col2 is used to specify a range of columns. |
| 5 | Delete row. If BlockMode is True, Row2 is used to specify a range of rows. |
| 6 | Insert column. If BlockMode is True, Col2 is used to specify a range of columns. |
| 7 | Insert row. If BlockMode is True, Row2 is used to specify a range of rows. |
| 8 | Load spreadsheet data using FileNum. |
| 9 | Save the current spreadsheet using FileNum. |
| 10 | Save only the text of the current spreadsheet using FileNum. |
| 11 | Perform manual recalculation on every formula in the spreadsheet. |
| 12 | Remove data from cell, row, column, or entire grid control. |
| 13 | Print the spreadsheet using the associated print properties. |
| 14 | Deselect a block of cells if one was previously selected. |
| 15 | Save all records in a bound grid that have been modified if DAutoSave is False. |
| 16 | Set a border around a cell or group of cells. |
| 17 | Add a selected block of cells if AllowMultiBlocks is True. |
| 18 | Retrieve the currently selected blocks of cells if AllowMultiBlocks property is True. |
| 19 | Copy a range of cells to another location. |
| 20 | Move a range of cells to another location. |
| 21 | Swap a range of cells with another block of cells. |
| 22 | Copy the currently selected block of cells to the Clipboard. |
| 23 | Cut the currently selected block of cells to the Clipboard. |
| 24 | Paste data from the Clipboard to the currently selected block of cells. |
| 25 | Sort the specified cells within the spreadsheet. |

| SETTING | DESCRIPTION |
|---------|-------------|
| 26 | Clear the contents (all items) of a combo box cell. |
| 27 | Remove an item from a combo box in a ComboBox cell. |
| 28 | Clear and reset all attributes of the grid back to the default settings. |
| 29 | Deselect all the selections of a spreadsheet in multiselect list box mode. |
| 30 | Discard current data and rerequest the data currently in the buffer. This Action must be used with Virtual mode. |
| 31 | Force the data to be refreshed from the database. This Action is used when grid is bound to the Q+E /Lib database. |
| 32 | Print the spreadsheet using smart printing provided by the spreadsheet. |

Specifying the attributes for individual cells is easy both at design time and run time. At design time, double-clicking the *InterfaceDesigner* property launches the Interface Designer, which allows you to specify the attributes of individual cells quickly and easily. Attributes include things like font information, editability, and *CellType*. The *CellType* determines the type of data displayed in a cell (Table 2-25). You can set the *CellType* for an entire row or column as easily as for a single cell, as the example program demonstrates.

**Table 2-25** Spread/VBX CellType property values

| SETTING | DESCRIPTION | SYMBOLIC CONSTANT |
|---------|-------------|-------------------|
| 0 | Date | SS_CELL_TYPE_DATE |
| 1 | Edit | SS_CELL_TYPE_EDIT |
| 2 | Float | SS_CELL_TYPE_FLOAT |
| 3 | Integer | SS_CELL_TYPE_INTEGER |
| 4 | PIC | SS_CELL_TYPE_PIC |
| 5 | Static text | SS_CELL_TYPE_STATIC_TEXT |
| 6 | Time | SS_CELL_TYPE_TIME |
| 7 | Button | SS_CELL_TYPE_BUTTON |
| 8 | Combo box | SS_CELL_TYPE_COMBOBOX |
| 9 | Picture | SS_CELL_TYPE_PICTURE |
| 10 | Check box | SS_CELL_TYPE_CHECKBOX |
| 11 | Owner drawn | SS_CELL_TYPE_OWNER_DRAWN |

**Formulas**   The *Formula* property defines a spreadsheet formula for a cell. Spread/VBX provides a few intrinsic functions that may be used in formulas (Table 2-26) plus the capability to define custom functions, which reside in DLLs, that may be used in formulas.

**Table 2-26** Spread/VBX intrinsic spreadsheet functions

| INTRINSIC SPREADSHEET FUNCTIONS | | |
|---|---|---|
| ABS | IF | ISEMPTY |
| NEG | NOT | ROUND |
| ROUNDUP | TRUNCATE | |

Custom functions have a number of supporting Spread/VBX functions and require a bit of work to implement. First you must define the function, either in a DLL or with VB code. Next you must define the function for use in the spreadsheet with the *SpreadAddCustomFunction* function. This function takes three parameters: the spreadsheet for which the function is being defined, the name of the function, and the number of arguments the function requires. Now you wait until a *CustomFunction* event fires, indicating that a custom function is being evaluated in a cell. Within the *CustomFunction* event, you use *SpreadCFGetParamInfo* to retrieve information about each parameter. *SpreadCFGetParamInfo* tells you the status (OK, Error, or Empty) and data type (Long, Double, or String) of each parameter. If the status is OK, based on the data type, you call *SpreadCFGetDoubleParam*, *SpreadCFGetLongParam*, or *SpreadCFGetStringParam* to retrieve the parameter. Once you have all the parameters, you can pass them to your custom function. Finally, to return the result of the custom function, you call *SpreadCFSetResult*.

# Example

The sample program (Figure 2-7) uses the *Action* property to load and save files in Spread/VBX's proprietary binary format. Its sample spreadsheet shows how flexible Spread/VBX is when it comes to the content and formatting of cells. Full Clipboard support is also provided via the *Action* property. The grid lines, row headers, and column headers can also be turned on and off simply by switching a property from *True* to *False*.

| Spread/VBX Demo | |
|---|---|
| **File Edit Display** | |
| **Test Cell** | **CellType (Notes)** |
| 12/04/94 | Date (MM/DD/YY, 01/01/90 - 01/01/95) |
| CA | Edit (2 Char max, Uppercase only) |
| $100000.00 | Float (Money, $0.00 - $1,000,000.00) |
| 35 | Integer (0 - 500) |
| Waite | PIC (First Char upper, Alpha only) |
| 09:34am | Time (12:00am - 12:00pm) |
| OK | Button |
| Item 3 | ComboBox (4 items, editable) |
| | Picture |
| I like it! | Check Box |

**Figure 2-7** Spread/VBX sample program

## Steps

1. Create a new project called SPREDVBX.MAK. Create a new form with the objects and properties shown in Table 2-27. Save this form as SPREDVBX.FRM.

**Table 2-27** Spread/VBX main form's objects and properties

| OBJECT | PROPERTY | SETTING |
|---|---|---|
| SpreadSheet | Name | spdMain |
| Form | FormName | frmMain |
| | Caption | "Spread/VBX Demo" |
| | ScaleMode | 3 'Pixel |

2. Add a menu to the SPREDVBX.FRM form using the Visual Basic Menu Design window, setting the captions and names as shown in Table 2-28. Note that the menus are set up as control arrays.

**Table 2-28** Menu definition for SPREDVBX.FRM

| CAPTION | NAME | INDEX | CHECKED |
|---|---|---|---|
| &File | mnuMain | 0 | |
| ––––&Open | mnuFile | 0 | |
| ––––––––&1. CellTypes | mnuFileOpen | 0 | |
| ––––––––&2. Test File | mnuFileOpen | 1 | |
| ––––&Save | mnuFile | 1 | |
| ––––&Close | mnuFile | 2 | |
| –––– | mnuFile | 3 | |
| ––––E&xit | mnuFile | 4 | |
| &Edit | mnuMain | 1 | |
| ––––Cu&t | mnuEdit | 0 | |
| ––––&Copy | mnuEdit | 1 | |
| ––––&Paste | mnuEdit | 2 | |
| &Display | mnuMain | 2 | |
| ––––&Grid Lines | mnuDisplay | 0 | True |
| ––––&Column Headers | mnuDisplay | 1 | True |
| ––––&Row Headers | mnuDisplay | 2 | True |

3. Add the following code to the SPREDVBX.FRM.

```
Sub Form_Resize ()

    spdMain.Width = frmMain.ScaleWidth
    spdMain.Height = frmMain.ScaleHeight

End Sub
```

(continued on next page)

*(continued from previous page)*

```vb
Sub mnuDisplay_Click (Index As Integer)

    mnuDisplay(Index%).Checked = Not (mnuDisplay(Index%).Checked)

    Select Case Index%
        Case MNU_DISPLAY_GRID_LINES
            spdMain.GridShowHoriz = Not (spdMain.GridShowHoriz)
            spdMain.GridShowVert = Not (spdMain.GridShowVert)
        Case MNU_DISPLAY_COL_HEADERS
            spdMain.DisplayColHeaders = Not (spdMain.DisplayColHeaders)
        Case MNU_DISPLAY_ROW_HEADERS
            spdMain.DisplayRowHeaders = Not (spdMain.DisplayRowHeaders)
    End Select

End Sub

Sub mnuEdit_Click (Index As Integer)

    Select Case Index%
        Case MNU_EDIT_CUT
            spdMain.Action = SS_ACTION_CLIPBOARD_CUT
        Case MNU_EDIT_COPY
            spdMain.Action = SS_ACTION_CLIPBOARD_COPY
        Case MNU_EDIT_PASTE
            spdMain.Action = SS_ACTION_CLIPBOARD_PASTE
    End Select

End Sub

Sub mnuFile_Click (Index As Integer)

    Select Case Index%
        Case MNU_FILE_OPEN
            '-- See mnuFileOpen_Click event
        Case MNU_FILE_SAVE
            Call FileSave
        Case MNU_FILE_CLOSE
            Call FileClose
        Case MNU_FILE_EXIT
            Call FileExit
    End Select

End Sub

Sub mnuFileOpen_Click (Index As Integer)
    Dim Filename$

    Select Case Index%
        Case MNU_FILE_OPEN_CELLTYPE
            Filename$ = App.Path & "\CELLTYPE.SS"
        Case MNU_FILE_OPEN_TESTFILE
            Filename$ = App.Path & "\TESTFILE.SS"
    End Select

    Call FileOpen(Filename$)

End Sub
```

4. Create a new module called SPREDVBX.BAS and add the following code to the declarations section.

```
Option Explicit
DefInt A-Z

'-- General Declarations
Global Const MB_OK = 0
Global Const MB_ICONSTOP = 16

'-- Spread/VBX Declarations
Global Const SS_ACTION_CLEAR = 3
Global Const SS_ACTION_LOAD_SPREAD_SHEET = 8
Global Const SS_ACTION_SAVE_ALL = 9
Global Const SS_ACTION_CLIPBOARD_COPY = 22
Global Const SS_ACTION_CLIPBOARD_CUT = 23
Global Const SS_ACTION_CLIPBOARD_PASTE = 24
Global Const SS_ACTION_RESET = 28

'-- Sample Program Declarations
Global Const MNU_FILE_OPEN = 0
Global Const MNU_FILE_SAVE = 1
Global Const MNU_FILE_CLOSE = 2
Global Const MNU_FILE_EXIT = 4

Global Const MNU_FILE_OPEN_CELLTYPE = 0
Global Const MNU_FILE_OPEN_TESTFILE = 1

Global Const MNU_EDIT_CUT = 0
Global Const MNU_EDIT_COPY = 1
Global Const MNU_EDIT_PASTE = 2

Global Const MNU_DISPLAY_GRID_LINES = 0
Global Const MNU_DISPLAY_COL_HEADERS = 1
Global Const MNU_DISPLAY_ROW_HEADERS = 2

Dim mFilename$  '-- Current File

Sub FileClose ()

    If Len(mFilename$) Then
        mFilename$ = ""
        frmMain!spdMain.FileNum = 0
        frmMain!spdMain.Action = SS_ACTION_RESET
        frmMain!mnuFile(MNU_FILE_SAVE).Enabled = False
        frmMain!mnuFile(MNU_FILE_CLOSE).Enabled = False
    End If

End Sub

Sub FileExit ()

    Call FileClose
    Unload frmMain
    End

End Sub

Sub FileOpen (Filename$)
    Dim hFile%
```

*(continued on next page)*

*(continued from previous page)*

```
    '-- If a file is open, close it before
    '   opening a new file.
    Call FileClose

    On Error GoTo FileOpenErr
        hFile% = FreeFile
        Open Filename$ For Binary As #hFile%
            mFilename$ = Filename$
            frmMain!spdMain.FileNum = hFile%
            frmMain!spdMain.Action = SS_ACTION_LOAD_SPREAD_SHEET
        Close #hFile%
        frmMain!spdMain.ChangeMade = False
        frmMain!mnuFile(MNU_FILE_SAVE).Enabled = True
        frmMain!mnuFile(MNU_FILE_CLOSE).Enabled = True
    On Error GoTo 0

FileOpenExit:
    Exit Sub

FileOpenErr:
    MsgBox "Error in FileOpen", MB_OK + MB_ICONSTOP, Error$(Err)
    mFilename$ = ""
    Resume FileOpenExit

End Sub

Sub FileSave ()
    Dim hFile%

    If Len(mFilename$) Then
        On Error GoTo FileSaveErr
            hFile% = FreeFile
            Open mFilename$ For Binary As #hFile%
                frmMain!spdMain.FileNum = hFile%
                frmMain!spdMain.Action = SS_ACTION_SAVE_ALL
            Close #hFile%
            frmMain!spdMain.ChangeMade = False
        On Error GoTo 0
    End If

FileSaveExit:
    Exit Sub

FileSaveErr:
    MsgBox "Error in FileSave", MB_OK + MB_ICONSTOP, Error$(Err)
    Resume FileSaveExit

End Sub
```

# Tips and Comments

Spread/VBX is extremely flexible when it comes to cell formatting and appearance, which is critical with the importance now attached to user interface design. It is a large control (just over 500K), but it performs well and the manual gives optimization tips to help improve performance if necessary. Spread/VBX's ability to bind to the Q+E/Lib database also gives it an extra edge over other bound controls on the market.

# TrueGrid (TRUEGRID.VBX)

| USAGE: | Bound/Unbound Data Grid |
|---|---|
| MANUFACTURER: | Apex Software |
| COST: | $149 |

TrueGrid is a fully editable bound data grid that provides VB developers with a wealth of power and flexibility. You can build a full database editor/browser without writing a single line of code, or you can customize and control TrueGrid's appearance and operation to suit your needs. TrueGrid can also operate in callback (unbound) mode, in which case the developer is in charge of the data and TrueGrid handles display of the data and user interaction.

## Syntax

TrueGrid provides over 100 custom properties and 25 custom events (Table 2-29). It's not this sheer volume that makes TrueGrid powerful, however but the fact that it is a well-designed control that works the way you expect it to. Initially its mode of operation may seem a bit different than other grid controls, but it works well and helps TrueGrid to provide excellent performance in both Database (bound) and Callback (unbound) modes.

**Table 2-29** TrueGrid nonstandard properties and events

### PROPERTIES

| | | |
|---|---|---|
| About | Active | AddRegexAttr |
| AllowArrows | AllowTabs | BookmarkCount |
| BookmarkList | BottomRow | BookmarkCount |
| BookmarkList | BottomRow | CellRectHeight |
| CellRectLeft | CellRectTop | CellRectWidth |
| ColumnAddRegexAttr | ColumnAtPoint | ColumnBackColor |
| ColumnButton | ColumnCellAttr | ColumnChanged |
| ColumnComboMaxItems | ColumnExpression | ColumnFetchMargins |
| ColumnField | ColumnFontStyle | ColumnForeColor |
| ColumnHasRegexAttr | ColumnHeadFontStyle | ColumnIndex |
| ColumnName | ColumnOrder | ColumnRectLeft |
| ColumnRectWidth | Columns | ColumnSetStatusAttr |
| ColumnSize | ColumnStyle | ColumnSum |
| ColumnSumEnable | ColumnText | ColumnType |
| ColumnVertScroll | ColumnVisible | ColumnWidth |
| ColumnWordWrap | Configurable | CurCellVisible |
| DataChanged | DataMode | DataSource |

*(continued on next page)*

## PROPERTIES

*(continued from previous page)*

| | | |
|---|---|---|
| DataSourceHwnd | Editable | EditActive |
| EditBackColor | EditDropDown | EditForeColor |
| EditMask | ExposeCellMode | ExtendRightCol |
| FetchMode | HasRegexAttr | HeadBackColor |
| HeadFontStyle | HeadForeColor | HeadingHeight |
| Headings | HorzColor | HorzLines |
| HorzScrollbar | HwndEdit | InactiveBackColor |
| InactiveForeColor | InsertSplit | Layout |
| LayoutIndex | LeftColumn | LinesPerRow |
| MarqueeStyle | MarqueeUnique | Modified |
| ParamBackColor | ParamFontStyle | ParamForeColor |
| ParamStatus | Picture | PointX |
| PointY | ReferenceRow | RefreshColumn |
| RefreshRow | RemoveSplit | RightColumn |
| RowAtPoint | RowIndex | Rows |
| SelectedBackColor | SelectedForeColor | SelectMode |
| SelectZoneWidth | SelLength | SelStart |
| SelText | SetStatusAttr | SplitEditable |
| SplitGroup | SplitIndex | SplitLocked |
| SplitPropsGlobal | Splits | SplitSelectable |
| SplitSize | SplitSizeMode | SplitTabMode |
| TabCapture | Text | TopRow |
| Version | VertColor | VertLines |
| VertScrollbar | VlistColumn | VlistCount |
| VlistData | VlistDefault | VlistPicture |
| VlistStyle | VlistText | WrapCellPointer |

## EVENTS

| | | |
|---|---|---|
| Append | CellChange | Change |
| CheckRows | ClickButton | ColumnChange |
| ColumnSumChange | ComboSelect | DragCell |
| EnterEdit | ExitEdit | Fetch |
| FetchMargins | LeftColChange | LayoutChange |
| MarkChange | QueryMark | RequestEdit |
| RowChange | SplitChange | TopRowChange |
| UnboundFetch | Update | Validate |
| ValidateError | | |

When you bind a TrueGrid to a data control it can configure itself automatically based on the contents of the data source. Alternatively, you can configure it using the

Layout Editor, which you launch by double-clicking on the grid at design time. With the Layout Editor, you configure the grid via a pop-up menu by right-clicking on the column whose properties you wish to change. From the pop-up menu, you can set properties directly or open the Column Properties dialog (Figure 2-8) for more control. If the data source changes, TrueGrid can automatically reconfigure itself.

The configuration information is stored in the *Layout* property. You can store and retrieve multiple layouts by changing the *LayoutIndex* property. If the *Layout* changes, TrueGrid fires a *LayoutChange* event telling you why it changed (user action, data source changed, *Layout* or *LayoutIndex* changed).

**Show and Tell**   When TrueGrid's *DataMode* property is set to 0 (*Database*), the grid operates in bound mode. If *DataMode* is set to 1 (*Callback*), the grid operates in unbound mode. In *Database* mode, TrueGrid displays data automatically. In *Callback* mode, it fires a *Fetch* event to request data for display. The *Fetch* event parameters are *Row*, *Col*, and *Value*. *Row* and *Col* tell you which cell the data is for, and *Value* is a string parameter that you fill with the data you want TrueGrid to display in that cell. In *Callback* mode, TrueGrid doesn't actually maintain the data; it just requests and displays it. You can also mix the two by using *Database* mode but specifying that certain columns operate in unbound mode. In this case, an *UnboundFetch* event fires to request data for unbound columns. You can force TrueGrid to rerequest data with the *RefreshRow* and *RefreshColumn* properties.

In both *Database* and *Callback* modes, when the user clicks or starts typing in a cell, a *RequestEdit* and an *EnterEdit* event fires, in that order. You can deny the request to edit in *RequestEdit,* in which case *EnterEdit* does not fire. On the other end, when the user is done editing *Validate*, *Update*, and *ExitEdit* events fire, in that order. The user can be kept in edit mode until the data is valid through use of the *Validate* event. In *Callback* mode, the *Update* event would be used as your trigger to save the data in the cell. In *Database* mode, updates are handled automatically.

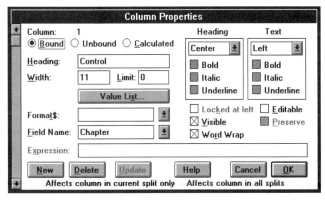

**Figure 2-8** TrueGrid Column Properties dialog

TrueGrid allows the user to select multiple rows if the *SelectMode* property is set to enabled. In *Database* mode, the record set must be bookmarkable but TrueGrid maintains the list of selected items automatically in its *BookmarkCount* and *BookmarkList* properties. *BookmarkList* is an array that contains a list of selected rows, identified by their bookmarks. In *Callback* mode, the developer is responsible for tracking and maintaining the selected items through use of the *MarkChange* and *QueryMark* events.

**More Power**   One of TrueGrid's most outstanding features is its ability to display the grid as multiple split windows, or *splits*, as can Excel and other spreadsheets. Splits allow you to lock columns at the left, scroll splits independently, set colors and fonts for specific splits, and on and on. In some ways you can think of each split as an independent grid within the main grid. Splits are one of TrueGrid's more complex features, but it is worth your time to master them.

*Value lists* are another feature worth noting. You can think of a value list as containing two columns. The first column is the actual data that is being manipulated, and the second column is the associated list of items (the user list) that will be displayed. For example, the data might be two-character state codes but the user list would be the names of the states, spelled out completely. You can also display pictures, check boxes, and option buttons in a value list.

# Example

The sample program (Figure 2-9) shows off TrueGrid's excellent support for drag and drop, dynamic configurability, and the use of splits. It also shows how you can use a

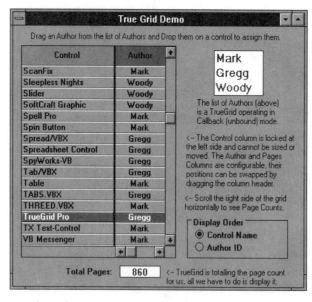

**Figure 2-9** TrueGrid sample application

TrueGrid to simulate a list box, operating in *Callback* mode, and how you can support calculated columns with the *ColumnSumChange* event.

TrueGrid's approach to support for drag and drop integrates nicely with the standard VB *DragOver* and *DragDrop* events. You can locate a cell based on its coordinates by using the *PointX*, *PointY*, *RowAtPoint*, and *ColumnAtPoint* properties. As you can see in the sample code, it's very easy to use the standard VB *DragOver* event, which provides the necessary coordinates,  to set these properties and determine which cell is the drop target. When the drag operation begins, TrueGrid fires a *DragCell* event, which allows us to change the DragIcon based on which cell is being dragged. Also note that the Author column in the main grid uses a value list and the actual author's name is retrieved with the *VlistText* property.

## Steps

1. Create a new project called TGDEMO.MAK. Create a new form with the objects and properties shown in Table 2-30. Save this form as TGDEMO.FRM.

**Table 2-30** TrueGrid main form's objects and properties

| OBJECT | PROPERTY | SETTING |
| --- | --- | --- |
| Form | FormName | frmMain |
| | BackColor | &H00C0C0C0& |
| | Caption | "True Grid Demo" |
| | ScaleMode | 3 'Pixel |
| Frame | Name | fraDisplayOrder |
| | BackColor | &H00C0C0C0& |
| | Caption | "Display Order" |
| Label | Name | lblDragIcon |
| | Caption | "Mark's DragIcon" |
| | DragIcon | (set at design time in Properties window) |
| | Index | 0 |
| | Visible | 0 'False |
| Label | Name | lblDragIcon |
| | Caption | "Gregg's DragIcon" |
| | DragIcon | (set at design time in Properties window) |
| | Index | 1 |
| | Visible | 0 'False |
| Label | Name | lblDragIcon |
| | Caption | "Woody's DragIcon" |
| | DragIcon | (set at design time in Properties window) |
| | Index | 2 |
| | Visible | 0 'False |

*(continued on next page)*

| OBJECT | PROPERTY | SETTING |
|--------|----------|---------|
| *(continued from previous page)* | | |
| Label | Name | lblTotalPages |
| | Alignment | 1 'Right Justify |
| | BackStyle | 0 'Transparent |
| | Caption | "Total Pages:" |
| Label | Name | lblPageCount |
| | Alignment | 2 'Center |
| | BorderStyle | 1 'Fixed Single |
| | FontSize | 9.75 |
| | ForeColor | &H00FF0000& |
| Label | Name | lblInfoPageCount |
| | BackStyle | 0 'Transparent |
| | Caption | "<-- TrueGrid is totalling the page count for us; all we have to do is display it." |
| | FontBold | 0 'False |
| Label | Name | lblInfoAuthor |
| | BackStyle | 0 'Transparent |
| | Caption | "The list of Authors (above) is a TrueGrid operating in Callback (unbound) mode." |
| | FontBold | 0 'False |
| Label | Name | lblInfoDrag |
| | BackStyle | 0 'Transparent |
| | Caption | "Drag Authors from the list of authors and drop them on a control to assign them." |
| | FontBold | 0 'False |
| Label | Name | lblInfo |
| | BackStyle | 0 'Transparent |
| | Caption | "<-- The Control column is locked at the left side and cannot be sized or moved. The Author and Pages columns are configurable; their positions can be swapped by dragging the column header." |
| | FontBold | 0 'False |
| | Index | 0 |
| Label | Name | lblInfo |
| | BackStyle | 0 'Transparent |
| | Caption | "<-- Scroll the right side of the grid horizontally to see page counts." |
| | FontBold | 0 'False |

2 ◄

| OBJECT | PROPERTY | SETTING |
|--------|----------|---------|
| | Index | 1 |
| TrueGrid | Name | tgAuthor |
| | AllowArrows | -1 'True |
| | AllowTabs | -1 'True |
| | DragIcon | (set at design time in Properties window) |
| | Editable | -1 'True |
| | EditDropDown | -1 'True |
| | ExposeCellMode | 0 'Expose upon selection |
| | FetchMode | 0 'By cell |
| | FontSize | 12 |
| | HeadingHeight | 1 |
| | HorzLines | 0 'None |
| | Layout | (set at design time in Properties window) |
| | LayoutIndex | 1 |
| | LinesPerRow | 1 |
| | MarqueeUnique | -1 'True |
| | SplitPropsGlobal= | 'True |
| | SplitTabMode | 0 'Don't tab across splits |
| | TabCapture | 0 'False |
| | UseBookmarks | -1 'True |
| | WrapCellPointer | 0 'False |
| Data | Name | Data1 |
| | Caption | "Data1" |
| | Connect | " " |
| | DatabaseName | "CTLDB.MDB" |
| | Exclusive | 0 'False |
| | Options | 0 |
| | ReadOnly | 0 'False |
| | RecordSource | " " |
| | Visible | 0 'False |
| TrueGrid | Name | tgControl |
| | AllowArrows | -1 'True |
| | AllowTabs | -1 'True |
| | BackColor | &H00C0C0C0& |
| | DataSource | "Data1" |
| | Editable | -1 'True |
| | EditDropDown | -1 'True |
| | ExposeCellMode | 0 'Expose upon selection |
| | FetchMode | 0 'By cell |
| | HeadingHeight | 2 |

*(continued on next page)*

| OBJECT | PROPERTY | SETTING |
|--------|----------|---------|
| *(continued from previous page)* | | |
| | HorzLines | 2 '3D |
| | Layout | (set at design time in Properties window) |
| | LayoutIndex | 1 |
| | LinesPerRow | 1 |
| | MarqueeUnique | -1 'True |
| | SplitPropsGlobal= | 'False |
| | SplitTabMode | 0 'Don't tab across splits |
| | TabCapture | 0 'False |
| | UseBookmarks | -1 'True |
| | WrapCellPointer | 0 'False |

2. Place the controls shown in Table 2-31 within the fraDisplayOrder Frame control.

**Table 2-31** TrueGrid fraDisplayOrder child objects and properties

| OBJECT | PROPERTY | SETTING |
|--------|----------|---------|
| OptionButton | Name | optDisplayOrder |
| | BackColor | &H00C0C0C0& |
| | Caption | "Control Name" |
| | Index | 0 |
| | Value | -1 'True |
| OptionButton | Name | optDisplayOrder |
| | BackColor | &H00C0C0C0& |
| | Caption | "Author ID" |
| | Index | 1 |

3. Add the following code to the TGDEMO form.

```
Option Explicit
DefInt A-Z

' Colors
Const BLACK = &H0
Const RED = &HFF&
Const WHITE = &HFFFFFF
Const BLUE = &HFF0000

' Drag (controls)
Const BEGIN_DRAG = 1

' MsgBox parameters
Const MB_YESNO = 4              ' Yes and No buttons
Const MB_ICONQUESTION = 32     ' Warning query
Const IDYES = 6                ' Yes button pressed
```

```
Sub Form_Load ()

    Data1.DatabaseName = App.Path & "\" & "CTLDB.MDB"
    Data1.RecordSource = "Select * From ChapterData ORDER BY Chapter"

    '-- This will cause a ColumnSumChange event to
    '    fire whenever the total of Column 3 (Pages)
    '    changes.
    tgControl.ColumnSumEnable(3) = True

    '-- The Author column is the only one using a
    '    Value List, so we'll set it here and then
    '    forget about it.
    tgControl.VlistColumn = 2

    '-- This will cause a FetchAttributes event to
    '    fire for Column 1 in the Author Grid.
    tgAuthor.ColumnCellAttrs(1) = True

    '-- The Author Grid is unbound so we need to
    '    tell TrueGrid how many rows we want.
    tgAuthor.Rows = 3

End Sub

Sub optDisplayOrder_Click (Index As Integer)

    Select Case Index%
        Case 0
            Data1.RecordSource = "Select * From ChapterData ORDER BY Chapter"
        Case 1
            Data1.RecordSource = "Select * From ChapterData ORDER BY AuthorID"
    End Select

    Data1.Refresh

End Sub

Sub tgAuthor_DragCell (Split As Integer, Row As Long, Col As Integer)

    '-- Set our reference position so we know which
    '    Author was dragged off.
    tgAuthor.RowIndex = Row&
    tgAuthor.ColumnIndex = Col%

    '-- Load the Mark, Gregg, or Woody drag icon.
    tgAuthor.DragIcon = lblDragIcon(Row& - 1).DragIcon

    tgAuthor.Drag BEGIN_DRAG

End Sub

Sub tgAuthor_Fetch (Row As Long, Col As Integer, Value As String)

    '-- The Author Grid is unbound so when TrueGrid
    '    asks us for data, we supply it.
    Select Case Row&
        Case 1
            Value$ = "Mark"
```

*(continued on next page)*

*(continued from previous page)*

```
            Case 2
                Value$ = "Gregg"
            Case 3
                Value$ = "Woody"
        End Select

End Sub

Sub tgAuthor_FetchAttributes (Status As Integer, Split As Integer, Row As Long, Col As Integer,
FgColor As Long, BgColor As Long, FontStyle As Integer)

    Select Case Row&
        Case 1
            FgColor& = BLACK
            'BgColor& = &HFFFFFF
        Case 2
            FgColor& = BLUE
            'BgColor& = &HC0C0C0
        Case 3
            FgColor& = RED
            'BgColor& = &H808080
    End Select

End Sub

Sub tgControl_ColumnSumChange (Col As Integer)

    lblPageCount.Caption = Format$(tgControl.ColumnSum(3), "0")

End Sub

Sub tgControl_DragDrop (Source As Control, X As Single, Y As Single)
    Dim mbRtn      As Integer
    Dim Msg        As String
    Dim MsgCaption As String
    Dim OldAuthor  As String
    Dim NewAuthor  As String
    Dim AuthorID%

    On Error Resume Next
        AuthorID% = CInt(tgControl.ColumnText(2))
        OldAuthor$ = Trim$(tgControl.VlistText(AuthorID%))
    On Error GoTo 0
    If Len(OldAuthor$) Then
        NewAuthor$ = Trim$(tgAuthor.ColumnText(1))
        Msg$ = "Are you sure you want to replace " & OldAuthor$ & " with " & NewAuthor$ & "?"
        mbRtn% = MsgBox(Msg$, MB_YESNO + MB_ICONQUESTION, "Change Authors")
        If mbRtn% = IDYES Then
            tgControl.ColumnText(2) = tgAuthor.RowIndex
            Data1.Recordset.Update
        End If
    Else
        tgControl.ColumnText(2) = tgAuthor.RowIndex
        Data1.Recordset.Update
    End If

End Sub
```

```
Sub tgControl_DragOver (Source As Control, X As Single, Y As Single, State As Integer)

    tgControl.PointX = X
    tgControl.PointY = Y
    If tgControl.RowAtPoint > 0 Then
        tgControl.RowIndex = tgControl.RowAtPoint
    End If
    If tgControl.ColumnAtPoint Then
        tgControl.ColumnIndex = tgControl.ColumnAtPoint
    End If

End Sub
```

## Tips and Comments

While some grid controls attempt to act as both data grids and spreadsheets, TrueGrid strives to be the best data grid it can be. One result of this is that TrueGrid is perhaps the fastest grid on the market. It will appeal to both the novice and the expert and will allow you to exert more control as your skills develop. Start by letting TrueGrid do all the work (the "No Code" approach) and then customize your app's appearance and operation as you see fit.

TrueGrid comes with a broad selection of well-written sample applications to help get you acquainted with the various aspects of its operation. All vendors would do well to provide samples of this caliber. The documentation and online help are also a cut above average and Apex has detailed how TrueGrid interacts with the data control in bound mode, which should eliminate a lot of confusion. With controls as large and complex as the current crop of grids, good supporting tools are essential.

# 3
# WORD PROCESSORS AND TEXT EDITORS

Since the advent of computers in the business world, the role of text processing has been an important, if often ignored, function. Even though today computers can talk, make music, show works of art, play games, and display movies, their central use is to present textual information. This is not surprising, since our society has for thousands of years preserved its thoughts through the written word. So it's natural that the burgeoning market for software components includes tools for the preparation of documents.

The controls covered in this chapter fall loosely into the category of word processors. They range from relatively "light" controls intended to address the limitations of the standard text box control, all the way to controls that possess many of the same features as commercial word processing packages. All of these controls take a slightly different slant on the problem, and each has a different "feel."

When evaluating these controls, don't fall into the trap of merely selecting the control with the most features. It is crucial to pick the right set of features for your particular problem. For example, each of these controls handles data in a different way. Will your data be stored in separate text files, as records in a database, or in some other format entirely? You should first decide how you want to handle data, and then select a control that will meet your needs. Unwanted features can be at least as big a problem as missing features, if you can't easily disable those features. The following controls are discussed in this chapter:

▲ **ALLText HT/Pro**  ALLText is a word processing control that also supports special text formats that let you create and view hypertext or hypermedia documents. The concept of hypertext should be familiar to anyone who has used Windows Help. The user is presented with text that contains embedded hot spots. These are words, phrases, or pictures that, when selected, display a related topic. Hypertext is not limited to help systems. (In fact, if you need to create a help system you should probably stick with conventional Windows Help tools.) Rather, you can use hypertext controls to build any number of applications, including games, reference works, training aids, and more. You'll use ALLText HT/Pro to make a text adventure game engine using a hypertext engine.

▲ **Early Morning Editor**  The Early Morning Editor can easily serve as a replacement for the conventional multiline text box control. This control is a text processor, not a word processor, so it handles only ASCII text. Unlike the text box, however, it can handle a lot of text. This is important in applications that deal with a great deal of text but have no need for multiple fonts or formatting features. You'll use this control to build a replacement for Windows Notepad that doesn't have the 32K text limitations.

▲ **RavenWrite**  RavenWrite is another word processing control that supports hypertext. As a word processor, it supports Rich Text Format, ASCII text, and its own word processing file format. The example will exploit RavenWrite's hypertext abilities to create a program that administers and scores tests.

▲ **VBViewer**  VBViewer doesn't allow you to edit documents; it only lets you view them. But look at what you can view: In addition to Microsoft Word and Write, WordPerfect, AMI, and Microsoft Works documents, this control can display ASCII text; hexadecimal dumps; a half dozen graphics formats including GIF, TIF, and WMF; icon files; dBASE, Paradox, and MS Works database files, Lotus, Excel, and Quattro Pro spreadsheet; files, and a variety of other file formats. This control even detects the format of a file automatically. This feature could be very useful if you needed a document archiving application that indexed and displayed documents in several formats. You'll use VBViewer to build a universal file browser that can view virtually any type of file, and that supports drag and drop from File Manager.

# ALLText HT/Pro (ATX30H.VBX)

| USAGE: | Word Processing and Hypertext |
| --- | --- |
| MANUFACTURER: | Bennet-Tec Information Systems |
| COST: | $350 |

ALLText HT/Pro is a text processing and hypertext control. You can use ALLText as a conventional word processing control, with support for multiple fonts, text colors, and paragraph formatting. You can also use it to create documents or databases with hypertext links. ALLText is a data-aware control, and can be bound to a database using the Visual Basic data control. ALLText also supports embedded OLE 1 objects.

ALLText HT/Pro is Bennet-Tec's high-end text processing control; they also provide a less powerful version of ALLText that lacks the hypertext, database, and OLE capabilities. Here ALLText refers to the more powerful ALLText HT/Pro control.

## Syntax

Most of the ALLText control's features can be accessed by properties, either at design time or run time. A few functions and events are used to implement special features. These properties, events, and functions are listed in Table 3-1.

**Table 3-1** Nonstandard properties, events, and functions for ALLText

### PROPERTIES

| | | |
| --- | --- | --- |
| Alignment | BackPicture | BackPictureX |
| BackPictureY | BackPictureRefresh | Border |
| BottomIndent | CaretWidth | ClearAll |
| CurChar | CurPar | DataType |
| DocHeight | DocWidth | FileName |
| FileLoad | FileSave | FirstLineIndent |
| FontBold | FontColor | FontFamily |
| FontItalic | FontIndex | FontName |
| FontShadow | FontSize | FontStrike |
| FontSubSup | FontTableSize | FontUnder |
| FontWidth | FormatPaste | F2On |
| LeftIndent | LineSpacing | NumParagraphs |
| OverType | RightIndent | ScrollBarH |
| ScrollBarV | ScrollHorz | ScrollVert |
| SelToPar | SelToChar | Select |
| SelFText | SelLength | SelStart |
| SelText | TabStep | Text |
| TextLength | TopIndent | WriteProtect |

*(continued on next page)*

*(continued from previous page)*

### EVENTS

| | |
|---|---|
| ATXGet | ATXPut |

### FUNCTIONS

| | | |
|---|---|---|
| Get_Border | Get_Shadow | Get_Underline |
| Make_Border | Make_Shadow | Make_Underline |

**Text Formats** ALLText supports three text file formats: plain ASCII text files, ALLText's proprietary format (there are actually two variants of this), and Rich Text Format (RTF).

The ALLText format is a hybrid version of RTF. It contains a subset of some of the RTF formatting codes, and also includes additional codes unique to ALLText. ALLText's support for the RTF format is extended as well. Special \ATF operators have been added to enhance ALLText's support for hypertext tags and extended font shadowing and underlining features. This does not prevent other word processors from reading documents created by ALLText's RTF format, as these extended operators are ignored.

You use the *DataType* property to determine how a document is loaded or saved by the ALLText control. You can set this integer property to one of the values shown in Table 3-2.

**Table 3-2** Values for the DataType property

| VALUE | MEANING |
|---|---|
| 0 | Text only (the default) |
| 1 | ALLText special format |
| 2 | ALLText full format |
| 3 | Rich Text Format (RTF) |

You usually load text files into the ALLText control by first setting the *DataType* property to one of the values just described. Next, you set the control's *FileName* property to the full path of the document file to be loaded. Finally, you set the *FileLoad* property to one of first three values shown in Table 3-3. ALLText includes a data constants file, ATXCNSTH.TXT, and the documentation generally refers to these constants rather than numeric values. For that reason, many of the property value tables in this section refer to these constant names in ATXCNSTH.TXT.

**Table 3-3** Values for the FileLoad property

| VALUE | MEANING |
|---|---|
| ATX_IO_FAST | Fast file loading is started. |
| ATX_IO_STANDARD | Standard file loading mode is started. |
| ATX_IO_LOWLEVEL | Low-level file loading is started. |
| ATX_IO_COMPLETED | File loading was successful (read-only value). |

In fast file loading mode, setting the *FileLoad* property initiates the loading process, and no other program intervention is required until the file is loaded. In standard and low-level file loading mode, a special event, *ATXGet,* is triggered. In standard file loading mode, *ATXGet* is fired once for each "chunk" of the file that's loaded. This chunk (which is currently defined as approximately 2,000 characters) is passed as a string parameter to *ATXGet.* This parameter can be altered within the event routine, allowing the programmer to preprocess data as it is read. *ATXGet* also receives a *Flag* parameter, which is set to *False* when the end of the input file is reached. The programmer can also set *Flag* to *False* within the event routine, which causes ALLText to stop the file loading process.

If low-level file loading is selected, ALLText does not read from the file, but merely triggers the *ATXGet* event, where the programmer must handle data input. This provides a flexible method for loading data from a file or other source.

Documents are saved using routines similar to those used for loading. The *FileSave* property is used to initiate file saving in a manner similar to *FileLoad. FileSave* saves only the currently selected area of text in an ALLText control, not the entire document. The text to be saved can be selected in the program using the *SelStart* and *SelLength* properties, which are basically the same as the properties of the same names used in the standard text box.

**Formatting Text**  Most formatting operations, such as changing a font to bold, affect only text that is currently selected. The user can select text by highlighting (dragging the mouse over a region of text), or text can be selected in the program code using the selection properties.

ALLText supports the standard *SelStart, SelLength,* and *SelText* properties, as well as some extended properties. *SelFText* is similar to *SelText,* except that *SelFText* interprets any special formatting codes. This means you can use *SelFText* to copy blocks of text with their formatting intact. The read-only Boolean *Select* property returns a *True* if some area of text is currently selected. The *SelToPar* and *SelToChar* properties determine the paragraph number, and the position within that paragraph, of the end of a selected region.

The Boolean *FormatPaste* property determines whether formatting codes are interpreted when data is pasted from the Windows Clipboard. If this property is set to *False,* any formatting codes are treated as plain text.

Two properties, *CurPar* and *CurChar,* set the caret (text cursor) position within an ALLText control. You can use *CurPar* to set the caret to the beginning of a paragraph, and you can use *CurChar* to set the caret at an integer offset within a paragraph. You can use these properties to determine the current caret location, but bear in mind that when the *Selected* property is *True* the properties refer to the beginning of a selected block of text, not the current caret position.

**Printing**  The ALLText control provides two functions and one special control accelerator key for printing text. The two functions allow printing of specified pages or paragraphs within the control, while the accelerator, or hot key ((F3)), prints the entire contents of the control.

*Print_ATextPages* can be used to print specified pages. An example of this function is shown here:

```
result = Print_ATextPages (AllText1, TopMargin, BottomMargin, LeftMargin,
LineLength, PageMask, Flag)
```

The first parameter is the name of the ALLText control being printed, and the margin and line length parameters are used to specify the printing area in twips. *PageMask* is a string that is used as a mask to indicate which pages are to be printed. Each character in the string corresponds to a page of the document, with the first character representing the first page. Nonblank characters in the string indicate pages that should be printed, while blank characters indicate pages to skip. The *Flag* parameter is set to *True* if the control's background bitmap is to be printed.

The *Print_AText* function works in a similar way, as shown here:

```
result = Print_AText (AllText1, TopMargin, BottomMargin, LeftMargin, LineLength,
FromPara, ToPara, Flag)
```

The *FromPara* and *ToPara* parameters specify the starting and ending paragraphs to be printed.

**Hypertext Tags**   Anyone who has ever used Windows Help will be familiar with hypertext. By clicking on predefined hot spots a user can move between related topics within a document. So that you can build hypertext documents, ALLText lets you create *tagged fields*, areas of text within a document that react in special ways. You can tag areas of text in much the same way that you reformat them. The area of text is selected, and then the *HTag* property is set to an integer value. In code, you do this by simply assigning the property, as shown here:

```
AllText1.HTag = 3
```

A text field tagged in this way displays a special mouse pointer, or cursor, when the mouse pointer moves over the field. You can set this cursor to any of a variety of predetermined shapes by assigning a value to the special *MouseHPointer* property. This special cursor gives the user visual feedback that a phrase is a hypertext hot spot.

When the user clicks or double-clicks on a tagged hot spot, the *HTag* property is set to the corresponding fields tag value, which can then be inspected within the event subroutine, and appropriate action can be taken.

Since ALLText can serve as a bound data control, you can store ALLText text, including its formatting, within a database. This lets you create hypertext databases, where the *HTag* integer property specifies a record key with the database. You will examine such a database in the example program.

# Example

The example program creates a short Adventure-style text adventure, using the hypertext capabilities of ALLText. The ALLText HT/Pro control comes with a demo program that includes a hypertext database designer, which is used to create the database in this example. The example then creates a custom hypertext viewer program to present the hypertext game. The example program is shown in Figure 3-1.

The idea behind the hypertext game is simple. The game describes a situation to the player, who is then presented with one or more courses of action, in the form of hypertext links. When an action is selected, that action's *HTag* property is inspected, and the integer value is interpreted as the key to another document stored in the database. This new text is retrieved, and replaces the first. The new text now describes the current situation, with its own set of action choices. The game progresses until the player wins or is defeated.

## Steps

1. Use the HT_DEMO demo program that comes with the ALLText HT/Pro control to create a hypertext database. You can do this by deleting or editing the records that are stored in the demo database. Designing the game is straightforward, but it helps to do a little planning. In general, each record in the hypertext game database will consist of some text explaining the player's current situation, followed by a series of choices that contain hypertext tags. The *HTag* value of each choice should reference the index of another record that moves the action of the game forward. Once the database is

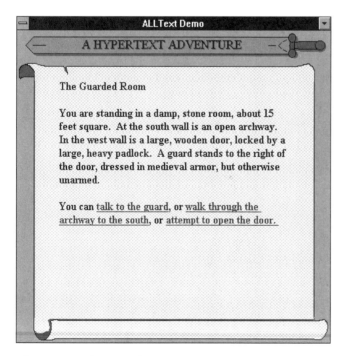

**Figure 3-1** The example ALLText program

completed, copy the Microsoft Access database file (which will be named HT_DEMO.MDB) to the directory where you will be building your project, and rename it ALLTEXT.MDB.

2. Create a new project called ALLTEXT.MAK. Add the ATX30H.VBX control to the project. Create a new form with the objects and properties described in Table 3-4. Save this form as ALLTEXT.FRM.

**Table 3-4** Objects and properties for ALLTEXT.FRM

| OBJECT | PROPERTY | SETTING |
|--------|----------|---------|
| Form | FormName | frmALLText |
| | BackColor | &H00C0C0C0& |
| | BorderStyle | 1 'Fixed Single |
| | Caption | "ALLText Demo" |
| | MaxButton | 0 'False |
| Line | Name | Line1 |
| | Index | 0 |
| | X1 | 390 |
| | X2 | 390 |
| | Y1 | 1080 |
| | Y2 | 6150 |
| Line | Name | Line1 |
| | Index | 1 |
| | X1 | 6780 |
| | X2 | 6780 |
| | Y1 | 1050 |
| | Y2 | 6120 |
| Image | Name | Image2 |
| | Picture | (set at design time in Properties window) |
| Image | Name | Image3 |
| | Picture | (set at design time in Properties window) |
| ATX3h | Name | AllText1 |
| | BackColor | &H0080FFFF& |
| | BackStyle | 1 'Opaque |
| | BorderStyle | 0 'None |
| | CaretWidth | 0 |
| | DataField | "Content" |
| | DataSource | "Data1" |
| | DataType | 2 'ATXf - AllText full format |
| | F2ON | 0 'False |
| | F3ON | 0 'False |
| | MouseHPointer | 13 '13 Finger |

| OBJECT | PROPERTY | SETTING |
|--------|----------|---------|
| | ScrollBarH | 1 ' 1 - Invisible |
| | ScrollBarV | 0 ' 0 - Auto |
| | TabEnabled | -1 'True |
| | WriteProtect | -1 |
| Data | Name | Data1 |
| | DatabaseName | "ALLTEXT.MDB" |
| | RecordSource | "Table1" |
| | Visible | 0 'False |

3. Add the following code to the declarations section of ALLTEXT.FRM.

```
Option Explicit
'----------------------------------------------------
' Constants and declarations for the ALLText example.
'----------------------------------------------------

' The ASCII value for a Tab character.
Const ATAB = 9

' Constants for the MousePointer.
Const CSR_DEFAULT = 0
Const CSR_HOURGLASS = 11
Const CSR_HAND = 13

' Hypertext function.
Declare Function find_htag Lib "atx30h" (alltext As Any, ByVal HTag&, ByVal skipcount&) As Long

Declare Function Print_ATextPages Lib "atx30h" (alltext As Any, ByVal ptop&, ByVal pbottom&,
ByVal pleft&, ByVal pwidth&, ByVal pages$, ByVal Flags%) As Integer
Declare Function Print_AText Lib "atx30h" (alltext As Any, ByVal ptop&, ByVal pbottom&, ByVal
pleft&, ByVal pwidth&, ByVal start_par%, ByVal end_par%, ByVal Flags%) As Integer
```

4. Add the following subroutines to ALLTEXT.FRM. Make sure to put event code into the
   proper subroutines. You'll notice that this application requires very little code. Since most
   of the "logic" of the game is stored in the database, all the program needs to do is move
   from hypertext page to hypertext page.

```
Sub AllText1_Click ()
'----------------------------------------------------
' If the user clicks on a hypertext tag, jump to
' the record referenced by that tag.
'----------------------------------------------------

    If AllText1.HTag  0 Then
      If AllText1.HTag = 999 Then End
      AllText1.MouseHPointer = CSR_HOURGLASS

      ' Temporarily disable the ALLText control until new record is loaded.
      AllText1.Enabled = False

      ' Find the database record with the matching hypertext tag.
      Data1.Recordset.FindFirst ("Htag=" & Str$(AllText1.HTag))
    End If
```

(continued on next page)

*(continued from previous page)*

```
End Sub

Sub AllText1_KeyPress (Key As Integer)
'----------------------------------------------------
' Allow the user to tab between hypertext hot spots.
'----------------------------------------------------
Dim retcode As Integer

    If Key = ATAB Then
      retcode = find_htag(AllText1, 5, 1)
    End If
End Sub

Sub Data1_Reposition ()
'----------------------------------------------------
' Re-enable the ALLText control.
'----------------------------------------------------

    AllText1.MouseHPointer = CSR_HAND
    AllText1.Enabled = True
End Sub

Sub Form_Load ()
'----------------------------------------------------
' Center the form and set the data control to
' point to the database in the project's directory.
'----------------------------------------------------

    ' Center the form on the screen.
    Me.Move (Screen.Width - Me.Width) \ 2, (Screen.Height - Me.Height) \ 2

    ' Set the database file name.
    Data1.DatabaseName = App.Path & "\ALLTEXT.MDB"
End Sub
```

## Tips and Comments

You can use the ALLText control for a variety of applications, from a high-capacity replacement for the standard text box control, to a word processor embedded within an application, to a hypertext engine. The control's ability to bind to a data control makes it particularly attractive for hypertext, as witnessed by the trivial amount of code required to create the example hypertext game.

# Early Morning Editor (EMEDIT.VBX)

| USAGE: | Text Editor |
|---|---|
| MANUFACTURER: | Early Morning Software |
| COST: | $30 (available on CompuServe) |

The Early Morning Editor control is a high-powered, multiline text editing control. It can handle more than 32K of text, the approximate limit of the standard Visual Basic text control. This makes it quite useful when you need more power than the text control, but when a full-blown word processing control would be overkill.

# Syntax

The Early Morning Editor control is similar in appearance to the standard text box, with several additional features that make it easier to process files and manipulate text. The control's nonstandard properties and events are listed in Table 3-5.

**Table 3-5** Nonstandard properties and events for Early Morning Editor

**PROPERTIES**

| | | |
|---|---|---|
| Action | Count | CaretX |
| CaretY | FileOpen | FileSave |
| InsertMode | IsDirty | LeftHi |
| ReadOnly | Redraw | RightHi |
| ScrollBars | SelDefaultType | SelEndX |
| SelEndY | SelMark | SelStartX |
| SelStartY | SelText | Text |
| TopY | | |

**EVENTS**

| | | |
|---|---|---|
| BeginMessage | EndMessage | ProcessMessage |

Unlike a standard text control, the Early Morning Editor control is always multiline. You can select whether it displays scroll bars by setting the integer *ScrollBars* property to one of the values listing in Table 3-6.

**Table 3-6** Values for the ScrollBars property

| VALUE | MEANING |
|---|---|
| 0 | No scroll bars (default) |
| 1 | Horizontal scroll bars |
| 2 | Vertical scroll bars |
| 3 | Both horizontal and vertical scroll bars |

You determine the location of the text cursor, or caret, in the editor with the *CaretX* and *CaretY* properties. These integer properties give the column and row of the caret, and can be both read and set at run time. This allows you to move the caret under program control.

**Overcoming the Standard Text Box's Limitations** The *Text* property is handled differently in the Early Morning Editor than in a standard text control. The standard multiline text box lacks an easy way to get information about a specific line of text. The editor solves this problem by introducing *TextIndex* and *Count* properties. *TextIndex* is analogous to the *ListIndex* property of standard list boxes; it indicates which line of text in the editor is currently stored in *Text.* Likewise, *Count* shows how many lines are in the editor. As an illustration, the following code scans the contents of an editor control for the first line that starts with the letter "Z."

```
For i=1 to Editor1.Count
    Editor1.ListIndex = i
    If Left$(Editor1.Text, 1) = "Z" Then
        Label1 = "Found 'Z' at Line " & Format$(i)
        Exit For
    End If
Next
```

The standard text box also provides no good way to disable text editing. This problem is solved by the *ReadOnly* property of the Early Morning Editor control. Setting this property to *True* prevents the user from editing text. Text can still be changed from within the program.

Program control of cut and paste operations is handled by the *Action* property. Actions are only related to Windows Clipboard operations, and are summarized in Table 3-7.

**Table 3-7** Values for the Action property

| VALUE | MEANING |
| --- | --- |
| 0 | No action |
| 1 | Copy selected text to the Windows Clipboard |
| 2 | Paste text from the Clipboard to current caret position |
| 3 | Cut selected text to the Windows Clipboard |
| 4 | Delete selected text from editor |

Yet another problem with the standard text control is its lack of an overstrike mode. You can insert text, but can't type over existing text without resorting to the addition of code in *Key* events. You can overcome this problem by the addition of a Boolean *InsertMode* property. If you set this property to *True,* which is the default value, the editor behaves as a standard text box. If you set it to *False,* text in the control can be overtyped.

The Early Morning Editor control provides several options for selecting text in the editor. You choose these options by setting the *SelDefaultType* property. By default, text is selected as a "stream"—that is, selected text can start in the middle of one line and end in the middle of another. This is the normal behavior most users expect from the standard text box or the Windows Notepad. "Line" selection allows only entire text lines to be selected. This is the way text is selected in the Visual Basic code windows. "Column" selection allows text to be highlighted in columns, a great feature when you're trying to extract a column of figures from the middle of a table of data. The values used to set *SelDefaultType* are shown in Table 3-8.

**Table 3-8** Values for the SelDefaultType property

| VALUE | MEANING |
|---|---|
| 0 | Text cannot be selected |
| 1 | Stream text selection |
| 2 | Line text selection |
| 3 | Column text selection |

The *SelMark* property indicates the selection type of the currently selected text. It returns the same values as *SelDefaultType,* except that a value of 0 indicates that no text is currently selected.

The four properties *SelStartX, SelStartY, SelEndX,* and *SelEndY,* indicate the area of text that is currently selected. These properties give the beginning column and row, and the ending column and row, of the selected text area. You can also select text by assigning values to these properties in your program.

The *SelText* property returns the selected text for the row referred to by *TextIndex.* If a value is assigned to *SelText,* the entire selected text area is replaced by the new value in *SelText.*

Reading and saving text from text files is trivial with the Early Morning Editor control. When the *FileOpen* property is set to a valid file name, that file is loaded into the Editor control. Likewise, when the *FileSave* property is assigned a valid file name, a file is created, or an existing one replaced, under that file name. It is the programmer's responsibility to make sure the file name is valid.

The *IsDirty* property is set to *True* automatically whenever the text in an editor changes. The programmer can set it to *False,* and it is also set to *False* when a new file is loaded using the *FileOpen* property. *IsDirty* is very useful when determining whether the contents of the editor need to be saved.

A Boolean *Redraw* property allows you to disable screen updates when a lengthy set of operations is taking place. Setting this property to *False,* suppresses screen updating and caret movements until the *Redraw* property is reset to *True.* This gives a smoother appearance to screen updates. *Redraw* is set to *True* by default.

The Early Morning Editor control provides three events—*BeginMessage, ProcessMessage,* and *EndMessage,* that serve as generic events for message handling. Windows messages are sent to these events, which allow you to tailor your handling of events sent to the editor. These events are very handy for providing features such as "line/column" indicators to programs that use the Editor control.

# Example

The Early Morning Editor example program is a complete text editing program. In several ways, this program is better than the Windows Notepad. It handles large amounts of text, you can toggle between insert and overstrike modes, you can select the font, and the program displays your line and column location. The program is shown in Figure 3-2.

```
┌─────────────────────────────────────────────────────────┐
│ ═    Early Morning Editor Demo - C:\VB30\CONSTANT.TXT  ▼ ▲│
│ File  Edit                                                │
│ ┌─────────┬──────────────────────┬────────────────────┐  │
│ │ Find:  │ mb_                  │ Fonts: Fixedsys    ▼ │  │
│ ├─────────┴──────────────────────┴────────────────────┤  │
│ │Global Const MB_OK = 0           ' OK button only    ▲│  │
│ │Global Const MB_OKCANCEL = 1     ' OK and Cancel bu   │  │
│ │Global Const MB_ABORTRETRYIGNORE = 2 ' Abort, Retry, an│  │
│ │Global Const MB_YESNOCANCEL = 3  ' Yes, No, and Can   │  │
│ │Global Const MB_YESNO = 4        ' Yes and No butto   │  │
│ │Global Const MB_RETRYCANCEL = 5  ' Retry and Cancel   │  │
│ │                                                      │  │
│ │Global Const MB_ICONSTOP = 16    ' Critical message   │  │
│ │Global Const MB_ICONQUESTION = 32 ' Warning query     │  │
│ │Global Const MB_ICONEXCLAMATION = 48 ' Warning message│  │
│ │Global Const MB_ICONINFORMATION = 64 ' Information mess│  │
│ │                                                      │  │
│ │Global Const MB_APPLMODAL = 0    ' Application Moda    │  │
│ │Global Const MB_DEFBUTTON1 = 0   ' First button is    │  │
│ │Global Const MB_DEFBUTTON2 = 256 ' Second button is   │  │
│ │Global Const MB_DEFBUTTON3 = 512 ' Third button is    │  │
│ │Global Const MB_SYSTEMMODAL = 4096 'System Modal     ▼│  │
│ │◄                                                   ►  │  │
│ ├──────────────────────────────────────────────┬──────┤  │
│ │Line 322, Column 17                            │ INS  │  │
│ └──────────────────────────────────────────────┴──────┘  │
└─────────────────────────────────────────────────────────┘
```

**Figure 3-2** The Early Morning Editor demo program

It's also worth noting that this program is implemented entirely within one form and requires only two nonstandard controls (the Editor and the Common Dialog controls).

## Steps

1. Create a new project called EMEDIT.MAK. Add the EMEDIT.VBX and the CMDIALOG.VBX (Common Dialog) controls to this project. Create a new form with the objects and properties described in Table 3-9. Save this form as EMEDIT.FRM.

**Table 3-9** Objects and properties for EMEDIT.FRM

| OBJECT | PROPERTY | SETTING |
|--------|----------|---------|
| Form | FormName | frmEMedit |
| | AutoRedraw | -1 'True |
| | BackColor | &H00C0C0C0& |
| | Caption | "Early Morning Editor Demo" |
| Label | Name | Label1 |
| | Alignment | 1 'Right Justify |
| | BackStyle | 0 'Transparent |
| | Caption | "Fonts:" |
| | ForeColor | &H00000000& |
| Editor | Name | Editor1 |
| | FileOpen | " " |
| | FontBold | 0 'False |
| | FontName | "Fixedsys" |

| OBJECT | PROPERTY | SETTING |
|---|---|---|
| | FontSize | 9 |
| | InsertMode | -1 'True |
| | Password | 0 |
| | ReadOnly | 0 'False |
| | ScrollBars | 3 'Both |
| | SelDefaultType | 1 'Stream |
| CommonDialog | Name | CMDialog1 |
| | Filter | "*.TXT" |
| | FilterIndex | 1 |
| PictureBox | Name | picStatLine |
| | Align | 2 'Align Bottom |
| | BackColor | &H00C0C0C0& |
| | BorderStyle | 0 'None |
| ComboBox | Name | cmbFonts |
| | Sorted | -1 'True |
| | Style | 2 'Dropdown List |
| CommandButton | Name | btnFind |
| | Caption | "Find:" |
| TextBox | Name | txtSearchWord |
| | BackColor | &H00FFFFFF& |

2. Place the controls shown in Table 3-10 inside the picStatLine Picture control. Make sure to select the picStatLine control on the form before placing each of these controls.

**Table 3-10** Controls contained inside the picStatLine PictureBox control

| OBJECT | PROPERTY | SETTING |
|---|---|---|
| Line | Name | linLeft |
| | BorderColor | &H00808080& |
| | X1 | 30 |
| | X2 | 30 |
| | Y1 | 45 |
| | Y2 | 270 |
| Line | Name | linTop |
| | BorderColor | &H00808080& |
| | X1 | 30 |
| | X2 | 810 |
| | Y1 | 30 |
| | Y2 | 30 |
| Line | Name | linBottom |

(continued on next page)

| OBJECT | PROPERTY | SETTING |
|--------|----------|---------|
| *(continued from previous page)* | | |
| | BorderColor | &H00FFFFFF& |
| | X1 | 30 |
| | X2 | 810 |
| | Y1 | 270 |
| | Y2 | 270 |
| Line | Name | linRight |
| | BorderColor | &H00FFFFFF& |
| | X1 | 810 |
| | X2 | 810 |
| | Y1 | 45 |
| | Y2 | 270 |
| Label | Name | lblStatLine |
| | BackStyle | 0 'Transparent |
| | ForeColor | &H00800000& |
| Label | Name | lblInsertMode |
| | Alignment | 1 'Right Justify |
| | BackStyle | 0 'Transparent |
| | Caption | "INS" |
| | ForeColor | &H00800000& |

3. Add a menu to the EMEDIT.FRM using the Visual Basic Menu Design window, setting the captions and names as shown in Table 3-11.

**Table 3-11** Menu definition for EMEDIT.FRM

| CAPTION | NAME |
|---------|------|
| &File | File |
| – – – – &New | FileNew |
| – – – – &Open | FileOpen |
| – – – – &Save | FileSave |
| – – – – Save &As... | FileSaveAs |
| – – – – | FileSep1 |
| – – – – E&xit | FileExit |
| &Edit | Edit |
| – – – – Cu&t | EditCut |
| – – – – &Copy | EditCopy |
| – – – – &Paste | EditPaste |
| – – – – &Delete | EditDelete |
| – – – – | EditSep1 |
| – – – – &Find | EditFind |

4. After creating the form, add the following code to EMEDIT.FRM's declarations section.

```
Option Explicit
'---------------------------------------------------
' Early Morning Editor control demo program.
'---------------------------------------------------

' Constants used to set the ScrollBar property of the editor.
Const SB_NONE = 0
Const SB_HORIZONTAL = 1
Const SB_VERTICAL = 2
Const SB_BOTH = 3

' Constants used for the editor's Action property.
Const ACTION_COPY = 1
Const ACTION_PASTE = 2
Const ACTION_CUT = 3
Const ACTION_DELETE = 4

' Constants used by the Common Dialog's Action property.
Const CD_FILEOPEN = 1
Const CD_FILESAVEAS = 2

' Constants for key presses.
Const ESCAPE = 27
Const ENTER = 13
Const INSERT = &H2D

' Default file name.
Const DEFAULT_FILE = "[Untitled]"

' Window title.
Const WINDOW_TITLE = "Early Morning Editor Demo"

' Current file name.
Dim CurrentFile As String

' WindowState constants.
Const MINIMIZED = 1

' Color constants.
Const DARK_GRAY = &H808080
Const WHITE = &HFFFFFF

' MsgBox parameters.
Const MB_YESNOCANCEL = 3         ' Yes, No, and Cancel buttons
Const MB_YESNO = 4               ' Yes and No buttons

Const MB_ICONSTOP = 16           ' Critical message
Const MB_ICONQUESTION = 32       ' Warning query

' MsgBox return values.
Const IDCANCEL = 2               ' Cancel button pressed
Const IDYES = 6                  ' Yes button pressed
Const IDNO = 7                   ' No button pressed

' Cursor shape constants.
Const CSR_NORMAL = 0
Const CSR_HOURGLASS = 11
```

(continued on next page)

*(continued from previous page)*

```
' Globals used by BeginMessage and EndMessage events.
Dim BeginCaretX As Long
Dim BeginCaretY As Long
Dim BeginCount As Long
Dim MessageNesting As Integer

' Used to tell if "Save As" operation was canceled.
Dim SaveAsCanceled As Integer
```

5. Add the following subroutines to the EMEDIT.FRM form. Rather than have the text search option as just a menu event, we place this function on the "option bar" under the menu. The Find menu option merely simulates pressing the Find button. This eliminates the need for another form to enter search criteria. Font selection is also accessed via a combo box in the option bar.

   The *BeginMessage* and *EndMessage* events track the current row and column position for the editor caret. These values are then displayed on the status line.

```
Sub btnFind_Click ()
'-----------------------------------------------------
' Search down from the current cursor position for
' the string entered in lblSearchWord.
'-----------------------------------------------------
Dim row As Integer, col As Integer
Dim ALine As String
Dim pos As Integer

    col = Editor1.CaretX
    Screen.MousePointer = CSR_HOURGLASS
    ' Search down row by row.
    For row = Editor1.CaretY To Editor1.Count
      Editor1.TextIndex = row
      ALine = Mid$(Editor1.Text, col)
      pos = InStr(LCase$(ALine), LCase$(txtSearchWord))
      ' We've found a match.
      If pos > 0 Then
          pos = pos + col - 1
          If row > Editor1.TopY Then Editor1.TopY = row
          ' Highlight it.
          Editor1.SelMark = 0 ' Unmark any existing block mark, if any.
          Editor1.SelMark = 1 ' Start a stream block.
          Editor1.SelStartY = row
          Editor1.SelStartX = pos
          Editor1.SelEndY = row
          Editor1.SelEndX = pos + Len(txtSearchWord)

          ' Move caret to end of matched string.
          Editor1.CaretY = row
          Editor1.CaretX = pos + Len(txtSearchWord)
          Editor1.SetFocus

          Screen.MousePointer = CSR_NORMAL
          Exit Sub
      End If
      col = 1
    Next
```

```
      Screen.MousePointer = CSR_NORMAL
      lblStatLine = "String not found."
      Beep
  End Sub

  Sub ClearEditor (AnEditor As Editor)
  '-----------------------------------------------------
  ' Clear all data from the editor.
  '-----------------------------------------------------
      AnEditor.SelMark = 0 ' unmark any existing block mark, if any
      AnEditor.SelMark = 2 ' start a line block
      AnEditor.SelStartX = 1
      AnEditor.SelStartY = 1
      AnEditor.TextIndex = Editor1.Count
      AnEditor.SelEndY = Editor1.Count
      AnEditor.SelEndX = Len(Editor1.Text)
      AnEditor.Action = ACTION_DELETE
      AnEditor.IsDirty = False
      AnEditor.SetFocus
  End Sub

  Sub cmbFonts_Click ()
  '-----------------------------------------------------
  ' Change the current editor font.
  '-----------------------------------------------------
      If cmbFonts.ListIndex >= 0 Then
        Editor1.FontName = cmbFonts.List(cmbFonts.ListIndex)
        Editor1.FontBold = False
        Editor1.FontItalic = False
        Editor1.FontUnderline = False
        Editor1.FontSize = 9
      End If
  End Sub

  Sub EditCopy_Click ()
  '-----------------------------------------------------
  ' Copy the selection to the Clipboard.
  '-----------------------------------------------------
      Editor1.Action = ACTION_COPY
      Editor1.SelMark = 0 ' Unmark any existing block mark, if any.
  End Sub

  Sub EditCut_Click ()
  '-----------------------------------------------------
  ' Cut the current selection and put in Clipboard.
  '-----------------------------------------------------
      Editor1.Action = ACTION_CUT
  End Sub

  Sub EditDelete_Click ()
  '-----------------------------------------------------
  ' Delete current selection from editor.
  '-----------------------------------------------------
      Editor1.Action = ACTION_DELETE
  End Sub

  Sub EditFind_Click ()
```

*(continued on next page)*

*(continued from previous page)*

```vb
'------------------------------------------------------
' Selecting Find menu option simulates pushing
' the Find button.
'------------------------------------------------------
    btnFind.Value = 1
End Sub

Sub Editor1_BeginMessage (HControl As Long, HWindow As Integer, Message As Integer, WParam As
Integer, LParam As Long, fProcessMessage As Integer)
'------------------------------------------------------
' Event used to track caret position.
'------------------------------------------------------
    If MessageNesting = 0 Then
       BeginCaretY = Editor1.CaretY
       BeginCaretX = Editor1.CaretX
       BeginCount = Editor1.Count
    End If
    MessageNesting = MessageNesting + 1
End Sub

Sub Editor1_EndMessage (HControl As Long, HWindow As Integer, Message As Integer, WParam As
Integer, LParam As Long)
'------------------------------------------------------
' Event used to track caret position.
'------------------------------------------------------
    If MessageNesting = 1 Then
       If BeginCaretX  Editor1.CaretX Or BeginCaretY  Editor1.CaretY Or BeginCount 
Editor1.Count Then
             UpdateStatusLine
       End If
    End If
    MessageNesting = MessageNesting - 1
End Sub

Sub Editor1_KeyDown (KeyCode As Integer, Shift As Integer)
'------------------------------------------------------
' Event used to switch from Insert to Overstrike mode.
'------------------------------------------------------
    If KeyCode = INSERT And Shift = 0 Then
       Editor1.InsertMode = Not Editor1.InsertMode
       If Editor1.InsertMode Then
           lblInsertMode = "INS"
       Else
           lblInsertMode = "OVR"
       End If
    End If
End Sub

Sub EditPaste_Click ()
'------------------------------------------------------
' Paste from Clipboard to current caret location.
'------------------------------------------------------
    Editor1.Action = ACTION_PASTE
End Sub

Sub FileExit_Click ()
'------------------------------------------------------
' Try to unload main form.
'------------------------------------------------------
```

```
    Unload Me
End Sub

Sub FileNew_Click ()
'----------------------------------------------------
' Menu option to start fresh file.
'----------------------------------------------------

    If Not SavedCurrentFile() Then Exit Sub

    ClearEditor Editor1
    Editor1.SetFocus
End Sub

Sub FileOpen_Click ()
'----------------------------------------------------
' Open a new file.
'----------------------------------------------------
    If Not SavedCurrentFile() Then Exit Sub

    CMDialog1.DefaultExt = "TXT"
    CMDialog1.Filter = "Text (*.TXT)|*.txt"
    CMDialog1.FilterIndex = 1
    CMDialog1.Action = CD_FILEOPEN
    If CMDialog1.Filename  "" Then
      ClearEditor Editor1
      CurrentFile = CMDialog1.Filename
      Editor1.FileOpen = CurrentFile
      Me.Caption = WINDOW_TITLE & " - " & CurrentFile
    End If
    Editor1.SetFocus
End Sub

Sub FileSave_Click ()
'----------------------------------------------------
' Menu option to save the current file.
'----------------------------------------------------
    If CurrentFile = DEFAULT_FILE Then
      FileSaveAs_Click
    Else
      Editor1.FileSave = CurrentFile
      lblStatLine = "File saved."
    End If
    Editor1.SetFocus
End Sub

Sub FileSaveAs_Click ()
'----------------------------------------------------
' Menu option to save file by name.
'----------------------------------------------------
    CMDialog1.DefaultExt = "TXT"
    CMDialog1.Filter = "Text (*.TXT)|*.txt"
    CMDialog1.FilterIndex = 1
    CMDialog1.Action = CD_FILESAVEAS
    If CMDialog1.Filename  "" Then
        CurrentFile = CMDialog1.Filename
        Editor1.FileSave = CurrentFile
        Me.Caption = WINDOW_TITLE & " - " & CurrentFile
        lblStatLine = "File saved."
        SaveAsCanceled = False
```

3 ◀

*(continued on next page)*

*(continued from previous page)*

```
    Else
            SaveAsCanceled = True
    End If
End Sub

Sub Form_Load ()
'----------------------------------------------------
' Initialize form data and position form on screen.
'----------------------------------------------------
Dim i As Integer

    Me.Move (Screen.Width - Me.Width) \ 2, (Screen.Height - Me.Height) \ 2

    For i = 0 To Screen.FontCount - 1
      cmbFonts.AddItem Screen.Fonts(i)
      If Screen.Fonts(i) = Editor1.FontName Then
          cmbFonts.ListIndex = cmbFonts.NewIndex
      End If
    Next

    Me.Show
    CurrentFile = DEFAULT_FILE
    Me.Caption = WINDOW_TITLE & " - " & CurrentFile

    UpdateStatusLine
    Make3D frmEMedit, cmbFonts
    Make3D frmEMedit, txtSearchWord
End Sub

Sub Form_QueryUnload (Cancel As Integer, UnloadMode As Integer)
'----------------------------------------------------
' Try to clean up before exiting.
'----------------------------------------------------
    If Not SavedCurrentFile() Then Cancel = True
    Editor1.SetFocus
End Sub

Sub Form_Resize ()
'----------------------------------------------------
' Adjust all controls to the new form size.
'----------------------------------------------------
Dim FarRight As Integer
Dim ToolBarHeight As Integer

    On Error GoTo Resize_Error
    If Me.WindowState = MINIMIZED Then Exit Sub

    ' Adjust the 3D lines of the status line border.
    FarRight = Me.ScaleWidth - (linLeft.X1 * 2)
    linTop.X2 = FarRight
    linBottom.X2 = FarRight
    linRight.X1 = FarRight
    linRight.X2 = FarRight

    ' Adjust the editor control.
    ToolBarHeight = btnFind.Height + (btnFind.Top * 2) + 10
    Editor1.Move 0, ToolBarHeight, Me.ScaleWidth, Me.ScaleHeight - picStatLine.Height -
ToolBarHeight
```

```
     ' Adjust the "Insert/Overstrike" label.
     lblInsertMode.Move Me.ScaleWidth - lblInsertMode.Width - (linLeft.X1 * 2)
Exit Sub

Resize_Error:
     Me.Width = Screen.Width / 2
     Me.Height = Screen.Height / 2
     Exit Sub
End Sub

Sub Make3D (pic As Form, ctl As Control)
'---------------------------------------------------
' Wrap a 3D effect around a control on a form.
'---------------------------------------------------
Dim AdjustX As Integer, AdjustY As Integer

     AdjustX = Screen.TwipsPerPixelX
     AdjustY = Screen.TwipsPerPixelY

     ' Set the top shading line.
     pic.Line (ctl.Left - AdjustX, ctl.Top - AdjustY)-(ctl.Left + ctl.Width, ctl.Top - AdjustY),
DARK_GRAY
     pic.Line -(ctl.Left + ctl.Width, ctl.Top + ctl.Height), WHITE
     pic.Line -(ctl.Left - AdjustX, ctl.Top + ctl.Height), WHITE
     pic.Line -(ctl.Left - AdjustX, ctl.Top - AdjustY), DARK_GRAY
End Sub

Function SavedCurrentFile () As Integer
'---------------------------------------------------
' Try to save current file if it has been changed.
'---------------------------------------------------
Dim answer As Integer
Dim Msg As String

     If Editor1.IsDirty Then
          Msg = "The text in file " & CurrentFile
          Msg = Msg & " has changed." & Chr$(13) & Chr$(13) & "Do you want to save the changes?"
          answer = MsgBox(Msg, MB_YESNOCANCEL Or MB_ICONQUESTION, WINDOW_TITLE)
          If answer = IDYES Then
               SaveAsCanceled = False
               FileSave_Click
               If SaveAsCanceled Then
                 SavedCurrentFile = False
                 Exit Function
               End If
          ElseIf answer = IDCANCEL Then
               SavedCurrentFile = False
               Exit Function
          End If
     End If
     SavedCurrentFile = True
End Function

Sub txtSearchWord_KeyPress (KeyAscii As Integer)
'---------------------------------------------------
' Initiate or continue the search when Enter key
' is pressed.
'---------------------------------------------------
```

*(continued on next page)*

*(continued from previous page)*

```
    If KeyAscii = ENTER Then
      KeyAscii = 0
      btnFind.Value = 1
      txtSearchWord.SetFocus
    End If
End Sub

Sub UpdateStatusLine ()
'----------------------------------------------------
' Update the cursor position info. on status line.
'----------------------------------------------------
    lblStatLine = "Line " & Format$(Editor1.CaretY) & ", Column " & Format$(Editor1.CaretX)
End Sub
```

## Tips and Comments

The Early Morning Editor provides a good alternative to the standard text control. Early Morning Software provides a demo program with the control that implements a complete MDI text editing program. Their demo goes into more depth than our example program, and is a good source of information when using this control.

# RavenWrite (RAVENW.VBX)

| USAGE: | Word Processing and Hypertext |
| --- | --- |
| MANUFACTURER: | Looking Glass Software |
| COST: | $295 |

RavenWrite is a combination word processing and hypermedia control. It supports documents in Rich Text Format (.RTF), standard ASCII text, or RavenWrite's own "tagged" text file format. It also supports ViperWrite (.HPW) files. RavenWrite supports the display of multiple fonts, colors, and bitmaps within a single document, and can display documents with multiple columns and transparent backgrounds. When used as a word processor, RavenWrite can display function bars that give users access to text formatting features.

## Syntax

RavenWrite's features are controlled primarily by a large set of properties. These special properties, along with RavenWrite's special control events, are listed in Table 3-12. Each text processing control puts its own unique slant on the business of manipulating and accessing documents, and RavenWrite is no exception. One unusual feature of this control is the concept of formatting *layers,* each of which defines a set of formatting attributes. Layering allows you to display text as, for example, bold in one layer and italic in another. You can selectively activate or deactivate layers at run time. For example, let's say you have a formatting layer that underlines a set of keywords. If you activate this layer, all your keywords appear underlined. To turn off the underlining, you deactivate the layer again.

**Table 3-12** Nonstandard properties and events for RavenWrite control

**PROPERTIES**

| | | |
|---|---|---|
| About | Changed | ColumnSpacing |
| Copy | Cut | Erase |
| Find | FindBookMark | FindIndex |
| FunctionBars | GetWord | GetWordNumber |
| IndexNext | IndexOfBookmarkNext | IndexOfBookmarkPrevious |
| IndexPrevious | IndexStartOfNextParagraph | IndexStartOfNextWord |
| Keyboard | Layer | Length |
| Mode | New | NumberOfColumns |
| NumberOfPages | NumberOfWords | Open |
| OpenRTF | OpenTagged | OutlineAll |
| Outlining | Page | PageOfIndexPaste |
| Picture | PrintDocument | RecalcDocument |
| RedrawDocument | RedrawTransparent | RulerAlignment |
| RulerIndentFirstLine | RulerIndentLeft | RulerIndentRight |
| RulerLineSpacing | RulerSpaceAfter | RulerSpaceBefore |
| Save | ScrollMax | ScrollPosition |
| ScrollTo | SelectedText | SelectEnd |
| SelectStart | ShowBookMarks | ShowHidden |
| ShowInvisibleChars | StyleBevelColorBottom | StyleBevelColorLeft |
| StyleBevelColorRight | StyleBevelColorTop | StyleBevelHeight |
| StyleBevelWidth | StyleBold | StyleColorBack |
| StyleColorFore | StyleDottedUnderline | StyleFont |
| StyleHidden | StyleItalic | StyleKerning StylePlain |
| StyleShadowColor | StyleShadowHor | StyleShadowVer |
| StyleShift | StyleSize | StyleStrikeThrough |
| StyleUnderline | StyleUserFile | StyleUserID |
| Transparent | Undo | UserDefinedCharacter |
| UserDefinedCharacterBottom | UserDefinedCharacterLeft | UserDefinedCharacterRight |
| UserDefinedCharacterTop | | |

**EVENTS**

| | | |
|---|---|---|
| ChangeNumberOfPages | DrawUserDefinedCharacter | Scroll |
| ScrollEnd | SingleWordClicked | TextSelected Trash |
| UserFileClicked | UserIDClicked | |

The RavenWrite control can operate in one of four modes: edit mode, hot link mode, hot word mode, and select mode. Use the *Mode* property to set the current mode at design or run time. Select the edit mode when the control is to be used as a word processor. In hot link mode, text that has been previously tagged as hypertext hot spots becomes active; when the user clicks on these hot spots the control triggers special events. In hot word mode, each word is automatically a hot spot, and a special event lets you determine what word has been clicked. The select mode does not allow the user to enter or delete text, but the user can highlight text to be copied. In this mode, a special *TextSelected* event is fired whenever a new text selection is made.

**Using RavenWrite As a Word Processor**   As a word processor, RavenWrite can display a style bar and ruler similar to those in commercial packages such as Microsoft Word (see Figure 3-3). These features are optional, and you can control them by setting the *FunctionBars* property to one of the values shown in Table 3-13.

The style bar allows the user to change font style and attributes, as well as line spacing and text alignment. The ruler is used to display and set margins and tabs.

**Table 3-13** Values for the FunctionBars property

| VALUE | MEANING |
| --- | --- |
| 0 | No format bars are displayed (the default). |
| 1 | The style bar is displayed. |
| 2 | The ruler is displayed. |
| 3 | Both style bar and ruler are displayed. |

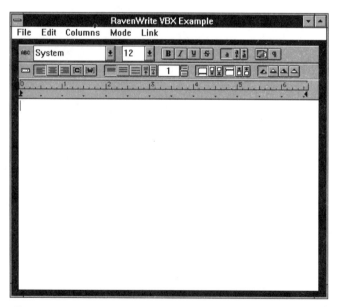

**Figure 3-3** A RavenWrite program showing both the ruler and style bars

RavenWrite uses variations on the conventional text selection properties to implement selection functions. The standard *SelStart, SelLength,* and *SelText* used in conventional text box controls have been replaced by RavenWrite's *SelectStart, SelectEnd,* and *SelectedText.* These are similar to the conventional properties, with the main difference being that *SelectEnd* returns the character index for the end of the selected text, where the conventional *SelLength* returns the number of selected characters. When the *SelectedText* property is assigned a string value, that string replaces the selected text. Most of the style and formatting properties affect only the currently selected text.

RavenWrite has three separate properties for opening document files. The *Open* property opens text (.TXT), RavenWrite (.RW), or HyperWrite (.HPW) files, and loads their contents into the control. The *OpenRTF* property loads files saved in Rich Text Format (.RTF), and the *OpenTagged* property loads files stored in "tagged" text format. Each of these three properties initiates file loading when assigned a valid file name. These properties also trigger the *Trash* event. *Trash* is fired whenever an existing document is about to be cleared, and can be used to check if the current document needs to be saved.

To determine whether an existing document has been modified, you can inspect the Boolean *Changed* property. This property is automatically set to *False* when a new document is loaded, and to *True* when changes are made.

You can use the *Save* property to save files in the text (.TXT), RavenWrite (.RW), RavenText (.RW), or HyperWrite (.HPW) format. Note that if you are using the *Changed* property to track when documents should be saved, you must explicitly set it to *False* after saving a document.

## Using RavenWrite As a Hypermedia Engine

Hypertext and hypermedia are popular formats for displaying sets of interrelated information. The ability to jump from one topic to another via hot spots makes hypertext popular for applications such as help systems (such as the Windows Help engine), document retrieval systems, games, and online reference works. When RavenWrite is set to hot link mode, it can be used as a hypertext engine. RavenWrite lets you create hypertext documents, and supports an interesting "tagged" text file format that allows you to create hypermedia documents using an ordinary text editor such as Windows Notepad.

The tagged text format is simply a text file with special control tokens interspersed into the plain ASCII text. These tokens are text themselves; they begin and end with backslash characters (\). The first backslash is followed by a two-letter token tag, which may be followed by optional parameters. Tokens can indicate anything from a font style change to a hypertext jump to another file to a command to embed a graphic. A short example helps to explain the format:

```
\fnArial\\sz12\This is an \fb1\example\fb0\ of a \ui23\tagged\ui\ text file.
```

In this example, the first token, *\fnArial\,* consists of the tag *fn,* which indicates a font style change, and the parameter *Arial,* which indicates the new font style. The second token, *\sz12\,* changes the font size to 12 points. The two tokens on either side of the word "example," \fb1\ and \fb0\, turn boldfacing on and off. The preceding example would be displayed as:

## This is an **example** of a tagged text file.

The last set of tokens, around the word "tagged," enable you to use this format for hypertext applications. The \ui23\ token sets a user ID tag for the text that follows, and the \ui\ token indicates the end of the tagged field. In hypertext mode, the word "tagged" becomes a hot spot that generates a *UserIDClicked* event. This event receives the ID, in this case the value 23, for the item that was clicked on, and can use this value to take appropriate action.

Another similar token is *uf,* which stands for "user file." This token lets you tag text with a file name. When the hot spot is clicked on, RavenWrite attempts to load the file into the control, replacing the existing text, and then generates a *UserFileClicked* event. This provides a simple method for moving from one hypertext file to another. Because the *UserFileClicked* event is generated even if the file cannot be loaded, the user file tag has an additional undocumented ability: you can use the tag to embed hidden text strings. The *UserFileClicked* event returns the hidden text string in its *ClickedFile* parameter. You can then process this string however you wish. You could use the text to update the text in a separate status line. For example, suppose you have this string of text:

```
This \ufHidden Text\is\uf\ a test.
```

This sentence would be displayed as

### This is a test

with the word "is" as a tagged field. Clicking on the word "is" fires a *UserFileClicked* event. This event receives the string "Hidden Text" in its *ClickedFile* parameter. "Hidden Text" is not a valid file name, so no new file is loaded and you can use the *ClickedFile* string for your own purposes.

**Reading and Writing Text**  If you want to read text into or extract text from the RavenWrite control, you must use the Windows API *SendMessage* function, and you should have some previous understanding of Windows messages. RavenWrite defines two messages, RWM_GETDATA and RWM_SETDATA, and a special data structure that holds the window handles to the data.

If you don't need to access the formatting of a document, and just need to access the text, you can use the *SelectStart* and *SelectEnd* properties to select a region of text, and then inspect the text by evaluating the contents of the *SelectText* property.

# Example

The example program shown in Figure 3-4 administers and scores tests. Information about each question is stored in a separate file in the tagged text format. You can create and edit these files with any text editor; Windows Notepad was used to create the sample questions.

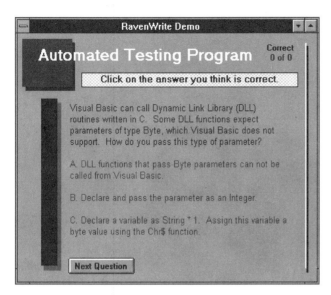

**Figure 3-4** The RavenWrite example program

Questions are in multiple-choice format, with each answer tagged as a separate hypertext field with its own ID. To simplify program processing, each tag value is "intelligent." It contains information about what answer it refers to, and which answer is the correct answer. For example, a multiple-choice question might have three answers tagged 201, 202, and 203. The last digit of each number indicates the question: 1 for choice A, 2 for choice B, and so on. The digit in the hundreds column corresponds to the correct answer, and will be the same for all answers. In our example, this digit is 2, which means that the correct answer is B.

The example program also uses RavenWrite's format layering features. Formatting differences can be applied in "layers" within a document, and you can switch these layers simply by setting the numeric *Layer* property. The base layer, which is always numbered 0, is used for default formatting, with other layers overriding this default formatting. In the example, this feature is used to change the text color of the correct answer to white after the question is answered.

## Steps

1. Create a series of tagged text files, and name them TEST*nnn*.TXT, where *nnn* is the question number. Your first question file should be named TEST001.TXT. Use the hypertext tag ID scheme described earlier to designate the correct answer to the question. You can also use the text layering token, *ly,* to change the appearance of the correct answer. Any formatting attributes that fall between the \\*ly1*\\ and \\*ly0*\\ tokens are displayed only after an answer has been selected. You can accomplish this in the program code by setting the *Layer* property to 1, and resetting the *Layer* property to 0 before the

next question file is loaded. In the example, the font color is set to white, and boldfacing is turned on for answer B when layer 1 is active. The example program expects five questions, but you can easily change this by resetting the LAST_QUESTION constant in the program code. The tagged files should follow the format shown here:

```
\fnArial\\sz10\\fb0\\fc0000FF\This is the first question?
\fcFF0000\
\ui201\A. First incorrect answer.\ui\

\ui202\\ly1\\fcFFFFFF\\fb1\B. This answer is correct.\ly0\\ui\

\ui203\C. Second incorrect answer.\ui\
```

2. Create a new project called RAVENWRT.MAK. Add the RAVENW.VBX control to this project. Create a new form with the objects and properties described in Table 3-14. Save this form as RAVENWRT.FRM.

**Table 3-14** Objects and properties for the RavenWrite control

| OBJECT | PROPERTY | SETTING |
| --- | --- | --- |
| Form | FormName | frmRavenWrt |
| | BackColor | &H00FFFFFF& |
| | Caption | "RavenWrite Demo" |
| | Picture | (set at design time in Properties window) |
| Label | Name | lblStatusLine |
| | Alignment | 2 'Center |
| | BackColor | &H0080FFFF& |
| | BorderStyle | 1 'Fixed Single |
| | Caption | "Click on the answer you think is correct." |
| | FontSize | 9.75 |
| Label | Name | Label2 |
| | Alignment | 2 'Center |
| | BackStyle | 0 'Transparent |
| | Caption | "Correct" |
| Label | Name | lblScore |
| | Alignment | 2 'Center |
| | BackStyle | 0 'Transparent |
| | Caption | "0 of 0" |
| | ForeColor | &H000000FF& |
| RavenWrite | Name | Raven1 |
| | BackColor | &H00FFFFFF& |
| | BorderStyle | 0 'None |
| | ColumnSpacing | 0 |
| | FunctionBars | 0 'None |
| | Keyboard | 0 'False |

| OBJECT | PROPERTY | SETTING |
|---|---|---|
| | Layer | 0 |
| | Mode | 1 'Hot Link Mode |
| | OutlineAll | 0 'False |
| | Outlining | 0 'False |
| | Transparent | -1 'True |
| CommandButton | Name | btnNext |
| | Caption | "Next Question" |
| | Visible | 0 'False |
| CommandButton | Name | btnBegin |
| | Caption | "Begin" |

3. After creating the form, add the following code to its declarations section.

```
Option Explicit

'---------------------------------------------------
' Variables and constants used in the RavenWrite
' example.
'---------------------------------------------------

' Stores the default status line string.
Dim DefStatus As String

' This Boolean prevents the user from answering a question twice.
Dim QuestionAnswered As Integer

' How many questions have been asked,
' and how many were answered correctly?
Dim NumQuestions As Integer
Dim NumCorrect As Integer

' The total number of questions in the test.
Const LAST_QUESTION = 5
```

4. Add the following subroutines to the RAVENWRT.FRM form. This code processes the *UserIDClick* event when the user selects an answer by clicking on a hot spot. The ID value is evaluated to determine whether the answer is correct. The *Layer* property is changed to 1 to highlight the correct answer, and the score is updated.

When the user clicks on the Next Question button, a new tagged text file is loaded into the RavenWrite control. When all questions have been answered, the user is presented with his or her score, and the test can be started again.

```
Sub btnBegin_Click ()
'---------------------------------------------------
' Initialize variables needed to start the test,
' and load the first question.
'---------------------------------------------------

    btnNext.Visible = True
    btnBegin.Visible = False
```

*(continued on next page)*

*(continued from previous page)*

```vb
    QuestionAnswered = False
    lblScore = "0 of 0"

    ' Display default status line text.
    lblStatusLine = DefStatus

    ' Initialize score counters.
    NumCorrect = 0
    NumQuestions = 1

    ' Load first question.
    ChDir App.Path
    Raven1.OpenTagged = App.Path & "\test" & Format$(NumQuestions, "000") & ".txt"
End Sub

Sub btnNext_Click ()
'----------------------------------------------------
' Present the next test question.
'----------------------------------------------------

    ' Question has not yet been answered.
    QuestionAnswered = False
    NumQuestions = NumQuestions + 1

    ' Reset the text formatting to "base" layer.
    Raven1.Layer = 0

    ' Have we already asked the last question?
    If NumQuestions > LAST_QUESTION Then
        TestCompleted
    Else
        ' Load next question.
        ChDir App.Path
        Raven1.OpenTagged = App.Path & "\test" & Format$(NumQuestions, "000") & ".txt"
    End If
End Sub

Sub Form_Load ()
'----------------------------------------------------
' Save the default status line, and center the
' form on the screen.
'----------------------------------------------------

    DefStatus = lblStatusLine.Caption
    lblStatusLine.Caption = "Press BEGIN button to take the test."

    Me.Move (Screen.Width - Me.Width) \ 2, (Screen.Height - Me.Height) \ 2
End Sub

Sub Raven1_UserIDClicked (ClickedID As Long, StartIndex As Long, EndIndex As Long)
'----------------------------------------------------
' Determine if the selected answer is correct,
' tell the user, show him or her the correct answer,
' and update the score.
'----------------------------------------------------
Dim Correct As Integer
Dim Chosen As Integer
```

```
    ' Don't let the user answer a question twice.
    If QuestionAnswered Then
        lblStatusLine = "You have already answered this question."
        Beep
        Exit Sub
    End If
    QuestionAnswered = True

    ' Get the correct and chosen answers from the tag ID.
    Correct = (ClickedID \ 100)
    Chosen = ClickedID - (Correct * 100)

    ' Tell the user if he or she was correct.
    If Chosen = Correct Then
        lblStatusLine = "Correct!"
        NumCorrect = NumCorrect + 1
        lblScore = Format$(NumCorrect) & " of " & Format$(NumQuestions)
    Else
        lblStatusLine = "Incorrect. The correct answer was " & Chr$(Asc("A") + (Correct - 1)) & "."
    End If

    ' Update the score display.
    lblScore = Format$(NumCorrect) & " of " & Format$(NumQuestions)

    ' Show any formatting that's "hiding" in Layer 1.
    Raven1.Layer = 1

    ' If we're out of questions then show user his or her score and reset.
    If NumQuestions = LAST_QUESTION Then
        TestCompleted
    End If
End Sub

Sub TestCompleted ()
'-------------------------------------------------
' Reset to our starting state when test is over.
'-------------------------------------------------
    btnBegin.Visible = True
    btnNext.Visible = False
    lblStatusLine = "Test Completed. Final score: " & Format$(NumCorrect / NumQuestions, "##0%")
End Sub
```

# Tips and Comments

RavenWrite's tagged text file format makes it quite simple to develop hypertext applications, and to modify them on the fly with no more than a conventional text editor. You could easily extend our example program into a full-featured testing application, with little more than the RavenWrite control and a bit of work.

RavenWrite's support for text format "layering" also presents a wealth of possibilities. You can use this feature to make text disappear by setting its color to the background color. Using RavenWrite's layering and hypertext abilities, you can quickly begin building a variety of hypertext-based applications.

# VBViewer (MHVIEW.VBX)

| USAGE: | Multi-Format File Viewing |
|---|---|
| MANUFACTURER: | MicroHelp, Inc. |
| COST: | $99 |

The popularity of personal computers has led to the development of a huge number of commercial software packages. These software packages need to store their data on disk in an efficient way, so along with this wave of software has come an explosion in the number of file formats. Some of these formats have become standards. Other vendors must support that to remain competitive. Developers must also contend with myriad file formats. That is what VBViewer is geared for: automatically detecting and displaying the content of files. VBViewer recognizes several word processing, database, spreadsheet, file compression, and graphics file formats. It can also automatically receive and display files dropped from the Windows File Manager.

## Syntax

VBViewer consists of a control (.VBX) and multiple dynamic link libraries (.DLLs); each DLL handles the translation of a different file format. If you only need to support a single file format, you can just distribute its DLL and the VBX. The nonstandard properties and events used by VBViewer are listed in Table 3-15.

**Table 3-15** Nonstandard properties and events for the VBViewer control

### PROPERTIES

| AutoFileType | BevelStyle | BevelWidth |
|---|---|---|
| BorderColor | BorderStyle | DropFiles |
| DroppedCount | DroppedFiles | FileName |
| FileType | FillColor | FindCase |
| FindString | hWndView | LightColor |
| ScreenUpdate | SearchDialog | SearchHelp |
| ShadowColor | TextColor | TotalBytes |

### EVENTS

| ErrorLoad | FileChange | FileDrop |
|---|---|---|
| SearchHelp | SearchRequest | SearchResult |
| ViewerFormatSet | ViewNotFound | |

When using VBViewer, you must first decide what type of file your application will be displaying. The *FileType* property lets you pick the supported file type by setting an integer value. Table 3-16 shows the supported types along with their *FileType* values.

**Table 3-16** Values for the FileType property

| VALUE | MEANING |
|---|---|
| 0 | Automatically detect file type |
| 1 | ASCII text |
| 2 | Hexadecimal |
| 3 | Graphics (.BMP, .GIF, .ICO, .PCX, .TIF, .WMF) |
| 4 | Icon files |
| 5 | Microsoft Word/Microsoft Write |
| 6 | WordPerfect |
| 7 | AMI |
| 8 | dBASE |
| 9 | Paradox |
| 10 | Lotus |
| 11 | Excel |
| 12 | Lotus .WK3 spreadsheets |
| 13 | .ZIP compressed files |
| 14 | .LZH compressed files |
| 15 | Quattro Pro for Windows |
| 16 | Windows .WAV sound files |
| 17 | Windows Meta Files |
| 18 | Q&A for Windows |
| 19 | Q&A for DOS |
| 20 | Microsoft Works documents |
| 21 | Microsoft Works databases |

File type 0, which is the default, is appropriate for generic file browsing utilities or applications where multiple formats are supported. Once the file type is set, you load a file by assigning a name to the *FileName* property. If the file is found, its contents are automatically displayed in the VBViewer control.

If *FileType* is set to automatic detection (a value of 0), the *ViewerFormatSet* event is called after the actual file type is determined but before the file is displayed. This event allows you to change the *FileType* property to a generic file type such as ASCII or Hexadecimal and prevent VBViewer from using a particular viewer. This feature would be useful, for example, in a utility that displayed files in hex format, but was intelligent enough to display text files in ASCII format.

**Error Detection and Handling**   If an error occurs while VBViewer is loading a file, the *ErrorLoad* event is fired and an *ErrorCode* parameter is passed to the event routine. The common file loading errors are shown in Table 3-17.

**Table 3-17** Possible ErrorCode values passed to the ErrorLoad event

| VALUE | MEANING |
|-------|---------|
| 1 | Display DLL not found |
| 2 | Unable to create viewer window |
| 3 | Incorrect file format |
| 4 | Name refers to a subdirectory, not a file |
| 259 | File not found |

If a file can't be loaded because a particular Viewer DLL is not available, VBViewer fires a *ViewerNotFound* event. This event is passed a *FileType* parameter that indicates which type of file caused the error. In the event routine, the *FileType* property (not the parameter) can be changed to a "generic" viewer type, such as ASCII or Hexadecimal, to display the file.

**Loading Files Using File Manager** The Boolean *DropFiles* property lets VBViewer automatically load files dragged from the Windows File Manager. Setting *DropFiles* to *False* disables this feature. When files are dragged from File Manager and dropped over the VBViewer control, the first file in the group is loaded automatically.

The *DroppedFiles* property array contains the names of the files the user dropped; the *DropCount* property contains the number of files.

**Working with Files** Once a file is loaded, you can determine its type using the *AutoFileType* property. This read-only property returns integers that correspond to the *FileType* values shown in Table 3-16, except that with *AutoFileType,* a value of 0 means that no file is currently loaded.

**File Searching** The user can scroll through or search text-oriented files. When your program assigns the *SearchDialog* property a text string, a Find dialog appears with the assigned text highlighted in a Find What text box. The user clicks the Find Next button, and the control highlights the text in the VBViewer control while the Search dialog box remains persistently on top. This allows the user to repeatedly press the Find Next button while seeing the results of the search in the window underneath.

If you prefer to create your own Find dialog, or want more control over your search functions, use the *FindString* property. Assign a string to this property and the VBViewer window scrolls forward to the next occurrence of the string. You can force *FindString* to start a search at the beginning of a file by first setting it to a null string (""), and then setting it to the desired search string.

The *FindCase* property determines whether a search is case-sensitive. When this property is set to *True,* searches must match strings exactly; when it's set to *False,* case is ignored. You can change this property with your program code, or the user can set the value by checking the Match Case check box on the Search Dialog box.

The beginning and end of each search is bracketed by two events, *SearchRequest* and *SearchResult. SearchRequest* is fired immediately after a search is initiated, by assigning a value to either the *FindString* property or the *SearchDialog* property. When a search is completed—either by finding the requested string or by reaching the end of the file—the *SearchResult* event is fired. This event is passed a *Found* parameter, which when *True* indicates that the search was successful.

**VBViewer Aesthetics** In design mode, a VBViewer control looks like an innocuous rectangle on your Visual Basic form. Figure 3-5 shows the VBViewer control used in the example program. You can give the control a 3D appearance with the *BevelStyle* (0 for a raised border, 1 for a lowered border) and *BevelWidth* properties. If *BevelWidth* is set to 0, the border has no 3D effect. You can control the shading color of the 3D effect using the *LightColor* and *ShadowColor* properties, so you needn't settle for dark gray shadows and white highlights.

You control the border itself with the *BorderStyle* and *BorderColor* properties. In addition to the standard style (no border or a single-line border), VBViewer provides a rounded-corner border style.

While the VBViewer's properties include the standard *ForeColor* and *BackColor*, you actually set the text and background colors using the special properties *TextColor* and *FillColor*. You should use these two properties in place of the standard properties, which have no visible effect on the control when set.

# Example

The example program is a general-purpose file viewer that can receive and view files from the Windows File Manager. The user can search for strings in file formats that support VBViewer's search features. Figure 3-6 shows the VBViewer example program.

To view multiple files using the Windows File Manager, select the files in File Manager, and then drag and drop them over the VBViewer control.

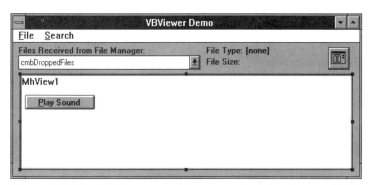

**Figure 3-5** The VBViewer example program showing the control at design time

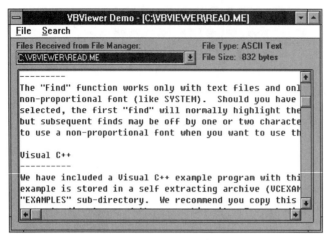

**Figure 3-6** The VBViewer example program

## Steps

1. Create a new project called VBVIEW.MAK. Add the Visual Basic Common Dialog control (CMDIALOG.VBX) and MicroHelp's VBViewer control (MHVIEW.VBX) to the project. Create a new form with the objects and properties shown in Table 3-18. Save this form as VBVIEW.FRM.

**Table 3-18** Objects and properties for VBVIEW.FRM

| OBJECT | PROPERTY | SETTING |
|--------|----------|---------|
| Form | FormName | frmVBView |
| | BackColor | &H00C0C0C0& |
| | Caption | "VBViewer Demo" |
| Label | Name | Label1 |
| | BackStyle | 0 'Transparent |
| | Caption | "File Type:" |
| | ForeColor | &H00000080& |
| Label | Name | lblFileType |
| | BackStyle | 0 'Transparent |
| | Caption | "[none]" |
| | ForeColor | &H00800000& |
| Label | Name | Label2 |
| | BackStyle | 0 'Transparent |
| | Caption | "File Size:" |
| | ForeColor | &H00000080& |
| Label | Name | lblFileSize |

| OBJECT | PROPERTY | SETTING |
|---|---|---|
|  | BackStyle | 0 'Transparent |
|  | ForeColor | &H00800000& |
| Label | Name | Label3 |
|  | BackStyle | 0 'Transparent |
|  | Caption | "Files Received from File Manager:" |
|  | ForeColor | &H00000080& |
| MhView | Name | MhView1 |
|  | BackColor | &H0080FFFF& |
|  | BevelWidth | 2 |
|  | BorderColor | &H80000006& |
|  | BorderStyle | 2 'Single Line with rounded corners |
|  | Caption | "MhView1" |
|  | DropFiles | -1 'True |
|  | FillColor | &H00FFFFFF& |
|  | ForeColor | &H00FFFFFF& |
|  | LightColor | &H00C0C0C0& |
|  | ScrollBars | 3 'Both |
|  | ShadowColor | &H80000010& |
|  | TextColor | &H00800000& |
| ComboBox | Name | cmbDroppedFiles |
|  | FontBold | 0 'False |
|  | Style | 2 'Dropdown List |
| CommonDialog | Name | CMDialog1 |
| CommandButton | Name | btnPlaySound |
|  | Caption | "&Play Sound" |
|  | Visible | 0 'False |

2. Add a menu to the VBVIEW.FRM form using the Visual Basic Menu Design window, setting the captions and names as shown in Table 3-19.

**Table 3-19** Menu definition for VBVIEW.FRM

| CAPTION | NAME |
|---|---|
| &File | mnuFile |
| − − − − &Open | mnuFileOpen |
| − − − − | mnuFileSep1 |
| − − − − E&xit | mnuFileExit |
| &Search | mnuSearch |

3. After creating the VBVIEW.FRM form, add the following code to its declarations section.

```
Option Explicit
'----------------------------------------------------
' Constants used by the VBViewer example program.
'----------------------------------------------------

' MsgBox Flags
Const MB_OK = &H0
Const MB_OKCANCEL = &H1
Const MB_ABORTRETRYIGNORE = &H2
Const MB_YESNOCANCEL = &H3
Const MB_YESNO = &H4

Const MB_ICONHAND = &H10
Const MB_ICONQUESTION = &H20
Const MB_ICONEXCLAMATION = &H30
Const MB_ICONASTERISK = &H40
Const MB_ICONINFORMATION = MB_ICONASTERISK
Const MB_ICONSTOP = MB_ICONHAND

' File Common Dialog constant
Const OFN_HIDEREADONLY = &H4
```

4. Add the following subroutines to the VBVIEW.FRM form. Make sure to put event code into the appropriate subroutines. This is the main program for the VBViewer demo; it contains all the code needed to create a generic file viewer using the VBViewer. Search features are implemented using VBViewer's built-in search dialog. This dialog is invoked through the *mnuSearch* menu event. Whenever files are received from File Manager, the *FileDrop* event updates the list in the *cmbDroppedFiles* combo box.

```
Sub btnPlaySound_Click ()
'----------------------------------------------------
' Forcing a change in the ScrollBars property
' causes the sound to play again.
'----------------------------------------------------
Dim CurFileName As String

    ' Cycle through possible scrollbar settings.
    MHView1.ScrollBars = (MHView1.ScrollBars + 1) Mod 4
End Sub

Sub cmbDroppedFiles_Click ()
'----------------------------------------------------
' Load the file selected from the combo box into
' the Viewer.
'----------------------------------------------------
    MHView1.FileName = cmbDroppedFiles.Text
End Sub

Sub Form_Load ()
'----------------------------------------------------
' Center the form on the screen.
'----------------------------------------------------
    Me.Move (Screen.Width - Me.Width) \ 2, (Screen.Height - Me.Height) \ 2
End Sub
```

```
Sub Form_Resize ()
'----------------------------------------------------
' Adjust the size of the Viewer to the size of the
' Window.
'----------------------------------------------------
    ' Don't resize controls if window is being minimized.
    If WindowState = 1 Then Exit Sub

    ' Don't allow the window to shrink too small.
    If (Me.Width < (150 * Screen.TwipsPerPixelX)) Then
        Me.Width = 150 * Screen.TwipsPerPixelX
    End If
    If (Me.Height < (150 * Screen.TwipsPerPixelY)) Then
        Me.Height = 150 * Screen.TwipsPerPixelY
    End If

    ' Adjust Viewer size.
    MHView1.Move MHView1.Left, MHView1.Top, Me.ScaleWidth - (MHView1.Left * 2), Me.ScaleHeight
- MHView1.Top - MHView1.Left
End Sub

Sub MhView1_ErrorLoad (ErrorCode As Integer)
'----------------------------------------------------
' If an error occurs while loading a file, display
' an appropriate error message.
'----------------------------------------------------
Dim ErrMsg As String

    Select Case ErrorCode
        Case 259: ErrMsg = "File Not Found."
        Case 1: ErrMsg = "Can't find display DLL."
        Case 2: ErrMsg = "Can't create viewer window."
        Case 3: ErrMsg = "Can't view this file."
        Case 4: ErrMsg = "Can't view this subdirectory."
        Case Else: ErrMsg = "Error No. " & Format$(ErrorCode) & " occurred while trying to load
file."
    End Select
End Sub

Sub MhView1_FileChange ()
'----------------------------------------------------
' Update controls and properties when a new file
' is loaded.
'----------------------------------------------------
    ' Set the default font to use with this viewer.
    MHView1.FontName = "FIXEDSYS"
    MHView1.FontBold = False
    MHView1.FontSize = 9

    ' Searching is enabled unless we override below.
    mnuSearch.Enabled = True

    ' Set the scroll bar with special consideration for
    ' Sound Files.
    If MHView1.AutoFileType  16 Then
        MHView1.ScrollBars = 3 'Both vertical and horizontal
    End If
```

*(continued on next page)*

*(continued from previous page)*

```
    ' Make sure the Play Sound button is hidden.
    btnPlaySound.Visible = False

    ' Set information related to specific file types.
    Select Case MHView1.AutoFileType
        Case 0: lblFileType = "[No File]"
        Case 1: lblFileType = "ASCII Text"
        Case 2: lblFileType = "Hexidecimal"
        Case 3: lblFileType = "Graphic"
                mnuSearch.Enabled = False
        Case 4: lblFileType = "Icon"
                mnuSearch.Enabled = False
        Case 5: lblFileType = "MS Word/Write Document"
        Case 6: lblFileType = "WordPerfect Document"
        Case 7: lblFileType = "AMI Document"
        Case 8: lblFileType = "dBASE Database"
        Case 9: lblFileType = "Paradox Database"
        Case 10: lblFileType = "Lotus Spreadsheet"
                mnuSearch.Enabled = False
        Case 11: lblFileType = "Excel Spreadsheet"
                mnuSearch.Enabled = False
        Case 12: lblFileType = "Lotus (WK3) Spreadsheet"
                mnuSearch.Enabled = False
        Case 13: lblFileType = "ZIP Compressed"
        Case 14: lblFileType = "LZH Compressed"
        Case 15: lblFileType = "Quattro Pro (Win) Spreadsheet"
                mnuSearch.Enabled = False
        Case 16: lblFileType = "Windows Sound File"
                mnuSearch.Enabled = False
                btnPlaySound.Visible = True
        Case 17: lblFileType = "Windows Meta File"
                mnuSearch.Enabled = False
        Case 18: lblFileType = "Q&A for Windows"
                mnuSearch.Enabled = False
        Case 19: lblFileType = "Q&A for DOS"
                mnuSearch.Enabled = False
        Case 20: lblFileType = "MS Works Document"
        Case 21: lblFileType = "MS Works DataBase"
        Case Else: lblFileType = "Unknown File Type"
    End Select

    lblFileSize = Format$(FileLen(MHView1.FileName), "#,###,##0") & " bytes"

    ' Update the caption with the new file name.
    Caption = "VBViewer Demo - [" & MHView1.FileName & "]"
End Sub

Sub MhView1_FileDrop (Cancel As Integer)
'-------------------------------------------------
' When a new group of files is loaded into the
' Viewer, list them in the combo box.
'-------------------------------------------------
Dim i As Integer

    cmbDroppedFiles.Clear
    ' Load all the new file names received from File Manager.
    For i = 0 To MHView1.DroppedCount - 1
        cmbDroppedFiles.AddItem MHView1.DroppedFiles(i)
    Next
    cmbDroppedFiles.ListIndex = 0
```

```
End Sub

Sub MhView1_SearchResult (Found As Integer)
'--------------------------------------------------
' If no more matches are found, show a message and
' force the Find window closed with SendKeys.
'--------------------------------------------------
    If Not Found Then
        MsgBox "No more occurrences found", MB_OK Or MB_ICONEXCLAMATION, "Search for '" &
MHView1.FindString & "'"
        SendKeys "%{F4}", True
    End If
End Sub

Sub mnuFileExit_Click ()
'--------------------------------------------------
' Exit the program.
'--------------------------------------------------
    Unload Me
End Sub

Sub mnuFileOpen_Click ()
'--------------------------------------------------
' Use the common dialog to get a new file to load
' into the Viewer.
'--------------------------------------------------
Dim Canceled As Integer

    Canceled = False
    On Error GoTo mnuFileOpen_Error

    CMDialog1.DialogTitle = "Select a File"
    CMDialog1.Flags = OFN_HIDEREADONLY
    CMDialog1.Filter = "All Files (*.*) | *.*"
    CMDialog1.Action = 1
    If Not Canceled Then
        cmbDroppedFiles.Clear
        MHView1.FileName = CMDialog1.Filename
    End If

mnuFileOpen_Error:
    If Err = 32755 Then Canceled = True
    Resume Next
End Sub

Sub mnuSearch_Click ()
'--------------------------------------------------
' Start a search at the beginning of the file.
'--------------------------------------------------
Dim PrevString As String

    ' Save previous search text.
    PrevString = MHView1.FindString

    ' This ensures the search starts at top of file.
    MHView1.FindString = ""

    ' This initiates the search.
    MHView1.SearchDialog = PrevString
End Sub
```

## Tips and Comments

While the example shows how you can use VBViewer as a generic file viewer, other applications may only need a subset of its capabilities. For example, you could create a word processing document manager that would allow text searching on Word, Write, WordPerfect, AMI, and Works documents.

When working with VBViewer, make sure you provide error-handling for missing Viewer DLLs. VBViewer provides an easy method for handling these occurrences with the *ViewerNotFound* event.

# CONTROL LIBRARIES

Many manufacturers bundle several Visual Basic controls together. Some of these control libraries are designed to serve a specific purpose, while others are a hodgepodge of Widgets. In either case, these libraries are often convenient and cost-effective alternatives to individual controls.

Most of the libraries covered in this chapter are collections of Widgets. Some control libraries that concentrate on a special purpose are covered in other chapters. For example, Sheridan's Data Widgets is covered in Chapter 11, which discusses databases.

For the most part, the libraries described here are designed to improve the appearance of your applications. You'll find everything from 3D check boxes to playing card controls. Somewhere in between, you'll certainly find the solution to one of your programming problems.

▲ **3D Controls**  This set of controls, which comes with Visual Basic 3.0 Professional, includes 3D replacements for the standard option button, check box, command button, and frame control.

▲ **3-D Widgets**  This package of three VBXs includes enhanced list and combo boxes, file and drive lists, and an enhanced menu control.

▲ **CCF-Cursors**  This combination of a dynamic link library (DLL) and a custom control lets you create custom and animated Visual Basic mouse pointers. It also provides special functions for manipulating the cursor.

▲ **Custom Control Factory**  The Custom Control Factory lets you design and create your own widget-style controls.

▲ **Designer Widgets**  This bundled set of three controls includes a dockable toolbar; an index tab control; and a control that lets you add special effects to a form's caption, border, and client areas.

▲ **QuickPak Professional for Windows**  This set of over 30 controls and 400 functions provides everything from standard dialog controls to calendar controls.

▲ **VBTools 4.0**  This is another large set of over 50 controls, ranging from histograms to circular dials to a control that implements Windows callback functions.

▲ **WsHelp**  This set of controls provides several different forms of context-sensitive help, including balloon help, pop-up help activated by mouse clicks, and status bar help when the mouse moves over a control.

▲ **Aware/VBX**  This set of 13 controls includes a memo control that handles large amounts of text, a data-aware Alarm clock, and an enhanced masked edit control.

> Sample programs featuring these libraries are included on the CD included with this book. Due to their length, however, the code for these samples will not appear in this chapter.

# 3D Controls (THREED.VBX)

| | |
|---|---|
| USAGE: | Provides 3D Replacements for Standard Controls |
| MANUFACTURER: | Sheridan Software Systems, Inc. |
| COST: | Provided with Visual Basic 3.0 Professional Edition |

This set of six controls provides 3D replacements for the standard option button, check box, command button, and frame controls. In addition, it provides a versatile 3D panel control that can serve as a toolbar, status line, or percent meter indicator.

## Syntax

You can use these six controls to give a 3D appearance to an application. Most of these controls are designed to be placed on a light gray background.

**3D Option Button and 3D Check Box**   The 3D Option Button and 3D Check Box controls, SSOption and SSCheck, are replacements for the standard Windows option button and check box. Table 4-1 shows the nonstandard properties and event for the 3D Check Box, and Table 4-2 shows the nonstandard properties and events for the 3D Option Button. The only noteworthy difference is the *Font3D* property, which is common to most of these controls. (The 3D Group Push Button control has no *Caption* property, so it has no need for the *Font3D* property.) This property determines the type of 3D shading effect used to display the *Caption* text. These controls can be displayed with heavy or light shading, and with either an inset or raised appearance.

**Table 4-1** Nonstandard properties and event of the 3D Check Box control

| PROPERTIES | |
|---|---|
| Alignment | Font3D |
| **EVENT** | |
| Click | |

**Table 4-2** Nonstandard properties and events of the 3D Option Button control

| PROPERTIES | |
|---|---|
| Alignment | Font3D |
| **EVENTS** | |
| Click | DblClick |

**3D Frame**   The 3D Frame control, SSFrame, is a replacement for the standard Frame control. Table 4-3 lists this control's nonstandard properties. In addition to the *Font3D* property, this control provides an *Alignment* property for setting the position of

4 ◀

the text caption at the top of the frame. You can change the 3D appearance of the frame border by setting the *ShadowColor* property to either dark gray (the default) or black, and by setting the *ShadowStyle* property to either inset (the default) or raised.

**Table 4-3** Nonstandard properties of the 3D Frame control

| | | |
|---|---|---|
| Alignment | Font3D | ShadowColor |
| ShadowStyle | | |

### 3D Group Push Button

**3D Group Push Button**  Table 4-4 lists the 3D Group Push Button's nonstandard properties and event. The 3D Group Push Button, SSRibbon, provides a way to simulate the toolbar buttons found in many current Windows applications. For example, both Microsoft Excel and Microsoft Word place this style of button on their toolbars to indicate the font style of the currently selected text. Three buttons represent the three possible styles: bold, italic, and underline. Each of these buttons can be in the up position, indicating that the option is not in effect, or in the down position, indicating that the option is active. These buttons can also be in a disabled state, indicating that an option is not available.

**Table 4-4** Nonstandard properties and event of the 3D Group Push Button control

| PROPERTIES | | |
|---|---|---|
| AutoSize | BevelWidth | GroupAllowAllUp |
| GroupNumber | Outline | PictureDisabled |
| PictureDn | PictureDnChange | PictureUp |
| PictureCorners | | |
| **EVENT** | | |
| Click | | |

The 3D Group Push Button does not provide a *Caption* property, so the purpose of the button is determined by the picture displayed on the button's face. There are four properties for defining the bitmap displayed on the button, *PictureUp, PictureDn,* and *PictureDisabled.* Each are assigned a bitmap name, and determine the button's appearance when it is in the up position, down position, or has been disabled, respectively. A fourth property, *PictureDnChange*, determines how the button appears in the down position if no bitmap has been specified in the *PictureDn* property.

The *GroupNumber* property determines how multiple 3D Group Push Buttons act on a form or within a frame. Buttons with the same *GroupNumber* property can act much like normal Windows option buttons: When one is selected all other buttons in the same group are deselected. This property makes it easy to program mutually exclusive options. Unlike conventional Windows options buttons, 3D Group Push Buttons can be set so that *all* buttons are deselected. You accomplish this with the *GroupAllowAllUp* property, which when set to *True* allows all buttons to be in the up position.

**3D Command Button**   The 3D Command Button, SSCommand, operates almost identically to a conventional Windows command button, but the button can display its text in different colors and with a 3D effect, and the button face can display a bitmapped picture. Table 4-5 lists its nonstandard properties.

**Table 4-5**  Nonstandard properties of the 3D Command Button control

| AutoSize | BevelWidth | Font3D |
|---|---|---|
| Outline | Picture | RoundedCorners |

Use the *Picture* property of the 3D Command Button to assign a bitmap, in either BMP or ICO format, to the control. This picture appears centered above any text specified with the button's *Caption* property. You can use an *AutoSize* property to either scale the picture to the size of the button or scale the button to the size of the bitmap. By default, no scaling is performed.

You can use the *BevelWidth* property to vary the raised 3D effect around the outer edge of the 3D Command Button. You can vary this property from 0 to 10. Values outside of this range cause trappable run-time error 30004.

**3D Panel**   Table 4-6 lists the nonstandard properties of the 3D Panel, SSPanel. As a container for other controls, the 3D Panel works in the same fashion as a frame control: Controls placed on the panel's surface have *Left* and *Top* properties relative to the upper-left corner of the 3D Panel. This control can also serve as a progress meter gauge.

**Table 4-6**  Nonstandard properties of the 3D Panel control

| Alignment | AutoSize | BevelInner |
|---|---|---|
| BevelOuter | BevelWidth | BorderWidth |
| FloodColor | FloodPercent | FloodShowPct |
| FloodType | Font3D | Outline |
| RoundedCorners | ShadowColor | |

When you set the *FloodType* property to a valid value greater than 0 (shown in Table 4-7), you can use the 3D Panel as a percentage meter to show how much of a process has completed. For example, you could indicate the percentage complete of a disk copy process or the percent of hard disk space available. There are two basic meter styles: bar graph or widening circle. When you use the 3D panel as a percentage meter display, the interior of the panel is painted with a colored bar or circle indicating a percentage. Change the value of the *FloodPercent* property to adjust this painted section of the control. *FloodPercent* values must be between 0 and 100; values outside that range trigger trappable run-time error 30006.

**Table 4-7** 3D Panel's FloodType property values

| VALUE | MEANING |
| --- | --- |
| 0 | No percentage meter is displayed, use as 3D frame |
| 1 | Percentage is displayed as a bar that expands from left to right |
| 2 | Percentage is displayed as a bar that expands from right to left |
| 3 | Percentage is displayed as a bar that expands from top to bottom |
| 4 | Percentage is displayed as a bar that expands from bottom to top |
| 5 | Percentage is displayed as an expanding filled circle |

The *FloodShowPct* property is a Boolean value that determines whether the current percentage value is displayed at the center of the control. The *FloodColor* property determines the color of the painted bar or circle; the default color is bright blue.

You can change the panel border's appearance by adjusting the three bevel properties—*BevelInner, BevelOuter,* and *BevelWidth*, and the *BorderWidth* property.

# Example

The example program, shown in Figure 4-1, uses the 3D Controls in a variety of ways to demonstrate how they provide a 3D effect.

The program uses five 3D Panels to illustrate the basic uses of this versatile control.

The first panel, sspanToolBar, is positioned directly below the window's title bar, and runs the entire width of the window. This panel is a container for other controls, in this case the alignment buttons and the Use 3D Fonts check box. A second panel was placed behind the alignment buttons to give them a 3D raised appearance.

The third panel, sspanStatusLine, is positioned at the bottom of the window. By setting its *Caption* property, you can have it serve as a simple status bar. By using the *Align* property, you can automatically position the panel at the top or bottom of the window. When the window is resized, the panel will then automatically expand or contract to match the new window size.

**Figure 4-1** The 3D Controls demo program

The fourth panel, sspanBarMeter, displays a percentage meter near the bottom of the window. The program changes this control's *FloodType* property to change the style used to graphically display the percentage. In the example, the user selects a different *FloodType* from the set of 3D Option Buttons and presses the Run button to make the sspanBarMeter and sspanCircleMeter controls cycle from 0 to 100 percent.

Another 3D Panel is placed on top of the sspanToolBar control, surrounding the 3D Group Push Buttons. This panel was placed solely to provide a 3D raised effect to the group of buttons.

The user sets the 3D Group Push Buttons to select the alignment of the text in the status bar. Note that the *GroupAllowAllUp* property has been set to *False*, so at least one button must be in the down position.

## Tips and Comments

Because the 3D Command Button lacks the *Default* and *Cancel* properties of the standard Windows command button, you can't use it when you need to emulate the exact functionality of the standard command button.

The 3D Panel is one of the few controls that you can place within the client area of an MDI form (another is the Picture control). While the appearance and function of the control are quite versatile, it processes only two events: *DragDrop* and *DragOver*. The absence of either a *Click* or *DblClick* event is a shortcoming. A workaround is to place a Label control—with its *BackStyle* property set to 0 (transparent) and no *Caption* string— over the Panel control. The Label can then be used to process events for the 3D Panel.

# 3-D Widgets

| USAGE: | 3D Enhancements and Additions to Standard Controls |
|---|---|
| MANUFACTURER: | Sheridan Software Systems, Inc. |
| COST: | $109 |

This is a package of three VBXs, called 3-D Widgets/1, 2, and 3. 3-D Widgets/1 is essentially the same as the THREED.VBX controls that come with Visual Basic 3.0 Professional Edition. 3-D Widgets/2 contains five controls: 3D replacements for the list box, combo box, file list box, directory list box, and drive list box. 3-D Widgets/3 contains an enhanced menu control. Each of these controls provides new capabilities beyond their ability to display 3D effects.

## Syntax

Since 3-D Widgets/1 was covered in the earlier section on THREED.VBX, this section covers the capabilities of the other two VBXs. Each control's object name is prefaced by an *SS,* which distinguishes it as a Sheridan Systems control.

The 3-D Widgets/2 controls, which are all variations on list or combo boxes, share many common properties and events. This makes them easier to learn, as they tend to act in a consistent manner.

**SSList Control**   The SSList control replaces the standard Visual Basic list box. Its nonstandard properties and event are listed in Table 4-8. You can use this control to create multicolumn list boxes, with pictures assigned to individual list items. The control features built-in search capabilities, the ability to set hard and soft tabs, and scroll events that allow you to "synchronize" the scrolling of multiple list boxes.

**Table 4-8** Nonstandard properties and event for SSList

**PROPERTIES**

| | | |
|---|---|---|
| (About) | (TabsSettings) | AllowForPicture |
| BorderStyle | Case | ColumnWidth |
| DividerStyle | EmptyList | FindFirst |
| FindNext | Font3D | Hwnd |
| IntegralSize | LastAdded | LastFound |
| LastReplaced | ListIndexMulti | ListStyle |
| MultiColumn | Picture | RefreshOnUpdate |
| ScrollHorizontal | ScrollVertical | SelectCount |
| Selected | SelectionType | ShadowColor |
| TabCharacter | TabPos | TabScale |
| TabType | TopIndex | |

**EVENT**

TopIndexChange

A nice feature of SSList is its *IntegralSize* property. This Boolean property, when set to *False,* allows the last list box entry to be clipped. When it's set to *True*, the default, SSList acts like a conventional list box, which is automatically shortened so that no list entries are obscured.

SSList also provides automatic searching capabilities through the *FindFirst, FindNext,* and *LastFound* properties. You assign *FindFirst* a string value, and then evaluate the *LastFound* property. If a match is found in the list box, *LastFound* is set to the index of the matching item; if no match is found, the property is set to -1. *FindNext* continues a search, and when assigned a string it searches beginning with the list item that follows the last match. Matches need not be exact; a match is any string that begins with the search string.

**SSCombo Control**   The SSCombo control replaces the standard Visual Basic combo box control. Like SSList, this control supports pictures for individual list items, item text searching, hard and soft tabs for list items, and a variety of 3D effects. The nonstandard properties supported by SSCombo are listed in Table 4-9.

**Table 4-9** Nonstandard properties of SSCombo

| (About) | (TabSettings) | AutoHScroll |
|---|---|---|
| Case | DividerStyle | EmptyList |
| FindFirst | FindNext | Font3D |
| Hwnd | Indent | LastAdded |
| LastFound | LastReplaced | ListStyle |
| MaxDropDnItems | ScrollVerticalShadowColor | TabCharacter |
| TabPos | TabScale | TabType |
| TextLimit | | |

SSCombo has a *TextLimit* property that allows you to limit the number of characters that the user can enter into the text box section of the control. This property works just like a conventional text control's *MaxLength* property. When *TextLimit* is set to 0, there is no preset limit to the number of characters.

The *MaxDropDnItems* property lets you set the number of items that are displayed when the drop-down list is shown. If there are more items in the list than can be shown, you can place an optional vertical scroll bar on the list by setting the *ScrollVertical* property to *True*.

**SSFile Control** The SSFile control replaces the conventional file list, which is used to show some or all of the files in a selected directory. This control is basically a specialized version of the SSList control, and shares many of the same properties and event, as shown in Table 4-10.

**Table 4-10** Nonstandard properties and event of SSFile

**PROPERTIES**

| (About) | BorderStyle | Case |
|---|---|---|
| ColumnWidth | DividerStyle | EmptyList |
| FileTypePics | FindFirst | FindNext |
| Font3D | Hwnd | IntegralSize |
| LastFound | ListIndexMulti | ListStyle |
| MultiColumn | ScrollHorizontal | ScrollVertical |
| SelectCount | Selected | SelectionType |
| ShadowColor | TopIndex | |

**EVENT**

TopIndexChange

The SSFile control improves upon the standard list box by allowing for multicolumn lists. The control also has the built-in ability to display file type graphics similar to those shown in the Windows File Manager file lists. SSFile also shares a unique ability with SSList and SSDir: The *BorderStyle* property allows you to add caption bars and sizable borders to these controls. This allows the user to move or resize these controls within a form at run time.

**SSDir Control**  SSDir replaces the standard Visual Basic directory list box. Table 4-11 shows its nonstandard properties and event. This control can indicate the presence of subdirectories; setting the *FlagSubDirs* property to *True* causes a plus sign (+) to be shown within the file graphic of any directory that contains other subdirectories.

**Table 4-11** Nonstandard properties and event of SSDir

### PROPERTIES

| | | |
|---|---|---|
| (About) | BorderStyle | Case |
| DividerStyle | EmptyList | FlagSubDirs |
| Font3D | Hwnd | IntegralSize |
| ListStyle | ScrollHorizontal | ScrollVertical |
| Selected | ShadowColor | TopIndex |

### EVENT

TopIndexChange

**SSDrive Control**  SSDrive is a replacement for the standard drive list control. Table 4-12 shows its nonstandard properties. This control lets you choose what types of drives to display in the drive list. By default, all types of drives are shown, but by setting the four *Drive* properties to *False* you can selectively exclude fixed, RAM, remote, or removable drives from the list.

**Table 4-12** Nonstandard properties for SSDrive

| | | |
|---|---|---|
| (About) | Case | DividerStyle |
| DriveFixed | DriveRam | DriveRemote |
| DriveRemovable | Font3D | Hwnd |
| ListStyle | MaxDropDnItems | |
| ScrollVertical | ShadowColor | |

**SSMenu**  The SSMenu control is a replacement for the standard Visual Basic menus. The only control in 3-D Widgets/3, its properties and events are shown in Table 4-13.

**Table 4-13** Nonstandard properties and events for SSMenu

### PROPERTIES

| | | |
|---|---|---|
| About | BevelDropdown | BevelSection |
| BevelTopMenu | DividerStyle | Font3D |
| SelectionStyle | ShadowColor | TopMenuStyle |
| TopPicAlignment | TopPicItemName | |
| TopPicture | | |

**EVENTS**

FunctionKeyPressed    ItemSelected

The SSMenu control radically changes the appearance of Visual Basic menus. The control is very simple to use; you simply place an instance of the SSMenu control on your form. This control is invisible at run time. You still design the form's menu in the conventional way, using the Visual Basic menu designer. At run time, the menu can display a variety of 3D effects and styles. You can change fonts, make menu options appear as buttons or 3D panels, add pictures to menu items, and add shading effects to fonts.

Menu processing is enhanced by the *ItemSelected* event, which is triggered when an item is highlighted, not just when it is clicked. This lets you easily add, for example, status line help when the user is moving through menu items.

# Example

The example program, shown in Figure 4-2, uses several of the controls from 3-D Widgets/2 and 3-D Widgets/3 to build a File Manager-style application. The 3D replacements for the drive list, directory list, and file list are particularly well-suited for the task, and the SSMenu control is included as well to show how it changes the appearance of conventional menus.

The example program is easy to use. Selecting a new drive affects the directory and file lists, and changing a directory affects the file list. The file list shows the multicolumn and picture features of the SSFile control. The View menu lets the user select between seeing all files and seeing just the executable files.

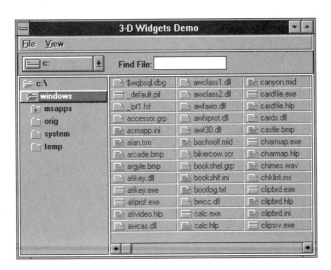

**Figure 4-2** The 3-D Widgets example program

To see the built-in searching features of the SSFile control, start typing a file name into the Find File text box. The matching file name in the file list is highlighted as you entered text. The program uses the *FindFirst* property to automatically search the file list in the text box's *Change* event.

## Tips and Comments

All the 3-D Widget controls do more than provide a 3D replacement for their standard Visual Basic counterparts. All add significant abilities that can warrant their inclusion in a project. As you saw in the example program, the multicolumn and picture abilities of the file list make it easy to begin building your own File Manager-style application. It would be a fairly simple exercise to extend the example to check file associations and launch the associated application, or to build support for the display of bitmap files.

 # CCF-Cursors

| USAGE: | Custom and Animated Mouse Pointers |
|---|---|
| MANUFACTURER: | Desaware |
| COST: | $35 |

One of the glaring deficiencies in Visual Basic is its poor support for cursors, which Visual Basic calls mouse pointers. Sure, you can set different cursors for controls, and Visual Basic will automatically change the cursor when it's positioned over that control. But beyond that, you have little control. Visual Basic gives you a stock set of 12 cursor shapes from which to choose. If none of these are to your liking, you're stuck. And that's where CCF-Cursors comes in. This package, which is a combination of dynamic link libraries (DLLs) and a Visual Basic control, lets you create and use your own cursors, as well as providing special functions for manipulating the cursor. You can even create animated cursors that appear to move, and convert existing icons into cursors.

## Syntax

CCF-Cursors can associate a custom cursor with just about any Visual Basic control or form. This cursor can be stored in a cursor file (in a special cursor file format, usually with a .CUR extension), or stored as a resource in an executable file (.EXE) or dynamic link library (.DLL). This means that you can design your own cursors with a Windows resource editor (such as Borland's Resource WorkShop), or "borrow" a cursor from another program or library.

Cursors are very much like Windows icons, but they can only include the three colors: black, white, and transparent. Cursors usually have the same dimensions as icons, 32x32 pixels. One unique feature of cursors is their *hot spot*—the point inside the cursor determines the precise location it is pointing to. With arrow pointers, for example, the hot spot is usually set to the tip of the arrow.

Using a custom cursor is basically a three-step process. First, you have to load the cursor from wherever it's stored. Then you have to associate, or set, the cursor to a particular Visual Basic control or form. Finally, when you're finished with a cursor, you may need to dispose of it so that it doesn't continue to eat up Windows system resources.

**Creating Cursors**   As mentioned, one way to create a cursor is to draw one using a resource editor and then save it to a file. CCF-Cursors provides another way. A program called Icon2Cur takes a Windows icon (.ICO) file and creates a cursor file. This program was written in Visual Basic, and full source code is provided. CCF-Cursors lets you convert icons to cursors in your program, on the fly, using the *dwCreateCursorFromIcon()* function. Any nonwhite colors in an icon are converted to black. Both the Icon2Cur program and the *dwCreateCursorFromIcon()* function let you set the hot spot location when saving the cursor.

**Loading Cursors**   Once a cursor has been created, you need to load it into the program so it can be used. How you load the cursor depends on whether it's stored in a file or as a resource inside another program or library.

If the cursor is in a .CUR file, loading is easy: Just call the *dwLoadCursorFile()* function. The following example shows the syntax for this call.

```
Dim ACursor as integer
ACursor = dwLoadCursorFile("C:\MYDIR\MYCURSOR.CUR")
```

The integer value returned by this function is a cursor handle. You can use this handle to set the cursors of more than one form or control. The function is passed the full file name of the cursor file to be loaded. If it can't find the file, or some other error occurs, the function returns a value of 0.

If you load a cursor from a file, you must remember to discard it properly when it's no longer needed. These cursors use Windows system resources, and unless you remember to clean up your old cursors, the resources they use will be lost until your user terminates the Windows session. Use the *dwDestroyCursor()* function to free the resources used by a cursor that was loaded from a file.

If a cursor is stored in another program, or in a dynamic link library, extracting it is a two-step process. First, you've got to find the module handle of the .EXE or .DLL that contains the cursor. CCF-Cursors provides dozens of cursors inside a library called CCFCURS.DLL. A special function, *dwGetCursorModule()*, returns the handle of this module. If you want to extract a cursor from another module, you can use the Windows API call *GetModuleHandle()*. Pass this function a valid file name of your .EXE or .DLL, and it will return the corresponding module handle. CCF-Cursors provides the function declaration for this and a number of other API calls in .BAS source file called CCFCURS.BAS.

Once the module handle has been retrieved, the second step is to get the handle to a cursor by calling the *dwLoadCursorByNum()* function. The one catch is that you need to know the resource number of the desired cursor. If you have a resource editor such as Borland's Resource WorkShop, you can inspect executable files to view the various resources, including cursors, and note the resource numbers for any cursors you might want. For example, the following code extracts a cursor from Word for Windows 2.0.

```
Dim LibHandle As Integer
Dim ModuleName As String
Dim ACursor as integer

ModuleName = "c:\winword\winword.exe"
LibHandle = GetModuleHandle(ModuleName)
ACursor = LoadCursorByNum(LibHandle, 7)
```

### Associating a Cursor with a Form or Control

Now that the cursor is loaded, you want to be able to use it in your Visual Basic program. In standard Visual Basic, you do this by assigning a value to a control's *MousePointer* property, as in

```
Form1.MousePointer = 11
```

which sets the cursor to an hourglass.

To use CCF-Cursors, you must employ a different approach. To set the cursor for Form1 to a previously loaded cursor, use the *dwSetCursor()* or *dwSetHwndCursor()* function, as in this example.

```
Dim OldCursor as integer
Dim SetChildren as integer

SetChildren = True
OldCursor = dwSetCursor (Form1, ACursor, SetChildren)
```

In this example, the cursor *ACursor* becomes the default cursor for *Form1,* whenever the mouse pointer is over that form. The *SetChildren* parameter is a Boolean value used to indicate whether child controls placed on *Form1* should also use this cursor. If *SetChildren* is set to *True,* child controls will use *Form1*'s cursor unless they have specified their own cursor using the Visual Basic *MousePointer* property or CCF-Cursors.

The *dwSetHwndCursor()* function serves the same purpose as *dwSetCursor(),* but uses a slightly different syntax. In the preceding example, replace the last line with

```
OldCursor = dwSetHwndCursor (Form1.HWnd, ACursor, SetChildren)
```

These two functions can be used interchangeably. The only difference is that one takes a Form argument and the other takes an hWnd argument.

The return value from these functions, shown as *OldCursor* in the examples, is the handle of the previous cursor, if the cursor was set using CCF-Cursors. If it had not previously been set, or was set using the Visual Basic *MousePointer* property, the return value will be 0.

### Animating Cursors

Animated cursors can provide a dramatic visual impact and can help to draw the eye to a specific location on the screen. Animated cursors are just a set of two or more cursors that are displayed in sequence, with a slight time delay in between, like the frames in an animated cartoon. CCF-Cursors provides a set of hourglasses that are designed for this purpose. When animated, the hourglass appears to constantly rotate. With a resource editor, it's quite easy to draw your own animated cursors. Just create two or more cursors to serve as frames.

Once you've designed your set of "frame" cursors, either in cursor files or as a resource in a program or library, you simply load the cursors using the techniques described earlier. Load the cursor handles into an array, where each element of the array represents one frame of the cursor animation. Then simply call the *dwCreateAniCursor()* function, as in this example:

```
Dim AnimHandle as integer

For i=0 to 6
    MyAnim(i) = dwLoadCursorFile("ANIM" & Format$(i) & ".CUR")
Next
AnimHandle = dwCreateAniCursor(MyAnim(), 100)
```

This example loads seven cursors from the files ANIM0.CUR through ANIM6.CUR. The array of cursor handles, *MyAnim*, is then passed to the *dwCreateAniCursor()* function, along with an interval value (100 in the example) in milliseconds. This interval is the amount of delay inserted between the individual frames of the animation.

Once you've successfully loaded an animated cursor, you can assign it to a form or control just as you would any other cursor, using *dwSetCursor* or *dwSetHwndCursor*.

When you've finished using an animated cursor, you need to dispose of it properly so that you don't eat up system resources. CCF-Cursors has a special function, *dwDestroyAniCursor(),* just for this purpose.

**The CCMouse Control**   CCF-Cursors includes a special control, CCMOUSE.VBX, designed to detect mouse and menu events. To use the control, drag an instance of it from the Visual Basic toolbox into a form. This control displays as a small icon that is invisible at run time. The nonstandard properties and events of CCMouse are listed in Table 4-14.

**Table 4-14** Nonstandard properties and events of the CCMouse control

| PROPERTIES | | |
| --- | --- | --- |
| hWndParam | ControlParam | PostEvent |
| NoMouseEvents | | |
| **EVENTS** | | |
| DelayedEvent | MenuSelect | MenuChar |
| WndMouseUp | WndMouseDown | WndMouseMove |
| WndDblClick | | |

At run time, you associate a CCMouse control with a form or control using the *hWndParam* property. Part of the power of CCMouse is that it can detect mouse events for controls that don't support mouse events on their own. Assign the *hWnd* parameter of the form or control you want to link to CCMouse, as shown below.

```
CCMouse1.hWndParam=Form1.hWnd
```

Four events, *WndMouseUp()*, *WndMouseDown()*, *WndMouseMove()*, and *WndDblClick()*, similar to the like-named Visual Basic events, provide feedback on mouse movement.

If you want to intercept detailed information on menu items, CCMouse gives you what you need. The *MenuSelect* event is triggered whenever you select a menu item, not just when you click on it. The event is declared as

```
MenuSelect (MenuName As String, Position As Integer, MenuFlags As Integer)
```

*MenuName* is the string for the current menu item, including any embedded ampersands (for example, &File). *Position* is the displacement of the selected item from the top of the current menu, where the first item is 0. *MenuFlags* is an integer containing additional information such as whether the current menu item is disabled, grayed, part of a pop-up menu, or part of the system menu.

# Example

The example program, shown in Figure 4-3, builds the framework for a graphical equipment inventory system. A floor plan is displayed, with equipment items shown as icons within different rooms. Moving the cursor around the floor plan changes the cursor: When it is inside an office, it appears as a large arrow; when it is in the hallway, it

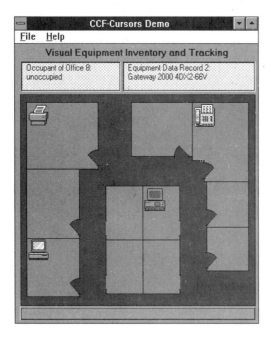

**Figure 4-3** The CCF-Cursors example program

looks like an international "not" symbol; and when it is over an equipment icon, it turns into an animated, grasping hand.

You can drag items from room to room by holding down the left mouse button while over an item, and then moving it to a new location. You cannot move items to an invalid location; if you try, they jump back to their original office.

Also notice that you cannot drag an item outside the floor plan area. This is accomplished using the CCF-Cursors *dwClipCursor()* function, which can restrict the movement of the cursor to a rectangular area within a specified window or control.

The example uses one CCMouse control to get feedback on mouse movements while moving equipment items. Another CCMouse control gets menu information, in particular the name of the current menu option, that is displayed on the bottom status line.

## Tips and Comments

The example shows how custom cursors can improve the appearance of an application and make it more intuitive to use at the same time. With the framework provided on the CD, you could begin to build your own visual inventory system. The use of icons for items provides immediate feedback for the location of items, and the custom cursors supply constant visual cues telling you what can be moved and where.

CCF-Cursors includes a number of routines not covered here in detail, including routines to set the position of the cursor to a specific location on the screen, and the ability to extract cursors stored in controls created with Desaware's Custom Control Factory.

# Custom Control Factory (CCBUTTON.VBX)

| USAGE: | MultiState/Animated Buttons, Toolbar Buttons |
|---|---|
| MANUFACTURER: | Desaware |
| COST: | $48 |

Desaware's Custom Control Factory (CCF) looks, at first glance, as if it should be classified as an enhanced button right alongside the animated button control that comes with the Professional Edition of VB. (In fact, the animated button was derived from CCF.) However, this control is more powerful than ANIBUTON.VBX with advanced features such as 3D bevels and picture compression.

## Syntax

The standard VB command button should help give you an idea how CCF buttons work. You can think of the standard command button as having two states: up and down. When you click on the button, the picture changes from the up picture to the down picture and back to up again. Custom Control Factory button controls work the same way, sort of. A CCF button can have as many pictures as you want and it can display those pictures in any order. The pictures can be bitmaps, icons, or metafiles. Custom Control Factory buttons can also have a caption just like regular command buttons, but CCF offers more control over the appearance of the caption. There are 42 custom properties that give you control over every aspect of how the control operates. Here the properties are covered in functional groups. Table 4-15 lists the nonstandard properties and events for Custom Control Factory buttons.

**Table 4-15** Custom Control Factory nonstandard properties and events

### PROPERTIES

| | | |
|---|---|---|
| About | Alignment | CaptionMoveX |
| CaptionMoveY | cc3DBevel | cc3DBorder |
| cc3DDownFrame | cc3DHighlight | cc3DShadow |
| CCBFileLoad | CCBFileSave | ClearFirst |
| ClickFilter | ClickLocPic | ClickOnPress |
| Compression | Cycle | DontGreyText |
| Frame | FrameCount | HideFocusBox |
| HotX | HotY | ImageMoveX |
| ImageMoveY | MetaHeight | MetaWidth |
| MetaToDIB | OptionMode | PaletteFrame |
| PalettePicture | Picture | PictDrawMode |
| PictureXpos | PictureYpos | SpecialOp |
| Speed | SyncEnable | TextPosition |
| TextXpos | TextYpos | Value |

### EVENTS

| | |
|---|---|
| NextFrame | Sync |

**Oh Caption, My Caption!** There are a number of caption-related properties. The position of the caption is controlled by the *TextPosition*, *TextXPos*, and *TextYPos* properties. *TextPosition* defines the area where the caption appears relative to the picture on the control. The values for *TextPosition* are defined in Table 4-16.

**Table 4-16** TextPosition values

| VALUE | MEANING |
|---|---|
| 0 | Caption overlays the picture |
| 1 | Caption is placed to the right of the picture |
| 2 | Caption is placed to the left of the picture |
| 3 | Caption is placed above the picture |
| 4 | Caption is placed below the picture |

*TextXPos* and *TextYPos* define exactly where the caption appears within its defined area. They are both expressed as a percentage of how far the caption appears from the upper-left corner of its defined area. If both of these properties are set to 0, the caption appears in the upper-left corner of the caption area. If they are set to 100, the caption appears in the lower-right corner of the caption area. The *Alignment* property affects whether multiline captions are left-, center-, or right-aligned. Setting the *DontGreyText* property to *True* keeps the caption from being grayed when the button is disabled. Standard command buttons draw a focus rectangle around the caption when the button has the focus. CCF buttons allow you to override this behavior by setting the *HideFocusBox* property to *True*. When command buttons are pushed in, the caption is moved down and to the left slightly to make them looked pushed in. CCF buttons allow you to specify how far the caption moves in each direction by setting the *CaptionMoveX* and *CaptionMoveY* properties.

### Headin' for the Border

There are also several border-related properties. Most standard controls give you two choices: no border or a single black line. Once again, CCF buttons offer quite a bit more.

By default, CCF buttons are not 3D. To get the 3D effect you use the *cc3DBevel* property. The value of *cc3DBevel* defines the 3D bevel width. A value of 2 gives you the appearance of a standard command button, but you can set *cc3DBevel* to any value you want. You use *cc3DBorder* to reserve some space between the picture or caption and any bevel you might have specified. *cc3DHighlight* and *cc3DShadow* control the colors used to draw the bevel specified with *cc3DBevel*. You're not limited to the shades of gray used by standard controls. *cc3DHighlight* defines the color for the top and left bevels. *cc3DShadow* does the same for the bottom and right bevels.

### Get the Picture

Picture handling is really CCF buttons' forte. Some controls let you put a picture on them, but that's about it. Not CCF buttons. For example, *ImageMoveX* and *ImageMoveY* tell the button how far to move the picture when the button is pushed in. Set them to the same values as their caption counterparts to create a professional 3D appearance. Similarly, *PictureXpos* and *PictureYpos* parallel *TextXpos* and *TextYpos*, defining exactly where the picture appears in its defined area.

Bitmaps can take up a lot of space, so CCF buttons offer a *Compression* property that stores the bitmaps used on a CCF button in compressed format without any further intervention on your part. What's more, you can tell the Custom Control Factory button whether the bitmaps should be compressed in the forms but not in memory for better performance, or both in forms and memory for maximum space savings. *PictDrawMode* tells the CCF button if it should resize the picture to match the button, the button to match the picture, or not to resize anything. Table 4-17 shows the possible values for *PictDrawMode*.

**Table 4-17** PictDrawMode values

| VALUE | MEANING |
|---|---|
| 0 | Use PictureXPos and PictureYPos to position picture |
| 1 | Size CCF button to fit picture or caption |
| 2 | Stretch picture to fit the size of the CCF button |

CCF buttons support metafiles and provide some extra properties for dealing with them. Use *MetaHeight* and *MetaWidth* to specify the size of the metafile as a percentage of the picture area. By default, CCF buttons convert metafiles to bitmaps, (DIBs, or Device Independent Bitmaps to be precise), but by setting the *MetaToDIB* property to *False* you can force CCF buttons to keep the metafiles in their native format. Metafiles are slower to draw but generally take up less space than an equivalent bitmap. *MetaToDIB* doesn't have any effect when applied at run time; you have to specify it when you load pictures into the CCF button.

If you're displaying 256 color bitmaps, you will be glad to hear that CCF buttons give you some control over palettes—not a lot, but some. All frames in a CCF button use the same palette (remember, CCF buttons can have more than one picture), but you can choose which palette with the *PaletteFrame* property. Simply set *PaletteFrame* to the number of the frame whose palette you want the control to use. If you load a bitmap into the *PalettePicture* property, its palette is used by the control. This lets you create a bitmap that you can use specifically for its palette.

Each CCF button can hold more than one picture, although you can only view one picture at any given time. Each picture is referred to as a frame; frames shown in sequence can create the appearance of movement on the screen. CCF buttons allow you to specify in what order the frames should be shown. You can show all of them, some of them, or just one of them. It's up to you.

The *Picture* property acts like the standard *Picture* property found in many controls, but it is dependent on the *Frame* property to tell it which frame to put the current picture in. There is a special dialog (Figure 4-4) for adding pictures to frames. It appears when you select the *Frame* property from the Properties window at design time. From this dialog, you can load pictures into individual frames using the Load button and step from frame to frame using the scroll bar. You can use the *FrameCount* property at run time to find out how many frames are in a CCF button. You can save all the frames into a special .CCB (Custom Control button) file via the *ccbFileSave* property and load them again via the *ccbFileLoad* property. This allows you to store groups of images in disk files that can be loaded at run time.

You control the order in which the frames are displayed with the *Cycle* property. There are eight standard cycles to choose from, plus a *Custom* setting that puts you in complete control of the order in which the frames are displayed. You can adjust how quickly the frames are displayed with the *Speed* property. If the *ClearFirst* property is set to *True,* the CCF button is cleared between frames. This property is available strictly for aesthetics; it improves the appearance of the animation if there are significant changes between the pictures in two frames.

There are only two events for CCF buttons and both are tied to properties. If the *SyncEnable* property is *True,* the CCF button fires a *Sync* event before each frame is drawn. The *Sync* event tells you which frame is being drawn and allows you to skip that frame, or all remaining frames. If the *Cycle* property is set to *Custom,* the *NextFrame* event fires whenever the control requires redrawing. Not only can you tell it which frame

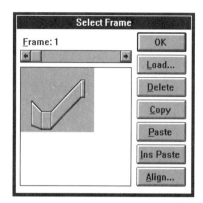

**Figure 4-4** CCF Select Frame dialog

to draw, but you can do all your own drawing with Windows GDI commands as if the CCF button were an owner draw control.

You can control the behavior of a CCF button as well as its appearance. *OptionMode* makes a CCF button act like an option button. *ClickFilter* determines what part of the control will detect mouse clicks (see Table 4-18 for values).

**Table 4-18** ClickFilter values

| VALUE | MEANING |
| --- | --- |
| 0 | Mouse clicks are detected anywhere in the control window. |
| 1 | Mouse clicks must be on the caption text or image frame. |
| 2 | Mouse clicks must be on the image frame. |
| 3 | Mouse clicks must be on the caption text. |

*ClickLocPic* tells you the coordinates of the last mouse click so you can execute different code based on where in the button the mouse was clicked. If *ClickOnPress* is set to *True,* the *Click* event fires when the mouse button is pressed, rather than when it's released. You can use the *SpecialOp* property to simulate a click, generate continuous animation, or redraw the control.

Now you can see why it's called the Custom Control Factory. You can make it look and act any way you want it to.

# Example

The CCF sample programs take advantage of the animation capabilities provided by CCF. The first sample uses ten CCF buttons to emulate an LED display (Figure 4-5).

Each vertical bar in the LED display is a CCF button. Each CCF button contains eight frames, showing the bar filled to a higher level (Figure 4-6).

The CCF buttons have *Cycle* set to Custom (8) so we're in control of what frames are displayed. The animation is driven from a timer. The *Timer* event sets the *SpecialOp* property to 2 (SPECIAL_OP_TRIGGER), causing the control to fire a *NextFrame* event, which is where we tell it what frame to display. The sample selects a frame at random, but you can use whatever criteria you want to determine which frame to display. That's all there is to it; the CCF buttons handle the rest. The scroll bar is used to adjust the timer interval that changes the speed of the animation.

The second sample (Figure 4-7) uses a cycle of 2 (Forward on Press) to play all the frames from start to finish. Setting the *SpecialOp* property to 2 (SPECIAL_OP_TRIGGER) starts the animation. Sample 2 also makes use of the *ClickFilter* property. The animation should only be started from the *DragDrop* event, but a *Click* event would also start it, so the *ClickFilter* property is set to 3 (Text Only). Since there is no text (*Caption*) on the CCF button this effectively filters out all *Click* events.

## Tips and Comments

Custom Control Factory is the commercial version of the ANIBUTON.VBX that comes with VB 3.0 Professional Edition and, as such, it has many capabilities beyond those of ANIBUTON. There are 42 custom properties, versus 17 for ANIBUTON, and 2 events, versus 0 for ANIBUTON. If you save CCB files with ANIBUTON (using *ccbFileSave*), CCF can read them just fine. If you had to choose just one control in the button family, you won't find one more flexible than Custom Control Factory.

# Designer Widgets

| USAGE: | Dockable Toolbar, Index Tab, and Special Form Effects |
|---|---|
| MANUFACTURER: | Sheridan Software Systems |
| COST: | $129 |

Designer Widgets is a bundled set of three controls. You can use the Dockable Toolbar control in both MDI and non-MDI applications to complement or replace menu

**Figure 4-5** CCF sample 1

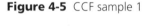

**Figure 4-6** CCF sample 1 frames

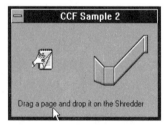

**Figure 4-7** CCF sample 2

functions. The Index Tab control provides the increasingly popular tabbed file folder look. The last control, called FormFX, allows you to add special effects to a form's caption, border, and client area.

# Syntax

Each of the three Designer Widgets controls is stand-alone. They are covered in separate sections, and the example project makes use of all three.

**Dockable Toolbar** This Dockable Toolbar control lets you create a toolbar with a diverse group of features. Each toolbar can have multiple logical groups of buttons, each button can automatically display balloon help when the mouse is held over it, and you can specify a shortcut (accelerator) key for each toolbar button. Toolbars placed on an MDI form, can be docked at the left, right, top, or bottom of the MDI parent window. The user can also detach and drag the toolbar off the form, making it a floating toolbar.

The special properties and events for the Dockable Toolbar control are shown in Table 4-19. You can customize the Toolbar control using the ToolbarDesigner application, which you launch by selecting (ToolbarDesigner) from the Visual Basic properties window. This application lets you design and customize much of the behavior of a toolbar at design time.

**Table 4-19** Nonstandard properties and events for the Dockable Toolbar control

### PROPERTIES

| | | |
|---|---|---|
| (About) | (ToolbarDesigner) | AllowToolbarDockBottom |
| AllowToolbarDockLeft | AllowToolbarDockRight | AllowToolbarDockTop |
| AllowToolbarFloat | AllowToolbrMove | BackColorDock |
| BackColorHelp | BalloonHelp | BalloonHelpDelay |
| BevelColorFace | BevelColorHighlight | BevelColorShadow |
| BevelInner | BevelOuter | BevelWidth |
| BorderWidth | BtnEnabled | BtnGroupSpacing |
| BtnHeight | BtnMarginX | BtnMarginY |
| Btns | BtnSpacing | BtnToolNum |
| BtnValue | BtnVisible | BtnWidth |
| DockRank | DockRankSeq | DockStatus |
| FloatingCaption | FloatingCaptionType | FloatingControlBox |
| FloatingLeft | FloatingSizable | FloatingTop |
| FloatingWidthInBtns | ForeColorHelp | Outline |
| Toolbar3D | ToolsetName | ToolsetNumBtnStates |
| ToolsetNumTools | ToolsetPicture | ToolsetAllowAllUp |
| ToolsetToolDesc | ToolsetToolExclusive | ToolsetToolGroup |
| ToolsetToolHelp | ToolsetToolID | ToolsetToolMnemonic |
| ToolsetToolPicDnDis | ToolsetToolPicDn | ToolsetToolPicUp |
| ToolsetToolPicUpDis | ToolsetToolType | |

(continued on next page)

*(continued from previous page)*

**EVENTS**

| Click | DockStatusChanged | Help |
| MouseEnter | MouseExit | ToolbarClosed |
| ToolbarResized | | |

*Toolsets* are collections of buttons that you use to create your toolbar. These toolsets are built and maintained by the ToolbarDesigner program. To create a new toolset, you first need to design a set of buttons using a bitmap editor such as Windows Paintbrush. An example of a toolset bitmap is shown in Figure 4-8. These bitmaps are similar to the type used by the Visual Basic Picture Clip control, where several pictures are arranged in rows and columns within a single bitmap.

A single toolset bitmap will define multiple buttons. Using the ToolbarDesigner's Edit Toolset command, you specify details about each button: a text description of the button, an accelerator key, a string identifier, the text used for the balloon help option, and the logical group number for the button. You can also specify whether the tool is a conventional push button or a toggle button that remains in either an up or down state.

You can supply up to four state bitmaps for each button—one for the up position, another for the down position, and two optional bitmaps for disabled up and down positions.

Once you have designed a toolset, you can place individual buttons on your toolbar using ToolbarDesigner.

By default, a docked toolbar on an MDI parent form can be "grabbed" with the mouse and dragged anywhere on the screen. The toolbar is also "intelligent." It detects when it is over one of the MDI parent's borders and attaches, or docks, itself to that side of the MDI parent if the button is released. You can disable the ability to detach the toolbar by setting the *AllowToolbarFloat* property to *False*.

Several properties control the behavior of the toolbar when it is floating as a detached window. *FloatingSizable* is a Boolean that determines whether the toolbar can be resized. *FloatingLeft* and *FloatingTop* return the current position of the toolbar relative to the upper-left corner of the MDI form's client area. A *FloatingCaption* property specifies what text appears on the toolbar's caption, if it has one.

Individual buttons on the toolbar can be disabled or rendered invisible, just as other controls can. You do this by using the special *BtnEnabled()* and *BtnVisible()* property arrays. Each element of these arrays corresponds to a button on the toolbar, with the first

**Figure 4-8** A sample toolset bitmap

(far left) button designated as element 0. A *Btns* property returns the total number of buttons in the toolbar.

There are numerous other properties for handling button spacing, returning toolset information, and giving the toolbar a 3D appearance.

A *DockStatusChanged* event is fired whenever a toolbar is docked or detached from an MDI form. When the toolbar is detached and floating, a *ToolbarClosed* event is fired when the toolbar window is closed using its system menu. A *ToolbarResized* event is triggered whenever the user resizes a detached toolbar.

When balloon help is activated for a button, a *Help* event is fired, and the *MouseEnter* and *MouseExit* events are fired when the mouse pointer enters or leaves a particular button. These events can be used to update help information on a status line when the mouse moves over each button.

The toolbar uses a modified *Click* event. Regardless of which button is clicked on, the same *Click* event is fired. This event passes information about the specific button pressed, and specific processing is usually handled using a Visual Basic *Select Case* statement.

**Index Tab**  The Index Tab is a container control that allows you to pack a lot of information into a single form. This style of control is becoming increasingly popular because it provides the user with an immediately understandable visual metaphor: the tabbed file folder. The Index Tab control supports multiple tab rows, and you can easily place child controls on individual tabs at design time. The nonstandard properties and event for the Index Tab control are listed in Table 4-20.

**Table 4-20**  Nonstandard properties and event for the Index Tab control

| PROPERTIES | | |
|---|---|---|
| (About) | ActiveTabBackColor | ActiveTabFontBold |
| ActiveTabFontItalic | ActiveTabFontStrikeThru | ActiveTabFontUnderline |
| ActiveTabForeColor | ActiveTabPicture | AlignmentCaption |
| AlignmentPicture | BevelColorFace | BevelColorHighlight |
| BevelColorShadow | Font3D | Picture |
| Redraw | Rows | ShowFocusRect |
| Tab | TabBackColor | TabCaption |
| TabCutSize | TabEnabled | TabForeColor |
| TabHeight | TabHwnd | TabMaxWidth |
| TabOrientation | TabPicture | TabPictureMetaHeight |
| TabPictureMetaWidth | TabRowOffset | Tabs |
| Tabs3D | TabSelectType | TabsPerRow |
| TabStart | TabVisible | |
| **EVENT** | | |
| Click | | |

Once you have placed an Index Tab control on a form, you can set the total number of tabs to display by setting the *Tab* property. If you want to display the tabs in multiple rows, set the *TabsPerRow* property, and Index Tab will automatically organize the rows.

The Index Tab is a container control in that it can hold other controls within it. Actually, the Index Tab serves as multiple containers, one for each tab. To place controls within a particular tab at design time, first select the tab by clicking on it, and then drag the "child" control from the Visual Basic toolbox and place it within the tab desired.

The Index Tab can only hold other controls that have an *hWnd* property. This means that you cannot place standard controls such as the Label, Image, Line, and Shape directly on the Index Tab control. To use these controls, you must place them within a container control such as a Frame or Picture control.

Each separate tab has its own window handle property, accessible through the *TabHwnd()* property array. There is one element for each tab in the control, with the first (front left) tab numbered 0. Two other property arrays, *TabEnabled()* and *TabVisible()*, let you determine whether a tab can be moved to or seen.

Numerous properties allow you to change the appearance of the Index Tab control. These include *TabOrientation* (see Table 4-21), which allows you to specify if the tabs should be displayed at the top, bottom, left, or right of the control. You can give both the tab fonts and the tabs themselves a 3D appearance, and you can specify different colors for active and inactive tabs.

**Table 4-21** Values for the TabOrientation property

| VALUE | MEANING |
|---|---|
| 0 | Tabs on top of the control (the default) |
| 1 | Tabs on bottom of the control |
| 2 | Tabs on left side of control |
| 3 | Tabs on right side of control |

Only one special event is provided by Index Tab, a modified *Click* event that passes the previous tab's numeric value (as stored in the *Tab* property) as a parameter. The *Click* event can be useful for setting "persistent," or shared, child controls. A persistent control is only placed on one tab, but by using the *SetParent* Windows API call, you can have the control shared by several or all of the other tabs by resetting the child control's parent to the current tab within the Index Tab *Click* event. You declare the *SetParent* function in a form or module's declarations section like this:

```
Declare Function SetParent Lib "USER.EXE" (ByVal hWndChild As Integer, ByVal hWndParent As Integer) As Integer
```

If you had a command button named btnOK inside one tab of the control tabTest, you could have it display on other tabs by adding this code to tabTest's *Click* event:

```
Dim NewTab As Integer
Dim retcode As Integer

NewTab = tabTest.Tab
retcode = SetParent (btnOK.Hwnd, tabTest.TabHwnd(NewTab))
```

**FormFX**  FormFX lets you control the appearance of window captions and borders, areas that are off limits to standard Visual Basic applications. Figure 4-9 shows how this control lets you use different fonts on caption titles, customize the appearance of caption buttons, and in general break most of the rules about what a window normally looks like. You can produce these effects by placing a FormFX control on your Visual Basic form, and then setting any of numerous properties to create special window effects. These properties are listed in Table 4-22.

**Table 4-22**  Nonstandard properties for the FormFX control

| | | |
|---|---|---|
| (About) | AlignmentCaption | AlignmentPicture |
| AlwaysOnTop | BackColorActive | BackColorInactive |
| BevelColorFace | BevelColorHighlight | BevelColorShadow |
| Border3D | Caption | Caption3D |
| CaptionBevelInner | CaptionBevelOuter | CaptionBevelWidth |
| CaptionBorderWidth | CaptionButtonsPic | CaptionHeight |
| CaptionMultiLine | CaptionPicture | CaptionPictureMetaHeight |
| CaptionPictureMetaWidth | CaptionPictureX | CaptionPictureY |
| Client3D | ClientBevelInner | ClientBevelOuter |
| ClientBevelWidth | ClientBorderWidth | ClientMove |
| ControlBox3D | Font3D | ForeColorActive |
| ForeColorInactive | InstantClose | LockCtlKeyOverride |
| LockMove | LockSize | MaximizeHeight |
| MaximizeTop | MaximizeLeft | MaximizeWidth |
| Redraw | SizeMaxHeight | SizeMaxWidth |
| SizeMinHeight | SizeMinWidth | StdButtonHeight |
| StdCaption | StdCaptionHeight | |

As you can see from the table, the FormFX properties are divided into several large categories, most related to some area of a form: captions, borders, control boxes, and client area.

There are other properties that handle other aspects of form, and these require a bit more explanation. The three Boolean *Lock* properties restrict the movement and resizing of forms. When *LockMove* is set to *True*, the user cannot move a form; it's effectively "locked down." Likewise, when *LockSize* is set to *True,* the user cannot resize a form. The *LockCtlKeyOverride* property, when set to *True,* allows the user to override the other two properties and move or resize forms by holding down the (CTRL) key while using the mouse to resize or move the window.

The four *Maximize* properties set the size of the window when maximized, allowing you to opt for a size other than full screen. The *SizeMax* and *SizeMin* properties let you control the maximum and minimum dimensions to which a window can be resized.

**Figure 4-9** The FormFX control modifies the caption and borders of forms

# Example

The example program uses all three Designer Widgets controls to build an MDI File Browsing utility. It uses the Dockable Toolbar control to replace the traditional menu options, the FormFX control to design a directory selection window with several special features, and the Index Tab control to organize the information displayed in MDI child windows.

The example program is shown in Figure 4-10. The dockable toolbar contains five buttons. Holding the mouse pointer over these buttons displays a short balloon help message explaining what the button does. You can detach the toolbar from the top of the MDI parent window by grabbing a non-button area and dragging with the mouse.

When the leftmost toolbar button is pressed, you'll see a directory selection window that lets you navigate through directory structures. The window itself contains several special effects courtesy of the FormFX control. Try resizing the control and you will notice that, while you can make it taller, you cannot make it wider. This is accomplished by setting the FormFX *SizeMax* and *SizeMin* properties when the form is loaded. Also notice that the border, caption, control button, and client area all contain 3D or nonstandard visual features. For example, the caption bar is shorter than a standard caption bar, and the text within it is left-justified rather than centered. Also, a single click on the upper-left control box closes the window, and the window always remains on top of other windows, even if those other windows have the focus.

The MDI child window shows a use of the Index Tab control, in this case showing three different groups of files for a selected directory.

# Tips and Comments

These three controls pack a lot of power. The Dockable Toolbar control is extremely flexible when used in MDI forms, and the FormFX control encapsulates several features, such as control over form resizing limits, that are often needed in applications. The Index

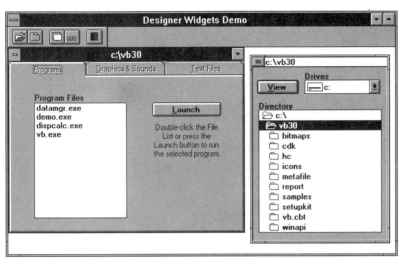

**Figure 4-10** The Designer Widgets example program

Tab control's inability to place "graphical" controls directly on a tab is unfortunate, particularly as it hinders the natural use of Label controls within the control.

# QuickPak Professional for Windows

| USAGE: | Function Library, Multiple Custom Controls |
|---|---|
| MANUFACTURER: | Crescent Software |
| COST: | $199 |

If you like one-stop shopping, you've come to the right place with Crescent's QuickPak Professional for Windows. With more than 30 custom controls and a DLL with over 400 functions, QuickPak provides a very healthy toolbox. Most of the custom controls are enhanced versions of the standard VB controls but a few unique controls, such as hypertext control and a form subclassing control, have no peer in the standard VB toolbox. QuickPak also comes with utilities like a data entry form wizard that can make your job a little easier.

## Syntax

Since there are so many custom controls in QuickPak Professional, each one is discussed separately.

**CSDIALOG.VBX** The CSDIALOG.VBX file contains five custom controls, each one a common dialog with a specific purpose. Where the standard VB CMDIALOG.VBX uses a single control to access all common dialogs, Crescent has opted to separate them. There are two sets of common dialogs that share a control: the

FileOpen and FileSave dialogs share the CSDIALOG and the Find and Replace dialogs (Figure 4-11).

For the File dialog and Find dialog there are two possible values for the *Action* property, which activates the dialog (Table 4-23). For the Color, Font, and Print dialogs there is only one value.

**Table 4-23** QuickPak Pro File dialog and Find dialog Action property values

| VALUE | MEANING |
|---|---|
| | **File Dialog** |
| 1 | Activate the File Open common dialog |
| 2 | Activate the File Save common dialog |
| | |
| | **Find Dialog** |
| 1 | Activate the Find Text common dialog |
| 2 | Activate the Replace Text common dialog |

You can use the *DialogLeft* and *DialogTop* properties to position the dialog on the screen, which CMDIALOG.VBX doesn't allow. The Find and Replace dialogs aren't available at all in the standard VB control. Find/Replace are modeless dialogs, whereas all the other dialogs are modal. The dialogs don't perform any automatic processing but instead fire *Cancel, Find,* or *Replace* events, which allow you to perform the necessary processing. The Crescent version of the Print dialog offers a great deal more information than the standard VB version, including the currently selected bin (*DefaultSource*), device driver name *(DevName),* paper size *(PaperLength, PaperSize, PaperWidth), Orientation, PrintQuality,* and *PrintScale.*

**CSCALNDR.VBX**   The Calendar control has no equivalent standard control. It is a pop-up calendar that can be used to select and/or display dates. It can also be used as a bound control. The calendar can be navigated with the keyboard if the *GetArrows* property is *True,* which is a nice feature. The calendar also supports drag and drop. The *Date* property reflects the date where the drag operation began or the drop occurred.

If you need to restrict the range of available dates, you can set the *MinDate* and *MaxDate* properties to avoid out of range errors. There are six *MarkColor* properties *(MarkColor1, MarkColor2,* and so on), which work in conjunction with the *MarkType*

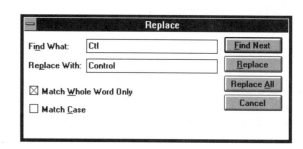

**Figure 4-11** QuickPak Pro Replace dialog

property to mark dates in the current month with up to six different colors. For example, if your application handled appointment scheduling, you could mark days whose schedule was full with a specific color to indicate that fact.

**CSCAPT.VBX** The CSCaption control is a variation on the standard VB frame. Rather than multiple child controls, CSCaption is designed to have one child control placed inside it. It then acts like a label that is associated with, or tied to, that child control. By adjusting the *LabelAlignment, LabelPosition, LabelLeft, LabelTop, LabelHeight,* and *LabelWidth* properties, you can place the *caption* where you want, in relation to the child control that's inside the CSCaption. You can also adjust the margins and distance between the *caption* and child control. If you don't want to go to all that trouble, you can use the *AutoAdjust* and *LabelAutoSize* properties, letting CSCaption decide what looks best. You can also give the child control a 3D appearance by using the CSCaption control's *ChildBorderEffect* property.

**CSCHK.VBX** The CSCheckList control is just what the name implies: a list of items that may be checked. These items look like individual check boxes but act like a cohesive group. To set the number of check boxes and their captions, you use the *Contents* property at design time. Each line in the *Contents* property should contain a *value* and a *caption,* separated by a semicolon. If you don't specify values, default values are used. The *Caption* property determines the caption of the frame and the *Value* property contains the value for all check boxes that appear in the frame. The *Value* property is a bit-coded long integer and each check box, represents one bit (on or off). To change the caption or value of a single check box, use the *ItemCaption* and *ItemValue* properties.

**CSCMD.VBX** The CSCmd control is an enhanced command button that allows you to display pictures (bitmaps or icons), size those pictures (if they're bitmaps), and control their position relative to the caption (above, below, left, or right of the *caption*). All the colors of the button (Border, Face, Highlight, and Shadow) can be changed as can the *BevelWidth* and *BorderWidth*. You can use the *DataMethod* property to make the CSCmd perform a specific data operation automatically; Table 4-24 contains its possible values and their associated data operations.

**Table 4-24** CSCmd DataMethod values

| VALUE | MEANING |
| --- | --- |
| 0 | None |
| 1 | Add new record |
| 2 | Delete record |
| 3 | Update record |
| 4 | Move to bookmark |
| 5 | Move to first record |
| 6 | Move to last record |
| 7 | Move to next record |
| 8 | Move to previous record |

**CSCOMBO.VBX**   The CSCombo control has far more capabilities than the standard VB combo box. Not only can it be bound to a data control, but it can perform aliasing automatically, using a value list that you define. For example, you could store two-letter state codes in your database but the combo box could display the full state names for you to choose from. The text portion and the list portion of CSCombo may be bound to separate data controls so the list can act as a pick list from a secondary table. It's easy to search the list thanks to the *AutoSearch* property, which can search for a complete match in the list (based on what the user types in the text portion) or can perform incremental searching (looking through the list for matching prefixes).

**CSTEXT.VBX**   The CSText.VBX file hosts six custom text box controls, each of which is tailored to a specific kind of data input: currency, date, double-precision numbers, long integers, time, and general masked input. Each control lets you mask keystrokes and format the text automatically and also lets you access the unformatted data via the *RawData* property. For numeric text boxes, you can specify a *MinValue* and *MaxValue* and the text box will fire an *OutOfRange* event if the value of the data falls outside those values. All the text boxes can also toggle between Insert and Overstrike mode, which standard VB text boxes cannot.

**CSFORM.VBX**   CSForm is used to enhance VB forms themselves. Simply placing a CSForm control on a Visual Basic form effectively adds new properties and events to that form. If the *AcceptFiles* property is *True,* the form will accept files dropped from File Manager and will fire a *DropFiles* event and load the *DropFile* array property if that occurs. By assigning a bitmap to the *BackgroundBrush* property, you can give your forms a new background pattern. You can make the form virtual and scrollable with the *VirtualHeight, VirtualWidth,* and *Scrollbars* properties. This allows you to create scrollable forms that are larger than the display. If *LockIcon* is *True,* the form will be locked as an icon on the screen. Table 4-25 lists the nonstandard events fired by the CSForm control.

**Table 4-25** CSForm nonstandard events

| EVENTS | | |
| --- | --- | --- |
| AppActivate | AppDeactivate | ClipBoardChange |
| Compacting | CtlColor | CtlNotify |
| DevModeChange | DropFiles | FMDragEnter |
| FMDragLeave | FontChange | MaxInfo |
| MenuBrowse | MouseEnter | Move |
| Moving | PaintIcon | PowerRestore |
| PowerSuspend | PrintQueue | RegisteredMessage |
| SysColorChange | SysMenuClick | TimeChange |
| TrackInfo | UserMsg | WinIniChange |

New events inform you when the application is being activated or deactivated, when the Clipboard contents or the default device-mode settings change, and when the form is moved or resized (so you can prevent resizing of the form before it occurs).

**CSGROUP.VBX** The CSGroup control is much like the standard VB Frame control but provides an inset 3D appearance for the main area and lets you have the caption appear as a raised panel.

**CSHT.VBX** The CSHyperText control allows you to display text using multiple styles and colors and, indeed, lets you create hypertext that the user can navigate. The text must be formatted with special codes, much like a RichTextFormat (.RTF) file. *Jump* and *Popup* events are fired when the user clicks on text defined as *Jump* or *Popup* text. When those events occur you change the *Text* contained in the CSHyperText control to reflect the *Jump* destination or display *Popup* information. CSHyperText doesn't perform automatic navigation of hypertext; it simply provides the events that make this possible.

**CSINVIS.VBX** Think of the CSInvisible control as a big, invisible button that you can place on your forms, or inside another control like a picture box. You can use it to create hot spots to be clicked on. Rather than checking the X and Y coordinates in the *MouseDown* event of the picture box and trying to figure out what region was hit, you can simply place a CSInvisible control in each region and act on its *Click* event.

**CSMETER.VBX** The CSMeter control is an enhanced version of the 3D panel that comes with VB Professional. It can display the percentage information in any of four directions, based on the *FillType* property. It also allows you to define a *MinValue*, *MaxValue*, and *UserValue* so you don't have to perform percentage calculations yourself.

**CSOPT.VBX** The CSOptionList control works much like the CSCheckList control. However, instead of assigning bit values, each option button, when selected, assigns its value to the *Value* property of the control. This behavior eliminates all the code you need to write to find out which option button out of a group of option buttons is selected.

**CSPICT.VBX** The CSPict control does for picture boxes what the CSForm control does for forms. The added properties and events are virtually the same as CSForm but some form-specific properties and events (*MainForm, SystemModal, LockIcon,* and so on) do not apply.

**CSPICTUR.VBX** If you think the VB Picture Box control should support more file formats, you'll like CSPicture. It supports Windows Bitmap (.BMP), Graphics Interchange Format (.GIF), PC-Paintbrush (.PCX), and Targa (.TGA) files. Images loaded into a CSPicture can be scaled, panned, and printed via property access. CSPicture also provides details *(PicHeight, PicWidth,* and *PicColorBits)* about the image that is loaded.

**CSSPIN.VBX** The CSSpin control provides some enhancements over the spin button that comes with VB. You can set the *Increment* value and the spin button will react as quickly as you can click on it. (The spin button that comes with VB Pro may ignore mouse clicks if you click too quickly.) It can also provide a *ValueDisplay,* which displays the current value of the spin button. CSSpin reacts to the arrow keys when it has focus, which is a nice touch.

▲ **CSVLIST.VBX** CSVList is a virtual list box. In bound mode it only loads the data it needs to display; in manual (unbound) mode rather than loading the list with data, you control the data and CSVList and then asks for data when it needs to display it. CSVList does this by firing a *QueryItem* event, and then providing you with the number of the item it needs and a string variable that you fill with the data to be displayed.

▲ **CURTIME.VBX** The CurTime control automatically displays the current time in its caption, in either 12-hour or 24-hour format. It also allows you to set a value into its *AlarmTime* property. When that time is reached, an *Alarm* event fires that you can react to. There's no snooze button though.

▲ **QPSCROLL.VBX** The QPScroll controls provided enhanced capabilities over the standard scroll controls in VB 1.0. Their functionality is now built into the standard VB scroll controls.

▲ **QPLIST.VBX** The QPList control is an enhanced version of the VB list box. It can also act like the VB File, Directory, and Drive List controls. It allows fast searching of the list and supports tab stops in the list as well.

▲ **QPRO200.DLL** QPRO200.DLL is a library of over 400 functions that your VB application can use. There isn't space to discuss each function in detail, so this section just briefly discusses related groups of functions. Much of QPRO200.DLL was written in assembly language and is extremely fast. QuickPak Pro comes with a file called PRODECL.BAS, which contains the declarations for all the functions available in QPRO200.DLL.

There are approximately 80 array routines that allow you to sort and search arrays in a variety of ways. You can either sort the actual array or an array of integers that act as pointers to the array elements. You can sort any type of array, including arrays of variants and user-defined types. There are routines for manipulating bit arrays as well. *Min, Max,* and *Insert* functions are much faster than the equivalent VB code would be.

DOS services (more than 85 functions) provide low-level access to the underlying operating system allowing you to do things not possible with VB alone. For example, a function called *DOSCall* lets you call DOS Interrupt &H21. Many of the functions are file related. In addition to basic file I/O functions, QPRO200 provides functions for reading and writing entire arrays with one function call. One of the biggest advantages of the QPRO functions is that they return an error code directly, so you don't have to use On Error for error handling.

Keyboard related functions permit you to turn on and off the (CAPS LOCK), (NUM LOCK), and (SCROLL LOCK) keys and set up system-wide keyboard hooks and hot keys.

In case VB doesn't have enough string manipulation functions for you, QuickPak adds a few more to your arsenal. There are functions for encrypting and decrypting strings, counting the number of times a character or substring appears in a string, replacing a substring, and trimming NULL-terminated strings.

Other functions, more than 200 of them, perform string parsing, convert numbers to and from their binary representation in string format. Other functions perform financial, mathematical, and statistical calculations, which would come in handy if you were writing any type of spreadsheet application.

## Example

The example program on the CD (Figure 4-12) illustrates a good number of the controls available in QuickPak Professional, but doesn't push the limits of the controls by any means. QuickPak comes with almost 3 megabytes of sample code to show off the controls. The example program just gives you the "flavor" of the controls. You'll see that very little code is involved.

## Tips and Comments

QuickPak Professional should satisfy the appetite of the most voracious VB developer, providing a large library of functions and a broad selection of custom controls. The only thing missing from this otherwise superb package is an online .HLP file.

 # VBTools 4.0

| USAGE: | Visual Basic Tools |
|---|---|
| MANUFACTURER: | MicroHelp |
| COST: | $129 |

Microhelp's latest release of VBTools, version 4.0, combines their 3D Gizmos package with the previous release of VBTools to create a package of more than 50 controls that do everything from tell time and ring alarms to subclass Windows messages.

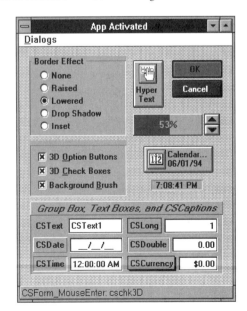

**Figure 4-12** QuickPak Professional sample program

Some of these controls have been in existence since VBTools Version 1.0 and are included only for compatibility with previous releases of VBTools. MhMDI is basically obsolete, having been replaced by the MDI parent and children forms. However, most of the controls are very useful. VBTools includes a full set of input controls: 3D bound replacements for all of the standard VB controls, many different kinds of buttons and check/option boxes, a replacement for the common dialog control that allows you to add your own controls to the dialog box, a tab control, an outline control, a calendar control, and the list goes on and on. One of the coolest controls is Mh3dOutOfBounds. Most VBTools controls are bound, but you may want to bind something that's not normally bound, for example, a menu caption. Using Mh3dOutOfBounds, you can handle this with just a few mouse clicks in a custom dialog box. See Figure 4-13 for a picture of the dialog.

Two of the controls are rather silly. MhCard is a VBX and DLL combination that gives you card backs for any card games you might want to play. MhDice does the same thing for any dice games.

As a bonus of sorts, MicroHelp also ships a copy of FarPoint's Grid/VBX Version 1.0 with VBTools. You can use this control in any of your projects, or if you really need power, FarPoint offers an upgrade to their powerful Spread/VBX spreadsheet control.

## Syntax

All the MicroHelp controls share some convenient features. They all can bring up help when you highlight the control and press the help key. Many of the 3D controls let you resize the inside of the control using the right mouse button. Many of the controls also feature properties for very precise positioning of any pictures used in the control, and most have full color control. You can also set 3D effects for any text displayed in many of the VBTools controls. See Table 4-26 for a list of the 3D properties.

**Figure 4-13** Mh3dOutOfBounds control dialog

**Table 4-26** MicroHelp 3D properties

| | | |
|---|---|---|
| BevelSize | BevelSizeInside | BevelStyle |
| BorderColor | BorderStyle | InnerBottom |
| InnerLeft | InnerRight | InnerTop |
| LightColor | OuterFillColor | ReverseFill |
| ShadowColor | | |

The upcoming section covers some of the more interesting controls in VBTools and their properties.

**Command, Check, and Option Buttons** VBTools has an amazing number of button controls that are very similar in their capabilities. See Table 4-27 for a list of the controls, icons, and VBXs.

**Table 4-27** VBTools button controls

| CONTROL | ICON | VBX |
|---|---|---|
| Mh3dButn | | MH3B200.VBX |
| Mh3dCheck | | MHGCHK.VBX |
| Mh3dCommand | | MHGCMD.VBX |
| Mh3dGroup | | MHGGRP.VBX |
| Mh3dOption | | MHGOPT.VBX |
| MhCommand | | MHCM200.VBX |
| MhMulti | | MHML200.VBX |

All these controls can display custom pictures and multiline captions. They all either can be or are state buttons. That is, you can have a command button act like a check box, where it stays depressed until you "unclick" it. Most of these controls can be combined into groups so they can act like radio buttons. All have 3D properties as well. You can also combine several sets of option buttons on one container control, rather than using one container for each set of option buttons.

The only unusual control in the group is MhMulti, which is a two-, three- or four-state button. This means you can use it to represent up to five different values by itself, rather than using a group of option buttons. For example, in a scheduling program where you have a daily, weekly, monthly, and yearly view, you could use one MhMulti control rather than 4 option buttons or some other combination of multiple hidden buttons or picture controls.

**Input Controls**  VBTools comes with a variety of controls to make it easy to accept formatted input from the user. See Table 4-28 for a list of these controls.

**Table 4-28**  VBTools input controls

| CONTROL | ICON | VBX |
|---|---|---|
| Mh3dText | | MHGTXT.VBX |
| MhDateInput | | MHINDAT.VBX |
| MhInput | | MHIN200.VBX |
| MhIntInput | | MHININT.VBX |
| MhMaskInput | | MHINMSK.VBX |
| MhRealInput | | MHINREL.VBX |

Mh3dText is the simplest of the input controls. Aside from its 3D appearance, it is basically the same as a standard text box.

Unlike the other input controls, MhMaskInput has its own .INI file that contains settings the control uses to establish the input mask, default value, and valid characters for the controls. Each instance of the control can have its own section and values, as designated by the *SectionName* property. MicroHelp includes a program for controlling the .INI files, or you can do it yourself using the *Get* and *SetPrivateProfile* API calls.

The other four controls allow you to set filters on the data. You can set minimum and maximum values based on the type of control. For example, MhDateInput lets you set the mininum and maximum date, MhIntInput permits you to set the minimum and maximum integer, and so on. These controls also have an optional spin button you can use as an alternate method of input. Table 4-29 lists the custom properties and events for the input controls.

**Table 4-29** Mh...Input nonstandard properties and events for controls

**PROPERTIES**

| | | |
|---|---|---|
| CaretColor | CaretHeight | CaretInterval |
| CaretStyle | CaretVAlign | CaretVisible |
| CaretWidth | Max | MaxReal |
| MaxDay | MaxMonth | MaxYear |
| Min | MinReal | MinDay |
| MinMonth | MinYear | ReadOnly |
| Spin | SpinChange | SpinDelay |
| SpinSpeed | Undo | VAlignment |
| Value | | |

**EVENTS**

| | |
|---|---|
| InvalidEntry | InvalidSetText |

**4** ◀

**Mh3dCalendar**  The Mh3dCalendar (MHGCAL.VBX) control is a fully featured, data-aware calendar control. You have full control over the appearance of the calendar, including any colors or sizes of boxes, and so on. You can load a picture in as the background of the control. Alternatively, you can load it like a garage pinup calendar, with the picture on the top half and the dates on the bottom half. It can be bound to a Date/Time column in an Access database. It can also work with the date format specified in the WIN.INI file or you can override with a format of your own choosing. Mh3dCalendar also has properties for making drag and drop easier to use by reporting the specific day something was dropped on. See Table 4-30 for a list of Mh3dCalendar's custom properties and events.

**Table 4-30** Mh3dCalendar custom properties and events

**PROPERTIES**

| | | |
|---|---|---|
| Alignment | Autosize | CalendarStyle |
| CalStatic | Date | DateArr |
| DayDropped | DayMath | DaySel |
| DayStart | Month | MonthArr |
| MonthSel | MonthText | MonthTextArr |
| MultiSelect | MultiStatic | SelectedCount |
| TitleFont | TitleFontBold | TitleFontItalic |
| TitleFontName | TitleFontSize | TitleFontStrike |
| TitleFontStyle | TitleFontUnder | TitleHeight |
| WallPaper | WeekDay | WeekDayArr |
| WeekDayText | WeekDayTextArr | Year |
| YearArr | YearSel | |

**EVENTS**

| | | |
|---|---|---|
| DayChange | MonthChange | YearChange |

**Mh3dCombo and Mh3dList**   The Mh3dCombo (MHGCMB.VBX) and Mh3dList (MHGLBX.VBX) controls are data-aware list and combo box controls. You have full control over the appearance of these controls, including the foreground, shadow, and line colors for both title and box body. You also control the height and width of the columns title. They are multicolumn as well. The controls allow you to virtualize the data access, so they don't try to load your billion row customer table from SQLServer all at once. Instead, the control fetches a subset of the selected rows of data, speeding up response time. As you move back and forth in the selected rows, the control loads in the rows needed for display. Both feature the dialog box shown in Figure 4-14 to allow easy column setup.

The Gizmo button on the Column Width Settings dialog box brings up the Data Field configuration dialog box shown in Figure 4-15, which lets you set up the data access information.

Both controls permit you to embed pictures in a cell of the list box. You can set the control to display one picture for selected lines and one for unselected lines.

The Mh3dCombo control allows you to bind the list portion of the control separately from the text portion of the control. This gives you great flexibility in handling database access. For instance, you can bind the text portion of the control to the State column of a mailing address and either use AddItem or a database to build an accepted list of states. Or you could bind the list portion to a table containing valid values but leave the text portion unbound. This lets you use a data access object to the actual database updates under program control but still have the ease of use of the data control for read-only access.

Mh3dCombo and Mh3dList also let you search the list box. You can search for values across all the columns or search a specific column.

See Table 4-31 for a list of custom properties and events for Mh3dCombo and Mh3dList.

**Table 4-31** Mh3dList and Mh3dCombo custom properties and events

**PROPERTIES**

| | | |
|---|---|---|
| AutoHScroll | BufferSize | Case |
| ClearBox | Col | ColAlignment |
| ColCharacter | ColDataField | ColFormat |
| ColInstr | ColList | ColText |
| ColTitle | ColWidth | DataSourceList |
| DataStyleList | FindInstr | FindString |
| FoundIndex | LastAdded | LastReplaced |
| ListData | ListPicture | ListPictureSel |
| MaxDop | PictureHeight | PictureWidth |
| Title Bevel Size | Title Bevel Style | Title Color |
| Title Fill Color | Title Font Bold | Title Font Italic |
| Title Font Name | Title Font Size | Title Font Strike |

**PROPERTIES**

| Title Font Style | Title Font Under | Title Height |
|---|---|---|
| VirtualList | Wallpaper | |

**EVENTS**

| CloseUp | DataLoadStart | DataLoadComplete |
|---|---|---|

**Mh3dMultiLabel**  Mh3dMultiLabel (MHGMUL.VBX) is a cool control that allows you to place an easy-to-use multicelled status bar on a form. The control can handle up to 100 different cells, each with different properties. Mh3dMultiLabel supports the *Align* property so you can place it on an MDI parent form as well as a normal form. It can be bound to a data control, with each segment getting a different field. You can also use a cell on Mh3dMultiLabel as a gauge or percentage compete indicator. You can set the control to update the size of the cells automatically as the form resizes, or to leave the cells unchanged. Finally, you can display a picture in the control itself and pictures in each individual cell. Table 4-32 lists the custom properties for Mh3dMultiLabel.

**Table 4-32**  Mh3dMultiLabel custom properties

| Align | AutoSize | SegAlignment |
|---|---|---|
| SegAutosize | SegCaption | SegDataField |
| SegFormat | SegMax | Segment |
| Segments | SegMultiLine | SegPicture |
| SegWallpaper | | |

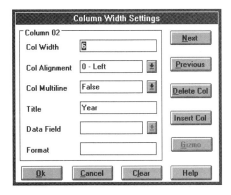

**Figure 4-14** Column Width Settings dialog box

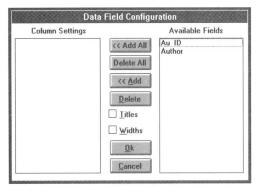

**Figure 4-15** Data Field Configuration dialog box

**Mh3dMenu**   The Mh3dMenu (MHGMEN.VBX) control gives you control over the appearance and selection of the menu in your Visual Basic program. Using Mh3dMenu, you can give your menus a 3D appearance or can track menu selection. If you track menu selection, you can display menu help while the users are clicking on menus, and not just when they actually select a menu item. This ability to provide feedback has become a standard feature for Windows applications like Microsoft Office or WordPerfect for Windows.

You can also use Mh3dMenu to create a pop-up menu. The process uses a standard VB menu structure that Mh3dMenu takes control of. The process isn't perfect; sometimes you see a flicker as the menu appears and then moves into the position you specify. The menu *Click* events fire as they would normally.

You can use the same process to remove and then replace the standard system menu with either a 3D or custom menu. Once you've removed the system menu, you have to add back any system functions plus any custom items you want in the system menu.

Table 4-33 lists the custom properties and event for Mh3dMenu.

**Table 4-33** Mh3dMenu custom properties and event

**PROPERTIES**

| | | |
|---|---|---|
| CheckHeight | CheckWidth | Events |
| Item | ItemAlignment | ItemAutosize |
| ItemMultiLine | ItemPictureChecked | ItemPictureUnchecked |
| PopupAlignment | PopupCreate | PopupLeft |
| PopupTop | PopupVisible | SelCaption |
| SystemCreate | WhichEvent | |

**EVENT**

Closed

**MhCallBack**   The MhCallBack (MHCB200.VBX) control lets you use Windows callback functions and intercept Windows messages. MhCallBack has direct support for enumerated lists of screen fonts, printer fonts, the child window handles for your application, and the formats supported by the Windows Clipboard.

MhCallBack also supports general Windows subclassing. Briefly, subclassing involves trapping messages destined for one window and doing additional processing based on information contained in that message. You can set the level of messages you're interested in and which particular message or messages you'd like to trap for which (.hWnd).

Table 4-34 lists the custom properties and events for MhCallBack.

**Table 4-34** Mh3dCallBack custom properties and events

**PROPERTIES**

| | | |
|---|---|---|
| HWndSubclass | MsgLst | MsgPassage |
| Style | | |

**EVENTS**

| | | |
|---|---|---|
| ClipboardFormatChanged | GetMessageHook | KeyboardHook |
| MsgFilterHook | SubclassMsg | SysMsgFilterHook |

**MhFileDisplay**   The MhFileDisplay (MHPFST.VBX) control enables you to display and search ASCII files. You can set it to expand tabs and also to allow copying specified portions of files to the Clipboard. When the file is first read in, it's processed for line numbers. This may cause an initial hesitation before the file is displayed. By using the line numbers for positioning, however, you can get very fast file movement. The MhFileDisplay control also includes a Find dialog that you can use to search the ASCII file. In addition you can also use the *FindString* property to search under program control. See Figure 4-16 for an example of the Find dialog.

Table 4-35 lists the custom properties and event for MhFileDisplay.

**Table 4-35**  MhFileDisplay custom properties and event

**PROPERTIES**

| | | |
|---|---|---|
| CheckHeight | CheckWidth | Events |
| Item | ItemAlignment | ItemAutosize |
| ItemMultiLine | ItemPictureChecked | ItemPictureUnchecked |
| PopupAlignment | PopupCreate | PopupLeft |
| PopupTop | PopupVisible | SelCaption |
| SystemCreate | WhichEvent | |

**EVENT**

Closed

**MhTab**   The MhTab (MHTAB.VBX) control is a tabbed container object that allows you to put multiple controls on each "folder" of the control. During design time, you can activate the individual folders by right-clicking on them. Once you've brought up the desired tab folder, you can put controls on it just as you can put controls on a Frame control. You have the option of associating controls with individual pages or just treating the control as one frame and using the tabs more as a visible queue. If you need to add controls at run time, you need to use the Windows *SetParent* API call. The tab control can display tabs on all four sides of the control. If you do choose to rotate the control,

**Figure 4-16**  Find dialog for MhFileDisplay

you need to use *FontEscapement* and *FontOrientation* to rotate the font and text so it is facing in the proper direction.

Table 4-36 lists the custom properties and events for MhTab.

**Table 4-36** MhTab custom properties and events

**PROPERTIES**

| | | |
|---|---|---|
| Folder | Folders | FontEscapement |
| FontOrientation | PagePicture | PageWallpaper |
| PictureAlignment | PictureHeight | PictureWidth |
| TabCaption | TabFormat | TabsPerRow |
| TabVAlignment | | |

**EVENTS**

| | |
|---|---|
| TabChanged | TabChanging |

**MhTip**   The MhTip (MHTIP.VBX) control is a 3D balloon help control. MhTip allows you to supply the same sort of pop-up help that is available in such applications as Microsoft Word. You can set up the control so it looks just like Microsoft's help, or you can create imaginative pop-ups using the 3D and color properties. MhTip only works for controls that have the same parent as MhTips, so if you have a form with many container controls you need an MhTip control for each container.

Table 4-37 lists the custom properties and event for MhTab.

**Table 4-37** MhTab custom properties and event

**PROPERTIES**

| | | |
|---|---|---|
| AutoSize | AutoSizeToText | Caption |
| Interval | MultiLine | MultiLine |
| Picture | TipOffsetLeft | TipOffsetTop |
| WallPaper | | |

**EVENT**

| |
|---|
| SetCaption |

**MhCommonDialog**   MhCommonDialog (MHCOMD.VBX) is a drop-in replacement for the CMDialog control that ships with Visual Basic. MhCommonDialog has several enhancements to make common dialogs more flexible. You can position and resize the common dialog boxes. Being able to resize the dialog box is important because MhCommonDialog allows you to add your own controls to the common dialogs. In addition, the File Open and File Save dialogs use the *FileNameChange* event to notify you as the user scrolls though the file listings. This lets you display the file or perform some other action to indicate that this is the right file.

Before you jump in head first, note that the VBTools manual includes a whole page of dos and don'ts about adding controls to the common dialogs.

Table 4-38 lists the custom properties and events for MhCommonDialog.

**Table 4-38** MhCommonDialog custom properties and events

**PROPERTIES**

| | | |
|---|---|---|
| AddControl | CancelError | DialogDefaultHeight |
| DialogDefaultLeft | DialogDefaultTop | DialogLeft |
| DialogTop | DialogWidth | RemoveControl |

**EVENTS**

| | | |
|---|---|---|
| CommonDialogClosed | CommonDialogOpened | FileNameChange |

## Example

This sample program on the CD (shown in Figure 4-17) illustrates some of the features of about 20 of the controls in VBTools. It makes extensive use of the Tab control. Most of the tabs feature an Mh3dLabel control explaining the use of the control or controls on the tab. The demo app also features 3D menu effects courtesy of the Mh3dMenu control.

## Tips and Comments

VBTools is packed with controls that vary from extremely useful to barely meaningful. Some of them, MhMDI, for example, are left over from the days of Visual Basic Version 1. Several such as MhCallBack and Mh3dMenu, perform services that you can't do from VB. Controls like Mh3dCalendar, MhTab, MhTip, Mh3dOutOfBounds, and some others show how much time a well-written VBX can save programmers. They give your program the appearance and ease of use that customers are expecting from a professional application.

# WsHelp (WSHELP.VBX)

| | |
|---|---|
| USAGE: | Pop-Up and Status Bar Help |
| MANUFACTURER: | Weimar Software |
| COST: | $45, with three other controls |

WsHelp is part of the WSIHelp package, which includes Balloon, RTMouse, STMouse, and WsHelp itself. Balloon gives pop-up help balloons as the mouse cursor passes over a control, RTMouse gives pop-up help when the right mouse button is clicked on a control, and STMouse gives status bar help when the mouse cursor passes over a control. WsHelp combines the functionality of RTMouse, STMouse, and Balloon and adds timed help balloons, allowing you to simulate the help in the Microsoft Office package.

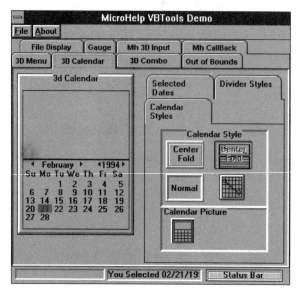

**Figure 4-17** The VBTools example program

These easy-to-use controls let you add the latest in user interface features using the custom events from the WsHelp controls and the *hWnd* of the controls on your form.

# Syntax

The WsHelp control is visible at design time only, so you can place it anywhere on the form. You do need one instance of WsHelp for each form.

You can control all the attributes of the appearance of the pop-up balloon, including color, size, shape, relative location to the control, and whether an "arrow" pointing to the control is shown. *BackColor* is the standard VB property controlling the color of the pop-up balloon. *BalloonHorizontalOffset* and *BalloonVerticalOffset* designate where the pop-up balloon appears in relation to the control WSHelp points to.

WsHelp also has a number of nonstandard properties used to control the actions of the control while the application is running, as listed in Table 4-39.

**Table 4-39** WsHelp nonstandard properties

| Action | BackColor | BalloonType |
|---|---|---|
| BalloonArrow | BalloonHorizontalOffset | BalloonReferencePoint |
| BalloonVerticalOffset | DTBOnceOnly | DelayPopup |
| DelayRemove | Inverse Video | MessageText |
| Timeout | | |

The *Action* property controls the starting and stopping of the various types of helps at run time. *DelayPopup* and *DelayRemove* specify the amount of time in milliseconds that the cursor has to sit on a control before a pop-up balloon pops up and expires, respectively. The minimum time is 1,000 milliseconds (1 second), the maximum is 32 seconds, and the default is 10 seconds (10,000 milliseconds). *InverseVideo* reverses the color of the control receiving help, giving a visual clue to the user. The *Timeout* property is to balloon help what *DelayRemove* is to timed balloon help: It determines how long the balloon remains visible without mouse movement or keyboard action.

The *MessageText* property is the message the balloon help displays. You set *MessageText* in one of the four custom events (shown in Table 4-40) that come with WsHelp. When you set *MessageText* in *BalloonClick, DTBalloonClick,* and *RTMouseClick* a help balloon appears. If you don't set *MessageText*, WSHelp goes back to sleep. The fourth event, *STMouseClick,* is used for status bar help, and it is up to you to provide the message and a status bar to display it. See the example program for sample code.

**Table 4-40** WsHelp nonstandard events

| |
|---|
| BalloonClick |
| DTBalloonClick |
| RTMouseClick |
| STMouseClick |

WsHelp also exports four functions listed in Table 4-41 to give you access to the control name, help id, tab index, and *tag* property of a control based on its *hWnd*, listed in Table 4-41.

**Table 4-41** WsHelp exported functions

| |
|---|
| Hwnd2ControlTabIndex |
| Hwnd2CtlName |
| Hwnd2HelpContextID |
| Hwnd2TagText |

# Example

The example program on the CD (see Figure 4-18) shows a concentration-type game that gives hints using the WsHelp control. The buttons on the command bar let you control help functions and the game board size. There's also a Start/Stop button to begin and end the game, a Help button to display the standard About form, an Exit button to end the program, and a vertical scroll bar that controls how long the pop-up balloon waits before it pops up. The 3D buttons on the command bar are implemented using VB code, as is the status bar at the bottom of the screen.

All controls on the form have help text built into their tag properties, since that's one of the easiest ways to use the WsHelp controls. You could also determine what help to pop up by using a *Select Case* statement with the *hWndatMouse* parameter returned in the WsHelp custom events and the *hWnd* property of the controls on the form.

## Tips and Comments

You can use Balloon, RTMouse, STMouse, and WsHelp to make your program much friendlier for novices and give it that professional Microsoft Office appearance. The controls are easy to use and fairly flexible. WSHelp and its siblings, Balloon, RTMouse, and STMouse, let you do things that are difficult to do in VB alone, which makes them fairly unique as custom controls go.

One word of warning: The WsHelp control that accompanies this book is a design-time only control, for evaluation purposes only. This means that you can only see the program run from the VB development environment.

 # Aware/VBX

| USAGE: | Data-Aware 3D Replacements for Standard Controls |
|---|---|
| MANUFACTURER: | FarPoint Technologies |
| COST: | $149 |

Aware/VBX is a set of 13 nonstandard controls that replaces and augments the standard set of tools distributed with Visual Basic Professional. The controls include fpBinary, an enhanced picture box; fpBoolean, an enhanced command/check/option button; fpCalendar, a data-aware calendar control; fpClock, a data-aware alarm clock; fpComboBox, an enhanced data-aware combo box; fpListBox, an enhanced data-aware list box; fpMask, an enhanced masked edit control; and fpMemo, a text control that handles more than 64K of data. Additionally, fpCurrency, fpDateTime, fpDoubleSingle, fpLongInteger, and fpText are all specialized data-entry controls.

## Syntax

The 13 Aware/VBX controls are contained in six different VBXs. You can change the appearance of the Aware/VBX controls as they receive and lose focus, control the

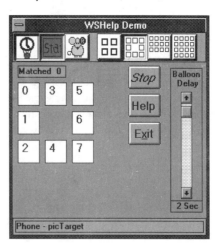

**Figure 4-18** The WSHLP example program

appearance of the insertion point (or caret), and change the display of data based on the data's validity. Each of the data-entry controls also allows for a button to control data input. The button can be one of several types controlled by the Button Style property, including a spinner, slide button, or just a plain vanilla command button. Valid values for *ButtonStyle* are listed in Table 4-42.

**Table 4-42** Values for ButtonStyle property

| VALUE | MEANING |
| --- | --- |
| 0 | None |
| 1 | Spin |
| 2 | Pop-up |
| 3 | Drop down |
| 4 | Slide |

All the Aware/VBX controls can have a 3D appearance. You control the 3D appearance using the properties listed in Table 4-43.

**Table 4-43** Nonstandard 3D properties for Aware/VBX

| PROPERTIES | | |
| --- | --- | --- |
| BorderGrayAreaColor | BorderStyle | BorderWidth |
| DropShadowColor | DropShadowWidth | OnFocusInvert3D |
| OnFocusShadow | ThreeDInsideStyle | ThreeDInsideWidth |
| ThreeDInsideHighlightColor | ThreeDOutsideStyle | ThreeDOutsideWidth |
| ThreeDInsideShadowColor | ThreeDTextOffset | ThreeDText |
| ThreeDTextHighlightColor | ThreeDFrameWidth | |
| ThreeDOutsideShadowColor | ThreeDOutsideHighlightColor | |

Another property shared by the data-entry controls is *AutoAdvance*. *AutoAdvance* is a Boolean property that tells the controls to automatically jump to the next or previous control in tab order when the user reaches the beginning or end of the text in a control. For example, if the user typed THEEND into an fpText control and then pressed the → key, the fpText control would automatically set focus to the next control, assuming *AutoAdvance* was set to *True*. If the insertion point is at the begining of a control and the user presses the ← key, focus is set to the previous control in tab order.

What follows is a brief description of each control in Aware/VBX. An example program at the end of this section features many of these Aware/VBX controls.

**fpBinary** fpBinary (AWAREBB.VBX) is a replacement for the Visual Basic Picture control. Besides providing the standard Picture control properties, it lets you size a picture to the control and display scroll bars if the picture is too big to fit into fpBinary. fpBinary is data aware. fpBinary can have an (optional) 3D appearance.

See Table 4-44 for a list of the nonstandard properties and events for fpBinary.

**Table 4-44** Nonstandard properties and events for fpBinary

**PROPERTIES**

| | | |
|---|---|---|
| About | BinaryStyle | DataChanged |
| ScrollBars | | |

**EVENTS**

| | |
|---|---|
| Advance | UserError |

**fpBoolean** fpBoolean (AWAREBB.VBX) is a data-aware replacement for the Visual Basic Option, Check, and Command controls, depending on how the control's *BooleanPicture* and *BooleanMode* properties are set. See Tables 4-45 and 4-46 for the values. The user-defined value allows you to load custom bitmaps for the various button states. See Figure 4-19 for an example of fpBoolean.

**Table 4-45** Values for BooleanPicture

| VALUE | MEANING |
|---|---|
| 0 | Check box |
| 1 | Option button |
| 2 | 3D check box |
| 3 | 3D option |
| 4 | User-defined |

**Table 4-46** Values for BooleanMode

| VALUE | MEANING |
|---|---|
| 0 | Two-state button (option button) |
| 1 | Three-state button (check box) |
| 2 | Command button |

You can group fpBoolean controls using the *Group* properties. You use the *GroupId* property to group sets of option buttons on one parent container. This means you don't need to group sets of option buttons in separate parent controls. The *GroupSelect* property allows you to determine how sets of *fpBoolean* controls act.

*GroupValue* is a Long that contains the value of the group of fbBoolean controls. You can assign a value to each control in a group using the *GroupTag* property. As the user turns members of the fbBoolean group on or off, the *GroupTag* of each individual control is ANDed with the value of *GroupValue*, giving the group of fbBooleans a value. You can use *GroupValue* to update a numeric column in a bound table.

fpBoolean also has a set of *Picture* properties that you can use to assign custom pictures to the values of an fpBoolean control.

Table 4-47 lists the nonstandard properties and events for fpBoolean.

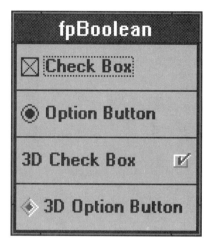

**Figure 4-19** fpBoolean examples

**Table 4-47** Nonstandard properties and events for fpBoolean

**PROPERTIES**

| | | |
|---|---|---|
| AlignPictureH | AlignPictureV | AlignTextH |
| AlignTextV | AutoToggle | BooleanMode |
| BooleanPicture | BooleanStyle | GroupSelect |
| GroupTag | GroupValue | MarginBottom |
| MarginLeft | MarginRight | MarginTop |
| PictureFalse | PictureFalseDisabled | PictureFalseDown |
| PictureTrue | PictureTrueDisabled | PictureTrueDown |
| TextDisabled | TextFalse | TextTrue |
| ToggleFalse | ToggleTrue | |

**EVENTS**

| | |
|---|---|
| Advance | UserError |

**fpCalendar**   fpCalendar (AWARECC.VBX) is a complete drop-in data-aware calendar. See Figure 4-20 for an example of fpCalendar.

You can bind fpCalendar to a text or a date/time column. You have control over the colors and appearance of the control. Rather than having a large number of custom properties, fpCalendar allows you to customize the visual attributes of the control using the *Element* and *ElementIndex* properties. See Table 4-48 for the values of *Element*. You use *Element* to choose which aspect of fpCalendar you'd like to customize. You can change the appearance and value of individual weekdays and days of the month by setting *Element* to 5 (WeekDayIndex) or 6 (DayIndex), and then setting *ElementIndex* to the appropriate day (1 through 7) or date (1 through 31).

**Table 4-48** Values for Element

| VALUE | MEANING |
|---|---|
| 0- | Default—(sets the default properties for color, style, and so on) |
| 1- | Month—(selects the month title) |
| 2- | Days—(all days of the month) |
| 3- | Year—(selects the Year title) |
| 4- | WeekDays—(selects the WeekDay titles) |
| 5- | WeekDayIndex—(used to change the individual weekday names) (Use the ElementIndex to choose a specific day) |
| 6- | DaysIndex—(used to change the individual day numbers) (Use ElementIndex to choose a specific number) |
| 7- | DropDown—(provides an optional DropDown button for the month and/or year titles) |

The date displayed on fpCalendar is set or returned using the *CurrentDate* property. The individual parts of the date are accessible using *Day, Month,* or *Year* properties. Table 4-49 lists the nonstandard properties for fpCalendar.

**Table 4-49** Nonstandard properties for fpCalendar

| | | |
|---|---|---|
| About | BorderGrayAreaColor | BorderStyle |
| BorderWidth | CurrentDate | DateMax |
| DateMin | Day | DropShadowColor |
| DropShadowWidth | Element | Element3DHighlightColor |
| Element3DShadowColor | Element3DShadowWidth | Element3DStyle |
| Element3DText | ElementBackColor | ElementForeColor |
| ElementIndex | FirstDayOfWeek | HeaderStyle |
| Month | MonthHeaderStyle | WeekDayHdr |
| Year | YearHeaderStyle | |

**Figure 4-20** fpCalendar example

**fpClock**   fpClock (AWARECC.VBX) is a data-aware clock control. You can display either a digital clock, an analog clock, or the default "text" time display. When displaying the analog clock, you can control how the numbers are displayed and the shape of the hands. You can build custom hands for the analog version of fpClock using the *Analog* properties, which give you very exact control over the size and shape of each hand.

You can use fpClock to display the time or as a stop watch or alarm clock. If you use fpClock in analog mode, you can allow the user to drag the hands to set the time. When the user moves the clock hands, the control sets the *CurrentTime* property to the time on the clock and then the *MoveHandEvent* fires.

To make fpClock act as an alarm clock, set the *AlarmTime* property to the time you'd like the alarm to go off. When the time in *AlarmTime* is reached, the *Alarm* event fires. fpClock has no snooze feature built in; you'll have to add snooze if you want it.

Table 4-50 lists the custom properties and events for fpClock.

**Table 4-50**  Nonstandard properties and events for fpClock

**PROPERTIES**

| | | |
|---|---|---|
| About | AlarmTime | AllowMoveHand |
| AnalogFace | AnalogHourFill | AnalogHourFillColor |
| AnalogHourHandAngle | AnalogHourHandColor | AnalogHourHandPts |
| AnalogHourHandRadius | AnalogMinFill | AnalogMinFillColor |
| AnalogMinHandAngle | AnalogMinHandColor | AnalogMinHandPts |
| AnalogMinHandRadius | AnalogSecFill | AnalogSecFillColor |
| AnalogSecHandAngle | AnalogSecHandColor | AnalogSecHandPts |
| AnalogSecHandRadius | AnalogTickFillColor | AnalogTicks |
| AnalogTickShadowColor | AutoSet | AutoUpdate |
| ClockMode | ClockStyle | CurrentTime |
| ElapsedTime | Hour | Interval |
| LeadZero | Left | Min |
| Sec | Seconds | Separator |
| StartTime | TimeScale | TimeString1159 |
| TimeString2359 | | |

**EVENTS**

| | | |
|---|---|---|
| Alarm | MoveHandEvent | Timer |

**fpComboBox**   fpComboBox (AWARECB.VBX) is an enhanced, multicolumn, data-aware version of the Visual Basic ComboBox control. Like the other controls in Aware/VBX, fpComboBox can take on a 3D appearance.

There are three ways to use fpComboBox with a data control. You can bind the text portion to a data control, bind the list portion to a data control, or bind the text portion to one data control and the list portion to a second data control.

As with all combo boxes, you can use the drop-down list portion to hold valid values for the field. This feature lets you use a database table to store the valid values for the column bound to the text portion of fpComboBox. You might use this feature to store a table of valid states for a state column. Using a bound list portion with an unbound text portion gives you the best of both worlds. The data control makes it easy to populate the list box, while a Data Access Object gives you fine control over updating your database.

fpComboBox also supports multiple columns in the list portion of the control. You might use multiple columns to display a coded value in the text portion, and display the code and its value when the user drops down the list box. Although you can change the properties controlling the multiple columns at design time, with fpComboBox multiple columns are probably best handled via code. The following code is an example of how to control multiple columns.

```
fpcombobox1.Col = 0
fpcombobox1.ColDataField = "aptTextDate"
fpcombobox1.ColHeaderText = "Date"
fpcombobox1.ColFormat = "&&&&/&&/&&"
fpcombobox1.ColWidth = 11
fpcombobox1.Col = 1
fpcombobox1.ColHeaderText = "Location"
fpcombobox1.ColDataField = "aptLocation"
fpcombobox1.ColWidth = 10
```

fpComboBox has two custom events, *CloseUp* and *SelChange*. *CloseUp* is fired when the list box portion of the control is hidden. *SelChange* is fired when the user selects a new item in the list portion of the control.

Table 4-51 lists the nonstandard properties and events for fpComboBox.

**Table 4-51** Nonstandard properties and events for fpComboBox

**PROPERTIES**

| | | |
|---|---|---|
| Col | ColAlignH | ColDataField |
| ColFieldType | ColFormat | ColHeaderAlignH |
| ColHeaderText | ColHide | ColList |
| ColSortSequence | ColText | ColumnEdit |
| Columns | ColumnSeparatorChar | ColumnWidthScale |
| ColWidth | ComboListWidth | DataFieldList |
| DataSourceList | FieldType | Header3DStyle |
| Header3DText | Header3DTextOffset | Header3DTextHighlightColor |
| Header3DWidth | HeaderBackColor | Header3DTextShadowColor |
| HeaderFontBold | HeaderFontItalic | HeaderFontName |
| HeaderFontSize | HeaderFontStrike | HeaderFontUnder |
| ColSorted | HeaderForeColor | HeaderHeight |
| HeaderShow | LineColor | LineHighlightColor |
| LineShadowColor | LineStyleH | LineStyleV |
| LineWidth | List3DText | List3DTextHighlightColor |
| MaxDrop | List3DTextOffset | List3DTextShadowColor |

### PROPERTIES

| | | |
|---|---|---|
| Row | Sel3DHighlightColor | Sel3DShadowColor |
| Sel3DStyle | Sel3DWidth | SelBackColor |
| SelDrawFocusRect | SelForeColor | SelLength |
| SelStart | TopIndex | VirtualMode |
| VirtualScrollMax | | |

### EVENTS

| | |
|---|---|
| CloseUp | SelChange |

**fpCurrency** fpCurrency (AWARE.VBX) is a specialized data-aware data-entry control with 3D properties. It's specifically designed to handle currency input and output. Unless you otherwise specify, fpCurrency defaults to the international settings specified in the WIN.INI file.

Table 4-52 lists the custom properties and events for fpCurrency.

**Table 4-52** Nonstandard properties and events for fpCurrency

### PROPERTIES

| | | |
|---|---|---|
| About | Action | AlignTextH |
| AlignTextV | AllowNull | AutoAdvance |
| AutoBeep | BorderWidth | ButtonDefaultAction |
| ButtonDisable | ButtonHide | ButtonIncrement |
| ButtonIndex | ButtonMax | ButtonMin |
| ButtonStyle | ButtonWidth | ButtonWrap |
| CaretInsert | CaretOverWrite | CharPositionLeft |
| CharPositionRight | ControlType | CurrencyDecimalPlaces |
| CurrencyNegFormat | CurrencyPlacement | CurrencySymbol |
| CurrentPosition | DecimalPoint | DropShadowColor |
| DropShadowWidth | FixedPoint | FontBold |
| HideSelection | hWnd | IncDec |
| IncInt | Index | InvalidColor |
| InvalidOption | IsNull | IsValid |
| LeadZero | MarginBottom | MarginLeft |
| MarginRight | MarginTop | MaxValue |
| MinValue | NegToggle | NoSpecialKeys |
| NullColor | OnFocusAlignH | OnFocusAlignV |
| Separator | Text | UnFmtText |
| UserEntry | UseSeparator | Value |

### EVENTS

| | | |
|---|---|---|
| Advance | ButtonHit | Change |
| ChangeMode | InvalidData | UserError |

**fpDateTime**   fpDateTime (AWARE.VBX) is a specialized data-aware data-entry control with 3D properties. It's specifically designed to handle date and time input and output. It can be connected with a date/time column or a text column in a database. Of course, if you connect fpDateTime to a text column, you need to make sure the data stored in the column is in valid date or time format.

fpDateTime lets you handle either a date, time, or date and time at the same time. You can have fpDateTime guess the correct values for an input date or time based on the current date and time. You can use fpDateTime in conjunction with the fpCalendar control.

Table 4-53 lists the nonstandard properties and events for fpDateTime.

**Table 4-53** Nonstandard properties and events for fpDateTime

**PROPERTIES**

| | | |
|---|---|---|
| About | Action | AlignTextH |
| AlignTextV | AllowNull | AutoAdvance |
| AutoBeep | BorderGrayAreaColor | BorderColor |
| BorderStyle | ButtonDefaultAction | BorderWidth |
| ButtonDisable | ButtonHide | ButtonIncrement |
| ButtonIndex | ButtonMax | ButtonMin |
| ButtonStyle | ButtonWidth | ButtonWrap |
| CaretInsert | CaretOverWrite | CharPositionLeft |
| CharPositionRight | ControlType | CurrentPosition |
| DataSource | DateCalcMethod | DateDefault |
| DateMax | DateMin | DateTimeFormat |
| DateValue | Day | DropShadowColor |
| DropShadowWidth | HideSelection | Hour |
| InvalidColor | InvalidOption | IsNull |
| IsValid | MarginBottom | MarginLeft |
| MarginRight | MarginTop | Min |
| Month | NoSpecialKeys | NullColor |
| OnFocusAlignH | OnFocusAlignV | OnFocusNoSelect |
| OnFocusPosition | OnFocusShadow | Sec |
| TimeDefault | TimeMax | TimeMin |
| TimeString1159 | TimeString2359 | TimeStyle |
| TimeValue | UnFmtText | UserDefinedFormat |
| UserEntry | Year | |

**EVENTS**

| | | |
|---|---|---|
| Advance | ButtonHit | ChangeMode |
| InvalidData | UserError | |

**fpDoubleSingle** fpDoubleSingle (AWARE.VBX) is a specialized data-aware data-entry control with 3D properties. It's specifically designed to handle real number input and output. Unless you specify otherwise, fpDoubleSingle defaults to the international settings in the WIN.INI file.

Table 4-54 lists the nonstandard properties and events for fpDoubleSingle.

**Table 4-54** Nonstandard properties and events for fpDoubleSingle

### PROPERTIES

| | | |
|---|---|---|
| About | Action | AlignTextH |
| AlignTextV | AllowNull | AutoAdvance |
| AutoBeep | BackColor | BorderColor |
| BorderGrayAreaColor | BorderStyle | BorderWidth |
| ButtonDefaultAction | ButtonDisable | ButtonHide |
| ButtonIncrement | ButtonIndex | ButtonMax |
| ButtonMin | ButtonStyle | ButtonWidth |
| ButtonWrap | CaretInsert | CaretOverWrite |
| CharPositionLeft | CharPositionRight | ControlType |
| CurrentPosition | DecimalPlaces | DecimalPoint |
| DropShadowColor | DropShadowWidth | FixedPoint |
| HideSelection | IncDec | IncInt |
| InvalidColor | InvalidOption | IsNull |
| IsValid | LeadZero | Left |
| MarginBottom | MarginLeft | MarginRight |
| MarginTop | MaxValue | NegFormat |
| NegToggle | NoSpecialKeys | NullColor |
| OnFocusAlignH | OnFocusAlignV | OnFocusInvert3D |
| OnFocusNoSelect | Separator | Text |
| UnFmtText | UserEntry | UseSeparator |
| Value | | |

### EVENTS

| | | |
|---|---|---|
| Advance | ButtonHit | ChangeMode |
| InvalidData | UserError | |

**fpListBox** fpListBox (AWARELB.VBX) is an enhanced version of the standard Visual Basic list box. fpListBox is multicolumn, multiselect, 3D, and data aware. It also allows you to specify the amount of data returned from the data control so the list box can display more than the standard 64K of data. fpListBox permits you to sort on one or more columns in the list box. As with fpComboBox, although you can access the properties for the individual columns at design time, it is easier to set the column properties at run time.

Table 4-55 lists the nonstandard properties and event for fpListBox.

**Table 4-55** Nonstandard properties and event for fpListBox

### PROPERTIES

| | | |
|---|---|---|
| About | BackColor | Col |
| ColAlignH | ColDataField | ColFieldType |
| ColFormat | ColHeaderAlignH | ColHeaderText |
| ColHide | ColList | ColSorted |
| ColSortSequence | Columns | ColumnSeparatorChar |
| ColumnWidthScale | ColWidth | DragMode |
| FieldType | Header3DStyle | Header3DText |
| Header3DTextHighlightColor | Header3DTextOffset | Header3DWidth |
| Header3DTextShadowColor | HeaderBackColor | HeaderFontBold |
| HeaderFontItalic | HeaderFontName | HeaderFontSize |
| HeaderFontStrike | HeaderFontUnder | HeaderForeColor |
| HeaderHeight | HeaderShow | LineColor |
| LineHighlightColor | LineShadowColor | LineStyleH |
| LineStyleV | LineWidth | List |
| List3DText | List3DTextOffset | List3DTextHighlightColor |
| List3DTextShadowColor | ListIndex | MultiSelect |
| Row | ScrollBars | Sel3DHighlightColor |
| Sel3DShadowColor | Sel3DStyle | Sel3DWidth |
| SelBackColor | SelCount | SelDrawFocusRect |
| SelForeColor | SelMax | Sorted |
| Text | | |

### EVENT

SelChange

**fpLongInteger**  fpLongInteger (AWARE.VBX) is a specialized data-aware data-entry control with 3D properties. It's specifically designed to handle integer number input and output. Unless you specify otherwise, fpLongInteger  defaults to the international settings in the WIN.INI file.

Table 4-56 lists the nonstandard properties and events for fpLongInteger.

**Table 4-56** Nonstandard properties and events for fpLongInteger

### PROPERTIES

| | | |
|---|---|---|
| About | Action | AlignTextH |
| AlignTextV | AllowNull | AutoAdvance |
| AutoBeep | BorderColor | BorderGrayAreaColor |
| BorderStyle | BorderWidth | ButtonDefaultAction |

## PROPERTIES

| | | |
|---|---|---|
| ButtonDisable | ButtonHide | ButtonIncrement |
| ButtonIndex | ButtonMax | ButtonMin |
| ButtonStyle | ButtonWidth | ButtonWrap |
| CaretInsert | CaretOverWrite | CharPositionLeft |
| CharPositionRight | ControlType | CurrentPosition |
| HideSelection | IncInt | InvalidColor |
| InvalidOption | IsNull | IsValid |
| MarginBottom | MarginLeft | MarginRight |
| MarginTop | MaxValue | MinValue |
| NegFormat | NegToggle | NoSpecialKeys |
| NullColor | OnFocusAlignH | OnFocusAlignV |
| OnFocusNoSelect | OnFocusPosition | Separator |
| Text | UnFmtText | UserEntry |
| UseSeparator | Value | Width |

## EVENTS

| | | |
|---|---|---|
| Advance | ButtonHit | ChangeMode |
| InvalidData | UserError | |

**fpMask**  fpMask (AWARE.VBX) is an enhanced version of the Masked Edit control supplied with Visual Basic. It is data aware and has 3D properties.

fpMask lets you define custom masks for data input and display. Once the mask is defined, the user can only enter correctly formatted data. Any attempt to enter invalid data causes the *UserError* event to fire. The mask can contain literal data, such as parentheses or dashes, and placeholder data to indicate the valid data. The *DataFormat* property lets you write the data to a bound database either unformatted or using the defined mask.

Table 4-57 lists the nonstandard properties and events for fpMask.

**Table 4-57** Nonstandard properties and events for fpMask

### PROPERTIES

| | | |
|---|---|---|
| About | Action | AlignTextH |
| AlignTextV | AllowNull | AllowOverflow |
| AutoAdvance | AutoBeep | AutoCase |
| BestFit | ButtonDisable | ButtonHide |
| ButtonIncrement | ButtonIndex | ButtonMax |
| ButtonMin | ButtonStyle | ButtonWidth |
| ButtonWrap | CaretInsert | CaretOverWrite |
| CharPositionLeft | CharPositionRight | ClipMode |

*(continued on next page)*

**PROPERTIES**

*(continued from previous page)*

| | | |
|---|---|---|
| CurrentPosition | HideSelection | InvalidColor |
| InvalidOption | IsNull | IsValid |
| MaskChar | MousePointer | NoSpecialKeys |
| NullColor | OnFocusAlignH | OnFocusAlignV |
| OnFocusNoSelect | OnFocusPosition | OnFocusShadow |
| PromptChar | PromptInclude | RequireFill |
| SelLength | UnFmtText | UserEntry |

**EVENTS**

| | | |
|---|---|---|
| Advance | ButtonHit | ChangeMode |
| InvalidData | UserError | |

**fpMemo**   fpMemo (AWAREMM.VBX) is an enhanced version of the Text control supplied with Visual Basic. It is data aware and has 3D properties.

fpMemo has several enhancements over the standard VB text box. fpMemo breaks the 64K memory barrier of the standard text box, making it useful for apps that must handle large text files. You control how fbMemo handles the data using the *TextMode* property, whose values are listed in Table 4-58.

**Table 4-58** Values for TextMode

| VALUE | MEANING |
|---|---|
| 0 | Normal (64K max) |
| 1 | Read a 64K block of text as needed, replacing the current contents |
| 2 | New text is appended to existing text, or a new block of text is read as the user scrolls or types into the control |
| 3 | Read a specific line based on the LineIndex property |

The fpMemo control also has several basic word processing features not found in most text box replacement controls. *PageWidth* sets the width of the "printed" page. *WordWrap* turns on or off word wrap. *ShowEOL* lets you display the end of sentence markers (usually CRLF) as a paragraph mark.

Table 4-59 lists the nonstandard properties and events for fpMemo.

**Table 4-59** Nonstandard properties and events for fpMemo

**PROPERTIES**

| | | |
|---|---|---|
| Action | AlignTextH | AlignTextV |
| AllowNull | AutoAdvance | AutoBeep |
| ButtonDefaultAction | ButtonDisable | ButtonHide |

## PROPERTIES

| | | |
|---|---|---|
| ButtonIncrement | ButtonIndex | ButtonMax |
| ButtonMin | ButtonStyle | ButtonWidth |
| ButtonWrap | CaretInsert | CaretOverWrite |
| CharPositionLeft | CharPositionRight | ControlType |
| CurrentPosition | DataChanged | DataField |
| DataSource | DragIcon | DragMode |
| DropShadowColor | DropShadowWidth | Enabled |
| HideSelection | InvalidColor | InvalidOption |
| IsNull | IsValid | Left |
| LineCount | LineIndex | LineLimit |
| MarginBottom | MarginLeft | MarginRight |
| MarginTop | MousePointer | Name |
| NoSpecialKeys | NullColor | OnFocusAlignH |
| OnFocusAlignV | OnFocusPosition | OnFocusShadow |
| PageWidth | ShowEOL | TabStop |
| TextMode | Top | UserEntry |
| Visible | Width | WordWrap |

## EVENTS

| | | |
|---|---|---|
| Advance | ButtonHit | ChangeMode |
| InvalidData | UserError | |

**fpText**  fpText (AWARE.VBX) is an enhanced version of the Text control supplied with Visual Basic. It is data aware and has 3D properties.

fpText has several enhancements over the standard VB text box. You can limit the user to a subset of the keyboard using the *CharValidationText* and *UserEntry* properties. For example, if you set *CharValidationText* to "AEIOU" and set *UserEntry* to 0, Formatted, the user could only enter vowels. Setting *UserEntry* to 1, FreeFormat, tells fpText to ignore the setting of *CharValidationText*. *CharValidationText* is case sensitive, so "aeiou" would not be valid.

You can control the case of the text input using the *AutoCase* property. Table 4-60 lists the valid values for *AutoCase*.

**Table 4-60** Values for AutoCase

| VALUE | MEANING |
|---|---|
| 0 | No automatic case setting |
| 1 | Sets all characters to uppercase |
| 2 | Sets all characters to lowercase |
| 3 | Sets proper case |
| 4 | Sets proper case, but allows embedded uppercase letters |

Table 4-61 lists the nonstandard properties and events for fpText.

**Table 4-61** Nonstandard properties and events for fpText

### PROPERTIES

| | | |
|---|---|---|
| Action | AlignTextH | AlignTextV |
| AllowNull | AutoAdvance | AutoBeep |
| AutoCase | ButtonDefaultAction | ButtonDisable |
| ButtonHide | ButtonIncrement | ButtonIndex |
| ButtonMax | ButtonMin | ButtonStyle |
| ButtonWidth | ButtonWrap | CaretInsert |
| CaretOverWrite | CharPositionLeft | CharPositionRight |
| CharValidationText | CurrentPosition | HideSelection |
| IncHoriz | InvalidColor | InvalidOption |
| IsNull | IsValid | MarginBottom |
| MarginLeft | MarginRight | MarginTop |
| MaxLength | NoSpecialKeys | NullColor |
| OnFocusAlignH | OnFocusAlignV | PasswordChar |
| UserEntry | | |

### EVENTS

| | | |
|---|---|---|
| Advance | ButtonHit | ChangeMode |
| InvalidData | UserError | |

# Example

The example program on the CD (shown in Figure 4-21) is a basic appointment scheduler. It uses an fpMemo control to record the description, fpClock and fpCalendar controls to determine the date and time of the appointment, and other FarPoint controls to enter other interesting or uninteresting information, including a totally gratuitous use of the fpDoubleSingle control.

# Tips and Comments

The controls included in Aware/VBX make it easy to do simple database programs. The fpCalendar and fpClock controls simplify working with dates and times. The fpMemo control is also useful if you need a way to edit more than 64K of text at once. The addition of the buttons to the input controls gives you a flexibility that isn't found in most competing packages. Being able to automatically show invalid data graphically is also very useful.

This package has some rough edges, as you might expect from version 1 of any software, but there aren't any show stoppers. Make sure to download the latest release of the controls from FarPoint's BBS or CompuServe forum. This will fix many of the more flagrant glitches.

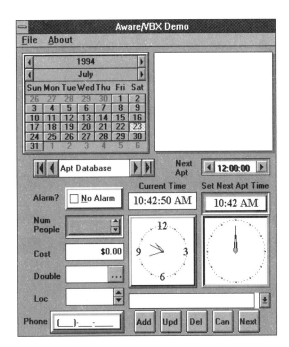

**Figure 4-21** The Aware/VBX
example program

# COMMUNICATIONS

One increasingly critical function of the PC is communicating with other computers, from small BBS systems to online services like CompuServe to the largest mainframe systems. The controls covered in this chapter—Microsoft MSComm and Crescent PDQ Comm— enable Visual Basic to communicate with the outside world in a variety of ways.

Microsoft MSComm is the lightest of the two packages covered here, offering only basic communications with the modem in an event-driven fashion. MSComm has no built-in terminal emulations or downloading capabilities. Crescent's PDQComm has a broader range of terminal emulations and an equal range of file transfer protocols, and also offers an event-driven user interface that makes it somewhat easier to use.

Using the controls covered in this chapter, you'll learn how to:

▲ Build an autodialer

▲ Dial into another computer and emulate an ANSI or TTY terminal using a timer to handle sending and receiving data

▲ Dial into another computer and emulate a VT52, VT100, ANSI, or TTY terminal using the event-driven Visual Basic model

# Microsoft MSComm (MSCOMM.VBX)

| USAGE: | Windows Communication Software |
| --- | --- |
| MANUFACTURER: | Microsoft |
| COST: | Included with Visual Basic 3.0 Professional Edition |

MSCOMM.VBX lets you deal with modems using the event-driven model with which Visual Basic programmers have become familiar. Besides supplying custom properties for controlling the modem's features and settings, MSComm gives you an easy way to deal with modem communications.

Unlike some of the other communications custom controls, MSComm doesn't have any built-in terminal emulation or file transfer capabilities, so if you need those capabilities you'll have to "roll your own." MSComm does support all the features of the average modem, including Data Terminal Ready (DTR), Data Set Ready (DSR), Clear to Send (CTS), Carrier Detect (CD), and RTS (Ready to Send). MSComm also supports the full range of baud rates that COMM.DRV or any compatible replacement supports.

## Syntax

MSComm has a full range of properties and one event for controlling the modem, as listed in Table 5-1.

**Table 5-1** Custom properties and event of the MSComm control

### PROPERTIES

| | | |
| --- | --- | --- |
| CDHolding | CDTimeout | CommEvent |
| CommID | CommPort | CTSHolding |
| CTSTimeout | DSRHolding | DSRTimeOut |
| DTREnable | HandShaking | InBufferCount |
| InBufferSize | Input | InputLen |

## PROPERTIES

| | | |
|---|---|---|
| Interval | NullDiscard | OutBufferCount |
| Output | OutBufferSize | ParityReplace |
| PortOpen | RThreshold | RTSEnable |
| Settings | SThreshold | |

## EVENT

OnComm

MSComm has one custom event, *OnComm*, that fires whenever something significant happens with the modem. *OnComm* fires for incoming or outgoing data, change in modem status, and some modem errors. You must read the *CommEvent* property to determine what caused *OnComm* to fire. The *CommEvent* property contains the most recent communications event or error, and can take on the values listed in Table 5-2.

**Table 5-2** Values for the CommEvent property

| CONSTANT | VALUE | MEANING |
|---|---|---|
| MSCOMM_EV_SEND | 1 | There are fewer than SThreshold characters in the output buffer |
| MSCOMM_EV_RECEIVE | 2 | Received RThreshold characters |
| MSCOMM_EV_CTS | 3 | Change in Clear to Send (CTS) |
| MSCOMM_EV_DSR | 4 | Change in Data Set Ready (DSR) |
| MSCOMM_EV_CD | 5 | Change in Carrier Detect (CD) |
| MSCOMM_EV_RING | 6 | Ring detected |
| MSCOMM_EV_EOF | 7 | End of File received |
| MSCOMM_ER_BREAK | 1001 | Break detected |
| MSCOMM_ER_CTSTO | 1002 | Clear to Send timeout |
| MSCOMM_ER_DSRTO | 1003 | Data Set Ready timeout |
| MSCOMM_ER_FRAME | 1004 | Framing error |
| MSCOMM_ER_OVERRUN | 1006 | Port Overrun error |
| MSCOMM_ER_CDTO | 1007 | Carrier Detect timeout |
| MSCOMM_ER_RXOVER | 1008 | Receive overflow |
| MSCOMM_ER_RXPARITY | 1009 | Parity error |
| MSCOMM_ER_TXFULL | 1010 | Transmit buffer full |

The *Settings* property is where you load the parameters controlling the baud rate, parity, data bits, and stop bits for the computer you're dialing into. You set the *PortOpen* property to *True* to open or *False* to close the port specified by *CommPort*.

5

Data is sent to the modem using the Output property and data is retrieved from the modem using the Input property. Each has an associated BufferSize and BufferCount property. BufferCount tells how many characters are waiting to be sent or received and BufferSize is the raw size of the buffer in bytes.

*RThreshold* controls how often *OnComm* fires when characters are received. Setting it to 0 turns it off. The *InTimeout* property in combination with the *RThreshold* property govern how often MSComm notifies you that you have input data. *CommEvent* fires either to notify you that the specified number of characters have arrived from the communications port, or that data is there but the timer expired before you reached your specified threshold.

*SThreshold* sets how many characters or less remain in the output buffer when *OnComm* fires. For example, if you set *SThreshold* to 10, when *OutputBufferCount* goes below 10 *OnComm* fires with a *CommEvent* value of MSCOMM_EV_SEND. This lets you know you can place more data in the output buffer for processing. If *SThreshold* is set to 1, *OnComm* fires when *OutputBufferCount* reaches 0; and if *SThreshold* is set to 0, *OnComm* never fires with an output buffer event.

# Example

This example program shows how to use MSComm to create the autodialer in Figure 5-1. This program allows you to save and update numbers stored in an .INI file in your Windows directory. The Delete Ini File menu option deletes the .INI file, allowing you to keep your Windows directory neat and clean.

## Steps

1. Create a new project called MSCOMM.MAK and add MSCOMM.VBX. Create a new form with the objects and properties shown in Table 5-3. Save this form as MSCOMM.FRM.

**Figure 5-1** The MSCOMM example program

**Table 5-3** The MSCOMM form's objects and properties

| OBJECT | PROPERTY | SETTING |
|---|---|---|
| Label | Name | lblStatus |
| | Caption | "Status" |
| Label | Name | Label1 |
| | Caption | "Number:" |
| Label | Name | lblCommPort |
| | Caption | "Comm 1" |
| CommandButton | Name | cmdDial |
| | Caption | "Dial" |
| | Default | -1 'True |
| MSComm | Name | Comm1 |
| | CommPort | 2 |
| | Interval | 1000 |
| | RTSEnable | -1 'True |
| CommandButton | Name | cmdQuit |
| | Cancel | -1 'True |
| | Caption | "Quit" |
| CommandButton | Name | cmdCancel |
| | Caption | "Cancel" |
| | Enabled | 0 'False |
| ComboBox | Name | cmbDirectory |
| TextBox | Name | txtNumber |
| CommandButton | Name | cmdSave |
| | Caption | "Save" |
| VScrollBar | Name | vscrPort |
| | Max | 4 |
| | Min | 1 |
| | Value | 1 |
| Form | FormName | MSCOMM1 |
| | BorderStyle | 3 'Fixed Double |
| | Caption | "MSComm Phone Dialer" |
| | MaxButton | 0 'False |
| | MinButton | 0 'False |

2. Add the following definitions to the declarations section of the MSCOMM form. This code sets up any declarations needed in the MSCOMM form and adds code to handle any specific events caused by controls on the form.

```
'-- This flag is set when Cancel is pressed.
Dim CancelFlag As Integer
```

(continued on next page)

*(continued from previous page)*

```
    '
    ' Used in StringFromINI function.
    Declare Function GetProfileString Lib "Kernel" (ByVal Section As String, ByVal KeyName As
String, ByVal Default As String, ByVal ReturnedString As String, ByVal nSize As Integer) As
Integer
    Declare Function GetPrivateProfileString Lib "Kernel" (ByVal Section As String, ByVal
KeyName As String, ByVal Default As String, ByVal ReturnedString As String, ByVal MaxSize%,
ByVal FileName As String) As Integer          .

    ' Used to get all section names.
    Declare Function GetPrivProfSections Lib "Kernel" Alias "GetPrivateProfileString" (ByVal
Section As String, ByVal KeyName As Any, ByVal Default As String, ByVal ReturnedString As
String, ByVal MaxSize%, ByVal FileName As String) As Integer
    '
    ' Used in StringToINI Sub.
    Declare Function WritePrivateProfileString Lib "Kernel" (ByVal sectname As String, ByVal
KeyName As String, ByVal NewString As String, ByVal FileName As String) As Integer
    '
    ' Used in Windir() function.
    Declare Function GetWindowsDirectory Lib "Kernel" (ByVal lpBuffer As String, ByVal nSize As
Integer) As Integer

    ' Used for .INI file processing.
    Const INIFILENAME = "MSCMDIAL.INI"
    Const APPNAME = "Directory"
    Const NUMBERSECT = "Number"
    Const PORTSECT = "Port"
```

3. Add the following code to MSCOMM.FRM. The code in this form handles loading the combo box with directory names from the database .INI file, updating the name comm port and phone number for a specific listing, opening the comm port, dialing, and detaching the modem so the person you're calling doesn't get an earful of modem whine.

```
Sub cmbDirectory_Click ()
    '--------------------------------
    ' Get the phone number and modem port
    'based on the data in the combo box.
    '--------------------------------
    Dim Number As String

    txtNumber = StringFromINI((cmbDirectory.Text), NUMBERSECT, "", INIFILENAME)
    vscrPort = Val(StringFromINI((cmbDirectory.Text), PORTSECT, "2", INIFILENAME))
End Sub

Sub cmdCancel_Click ()

    '--------------------------------
    ' CancelFlag tells the Dial routine to exit.
    '--------------------------------
    CancelFlag = True

    cmdCancel.Enabled = False

End Sub

Sub cmdDial_Click ()
```

```
'----------------------------
' Dial the phone.
'----------------------------
Dim Number$, Temp$

cmdDial.Enabled = False
cmdQuit.Enabled = False
cmdCancel.Enabled = True

'----------------------------
' Get the number to dial.
'----------------------------
Number$ = txtNumber

Temp$ = lblStatus
lblStatus = "Dialing - " + Number$

'----------------------------
' Dial the selected phone number.
'----------------------------
Dial Number$

cmdDial.Enabled = True
cmdQuit.Enabled = True
cmdCancel.Enabled = False

lblStatus = Temp$

End Sub

Sub cmdQuit_Click ()
    Unload frmabout
    Unload Me
End Sub

Sub cmdSave_Click ()
    '----------------------------
    ' Update the dialing directory database.
    '----------------------------

    Dim res As Integer

    res = StringToINI(APPNAME, (cmbDirectory.Text), (cmbDirectory.Text), INIFILENAME)

    res = StringToINI((cmbDirectory.Text), NUMBERSECT, (txtNumber), INIFILENAME)
    res = StringToINI((cmbDirectory.Text), PORTSECT, Format$(vscrPort), INIFILENAME)

End Sub

Sub Dial (Number$)
    '----------------------------
    ' Dial the phone using Number$ from above.
    '----------------------------

    Dim DialString As String
    Dim FromModem As String
    Dim StopString As String
    Dim Dummy As Integer
    Dim Delay As Double
```

*(continued on next page)*

5

*(continued from previous page)*

```
'------------------------------
' The semicolon tells the modem to return to
' command mode after it executes the command.
'------------------------------
DialString$ = "ATDT" + Number$ + ";" + Chr$(13)


'------------------------------
' Hang up - or more accurately, disconnect the modem.
'------------------------------
StopString = "ATHO" + Chr$(13)
comm1.CommPort = vscrPort
comm1.Settings = "300,N,8,1"


'------------------------------
' Open the comm port.
'------------------------------
On Error Resume Next
comm1.PortOpen = True
If Err Then
    MsgBox "Couldn't open comm port - error: " & Error$(Err)
    Exit Sub
End If


comm1.InBufferCount = 0

' Dial.
comm1.Output = DialString$


'------------------------------
' Wait for OK to come back from the modem.
'------------------------------
Do
    Dummy = DoEvents()
    '------------------------------
    ' If there is data in the buffer, then read it.
    '------------------------------
    If comm1.InBufferCount Then
        FromModem$ = FromModem$ + comm1.Input
        ' Check for OK.
        If InStr(FromModem$, "OK") Then
            ' Notify the user to pick up the phone.
            FromModem = ""
            Beep
            MsgBox "Please pick up the phone and either press Enter or click OK"
            Exit Do
        End If
    End If

    ' Was Cancel pressed?
    If CancelFlag Then
        CancelFlag = False
        Exit Do
    End If
Loop

' Disconnect the modem.
comm1.Output = StopString

' Wait a second.
```

```
    Delay = Timer
    While Delay + 1 > Timer
        Dummy = DoEvents()
    Wend

    '------------------------------
    ' Setting DTREnable to false hangs up the phone.
    ' In this case, it should detach the modem.
    '------------------------------

    comm1.DTREnable = False
    Delay = Timer
    While Delay + 1 > Timer
        Dummy = DoEvents()
    Wend

    '------------------------------
    ' Set it back to on so MSComm can track status of
    ' connection.
    '------------------------------
    comm1.DTREnable = True

    '------------------------------
    ' Finally, close the port.
    '------------------------------
    comm1.PortOpen = False

End Sub

Sub Form_Load ()

    '------------------------------
    ' Center the form in the screen.
    '------------------------------
    Me.Move (Screen.Width - Me.Width) \ 2, (Screen.Height - Me.Height) \ 2

    LoadDirCombo cmbDirectory

    '------------------------------
    ' Initialize scroll bar that holds the comm port.
    '------------------------------
    vscrPort = 1

    '------------------------------
    ' Set this to 0 so we get "instant response" when
    ' the modem responds to our commands.
    '------------------------------
    comm1.InputLen = 0

End Sub

Sub Form_QueryUnload (Cancel As Integer, UnloadMode As Integer)
    '------------------------------
    ' Close the comm port if we're exiting.
    '------------------------------
    If comm1.PortOpen = True Then comm1.PortOpen = False
End Sub

Sub LoadDirCombo (cmbDirectory As Control)
```

*(continued on next page)*

**5**

311

*(continued from previous page)*

```
'------------------------------
' Get the "dialing directory" from the .INI file.
'------------------------------

    Dim HoldDirectory As String
    Dim SearchStr  As String
    Dim res As Integer
    Dim Stringpointer As Integer
    Dim LastPointer As Integer

    cmbDirectory.Clear
    SearchStr = Chr(0)
    '------------------------------
    ' We're going to put the entire dialing directory here,
    ' or at least 4K of it.
    '------------------------------
    HoldDirectory = String$(4001, 0)

    res = GetPrivProfSections(APPNAME, 0&, "", HoldDirectory, 4000, INIFILENAME)
    '------------------------------
    ' res = total number of characters returned.
    ' "Prime" the pump, so to speak.
    '------------------------------
    Stringpointer = InStr(1, HoldDirectory, SearchStr)
    LastPointer = 1
    Do While Stringpointer <= res
        cmbDirectory.AddItem Mid$(HoldDirectory, LastPointer, Stringpointer - 1)
        LastPointer = Stringpointer + 1 'point past the null
        Stringpointer = InStr(LastPointer, HoldDirectory, SearchStr)
        '------------------------------
        ' Returned string terminated by two nulls.
        '------------------------------
        If Stringpointer = LastPointer + 1 Then Exit Do
    Loop

End Sub

Sub mnuAbout_Click ()
    frmabout.Show 1
End Sub

Sub mnuDeleteINIFile_Click ()
    '------------------------------
    ' Delete the .INI file.
    '------------------------------

    On Error Resume Next ' Turn error handling off.
    Dim WinDirectory As String

    WinDirectory = WinDir()

    Kill WinDirectory & "\" & INIFILENAME

    On Error GoTo 0 ' Reset error handling.
End Sub

Sub mnuExit_Click ()
    Unload frmabout
    Unload Me
```

```
End Sub

Function StringFromINI (Section As String, KeyName As String, Default As String, FileName As
String) As String
    '-----------------------------
    ' Function reads the .INI file passed.
    '-----------------------------

    Dim MaxStringLen%, ReturnedStr$, result%, ResultStr$

    MaxStringLen% = 255
    ReturnedStr$ = Space$(MaxStringLen%)

    '-----------------------------
    ' Note that result% is the length of the string returned.
    '-----------------------------
    result% = GetPrivateProfileString(Section, KeyName, Default, ReturnedStr$, MaxStringLen%,
FileName)

    ResultStr$ = Left$(ResultStr$, result%)
    StringFromINI = Trim$(ResultStr$)
End Function

Function StringToINI (sectname As String, KeyName As String, DataString As String, INIFILENAME
As String) As Integer
    '-----------------------------
    ' Writes the passed string to the specified section of the specified .INI file.
    '-----------------------------
    StringToINI = WritePrivateProfileString(sectname, KeyName, DataString, INIFILENAME)
End Function

Sub vscrPort_Change ()
    lblCommPort = "Comm " & Format$(vscrPort)
End Sub

Function WinDir () As String
    '-----------------------------
    ' Returns the name of the Windows directory.
    '-----------------------------

    Dim Buff As String
    Dim Tchars As Integer

    Buff = Space$(255)
    Tchars = GetWindowsDirectory(Buff$, 255)
    WinDir = Left$(Buff$, Tchars)
End Function
```

## Tips and Comments

MSCOMM.VBX lets you write communications programs where you control all the action with incoming and outgoing data. MSComm handles most of the chores of managing Comm ports and setting modem parameters. The *OnComm* event provides notification for modem errors or status changes, such as receipt of data or the clearing of the output buffer. Once you are notified about modem events, your program can send data to a window or capture it to a file, or load more data into the output buffer.

MSComm would be ideal for reading data from a bar code reader hooked to a comm port, or possibly some sort of point of sale terminal, or reading data from an industrial machine that sends specific chunks of data. You probably wouldn't want to use MSComm when you were doing terminal emulation, because products like PDQComm from Crescent and VBComm from MicroHelp handle some types of terminal emulation automatically. One interesting point is that PDQComm is entirely compatible with MSComm because Crescent wrote MSComm and licensed it to Microsoft.

It is important to make liberal use of DoEvents while you are sending and receiving data from the modem. If you don't, Visual Basic keeps on rolling, ignoring any messages that might be waiting for it until it finishes executing.

# Crescent PDQComm (PDQCOMM2.VBX)

| USAGE: | Windows Communication Software |
|---|---|
| MANUFACTURER: | Crescent Software |
| COST: | $149 |

Communications software and modems are very complex. Crescent Software's PDQComm hides some of the complexity from you, even if using this package is still not as easy as dropping a phone icon on your form and having an instantly usable package.

PDQCOMM2.VBX features four built-in terminal emulations: ANSI BBS, TTY, VT52, and VT100. PDQComm also has eight types of file transfer protocols: three kinds of XModem, two kinds of YModem, ZModem, Kermit, and CompuServe B+. PDQComm has a built-in file transfer status dialog box, and all file transferring is done in the background so the user can continue working in other applications while the file transfer runs. PDQComm handles the full range of the modem alphabet, including Data Terminal Ready (DTR), Data Set Ready (DSR), Clear to Send (CTS), Carrier Detect (CD), and RTS (Ready to Send).

PDQComm can be operated under direct program control or automatically. The direct program mode is exactly like MSCOMM.VBX, which makes sense since Crescent wrote MSCOMM.VBX for Microsoft. The automatic mode is by far the easiest way to use PDQComm, because it handles all the translation of codes for whichever terminal emulation you've chosen.

PDQComm supports the full range of baud rates that COMM.DRV or any compatible replacement supports. PDQComm comes with a very useful set of sample code and a library of functions for determining modem statuses, setting variable baud rates, and so on.

Although the PDQComm manual contains some good information on how modems work, it predates the wide acceptance of 14,400 and faster modems.

# Syntax

In addition to the standard set of properties and events, PDQComm has one custom event and a full range of properties for controlling the modem, as listed in Table 5-4.

**Table 5-4** PDQCOMM2's custom properties and event

### PROPERTIES

| | | |
|---|---|---|
| AutoProcess | AutoScroll | AutoSize |
| CaptureMode | Columns | CaptureFileName |
| CDHolding | CDTimeout | CommEvent |
| CommID | CommPort | CTSHolding |
| CTSTimeout | CursorColumn | CursorRow |
| Disp | DownLoad | DSRHolding |
| DSRTimeOut | DTREnable | Echo |
| Emulation | HandShaking | Rows |
| InBufferCount | InBufferSize | Input |
| Interval | InTimeout | NullDiscard |
| Output | OutBufferSize | OutBufferCount |
| ParityReplace | PortOpen | Rows |
| RThreshold | RTSEnable | ScrollRows |
| ScrollText | Settings | SThreshold |
| Text | Upload | XferStatusDialog |
| XferFileSize | XferMessage | XferDestFilename |
| XferProtocol | XferStatus | XferTransferred |
| XferSourceFilename | | |

### EVENT

OnComm

The *OnComm* event is fired whenever something significant happens with the modem, including incoming or outgoing data, change in modem status, and some modem errors. You must read the *CommEvent* property to determine what caused *OnComm* to fire. The *CommEvent* property contains the most recent communications event or error, and can take on the valves listed in Table 5-5.

**Table 5-5** Values for the CommEvent property

| CONSTANT | VALUE | MEANING |
|---|---|---|
| PDQ_EV_SEND | 1 | There are fewer than SThreshold characters in the output buffer |
| PDQ_EV_RECEIVE | 2 | Received RThreshold characters |
| PDQ_EV_CTS | 3 | Change in Clear to Send (CTS) |

*(continued on next page)*

| CONSTANT | VALUE | MEANING |
|---|---|---|
| *(continued from previous page)* | | |
| PDQ_EV_DSR | 4 | Change in Data Set Ready (DSR) |
| PDQ_EV_CD | 5 | Change in Carrier Detect (CD) |
| PDQ_EV_RING | 6 | Ring Detected |
| PDQ_EV_EOF | 7 | End of File received |
| PDQ_EV_XFER | 100 | File Transfer event; check the XferStatus property |
| PDQ_ER_BREAK | 1001 | Break was detected |
| PDQ_ER_CTSTO | 1002 | Clear to Send timeout |
| PDQ_ER_DSRTO | 1003 | Data Set Ready timeout |
| PDQ_ER_FRAME | 1004 | Framing error |
| PDQ_ER_INTO | 1005 | Input timeout before RThreshold characters received |
| PDQ_ER_OVERRUN | 1006 | Port Overrun error |
| PDQ_ER_CDTO | 1007 | Carrier Detect timeout |
| PDQ_ER_RXOVER | 1008 | Receive overflow |
| PDQ_ER_RXPARITY | 1009 | Parity error |
| PDQ_ER_TXFULL | 1010 | Transmit buffer full |

The *Settings* property is where you load the parameters controlling the baud rate, parity, data bits, and stop bits for the computer you're dialing up. The *PortOpen* property is set to *True* to open or *False* to close the port specified by *CommPort*. The *Echo* property controls whether characters sent should be echoed to the screen. Set *Echo* to *False* when the system you're communicating with returns the typed character (this is true of most bulletin board systems), and *True* when it doesn't.

You send data to the modem using the *Output* property and get data from the modem using the *Input* property. Each has an associated *BufferSize* and *BufferCount* property. *BufferCount* tells how many characters are waiting to be sent or received, and *BufferSize* is the raw size of the buffer. The *InTimeout* property governs how long PDQComm waits before it fires the *CommEvent* event.

*RThreshold* controls how often *OnComm* fires when characters are received. If *RThreshold* is set to 10, when *InputBufferCount* reaches 10 *OnComm* fires with *CommEvent* set to 2, PDQ_EV_RECEIVE. Setting *InputBufferCount* to 0 turns it off, and *OnComm* never fires for PDQ_EV_RECEIVE *CommEvent* messages.

*SThreshold* controls how many characters or less are in the output buffer when *OnComm* fires. If you set *SThreshold* to 10, when *OutputBufferCount* passes from 10 to 9 *OnComm* fires with a *CommEvent* value of 1, MSCOMM_EV_SEND. This lets you know you can place more data in the output buffer for processing. If *SThreshold* is set to 1, *OnComm* fires when *OutputBufferCount* reaches 0; and if *SThreshold* is set to 0, *OnComm* never fires with an output buffer event.

The *Xfer, Upload,* and *DownLoad* properties control file transfer. The *Upload* and *Download* properties actually initiate the file transfer. The various *Xfer* properties control the type of transfer and the sending and receiving file names. *XferStatus* gives status information while a transfer is taking place.

To use PDQCOMM2.VBX as a terminal emulator, you set the *Emulation* property to the type of terminal you'd like your computer to be. Table 5-6 shows the possible values for *Emulation.*

**Table 5-6** Values for the Emulation property

| VALUE | MEANING |
|---|---|
| 0 | None, the VB program handles all processing |
| 1 | TTY terminal |
| 2 | ANSI terminal |
| 3 | VT52 |
| 4 | VT100 |

The *Rows* and *Columns* properties control the size of the terminal window in characters. If you're not emulating a terminal, *Rows* and *Columns* are ignored. The *CursorColumn* and *CursorRow* properties either set or return the current cursor position in the terminal window. The *AutoSize* property tells PDQComm to automatically size the text window to match the *Rows* and *Columns* properties. The *AutoProcess* property tells PDQComm how to handle keystrokes. Its possible values are spelled out in Table 5-7.

**Table 5-7** Values for the AutoProcess property

| VALUE | MEANING |
|---|---|
| 0 | Leave all data handling to the VB program |
| 1 | Handle data coming in from the serial port |
| 2 | Handle all keyboard input |
| 3 | Handle both the serial and keyboard input |

The *AutoScroll* property controls scrolling of the terminal window. Valid values and their effects are listed in Table 5-8.

**Table 5-8** Values for the AutoScroll property

| VALUE | MEANING |
|---|---|
| 0 | No automatic scrolling |
| 1 | Automatic vertical scrolling |
| 2 | Automatic horizontal scrolling |
| 3 | Automatic horizontal and vertical scrolling |
| 4 | Automatic vertical scrolling, and horizontal scrolling when a key is pressed |

5 ◄

You can also have PDQComm automatically log data sent to the modem by using the *CaptureFilename* and *CaptureMode* properties. Set *CaptureFilename* to the file name and directory where you want to store your captured data. Set the *CaptureMode* to one of the values listed in Table 5-9. While PDQComm has the file open for output, you can open the file read-only to browse it, but PDQComm doesn't close the specified file until you set *CaptureFilename* to "".

**Table 5-9** Values for the CaptureMode property

| VALUE | MEANING |
| --- | --- |
| 0 | Data saved in the order it's received, with no formatting |
| 1 | All data is saved exactly as received by PDQComm |
| 2 | Data displayed on the terminal window is saved |

## Example

The example program for PDQComm is a communications program. See Figure 5-2 for a screen image. A dialog box (Figure 5-3) lets the user configure the Modem and set an initialization string. The user can save the control parameters and initialization string to an .INI file database using the same button on the Modem Setup dialog box. The Kill Ini File menu option removes the .INI file in the ComHWin2 File menu.

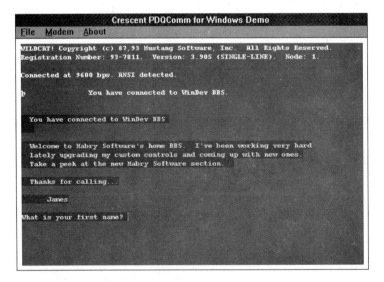

**Figure 5-2** The PDQComm example program

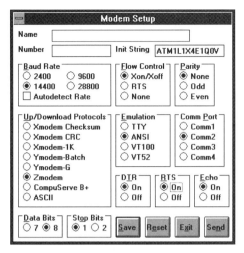

**Figure 5-3** The Modem Setup dialog box

## Steps

1. Create a new project called COM4WIN2.MAK and add PDQCOMM2.VBX. Create a new form with the objects and properties shown in Table 5-10. Save this form as COM4WIN2.FRM. This form contains the actual PDQCOMM2 control.

**Table 5-10** COM4WIN2 main form's objects and properties

| OBJECT | PROPERTY | SETTING |
|---|---|---|
| PDQComm | Name | Comm1 |
| | AutoProcess | 3 'Both |
| | AutoScroll | 3 'Both |
| | AutoSize | -1 'True |
| | BackColor | 1 |
| | Columns | 80 |
| | Echo | 0 'False |
| | Emulation | 1 'TTY |
| | FontName | "Courier New" |
| | ForeColor | 15 |
| | InBufferSize | 2048 |
| | Interval | 55 |
| | OutBufferSize | 2048 |
| | Rows | 25 |
| | RTSEnable | -1 'True |
| | ScrollRows | 0 |

*(continued on next page)*

| OBJECT | PROPERTY | SETTING |
|--------|----------|---------|
| *(continued from previous page)* | | |
| Form | FormName | com4win2 |
| | BorderStyle | 3 'Fixed Double |
| | Caption | "Crescent PDQComm for Windows Demo" |
| | ControlBox | 0 'False |
| | MaxButton | 0 'False |
| | MinButton | 0 'False |

2. Add a menu to COM4WIN2.FRM, setting the captions and names as shown in Table 5-11.

**Table 5-11** COM4WIN2 menu items

| CAPTION | NAME |
|---------|------|
| &File | mnuFile |
| – – – – &Dialing Directory | mnuDialingDirectory |
| – – – – – | |
| – – – – Kill Ini File | mnuKillIniFile |
| – – – – – | |
| – – – – E&xit | mnuExit |
| &Modem | mnuModem |
| – – – – &Hang Up | mnuHangUp |
| &About | mnuAbout |

3. Add the following code to the COM4WIN2 form. This code handles the PDQComm communications event processing.

```
Sub Comm1_OnComm ()

    '-----------------------------
    ' The OnComm event is triggered whenever a communications event or
    ' error occurs. The CommEvent property reflects the most recent
    ' communications event or error. In this case, we are printing
    ' a status message based on the error or event received.
    '-----------------------------

    Select Case Comm1.CommEvent
    Case PDQ_EV_SEND
    Case PDQ_EV_RECEIVE
    Case PDQ_EV_CTS
    Msg = "Change in CTS Detected"
    Case PDQ_EV_DSR
    Msg = "Change in DSR Detected"
    Case PDQ_EV_CD
    Msg = "Change in Carrier Detected"
    Case PDQ_EV_RING
    Msg = "Ring Detected"
    Case PDQ_EV_EOF
    Msg = "End of File Detected"
```

```
        Case PDQ_ER_BREAK
        Msg = "Break Detected"
        Case PDQ_ER_CTSTO
        Msg = "CTS Timeout"
        Case PDQ_ER_DSRTO
        Msg = "DSR Timeout"
        Case PDQ_ER_FRAME
        Msg = "Framing Error"
        Case PDQ_ER_INTO
        Msg = "Input Timeout"
        Case PDQ_ER_OVERRUN
        Msg = "Overrun Error"
        Case PDQ_ER_CDTO
        Msg = "Carrier Detect Timeout"
        Case PDQ_ER_RXOVER
        Msg = "Receive Overflow"
        Case PDQ_ER_TXFULL
        Msg = "Transmit Buffer Overflow"
        End Select

        If Len(Msg) Then
        '----------------------------
        ' Print the error message.
        '----------------------------
        StatusPrint Msg
        '----------------------------
        ' Allow the user to end the program if in an endless loop.
        '----------------------------
        DoEvents
        End If
End Sub

Sub Form_Load ()
        '----------------------------
        ' Center the form.
        '----------------------------
        Me.Move (Screen.Width - Me.Width) \ 2, (Screen.Height - Me.Height) \ 2
End Sub

Sub mnuAbout_Click ()
        frmAbout.Show
End Sub

Sub mnuDialingDirectory_Click ()
        dialing.Show
End Sub

Sub mnuExit_Click ()
        '----------------------------
        ' close the modem if it's open.
        '----------------------------
        If com4win2!Comm1.PortOpen = True Then com4win2!Comm1.PortOpen = False

        Unload dialing
        Unload frmAbout
        Unload ModemSetup
        Unload Me
End Sub

Sub mnuHangUp_Click ()
```

5 ◀

*(continued on next page)*

*(continued from previous page)*

```
'------------------------------
' Hang up the modem (if it's open).
'------------------------------
If Comm1.PortOpen = False Then Exit Sub

'-- Get the modem's attention.
Comm1.Output = "+++"
Pause 1 ' This may depend on modem and computer speed.

'-- Hang it up.
Comm1.Output = "ATH" + Cr$
Pause 1


End Sub

Sub mnuKillIniFile_Click ()
    '------------------------------
    ' Delete the .INI file - neatness counts!
    '------------------------------

    On Error Resume Next ' Turn error handling off.
    Dim WinDirectory As String

    WinDirectory = WinDir()

    Kill WinDirectory & "\" & INIFileName

    On Error GoTo 0 ' Reset error handling.
End Sub
```

4. Create a new form with the objects and properties shown in Table 5-12. Save this form as DIALING.FRM.

**Table 5-12** The Dialing form's objects and properties

| OBJECT | PROPERTY | SETTING |
|---|---|---|
| Label | Name | lblStatus |
| | Caption | "Status" |
| Label | Name | lblDisplay |
| | Caption | "Display" |
| Label | Name | lblCommSettings |
| | Caption | "Comm Settings" |
| Label | Name | Label3 |
| | Caption | "Init String" |
| CommandButton | Name | Command1 |
| | Caption | "Dial" |
| | FontSize | 24 |
| ComboBox | Name | cmbDialingDirectory |
| TextBox | Name | txtInitString |

| OBJECT | PROPERTY | SETTING |
|--------|----------|---------|
| Form | FormName | Dialing |
| | AutoRedraw | -1 'True |
| | Caption | "Dialing Directory" |

5. Add a menu to DIALING.FRM, setting the captions and names as shown in Table 5-13.

**Table 5-13** COM4WIN2 menu items

| CAPTION | NAME |
|---------|------|
| &File | mnuFile |
| − − − − &Configure Defaults | mnuConfigureDefaults |
| − − − − − | |
| − − − − E&xit | mnuExit |
| &Configure Modem | mnuConfigureModem |

6. Add the following code to DIALING.FRM. This form maintains the "dialing directory" and actually dials the modem. The dialing directory is an .INI file stored in the Windows directory. This file has two parts. The first part is a section that holds the names of all the bulletin boards, and so on for which you've saved parameters. The second part is a series of sections, one for each name in the first section. The dialing form's *Form_Load* event calls a sub in the COM4WIN2 module that uses the *GetPrivateProfileString* API call with no key name to retrieve all the key names in the first section. The key names are parsed out and loaded into the cmbDialingDirectory combo box. When the Dial command button is clicked on the modem parameters are fetched from the .INI file using the name in the combo box. Once these parameters have been fetched, they're used to set up the modem and the comm port is opened and dialed. Once the modem connects, control is returned to the COM4WIN2 form.

```
Option Explicit

Sub Command1_Click ()
    '----------------------------
    ' Dial the phone.
    '----------------------------
    If cmbDialingDirectory.Text = "" Then
        cmbDialingDirectory.SetFocus
        MsgBox "Please choose a number to dial!", MB_ICONEXCLAMATION, "Comm 4 Win 2 Demo"
    Else
        ModemParms.Name = cmbDialingDirectory.Text
        GetModemParms
        txtInitString = ModemParms.InitString
        If Com4Win2!Comm1.PortOpen = True Then
            Com4Win2!Comm1.PortOpen = False
        End If
    End If

    If ModemParms.Number = "" Then
```

*(continued on next page)*

*(continued from previous page)*

```vb
            ModemSetup.Show
            Exit Sub
        End If

    DialThePhone
    Com4Win2!Comm1.SetFocus
    Unload Me
End Sub

Sub Form_Load ()
    '----------------------------
    ' Center in the screen.
    '----------------------------
    Me.Move (Screen.Width - Me.Width) \ 2, (Screen.Height - Me.Height) \ 2


    '----------------------------
    ' Fill the combo box with the directory names.
    '----------------------------
    LoadDirCombo cmbDialingDirectory

    If cmbDialingDirectory.ListCount = 0 Then
        BuildIniFile
        LoadDirCombo cmbDialingDirectory
        '----------------------------
        ' Should do an error check here.
        '----------------------------
    End If

    If ModemParms.Name  "" Then cmbDialingDirectory.Text = ModemParms.Name
End Sub

Sub Form_Unload (Cancel As Integer)
    DialingNow = False
End Sub

Sub mnuConfigureDefaults_Click ()
    '----------------------------
    ' Configure the modem defaults.
    '----------------------------
    ModemParms.Name = "Default"

    GetModemParms

    ModemSetup.Show

End Sub

Sub mnuConfigureModem_Click ()
    '----------------------------
    ' Configure the modem.
    '----------------------------
    Dim i As Integer

    '----------------------------
    ' Prime the pump.
    '----------------------------
    ModemParms.Name = "Default"
```

```
'-----------------------------
' See if the text is in the list.
'-----------------------------
For i = 1 To cmbDialingDirectory.ListCount
    If cmbDialingDirectory.List(i) = cmbDialingDirectory.Text Then
        '-----------------------------
        ' If it is, prepare to get its parameters.
        '-----------------------------
        ModemParms.Name = cmbDialingDirectory.Text
        Exit For
    End If
Next i

' Get parameters.
GetModemParms

'-----------------------------
' If it's still equal to default, then this is a new
' entry - set up its name.
'-----------------------------
If ModemParms.Name = "Default" Then
    ModemParms.Name = cmbDialingDirectory.Text
End If

ModemSetup.Show
End Sub

Sub mnuExit_Click ()
    Unload ModemSetup
    Unload Me
End Sub
```

7. Create a new form with the objects and properties shown in Table 5-14. Save this form as MODEM.FRM.

**Table 5-14** The MODEM form's objects and properties

| OBJECT | PROPERTY | SETTING |
|--------|----------|---------|
| Label | Name | Label1 |
|  | Caption | "Name" |
| Label | Name | Label2 |
|  | Caption | "Number" |
| Label | Name | Label3 |
|  | Caption | "Init String" |
| Frame | Name | fraRTS |
|  | Caption | "&RTS" |
| Frame | Name | fraDTR |
|  | Caption | "D&TR" |
| Frame | Name | fraFlow |
|  | Caption | "&Flow Control" |

(continued on next page)

5

| OBJECT | PROPERTY | SETTING |
|---|---|---|
| *(continued from previous page)* | | |
| Frame | Name | fraCom |
| | Caption | "Com &Port" |
| Frame | Name | fraParity |
| | Caption | "&Parity" |
| Frame | Name | fraEcho |
| | Caption | "&Echo" |
| Frame | Name | fraStopBits |
| | Caption | "St&op Bits" |
| Frame | Name | fraDataBits |
| | Caption | "&Data Bits" |
| Frame | Name | fraBaud |
| | Caption | "&Baud Rate" |
| Frame | Name | fraTerminalType |
| | Caption | "&Emulation" |
| Frame | Name | fraProtocol |
| | Caption | "&Up/Download Protocols" |
| TextBox | Name | txtNumber |
| TextBox | Name | txtName |
| | Text | "Default" |
| CommandButton | Name | cmdSave |
| | Caption | "&Save" |
| | Default | -1 'True |
| CommandButton | Name | cmdCancel |
| | Cancel | -1 'True |
| | Caption | "R&eset" |
| CommandButton | Name | cmdExit |
| | Caption | "E&xit" |
| TextBox | Name | txtInitString |
| | Text | "ATM1L1X4E1Q0V1" |
| CommandButton | Name | cmdSend |
| | Caption | "Se&nd" |
| Form | FormName | ModemSetup |
| | BorderStyle | 3 'Fixed Double |
| | Caption | "Modem Setup" |
| | MaxButton | 0 'False |
| | MinButton | 0 'False |

8. Select the fraRTS frame and add the objects and properties shown in Table 5-15.

**Table 5-15** fraRTS properties

| OBJECT | PROPERTY | SETTING |
|---|---|---|
| OptionButton | Name | optRTS |
| | Caption | "Off" |
| | Index | 0 |
| OptionButton | Name | optRTS |
| | Caption | "On" |
| | Index | 1 |
| | Value | -1 'True |

9. Select the fraDTR frame and add the objects and properties shown in Table 5-16.

**Table 5-16** fraDTR properties

| OBJECT | PROPERTY | SETTING |
|---|---|---|
| OptionButton | Name | optDTR |
| | Caption | "On" |
| | Index | 1 |
| | Value | -1 'True |
| OptionButton | Name | optDTR |
| | Caption | "Off" |
| | Index | 0 |

10. Select the fraFlow frame and add the objects and properties shown in Table 5-17.

**Table 5-17** fraFlow properties

| OBJECT | PROPERTY | SETTING |
|---|---|---|
| OptionButton | Name | Flow |
| | Caption | "None" |
| | Index | 0 |
| OptionButton | Name | Flow |
| | Caption | "RTS" |
| | Index | 2 |
| OptionButton | Name | Flow |
| | Caption | "Xon/Xoff" |
| | Index | 1 |
| | Value | -1 'True |

11. Select the fraCom frame and add the objects and properties shown in Table 5-18.

5

**Table 5-18** fraCom properties

| OBJECT | PROPERTY | SETTING |
|---|---|---|
| OptionButton | Name | optPort |
| | Caption | "Com4" |
| | Index | 4 |
| OptionButton | Name | optPort |
| | Caption | "Com3" |
| | Index | 3 |
| OptionButton | Name | optPort |
| | Caption | "Com2" |
| | Index | 2 |
| OptionButton | Name | optPort |
| | Caption | "Com1" |
| | Index | 1 |
| | Value | -1 'True |

12. Select the fraParity frame and add the objects and properties shown in Table 5-19.

**Table 5-19** fraParity properties

| OBJECT | PROPERTY | SETTING |
|---|---|---|
| OptionButton | Name | optParity |
| | Caption | "Even" |
| | Index | 3 |
| | Tag | "E" |
| OptionButton | Name | optParity |
| | Caption | "Odd" |
| | Index | 2 |
| | Tag | "O" |
| OptionButton | Name | optParity |
| | Caption | "None" |
| | Index | 1 |
| | Tag | "N" |
| | Value | -1 'True |

13. Select the fraEcho frame and add the objects and properties shown in Table 5-20.

**Table 5-20** fraEcho properties

| OBJECT | PROPERTY | SETTING |
|---|---|---|
| OptionButton | Name | optEcho |
| | Caption | "On" |

| OBJECT | PROPERTY | SETTING |
|---|---|---|
| | Index | 1 |
| | Value | -1 'True |
| OptionButton | Name | optEcho |
| | Caption | "Off" |
| | Index | 0 |

14. Select the fraStopBits frame and add the objects and properties shown in Table 5-21.

**Table 5-21** fraStopBits properties

| OBJECT | PROPERTY | SETTING |
|---|---|---|
| OptionButton | Name | optStopBits |
| | Caption | "2" |
| | Index | 2 |
| OptionButton | Name | optStopBits |
| | Caption | "1" |
| | Index | 1 |
| | Value | -1 'True |

15. Select the fraDataBits frame and add the objects and properties shown in Table 5-22.

**Table 5-22** fraDataBits properties

| OBJECT | PROPERTY | SETTING |
|---|---|---|
| OptionButton | Name | optDataBits |
| | Caption | "8" |
| | Index | 8 |
| | Value | -1 'True |
| OptionButton | Name | optDataBits |
| | Caption | "7" |
| | Index | 7 |

16. Select the fraBaud frame and add the objects and properties shown in Table 5-23.

**Table 5-23** fraBaud properties

| OBJECT | PROPERTY | SETTING |
|---|---|---|
| OptionButton | Name | optBaud |
| | Caption | "28800" |
| | Index | 4 |

*(continued on next page)*

5 ◀

| OBJECT | PROPERTY | SETTING |
|---|---|---|
| *(continued from previous page)* | | |
| | Tag | "28800" |
| OptionButton | Name | optBaud |
| | Caption | "14400" |
| | Index | 3 |
| | Tag | "14400" |
| | Value | -1 'True |
| OptionButton | Name | optBaud |
| | Caption | "2400" |
| | Index | 1 |
| | Tag | "2400" |
| OptionButton | Name | optBaud |
| | Caption | "9600" |
| | Index | 2 |
| | Tag | "9600" |
| CheckBox | Name | chkAutoDetect |
| | Caption | "Autodetect Rate" |
| | Value | 1 'Checked |

17. Select the fraEmulation frame and add the objects and properties shown in Table 5-24.

**Table 5-24** fraEmulation properties

| OBJECT | PROPERTY | SETTING |
|---|---|---|
| OptionButton | Name | optEmulation |
| | Caption | "VT100" |
| | Index | 4 |
| OptionButton | Name | optEmulation |
| | Caption | "VT52" |
| | Index | 3 |
| OptionButton | Name | optEmulation |
| | Caption | "ANSI" |
| | Index | 2 |
| | Value | -1 'True |
| OptionButton | Name | optEmulation |
| | Caption | "TTY" |
| | Index | 1 |

18. Select the fraProtocol frame and add the objects and properties shown in Table 5-25.

**Table 5-25** fraProtocol properties

| OBJECT | PROPERTY | SETTING |
|---|---|---|
| OptionButton | Name | optProtocol |
| | Caption | "Xmodem Checksum" |
| | Index | 0 |
| OptionButton | Name | optProtocol |
| | Caption | "Xmodem CRC" |
| | Index | 1 |
| OptionButton | Name | optProtocol |
| | Caption | "Xmodem-1K" |
| | Index | 2 |
| OptionButton | Name | optProtocol |
| | Caption | "Ymodem-Batch" |
| | Index | 3 |
| OptionButton | Name | optProtocol |
| | Caption | "Ymodem-G" |
| | Index | 4 |
| OptionButton | Name | optProtocol |
| | Caption | "Zmodem" |
| | Index | 5 |
| | Value | -1 'True |
| OptionButton | Name | optProtocol |
| | Caption | "Compuserve B+" |
| | Index | 7 |
| OptionButton | Name | optProtocol |
| | Caption | "ASCII" |
| | Index | 6 |

19. Add the following code to the declarations section of the MODEM form. This code sets up any declarations needed in the MODEM form.

```
Option Explicit
    '----------------------------
    ' Used to restore modem info.
    '----------------------------
    Dim HoldModemName As String
```

20. Add the following code to MODEM.FRM. This code handles the modem parameters and the initialization string used to set up the modem before dialing and getting online. Clicking on the Send button allows the user to reset some modem parameters while the modem is connected. The Save button uses the *WritePrivateProfile* function to add data to the .INI file. The Reset button reloads data from the .INI file, acting like a single-level undo function.

```
Sub chkAutoDetect_Click ()
    If chkAutoDetect = CHECKED Then
        ModemParms.AdjustBaud = True
    Else
        ModemParms.AdjustBaud = False
    End If
End Sub

Sub cmdCancel_Click ()

    ModemParms.Name = HoldModemName

    GetModemParms

    LoadFormFromModemParms

End Sub

Sub cmdExit_Click ()
    Unload Me
End Sub

Sub cmdSave_Click ()

    ModemParms.Name = txtName
    ModemParms.Number = txtNumber
    ModemParms.InitString = txtInitString

    SaveModemParms

    SetModemParms

    Unload Me
End Sub

Sub cmdSend_Click ()
    ' Update modem parameters.

    SetModemParms

End Sub

Sub Form_Load ()
    Me.Move (Screen.Width - Me.Width) \ 2, (Screen.Height - Me.Height) \ 2

    LoadFormFromModemParms

End Sub

Sub LoadFormFromModemParms ()
    '-----------------------------
    ' Set up the form from the data in the
    ' modemparms user-defined variable.
    '-----------------------------

    Dim i As Integer

    txtName = ModemParms.Name
    txtNumber = ModemParms.Number
    HoldModemName = ModemParms.Name
    txtInitString = ModemParms.InitString
```

```
    For i = 1 To 4
        If optBaud(i).Tag = ModemParms.BaudRate Then
            optBaud(i) = True
            Exit For
        End If
    Next i

    For i = 1 To 3
        If optParity(i).Tag = ModemParms.Parity Then
            optParity(i) = True
            Exit For
        End If
    Next i

    optPort(ModemParms.port) = True

    If ModemParms.DTR = False Then
        optDTR(0) = True
    Else
        optDTR(1) = True
    End If

    If ModemParms.RTS = False Then
        optRTS(0) = True
    Else
        optRTS(1) = True
    End If

    If ModemParms.Echo = False Then
        optEcho(0) = True
    Else
        optEcho(1) = True
    End If

    optEmulation(ModemParms.Terminal) = True
    optDataBits(ModemParms.DataBits) = True
    optStopBits(ModemParms.StopBits) = True
    optProtocol(ModemParms.Protocol) = True

    If ModemParms.AdjustBaud = True Then
        chkAutoDetect = CHECKED
    Else
        chkAutoDetect = UNCHECKED
    End If

End Sub

Sub optBaud_Click (index As Integer)
    '------------------------------
    ' The baud rates are in the tag of the control.
    '------------------------------
    ModemParms.BaudRate = optBaud(index).Tag

End Sub

Sub optDataBits_Click (index As Integer)
    '------------------------------
    ' Note that we cleverly set the index of the control
    ' arrays to the proper value for databits.
    '------------------------------
```

*(continued on next page)*

*(continued from previous page)*

```
        ModemParms.DataBits = index
End Sub

Sub optDTR_Click (index As Integer)
    If index = False Then
        ModemParms.DTR = False
    Else
        ModemParms.DTR = True
    End If
End Sub

Sub optEcho_Click (index As Integer)
    If index = False Then
        ModemParms.Echo = False
    Else
        ModemParms.Echo = True
    End If
End Sub

Sub optEmulation_Click (index As Integer)
    ModemParms.Terminal = index
End Sub

Sub optParity_Click (index As Integer)
    '-----------------------------
    ' Preloaded the tag value with the parity value.
    '-----------------------------
    ModemParms.Parity = optParity(index).Tag
End Sub

Sub optPort_Click (index As Integer)
    ModemParms.port = index
End Sub

Sub optProtocol_Click (index As Integer)
    ModemParms.Protocol = index
End Sub

Sub optRTS_Click (index As Integer)
    If index = False Then
        ModemParms.RTS = False
    Else
        ModemParms.RTS = True
    End If
End Sub

Sub optStopBits_Click (index As Integer)
    '-----------------------------
    ' Control index = number of stop bits.
    '-----------------------------
    ModemParms.StopBits = index

End Sub
```

21. Add a new code module and save it as COM4WIN2.BAS. This module holds many of the subs and functions called from the forms, and also has the declarations of any API calls used in this program. The subs and functions in this module are used to load the

directory list, save and load the .INI file sections, and handle some of the comm functions. This includes dialing and resetting the baud rates for situations where you can't determine the baud rate ahead of time. This module also has an aliased version of the *GetPrivateProfileString* API call that gets the section headers for the directory.

```
Option Explicit

    Global CommSettings As String
    Global PortNum As Integer
    Global DialingNow As Integer

    Global Const MB_ICONEXCLAMATION = 48

    '------------------------------
    ' .INI section names.
    '------------------------------
    Global Const APPNAME = "VBGB Names"
    Global Const INIFileName = "VBGBC4W2.INI"
    Const NAMESECT = "Name"
    Const NUMBERSECT = "Number"
    Const BAUDRATESECT = "Baud Rate"
    Const INITSECT = "Init String"
    Const PORTSECT = "Port"
    Const PARITYSECT = "Parity"
    Const DTRSECT = "DTR"
    Const RTSSECT = "RTS"
    Const TERMINALSECT = "Terminal"
    Const DATABITSSECT = "Data Bits"
    Const STOPBITSSECT = "Stop Bits"
    Const ECHOSECT = "Echo"
    Const PROTOCOLSECT = "Protocol"
    Const ADJUSTBAUDSECT = "Adjust Baud"
    Global msg As String


    '------------------------------
    ' This holds the modem parameters.
    '------------------------------
    Type ModemParmstype
        Name As String
        Number As String
        BaudRate As String
        Parity As String
        InitString As String
        port As Integer
        DTR As Integer
        RTS As Integer
        Terminal As Integer
        DataBits As Integer
        StopBits As Integer
        Echo As Integer
        Protocol As Integer
        AdjustBaud As Integer
    End Type

    Global ModemParms As ModemParmstype

    Global cr As String
```

5 ◄

(continued on next page)

*(continued from previous page)*

```
    Global Const CHECKED = 1
    Global Const UNCHECKED = 0


    '----------------------------
    ' Used in StringToINI sub.
    '----------------------------
    Declare Function WritePrivateProfileString Lib "Kernel" (ByVal SectName As String, ByVal
KeyName As String, ByVal NewString As String, ByVal FileName As String) As Integer


    '----------------------------
    ' Used in StringFromINI function.
    '----------------------------
    Declare Function GetPrivateProfileString Lib "Kernel" (ByVal Section As String, ByVal
KeyName As String, ByVal Default As String, ByVal ReturnedString As String, ByVal MaxSize%,
ByVal FileName As String) As Integer
    Declare Function GetPrivProfSections Lib "Kernel" Alias "GetPrivateProfileString" (ByVal
Section As String, ByVal KeyName As Any, ByVal Default As String, ByVal ReturnedString As
String, ByVal MaxSize%, ByVal FileName As String) As Integer


    '----------------------------
    ' Used in Windir() function.
    '----------------------------
    Declare Function GetWindowsDirectory Lib "Kernel" (ByVal lpBuffer As String, ByVal nSize As
Integer) As Integer

Sub AdjustBaud ()
    '----------------------------
    ' Adjust the baud rate.
    '----------------------------

    Dim oldsettings As String
    Dim newsettings As String
    Dim received As String
    Dim baudpos As Integer
    Dim oldbaud As Integer
    Dim newbaud As Integer
    Dim connect As Integer
    Dim lenbaud As Integer
    Dim enter As Integer
    Dim comma As Integer
    Dim baud As String
    Dim in As String

    dialing!lblStatus = "Adjusting Baud Rate"


    '----------------------------
    ' Trim our received string so that is starts with CONNECT
    '----------------------------
    connect = InStr(in$, "CONNECT")
    received$ = Mid$(in$, connect)


    '----------------------------
    ' The first character of the baud rate is at position 8 in the string.
    '----------------------------
    baudpos = 8
    cr$ = Chr$(13)

    Do
```

```
          ' Do we have a carriage return?
          enter = InStr(received$, cr$)
          If enter Then
              ' Get the baud rate.
              lenbaud = enter - baudpos
              baud$ = Mid$(received$, baudpos, lenbaud)
              '----------------------------
              ' If we received just CONNECT, then we've connected at 300 baud.
              '----------------------------
              If Len(baud$) = 0 Then
              baud$ = "300"
              End If
              Exit Do
          Else
              ' We need more data.
              com4win2!Comm1.InTimeOut = 5000
              received$ = received$ + com4win2!Comm1.LineInput
          End If
          DoEvents
      Loop

      '----------------------------
      ' Get ready to adjust the settings.
      '----------------------------
      oldsettings$ = com4win2!Comm1.Settings
      comma = InStr(oldsettings$, ",")
      oldbaud = Val(Left$(oldsettings$, comma - 1))
      newbaud = Val(baud$)

      '----------------------------
      ' Only adjust the baud rate if the port
      ' was opened at 9600 or lower.
      '----------------------------
      If newbaud < oldbaud And newbaud <= 9600 Then
          newsettings$ = oldsettings$
          Mid$(newsettings$, 1, comma - 1) = LTrim$(Str$(newbaud))
          On Error Resume Next
          com4win2!Comm1.Settings = newsettings$
          If Err Then
              MsgBox "Error Adjusting Baud Rate"
              com4win2!Comm1.Settings = oldsettings$
          End If
      End If

End Sub

Sub BuildIniFile ()
      '----------------------------
      ' Initialized the .INI file.
      '----------------------------

      Dim res As Integer
      Dim defaultname As String

      defaultname = Space(30)

      res = GetPrivateProfileString(APPNAME, "Default", "Not Defined", defaultname, 30,
   INIFileName)

      If Left$(defaultname, Len(Trim$(defaultname)) - 1) = "Not Defined" Then
```

*(continued on next page)*

5

*(continued from previous page)*

```
        ModemParms.Name = "Default"
        ModemParms.Number = ""
        ModemParms.BaudRate = "14400"
        ModemParms.InitString = "ATM1L1X4E1Q0V1"
        ModemParms.Parity = "N"
        ModemParms.port = 2
        ModemParms.DTR = True
        ModemParms.RTS = True
        ModemParms.Terminal = PDQ_EMULATION_ANSI
        ModemParms.DataBits = 8
        ModemParms.StopBits = 1
        ModemParms.Echo = True
        ModemParms.Protocol = PDQ_ZMODEM
        ModemParms.AdjustBaud = False
        'build the ini file
        SaveModemParms
    End If

End Sub

Sub DialThePhone ()
    '-----------------------------
    ' This routine dials the phone.
    '-----------------------------

    Dim out As String
    Dim in As String ' Used with the modem.
    Dim tries As Integer
    Dim baudpos As Integer
    Dim lenbaud As Integer
    Dim connect As Integer
    Dim received As String
    Dim baud As String
    Dim oldsettings As String
    Dim newsettings As String
    Dim enter As Integer
    Dim oldbaud As Integer
    Dim newbaud As Integer
    Dim comma As Integer


    CommSettings = ModemParms.BaudRate & "," & ModemParms.Parity & "," & ⇒
Format$(ModemParms.DataBits) & "," & Format$(ModemParms.StopBits)

    dialing!lblCommSettings = CommSettings

    Debug.Print ModemParms.port
    Debug.Print ModemParms.Name

    PortNum = ModemParms.port

    SetModemParms

    If com4win2!Comm1.PortOpen = False Then
        '-----------------------------
        ' If it's not open, try to open it.
        '-----------------------------
        OpenComm CommSettings, PortNum
        '-----------------------------
```

```
    ' If it's STILL not open,
    '-----------------------------
    If com4win2!Comm1.PortOpen  True Then
        '-----------------------------
        ' couldn't open the comm port.
        '-----------------------------
        MsgBox "Can't open Comm port", MB_ICONEXCLAMATION
        Exit Sub
    End If
End If

'-----------------------------
' Set the Flag to show that we are currently dialing.
'-----------------------------
DialingNow = True                        .

dialing!lblStatus = "Dialing ..."

'-----------------------------
' This is the main dialing loop.
'-----------------------------
Do
    '-----------------------------
    ' In the Unload event, we set DialingNow to 0. So, if the form
    ' was unloaded, get out of here.
    '-----------------------------
    If DialingNow = False Then
        Exit Sub
    End If
    '-----------------------------
    ' Setting AutoProcess to 0 allows us to process the Communications
    'I/O manually.
    '-----------------------------
    com4win2!Comm1.AutoProcess = PDQ_AUTOPROCESS_NONE

    '-----------------------------
    ' Dial the number.
    '-----------------------------
    out$ = "ATDT" + ModemParms.Number + cr$
    com4win2!Comm1.Output = out$
    dialing!lblDisplay = out$
    '-----------------------------
    ' Wait until the transmit buffer is empty.
    '-----------------------------
    Do
        DoEvents
        If DialingNow = False Then Exit Sub
    Loop Until com4win2!Comm1.OutBufferCount = 0

    Pause 1

    '-----------------------------
    ' Flush the input buffer.
    '-----------------------------
    com4win2!Comm1.InBufferCount = 0

    '-----------------------------
    ' Loop to process the modem's response.
    '-----------------------------
    Do
```

*(continued on next page)*

*(continued from previous page)*

```
                DoEvents
                ' Bail out if not dialing.
                If DialingNow = False Then Exit Sub
                ' If we have a response...
                If com4win2!Comm1.InBufferCount Then
                    ' Wait half a second.
                    Pause 1
                    ' Get result code from the modem.
                    in$ = in$ + com4win2!Comm1.Input
                    ' Display the result code.
                    com4win2!Comm1.Disp = in$
                    ' Look for a response in the In$ string.
                    If InStr(in$, "BUSY") Then
                        ' Line was busy, redial.
                        in$ = ""
                        tries = tries + 1
                        dialing.Caption = "Redial" + Str$(tries)
                        Pause 1
                        ' Break out of this loop and try again.
                        com4win2!Comm1.InBufferCount = 0
                        com4win2!Comm1.OutBufferCount = 0
                        Exit Do
                    ElseIf InStr(in$, "CONNECT") Then
                        If ModemParms.AdjustBaud Then AdjustBaud
                        dialing!lblStatus = "Connected"
                        SetAutoProcess
                        Exit Sub
                    ElseIf InStr(in$, "NO CARRIER") Then
                        dialing!lblStatus = "No Carrier"
                        SetAutoProcess
                        Exit Sub
                    ElseIf InStr(in$, "NO DIALTONE") Then
                        dialing!lblStatus = "No Dialtone"
                        SetAutoProcess
                        Exit Sub
                    End If
                End If
            Loop
        Loop

        SetAutoProcess

End Sub

Sub GetModemParms ()
        '----------------------------
        ' Fetch the modem parameters from the .INI file.
        '----------------------------

    Dim workstr As String

    ModemParms.Number = StringFromINI(ModemParms.Name, NUMBERSECT, "", INIFileName)
    ModemParms.BaudRate = StringFromINI(ModemParms.Name, BAUDRATESECT, "14400", INIFileName)
    ModemParms.Parity = StringFromINI(ModemParms.Name, PARITYSECT, "N", INIFileName)
    ModemParms.InitString = StringFromINI(ModemParms.Name, INITSECT, "ATM1L1X4E1QOV1",⇒
INIFileName)
    workstr = StringFromINI(ModemParms.Name, DTRSECT, "-1", INIFileName)
    ModemParms.DTR = Val(workstr)
    workstr = StringFromINI(ModemParms.Name, PORTSECT, "2", INIFileName)
```

```
        ModemParms.port = Val(workstr)
        workstr = StringFromINI(ModemParms.Name, RTSSECT, "-1", INIFileName)
        ModemParms.RTS = Val(workstr)
        workstr = StringFromINI(ModemParms.Name, TERMINALSECT, Format$(PDQ_EMULATION_ANSI),
INIFileName)
        ModemParms.Terminal = Val(workstr)
        workstr = StringFromINI(ModemParms.Name, DATABITSSECT, "8", INIFileName)
        ModemParms.DataBits = Val(workstr)
        workstr = StringFromINI(ModemParms.Name, STOPBITSSECT, "1", INIFileName)
        ModemParms.StopBits = Val(workstr)
        workstr = StringFromINI(ModemParms.Name, ECHOSECT, "-1", INIFileName)
        ModemParms.Echo = Val(workstr)
        workstr = StringFromINI(ModemParms.Name, PROTOCOLSECT, Format$(PDQ_ZMODEM), INIFileName)
        ModemParms.Protocol = Val(workstr)
        workstr = StringFromINI(ModemParms.Name, ADJUSTBAUDSECT, "0", INIFileName)
        ModemParms.AdjustBaud = Val(workstr)

End Sub

Sub LoadDirCombo (cmbDialingDirectory As Control)
        '----------------------------
        ' Load the combo box from the .INI dialing directory.
        '----------------------------
        Dim HoldDirectory As String
        Dim SearchStr  As String
        Dim res As Integer
        Dim Stringpointer As Integer
        Dim LastPointer As Integer

        cmbDialingDirectory.Clear
        SearchStr = Chr(0)
        ' We're going to put the entire dialing directory here,
        'or atleast 4K of it.
        HoldDirectory = String$(4001, 0)

        res = GetPrivProfSections(APPNAME, 0&, "", HoldDirectory, 4000, INIFileName)
        ' res = total number of characters returned.
        ' "Prime" the pump, so to speak.
        Stringpointer = InStr(1, HoldDirectory, SearchStr)
        LastPointer = 1
        Do While Stringpointer <= res
            cmbDialingDirectory.AddItem Mid$(HoldDirectory, LastPointer, Stringpointer - 1)
            LastPointer = Stringpointer + 1 'point past the null
            Stringpointer = InStr(LastPointer, HoldDirectory, SearchStr)
            'returned string terminated by two nulls
            If Stringpointer = LastPointer + 1 Then Exit Do
        Loop

End Sub

Sub main ()
        '----------------------------
        ' Start the program here, initialize what needs
        ' to be initialized, and load the startup form.
        '----------------------------

        cr = Chr$(13)

        com4win2.Show
End Sub
```

5 ◄

(continued on next page)

*(continued from previous page)*

```vb
Sub OpenComm (Settings$, PortNum)

    '-------------------------------
    ' This routine opens the specified port.
    '-------------------------------

    Dim OldInputLen As Integer
    Dim errcode As Integer
    Dim received As String
    Dim ModemInit As String

    '-------------------------------
    ' Settings.
    '-------------------------------
    com4win2!Comm1.Settings = Settings$
    Debug.Print Settings

    '-------------------------------
    ' Save the InputLen property.
    '-------------------------------

    OldInputLen = com4win2!Comm1.InputLen

    If OldInputLen Then
        '-------------------------------
        ' In order for this routine to work, InputLen
        ' must be 0.
        '-------------------------------
        com4win2!Comm1.InputLen = 0
    End If

    '-------------------------------
    ' Trap VB errors.
    '-------------------------------
    On Error Resume Next

    com4win2!Comm1.CommPort = PortNum
    '-------------------------------
    ' Try to open the port.
    '-------------------------------

    com4win2!Comm1.PortOpen = True

    If Err = 0 Then
        '-------------------------------
        ' Initialize the modem.
        '-------------------------------
        ModemInit = dialing!txtInitString & cr ' "ATM1L1X4E1QOV1" & cr
        com4win2!Comm1.Output = ModemInit
        '-------------------------------
        ' Port opened OK. Now test for modem by sending AT.
        '-------------------------------
        com4win2!Comm1.Output = "AT" + Chr$(13)
        Debug.Print ModemInit
        '-------------------------------
        ' Wait up to 1 seconds to receive OK.
        '-------------------------------
        errcode = 0
```

```
        LeftOver$ = ""
        WaitFor com4win2!Comm1, "OK", 1, received$, errcode
        Debug.Print errcode
        If errcode = 0 Then
            '-------------------------------
            ' OK was received. There's a modem here!
            ' Initialize the modem.
            '-------------------------------
        Else
            '-------------------------------
            ' OK was not received. Close the port.
            '-------------------------------
            com4win2!Comm1.PortOpen = False
        End If
    End If


    '-------------------------------
    ' Reset error handler.
    '-------------------------------
    On Error GoTo 0

    If OldInputLen Then
        '-------------------------------
        ' Reset InputLen.
        '-------------------------------
        com4win2!Comm1.InputLen = OldInputLen
    End If


End Sub

Sub SaveModemParms ()
    '-------------------------------
    ' Update the phone directory database
    '-------------------------------
    Dim res As Integer

    ' Put the first section out there.
    res = StringToINI(APPNAME, ModemParms.Name, ModemParms.Name, INIFileName)
    ' Save its info.

    res = StringToINI(ModemParms.Name, NAMESECT, ModemParms.Name, INIFileName)
    res = StringToINI(ModemParms.Name, NUMBERSECT, ModemParms.Number, INIFileName)
    res = StringToINI(ModemParms.Name, BAUDRATESECT, ModemParms.BaudRate, INIFileName)
    res = StringToINI(ModemParms.Name, INITSECT, ModemParms.InitString, INIFileName)
    res = StringToINI(ModemParms.Name, PARITYSECT, ModemParms.Parity, INIFileName)
    res = StringToINI(ModemParms.Name, PORTSECT, Format$(ModemParms.port), INIFileName)
    res = StringToINI(ModemParms.Name, DTRSECT, Format$(ModemParms.DTR), INIFileName)
    res = StringToINI(ModemParms.Name, RTSSECT, Format$(ModemParms.RTS), INIFileName)
    res = StringToINI(ModemParms.Name, TERMINALSECT, Format$(ModemParms.Terminal), INIFileName)
    res = StringToINI(ModemParms.Name, DATABITSSECT, Format$(ModemParms.DataBits), INIFileName)
    res = StringToINI(ModemParms.Name, STOPBITSSECT, Format$(ModemParms.StopBits), INIFileName)
    res = StringToINI(ModemParms.Name, ECHOSECT, Format$(ModemParms.Echo), INIFileName)
    res = StringToINI(ModemParms.Name, PROTOCOLSECT, Format$(ModemParms.Protocol), INIFileName)
    res = StringToINI(ModemParms.Name, ADJUSTBAUDSECT, Format$(ModemParms.AdjustBaud), INIFileName)

End Sub

Sub SetAutoProcess ()
```

5 ◀

*(continued on next page)*

343

*(continued from previous page)*

```
    '----------------------------
    ' Reset autoproccessing and we're done.
    '----------------------------
    com4win2!Comm1.AutoProcess = PDQ_AUTOPROCESS_BOTH
    DialingNow = False
    dialing.Hide
    com4win2.Refresh
    com4win2!Comm1.SetFocus

End Sub

Sub SetModemParms ()
    '----------------------------
    ' Set the modem parameters.
    '----------------------------

    CommSettings = ModemParms.BaudRate & "," & ModemParms.Parity & "," &
Format$(ModemParms.DataBits) & "," & Format$(ModemParms.StopBits)

    dialing!lblCommSettings = CommSettings

    com4win2!Comm1.RTSEnable = ModemParms.RTS
    com4win2!Comm1.DTREnable = ModemParms.DTR
    com4win2!Comm1.Echo = ModemParms.Echo
    com4win2!Comm1.Emulation = ModemParms.Terminal
    com4win2!Comm1.XferProtocol = ModemParms.Protocol


End Sub

Sub StatusPrint (msg As String)
    dialing!lblDisplay = msg
End Sub

Function StringFromINI (Section As String, KeyName As String, Default As String, FileName As
String) As String
    '----------------------------
    ' Read the .INI file.
    '----------------------------

Dim MaxStringLen As Integer
Dim ReturnedStr As String
Dim result As Integer
Dim ResultStr As String

    MaxStringLen = 255
    ReturnedStr = Space$(MaxStringLen)

    result = GetPrivateProfileString(Section, KeyName, Default, ReturnedStr, MaxStringLen,
FileName)

    ResultStr = Left$(ResultStr, len(ResultStr) - 1)
    StringFromINI = ResultStr
End Function

Function StringToINI (SectName As String, KeyName As String, DataString As String, INIFileName
As String) As Integer
```

```
'-----------------------------
' Writes the passed string to the specified section of the specified .INI file.
'-----------------------------
   StringToINI = WritePrivateProfileString(SectName, KeyName, DataString, INIFileName)
End Function

Function WinDir () As String
   '-----------------------------
   ' Returns the name of the Windows directory.
   '-----------------------------

   Dim Buff As String, Tchars As Integer

   Buff = Space$(255)
   Tchars = GetWindowsDirectory(Buff$, 255)
   WinDir = Left$(Buff$, Tchars)
End Function
```

22. Finally (whew!) add the COMMCTRL.BAS file supplied by Crescent Software. This file holds the Constants and some utility functions provided by Crescent Software for use with PDQComm.

# Tips and Comments

PDQCOMM2.VBX makes writing communications programs easier, if not easy. The various properties and the *OnComm* event make interacting with the modem and the system you've dialed into simpler than handling it yourself using Windows API calls or MSCOMM.VBX. If you need a simple terminal emulation program or if you need more control over dialup than you get from a commercial program, you can use PDQComm and VB to do the job, as long as the four terminal emulations Crescent provides cover what you're trying to do. Also, the manual does a credible job of covering communications in general, so you'll probably come away from the project knowing more about communications than you did when you started.

Remember to make liberal use of DoEvents while you are sending and receiving data from the modem. That gives the modem a chance to respond and the Windows comm driver a chance to send the data to your program.

5

# 6

# CHARTING AND GRAPHING CONTROLS

O ne of the staples of the business world is the foot-tall
columnar report on traditional green-bar paper.
Intimidating and formidable, this type of report was
for years the best and only way to provide business
information. Most often only the total page was kept, and the
rest was thrown away. With the move towards Graphical
Interfaces, you can now distill the foot-tall report into a
single screen graph with detail available on request. This is
especially true in the Executive Information application
because the average executive is only worried about the
bottom line, and not the detail.

You can draw graphs in Visual Basic using the various controls, drawing tools, and API calls. It is much simpler, however, to hand data to a custom graphing control and let it do the work. Microsoft's GRAPH.VBX and its big brother from Bits Per Second software, ChartBuilder, handle all the standard types of graphs with ease.

GRAPH.VBX handles all the types of graphs you're likely to need, such as pie charts, bar charts, and area charts. Since it comes with Visual Basic Professional, the price is right too. GRAPH.VBX knows how to print itself, but only in a limited fashion.

ChartBuilder is similar to GRAPH.VBX, but ChartBuilder draws more kinds of graphs and, more significantly, lets you track mouse clicks on the graph. This enables you to give your favorite executive the summary she needs while providing the line supervisor the detail he needs to correct any problems or reward any exemplary behavior. ChartBuilder knows how to print itself with more flexibility than GRAPH.VBX.

The controls discussed in this chapter allow you to build a wide variety of graphs for all occasions. The demos in this chapter illustrate how to:

▲ Graph disk utilization by subdirectory or extension, print the results, and use mouse clicks to show which subdirectory or extension an area of the graph refers to

▲ Analyze and graph the use of controls in your Visual Basic project

# Graph (GRAPH.VBX)

| USAGE: | Charting/Graphing Software |
|---|---|
| MANUFACTURER: | Bits Per Second/Microsoft |
| COST: | Distributed with Visual Basic Professional |

Graph is a limited version of the ChartBuilder VBX distributed by Pinnacle Publishing. Although it's not as powerful as ChartBuilder, Graph is nothing to sneeze at. It allows you to display and print 11 different types of graphs. Each basic type of graph has its own set of options, giving you a wide variety of graphs with which to display your data.

Some Graph features make it easy for programmers to use, including the *AutoIncrement* property. After you tell Graph how many sets of data to expect and how many points of data are in each set, *AutoIncrement* lets you then load the data via any of Graph's array properties. Graph handles incrementing with the *ThisPoint* and *ThisSet* properties. Graph also knows how to print itself directly to the printer.

## Syntax

Table 6-1 lists nonstandard properties for Graph.

**Table 6-1** Nonstandard properties for Graph

### PROPERTIES

| | | |
|---|---|---|
| AutoInc | BottomTitle | ColorData |
| CtlVersion | DataReset | ExtraData |

## PROPERTIES

| | | |
|---|---|---|
| FontFamily | FontUse | GraphCaption |
| GraphData | GraphTitle | GraphType |
| GridStyle | ImageFile | ImageStyle |
| IndexStyle | LabelEvery | Labels |
| LabelText | LeftTitle | LegendText |
| LineStats | NumPoints | NumSets |
| Palette | PatternData | PatternedLines |
| PrintStyle | QuickData | RandomData |
| SeeThru | SymbolData | ThickLines |
| ThisPoint | ThisSet | TickEvery |
| Ticks | XposData | YAxisMax |
| YAxisMin | YAxisPos | YAxisStyle |
| YAxisTicks | | |

As mentioned, Graph can display 11 different types of graphs, including None. The graph type is controlled by the *GraphType* property. Table 6-2 lists the values for GraphType and the type of graph they produce.

**Table 6-2** Values for the GraphType property

| VALUE | MEANING |
|---|---|
| 0 | None |
| 1 | 2D pie |
| 2 | 3D pie |
| 3 | 2D bar (default) |
| 4 | 3D bar |
| 5 | Gantt |
| 6 | Line |
| 7 | Log/Lin |
| 8 | Area |
| 9 | Scatter |
| 10 | Polar |
| 11 | High, Low, Close Bars |

Each type of graph also has different display options, which are controlled by the *GraphStyle* property.

For example, you can use *GraphStyle* to use colored lines to connect the pie slices with their labels, or to show percentage labels or colored labels. For a bar graph you can have the bars appear horizontally rather than vertically, or be stacked rather than be next to each other.

Graph accepts input through the *GraphData* property. You set the amount of data Graph expects using the *NumPoints* and *NumSets* properties. If you set the *AutoInc* property to *True,* Graph automatically increments the *ThisPoint* and *ThisRow* counter properties as you enter array data, rolling *ThisPoint* back to one and adding one to *ThisRow* as indicated by the *NumPoints* property. If you prefer, you can also control *ThisPoint* and *ThisRow* directly—for instance, to change a specific data point.

Graph has a number of array properties that control the color, column legends, and other aspects of the graph. You use *ThisPoint* and *ThisRow* to refer directly to a specific point of data or any of the array properties of Graph. *LegendText* controls the legend for the data points or data sets, depending on the type of graph and data. *ColorData* uses the QBColor colors to set the color of the data points or data sets. When you are drawing a pie chart, *ExtraData* is used to explode slices of the pie. When you're drawing a 3D bar graph *ExtraData* sets the colors of the sides of the bars.

**Printing**   One of the big advantages of Graph is that it knows how to print itself. Using the *DrawMode* and *PrintStyle* properties, you can control how your graph is printed. Tables 6-3 and 6-4 show all values for *DrawMode* and *PrintStyle*.

**Table 6-3** Values for the DrawMode property

| VALUE | MEANING |
|---|---|
| 0 | No Action |
| 1 | Clear |
| 2 | Draw |
| 3 | Blit |
| 4 | Copy |
| 5 | Print |
| 6 | Write |

**Table 6-4** Values for the PrintStyle property

| VALUE | MEANING |
|---|---|
| 0 | Monochrome (default) |
| 1 | Color |
| 2 | Monochrome with border |
| 3 | Color with border |

As you can see, *DrawMode* is used for quite a bit more than just printing graphs. If you set this property to 0 (No action), the graph is left blank or cleared. A setting of 1 (Clear) repaints the graph in the graph's *BackGround* color. Setting *DrawMode* to 2 (Draw) causes the sections of the graph to be drawn individually on the control. If you set *DrawMode* to 3 (Blit) Graph builds a bitmap of the graph in memory and then bitblits the graph onto the window. Setting *DrawMode* to 5 (Print) causes the graph to print on the default printer based on the setting of the *PrintStyle* property. Setting *DrawMode* to 6 (Write) causes the graph to be saved to the file named in the *ImageFile* property. If *DrawMode* was previously set to 3 (Blit) a .BMP file is saved; otherwise, a Windows metafile is created. Setting *DrawMode* to 4 (Copy) copies the graph image to the Clipboard formatted as either a .WMF or .BMP, using the same rules as 6 (Write).

# Example

The example program shown in Figure 6-1 analyzes control use in a Visual Basic project. The user gives the program a .MAK or .FRM file to read. The program analyzes the controls used in the specified form or all forms in a project. Once the data is collected, the user can use the Graph Data menu to select which data to view.

The user can look at all the controls used across the project, all the controls used on a form, and all forms in a project. If the user chooses to display the controls used on a form, the combo box becomes active and the user chooses which form to view. No matter what option the user chooses, the list box shows a list of controls and how many of each type there are. The graph only displays up to 10 items, in order of appearance, due to space considerations.

## Steps

1. Create a new project called MSGRAPH.MAK and add GRAPH.VBX and CMDIALOG.VBX. Create a new form with the objects and properties shown in Table 6-5. Save this form as MSGRAPH.FRM.

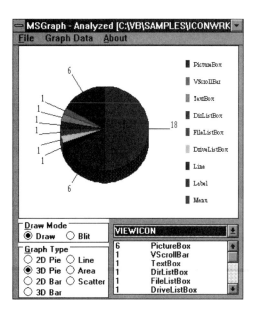

**Figure 6-1** The MSGraph example program

6

**Table 6-5** MSGraph main form's objects and properties

| OBJECT | PROPERTY | SETTING |
| --- | --- | --- |
| CommonDialog | Name | CMDialog1 |
| GRAPH | Name | Graph1 |
| | GraphType | 1 '2D Pie |
| ListBox | Name | lstControlList |
| ComboBox | Name | cmbFormCombo |
| | Enabled | 0 'False |
| | Style | 2 'Dropdown List |
| Frame | Name | fraDrawMode |
| | Caption | "&Draw Mode" |
| Frame | Name | fraGraphType |
| | Caption | "&Graph Type" |
| Form | FormName | frmMSGraph |
| | BackColor | &H00C0C0C0& |
| | BorderStyle | 3 'Fixed Double |
| | Caption | "MSGraph sample" |
| | MaxButton | 0 'False |

2. Add the objects and properties shown in Table 6-6 to the fraGraphType frame.

**Table 6-6** fraGraphType objects and properties

| OBJECT | PROPERTY | SETTING |
| --- | --- | --- |
| OptionButton | Name | OptGraphType |
| | Caption | "Scatter" |
| | Index | 9 |
| OptionButton | Name | OptGraphType |
| | Caption | "Area" |
| | Index | 8 |
| OptionButton | Name | OptGraphType |
| | Caption | "Line" |
| | Index | 6 |
| OptionButton | Name | OptGraphType |
| | Caption | "3D Bar" |
| | Index | 4 |
| OptionButton | Name | OptGraphType |
| | Caption | "2D Bar" |
| | Index | 3 |
| OptionButton | Name | OptGraphType |
| | Caption | "3D Pie" |
| | Index | 2 |

| OBJECT | PROPERTY | SETTING |
|---|---|---|
| OptionButton | Name | OptGraphType |
|  | Caption | "2D Pie" |
|  | Index | 1 |
|  | Value | -1 'True |

3. Add the objects and properties shown in Table 6-7 to the fraDrawMode frame.

**Table 6-7** fraDrawMode objects and properties

| OBJECT | PROPERTY | SETTING |
|---|---|---|
| OptionButton | Name | optDrawMode |
|  | Caption | "Blit" |
|  | Index | 3 |
| OptionButton | Name | optDrawMode |
|  | Caption | "Draw" |
|  | Index | 2 |
|  | Value | -1 'True |

4. Add the menu structure shown in Table 6-8 to the MSGRAPH form.

**Table 6-8** MSGRAPH menu structure

| CAPTION | NAME |
|---|---|
| &File | mnuFile |
| – – – – &Open | mnuOpen |
| – – – – – | mnuDash1 |
| – – – – E&xit | mnuExit |
| &Graph Data | mnuGraphData |
| – – – – &Graph Controls in Project | mnuGraph(0) |
| – – – – &Graph Forms in Project | mnuGraph(1) |
| – – – – &Graph Controls on a Form | mnuGraph(2) |
| &About | mnuAbout |

5. Add the following code to the MSGRAPH form. The MSGraph sample program processes VB .FRM files, counting the types of controls. You enter either a .MAK or .FRM file for MSGraph to process. Once you've entered a file for it to process, the program opens each file in turn, searching for control information using the BEGIN keyword from the .FRM to tell controls from code. The sample program uses the collected data to build several sets of tables. These tables hold the data displayed in the graph.

```
Option Explicit

Sub cmbFormCombo_Click ()
```

*(continued on next page)*

*(continued from previous page)*

```
    Dim i As Integer
    Dim FormSS As Integer

    If cmbFormCombo.ListIndex = -1 Then Exit Sub

    lstControlList.Clear

    FormSS = cmbFormCombo.ItemData(cmbFormCombo.ListIndex)

    graphthis FormSS

End Sub

Sub Form_Load ()
    '---------------------------------------------------------
    ' Center the form on the screen.
    '---------------------------------------------------------
    Me.Move (Screen.Width - Me.Width) \ 2, (Screen.Height - Me.Height) \ 2


    '---------------------------------------------------------
    ' Intialize some basic stuff.
    '---------------------------------------------------------
    ATab = Chr$(9)
    CRLF = Chr$(13) & Chr$(10)
    WhatToGraph = OPT_PROJ
    Graph1.DrawMode = G_CLEAR
    MaxPoints = 10
    MaxSets = 5

End Sub

Sub mnuAbout_Click ()
    frmabout.Show
End Sub

Sub mnuFileExit_Click ()
    Unload frmabout
    Unload Me
End Sub

Sub mnuFileOpen_Click ()
    '---------------------------------------------------------
    ' Get a file.
    '---------------------------------------------------------

    On Error GoTo mnuFileOpen_Error

    '---------------------------------------------------------
    ' Use common dialog to get a file name.
    '---------------------------------------------------------
    CmDialog1.Flags = OFN_HIDEREADONLY
    CmDialog1.Filter = "VB Project Files (*.mak)|*.mak|VB Form Files (*.frm)|*.frm"
    CmDialog1.DialogTitle = "Open Visual Basic File Source"
    CmDialog1.Action = DLG_FILE_OPEN
    If CmDialog1.Filename = "" Then Exit Sub
    If UCase$(Right$(CmDialog1.Filename, 3)) = "FRM" Then
        mnuGraph(OPT_PROJ).Enabled = False
        If mnuGraph(OPT_PROJ).Checked = True Then
```

```
            mnuGraph(OPT_FORM).Checked = True
            mnuGraph(OPT_PROJ).Checked = False
            WhatToGraph = OPT_FORM
    End If
Else
    mnuGraph(OPT_PROJ).Enabled = True
End If


'--------------------------------------------------
' Set the status indicator and switch the cursor to an hourglass.
'--------------------------------------------------
FrmMSGraph.Caption = "MSGraph - Analyzing [" & CmDialog1.Filename & "]"

Screen.MousePointer = CSR_HOURGLASS

FrmMSGraph!Graph1.DrawMode = G_CLEAR

cmbFormCombo.Clear


'--------------------------------------------------
' Just guesses. If your projects are larger or smaller, adjust as needed!
'--------------------------------------------------
FormsTop = 5
ControlsTop = 15
ProjectControlsTop = 15


'--------------------------------------------------
' Set up the arrays.
'--------------------------------------------------
ReDim FormInfo(1 To FormsTop)
ReDim ProjectControlsInfo(1 To ProjectControlsTop)

ProjectInfo.TotalControls = 0
ProjectInfo.TotalForms = 0
ProjectInfo.CountControls = 0


'--------------------------------------------------
' Decide what we're processing.
'--------------------------------------------------
If Right$(CmDialog1.Filename, 3) = "MAK" Then
    ProcessProject CmDialog1.Filename
Else
    ReDim ControlsInfo(1 To 1, 1 To 1)
    ProcessForm CmDialog1.Filename, 1, ControlsInfo()
End If


'--------------------------------------------------
' Switch the cursor back to normal and set the
' status indicator.
'--------------------------------------------------
Screen.MousePointer = CSR_NORMAL
FrmMSGraph.Caption = "MSGraph - Analyzed [" & CmDialog1.Filename & "]"

If WhatToGraph = OPT_FORM Then
    FrmMSGraph!cmbFormCombo.Enabled = True
    FrmMSGraph!cmbFormCombo.ListIndex = -1
    FrmMSGraph!cmbFormCombo.ListIndex = 0
Else
```

*(continued on next page)*

*(continued from previous page)*

```
            FrmMSGraph!cmbFormCombo.Enabled = False
            graphthis 0
        End If

Exit Sub

mnuFileOpen_Error:
        Screen.MousePointer = CSR_NORMAL
        Exit Sub
End Sub

Sub mnuGraph_Click (Index As Integer)

        '-------------------------------------------------
        ' Decide what to graph.
        '-------------------------------------------------
        Dim i As Integer

        For i = 0 To OPT_NUM_OPTS
            mnuGraph(i).Checked = False
        Next i

        mnuGraph(Index).Checked = True
        WhatToGraph = Index

        If WhatToGraph = OPT_FORM Then
            FrmMSGraph!cmbFormCombo.Enabled = True
        Else
            FrmMSGraph!cmbFormCombo.Enabled = False
        End If

        If FrmMSGraph!cmbFormCombo.ListCount = 0 Then Exit Sub

        If WhatToGraph = OPT_FORM Then
            '-----------------------------------------------------
            ' Fake it out; deselect and then select the first one.
            '-----------------------------------------------------
            FrmMSGraph!cmbFormCombo.ListIndex = -1
            FrmMSGraph!cmbFormCombo.ListIndex = 0
        Else
            graphthis 0
        End If
End Sub

Sub optGraphType_Click (Index As Integer)
        '---------------------------------------------------
        ' Set the graph type and draw the graph.
        '---------------------------------------------------
        Graph1.GraphType = Index

        If FrmMSGraph!optDrawMode(G_DRAW) = True Then
            FrmMSGraph!Graph1.DrawMode = G_DRAW
        Else
            FrmMSGraph!Graph1.DrawMode = G_BLIT
        End If

End Sub
```

6. Create a new .BAS module called MSGRAPH.BAS. Add the following types and global definitions. These types and definitions set up the tables and counters used to hold the graphing data.

```
Option Explicit
'--------------------------------------------------
' Define user types and global variables and constants.
'--------------------------------------------------

Type ProjectInfotype
      ProjectName As String
      TotalForms As Integer
      CountControls As Integer ' Count of individual controls in project.
      TotalControls As Integer ' Total controls in project.
End Type

Type FormInfotype
      FormName As String
      CountControls As Integer ' Count of individual controls on form.
      TotalControls As Integer ' Total controls on form.
End Type

Type ControlsInfoType
      ControlType As String ' Control type (picture, list box, etc.).
      TotalControls As Integer ' How many there are of this type on the form.
End Type

Global ProjectInfo As ProjectInfotype

Global FormInfo() As FormInfotype

Global ControlsInfo() As ControlsInfoType
Global ProjectControlsInfo() As ControlsInfoType

Global FormsTop As Integer
Global ControlsTop As Integer
Global ProjectControlsTop As Integer

Global ATab As String
Global CRLF As String

Global WhatToGraph As Integer
Global MaxPoints As Integer
Global MaxSets As Integer

Global Const OPT_PROJ = 0
Global Const OPT_FORM = 1
Global Const OPT_CNTL = 2
Global Const OPT_NUM_OPTS = 2

Global Const CSR_HOURGLASS = 11
Global Const CSR_NORMAL = 0

Global Const MINIMIZED = 1


'--------------------------------------------------
' MsgBox
'--------------------------------------------------
```

*(continued on next page)*

*(continued from previous page)*

```
Global Const MB_OK = 0                       ' OK button only
Global Const MB_OKCANCEL = 1                 ' OK and Cancel buttons
Global Const MB_ABORTRETRYIGNORE = 2         ' Abort, Retry, and Ignore buttons
Global Const MB_YESNOCANCEL = 3              ' Yes, No, and Cancel buttons
Global Const MB_YESNO = 4                    ' Yes and No buttons
Global Const MB_RETRYCANCEL = 5              ' Retry and Cancel buttons

Global Const MB_ICONSTOP = 16                ' Critical message
Global Const MB_ICONQUESTION = 32            ' Warning query
Global Const MB_ICONEXCLAMATION = 48         ' Warning message
Global Const MB_ICONINFORMATION = 64         ' Information message
Global Const MB_ICONSTOPLIGHT = 77           ' StopLight, Please Wait message

Global Const MB_DEFBUTTON1 = 0               ' First button is default
Global Const MB_DEFBUTTON2 = 256             ' Second button is default
Global Const MB_DEFBUTTON3 = 512             ' Third button is default

'---------------
' DialogBox ID
'---------------

Global Const IDOK = 1
Global Const IDCANCEL = 2
Global Const IDABORT = 3
Global Const IDRETRY = 4
Global Const IDIGNORE = 5
Global Const IDYES = 6
Global Const IDNO = 7

'----------------------------------------------------
' File Open/Save Dialog Flags
'----------------------------------------------------
Global Const OFN_READONLY = &H1&
Global Const OFN_OVERWRITEPROMPT = &H2&
Global Const OFN_HIDEREADONLY = &H4&
Global Const OFN_NOCHANGEDIR = &H8&
Global Const OFN_SHOWHELP = &H10&
Global Const OFN_NOVALIDATE = &H100&
Global Const OFN_ALLOWMULTISELECT = &H200&
Global Const OFN_EXTENSIONDIFFERENT = &H400&
Global Const OFN_PATHMUSTEXIST = &H800&
Global Const OFN_FILEMUSTEXIST = &H1000&
Global Const OFN_CREATEPROMPT = &H2000&
Global Const OFN_SHAREAWARE = &H4000&
Global Const OFN_NOREADONLYRETURN = &H8000&

Global Const DLG_FILE_OPEN = 1

'----------------------------------------------------
' Graph constants
' Draw Mode
'----------------------------------------------------
Global Const G_NO_ACTION = 0
Global Const G_CLEAR = 1
Global Const G_DRAW = 2
Global Const G_BLIT = 3
Global Const G_COPY = 4
Global Const G_PRINT = 5
Global Const G_WRITE = 6
```

7. Add the following code to MSGRAPH.BAS. These subroutines contain the actual code to read the .MAK and .FRM files and count the various controls.

```
Sub graphthis (FormSS As Integer)

    '-------------------------------------------------
    ' Decide what to graph.
    '-------------------------------------------------
    Dim i As Integer


    frmMSGraph!Graph1.NumSets = 1


    '-------------------------------------------------
    ' Set up the basic graph information and load the data
    ' based on the type of graph and what the user wants
    ' to look at/graph.
    '-------------------------------------------------
    Select Case WhatToGraph
        Case OPT_PROJ
        frmMSGraph!cmbFormCombo.Enabled = False
            If ProjectInfo.TotalForms < MaxPoints Then
                frmMSGraph!Graph1.NumPoints = ProjectInfo.TotalForms
            Else
                frmMSGraph!Graph1.NumPoints = MaxPoints
            End If
            For i = 1 To frmMSGraph!Graph1.NumPoints
                frmMSGraph!Graph1.GraphData = FormInfo(i).TotalControls
            Next i
            For i = 1 To frmMSGraph!Graph1.NumPoints
                frmMSGraph!Graph1.LegendText = FormInfo(i).FormName
            Next i
                frmMSGraph!lstControlList.Clear
            For i = 1 To ProjectInfo.TotalForms
                frmMSGraph!lstControlList.AddItem Format$(FormInfo(i).TotalControls) & ATab
& FormInfo(i).FormName
            Next i
        Case OPT_FORM
            If FormInfo(FormSS).CountControls < MaxPoints Then
                frmMSGraph!Graph1.NumPoints = FormInfo(FormSS).CountControls
            Else
                frmMSGraph!Graph1.NumPoints = MaxPoints
            End If
            If ProjectInfo.TotalForms < MaxSets Then
                frmMSGraph!Graph1.NumSets = ProjectInfo.TotalForms
            Else
                frmMSGraph!Graph1.NumSets = MaxSets
            End If
            For i = 1 To frmMSGraph!Graph1.NumPoints
                frmMSGraph!Graph1.GraphData = ControlsInfo(FormSS, i).TotalControls
            Next i
            For i = 1 To frmMSGraph!Graph1.NumPoints
                frmMSGraph!Graph1.LegendText = ControlsInfo(FormSS, i).ControlType
            Next i
                frmMSGraph!lstControlList.Clear
            For i = 1 To FormInfo(FormSS).CountControls
                frmMSGraph!lstControlList.AddItem Format$(ControlsInfo(FormSS,
i).TotalControls, "####") & ATab & ControlsInfo(FormSS, i).ControlType
```

*(continued on next page)*

*(continued from previous page)*

```
                Next i
        Case OPT_CNTL
                    frmMSGraph!cmbFormCombo.Enabled = False
                If ProjectInfo.CountControls < MaxPoints Then
                    frmMSGraph!Graph1.NumPoints = ProjectInfo.CountControls
                Else
                    frmMSGraph!Graph1.NumPoints = MaxPoints
                End If
                For i = 1 To frmMSGraph!Graph1.NumPoints
                    frmMSGraph!Graph1.GraphData = ProjectControlsInfo(i).TotalControls
                Next i
                For i = 1 To frmMSGraph!Graph1.NumPoints
                    frmMSGraph!Graph1.LegendText = ProjectControlsInfo(i).ControlType
                Next i
                    frmMSGraph!lstControlList.Clear
                For i = 1 To ProjectInfo.CountControls
                    frmMSGraph!lstControlList.AddItem
Format$(ProjectControlsInfo(i).TotalControls) & ₄Tab & ProjectControlsInfo(i).ControlType
            Next i
    End Select

    '------------------------------------------------------
    ' Draw the graph.
    '------------------------------------------------------
    If frmMSGraph!optDrawMode(G_DRAW) = True Then
            frmMSGraph!Graph1.DrawMode = G_DRAW
    Else
            frmMSGraph!Graph1.DrawMode = G_BLIT
    End If

End Sub

Sub ProcessForm (ByVal FormFile As String, FormPointer As Integer, ControlsInfo() As
ControlsInfoType)
    '------------------------------------------------------
    ' Process all the controls on a form.
    '------------------------------------------------------
    Dim astr As String
    Dim workstr As String
    Dim i As Integer

    Dim fnum As Integer

    Dim Done As Integer
    Dim EndSw As Integer

    Done = False
    EndSw = False

    fnum = FreeFile
    Open FormFile For Input As fnum

    While (Not EOF(fnum)) And (Not Done)
        DoEvents
        Line Input #fnum, astr
        astr = Trim$(astr)

        '------------------------------------------------------
        ' Figure out what we've read and, if it's a control name,
        ' count it.
        '------------------------------------------------------
```

```
    If UCase$(Left$(astr, 5)) = "BEGIN" Then
        workstr = Mid$(astr, 7, InStr(7, astr, " ") - 7)
        If UCase$(workstr) = "FORM" Then
            '----------------------------------------------------
            ' Returns everything starting at 12.
            ' 5 for begin, 1 for space, 4 for form, and 1 for space.
            '----------------------------------------------------
            FormInfo(FormPointer).FormName = Mid$(astr, 12)
        ElseIf UCase$(workstr) = "MDIFORM" Then
            '----------------------------------------------------
            ' Returns everything starting at 15.
            ' 5 for begin, 1 for space, 7 for MDIForm, and 1 for space.
            '----------------------------------------------------
            FormInfo(FormPointer).FormName = Mid$(astr, 15)
        Else
            i = 1
            '----------------------------------------------------
            ' Look for the control name in the array.
            '----------------------------------------------------
            Do While Not (ControlsInfo(FormPointer, i).ControlType = workstr Or
ControlsInfo(FormPointer, i).ControlType = "")
                i = i + 1
                '----------------------------------------------------
                ' See if we're at the end of the table.
                '----------------------------------------------------
                If i >= ControlsTop Then
                    '------------------
                    ' Make it bigger.
                    '------------------
                    ReDim Preserve ControlsInfo(1 To FormsTop, 1 To i)
                    ControlsTop = i
                    Exit Do
                End If
            Loop
            '----------------------------------------------------
            ' Count the control.  If it's not there, add it.
            '----------------------------------------------------
            If ControlsInfo(FormPointer, i).ControlType = "" Then
                ControlsInfo(FormPointer, i).TotalControls = 0
                ControlsInfo(FormPointer, i).ControlType = workstr
                FormInfo(FormPointer).CountControls = FormInfo(FormPointer).CountControls + 1
            End If
            ControlsInfo(FormPointer, i).TotalControls = ControlsInfo(FormPointer,
i).TotalControls + 1
            FormInfo(FormPointer).TotalControls = FormInfo(FormPointer).TotalControls + 1
            EndSw = False
        End If
    ElseIf UCase$(Left$(astr, 3)) = "END" Then
        EndSw = True
    ElseIf UCase$(Left$(astr, 6)) = "OPTION" Or UCase$(Left$(astr, 3)) = "SUB" Or
UCase$(Left$(astr, 8)) = "FUNCTION" Then
        '----------------------------------------------------
        ' Looking for the end this way will actually
        ' waste some reads, but it's probably more
        ' reliable that looking for some combination
        ' of ENDs or relying on the positioning of
        ' the last END.
        '----------------------------------------------------
        Done = True
    End If
```

(continued on next page)

*(continued from previous page)*

```
        Wend

        Close fnum

        Exit Sub

ProcessFormError:

        MsgBox "error while processing form " & FormFile & " - " & Error$(Err)

        Exit Sub

End Sub

Sub ProcessProject (ByVal ProjectFile As String)
        '----------------------------------------------------
        ' Process all the forms in a project.
        '----------------------------------------------------

        Dim astr As String

        Dim fnum As Integer
        Dim i As Integer
        Dim j As Integer
        Dim FormControlsSS As Integer

        On Error GoTo ProcessProjectError

        fnum = FreeFile
        Open ProjectFile For Input As fnum

        ProjectInfo.TotalForms = 0

        While (Not EOF(fnum))
                DoEvents
                Line Input #fnum, astr
                astr = Trim$(astr)

                '----------------------------------------------------
                ' Look for form names.
                '----------------------------------------------------
                If UCase$(Right$(astr, 3)) = "FRM" Then
                    ProjectInfo.TotalForms = ProjectInfo.TotalForms + 1
                    If ProjectInfo.TotalForms > FormsTop Then
                            FormsTop = ProjectInfo.TotalForms
                            ReDim Preserve FormInfo(1 To FormsTop)
                    End If
                    '----------------------------------------------------
                    ' If I find one, add it to the table and combo box.
                    '----------------------------------------------------
                    frmMSGraph!cmbFormCombo.AddItem Left$(astr, Len(astr) - 4)
                    frmMSGraph!cmbFormCombo.ItemData(frmMSGraph!cmbFormCombo.NewIndex) = ⇒
ProjectInfo.TotalForms
                End If
        Wend

        Close fnum

        i = 1
```

```
    ReDim ControlsInfo(1 To FormsTop, 1 To ControlsTop)

    While i <= ProjectInfo.TotalForms
        DoEvents
            '------------------------------------------------------
            ' Process the forms.
            '------------------------------------------------------
            ProcessForm frmMSGraph!cmbFormCombo.List(i - 1) & ".frm", i, ControlsInfo()
            ProjectInfo.TotalControls = ProjectInfo.TotalControls + FormInfo(i).TotalControls
            j = 1
            '------------------------------------------------------
            ' Process the controls on the form.
            '------------------------------------------------------
            For FormControlsSS = 1 To FormInfo(i).CountControls
                Do While Not (ProjectControlsInfo(j).ControlType = ControlsInfo(i,
FormControlsSS).ControlType Or ProjectControlsInfo(j).ControlType = "")
                    j = j + 1
                    If j >= ProjectControlsTop Then
                        ReDim Preserve ProjectControlsInfo(1 To j)
                        ProjectControlsTop = j
                        Exit Do
                    End If
                Loop
                If ProjectControlsInfo(j).ControlType = "" Then
                    ProjectControlsInfo(j).TotalControls = 0
                    ProjectControlsInfo(j).ControlType = ControlsInfo(i,
FormControlsSS).ControlType
                    ProjectInfo.CountControls = ProjectInfo.CountControls + 1
                End If
                ProjectControlsInfo(j).TotalControls = ProjectControlsInfo(j).TotalControls +
ControlsInfo(i, FormControlsSS).TotalControls
            Next FormControlsSS
            i = i + 1
    Wend


    Exit Sub

ProcessProjectError:

    MsgBox "error while processing the project " & Error$(Err)

    Exit Sub

End Sub
```

# Tips and Comments

GRAPH.VBX allows you to select a graph type that will display your data in a
meaningful fashion. Graph has many features that make it simple to use in your program,
including automatic data entry and the ability to print a graph directly to the printer or
save a graph as a .BMP or .WMF file.

# ChartBuilder (GRAPH.VBX)

| | |
|---|---|
| USAGE: | Charting/Graphing Software |
| MANUFACTURER: | Bits Per Second/Pinnacle Publishing |
| COST: | $149 |

ChartBuilder is the big brother to the Graph control that comes with Visual Basic Professional, because Bits Per Second licensed a limited version of ChartBuilder to Microsoft for VBPro. Anything Graph can do, ChartBuilder can do, and then some. Probably the biggest advance over Graph is ChartBuilder's *HotHit* custom event. This event allows the user to interact with the graph by clicking on it. When *HotHit* fires, it returns the data point and data set the user clicked on.

ChartBuilder also interfaces with Bits Per Second's Graphics Software Development Kit. Although a limited version of the Graphics SDK comes with ChartBuilder, the full Graphics SDK gives you total control over all your graphs by making available a large number of functions and activating several custom properties in ChartBuilder. You can also control the Graphics SDK via DDE. Usually, there is no need for this level of control over your graphing functions, but it's available if you do need it.

ChartBuilder has some very nice program interface features, including *AutoInc* property. After you tell ChartBuilder how many sets of data to expect and how many points of data there are in each set, *AutoInc* allows you to load the data via any of ChartBuilder's array properties. Like Graph, ChartBuilder knows how to print itself. You can either print a ChartBuilder graph directly to the printer or to VB's printer object. Both methods give you full printer resolution. Sending a graph to the printer object gives you control over the size and position of the graph on the page, while printing directly to the printer prints a screen-sized graph centered on the top of the page.

## Syntax

Table 6-9 lists the custom properties and events for ChartBuilder.

**Table 6-9** Custom properties and events for ChartBuilder

### PROPERTIES

| | | |
|---|---|---|
| About | AsciiForms | AutoInc |
| Backdrop | BackdropStyle | Background |
| BottomTitle | Color | ColorData |
| CtlVersion | CurveOrder | CurveSteps |
| CurveType | Data | DataReset |
| DrawMode | DrawStyle | Extra |
| ExtraData | FontFamily | FontName |
| FontSize | FontStyle | FontUse |
| Foreground | GraphCaption | GraphData |

## PROPERTIES

| | | |
|---|---|---|
| GraphStyle | GraphTitle | GraphType |
| GridStyle | Hot | ImageFile |
| IndexStyle | Label | LabelsEvery |
| Labels | LabelText | LeftTitle |
| Legend | LegendStyle | LegendText |
| LineStats | MousePointer | NumPoints |
| NumSets | Palette | Pattern |
| PatternData | PatternedLines | Picture |
| PrintInfo | PrintStyle | QuickData |
| RandomData | PrintStyle | SDKInfo |
| SDKMouse | SDKPaint | SeeThru |
| Symbol | SymbolData | SymbolSize |
| ThickLines | ThisPoint | ThisSet |
| TickEvery | Ticks | XAxisMax |
| XAxisMin | XAxisPos | XAxisStyle |
| XAxisTicks | XPos | XPosData |
| YAxisMax | YAxisMin | YAxisPos |
| YAxisStyle | YAxisTicks | |

## EVENTS

| | | |
|---|---|---|
| HotHit | SDKHit | SDKPaint |
| SDKPress | SDKTrack | |

Unlike the version of Graph that comes with Visual Basic Professional, ChartBuilder makes it easy to determine which section of the graph the user clicked on. You can do this using the *Hot* property and the *HotHit* event. Setting *Hot* to *On* causes ChartBuilder to fire the *HotHit* event whenever a region of the graph is clicked on. The *HotHit* event tells you which point and set your user clicked on. You can use these values as indexes to determine which data item was selected and then perform the appropriate action. You can turn *Hot* on and off at will, but once you turn it off, turning it back on won't have any affect until ChartBuilder redraws the graph.

You control the graph type using the *GraphType* property. ChartBuilder can display the 14 different base graphs listed in Table 6-10.

**Table 6-10** Values for the GraphType property

| VALUE | MEANING |
|---|---|
| 0 | None |
| 1 | 2D pie |
| 2 | 3D pie |
| 3 | 2D bar (default) |
| 4 | 3D bar |

*(continued on next page)*

| VALUE | MEANING |
|---|---|
| (continued from previous page) | |
| 5 | Gantt |
| 6 | Line |
| 7 | Log/Lin |
| 8 | Area |
| 9 | Scatter |
| 10 | Polar |
| 11 | HLC |
| 12 | Bubble |
| 13 | Tape |
| 14 | 3D area |

Each graph type has different style options, which are controlled by the *GraphStyle* property. For example, if you're displaying a pie chart, you can use the *GraphStyle* property to color the lines connecting the captions with the pie slices. You can also cause the pie captions to be displayed as percentages or to be displayed in color. If you are displaying a Gantt chart you can use the *GraphStyle* property to cause the bars to be spaced apart from each other or adjacent to each other.

*DrawMode* controls how the graph is drawn and what format the graph is stored in. See Table 6-11 for the values for *DrawMode*.

**Table 6-11** Values for the DrawMode property

| VALUE | MEANING |
|---|---|
| 0 | No Action |
| 1 | Clear |
| 2 | Draw |
| 3 | Blit |
| 4 | Copy |
| 5 | Print |
| 6 | Write |

If *DrawMode* is set to 0 (No action) then no graph will appear or the graph will be unchanged regardless of any properties you change. Setting *DrawMode* to 1 (Clear) clears the graph. Setting *DrawMode* to 2 (Draw) draws or redraws the graph. Setting *DrawMode* to 3 (Blit) also draws or redraws the graph, but using Blit causes the Graph control to build a hidden bitmap and copy the bitmap to screen using the Windows BitBlit function, where the 2 (Draw) setting allows Graph to build a Windows Metafile right in the control. When *DrawMode* is set to 2 the graph appears piece by piece. When *DrawMode* is 3 the graph appears all at once.

A *DrawMode* of 4 causes the graph to be copied to the Windows Clipboard. Depending on whether the graph was drawn with a *DrawMode* of 2 (Draw) or 3 (Blit), either a .WMF or .BMP is placed in the Clipboard. *DrawMode* 6 (Write) saves the graph to the file named in the *ImageFile* property. If the *ImageFile* property is not filled in then the graph is not saved. When *DrawMode* is 3 the graph appears all at once.

**Printing**    Setting *DrawMode* to *Print* causes ChartBuilder to print the graph. ChartBuilder prints the graph centered at the top of the page. If you set *DrawMode* to *Print* but don't use the *PrintInfo* property array, the *PrintInfo* property array lets you output the graph to the Visual Basic Print object. Table 6-12 lists the values possible for the array.

**Table 6-12** Values for the PrintInfo property array

| VALUE | MEANING |
| --- | --- |
| PrintInfo(1) | VB printer device context (set = Printer.hDC) |
| PrintInfo(2) | X coordinate of upper-left corner of graph |
| PrintInfo(3) | Y coordinate of upper-left corner of graph |
| PrintInfo(4) | Width of graph |
| PrintInfo(5) | Height of graph |
| PrintInfo(6) | Scale left (set = Printer.ScaleLeft) |
| PrintInfo(7) | Scale top (set = Printer.ScaleTop) |
| PrintInfo(8) | Scale width (set = Printer.ScaleWidth) |
| PrintInfo(9) | Scale height (set = Printer.ScaleHeight) |

By using the *PrintInfo* property array, you can position the graph where you need it for any report.

**Appearance**    ChartBuilder has a large number of custom properties for controlling the appearance of the graph and how the data is written to or read from the graph. The *NumPoints* and *NumSets* properties control the total number of data points ChartBuilder handles. *AutoInc* controls how the *ThisPoint* and *ThisSet* properties act as data is written to ChartBuilder. If *AutoInc* is *True* all the data properties automatically move from point to point and set to set. If it's *False*, you must control *ThisPoint* and *ThisSet* programmatically. You add labels to the data being plotted using the *LabelText* property. You can optionally set the colors for the graph elements using the *ColorData* property. ChartBuilder only understands the 16 QBColor colors.

In addition to properties controlled by *ThisPoint*, *ThisSet*, and *AutoInc,* ChartBuilder has equivalent array properties you can access only at run time. These properties—such as *Color, Data,* and *Label*—are accessed just like a standard Visual Basic array, and you can use them to set the appearance and data values for ChartBuilder using your own subscript rather than setting *ThisPoint.* The properties are only in one dimension, so if you have sets of data you still need to set *ThisSet* to access individual data points in a set of data. There is no advantage to using an individual property, such as *GraphData*, rather than an array property, such as *Data*, aside from programming style or programmer preference.

# Example

The example program shown in Figure 6-2 graphs disk usage for the disk space used in the subdirectories in a directory, or for all the files in a directory grouped by their extension. Select the desired graph options using the option buttons and check boxes, select the desired directory from the directories control, and choose the GO! option from the File menu.

The data is collected into a sorted list box just over the left border of the main form. You can resize the window before or during data collection to watch the data being collected. Once the data is collected, the number of data points you elected to graph is copied from the list box and handed to the graph. Once the graph is built, you can use the *HotHit* event to show which set of information you clicked on.

## Steps

1. Create a new project called GRAPH.MAK. Add GRAPH.VBX from ChartBuilder to the project. The ChartBuilder control has the same name as the control that ships with VB Professional, so make sure you get the right one. Create a new form with the objects and properties shown in Table 6-13. Save this form as GRAPH.FRM.

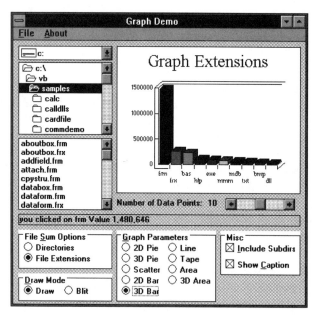

**Figure 6-2** The ChartBuilder example program

**Table 6-13** Graph main form's objects and properties

| OBJECT | PROPERTY | SETTING |
|---|---|---|
| Label | Name | lblDataPoints |
| | BackStyle | 0 'Transparent |
| | Caption | "Number of Datapoints:  10" |
| Label | Name | lblStatus |
| | BackStyle | 0 'Transparent |
| | BorderStyle | 1 'Fixed Single |
| DirListBox | Name | dirDirList |
| DriveListBox | Name | Drive1 |
| Frame | Name | fraGraphParameters |
| | Caption | "&Graph Parameters" |
| Frame | Name | fraFileSum |
| | Caption | "File &Sum Options" |
| GRAPH | Name | Graph1 |
| | GraphTitle | "Graph Directories" |
| | GraphType | 1 '2D Pie |
| | Hot | 1 'On |
| | NumPoints | 10 |
| Frame | Name | fraDrawMode |
| | Caption | "&Draw Mode" |
| ListBox | Name | lstTotalList |
| | FontBold | 0 'False |
| | Sorted | -1 'True |
| | TabStop | 0 'False |
| FileListBox | Name | filFileList |
| HScrollBar | Name | hscDataPoints |
| | Max | 15 |
| | Min | 5 |
| | Value | 10 |
| Frame | Name | fraMisc |
| | Caption | "Misc" |
| Form | FormName | frmGraph |
| | BackColor | &H00FFFF80& |
| | Caption | "Graph Demo" |

2. Add the objects and properties shown in Table 6-14 to the fraGraphParameters frame.

6

**Table 6-14** fraGraphParameters objects and properties

| OBJECT | PROPERTY | SETTING |
|---|---|---|
| OptionButton | Name | Option1 |
| | Caption | "2D Pie" |
| | Index | 1 |
| | Value | -1 'True |
| OptionButton | Name | Option1 |
| | Caption | "3D Pie" |
| | Index | 2 |
| OptionButton | Name | Option1 |
| | Caption | "2D Bar" |
| | Index | 3 |
| OptionButton | Name | Option1 |
| | Caption | "3D Bar" |
| | Index | 4 |
| OptionButton | Name | Option1 |
| | Caption | "Line" |
| | Index | 6 |
| OptionButton | Name | Option1 |
| | Caption | "Area" |
| | Index | 8 |
| OptionButton | Name | Option1 |
| | Caption | "Scatter" |
| | Index | 9 |
| OptionButton | Name | Option1 |
| | Caption | "3D Area" |
| | Index | 14 |
| OptionButton | Name | Option1 |
| | Caption | "Tape" |
| | Index | 13 |

3. Add the objects and properties shown in Table 6-15 to the fraFileSum frame.

**Table 6-15** fraFileSum objects and properties

| OBJECT | PROPERTY | SETTING |
|---|---|---|
| OptionButton | Name | optDrive |
| | Caption | "Directories" |
| | Index | 0 |
| | Value | -1 'True |
| OptionButton | Name | optDrive |

| OBJECT | PROPERTY | SETTING |
|---|---|---|
| | Caption | "File Extensions" |
| | Index | 1 |

4. Add the objects and properties shown in Table 6-16 to the fraDrawMode frame.

**Table 6-16** fraDrawMode objects and properties

| OBJECT | PROPERTY | SETTING |
|---|---|---|
| OptionButton | Name | optDrawMode |
| | Caption | "Draw" |
| | Index | 2 |
| | Value | -1 'True |
| OptionButton | Name | optDrawMode |
| | Caption | "Blit" |
| | Index | 3 |

5. Add the objects and properties shown in Table 6-17 to the fraMisc frame.

**Table 6-17** fraMisc objects and properties

| OBJECT | PROPERTY | SETTING |
|---|---|---|
| CheckBox | Name | chkSubDirs |
| | Caption | "&Include Subdirs" |
| | Value | 1 'Checked |
| CheckBox | Name | chkShowCaption |
| | Caption | "Show &Caption" |

6. Add the menu structure shown in Table 6-18 to the GRAPH form.

**Table 6-18** the GRAPH.FRM menu

| CAPTION | NAME |
|---|---|
| &File | mnuFile |
| − − − − &GO! | mnuGO |
| − − − − | mnuDash1 |
| − − − − &Print | mnuPrint |
| − − − − − − − − Print Monochrome | mnuGoPrint(0) |
| − − − − − − − − Print Color | mnuGoPrint(1) |
| − − − − − − − − Print Monochrome w/Border | mnuGoPrint(2) |
| − − − − − − − − Print Color w/ Border | mnuGoPrint(3) |
| − − − − − | mnuDash2 |
| − − − − E&xit | mnuExit |
| &About | mnuAbout |

6

7. Add the following code to the declarations section of the GRAPH form. These definitions set up constants used to control some of the graph properties and some control properties.

```
Option Explicit
Const CHECKED = 1
Const SUM_DIRECTORIES = 0
Const SUM_EXTENSIONS = 1
Const FormatString = "0000000000"

Const PRINTER_HDC = 1
Const X_TOP_LEFT = 2
Const Y_TOP_LEFT = 3
Const WIDTH_OF_GRAPH = 4
Const HEIGHT_OF_GRAPH = 5
Const SCALE_LEFT = 6
Const SCALE_TOP = 7
Const SCALE_WIDTH = 8
Const SCALE_HEIGHT = 9

Const GRAPH_DIRS = 0
Const GRAPH_EXTS = 1
```

8. Add the following code to the GRAPH form. These subroutines control the Graph form controls and also process the directory and subdirectory information. This sample program uses VB controls to get directory information and the list of files to process. You specify a subdirectory in the directory box and select whether to process all subdirectories or just the top level directory. The program sets the file list box path to the path from the directory box and reads each file in the list. If you're doing directory information only, the program just sums the file sizes. If you're doing extensions, the program searches the sorted list box for the extension of the file type(s) being processed. If the extension is in the list box, the list box entry is removed, the total for that extension is updated, and the list box entry is re-added to maintain the proper numeric sort order. This process is repeated for all subdirectories. Once all the subdirectories are processed, the data is fed to ChartBuilder and graphed according to the selected options. You can choose the graph type at any time, but some of the options only take effect when the graph is redrawn.

```
Sub Drive1_Change ()
    dirDirList.Path = drive1.Drive
End Sub

Sub Form_Load ()
    '----------------------------------------
    ' Center form in the screen and clear the graph.
    '----------------------------------------
    Me.Move (Screen.Width - Me.Width) \ 2, (Screen.Height - Me.Height) \ 2

    graph1.DrawMode = G_CLEAR

End Sub

Sub Graph1_HotHit (HitSet As Integer, HitPoint As Integer)
    '----------------------------------------
    ' just to demonstrate how HotHit works, display the
```

```
    ' caption of the graph area clicked on. You could
    ' do almost anything here with the data from the graph,
    ' such as focus the graph on the area selected (drilldown), etc.
    '-----------------------------------

    Dim Total As String
    Dim CaptionLen As Integer
    Dim ListIndex As Integer

    ListIndex = lstTotalList.ListCount - HitPoint
    CaptionLen = Len(lstTotalList.List(ListIndex)) - 10
    Total = Format$(Val(Left$(lstTotalList.List(ListIndex), 10)), "#,########")
    lblstatus = "you clicked on " & Right$(lstTotalList.List(ListIndex), CaptionLen) & " Value
" & Total

End Sub

Sub hscDataPoints_Change ()
    lblDataPoints = "Number of Datapoints: " & Str$(hscDataPoints)
    graph1.NumPoints = hscDataPoints
End Sub

Sub mnuAbout_Click ()
    frmabout.Show 1
End Sub

Sub mnuExit_Click ()
    Unload frmabout
    Unload Me
End Sub

Sub mnuGo_Click ()
    '-----------------------------------
    ' Start processing the file list.
    ' The static variable ensures we don't try
    ' processing if we've already started processing.
    '-----------------------------------
    Static processing As Integer

    If processing = True Then Exit Sub

    '-----------------------------------
    ' Initialize the list box holding the sorted totals.
    '-----------------------------------
    lstTotalList.Clear

    processing = True
    processdata
    processing = False
End Sub

Sub mnuGoPrint_Click (index As Integer)
    '-----------------------------------
    ' Print the data.
    '-----------------------------------
    graph1.PrintStyle = index

    graph1.PrintInfo(PRINTER_HDC) = printer.hDC
```

*(continued on next page)*

*(continued from previous page)*

```
'---------------------------------------
' Print the graph centered in the page, 10 pixels away
' from the edges.
'---------------------------------------
graph1.PrintInfo(X_TOP_LEFT) = 10
graph1.PrintInfo(Y_TOP_LEFT) = 10
graph1.PrintInfo(WIDTH_OF_GRAPH) = printer.Width - 20
graph1.PrintInfo(SCALE_LEFT) = printer.ScaleLeft
graph1.PrintInfo(SCALE_TOP) = printer.ScaleTop
graph1.PrintInfo(SCALE_WIDTH) = printer.ScaleWidth
graph1.PrintInfo(SCALE_HEIGHT) = printer.ScaleHeight

graph1.DrawMode = G_PRINT

printer.Print
printer.NewPage
printer.EndDoc

End Sub

Sub optDrive_Click (index As Integer)
    If index = GRAPH_DIRS Then
        graph1.GraphTitle = "Graph Directories"
    Else
        graph1.GraphTitle = "Graph Extensions"
    End If
End Sub

Sub Option1_Click (index As Integer)
    graph1.GraphType = index

    RedrawGraph
End Sub

Sub processdata ()
    '---------------------------------------
    ' Graph the data.
    '---------------------------------------


    Dim i As Integer
    Dim holdpath As String

    holdpath = dirDirList.Path
    For i = 0 To dirDirList.ListCount - 1
        SumData (dirDirList.List(i))
        dirDirList.Path = holdpath
    Next i

    If lstTotalList.ListCount < hscDataPoints Then
        graph1.NumPoints = lstTotalList.ListCount
    End If

    graph1.DataReset = G_ALL_DATA

    For i = lstTotalList.ListCount - 1 To lstTotalList.ListCount - graph1.NumPoints Step -1
        graph1.GraphData = Val(Left$(lstTotalList.List(i), 10))
    Next i
```

```
    If chkShowCaption = CHECKED Then
        For i = lstTotalList.ListCount - 1 To lstTotalList.ListCount - graph1.NumPoints Step -1
            graph1.LabelText = Right$(lstTotalList.List(i), Len(lstTotalList.List(i)) - 10)
        Next i
    End If

    RedrawGraph
End Sub

Sub RedrawGraph ()
    '--------------------------------------
    ' Draw the graph.
    '--------------------------------------
    If optDrawMode(G_DRAW).Value = True Then
        graph1.DrawMode = G_DRAW
    Else
        graph1.DrawMode = G_BLIT
    End If
End Sub

Sub SumData (DirName As String)
    '--------------------------------------
    ' Collect the data.
    '--------------------------------------
    Dim TotalSize As Long
    Dim DirNameSlash As String
    Dim i As Integer

    If Right$(DirName, 1) = "\" Then
        DirNameSlash = DirName
    Else
        DirNameSlash = DirName & "\"
    End If

    filFileList.Path = DirName
    For i = 0 To filFileList.ListCount - 1
        If optDrive(SUM_DIRECTORIES) = True Then
            TotalSize = FileLen(DirNameSlash & filFileList.List(i)) + TotalSize
            DoEvents
        Else
            SumExtension (filFileList.List(i)), DirNameSlash
        End If
    Next i

    If optDrive(SUM_DIRECTORIES) = True And TotalSize  0 Then
        lstTotalList.AddItem Format$(TotalSize, FormatString) & DirNameSlash
    End If

    '--------------------------------------
    ' Call myself recursively.
    '--------------------------------------
    If chkSubDirs = CHECKED Then
        dirDirList.Path = DirName
        For i = 0 To dirDirList.ListCount - 1
            SumData (dirDirList.List(i))
            dirDirList.Path = DirName
        Next i
    End If

End Sub
```

(continued on next page)

*(continued from previous page)*

```
Sub SumExtension (FileName As String, DirNameSlash As String)
    '------------------------------------
    ' Get the extension of the file name,
    ' see if it's in the sorted list box,
    ' and either add it if it's not there or
    ' update the list box if it is there.
    '------------------------------------

    Dim extension As String
    Dim HoldFileSize As Long
    Dim ExtensionTotal As Double'long
    Dim ExtensionLocation As Integer
    Dim i As Integer

    ExtensionLocation = InStr(FileName, ".")
    If ExtensionLocation = 0 Then
        extension = "    "
    Else
        extension = Format(Right$(FileName, Len(FileName) - ExtensionLocation), "@@@")
    End If

    For i = 0 To lstTotalList.ListCount - 1
        DoEvents
        If Right$(lstTotalList.List(i), 3) = extension Then
            ExtensionTotal = FileLen(DirNameSlash & FileName) + Val(Left$(lstTotalList.List(i), 10))
            lstTotalList.RemoveItem i
            lstTotalList.AddItem Format$(ExtensionTotal, FormatString) & extension
            Exit Sub
        End If
    Next i

    lstTotalList.AddItem Format$(FileLen(DirNameSlash & FileName), FormatString) & extension

End Sub
```

9. Create a new module and name it GRAPH.BAS. Load the GRAPH.TXT file that ships with ChartBuilder. This file includes all the constants and function definitions that are used to control the product.

## Tips and Comments

ChartBuilder is much more powerful than the Graph control that comes with Visual Basic. It gives you access to which region of the graph the user clicked on so you can give feedback based on where the click occurred. It also supplies several additional types of graphs.

ChartBuilder can also access VB's Printer object directly. This lets you position the graph where you need it on the page and print with full print quality.

If you are satisfied with Visual Basic Professional's Graph control, you probably don't need the power of ChartBuilder. However, its printing ability and the *HotHit* event make ChartBuilder an excellent tool. For true graphing power, you'll also want to add the

Graphics SDK, which gives you full control of your graph, letting you define additional hot hit areas and track the mouse while it's over the graph control. Bits Per Second is also working on an OCX version of ChartBuilder, and they include a sample OLE2 server version in the package for your programming pleasure.

6 ◀

# MULTIMEDIA

The set of controls covered in this chapter enable you to add the richness of multimedia sights and sounds to your Visual Basic applications. Multimedia can breathe life into educational programs, games, and training applications. This chapter reveals the strengths of several sets of multimedia controls. Keep in mind that the power of multimedia comes at a price: options like full-motion video can require a great deal of computational power and disk space.

▲ **FXTools/VB** This set of controls lets you design unusual transition effects when displaying images and text. You can have images slide onto the screen, gently fade to black, or dissolve into another image. There are dozens of effects from which to choose.

▲ **Multimedia MCI** This control, which comes with Visual Basic Professional 3.0, is a multimedia Swiss Army knife. It can play wave and MIDI audio files, control video disc and audio CD devices, show full-motion video (.AVI) files, and more.

▲ **MediaKnife** This set of controls and tools is specifically tailored to multimedia application design. The package contains its own MCI control, special sound and timer controls, a sprite control designed for creating arcade-style animated sprites, and a special image control. The tools include palette, sprite, and bitmap hot spot editors. This chapter uses MediaKnife to build an arcade-style application with animated sprites.

▲ **VBPlay** The AutoDesk Animator control, VBPlay, lets you display and control .FLI and .FLC format animation files. You can even optionally play a wave audio file as the animation runs. Here VBPlay is used to build a full-featured Autodesk Animator player, which can simultaneously play a sound file, adjust the playback speed, and step frame by frame through the animation.

# FXTools/VB

| USAGE: | Special Visual Effects for Images, Shapes, and Labels |
|---|---|
| MANUFACTURER: | ImageFX |
| COST: | $129 |

FXTools is a set of four custom controls that you can use in place of the standard label, shape, or image controls. All these controls can display themselves using any of dozens of special effects. Images can appear to slide in from the top or sides, fade in or out, or explode onto the screen. You can specify separate main, transition, and dissolve effects for a single control, and you can change effects at run time. A variety of autosizing and alignment options are provided, as well as 3D fonts and beveled border effects.

## Syntax

FXTools contains four separate controls: FXImage, FXLabel, FXShape, and FXRText. FXImage can replace a standard image or picture control. FXShape is similar to the standard shape control, but provides several more shape types. The FXLabel and FXRText controls can replace the standard label control; the FXRText control can display text rotated to any angle.

The main purpose of all the FXTools is to display their contents using some combination of special effects. These effects are divided into three distinct groups: main effects, transition effects, and dissolve effects. Some of the controls do not support all three effects.

**The FXImage Control**   You use the FXImage control to show sequences of images—for example, in a presentation slide show application. You might normally use an image or picture control to display images, loading new images by changing the control's *Image* or *Picture* property. This would create the transition from image to image that filmmakers refer to as a *cut,* where one image is quickly replaced by another. But filmmakers don't use only the cut for transitions; they use dissolves, fades, and a number of other editing tricks to change from one scene to the next. This is what the FXImage control provides: "tricks" that can make the transition between images more interesting.

The FXImage control shows an image using either a main or dissolve effect, either of which can be preceded by an optional transition effect.

The *transition effect* is always displayed first. This effect defines how the current image is removed before the new image is displayed. There are several dozen effect styles from which to choose. For example, you can remove images using left to right wipes, or by swirling in from the outer edges to the center of the image.

The *dissolve effect* allows the old image to remain as the new image replaces it. Dissolves can have up to three *passes,* and each pass can use a different effect style. During each pass, more of the new image is filled in. If a transition effect is being used, the transition effect is used to remove the old image before the dissolve effect begins.

The *main effect* displays the new image after the old one is removed (unlike the dissolve effect, where the previous image remains onscreen and is displaced by the new image). Like the dissolve effect, the main effect can optionally be preceded by a transition effect.

Table 7-1 lists the nonstandard properties of the FXImage control. To set a transition effect, you must first set the Boolean *TEnabled* property to *True.* All the transition effect properties are prefaced with the letter *T.* The integer *TGrain* property determines how much of the image to change during each step of an effect. For example, if you select the checkerboard transition effect, the size of each checkerboard square is determined by the value of *TGrain.* The *TDelay* property sets the amount of delay, in milliseconds, between each step of the effect. *TDelay* must be in the range from 0 to 255. You select the effect itself by using the enumerated integer *TEffect* property. There are 52 separate effect styles.

**7** ◄

**Table 7-1**  Properties for the FXImage control

| | | |
|---|---|---|
| AutoSize | BInnerColor1 | BInnerColor2 |
| BInnerStyle | BInnerWidth | BorderColor |
| BorderWidth | BOuterColor1 | BOuterColor2 |
| BOuterStyle | BOuterWidth | DEffect1 |
| DEffect2 | DEffect3 | DMode |
| FXHeight | FXWidth | MDelay |
| MEffect | MGrain | Multitask |
| Picture | TBackColor | TDelay |

*(continued on next page)*

*(continued from previous page)*

| TEffect | TEnabled | TForeColor |
|---------|----------|------------|
| TGrain | Transparent | TransparentColor |
| TStyle | UpdateImage | |

Main effects are handled in a similar way. The main effect properties all begin with the letter *M*. The *MGrain, MDelay,* and *MEffect* properties determine the appearance of the effect. The *MEffect* property has the same 52 effect styles used by the transitional effects.

Dissolve effects are handled in a slightly different way. Since a dissolve effect consists of up to three passes, FXImage provides three separate properties to define a dissolve: *DEffect1, DEffect2,* and *DEffect3.* You can assign each of these properties a different dissolve effect; the dissolve effects are a subset of the effects available for transitions and main effects. As mentioned, dissolves and main effects are not used together. To use a dissolve, you must set the *DMode* property to a value greater than 0 (the default) to indicate the number of passes to use in the dissolve effect. The dissolve effect uses the main effect's *MGrain* and *MDelay* properties to determine its resolution and speed.

Since you can set all these effects at design time, you can use the FXImage control to replace an image or picture control in an existing application with little or no change in code. You may have to make some changes if you are using the standard image control's *Stretch* property. FXImage replaces this property with an *AutoSize* property whose values are listed in Table 7-2.

**Table 7-2** Values for the FXImage AutoSize property

| VALUE | MEANING |
|-------|---------|
| 0 | The image is clipped to the size of the control. If the control is larger than the image, control is reduced to the image's size. |
| 1 | The control is resized to fit the image (the default) |
| 2 | The image is resized to fit the control. |

The FXImage control provides several 3D border effects. You can use these effects to give the control borders a raised or inset appearance. You can set the colors of the inner and outer bevels using the *BInnerColor1, BInnerColor2, BOuterColor1,* and *BOuterColor2* properties. You set the style (raised, inset, or none) of the bevel with the *BInnerStyle* and *BOuterStyle* properties. You define the width of the bevels with the *BInnerWidth* and *BOuterWidth* properties. The border is defined as the distance between the inner and outer bevels. You can set the width and color of this border with the *BorderWidth* and *BorderColor* properties.

When the *Transparent* property is set to *True,* the background of an image can be made transparent. The *TransparentColor* property determines which color in the image is considered the background color. When a transparent FXImage control is displayed over another FXImage or picture control, the underlying image shows through the transparent image's background, much as a background shows through the transparent areas of an icon. This feature can be useful when you need to display an irregular foreground image anywhere on a complex background image.

**The FXLabel Control**  The FXLabel control is similar to the FXImage control in that both can display the same transition, dissolve, and main effects, and both can define a 3D beveled border effect. Where FXImage is designed to display bitmaps, however, FXLabel is designed to display text, and can be used as a replacement for the standard label control. Its nonstandard properties are listed in Table 7-3.

**Table 7-3**  Nonstandard properties for the FXLabel control

| | | |
|---|---|---|
| Alignment | AutoSize | BInnerColor1 |
| BInnerColor2 | BInnerStyle | BInnerWidth |
| BorderColor | BorderWidth | BOuterColor1 |
| BOuterColor2 | BOuterStyle | BOuterWidth |
| DEffect1 | DEffect2 | DEffect3 |
| DMode | Font3D | FontBlockSize |
| FontDropX | FontDropY | FontShadowColor |
| MDelay | MEffect | MGrain |
| Multitask | Overlay | TBackColor |
| TDEffect1 | TDEffect2 | TDEffect3 |
| TDelay | TDMode | TEffect |
| TEnabled | TForeColor | TGrain |
| Transparent | TransparentColor | TStyle |
| UpdateLabel | WordWrap | |

The *Font3D* property lets you set a number of different shading effects, including raised and inset shading. Figure 7-1 shows the drop shadow *Font3D* effect, which creates the illusion of a shadow behind the font. You determine the "distance" between the font and its shadow by using the *FontDropX* and *FontDropY* properties, which you can set to values from -10 to 10. With the block shadow *Font3D* effect, the font appears to be carved from a solid block; you set the thickness of the block with the *FontBlockSize* property, which also has a range from -10 to 10. You set the color of block and drop shadows with the *FontShadowColor* property.

**The FXShape Control**  The FXShape control is designed as a replacement for the standard shape control, but it can be displayed using dissolve and main effects, and can be given an optional beveled border. Its nonstandard properties are listed in Table 7-4.

**Figure 7-1** FXLabel's drop shadow font effect

**Table 7-4** Nonstandard properties of the FXShape control

| | | |
|---|---|---|
| BInnerColor1 | BInnerColor2 | BInnerStyle |
| BInnerWidth | BOuterColor1 | BOuterColor2 |
| BOuterStyle | BOuterWidth | DEffect1 |
| DEffect2 | DEffect3 | DMode |
| MDelay | MEffect | MGrain |
| Multitask | ShadowColor | ShadowDropX |
| ShadowDropY | ShadowStyle | Shape |
| UpdateShape | | |

By setting the *Shape* property, you can have the FXShape control display 16 different shapes, including diamonds, pentagons, hexagons, stars, and five varieties of triangles. You can display these shapes with drop shadows by using the *ShadowDropX* and *ShadowDropY* properties to define the offset of the shadow.

**The FXRText Control** You can use the FXRText control to display TrueType fonts at any angle, as specified by the *Angle* property. This control can be displayed using the dissolve and main effects described earlier. It uses the same *Font3D* effects as the FXLabel control, but cannot display a border. Its nonstandard properties are listed in Table 7-5.

**Table 7-5** Nonstandard properties of the FXRText control

| | | |
|---|---|---|
| Angle | AutoSize | DEffect1 |
| DEffect2 | DEffect3 | DMode |
| Font3D | FontBlockSize | FontDropX |
| FontDropY | FontShadowColor | |
| MDelay | MEffect | MGrain |
| Multitask | UpdateText | |

All four controls have a *Multitask* Boolean property that allows other tasks to run concurrent with the various FXTools effects. This property is set to *False* by default, which prevents other tasks from being processed during an effect.

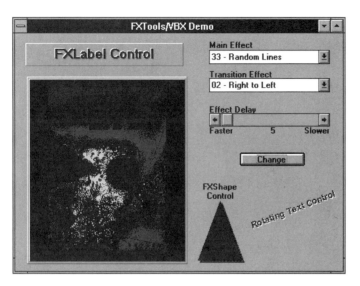

**Figure 7-2** The FXTools example program

# Example

The example program illustrates many of the key features of the FXTools controls. Drop-down combo boxes let the user select transition and main effects. The user can press the Change button to see the effect of different settings on the appearance of each control. Figure 7-2 shows the example program.

The FXImage control cycles through a set of images and changes the style of the image's border. The FXLabel control changes its border style as well. The FXShape control cycles through all available shapes and randomly selects a fill color. The FXRText control rotates 10 degrees each time the Change button is pressed, and also randomly changes text colors.

## Steps

1. Create a new project called FXTOOLS.MAK. Add the FXTools controls FXIMG130.VBX, FXLBL130.VBX, FXRTX130.VBX, and FXSHP130.VBX to the project. Create a new form with the objects and properties described in Table 7-6. Save this form as FXTOOLS.FRM.

**Table 7-6** Objects and properties of FXTOOLS.FRM

| OBJECT | PROPERTY | SETTING |
|--------|----------|---------|
| Form | FormName | frmFXTools |
| | BackColor | &H00C0C0C0& |

*(continued on next page)*

| OBJECT | PROPERTY | SETTING |
|--------|----------|---------|
| *(continued from previous page)* | | |
| | Caption | "FXTools/VBX Demo" |
| FXLabel | Name | FXLabel1 |
| | Alignment | 7 'Center - MIDDLE |
| | AutoSize | 0 'False |
| | BackColor | &H00C0C0C0& |
| | BackStyle | 1 'Opaque |
| | BInnerColor1 | &H00808080& |
| | BInnerColor2 | &H00FFFFFF& |
| | BInnerStyle | 1 'Inset |
| | BInnerWidth | 1 |
| | BorderColor | &H00C0C0C0& |
| | BorderWidth | 2 |
| | BOuterColor1 | &H00808080& |
| | BOuterColor2 | &H00FFFFFF& |
| | BOuterStyle | 0 'None |
| | BOuterWidth | 1 |
| | Caption | "FXLabel Control" |
| | FontSize | 13.5 |
| | ForeColor | &H00FF0000& |
| | MGrain | 3 |
| | Multitask | -1 'True |
| | Overlay | 0 'False |
| | TBackColor | &H00000000& |
| | TForeColor | &H00000000& |
| | TGrain | 5 |
| | TStyle | 0 'Solid |
| FXRText | Name | FXRText1 |
| | Angle | 0 |
| | AutoSize | -1 'True |
| | Caption | "Rotating Text Control" |
| | Font3D | 3 'Inset w/Light Shading |
| | FontName | "Arial" |
| | FontSize | 9.75 |
| | ForeColor | &H00000000& |
| | MGrain | 5 |
| | Multitask | -1 'True |
| FXShape | Name | FXShape1 |
| | BackColor | &H000000FF& |

| OBJECT | PROPERTY | SETTING |
|---|---|---|
| | BackStyle | 0 'Transparent |
| | FillColor | &H00808000& |
| | FillStyle | 0 'Solid |
| | MDelay | 0 |
| | MEffect | 0 'No Effect |
| | MGrain | 5 |
| | Multitask | -1 'True |
| | ShadowStyle | 0 'None |
| | Shape | 5 'Rounded Square |
| Label | Name | Label1 |
| | BackStyle | 0 'Transparent |
| | Caption | "Main Effect" |
| Label | Name | Label2 |
| | BackStyle | 0 'Transparent |
| | Caption | "Transition Effect" |
| Label | Name | Label3 |
| | BackStyle | 0 'Transparent |
| | Caption | "Effect Delay" |
| Label | Name | Label4 |
| | BackStyle | 0 'Transparent |
| | Caption | "Faster" |
| Label | Name | Label5 |
| | Alignment | 1 'Right Justify |
| | BackStyle | 0 'Transparent |
| | Caption | "Slower" |
| Label | Name | lblSpeed |
| | Alignment | 2 'Center |
| | BackStyle | 0 'Transparent |
| Label | Name | Label6 |
| | Alignment | 2 'Center |
| | BackStyle | 0 'Transparent |
| | Caption | " FXShape Control" |
| ComboBox | Name | cmbMeffect |
| | Style | 2 'Dropdown List |
| ComboBox | Name | cmbTEffect |
| | Style | 2 'Dropdown List |
| CommandButton | Name | btnChange |
| | Caption | "Change" |
| HScrollBar | Name | hscrSpeed |
| | LargeChange | 10 |

*(continued on next page)*

387

| OBJECT | PROPERTY | SETTING |
|---|---|---|
| *(continued from previous page)* | | |
| | SmallChange | 1 |
| | Max | 255 |
| | Min | 0 |
| | Value | 5 |
| PictureBox | Name | picPaletteFixer |
| | Visible | 0 'False |

2. After creating the form, add the following code to FXTOOLS.FRM's declarations section.

```
Option Explicit
'-------------------------------------------------
' Variables and constants used by FXTools example.
'-------------------------------------------------

' Array used to hold special effects descriptions
Dim Effects(52) As String

' Used to generate file name for image .BMP file
Dim ImageNum As Integer

' Number of last image file
Const LAST_IMAGE = 3
```

3. Add the following subroutines to FXTOOLS.FRM. The *btnChange_Click* event contains the code that changes the appearance of each control. Very little code is required to set any of the special effects. The scroll bar can be used to change the speed of effect changes.

```
Sub btnChange_Click ()
'-------------------------------------------------
' Change the appearance of the FXTools controls.
'-------------------------------------------------

    ' Change the rotating text control.
    FXRText1.Angle = (FXRText1.Angle + 10) Mod 360
    FXRText1.ForeColor = QBColor(Int(Rnd * 16))

    ' Change the Image control.
    ImageNum = (ImageNum + 1) Mod 3
    FXImage1.BInnerStyle = (FXImage1.BInnerStyle + 1) Mod 3
    FXImage1.BOuterStyle = (FXImage1.BOuterStyle + 1) Mod 3
    LoadImage ImageNum

    ' Change the Shape control.
    FXShape1.Shape = (FXShape1.Shape + 1) Mod 16
    FXShape1.FillColor = QBColor(Int(Rnd * 16))

    ' Change the Label control.
    FXLabel1.Caption = Trim$(FXLabel1.Caption)
    FXLabel1.Font3D = (FXLabel1.Font3D + 1) Mod 7
    FXLabel1.TStyle = (FXLabel1.TStyle + 1) Mod 7
    FXLabel1.BInnerStyle = (FXLabel1.BInnerStyle + 1) Mod 3
```

```
    FXLabel1.BOuterStyle = (FXLabel1.BOuterStyle + 1) Mod 3

End Sub

Sub cmbMeffect_Click ()
'-------------------------------------------------
' Change the main effect for all FXTools controls.
'-------------------------------------------------
    FXImage1.MEffect = cmbMEffect.ListIndex
    FXLabel1.MEffect = cmbMEffect.ListIndex
    FXShape1.MEffect = cmbMEffect.ListIndex
    FXRText1.MEffect = cmbMEffect.ListIndex
End Sub

Sub cmbTEffect_Click ()
'-------------------------------------------------
' Change the transition effect for the FXImage
' and FXLabel controls.
'-------------------------------------------------
    On Error GoTo cmbTEffect_Error

    FXImage1.TEffect = cmbTEffect.ListIndex
    FXLabel1.TEffect = cmbTEffect.ListIndex
Exit Sub
cmbTEffect_Error:
    cmbTEffect.ListIndex = FXImage1.TEffect
    Exit Sub
End Sub

Sub FixPalette ()
'-------------------------------------------------
' Loading an image into this invisible picture
' box forces palette shifting when other images
' are loaded into the FXImage control. This
' avoids unsightly palette shifting when the
' Change button is pressed.
'-------------------------------------------------
    picPaletteFixer.Visible = False
    picPaletteFixer.ZOrder 0
    picPaletteFixer.Picture = LoadPicture(App.Path & "\bl_000.bmp")
End Sub

Sub Form_Load ()
'-------------------------------------------------
' Initialize structures needed for FXTools example.
'-------------------------------------------------
Dim i As Integer
Dim xdir As Integer, ydir As Integer
Dim CurX As Integer, CurY As Integer

    ' Set the invisible picture box used to force palette shifts
    FixPalette

    ' Center the form.
    Me.Move (Screen.Width - Me.Width) \ 2, (Screen.Height - Me.Height) \ 2

    ' Initialize special effects combo boxes.
    InitEffectsArray
    For i = 0 To 51
        cmbMEffect.AddItem Effects(i)
```

7

*(continued on next page)*

*(continued from previous page)*

```
        cmbTEffect.AddItem Effects(i)
    Next
    cmbMEffect.ListIndex = 33
    cmbTEffect.ListIndex = 2

    ' Set the initial effect delay.
    lblSpeed = hscrSpeed
    hscrSpeed_Change

    ' Load the first picture.
    ImageNum = 0
    LoadImage ImageNum

    ' Adjust the label to the width of the image below it.
    FXLabel1.Width = FXImage1.FXWidth
End Sub

Sub hscrSpeed_Change ()
'----------------------------------------------------
' Change the main and transition effect delay
' values to change the speed of each transition.
'----------------------------------------------------
    lblSpeed = Format$(hscrSpeed)

    FXImage1.MDelay = hscrSpeed
    FXLabel1.MDelay = hscrSpeed
    FXRText1.MDelay = hscrSpeed
    FXShape1.MDelay = hscrSpeed

    FXImage1.TDelay = hscrSpeed
    FXLabel1.TDelay = hscrSpeed
End Sub

Sub InitEffectsArray ()
'----------------------------------------------------
' Initialize the Effects array with descriptions
' of FXTools special effects.
'----------------------------------------------------
    Effects(0) = "00 - No Effect"
    Effects(1) = "01 - Left to Right"
    Effects(2) = "02 - Right to Left"
    Effects(3) = "03 - Top to Bottom"
    Effects(4) = "04 - Bottom to Top"
    Effects(5) = "05 - Horizontal Wipe In"
    Effects(6) = "06 - Horizontal Wipe Out"
    Effects(7) = "07 - Vertical Wipe In"
    Effects(8) = "08 - Vertical Wipe Out"
    Effects(9) = "09 - Slide Up"
    Effects(10) = "10 - Side Down"
    Effects(11) = "11 - Push Up"
    Effects(12) = "12 - Push Down"
    Effects(13) = "13 - Diagonal TL - BR"
    Effects(14) = "14 - Diagonal BL - TR"
    Effects(15) = "15 - Diagonal TR - BL"
    Effects(16) = "16 - Diagonal BR - TL"
    Effects(17) = "17 - Double Diag. TL - BR"
    Effects(18) = "18 - Double Diag. TR - BL"
    Effects(19) = "19 - Diagonal Out TL - BR"
    Effects(20) = "20 - Diagonal Out TR-BL"
```

```
    Effects(21) = "21 - Diagonal Quad."
    Effects(22) = "22 - Explode"
    Effects(23) = "23 - Implode"
    Effects(24) = "24 - Zoom Out"
    Effects(25) = "25 - Zoom In"
    Effects(26) = "26 - Corners Out"
    Effects(27) = "27 - Horiz. Interlace"
    Effects(28) = "28 - Vert. Interlace"
    Effects(29) = "29 - Horiz. Double Pass 2"
    Effects(30) = "30 - Vert. Double Pass 2"
    Effects(31) = "31 - Horiz. Double Pass"
    Effects(32) = "32 - Vert. Double Pass"
    Effects(33) = "33 - Random Lines"
    Effects(34) = "34 - Horizontal Blind"
    Effects(35) = "35 - Vertical Blind"
    Effects(36) = "36 - Double Blind"
    Effects(37) = "37 - Swirl In"
    Effects(38) = "38 - Swirl Out"
    Effects(39) = "39 - Random Block"
    Effects(40) = "40 - Checkerboard"
    Effects(41) = "41 - Vert. Double Wipe"
    Effects(42) = "42 - Horiz. Double Wipe"
    Effects(43) = "43 - Kaleidoscope"
    Effects(44) = "44 - Double Wipe Out"
    Effects(45) = "45 - Double Wipe In"
    Effects(46) = "46 - Vert. Squash"
    Effects(47) = "47 - Vert. Pull"
    Effects(48) = "48 - Horiz. Squash"
    Effects(49) = "49 - Horiz. Pull"
    Effects(50) = "50 - Drip"
    Effects(51) = "51 - No Picture"
End Sub

Sub LoadImage (ByVal ImageNum As Integer)
'------------------------------------------------
' Build a file name using the ImageNum parameter
' and load image into FXImage1 control.
'------------------------------------------------
Dim AFile As String

    AFile = App.Path & "\BL_" & Format$(ImageNum, "000") & ".BMP"
    FXImage1.Picture = LoadPicture(AFile)
End Sub
```

# Tips and Comments

The FXTools controls allow you to build interesting special effects, but you'll need to experiment a bit to perfect the elements of an individual effect. In particular, the overall speed of an effect depends on the grain, delay, effects, and size of the image being displayed. Some more complex effects, such as swirl in or swirl out, can take a considerable amount of time, particularly if you use a small grain or large delay. The demonstration program that comes with FXTools provides a good way to experiment with different combinations of effects.

# Multimedia MCI (MCI.VBX)

| USAGE: | Display and Manipulation of Multimedia Files |
|---|---|
| MANUFACTURER: | Microsoft |
| COST: | Provided with Visual Basic 3.0 Professional Edition |

You can use the Multimedia MCI control to control multimedia devices such as sound boards, MIDI sequencers, audio CD players, and CD-ROM drives. You can also use it to play multimedia file formats that include wave audio (.WAV), MIDI (.MID), and Audio-Video Interleave (.AVI) formats.

The control, shown in Figure 7-3, looks like a set of VCR buttons that control playback and manipulation of multimedia devices or files. Each button corresponds to a function the control can perform: previous track, next track, play, pause, step back, step forward, stop, record, and eject.

## Syntax

For the MCI control to work properly, the proper Media Control Interface (MCI) services must be available. For example, to play wave audio files, the MCI control must be able to access the appropriate sound device through an installed Windows driver. If a device is available, it's easy to access its capabilities. This listing shows the code required to load a wave audio file.

```
MMControl1.Notify = False
MMControl1.Wait = True
MMControl1.Sharable = False
MMControl1.DeviceType = "WaveAudio"
MMControl1.FileName = "C:\WINDOWS\DING.WAV"
MMControl1.Command = "Open"
```

Each line of the code fragment sets a property of the MCI control, MMControl1. Table 7-7 lists the nonstandard properties and events of the MCI control. Since the process of controlling a media device is similar for most multimedia devices, let's look at some of these properties to see what they do.

**Table 7-7** Nonstandard properties and events of the Multimedia MCI control

### PROPERTIES

| | | |
|---|---|---|
| AutoEnable | ButtonEnabled | ButtonVisible |
| CanEject | CanPlay | CanRecord |
| CanStep | Command | DeviceID |
| DeviceType | DisplayhWnd | Enabled |
| Error | ErrorMessage | FileName |
| Frames | From | Length |
| Mode | Notify | NotifyMessage |

## PROPERTIES

| | | |
|---|---|---|
| Orientation | Position | RecordMode |
| Sharable | Silent | Start |
| TimeFormat | To | Track |
| TrackLength | TrackPosition | Tracks |
| UpdateInterval | UsesWindows | Visible |
| Wait | | |

## EVENTS

| | | |
|---|---|---|
| ButtonClicked | ButtonCompleted | ButtonGotFocus |
| ButtonLostFocus | StatusUpdate | |

The *Notify* property is set to *False* to indicate that the next MCI command should not fire a *Done* event. A *Done* event can be fired after an MCI command has completed, allowing the program to take any necessary action, such as moving back to the beginning of a wave audio file after the Play command has been completed. The *Done* event receives a *NotifyCode* parameter, a long integer that contains a completion code for the command. The possible values of *NotifyCode* are shown in Table 7-8.

**Table 7-8** Values for the NotifyCode parameter of the Done event

| VALUE | MEANING |
|---|---|
| 1 | The command completed successfully |
| 2 | Another command has superseded this command |
| 3 | The user aborted this command |
| 4 | The command failed |

The *Wait* property determines whether the MCI command should wait until the next command is completed before returning control to the Visual Basic program. Set this property to *True* to ensure that the next command completes before you allow processing to continue. Both the *Wait* property and the *Notify* property are only applicable for the next MCI command issued. You must reset these properties before each command; otherwise, their values are ignored.

The *Sharable* property indicates whether other programs should be able to share this device. Since you do not want anyone else to use the sound device, set this property to *False* to indicate that you want exclusive access.

The *DeviceType* property is a string that indicates what type of MCI device will be used. The valid string values for this property show the range of devices that the MCI

**Figure 7-3** The VCR-style buttons of the MCI control

control can handle: AVIVideo, CDAudio, DAT, MMMovie, Other, Overlay, Scanner, Sequencer, VCR, VideoDisk, and WaveAudio.

Use the *FileName* property when a disk resource such as a wave audio or digitized video file is to be processed. When you specify a file name and the device type can be determined by the file's extension, you don't strictly have to assign the *DeviceType* property.

### Controlling an MCI Device with the Command Property

The final line of the code example uses the *Command* property to open the specified device. The *Command* property is at the heart of the MCI control; it allows you to control devices programmatically.

You can control the MCI control in two different ways. If you set the *Visible* property of the MCI control to *False,* you must control devices entirely through *Command* property settings. This is useful when you want to control what commands are available to the user. The second method is to leave the MCI control visible. This approach allows the user to have access to the full capabilities of the device, and requires little program intervention. This second method doesn't prevent you from issuing commands within your program. As you'll see, it's possible to augment or even short-circuit the function of any of the MCI controls buttons. The following strings are valid for the *Command* property:

▲ **Open** Opens an MCI device. If the device uses a disk resource, such as a wave audio file, set the *FileName* property before issuing an Open command.

▲ **Close** Closes an MCI device. Issue this command before exiting a program, so that Multimedia resources can be released properly.

▲ **Play** Begins playing the MCI device.

▲ **Stop** Stops playing or recording with the MCI device.

▲ **Pause** Pauses the currently playing device, or, if the device is currently paused, resumes playing the MCI device.

▲ **Back** Steps back one frame.

▲ **Step** Steps forward one frame.

▲ **Prev** Seeks to the beginning of the current track.

▲ **Next** Seeks to the beginning of the next track.

▲ **Seek** Moves to a position specified by the *To* property.

▲ **Record** Begins recording using the current MCI device.

▲ **Eject** Ejects a media device, such as a CD player.

▲ **Sound** Plays a sound.

▲ **Save** Saves an open file, using the *FileName* property.

### Controlling the Control

As you can see, many of the *Command* property values perform the same tasks as some of the MCI control buttons. If you want the convenience of the MCI buttons, but want to control or disable some of the buttons, you can augment or override their usual behavior using the *Button* events. There are four of these events—*Button*Click, *Button*Completed, *Button*GotFocus, and *Button*LostFocus—for each of nine MCI buttons (Previous, Next, Play, Pause, Back, Step, Stop, Record, and Eject). For example, the *Click* event for the Play button is called *PlayClick*, its GotFocus event is *PlayGotFocus,* and so on.

The *Button*Click event is fired when the user presses and releases a button. This event is fired before the button's associated MCI command is performed. The event receives a *Cancel* parameter. The MCI command is disabled if Cancel is set to *True*.

The *Button*Completed event is fired after the MCI command has completed. The *Button*GotFocus and *Button*LostFocus events are fired whenever a particular button receives or loses the input focus. When any button on the MCI control has the focus, the keyboard's arrow keys can be used to shift focus to the left or right. Depending on the capabilities and the current state of a device, some buttons will be disabled, and so they won't receive the focus.

By default, the *AutoEnable* property is set to *True*. This lets the MCI control automatically enable only those MCI buttons whose functions are available. If you want more control over each button, set *AutoEnable* to *False* and use the *Button*Enabled and *Button*Visible properties. As with the button events, there is a separate property for each of the nine MCI buttons. Here is a short example of how this works.

```
' Turn off automatic button enabling.
MMControl1.AutoEnable = False

' Hide these buttons.
MMControl1.BackVisible = False
MMControl1.EjectVisible = False
MMControl1.RecordVisible = False
MMControl1.StepVisible = False

' Of the remaining buttons, only enable these.
MMControl1.PlayEnabled = True
MMControl1.PrevEnabled = True
MMControl1.NextEnabled = True
```

The first line of code turns off the automatic button enabling. Subsequent lines make several of the buttons invisible, leaving only the Previous, Next, Play, Pause, and Stop buttons displayed. Finally, the code explicitly enables the Play, Previous, and Next buttons. This results in a control resembling the one shown in Figure 7-4. The *Button*Enabled properties give you added control, but they also require you to take responsibility for enabling the proper buttons at the proper time. In the example, you

**Figure 7-4** MCI control modified using the ButtonEnabled and ButtonVisible properties

would need to enable the Stop button after the Play button is pressed, as well as disabling the Play button itself. You could do this in the *PlayClick* event discussed earlier.

### Getting Information About a Device

Different MCI devices can have radically different abilities, and you may need to determine just what the current device can do. The MCI control provides several *Can* properties, Booleans that indicate what functions are available. These functions are

▲ **CanEject,** which indicates whether the device can eject its media

▲ **CanPlay,** which is set to *True* if the current MCI device can play

▲ **CanRecord,** which indicates whether the current device is capable of recording

▲ **CanStep,** which indicates whether the current device can step frame by frame

The *TimeFormat* property is a long integer that indicates the time format the current device uses. The MCI control supports more than ten different time formats. For example, the *TimeFormat* for wave audio (.WAV) files is 0, which indicates that other timing information properties are returned in milliseconds. You must take into account the current time format when interpreting the *To, From, Length, Position, Start, TrackLength,* and *TrackPosition* properties.

### Graphical MCI Devices

Some MCI devices, such as MMMovie or AVIVideo, can have both an audio and a visual component. That video component must be displayed in a window. Some devices create their own separate window into which the video output is directed. In your program, however, you may want to direct the video output to your own window or to a control, such as a picture box, within a form. To determine if a device uses a window to display its output, examine the *UsesWindows* property, which returns *True* when a window is used. The example program that follows shows how to direct the video output of an .AVI file into a picture box control.

### Error Handling

Rather than issuing Visual Basic run-time errors, the MCI control sets a special *Error* property after each MCI command has completed. If no errors occurred during the previous command, this value is 0. Another special property, *ErrorMessage,* returns a string that explains the error that occurred. If no error occurred, this property returns the string "The specified command was carried out".

## Example

The example program is a small MCI viewer program that can control wave audio, MIDI, AVI video, and audio CD devices. This example shows how to load files, and in the case of the AVI video, how to redirect output to a picture box control. The program is shown in Figure 7-5.

**Figure 7-5** The MCI control example program

## Steps

1. Create a new project called MCI.MAK. Add the MCI control, MCI.VBX, and the Common Dialog control, CMDIALOG.VBX, to the project. Create a new form with the objects and properties described in Table 7-9. Save this form as MCIDEMO.FRM.

**Table 7-9** Objects and properties of MCIDEMO.FRM

| OBJECT | PROPERTY | SETTING |
|---|---|---|
| Form | FormName | Form1 |
| | BackColor | &H00C0C0C0& |
| | Caption | "MCI Demo" |
| | ForeColor | &H00000000& |
| | MaxButton | 0 'False |
| Label | Name | Label1 |
| | BackStyle | 0 'Transparent |
| | Caption | "Prev Next Play Pause Back Step Stop Rec Eject" |
| | FontBold | 0 'False |
| | FontName | "Small Fonts" |
| | FontSize | 6.75 |
| | ForeColor | &H00800000& |
| Label | Name | lblStatus |
| | Alignment | 2 'Center |
| | BackColor | &H0080FFFF& |
| | BorderStyle | 1 'Fixed Single |
| | FontBold | 0 'False |
| MMControl | Name | MMControl1 |
| PictureBox | Name | picAVIScreen |
| CommonDialog | Name | CMDialog1 |

7

2. Add a menu to MCIDEMO.FRM using the Visual Basic Menu Design window, setting the captions and names shown in Table 7-10.

**Table 7-10** Menu definition for MCIDEMO.FRM

| CAPTION | NAME |
|---|---|
| &File | mnuFile |
| – – – – &Open | mnuFileOpen |
| – – – – Play Audio &CD | mnuFilePlayCD |
| – – – – – | mnuFileSep1 |
| – – – – E&xit | mnuFileExit |

3. After creating the form, add the following code to MCIDEMO.FRM's declarations section.

```
Option Explicit
'--------------------------------------------------
' Variables, constants, and declarations used in the
' Multimedia MCI demo.
'--------------------------------------------------

' Stores the window handle of picture control.
' Used to display AVI file.
Dim HwndFrame As Integer

' Gets picture box window handle
Declare Function GetFocus Lib "User" () As Integer

' Stores the initial height and width of the form.
' Window cannot be resized smaller than this value.
Dim MinWinWidth As Integer
Dim MinWinHeight As Integer

' Color constants.
Const BLUE = &H800000
Const RED = &H80&
```

4. Add the following subroutines to the MCIDEMO.FRM form. Several techniques shown here can be useful when programming the MCI control. The *StatusUpdate* event updates the *lblStatus* label with the current mode of the open device (checking whether the device is playing, stopped, and so on). The *StatusUpdate* event is fired periodically, based on the setting of the *UpdateInterval* property. All you have to do in the event is update the label based on the current value of the *Mode* property.

For AVI videos, the program redirects the visual output to a picture box control, *picAVIScreen*. It does this by retrieving the window handle of the picture control in its *SetFocus* event, which is forced with a call to the *GetFocus()* Windows API call. This window handle is then assigned to the MCI control's *DisplayhWnd* property. This tells the MCI control to use the picture box as the video output window, rather than allowing a separate window to be created.

```
Sub EventDelay (LoopCount As Integer)
'------------------------------------------------------
' Delay, but allow events to still be processed.
' This is used to avoid MCI command timing problems.
'------------------------------------------------------
Dim i As Integer
Dim retcode As Integer

    ' Loop but allow events.
    For i = 1 To LoopCount
      retcode = DoEvents()
    Next
End Sub

Sub Form_Load ()
'------------------------------------------------------
' Center the form, and store the current width and
' height as minimum values.
'------------------------------------------------------
    Me.Move (Screen.Width - Me.Width) \ 2, (Screen.Height - Me.Height) \ 2

    MinWinWidth = Me.Width
    MinWinHeight = Me.Height
End Sub

Sub Form_Resize ()
'------------------------------------------------------
' Resize the picture box that displays AVI videos
' when the form is resized.
'------------------------------------------------------

    ' Make sure form is not sized too small.
    If Me.Width < MinWinWidth Then Me.Width = MinWinWidth
    If Me.Height < MinWinHeight Then Me.Height = MinWinHeight

    picAVIScreen.Width = Me.ScaleWidth - (picAVIScreen.Left * 2)
    picAVIScreen.Height = Me.ScaleHeight - picAVIScreen.Top - picAVIScreen.Left

    ' This forces a refresh of the video.
    If MMControl1.DeviceType = "AVIVideo" Then
        MMControl1.Refresh
    End If

    ' Update information about the file or CD.
    If LCase$(MMControl1.DeviceType) = "cdaudio" Then
        UpdateCDInfo
    ElseIf MMControl1.DeviceType  "" Then
        UpdateFileInfo
    End If

End Sub

Sub GetNewFileName (AFile As String)
'------------------------------------------------------
' Use the Common File Dialog to retrieve a file name.
'------------------------------------------------------
Dim Canceled As Integer

    Canceled = False
    On Error GoTo GetNewFileName_Error
```

7 ◄

*(continued on next page)*

*(continued from previous page)*

```
    ' Set up the Common File Dialog.
    CMDialog1.Filter = "Multimedia Files|*.wav;*.mid;*.avi"
    CMDialog1.DialogTitle = "Select Multimedia File"
    CMDialog1.CancelError = True

    ' Open the Common File Dialog.
    CMDialog1.Action = 1

    If Not Canceled Then
        AFile = CMDialog1.Filename
    Else
        AFile = ""
    End If
Exit Sub
GetNewFileName_Error:
    Canceled = True
    Resume Next
End Sub

Sub MMControl1_Done (NotifyCode As Integer)
'-------------------------------------------------------
' When a file is done playing, jump back to the
' first frame.
'-------------------------------------------------------

    If LCase$(MMControl1.DeviceType)  "cdaudeo" Then
        If MMControl1.Command = "Play" Then
            ' Two "Prev" commands within 3 seconds jumps
            ' back to the beginning.
            MMControl1.Command = "Prev"
            MMControl1.Command = "Prev"
            MMControl1.Command = "Step"
        End If
    End If
End Sub

Sub MMControl1_EjectClick (Cancel As Integer)
'-------------------------------------------------------
' Short-circuit the Eject button.
'-------------------------------------------------------
    Cancel = True
End Sub

Sub MMControl1_StatusUpdate ()
'-------------------------------------------------------
' The status label is updated to show the use
' of the StatusUpdate event.
'-------------------------------------------------------
Static TempStr As String

    ' Display the current mode.
    Select Case MMControl1.Mode
      Case 524: TempStr = "Not Open"
      Case 525: TempStr = "Stopped"
      Case 526: TempStr = "Playing"
      Case 527: TempStr = "Recording"
      Case 528: TempStr = "Seeking"
      Case 529: TempStr = "Paused"
```

```
      Case 530: TempStr = "Ready"
      Case Else: TempStr = "Unknown"
    End Select
    lblStatus = "MODE: " & TempStr
End Sub

Sub mnuFileExit_Click ()
'-------------------------------------------------
' Make sure we've closed whatever we have loaded.
'-------------------------------------------------
    MMControl1.Command = "CLOSE"
    Unload Me
End Sub

Sub mnuFileOpen_Click ()
'-------------------------------------------------
' Retrieve a media file name and attempt to load
' it into the MCI control.
'-------------------------------------------------
Dim OK As Integer
Dim FileExt As String
Dim AFileName As String

    OK = False
    GetNewFileName AFileName

    ' Extract the file's extension.
    If Len(AFileName) > 4 Then FileExt = Right$(AFileName, 4)

    ' Based on the extension, load the media file.
    Select Case FileExt
      Case ".WAV"
          OK = SetupWAVorMID(AFileName, MMControl1, "WaveAudio")
      Case ".MID"
          OK = SetupWAVorMID(AFileName, MMControl1, "Sequencer")
      Case ".AVI"
          OK = SetupAVI(AFileName, MMControl1, picAVIScreen)
    End Select

    If OK Then UpdateFileInfo
End Sub

Sub mnuFilePlayCD_Click ()
'-------------------------------------------------
' Attempt to load an audio CD to be played via
' the MCI control.
'-------------------------------------------------

    MMControl1.Notify = True
    MMControl1.FileName = ""
    MMControl1.Command = "Close"

    MMControl1.Notify = False
    MMControl1.Wait = True
    MMControl1.Shareable = False
    MMControl1.DeviceType = "CDAudio"

    EventDelay 150

    ' Open the CD Audio device.
```

7 ◀

(continued on next page)

*(continued from previous page)*

```
    MMControl1.Command = "Open"

    UpdateCDInfo
End Sub

Sub picAVIScreen_GotFocus ()
'------------------------------------------------------
' Get the window handle of control used to display
' AVI file.
'------------------------------------------------------
    HwndFrame = GetFocus()
End Sub

Function SetupAVI (ByVal AFileName As String, MMControl1 As MMControl, picAVIScreen As
PictureBox) As Integer
'------------------------------------------------------
' Attempt to load an Audio-Video Interleave (AVI)
' file into a picture box (picAVIScreen) for
' display.
'------------------------------------------------------

    On Error GoTo SetupAVI_Error
    SetupAVI = False

    ' Load the file into the MCI control.
    MMControl1.Command = "Close"
    If MMControl1.FileName  AFileName Then
        MMControl1.Notify = False
        MMControl1.Wait = True
        MMControl1.Shareable = False
        MMControl1.DeviceType = "AVIVideo"
        MMControl1.FileName = AFileName
    End If

    ' Display the picture control.
    picAVIScreen.Visible = True
    EventDelay 50

    ' Retrieve the hWnd of the Picture control.
    picAVIScreen.SetFocus
    EventDelay 50

    ' This causes the file to be displayed in the picture
    ' box, instead of the default pop-up window.
    MMControl1.hWndDisplay = HwndFrame

    ' Open the MCI WaveAudio device.
    MMControl1.Command = "Open"
    MMControl1.Command = "Step"

    SetupAVI = True
Exit Function
SetupAVI_Error:
    Exit Function
End Function

Function SetupWAVorMID (ByVal AFileName As String, MMControl1 As MMControl, ByVal DevType As
String) As Integer
```

```
'-------------------------------------------------
' Attempt to load a wave or MIDI audio file into
' the MCI control.
'-------------------------------------------------

    On Error GoTo SetupWAVorMID_Error
    SetupWAVorMID = False

    ' Load the file into the MCI control.
    MMControl1.Command = "Close"
    If MMControl1.FileName  AFileName Then
      MMControl1.Notify = False
      MMControl1.Wait = True
      MMControl1.Shareable = False
      MMControl1.DeviceType = DevType
      MMControl1.FileName = AFileName
    End If

    EventDelay 50

    ' Open the MCI WaveAudio or MIDI device.
    MMControl1.Command = "Open"

    SetupWAVorMID = True
Exit Function
SetupWAVorMID_Error:
    Exit Function
End Function

Sub UpdateCDInfo ()
'-------------------------------------------------
' This routine writes information about the
' CD directly onto the form.
'-------------------------------------------------
Dim LineHeight As Integer
Dim ATab As String

    ATab = Chr$(9)
    LineHeight = Me.TextHeight("Aj")

    Me.Cls

    Me.CurrentX = picAVIScreen.Left
    Me.CurrentY = Me.CurrentY + (LineHeight \ 2)
    Me.ForeColor = BLUE
    Me.Print "DeviceType:" & ATab;
    Me.ForeColor = RED
    Me.Print MMControl1.DeviceType;

    Me.CurrentX = picAVIScreen.Left
    Me.CurrentY = Me.CurrentY + LineHeight
    Me.ForeColor = BLUE
    Me.Print "Tracks:" & ATab;
    Me.ForeColor = RED
    Me.Print Format$(MMControl1.Tracks);
End Sub

Sub UpdateFileInfo ()
```

7 ◀

*(continued on next page)*

*(continued from previous page)*

```
'----------------------------------------------------
' This routine writes information about a media
' file directly onto the form.
'----------------------------------------------------
Dim LineHeight As Integer
Dim ATab As String

    ATab = Chr$(9)
    LineHeight = Me.TextHeight("Aj")

    Me.Cls

    Me.CurrentX = picAVIScreen.Left
    Me.CurrentY = Me.CurrentY + (LineHeight \ 2)
    Me.ForeColor = BLUE
    Me.Print "File Name:" & ATab;
    Me.ForeColor = RED
    Me.Print LCase$(MMControl1.FileName);

    Me.CurrentX = picAVIScreen.Left
    Me.CurrentY = Me.CurrentY + LineHeight
    Me.ForeColor = BLUE
    Me.Print "DeviceType:" & ATab;
    Me.ForeColor = RED
    Me.Print MMControl1.DeviceType;
End Sub
```

## Tips and Comments

The architecture of the MCI control is a good example of how to design an extensible control. In fact, you can play other media formats, such as AutoDesk Animator .FLI files, using the MCI control. The one drawback to almost all multimedia formats is the huge amount of disk space taken up by digitized audio and video. A 30-second AVI clip can eat up over 5 megabytes of space, and at only moderate resolution at that. Cheaper storage media, such as CD-ROM, and better compression techniques are helping to overcome this shortcoming.

##  MediaKnife/VBX

| USAGE: | Design of Multimedia Applications |
|---|---|
| MANUFACTURER: | Media Architects, Inc. |
| COST: | $299 |

MediaKnife/VBX is a collection of controls and tools designed to build multimedia applications using Visual Basic. The tools include palette, layout, and sprite editors. The controls include a timer, sprite, sound, MCI, text, and a special "window" or image control. You can use this toolset to build a wide range of programs, including interactive video games, stand-alone presentations or demos, and video-based training applications.

# Syntax

Most of the MediaKnife controls are designed to display some type of visual information. The display of graphics is handled by MediaKnife through the mkDisplay control. This control can create a special window, called an mkWindow, onto which graphics, sprites, and videos can be displayed. Since this control is pivotal to the use of many of the other controls, you'll look at mkDisplay first.

## The mkDisplay Control: A Wall Between You and Visual Basic

The mkDisplay control is placed on a Visual Basic form, but only appears as a small icon at design time. The mkDisplay control is manipulated by your program at run time to create a special window, mkWindow. This window acts as a surface onto which bitmaps, sprites, and others graphics can be displayed. Table 7-11 lists the nonstandard properties and events of the mkDisplay control.

**Table 7-11** Nonstandard properties and events of the mkDisplay control

### PROPERTIES

| | | |
|---|---|---|
| Action | AnimationColor | AnimationID |
| AnimationFlag | AutoLoad | AutoRemap |
| AutoSize | AutoTransfer | AutoUpdate |
| BkgFileName | BkgHasHDC | BkgHDC |
| BkgSelHeight | BkgSelLeft | BkgSelTop |
| BkgSelWidth | BufCount | BufFilename |
| BufHeight | BufID | BufLoaded |
| BufSelHeight | BufSelLeft | BufSelTop |
| BufSelWidth | BufSize | BufWidth |
| DrawStyle | DrawWidth | EventMask |
| FillColor | FillStyle | GetActionEvent |
| GetClick | GetCommand | GetKeyDown |
| GetKeyPress | GetKeyUp | GetHotSpotMove |
| GetHotSpotClick | GetKeyHook | GetMouseDown |
| GetMouseHook | GetMouseMove | GetMouseUp |
| GetPaint | GetUserEvent | Transparent |
| Version | WinBkgCreate | WinBkgForce8 |
| WinCaption | WinCaptionEnabled | |
| WinChildStyle | WinParent | WndActivate |
| WndAutoDrag | WndAutoErase | WndAutoRedraw |
| WndHeight | WndLeft | WndLockZOrder |
| WndState | WndTop | WndWidth |
| WndZOrder | | |

*(continued on next page)*

*(continued from previous page)*

## EVENTS

| | | |
|---|---|---|
| Action | Command | HotSpotClick |
| HotSpotMove | KeyHook | MouseHook |
| User | | |

You must understand two important concepts when working with an mkWindow: the buffers and the background. *Buffers* are areas of memory that mkDisplay uses to store bitmaps or palettes. The *background* is the area of the mkWindow that actually displays a picture. Let's look at what's required to create an mkWindow and display a picture on it.

```
' Make the mkWindow a child to a VB form.
mkDisplay1.WinParent = Me.hWnd

' Load a bitmap into the buffer.
mkDisplay1.BufFileName = app.Path & "\world5.bmp"
mkDisplay1.BufLoaded = True

' Use the picture to set the size of the mkWindow.
mkDisplay1.AutoSize = True

' Create the mkWindow.
mkDisplay1.Action = MK_CREATE

' Transfer current buffers palette to the background.
mkDisplay1.Action = MK_BUF_PAL_TO_BKG

' Transfer the current buffer to the background.
mkDisplay1.Action = MK_BUF_TO_BKG
```

The first line associates the mkWindow to be created with a specific Visual Basic form. This is required to easily display a picture within the boundaries of a form. Without this line, the picture would be displayed in the upper-left corner of the Windows desktop.

The next two lines assign a bitmap file and load it into an mkDisplay buffer. The *BufLoaded* property does not display the picture, but only loads it into an area of memory from disk. The subsequent line sets the *AutoSize* property to *True*. This tells the mkDisplay to make the mkWindow the same size as the loaded bitmap.

Next, the *Action* property creates the actual mkWindow. At this point, you still don't see the picture; you only see the black default background of the mkWindow. You use the *Action* property to perform a variety of mkWindow management functions, such as updating all or part of a window.

The last two code lines also use this *Action* property. The first statement tells mkDisplay to copy the palette of the bitmap previously loaded to the background. If you don't do this, the picture will be displayed using the existing background palette, and will probably be unrecognizable.

This problem is called *palette shifting*, where the palette from one picture is used to display another picture, often with unsatisfactory results. For example, 256-color mode can, as you would expect, display 256 colors simultaneously. The key word here is "simultaneously," because most video drivers can display many more than 256 colors. But 256-color mode will only display one set, or palette, of colors at a time.

The final line of code tells mkDisplay to copy the contents of the buffer to the background, which displays the bitmap to the user.

You can display pictures using a variety of special effects. The *mkWipe*, *mkMosaic*, and *mkMosaicArray* properties can make new images appear to slide, fade, sparkle, or push other images away.

**Sprites**   Sprites are animated bitmaps that are often used to design the elements of arcade-style games. The mkSprite control lets you display a sprite that has been created using MediaKnife's Sprite Editor tool. A sprite is a collection of one or more numbered frames similar to the individual frames of an animated movie. When the frames are displayed in sequence, an illusion of movement is created. Like a Windows icon, a sprite can be partially transparent; in these transparent areas the background bitmap will show through. Table 7-12 lists the nonstandard properties and events of the mkSprite control.

**Table 7-12** Nonstandard properties and events of the mkSprite control

**PROPERTIES**

| | | |
|---|---|---|
| ClassName | CrashByte | CrashMask |
| CurrentF | CurrentX | CurrentY |
| CursorHit | DragF | DragX |
| DragY | Enabled | FrameRoll |
| Frames | PathFilename | PathLoaded |
| PathSteps | Remap | Shadow |
| SpriteFilename | SpriteLoaded | TargetHandle |
| Version | | |

**EVENTS**

| | |
|---|---|
| Bounds | Crash |

Sprites are always displayed on a previously created mkWindow. You can move them about on the mkWindow surface simply by using the mkSprite's *Move* method. You supply the *Move* method with three parameters: the new x and y position of the sprite, and the sprite frame number to display.

You can program sprites to fire a *Crash* event when they collide with a part of the background that has a particular color. You set which colors cause a crash by assigning values to either the *CrashByte* property, which specifies a single crash color, or the *CrashMask* property, which can define a more complex set of crash colors.

A sprite can also detect when it has reached an edge boundary of the mkWindow. The *Bounds* event is fired whenever the sprite touches the edge of this window.

7

**The mkTimer Control**  The mkTimer control provides several enhancements over the standard Visual Basic timer control. The mkTimer control offers better timer resolution than the standard control, and can be used as a "one-shot" timer. It is also useful for controlling the movement of sprite animation. Table 7-13 lists the nonstandard properties and event of the mkTimer control.

**Table 7-13** Nonstandard properties and event of the mkTimer control

**PROPERTIES**

| | | |
|---|---|---|
| Enabled | Interval | MaxInterval |
| MinInterval | Periodic | Resolution |
| SystemTime | Version | |

**EVENT**

| |
|---|
| Timer |

*MaxInterval* and *MinInterval* are read-only properties that let you interrogate the timer capabilities of your system. You can then use this information to set the millisecond *Resolution* and *Interval* properties of mkTimer. The *Resolution* property sets the millisecond resolution used for timing events. The *Interval* property sets the number of milliseconds between each *Timer* event.

You can use the Boolean *Periodic* property to turn mkTimer into a one-shot timer. Setting this property to *False* causes the next *Timer* event to happen only once, and then become dormant. You can later reactivate the timer by setting mkTimer's *Enabled* property to *True.*

**The mkSound Control**  The mkSound control lets you play wave audio files and embed .WAV files directly in your Visual Basic executables. You can use multiple mkSound controls, each with its own associated sound file. You can also play sounds designated in the Windows WIN.INI [Sounds] section. Table 7-14 lists the nonstandard properties of the mkSound control.

**Table 7-14** Nonstandard properties of the mkSound control

| | | |
|---|---|---|
| Async | FileName | Loaded |
| Loop | Play | Preview |
| SoundName | Stop | Version |

You can load sounds at design time by clicking on mkSound's *Loaded* property in the Visual Basic Properties window. A file selection dialog lets you select a .WAV file, which will be stored with your Visual Basic project and embedded with your Visual Basic executable file when it's created. This means that you won't have to distribute individual .WAV files with your application, and that .WAV files won't have to load from disk each time they're played. Loading large audio files at design time significantly increases the size of your final executable file.

To play back a loaded .WAV file, you simply set the mkSound's *Play* property to *True.* You can control how a sound is played using the *Async* and *Loop* properties. When sounds are played asynchronously (the *Async* property is *True),* other tasks, such as window updating, can continue. The asynchronous sound begins playing, and then immediately returns control to the program. Synchronous sounds do not return control to the program until the entire sound is completed.

The *Loop* property, when set to *True,* causes a sound to repeat itself. This can be useful for creating constant background music or sound effects. You terminate a looping sound by playing another sound or setting the mkSound control's *Play* property to *False.*

**The mkMCI Control**   The mkMCI control serves the same purpose as the Microsoft MCI control: controlling multimedia devices. Where the Microsoft control attempts to encapsulate the MCI functions within a set of VCR-style buttons, the mkMCI control lets you send MCI string commands directly to a multimedia device. These devices include wave audio (.WAV) and MIDI (.MID) sound files, audio CD and laser disc players, and Audio-Video Interleave (.AVI files). The nonstandard properties and event of the mkMCI control are listed in Table 7-15.

**Table 7-15** Nonstandard properties and event of the mkMCI control

**PROPERTIES**

| ErrorMsg | ErrorNum | ReturnString |
|---|---|---|
| Send | Version | |

**EVENT**

Notify

The mkMCI control handles devices almost entirely through the *Send* property, which is used to pass a string command to an MCI device. For example, if you had an audio-capable CD-ROM attached to your computer, you could play an audio CD using the following sequence of commands:

```
mkMCI1.Send = "OPEN CDAUDIO ALIAS CD"
mkMCI1.Send = "PLAY CD FROM 4:32"
```

The first line opens the system's audio CD and tells it to accept other MCI commands using the alias of "CD". The second line starts playing the CD, beginning 4 minutes and 32 seconds from the beginning of the CD.

Three properties return information from MCI commands. The *ReturnString* property can be inspected after a *Send* if the MCI command returns a string. Likewise, the *ErrorMsg* and *ErrorNum* properties return an error message and message number if the last MCI command string resulted in an error.

**The mkText Control**   The mkText control can be used to display text within an mkWindow using a variety of effects and transitions. It can display the same effects as those used to display bitmap images with the mkDisplay control. The nonstandard properties of the mkText control are listed in Table 7-16.

**Table 7-16** Nonstandard properties of the mkText control

| Action | Alignment | TargetHandle |
|---|---|---|
| TextHigh | TextLeading | TextLeft |
| TextTop | TextWide | Version |

# Example

The example program, shown in Figure 7-6, is a variation on the old "pong" video game. The example shows the use of the mkDisplay, mkSound, mkTimer, and mkSprite controls. The ball and paddle displayed in this program are two sprites. The ball is controlled by an mkTimer control. The sound created when a ball hits the wall is produced with the mkSound control. The background bitmap is displayed within an mkWindow.

The ball sprite's *CrashByte* property is 251, which corresponds to yellow on the palette. Both the background bitmap and the paddle are bordered by this color, so when the ball sprite collides with them a *Crash* event is generated.

When a wall is hit, as determined by the X and Y coordinates returned by the *Crash* event, the ball's direction reverses. Collision with the paddle is handled in a similar fashion.

When you run the program, the screen contains only a blank picture box and the Go button. Strictly speaking, the picture box is not necessary; while mkDisplay will create an mkWindow and display a bitmap directly over the picture box, it is merely a convenience. In the *DefineMKWindow* subroutine, which creates the mkWindow, notice that the picture box control's dimensions and screen position serve as a guide for placement of the mkWindow. You could have instead hard-coded these values into the program, omitting the picture box. What the picture box provides is an area that you can resize easily at design time.

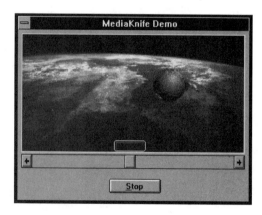

**Figure 7-6** The MediaKnife example program

The paddle sprite consists of only one frame, which you move by sliding the horizontal scroll bar. When the ball collides with the paddle, the ball bounces back and a "bonk" sound is produced.

To see how badly a palette can be mangled in 256-color mode, comment out the line in the *DefineMKWindow* subroutine that copies the buffer's palette to the background. Remember to restore the line before continuing.

## Steps

1. Create a new project called MEDIAKNF.MAK. Add MKDISPLY.VBX, MKSPRITE.VBX, and MKTOOLS.VBX, three of the MediaKnife controls, to the project. Also add MKCONST.BAS, the MediaKnife constants file (which comes with MediaKnife) to the project. Next, create a new form with the objects and properties described in Table 7-17. Save this form as MEDIAKNF.FRM.

**Table 7-17** Objects and properties of MEDIAKNF.FRM

| OBJECT | PROPERTY | SETTING |
|--------|----------|---------|
| Form | FormName | frmMediaKnife |
| | BackColor | &H00C0C0C0& |
| | BorderStyle | 3 'Fixed Double |
| | Caption | "MediaKnife Demo" |
| | ScaleMode | 3 'Pixel |
| MKSPRITE | Name | mkSpriteBall |
| | FrameRoll | -1 'True |
| | Frames | 4 |
| | Remap | -1 'True |
| | Shadow | 0 'False |
| MKSPRITE | Name | mkSpritePaddle |
| | Frames | 1 |
| | Remap | -1 'True |
| | Shadow | 0 'False |
| MKTIMER | Name | mkTimer1 |
| | Interval | 70 |
| | Periodic | -1 'True |
| | Resolution | 10 |
| MKSOUND | Name | mkSound1 |
| | Async | -1 'True |
| | Filename | " " |
| | Loop | 0 'False |
| MKSOUND | Name | mkSound2 |
| | Async | -1 'True |

*(continued on next page)*

411

| OBJECT | PROPERTY | SETTING |
|---|---|---|
| *(continued from previous page)* | | |
| | Filename | " " |
| | Loop | 0 'False |
| MEDIAK | Name | mkDisplay1 |
| | AnimationID | 0 |
| | AutoLoad | 0 'False |
| | AutoRemap | 0 'False |
| | AutoSize | 0 'False |
| | AutoTransfer | 0 'False |
| | AutoUpdate | 0 'False |
| | DrawStyle | 0 ' 0 - Solid |
| | DrawWidth | 1 |
| | EventMask | 0 |
| | FillColor | &H00000000& |
| | FillStyle | 1 ' 1 - Transparent |
| | Visible | -1 'True |
| PictureBox | Name | picSpriteWindow |
| | BackColor | &H0080FFFF& |
| HScrollBar | Name | hscrPaddle |
| | LargeChange | 10 |
| CommandButton | Name | btnStop |
| | Caption | "&Stop" |
| | Visible | 0 'False |

2. Use MediaKnife's Sprite Editor to create a 50x50-pixel, 8-frame ball sprite (a suitable ready-made sprite comes with MediaKnife) and a 48x26-pixel, 1-frame paddle sprite. Save these sprites as BALL.MKS and PADDLE.MKS.

3. After creating the form, add the following code to MEDIAKNF.FRM's declarations section.

```
Option Explicit
'-------------------------------------------------
' These are the variables and constants used in
' the MediaKnife example program.
'-------------------------------------------------

' The current x and y coordinates of the ball sprite.
Dim xpos As Integer
Dim ypos As Integer

' The speed and direction of the ball sprite.
Dim xinc As Integer
Dim yinc As Integer

' The current frame of the ball sprite.
```

```
Dim CurFrame As Integer

' The ball sprite width and height.
Const SPRITE_WIDTH = 50
Const SPRITE_HEIGHT = 50

' The paddle sprite width and height.
Const PADDLE_WIDTH = 48
Const PADDLE_HEIGHT = 18
```

4. Next, add the following subroutines to the MEDIAKNF.FRM form.

```
Sub btnGo_Click ()
'--------------------------------------------------
' When the Go button is pressed, build the mkWindow,
' load the sprites, and start the timer.
'--------------------------------------------------

    ' Turn the Stop button on and hide the Go button.
    btnStop.Visible = True
    btnGo.Visible = False

    ' Build the mkWindow that will hold the sprites.
    DefineMKWindow

    ' Set up the paddle sprite first. This is important
    ' to ensure the ball sprite can detect collisions
    ' with the paddle.
    SetupSprite2

    ' Set up the ball sprite.
    SetupSprite1

    ' Start the timer, which starts the ball moving.
    mkTimer1.Enabled = True

    ' Force an update of the paddle's x position by
    ' firing a scroller change event.
    hscrPaddle_Change
End Sub

Sub btnStop_Click ()
'--------------------------------------------------
' Clean up everything when the Stop button is pressed.
'--------------------------------------------------

    ' Turn on the Go button and hide the Stop button.
    btnGo.Visible = True
    btnStop.Visible = False

    ' Turn off the ball sprite's timer.
    mkTimer1.Enabled = False

    ' Dispose of the ball sprite.
    mkSpriteBall.Enabled = False
    mkSpriteBall.Refresh

    ' Dispose of the paddle sprite.
    mkSpritePaddle.Enabled = False
```

(continued on next page)

7 ◀

*(continued from previous page)*

```
    mkSpritePaddle.Refresh

    ' Dispose of the mkWindow.
    mkDisplay1.Action = MK_DESTROY
End Sub

Sub DefineMKWindow ()
'----------------------------------------------------
' Before we can display the sprites, we need to
' create a special mkWindow on which to display
' them.
'----------------------------------------------------

    ' Make the mkWindow a child to the main VB form.
    mkDisplay1.WinParent = Me.hWnd

    ' Because the mkWindow always uses pixel coordinates,
    ' make sure we're using the proper mode.
    picSpriteWindow.ScaleMode = 3 ' Pixels

    mkDisplay1.BufFileName = app.Path & "\world5.bmp"
    mkDisplay1.BufLoaded = True

    ' Set dimensions for mkWindow. We don't actually need
    ' the picture box; we only use it as a convienience
    ' to easily place the mkWindow where we want it.
    mkDisplay1.WndLeft = picSpriteWindow.Left
    mkDisplay1.WndTop = picSpriteWindow.Top
    mkDisplay1.WndWidth = picSpriteWindow.Width
    mkDisplay1.WndHeight = picSpriteWindow.Height

    ' Create the mkWindow.
    mkDisplay1.Action = MK_CREATE

    ' Transfer current buffers palette to the background.
    mkDisplay1.Action = MK_BUF_PAL_TO_BKG

    ' Transfer the current buffer to the background.
    mkDisplay1.Action = MK_BUF_TO_BKG
End Sub

Sub Form_Load ()
'----------------------------------------------------
' Set up the constants and control values needed
' by the example program.
'----------------------------------------------------

    ' Center the form on the screen.
    Me.Move (Screen.Width - Me.Width) \ 2, (Screen.Height - Me.Height) \ 2

    ' These variables control the speed and direction of the ball sprite.
    xinc = 5
    yinc = 5

    ' The scroller handles the movement of the paddle sprite.
    hscrPaddle.Min = 5
    hscrPaddle.Max = picSpriteWindow.Width - PADDLE_WIDTH - 5
    hscrPaddle.Value = (hscrPaddle.Max - hscrPaddle.Min) / 2
```

```
    ' We'll load this sound and use it when we hit the walls.
    mkSound1.Filename = app.Path & "\fingrpop.wav"
    mkSound1.Loaded = True

    ' We'll load this sound and use it when we hit the paddle.
    mkSound2.Filename = app.Path & "\paddlhit.wav"
    mkSound2.Loaded = True

    ' Situate the Stop button directly over the Go button.
    btnStop.Top = btnGo.Top
End Sub

Sub Form_Unload (Cancel As Integer)
'----------------------------------------------------
' If we are currently displaying sprites, then
' stop before exiting program.
'----------------------------------------------------

    If btnStop.Visible Then
        btnStop_Click
    End If
End Sub

Sub hscrPaddle_Change ()
'----------------------------------------------------
' Move the paddle sprite when the scroller moves.
'----------------------------------------------------

    If mkSpritePaddle.Enabled Then
        mkSpritePaddle.Move hscrPaddle, mkSpritePaddle.CurrentY
    End If
End Sub

Sub mkSpriteBall_Crash (X As Integer, Y As Integer, Frame As Integer)
'----------------------------------------------------
' React when the ball collides with the walls or
' paddle sprite, both of which are bordered by the crash
' color (yellow).
'----------------------------------------------------
Dim PaddleHit As Integer

    PaddleHit = True

    ' Collision with left or right wall.
    If ((X + SPRITE_WIDTH) >= mkDisplay1.WndWidth) Or (X = 0) Then
        xinc = -xinc
        PaddleHit = False
    End If

    ' Collision with top or bottom wall.
    If ((Y + SPRITE_HEIGHT) >= mkDisplay1.WndHeight) Or (Y = 0) Then
        yinc = -yinc
        PaddleHit = False
    End If

    ' Collision with paddle.
    If (yinc > 0) And (PaddleHit) Then
        yinc = -Abs(yinc)
    End If
```

*(continued on next page)*

7 ◀

*(continued from previous page)*

```
      ' Make a noise.
      If PaddleHit Then
          mkSound2.Play = True
      Else
          mkSound1.Play = True
      End If
End Sub

Sub mkTimer1_Timer (Calls As Integer, Errors As Integer)
'-----------------------------------------------------
' Move the ball sprite on each timer tick.
'-----------------------------------------------------

      ' Adjust the (x,y) coordinates.
      xpos = xpos + xinc
      ypos = ypos + yinc

      ' Set the next sprite animation frame.
      CurFrame = (CurFrame + 1) Mod 4

      ' Move the ball sprite.
      mkSpriteBall.Move xpos, ypos, CurFrame
      mkSpriteBall.Refresh
End Sub

Sub SetupSprite1 ()
'-----------------------------------------------------
' Load and display the ball sprite.
'-----------------------------------------------------

      ' Set the window that owns the sprite.
      mkSpriteBall.TargetHandle = mkDisplay1.hWnd

      ' Sprite first appears in upper-left corner.
      xpos = 15
      ypos = 15

      ' Start with first frame of sprite.
      CurFrame = 0

      ' Load the sprite from disk.
      mkSpriteBall.SpriteFilename = app.Path & "\BALL.MKS"
      mkSpriteBall.SpriteLoaded = True

      ' Create the sprite. It won't be displayed until
      ' "Refresh" is called.
      mkSpriteBall.Enabled = True

      ' Free up memory held by sprite.
      mkSpriteBall.SpriteLoaded = False

      ' Cause a "Crash" event when the sprite collides with
      ' anything "yellow" (palette entry 251).
      mkSpriteBall.CrashByte = 251
End Sub

Sub SetupSprite2 ()
'-----------------------------------------------------
' Load and display the paddle sprite.
'-----------------------------------------------------
```

```
    ' Set the window that owns the sprite.
    mkSpritePaddle.TargetHandle = mkDisplay1.hWnd

    ' Load the sprite from disk.
    mkSpritePaddle.SpriteFilename = app.Path & "\paddle.MKS"
    mkSpritePaddle.SpriteLoaded = True

    ' Create the sprite. It won't be displayed until
    ' "Refresh" is called.
    mkSpritePaddle.Enabled = True

    ' Free up memory held by sprite.
    mkSpritePaddle.SpriteLoaded = False

    ' Move the sprite to the bottom of the mkWindow.
    mkSpritePaddle.Move 1, picSpriteWindow.Height - PADDLE_HEIGHT
End Sub
```

## Tips and Comments

This section has only touched the surface of all the abilities of the MediaKinfe set of controls. You can also design backgrounds with hot spots that fire special events when the mouse moves or clicks over them, and give sprites predetermined paths that can be loaded from a file or loaded from a Visual Basic array. This package may be of greatest interest to game designers. It may take some effort to understand the sprite capabilities and mkWindow background programming features, but the flexibility of these tools makes them worthwhile to learn.

# VBPlay (VBPLAY.VBX)

| USAGE: | AutoDesk Animator File Viewer |
|---|---|
| MANUFACTURER: | AutoDesk |
| COST: | $25 |

The VBPlay Animation control was written by AutoDesk to allow viewing and manipulation of AutoDesk Animator files. These files, created with the AutoDesk Animator software, are a popular format for designing a variety of animations, from cartoons to digitized video clips.

## Syntax

AutoDesk Animator files are animation sequences stored in a file with either an .FLI or .FLC extension. The Animation control provides a "window" that you can place on a form and in which you can display an .FLI/.FLC file. The Animation control can be rather daunting because it provides so many options. However, the basic operation of the control is surprisingly simple, and requires only a few lines of code. This section starts with the basics, and then branches out into features such as fading, sound, and frame events. The nonstandard properties and events of the Animation control are listed in Table 7-18.

**Table 7-18** Nonstandard properties and events of the Animation control

### PROPERTIES

| | | |
|---|---|---|
| AllColors | Animation | AnimHeight |
| AnimSettings | AnimWidth | AnimWindow |
| AutoPlay | BeginFade | BeginFadeTime |
| ColorCycling | DesignSpeed | Device |
| EndFade | EndFadeTime | EndFrame |
| EndLoop | FrameCount | FrameEvents |
| FSDelay | FullScreen | Handle |
| Help | HideAnimation | LoopFrame |
| MemoryLoad | Pause | PauseAtEnd |
| Play | PositionFrame | PositionLoop |
| Sound | SoundDelay | SoundRepeats |
| Speed | StatusEvents | Type |
| XOrigin | YOrigin | |

### EVENTS

| | |
|---|---|
| AnimFrame | AnimStop |

Playing an animation involves only two steps; loading the animation file, which displays it in the Animation control's window, and starting the animation, as shown in the following piece of code.

```
Animation1.Play = false
Animation1.Animation = "c:\flifiles\bin7.fli"
Animation1.Play = true
```

Setting the *Animation* property to a file name associates the file with the control. The *Play* property, when set to *True,* runs the animation sequence. Also notice that the *Play* property was set to *False* before *Animation* was assigned a file name. You need to do this because the *Animation* property can only be set when an animation is not running.

That's all that's required for basic animation playing. Let's look at some of the other features of this control.

AutoDesk Animation files consist of sequences of *frames.* Each frame constitutes a separate image, slightly different from the frame before it and the one after it. These images are conceptually just like the individual frames of a motion picture. Displaying the frames in rapid succession generates the illusion of movement. The Animation control provides several frame-related properties.

The *FrameCount* property returns the total number of frames in the animation sequence. The *PositionFrame* property determines the current frame of animation. You can use this property to set an animation sequence to a particular frame, which can be particularly useful if you need to skip over a section of animation.

The *AnimFrame* event can be triggered at one or more specific frames. These frames must first be designated using a call to the aaPlay dynamic link library (AAPLAY.DLL). This library is required when using the Animation control, and should be installed in the Windows system directory. To set a frame to trigger an *AnimFrame* event, you must first make a call to the *aaNotify* function, which is declared here:

```
Declare Function aaNotify Lib "aaplay.dll" (ByVal hAa As Integer, ByVal lPosition As Long,
ByVal lParam As Long) As Integer
```

This function is passed the Animation control's *Handle* property as its first parameter. The second parameter, *lPosition,* is the frame at which an event is to be fired. The last parameter is a long integer value that is passed to the *AnimFrame* event when it's triggered. The function returns *True* if the notification was successfully set. To set an *AnimFrame* event to fire at the fifth frame of the current animation, you could use the following code:

```
If aaNotify(Animation1.Handle, 5, MyData) = 0 Then
    MsgBox "Notification was not set"
Else
    MsgBox "Notification was successfully set."
End If
```

The *AnimFrame* event has the following format:

```
Sub AnimFrame ([Index As Integer, ] User As Any)
```

*Index* is only used if the Animation control is part of a control array. *User* is the data that was passed to the *aaNotify* function in its *lParam* parameter. To determine what frame of the animation triggered the current *AnimFrame* event, check the *PositionFrame* property while in the event subroutine. Note that if you do not set up events at particular frames using *aaNotify,* you have no practical way to handle frame-level events effectively.

# Dimensions

Not all AutoDesk Animations have the same physical dimensions. If you've sized your Animation control too small, the animation will be clipped and you won't be able to see the bottom or right side of the animation sequence. If the Animation control is too large, the bottom and right side will be filled with unattractive white space. To avoid these problems, you must size the control based on the size of the loaded animation file, and the control provides several properties that allow just that.

The *AnimWidth* and *AnimHeight* properties provide the dimensions of the current animation file. These dimensions are always in pixel units. Visual Basic's default scale mode is twips, so when adjusting the Animation control's size you may need to convert between the two modes. (You can use the built-in Visual Basic *Screen.TwipsPerPixelX* and *Screen.TwipsPerPixelY* values for this conversion.)

The *XOrigin* and *YOrigin* properties control what part of the animation is displayed in the upper-left corner of the Animation control. These properties are very useful for "cropping" an animation that is larger than the area available for display. The upcoming example program uses these properties, as well as the *AnimWidth* and *AnimHeight* properties, to write a subroutine that always centers an animation within a frame,

7

centering the animation if it's too small, and cropping it equally on all sides if it is larger than the frame dimensions.

# Fades

Normally, when an animation sequence is played, the first frame abruptly appears and the animation begins. Sometimes, however, it's more effective to have the animation fade in when it starts, or fade out at the end. The Animation control provides properties for automatically performing these effects.

*BeginFade* and *EndFade* are integer properties that determine what type of fade effect is used at the beginning and end of an animation. Table 7-19 lists the possible values for these properties.

**Table 7-19** Values for BeginFade and EndFade

| VALUE | MEANING |
|---|---|
| 0 | No Fade. This is the default. |
| 1 | Fade from or to black. |
| 2 | Fade from or to white |

Associated with these two properties are *BeginFadeTime* and *EndFadeTime,* two properties that let you set the duration of the fade effect. The range is from 250 to 10,000 milliseconds. If *BeginFade* or *EndFade* are set to zero (no fade), the associated time property has no effect.

Silent animation sequences are like the old silent movies: artistic in their own right, but not living up to the full potential of the medium. Sound can greatly enhance your animation sequences, and the Animation control gives you a simple way to provide it.

The *Sound* property associates a digitized sound file or sound from an audio CD or video laser disc player. To associate a sound file with the animation, just assign its file name to the *Sound* property, like this:

```
Animation1.Sound = "DING.WAV"
```

A sound file can be in either WaveForm (.WAV) or MIDI (.MID) format.

Playing sound from an audio CD or video laser disc player is a two-step process. First, you must tell the Animation control what type of device will be used as the source for the sound, then you must tell the control what part of the CD or laser disc to play. You accomplish the first step by setting the *Device* property, a string property whose possible values are explained in Table 7-20.

**Table 7-20** Values for Device

| VALUE | MEANING |
|---|---|
| "WaveAudio" | .WAV format audio files |
| "CDAudio" | Audio compact disc player |
| "VideoDisc" | Audio from a video laserdisc player |
| "Sequencer" | .MID format audio files |

Notice that, while you can specify "WaveAudio" and "Sequencer" as devices for .WAV and .MID files, they are not required because the Animation control can determine the device by the file name specified in the *Sound* property.

The following section of code plays the first minute and a half of the third track of an audio CD when the animation is played:

```
Animation1.Device = "CDAudio"
Animation1.Sound = "from 3 to 3:1:30"
```

The string specified in the *Sound* property indicates the starting and stopping positions for the audio CD. The values can be specified in *tt:mm:ss:ff* format, which specifies the tracks, minutes, seconds, and frames of the audio sequence. Playing sound from a laser disc uses the same basic format, but the time is in *hh:mm:ss* format, which specifies hours, minutes, and seconds.

You use the *SoundDelay* property to determine when the sound begins in relation to the playing of the animation sequence. This property is a long integer value in the range –280,000,000 to +280,000,000 milliseconds, which amounts to –50 to +50 minutes. If the value is negative, the sound begins before the animation. If the value is positive, the sound begins the specified number of milliseconds after the animation begins. The default value for *SoundDelay* is 0, which indicates that the sound and animation should begin simultaneously.

If a sound is shorter than the animation sequence, you can use the *SoundRepeats* property to set the number of times to repeat the sound while the animation is in progress. By default, this value is 0, which causes the sound to repeat until the animation sequence has ended. To have the sound play only once, set this property to 1. The valid range for the *SoundRepeats* property is 0 to 1000.

When you design an AutoDesk Animation, the file stores a value to indicate how fast, in milliseconds per frame, the animation should be played. This value is stored in the read-only property *DesignSpeed*. You may want to play back an animation either slower or faster than its design speed, and you can accomplish this by setting the *Speed* property. Initially, *Speed* is set to the design speed when the animation is loaded, but you can subsequently reset this value to anywhere from 19 to 1,000 milliseconds per frame. Note that the lower the *Speed* value, the faster the animation speed.

You can greatly improve the performance and smoothness of an animation by storing the entire animation sequence in memory, rather than having to access it from disk storage. The *MemoryLoad* Boolean property tells the Animation control whether it should attempt to load the entire animation sequence into memory. By default, this property is set to *False*, which causes the control to retrieve each frame of the animation from disk when it's needed. For large animations, setting *MemoryLoad* to *True* can produce a significant time delay as the control attempts to read the entire animation sequence from disk, but will provide smoother display of the sequence.

The *Pause* property is a Boolean similar to the *Play* property. It allows the program to temporarily interrupt the playback of an animation sequence. Setting Pause to *False* causes the animation to begin again from the paused frame position.

The *PauseAtEnd* property indicates how many seconds to delay at the end of an animation sequence. This value can range from 0 milliseconds (the default) to 50,000 milliseconds (or 50 seconds).

The Boolean *HideAnimation* property is useful when you don't want the animation to be visible when it isn't playing. By default, *HideAnimation* is set to *False*. This causes the first frame of the animation to be visible in the Animation control when the animation is not playing. Setting this property to *True* causes the control to remain invisible when the animation is not in progress.

If you are using the Animation control to display only one animation file and you want to easily set and test many of the animation properties at design time, the *AnimSettings* property can be very useful. This property, which is only available at run time, displays the dialog box shown in Figure 7-7.

This dialog box is a convenient way to set properties, but can only be used if the *Animation* property has been set to a file name at design time.

If you would prefer to display the animation full screen instead of displaying it in the Animation control's "window," set the *FullScreen* property to *True*. The *FSDelay* property sets the amount of delay, in milliseconds, after the display changes video modes. The default is 1,500, or 1.5 seconds, and the maximum delay is 10,000 milliseconds.

If you want to have an animation play immediately, without using the *Play* property, set the *AutoPlay* property to *True*. This causes the animation to start as soon as it's loaded. Note that you can actually play an animation without a single line of Visual Basic code, just by setting the *Animation* and *AutoPlay* properties at design time.

---

**Animation Settings - d:\waite\e_shaft.flc**

☐ Load into **M**emory　　　　Frames:　　　74
☐ Use **F**ull Screen　　　　Design Speed:　8.8
☒ Loop Frame Present　　　　Duration:　　　8.436
☒ **C**olor Cycling OK　　　☐ **U**se All Colors

Animation Speed, Length, and Duration

Lock:　　　Speed Units:　○ **J**iffies　　◉ F**r**ames per Second

◉ **S**peed　　　　　　| 8.8 |　　←▮――――――→
○ **L**oops:Frames　　| Forever |　←――――――▮→
○ **D**uration　　　　| Forever |　←――――――▮→

**R**epeat Sound　　| Forever |　　←――――――▮→
Dela**y** Sound　　　| 0 |　　　　　←―――▮――――→
**P**ause at End　　| 1.000 |　　　←▮―――――――→

[ **Tr**ansitions ]　[ **T**est ]　[ OK ]　[ Cancel ]

**Figure 7-7** The Animation Settings dialog box

In a program, it's often necessary to know when an animation sequence has ended. For example, you may want to unload or hide the window that the animation was displayed in as soon as the animation has completed. To do this, use the Animation control's *AnimStop* event. This event is called when the animation ends normally or due to an error condition, but is not triggered when the *Play* property is set to *False*.

# Example

The example program implements an .FLI file viewer. The program allows you to load and play an .FLI or .FLC format animation file. It also lets you step through the animation frame by frame, set the playback speed, and attach a sound file to the animation.

The program, shown in Figure 7-8, automatically crops and centers the animation within the main form's upper frame. Controls used to set the various options appear below the frame.

Use the File menu's Attach Sound File option to associate a sound file with the current animation, and set the Play Sounds check box to enable the sound. Press the Play button to start the animation. When the animation is in progress, use the Stop button (which replaces the Play button) to stop the animation. You can use the scroller bars, combo boxes, and check boxes to adjust the various parameters.

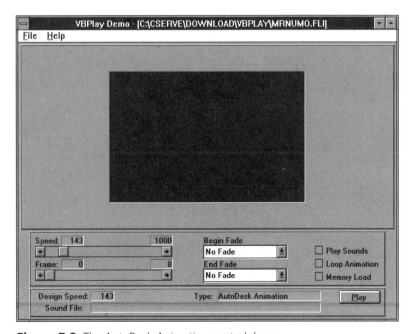

**Figure 7-8** The AutoDesk Animation control demo

## Steps

1. Create a new project called VBPLAY1.MAK. Add the Animation control, VBPLAY.VBX, and the common dialog control, CMDIALOG.VBX, to the project. Create a new form with the objects and properties described in Table 7-21. Save this form as VBPLAY1.FRM.

**Table 7-21** Objects and properties of VBPLAY1.FRM

| OBJECT | PROPERTY | SETTING |
|---|---|---|
| Form | FormName | frmVBPlay |
| | BackColor | &H00C0C0C0& |
| | Caption | "VBPlay Demo" |
| CommonDialog | Name | CMDialog1 |
| PictureBox | Name | picFLIFrame |
| | BackColor | &H00C0C0C0& |
| | Tag | "/3D/" |
| PictureBox | Name | picOptionsFrame |
| | BackColor | &H00C0C0C0& |
| PictureBox | Name | picStatusFrame |
| | BackColor | &H00C0C0C0& |

2. Place the controls shown in Table 7-23 inside the picFLIFrame PictureBox control. Make sure to select the picFLIFrame control on the form before placing these controls.

**Table 7-22** Controls contained inside the picFLIFrame PictureBox control

| OBJECT | PROPERTY | SETTING |
|---|---|---|
| VBAnimation | Name | Anim1 |
| | AllColors | 0 'False |
| | Animation | " " |
| | AutoPlay | 0 'False |
| | BackColor | &H00C0C0C0& |
| | BeginFade | 0 'Cut |
| | BeginFadeTime | 250 |
| | ColorCycling | -1 'True |
| | Device | " " |
| | EndFade | 0 'Cut |
| | EndFadeTime | 250 |
| | EndFrame | 0 |
| | EndLoop | 0 |
| | FrameEvents | -1 'True |
| | FSDelay | 1500 |

| OBJECT | PROPERTY | SETTING |
|---|---|---|
| | FullScreen | 0 'False |
| | HideAnimation | 0 'False |
| | LoopFrame | 0 'False |
| | MemoryLoad | 0 'False |
| | PauseAtEnd | 1000 |
| | Sound | " " |
| | SoundDelay | 0 |
| | SoundRepeats | 0 |
| | Speed | 0 |
| | StatusEvents | -1 'True |
| | XOrigin | 0 |
| | YOrigin | 0 |

3. Place the controls shown in Table 7-23 inside the picOptionsFrame PictureBox control. Make sure to select the picOptionsFrame control on the form before placing these controls.

**Table 7-23** Controls contained inside the picOptionsFrame PictureBox control

| OBJECT | PROPERTY | SETTING |
|---|---|---|
| Label | Name | lblMaxSpeed |
| | Alignment | 1 'Right Justify |
| | BackStyle | 0 'Transparent |
| | Caption | "1000" |
| | ForeColor | &H00800000& |
| | Tag | "/3D/" |
| Label | Name | lblSpeed |
| | Alignment | 1 'Right Justify |
| | BackStyle | 0 'Transparent |
| | ForeColor | &H00800000& |
| | Tag | "/3D/" |
| Label | Name | Label3 |
| | BackStyle | 0 'Transparent |
| | Caption | "Speed:" |
| | ForeColor | &H00800000& |
| Label | Name | lblFrameCount |
| | Alignment | 1 'Right Justify |
| | BackStyle | 0 'Transparent |
| | ForeColor | &H00800000& |
| | Tag | "/3D/" |
| Label | Name | lblFrame |

(continued on next page)

7 ◄

| OBJECT | PROPERTY | SETTING |
|---|---|---|
| *(continued from previous page)* | | |
| | Alignment | 1 'Right Justify |
| | BackStyle | 0 'Transparent |
| | ForeColor | &H00800000& |
| | Tag | "/3D/" |
| Label | Name | Label1 |
| | BackStyle | 0 'Transparent |
| | Caption | "Frame:" |
| | ForeColor | &H00800000& |
| Label | Name | Label5 |
| | BackStyle | 0 'Transparent |
| | Caption | "Begin Fade" |
| | ForeColor | &H00800000& |
| Label | Name | Label6 |
| | BackStyle | 0 'Transparent |
| | Caption | "End Fade" |
| | ForeColor | &H00800000& |
| HScrollBar | Name | hscrSpeed |
| | Enabled | 0 'False |
| | Max | 31 |
| | Min | 1 |
| | Value | 1 |
| HScrollBar | Name | hscrFrame |
| | Enabled | 0 'False |
| | Max | 31 |
| | Min | 1 |
| | Value | 1 |
| ComboBox | Name | cmbFade |
| | Index | 0 |
| | Style | 2 'Dropdown List |
| ComboBox | Name | cmbFade |
| | Index | 1 |
| | Style | 2 'Dropdown List |
| CheckBox | Name | chkPlaySound |
| | BackColor | &H00C0C0C0& |
| | Caption | "Play Sounds" |
| | ForeColor | &H00800000& |
| CheckBox | Name | chkLoop |
| | BackColor | &H00C0C0C0& |
| | Caption | "Loop Animation" |
| | ForeColor | &H00800000& |

| OBJECT | PROPERTY | SETTING |
|--------|----------|---------|
| CheckBox | Name | chkMemoryLoad |
| | BackColor | &H00C0C0C0& |
| | Caption | "Memory Load" |
| | ForeColor | &H00800000& |

4. Place the controls shown in Table 7-24 inside the picStatusFrame PictureBox control. Make sure to select the picStatusFrame control on the form before placing these controls.

**Table 7-24** Controls contained inside the picStatusFrame PictureBox control

| OBJECT | PROPERTY | SETTING |
|--------|----------|---------|
| Label | Name | lblDesignSpeed |
| | Alignment | 1 'Right Justify |
| | BackStyle | 0 'Transparent |
| | ForeColor | &H00800000& |
| | Tag | "/3D/" |
| Label | Name | Label2 |
| | Alignment | 1 'Right Justify |
| | BackStyle | 0 'Transparent |
| | Caption | "Design Speed:" |
| | ForeColor | &H00800000& |
| Label | Name | lblSoundFile |
| | BackStyle | 0 'Transparent |
| | ForeColor | &H00800000& |
| | Tag | "/3D/" |
| Label | Name | Label4 |
| | Alignment | 1 'Right Justify |
| | BackStyle | 0 'Transparent |
| | Caption | "Sound File:" |
| | ForeColor | &H00800000& |
| Label | Name | Label7 |
| | Alignment | 1 'Right Justify |
| | BackStyle | 0 'Transparent |
| | Caption | "Type:" |
| | ForeColor | &H00800000& |
| Label | Name | lblType |
| | BackStyle | 0 'Transparent |
| | ForeColor | &H00800000& |
| CommandButton | Name | btnPlay |
| | Caption | "&Play" |
| | Enabled | 0 'False |

7 ◄

5. Add a menu to VBPLAY1.FRM using the Visual Basic Menu Design window, setting the captions and names shown in Table 7-25.

**Table 7-25** Menu definition for VBPLAY1.FRM

| CAPTION | NAME |
| --- | --- |
| &File | mnuFile |
| – – – – &Open | mnuFileOpen |
| – – – – &Attach Sound File | mnuAttachSound |
| – – – – – | mnuFileSep1 |
| – – – – E&xit | mnuFileExit |

6. Add the following code to the form's declarations section.

```
Option Explicit
'-------------------------------------------------
' Constants, variables, and declarations used by the
' AutoDesk Animator VBPlay example.
'-------------------------------------------------

Dim Margin As Integer
Dim AnimMaxWidth As Integer
Dim AnimMaxHeight As Integer

' The minimum allowable size of the main form.
Dim MinWidth As Integer
Dim MinHeight As Integer

' WindowState constant.
Const MINIMIZED = 1

' Color constants.
Const DARK_GRAY = &H808080
Const WHITE = &HFFFFFF
Const BLACK = &H0

' Cursor shape constants.
Const CSR_NORMAL = 0
Const CSR_HOURGLASS = 11

' MsgBox parameters.
Const MB_OK = 0                    ' OK button only
Const MB_ICONEXCLAMATION = 48      ' Warning message

' 3D effect constants.
Const BORDER_INSET = 0
Const BORDER_RAISED = 1
```

7. Add the following functions and subroutines to the VBPLAY1.FRM form. This example program is fairly long because it develops a full-featured .FLI player that can automatically adjust the viewing window to the dimensions of the .FLI file being played. It also uses some simple Visual Basic techniques to give the application a 3D appearance

without the use of a separate control or link library. Look at the *Make3D* and *Make3DFrame* subroutines to see how this was accomplished.

```
Sub AdjustAnimationSize ()
'-------------------------------------------------
' Adjust the animation control within the frame.
'-------------------------------------------------
Dim AnimWidthTwips As Integer
Dim AnimHeightTwips As Integer
Dim FrameWidthPixels As Integer
Dim FrameHeightPixels As Integer

    Anim1.XOrigin = 0
    Anim1.YOrigin = 0

    ' Size the Animation control based on the Animation dimensions.

    AnimWidthTwips = Screen.TwipsPerPixelX * Anim1.AnimWidth
    AnimHeightTwips = Screen.TwipsPerPixelY * Anim1.AnimHeight
    FrameWidthPixels = AnimMaxWidth \ Screen.TwipsPerPixelX
    FrameHeightPixels = AnimMaxHeight \ Screen.TwipsPerPixelY

    ' If Animation is smaller than frame:
    If AnimWidthTwips < AnimMaxWidth Then
        Anim1.Width = AnimWidthTwips
        Anim1.Left = ((AnimMaxWidth - Anim1.Width) \ 2) + Margin
    End If
    If AnimHeightTwips < AnimMaxHeight Then
        Anim1.Height = AnimHeightTwips
        Anim1.Top = ((AnimMaxHeight - Anim1.Height) \ 2) + Margin
    End If

    ' If the Animation is larger than the frame, then center it.
    If AnimWidthTwips > AnimMaxWidth Then
        Anim1.Width = AnimMaxWidth
        Anim1.Left = Margin
        Anim1.XOrigin = (Anim1.AnimWidth - FrameWidthPixels) \ 2
    End If
    If AnimHeightTwips > AnimMaxHeight Then
        Anim1.Height = AnimMaxHeight
        Anim1.Top = Margin
        Anim1.YOrigin = (Anim1.AnimHeight - FrameHeightPixels) \ 2
    End If
End Sub

Sub Anim1_AnimStop (Reason As Long)
'-------------------------------------------------
' When the animation is finished, simulate clicking
' the Play button (which will be in Stop mode).
'-------------------------------------------------
    btnPlay_Click
End Sub

Sub btnPlay_Click ()
'-------------------------------------------------
' Depending on whether we're playing or not, either
' start the animation or stop the animation.
'-------------------------------------------------
    ' Play the animation.
    If btnPlay.Caption = "&Play" Then
```

7 ◀

*(continued on next page)*

*(continued from previous page)*

```
                btnPlay.Caption = "&Stop"
                hscrFrame.Enabled = False
                hscrSpeed.Enabled = False
                Anim1.Play = False
                Anim1.Play = True
        ' Stop the animation.
        Else
                Anim1.Play = False
                btnPlay.Caption = "&Play"
                hscrFrame.Enabled = True
                hscrSpeed.Enabled = True
                hscrFrame.Value = Anim1.PositionFrame
                Me.Refresh
                picFLIFrame.Refresh
        End If
        DoEvents
End Sub

Sub chkLoop_Click ()
'----------------------------------------------------
' Set the EndLoop property based on the value of
' the check box.
'----------------------------------------------------
        If chkLoop = 1 Then
                Anim1.EndLoop = 0
        Else
                Anim1.EndLoop = 1
        End If
End Sub

Sub chkMemoryLoad_Click ()
'----------------------------------------------------
' Set the MemoryLoad property based on the value
' of the check box.
'----------------------------------------------------
        If chkMemoryLoad = 1 Then
                Anim1.MemoryLoad = True
        Else
                Anim1.EndLoop = False
        End If

End Sub

Sub chkPlaySound_Click ()
'----------------------------------------------------
' Set the Sound property based on the value of the
' check box.
'----------------------------------------------------
        If chkPlaySound = 1 Then
                Anim1.Sound = lblSoundFile
        Else
                Anim1.Sound = ""
        End If
End Sub

Sub cmbFade_Click (Index As Integer)
'----------------------------------------------------
' Set the BeginFade or EndFade property when a new
' value is selected from its combo box.
'----------------------------------------------------
```

```
    If Index = 0 Then
        Anim1.BeginFade = cmbFade(Index).ListIndex
    Else
        Anim1.EndFade = cmbFade(Index).ListIndex
    End If

End Sub

Sub Form_Load ()
'-----------------------------------------------------
' Set initial values for the form and its controls.
'-----------------------------------------------------
Dim i As Integer

    Margin = Anim1.Left

    ' Set the limits on how small the form can get.
    MinWidth = Me.Width
    MinHeight = Me.Height

    ' Fill the Fade effect combo boxes.
    For i = 0 To 1
        cmbFade(i).AddItem "No Fade"
        cmbFade(i).AddItem "Fade To/From Black"
        cmbFade(i).AddItem "Fade To/From White"
        cmbFade(i).ListIndex = 0
    Next

    ' Center the form.
    Me.Move (Screen.Width - Me.Width) \ 2, (Screen.Height - Me.Height) \ 2
    Me.Show
    frmAbout.Show 1
End Sub

Sub Form_Paint ()
'-----------------------------------------------------
' Put a 3D border around any control tagged "3D".
'-----------------------------------------------------
    Make3DFrame picOptionsFrame, lblSpeed, BORDER_RAISED
    Make3DFrame picOptionsFrame, lblMaxSpeed, BORDER_RAISED
    Make3DFrame picOptionsFrame, lblFrame, BORDER_RAISED
    Make3DFrame picOptionsFrame, lblFrameCount, BORDER_RAISED
    Make3DFrame picOptionsFrame, cmbFade(0), BORDER_INSET
    Make3DFrame picOptionsFrame, cmbFade(1), BORDER_INSET

    Make3DFrame picFLIFrame, Anim1, BORDER_INSET

    Make3D Me, picFLIFrame, BORDER_RAISED
    Make3D Me, picOptionsFrame, BORDER_RAISED
    Make3D Me, picStatusFrame, BORDER_RAISED

    Make3DFrame picStatusFrame, lblDesignSpeed, BORDER_INSET
    Make3DFrame picStatusFrame, lblSoundFile, BORDER_INSET
    Make3DFrame picStatusFrame, lblType, BORDER_INSET
End Sub

Sub Form_Resize ()
```

7 ◄

(continued on next page)

431 ▶

*(continued from previous page)*

```
'------------------------------------------------------
' Adjust the placement and size of controls when
' the form is resized.
'------------------------------------------------------

    If WindowState = MINIMIZED Then Exit Sub

    If Me.Width < MinWidth Then
        Me.Width = MinWidth
        Exit Sub
    ElseIf Me.Height < MinHeight Then
        Me.Height = MinHeight
        Exit Sub
    End If

    picFLIFrame.Move Margin, Margin, Me.ScaleWidth - (Margin * 2), Me.ScaleHeight -
picOptionsFrame.Height - picStatusFrame.Height - (Margin * 4)

    picOptionsFrame.Move (Me.ScaleWidth - picOptionsFrame.Width) \ 2, picFLIFrame.Height +
(Margin * 2)
    picStatusFrame.Move picOptionsFrame.Left, Me.ScaleHeight - picStatusFrame.Height - Margin

    AnimMaxWidth = picFLIFrame.ScaleWidth - (Margin * 2)
    AnimMaxHeight = picFLIFrame.ScaleHeight - (Margin * 2)
    Anim1.Width = AnimMaxWidth
    Anim1.Height = AnimMaxHeight

    AdjustAnimationSize

    picFLIFrame.Refresh
    Me.Refresh
End Sub

Sub hscrFrame_Change ()
'------------------------------------------------------
' Change the currently displayed frame when the
' scroller value changes.
'------------------------------------------------------
    Anim1.PositionFrame = hscrFrame.Value
    lblFrame = hscrFrame.Value
End Sub

Sub hscrSpeed_Change ()
'------------------------------------------------------
' Change the animation playback speed when the
' scroller value change.
'------------------------------------------------------
    Anim1.Speed = hscrSpeed.Value
    lblSpeed = hscrSpeed.Value
End Sub

Sub Make3D (pic As Form, ctl As Control, ByVal BorderStyle As Integer)
'------------------------------------------------------
' Wrap a 3D effect around a control on a form.
'------------------------------------------------------
Dim AdjustX As Integer, AdjustY As Integer
Dim RightSide As Single
Dim BW As Integer, BorderWidth As Integer
Dim LeftTopColor As Long, RightBottomColor As Long
```

```
Dim i As Integer

    If Not ctl.Visible Then Exit Sub

    AdjustX = Screen.TwipsPerPixelX
    AdjustY = Screen.TwipsPerPixelY

    BorderWidth = 1

    Select Case BorderStyle
    Case 0: ' Inset
         LeftTopColor = DARK_GRAY
         RightBottomColor = WHITE
    Case 1: ' Raised
         LeftTopColor = WHITE
         RightBottomColor = DARK_GRAY
    End Select


    ' Set the top shading line.
    For BW = 1 To BorderWidth
       ' Top
       pic.CurrentX = ctl.Left - (AdjustX * BW)
       pic.CurrentY = ctl.Top - (AdjustY * BW)
       pic.Line -(ctl.Left + ctl.Width + (AdjustX * (BW - 1)), ctl.Top - (AdjustY * BW)),
LeftTopColor
       ' Right
       pic.Line -(ctl.Left + ctl.Width + (AdjustX * (BW - 1)), ctl.Top + ctl.Height + (AdjustY *
(BW - 1))), RightBottomColor
       ' Bottom
       pic.Line -(ctl.Left - (AdjustX * BW), ctl.Top + ctl.Height + (AdjustY * (BW - 1))),
RightBottomColor
       ' Left
       pic.Line -(ctl.Left - (AdjustX * BW), ctl.Top - (AdjustY * BW)), LeftTopColor
    Next
End Sub

Sub Make3DFrame (pic As Control, ctl As Control, ByVal BorderStyle As Integer)
'------------------------------------------------
' Wrap a 3D effect around a control in a control.
'------------------------------------------------
Dim AdjustX As Integer, AdjustY As Integer
Dim RightSide As Single
Dim BW As Integer, BorderWidth As Integer
Dim LeftTopColor As Long, RightBottomColor As Long
Dim i As Integer

    If Not ctl.Visible Then Exit Sub

    AdjustX = Screen.TwipsPerPixelX
    AdjustY = Screen.TwipsPerPixelY

    BorderWidth = 1
    BorderStyle = 0

    Select Case BorderStyle
    Case 0: ' Inset
         LeftTopColor = DARK_GRAY
         RightBottomColor = WHITE
```

*(continued on next page)*

*(continued from previous page)*

```
    Case 1: ' Raised
        LeftTopColor = WHITE
        RightBottomColor = DARK_GRAY
    End Select


    ' Set the top shading line.
    For BW = 1 To BorderWidth
        ' Top
        pic.CurrentX = ctl.Left - (AdjustX * BW)
        pic.CurrentY = ctl.Top - (AdjustY * BW)
        pic.Line -(ctl.Left + ctl.Width + (AdjustX * (BW - 1)), ctl.Top - (AdjustY * BW)),
LeftTopColor
        ' Right
        pic.Line -(ctl.Left + ctl.Width + (AdjustX * (BW - 1)), ctl.Top + ctl.Height +
(AdjustY * (BW - 1))), RightBottomColor
        ' Bottom
        pic.Line -(ctl.Left - (AdjustX * BW), ctl.Top + ctl.Height + (AdjustY * (BW - 1))),
RightBottomColor
        ' Left
        pic.Line -(ctl.Left - (AdjustX * BW), ctl.Top - (AdjustY * BW)), LeftTopColor
    Next

End Sub

Sub mnuAttachSound_Click ()
'----------------------------------------------------
' Menu option to associate a sound file with the
' animation.
'----------------------------------------------------

    On Error GoTo AttachSound_Error

    CMDialog1.Filename = ""
    CMDialog1.DialogTitle = "Open a Sound File"
    CMDialog1.Filter = "Sound Files|*.wav;*.mid"
    CMDialog1.Action = 1

    If CMDialog1.Filename = "" Then Exit Sub

    Anim1.Sound = CMDialog1.Filename

    lblSoundFile = CMDialog1.Filename
    If chkPlaySound = 1 Then
        Anim1.Sound = lblSoundFile
    Else
        Anim1.Sound = ""
    End If
Exit Sub

AttachSound_Error:
    MsgBox "The selected file was not in a valid Sound File Format.", MB_OK Or
MB_ICONEXCLAMATION, "Error Opening File"
    Exit Sub
End Sub

Sub mnuFileExit_Click ()
'----------------------------------------------------
' Stop playing the animation and exit the program.
'----------------------------------------------------
```

```
    Anim1.Play = False
    Unload Me
End Sub

Sub mnuFileOpen_Click ()
'-------------------------------------------------
' Load a new animation file and set controls and
' variables based on the new file's parameters.
'-------------------------------------------------

    On Error GoTo FileOpen_Error

    CMDialog1.Filename = ""
    CMDialog1.DialogTitle = "Open an Autodesk Animation File"
    CMDialog1.Filter = "Autodesk Animations|*.fli;*.flc"
    CMDialog1.Action = 1

    If CMDialog1.Filename = "" Then Exit Sub

    Anim1.XOrigin = 0
    Anim1.YOrigin = 0
    Anim1.Animation = CMDialog1.Filename
    Anim1.Sound = lblSoundFile
    Me.Caption = "VBPlay Demo — [" & CMDialog1.Filename & "]"

    If chkLoop = 1 Then
        Anim1.EndLoop = 0
    Else
        Anim1.EndLoop = 1
    End If

    Select Case Anim1.Type
        Case 1: lblType = "Autodesk Animation"
        Case 2: lblType = "Windows DIB Animation or Still"
        Case 3: lblType = "Animation Script"
    End Select

    btnPlay.Enabled = True

    hscrFrame.Enabled = True
    hscrSpeed.Enabled = True

    ' Set Frame Scroller.
    hscrFrame.Min = 0
    hscrFrame.Max = Anim1.FrameCount
    hscrFrame.Value = 0
    lblFrame = hscrFrame.Value
    lblFrameCount = hscrFrame.Max
    ' Set Speed Scroller.
    hscrSpeed.Min = 19
    hscrSpeed.Max = 1000
    hscrSpeed.Value = Anim1.DesignSpeed
    Anim1.Speed = Anim1.DesignSpeed
    lblSpeed = Anim1.Speed
    lblDesignSpeed = Anim1.DesignSpeed

    AdjustAnimationSize

Exit Sub
```

7 ◄

*(continued on next page)*

*(continued from previous page)*

```
FileOpen_Error:
    MsgBox "The selected file was not in a valid Animation Format.", MB_OK Or
MB_ICONEXCLAMATION, "Error Opening File"
    Exit Sub
End Sub

Sub mnuHelpAbout_Click ()
'--------------------------------------------------
' Show the About box.
'--------------------------------------------------
    frmAbout.Show 1
End Sub
```

## Tips and Comments

When you work with animations that use 256 or more colors, palette problems can occur. These are most noticeable when fade effects are enabled. The help file that comes with the Animation control has a useful section explaining ways of avoiding or minimizing these problems.

While this section only discusses how to play .FLI/.FLC format files, the Animation control also supports the playback of AutoDesk Animator Script (.AAS) files and Windows Device-Independent Bitmap (.DIB) files. To determine what type of file is currently loaded, you can use the *Type* property, whose values are listed in Table 7-26.

**Table 7-26** Values for Type

| VALUE | MEANING |
| --- | --- |
| 0 | No Animation file is loaded. |
| 1 | An AutoDesk Animator or Animator Pro file is loaded. |
| 2 | A Windows Device-Independent Bitmap file is loaded. |
| 3 | An AutoDesk Animator Script file is loaded. |

AAWIN.EXE, an animation player developed by AutoDesk, allows you to build .AAS script files, which let you play multiple .FLI/.FLC files, along with sound effects.

# 8

# BITMAP AND IMAGE PROCESSING

Before the popularity of Windows, most PC programs were written for MS-DOS running in text mode: 80 columns by 25 lines and 16 colors. Intrepid programmers ventured into other text modes (43-line EGA displays, 50-line VGA displays, and so on) and might occasionally flip into graphics mode to display a pie chart.

Microsoft Windows shifted PCs from a text-oriented into a graphical world. Now developers want to take advantage of this shift by including images in their programs. These images range from simple bitmaps to photographic renderings.

At the low-powered end of the image continuum, are the Visual Basic image and picture box controls. These controls are quite adequate for a wide range of images, but they fall short in several areas. First, they are designed strictly to display, not to manipulate these images. Second, they can only handle a few image file formats, although there are now dozens of image file "standards" available.

The controls in this chapter fill most of these gaps. Some handle a wider variety of image file formats, while others concentrate on applying special image effects.

▲ **ImageKnife** This control lets you apply complex image processing functions to your images, including image masking, edge extraction, color replacement, grayscaling, and color negation.

▲ **ImageMan/VB** This set of two controls supports image scanning, printing, and display. The example uses the ImageMan picBuf control to build a document imaging application that can store images of scanned documents as fields in a Microsoft Access database.

▲ **ImageStream - VB** This control can display and manipulate a wide range of image file formats, from CorelDraw to AutoCad. You'll use this control to optimize the palettes of multiple images to avoid annoying palette-shifting problems.

▲ **JPEG Image Compressor VBX** You will discover how to use this control to compress an image, significantly reducing the amount of disk storage required.

▲ **Picture Clip** You can use this control to extract a section of a large bitmap. In this chapter, you use it to build a smooth scrolling bitmap background like those used in arcade-style games.

▲ **Artist and PicScroll** The PicScroll control is an enhanced picture control that lets you display pictures in a scrollable area. The Artist control lets you create applications that allow the user to paint and manipulate bitmapped pictures.

 # ImageKnife (KNIFE.VBX)

| USAGE: | Complex Processing of Bitmapped Images |
|---|---|
| MANUFACTURER: | Media Architects, Inc. |
| COST: | $199 |

The ImageKnife control can display images in Windows Bitmap (.BMP), Windows Device Independent Bitmap (.DIB), CompuServe Graphics Interchange (.GIF), ZSOFT (.PCX), Tagged Image File (.TIF), and Targa (.TGA) formats, with JPEG image and TWAIN support available as an option. The control is data-aware, so you can use the data control to store images in Access databases. You can also store images in Access databases programmatically. The primary strength of this control is its extensive support for image processing, including image rotation to any angle, color negation, and matrix filtering.

# Syntax

The ImageKnife control's object name is PicBuf, which is how we will refer to it in this section. While the control has a number of nonstandard properties, most of the image processing effects are handled through a set of 44 function calls (see Table 8-1). These function calls are defined in a Visual Basic module called IMKCONST.TXT that is provided with the control.

**Table 8-1** Nonstandard properties and special functions of the PicBuf control

### PROPERTIES

| | | |
|---|---|---|
| AssignMode | AutoScale | AutoSize |
| Bitmap | ColorDepth | FullPicture |
| HeightPrint | HeightSelect | IMKVersion |
| LeftPrint | LeftSelect | Palette |
| Picture | PrinterhDC | ResizeMode |
| ScreenPalette | Selection | TopPrint |
| TopSelect | WidthPrint | WidthSelect |
| Xorigin | Xpan | Xresolution |
| Yorigin | Ypan | Yresolution |
| ZoomFactor | | |

### SUBROUTINES AND FUNCTIONS

| | | |
|---|---|---|
| imkAccessLoad | imkAccessStoreInit | imkAccessStoreGetData |
| imkAccessStoreDone | imkAppendTiff | imkBlur |
| imkBrightCont | imkColorReplace | imkCountImages |
| imkDuplicate | imkExtractEdges | imkForcePal |
| imkGamma | imkGetColor | imkGetColorCount |
| imkGetPalColor | imkGetPalette | imkGetScanLine |
| imkGrayScale | imkIncreaseColors | imkInit |
| imkLoad | imkLoadPal | imkMaskCopy |
| imkMatrixFilter | imkMirror | imkNegate |
| imkOptimizePal | imkPutScanLine | imkReduceColors |
| imkRemapPal | imkRotate | imkSetPalColor |
| imkSetPalette | imkSetScreenPal | imkSharpen |
| imkSoften | imkStore | imkStorePal |
| imkTwipsToXCoord | imkTwipsToYCoord | imkVerify |
| imkXCoordsToTwips | imkYCoordsToTwips | |

Unlike a conventional picture control, the image in a PicBuf control can be manipulated in various ways independent of the screen mode. This is because PicBuf stores the entire image and its palette in memory. This image can be referenced by the *FullPicture* property. This allows an image to retain its full color depth even when you use video modes that are incapable of displaying all the colors. This would allow you to manipulate 24-bit images using, for example, a 256-color Windows driver, even though you would not be able to see all the colors.

**Image Processing Effects**   You can apply a wide variety of effects, from the mundane to the esoteric, to an image. You'll take a look at each of these effects, and discover how they change an existing image.

The *imkBlur* function returns a blurred copy of an image passed to it as a parameter, as shown in the following line of code:

```
' Blur the PicBuf1 image.
PicBuf1.FullPicture = imkBlur (PicBuf1.FullPicture)
```

This example takes the image in PicBuf1, blurs it, and copies the blurred image back into PicBuf1. You could just as easily copy the blurred image into another PicBuf control by specifying it in the assignment statement. You can call the *imkBlur* function repeatedly to create an increasingly blurred image.

The functions *imkSoften* and *imkSharpen* are similar in some respects to *imkBlur*. While *imkBlur* blurs the entire image, *imkSoften* affects just the contrasting areas of the image. The *inkSharpen* function creates a sharper, more in-focus image.

The *imkBrightCont* function sets the brightness and contrast of an image. An example of this function is shown here:

```
' Increase the brightness, leave contrast unchanged.
PicBuf1 = imkBrightCont (PicBuf1, 0.75, 0.50)
```

The function accepts three parameters: the image to be changed, a brightness factor, and a contrast factor. Both these factors must be in the range 0.0 to 1.0. A value of 0.5 indicates that no change is to be made, values above 0.5 increase the brightness or contrast, values below 0.5 decrease them. Figure 8-1 shows an image of a car, and Figure 8-2 shows the same image after repeated adjustments to its contrast and brightness.

The *imkExtractEdges* function defines and "extracts" the edges within an image. Edges are the boundary lines between two highly contrasting areas. This function lets you specify the degree of edge extraction to apply, from 1 to 10. You can use this function very effectively in combination with other image functions to convert a full-color photograph to a rough equivalent of a black and white line drawing. Figure 8-3 shows the effects of applying edge extraction and image negation to the original image of the car from Figure 8-1.

You can use the *imkIncreaseColors* and *imkReduceColors* functions to increase and decrease the color depth of an image. The *imkIncreaseColor* function is the simpler of the two, as it only requires as parameters the image and a new color depth value. For example, the following code would convert PicBuf1 to a 24-bit image.

```
' Convert PicBuf1 to a 24-bit image.
PicBuf1 = imkIncreaseColors (PicBuf1, 24)
```

**Figure 8-1** The original car image before any processing

**Figure 8-2** A bitmap after contrast and brightness adjustments

**Figure 8-3** A bitmap after edge extraction and negation

8

The depth value must be either 4, 8, or 24, and the value must be greater than the current color depth of the image.

The *imkReduceColors* function is a bit more complicated because, unlike increasing colors, reducing colors requires that you intelligently discard some colors in the current image. The *imkReduceColors* function gives you several parameters for controlling the appearance of the resulting image.

```
' Reduce an image to 16 colors with an optimized palette,
' dithering, and reduced color bleeding.
Optimize = True
Dither = True
NoBleed = True
PicBuf1 = imkReduceColors (PicBuf1, 16, Optimize, Dither, NoBleed)
```

Dithering is the use of multiple colors to create a new color. For example, the standard set of 16 Windows colors doesn't include orange; however, a workable color can be simulated by mixing red and yellow on a 1-pixel checkerboard grid. If *Dither* is set to *True,* some colors in the resulting image will be created by dithering other colors. This can often provide a more realistic resulting image. The *NoBleed* parameter determines whether ImageKnife will attempt to reduce color bleeding in the resulting image.

The *imkMaskCopy* allows you to blend one image with another. A third image, called a *mask,* is used like a stencil. The mask image determines what sections of the first image will be copied onto the second image. All three images are composited to create the final image. One use for this function is to cut an irregular area from one image and overlay it onto a second image.

There are numerous other image processing functions. The *imkNegate* function changes all colors in an image into their opposites: white to black, yellow to blue, black to white, and so on. The *imkMirror* function lets you flip an image vertically or horizontally, and the *imkRotate* function can rotate an image to any angle. The *imkGrayScale* function converts a color image to its grayscale equivalent. The *imkColorReplace* function changes all pixels in an image from one color to another. You can use this function to "tint" an image.

### Displaying the Image

ImageKnife has several properties for displaying an image within the PicBuf control. You can use the Boolean *AutoScale* property to automatically scale an image to the size of the control. Aspect ratio is always maintained when this property is set to *True.* If *AutoScale* is *False,* the *ZoomFactor* property determines the size at which the image is displayed. By default, the *ZoomFactor* is 1.0, meaning that the image·is displayed at its actual size. Values greater than 1.0 cause the image to zoom in, while values less than 1.0 cause the image to zoom out.

### Loading and Saving Images

You handle loading an image file into a PicBuf control through the *imkLoad* function. The following example loads a .BMP file into a PicBuf control.

```
PicBuf1.FullPicture = imkLoad ("c:\windows\marble.bmp", 0, IMK_EXTENSION)
```

The first parameter is the file name of the image to be loaded. The second parameter is an image number. If the file format supports multiple images in a single file, as TIFF does, this parameter lets you choose which image will be loaded. The last parameter indicates the file format of the file. You can indicate a specific format using one of the defined constants. For example, to load the bitmap in the preceding example, you could have used the constant IMK_BITMAP. The IMK_EXTENSION constant used in the example tells ImageKnife to derive the file type by looking at the file's extension. This is useful when writing applications that handle multiple image file formats.

To save the contents of a PicBuf control, use the *imkStore* function. This function can save the image in the same or a different format from that of the originally loaded image. The following example shows how to save the entire contents of a PicBuf control to a TIFF file.

```
FileName = "c:\test\marble.tif"
imkStore Filename, PicBuf1.FullPicture, IMK_EXTENSION, 0
```

The first parameter is the name of the file you're saving to, the second parameter is the image you are saving. The example is saving the entire image, but you could have saved only a section of the image by using the *Selection* property instead of *FullPicture*. You can use *Selection*—in conjunction with the *TopSelect, LeftSelect, WidthSelect,* and *HeightSelect* properties—to specify a rectangular clipping region within the entire image. The third parameter is the file format to save the image as, and the last parameter indicates the compression method to use, if any.

# Example

The example program, shown in Figure 8-4, lets the user load an image and apply various image processing effects to it. The user can then save the modified image in the same or a different image file format.

The user initiates most of the functions using the buttons along the left edge of the form. The program stores two copies of the image. A small version of the image, displayed to the left, is never modified. Image effects are applied to the second copy of the image, stored in the large image control on the right. This second, main, image is always displayed at its actual size. You can use the Revert button at any time to discard effect changes and return the image to its original appearance. When you click on this button, the program simply copies the small image into the large image using their *FullPicture* properties as shown below:

```
PicBuf1.Full Picture = PicBufOriginal.FullPicture
```

The example program makes it easy to play with the special effects and radically change the appearance of an image.

**Figure 8-4** The ImageKnife example program

8

## Steps

1. Create a new project called IMAGEKNF.MAK. Add the ImageKnife image control, KNIFE.VBX, and the common dialog control, CMDIALOG.VBX, to the project. Also add the constants file, IMKCONST.TXT, to the project. This file comes with ImageKnife, and defines the constants and function declarations needed to perform many of the special image processing effects.

2. Create a new form with the objects and properties described in Table 8-2. Save this form as IMAGEKNF.FRM.

**Table 8-2** Objects and properties of IMAGEKNF.FRM

| OBJECT | PROPERTY | SETTING |
|---|---|---|
| Form | FormName | Form1 |
| | BackColor | &H00E0FFFF& |
| | Caption | "ImageKnife Demo" |
| PictureBox | Name | picContainer |
| | BackColor | &H00C0C0C0& |
| PicBuf | Name | PicBuf1 |
| | AssignMode | 0 'Complete Replacement |
| | AutoScale | 0 'False |
| | AutoSize | 0 'False |
| BackColor | &H00FFFFFF& | |
| | DataCompression | 0 |
| | DataFormat | 8 'Paintbrush OLE |
| | HeightPrint | 0 |
| | HeightSelect | 0 |
| | LeftPrint | 0 |
| | LeftSelect | 0 |
| | ResizeMode | 0 'Pixels Deleted, Fixed Aspect |
| | ScreenPalette | 0 'False |
| | TopPrint | 0 |
| | TopSelect | 0 |
| | WidthPrint | 0 |
| | WidthSelect | 0 |
| | Xorigin | 0 |
| | Xpan | 0 |
| | Yorigin | 0 |
| | Ypan | 0 |
| | ZZDIB | 0 |

3. Place the controls in Table 8-3 inside the picContainer PictureBox control. Make sure to select the picContainer control on the form before placing these controls inside it.

**Table 8-3** Controls contained within the picContainer PictureBox control

| OBJECT | PROPERTY | SETTING |
| --- | --- | --- |
| Label | Name | Label1 |
| | Alignment | 2 'Center |
| | BackStyle | 0 'Transparent |
| | Caption | "Brightness" |
| Label | Name | Label2 |
| | Alignment | 2 'Center |
| | BackStyle | 0 'Transparent |
| | Caption | "Contrast" |
| CommonDialog | Name | CMDialog1 |
| CommandButton | Name | btnOpenFile |
| | Caption | "&Open File" |
| CommandButton | Name | btnSaveFile |
| | Caption | "&Save File" |
| | Enabled | 0 'False |
| | Tag | "\disabled\" |
| PicBuf | Name | PicBufOriginal |
| | AssignMode | 0 'Total Replacement |
| | AutoScale | -1 'True |
| | AutoSize | 0 'False |
| | BackColor | &H00FFFFFF& |
| | DataCompression | 0 |
| | DataFormat | 8 'Paintbrush OLE |
| | HeightPrint | 0 |
| | HeightSelect | 0 |
| | LeftPrint | 0 |
| | LeftSelect | 0 |
| | ResizeMode | 0 'Pixels Deleted, Fixed Aspect |
| | ScreenPalette | 0 'False |
| | TopPrint | 0 |
| | TopSelect | 0 |
| | WidthPrint | 0 |
| | WidthSelect | 0 |
| | Xorigin | 0 |
| | Xpan | 0 |
| | Yorigin | 0 |

*(continued on next page)*

8 ◀

| OBJECT | PROPERTY | SETTING |
|---|---|---|
| *(continued from previous page)* | | |
| | Ypan | 0 |
| | ZZDIB | 0 |
| CommandButton | Name | btnRevert |
| | Caption | "&Revert" |
| | Enabled | 0 'False |
| | Tag | "\disabled\" |
| CommandButton | Name | btnRotate |
| | Caption | "Rotate" |
| | Enabled | 0 'False |
| | Tag | "\disabled\" |
| CommandButton | Name | btnGrayScale |
| | Caption | "GrayScale" |
| | Enabled | 0 'False |
| | Tag | "\disabled\" |
| CommandButton | Name | btnReduceColor |
| | Caption | "Reduce Colors" |
| | Enabled | 0 'False |
| | Tag | "\disabled\" |
| HScrollBar | Name | hscrBright |
| | Enabled | 0 'False |
| | LargeChange | 10 |
| | Max | 100 |
| | Tag | "\disabled\" |
| | Value | 50 |
| HScrollBar | Name | hscrContrast |
| | Enabled | 0 'False |
| | LargeChange | 10 |
| | Max | 100 |
| | Tag | "\disabled\" |
| | Value | 50 |
| CommandButton | Name | btnExtractEdges |
| | Caption | "Extract Edges" |
| | Enabled | 0 'False |
| | Tag | "\disabled\" |
| CommandButton | Name | btnNegate |
| | Caption | "Negate" |
| | Enabled | 0 'False |
| | Tag | "\disabled\" |
| CommandButton | Name | btnSharp |

| OBJECT | PROPERTY | SETTING |
|---|---|---|
|  | Caption | "Sharp" |
|  | Enabled | 0 'False |
|  | Tag | "\disabled\" |
| CommandButton | Name | btnSoften |
|  | Caption | "Soft" |
|  | Enabled | 0 'False |
|  | Tag | "\disabled\" |
| CommandButton | Name | btnPrint |
|  | Caption | "Print" |
|  | Enabled | 0 'False |
|  | Tag | "\disabled\" |

4. Add the following code to declarations section of the form.

```
Option Explicit
'---------------------------------------------------
' Constants and variables used in the ImageKnife
' example program.
'---------------------------------------------------

' WindowState constant.
Const MINIMIZED = 1

' Minimum dimensions for the main window.
Dim MinFormWidth As Integer
Dim MinFormHeight As Integer

' MsgBox constants.
Const MB_OK = 0
Const MB_YESNO = 4
Const MB_ICONINFORMATION = 64

Const IDOK = 1
Const IDYES = 6

' File Open/Save dialog flags.
Const OFN_READONLY = &H1&
Const OFN_HIDEREADONLY = &H4&
```

5. Add the following subroutines to IMAGEKNF.FRM form. The printing subroutine illustrates how to position and size an image while maintaining the image's proper aspect ratio.

```
Sub btnExtractEdges_Click ()
'---------------------------------------------------
' Extract the edges of the current image.
'---------------------------------------------------

   On Error Resume Next
   PicBuf1 = imkExtractEdges(PicBuf1, 5)
End Sub
```

*(continued on next page)*

8

*(continued from previous page)*

```
Sub btnGrayScale_Click ()
'-----------------------------------------------------
' Convert the current image to a grayscale image.
'-----------------------------------------------------

    On Error Resume Next
    PicBuf1 = imkGrayScale(PicBuf1)
End Sub

Sub btnNegate_Click ()
'-----------------------------------------------------
' Negate the colors in the current image.
'-----------------------------------------------------

    On Error Resume Next
    PicBuf1 = imkNegate(PicBuf1)
End Sub

Sub btnOpenFile_Click ()
'-----------------------------------------------------
' Open an image file and display it in the control.
'-----------------------------------------------------
Dim Canceled As Integer
Dim i As Integer

    On Error GoTo btnOpenFile_Error
    Canceled = False

    ' Set up and display the File Open dialog box.
    CMDialog1.Flags = OFN_HIDEREADONLY
    CMDialog1.CancelError = True
    CMDialog1.Filter = "Image Files|*.tif;*.tga;*.bmp;*.gif;*.dib;*.pcx"
    CMDialog1.DialogTitle = "Open an Image File"
    CMDialog1.Action = 1

    If Canceled Or (CMDialog1.Filename = "") Then Exit Sub

    ' First load the image into the small control; then copy it
    ' to the larger "working" control.
    PicBufOriginal.FullPicture = imkLoad(CMDialog1.Filename, 0, IMK_EXTENSION)
    PicBuf1.FullPicture = PicBufOriginal.FullPicture

    ' Change the caption to include the current file name.
    Me.Caption = "ImageKnife Demo - [" & CMDialog1.Filename & "]"

    ' Enable all the disabled controls.
    For i = 0 To Me.Controls.Count - 1
        If Me.Controls(i).Tag = "\disabled\" Then
            Me.Controls(i).Enabled = True
        End If
    Next
Exit Sub

btnOpenFile_Error:
    Canceled = True
    Beep
    Resume Next
End Sub

Sub btnPrint_Click ()
```

```
'------------------------------------------------------
' Print the image to the default printer.
'------------------------------------------------------
Dim margin As Integer

    Printer.ScaleMode = 3 ' Pixels
    Printer.Print " "

    margin = Printer.ScaleWidth / 10

    PicBuf1.LeftPrint = margin / 2
    PicBuf1.TopPrint = margin / 2

    ' Set the printer image's dimensions.
    PicBuf1.WidthPrint = PicBuf1.Xresolution * ((Printer.ScaleWidth - margin) / PicBuf1.Xresolution)
    PicBuf1.HeightPrint = PicBuf1.Yresolution * ((Printer.ScaleWidth - margin) / PicBuf1.Xresolution)

    PicBuf1.PrinterhDC = Printer.hDC
    Printer.EndDoc
End Sub

Sub btnReduceColor_Click ()
'------------------------------------------------------
' Reduce the color to a level specified by the user.
'------------------------------------------------------
Dim NewColors As Integer
Dim Optimize As Integer
Dim Dither As Integer
Dim NoBleed As Integer

    On Error GoTo btnReduceColor_Error

    ' Get the new, reduced color level.
    NewColors = Val(InputBox("Enter the new number of colors.", "Reduce Colors"))

    ' If we have more than 16 colors, optimize the palette.
    Optimize = NewColors >= 16

    ' Dither the resulting colors.
    Dither = True

    ' Reduce color bleeding in the resulting image.
    NoBleed = True

    ' Reduce the color level.
    PicBuf1 = imkReduceColors(PicBuf1, NewColors, Optimize, Dither, NoBleed)

Exit Sub
btnReduceColor_Error:
    MsgBox "The value '" & Format$(NewColors) & "' is not valid.", MB_OK Or MB_ICONINFORMATION, ⇒
"Invalid Number of Colors"
    Resume Next
End Sub

Sub btnRevert_Click ()
'------------------------------------------------------
' Revert back to the originally loaded image,
' stored in the PicBufOriginal control.
'------------------------------------------------------
Dim answer As Integer
```

*(continued on next page)*

*(continued from previous page)*

```
    answer = MsgBox("You will lose all changes made since the file was loaded. Do you want to
revert to original image?", MB_YESNO Or MB_ICONINFORMATION, "Revert To Original Image")
    If answer = IDYES Then
        hscrBright = 50
        hscrContrast = 50
        PicBuf1.FullPicture = PicBufOriginal.FullPicture
    End If
End Sub

Sub btnRotate_Click ()
'------------------------------------------------------
' Rotate the image by the degrees specified by
' the user.
'------------------------------------------------------
Dim degrees As Integer

    degrees = Val(InputBox("Enter number of degrees to rotate image.", "Rotate Image"))
    PicBuf1 = imkRotate(PicBuf1, degrees, 0)
End Sub

Sub btnSaveFile_Click ()
'------------------------------------------------------
' Save the current image. The image can be saved
' in a different file format than the original.
' The ImageKnife control will handle conversion
' automatically, based on file extension.
'------------------------------------------------------
Dim Canceled As Integer

    On Error GoTo btnSaveFile_Error
    Canceled = False

    ' Set up and display the Save File dialog box.
    CMDialog1.Flags = OFN_HIDEREADONLY
    CMDialog1.CancelError = True
    CMDialog1.DialogTitle = "Save An Image File"
    CMDialog1.Action = 1

    If Canceled Or (CMDialog1.Filename = "") Then Exit Sub

    ' Save the image to a file.
    imkStore CMDialog1.Filename, PicBuf1, IMK_EXTENSION, 0
Exit Sub

btnSaveFile_Error:
    Canceled = True
    Resume Next
End Sub

Sub btnSharp_Click ()
'------------------------------------------------------
' Sharpen the image.
'------------------------------------------------------

    On Error Resume Next
    PicBuf1 = imkSharpen(PicBuf1, 4)
End Sub

Sub btnSoften_Click ()
```

```
'-----------------------------------------------------
' Soften the image.
'-----------------------------------------------------

    On Error Resume Next

    PicBuf1 = imkSoften(PicBuf1, 4)
End Sub

Sub Form_Load ()
'-----------------------------------------------------
' Position the main form and initialize properties
' and variables.
'-----------------------------------------------------

    ' Center the window on the screen.
    Me.Move (Screen.Width - Me.Width) \ 2, (Screen.Height - Me.Height) \ 2

    ' The original form size is the smallest the form can get.
    MinFormWidth = Me.Width
    MinFormHeight = Me.Height

    ' The small image should be scaled to the control's size.
    PicBufOriginal.AutoScale = True
End Sub

Sub Form_Resize ()
'-----------------------------------------------------
' Resize the controls when the form resizes.
'-----------------------------------------------------
Dim margin As Integer

    ' If the window has been minimized, do nothing.
    If WindowState = MINIMIZED Then Exit Sub

    ' Make sure the window is not too small.
    If Me.Width < MinFormWidth Then Me.Width = MinFormWidth
    If Me.Height < MinFormHeight Then Me.Height = MinFormHeight

    ' Use the current left border as a margin for other calculations.
    margin = picContainer.Left

    ' Adjust the controls to the new window size.
    picContainer.Height = Me.ScaleHeight - picContainer.Top - margin
    PicBuf1.Height = Me.ScaleHeight - PicBuf1.Top - margin
    PicBuf1.Width = Me.ScaleWidth - PicBuf1.Left - margin

    If (Me.Width < Screen.Width) And (Me.Height < Screen.Height) Then
        ' Center the window on the screen.
        Me.Move (Screen.Width - Me.Width) \ 2, (Screen.Height - Me.Height) \ 2
    End If
End Sub

Sub hscrBright_Change ()
'-----------------------------------------------------
' Adjust the brightness of the image when the
' scroller is moved.
'-----------------------------------------------------

    PicBuf1 = imkBrightCont(PicBuf1, hscrBright / 100, hscrContrast / 100)
```

*(continued on next page)*

8 ◀

*(continued from previous page)*

```
    hscrBright = 50
End Sub

Sub hscrContrast_Change ()
'--------------------------------------------------
' Adjust the contrast of the image when the
' scroller is moved.
'--------------------------------------------------

    PicBuf1 = imkBrightCont(PicBuf1, hscrBright / 100, hscrContrast / 100)
    hscrContrast = 50
End Sub
```

## Tips and Comments

If you're not familiar with the image processing functions provided with ImageKnife, you'll have to experiment a bit to get up to speed, but the results are well worth it. Effects like color replacement, edge extraction, image masking, and palette manipulation are powerful functions not found in many other image controls.

The ability to dither an image during color reduction is quite useful, and can be used to reduce 24-bit color photographic images to 256 or even 16 colors while still retaining a realistic appearance.

# ImageMan/VB

| USAGE: | Image Scanning and Processing |
|---|---|
| MANUFACTURER: | Data Techniques, Inc. |
| COST: | $295 |

ImageMan/VB is a set of two controls that provide support for scanning, printing, and displaying images. Supported formats include Tagged Image File (.TIF), ZSOFT (.PCX), Intel-DCA Multiple Image File (.DCX), WordPerfect Graphics (.WPG), CompuServe Graphics (.GIF), Windows Bitmap (.BMP and .DIB), Targa (.TGA), GEM monochrome (.IMG), Aldus Placeable Metafile (.WMF), JFIF compliant (.JPG), and Encapsulated Postscript (.EPS) files. The scanner control supports the standard TWAIN interface, allowing you to include direct scanner support in your Visual Basic applications. This examination of ImageMan/VB focuses only on the image control, as the scanner control requires scanner hardware.

## Syntax

Table 8-4 lists the nonstandard properties and events of the ImageMan image control. The control can be used as a bound data control, so images can be stored in database fields. The control supports a wide range of image formats, including two multipage formats, DCX and TIFF. Support for these formats can simplify document imaging system development; you can store multipage documents in a single data file or database field.

**Table 8-4** Nonstandard properties and events of the ImageMan control

**PROPERTIES**

| | | |
|---|---|---|
| AutoDraw | AutoScale | Blue |
| Brightness | ClipboardCommand | DitherMethod |
| DoPrint | DstLeft | DstTop |
| DstRight | DstBottom | ErrCode |
| ErrString | Ext | ExtensionCount |
| Extensions | Gamma | GetFileName |
| Green | hDC | hDIB |
| hImage | ImageColors | ImageFlags |
| ImageHeight | ImageWidth | ImageXRes |
| ImageYRes | Magnification | Mirror |
| Pages | PageNumber | PaletteEntries |
| Picture | PrnHdc | Red |
| ReduceTo | Rotate | SaveAs |
| SaveOptions | ScaleHeight | ScaleWidth |
| ScaleLeft | ScaleTop | Scrollbars |
| Select | SrcLeft | ScrTop |
| SrcRight | SrcBottom | |

**EVENTS**

| | |
|---|---|
| Scroll | Select |

**Retrieving an Image**   To load images into the ImageMan control, you assign their file names to the *Picture* property. The control automatically detects the image file type, and displays the image in the ImageMan control, which looks much like a standard image or picture box control.

The *GetFileName* property provides built-in support for the File Open common dialog box. At run time, this property, when set to 1, displays the File Open dialog, with the masks of all supported file extensions already set for you. Selecting an image file and pressing the OK button loads the image file automatically.

You can also store an image as a field in a database. You can use the ImageMan control as a bound data control, and tie it automatically to a binary field of a database. To do this, assign the *DataSource* and *DataField* properties of the control to the associated data control and database field.

**Manipulating Images**   The ImageMan control provides several properties for manipulating the loaded image. Table 8-5 shows the possible values for the *AutoScale* property, which determines if an image is scaled to fit the size of the control. By default, the control performs no automatic scaling. The control provides two methods of automatic scaling, one that retains the aspect ratio of the image, and the other that stretches the image to fill the entire control.

8 ◄

**Table 8-5** Values for the AutoScale property

| VALUE | MEANING |
| --- | --- |
| 0 | The image is not automatically scaled |
| 1 | The image is scaled to the control with aspect ratio maintained |
| 2 | The image is stretched to fit the control |

If you choose no automatic scaling, the *Magnification* property determines how the image is scaled. A magnification level of 100 displays the image at its actual size, while values of 50 and 200 display the image at half and twice its normal size, respectively.

You can use the *ScaleHeight* and *ScaleWidth* properties to crop the right and bottom portions of the displayed image. The *ScaleLeft* and *ScaleTop* properties determine how much of the left and top sides of the image are cropped. You can use these two properties to scroll the image. The control automatically displays scroll bars as necessary when the *ScrollBars* property is *True*. When the user scrolls images using the scroll bars, the control automatically updates the *ScaleLeft* and *ScaleTop* properties.

The image itself can be processed in a variety of ways, including color reduction, rotation, and mirroring. Use the *ReduceTo* property to color reduce an image. You set this property to the number of colors the resultant image should have. The values for *ReduceTo* are shown in Table 8-6.

**Table 8-6** Values for the ReduceTo property

| VALUE | MEANING |
| --- | --- |
| 1 | 1-bit (black and white) |
| 2 | 8-bit (256-level grayscale) |
| 3 | 4-bit (16 colors) |
| 4 | 8-bit (256 colors) |

You can use the *ReduceTo* property in conjunction with the *DitherMethod* property, which defines what dithering algorithm (Bayer, Burkes, Floyd-Steinberg, or none) should be applied when reducing the color.

Use the *Rotate* property to rotate an image in multiples of 90 degrees (90, 180, or 270). Rotation values are cumulative, so setting the *Rotate* property to 90 four times will bring the image back to its original orientation. To horizontally or vertically flip the image, use the *Mirror* property.

**Determining Supported Image Formats**  Rather than hard-coding the image formats your program supports into your application, you can query the *Extensions* property array. This array of strings lists the image file extensions supported by ImageMan. The number of extensions in the list is returned by the *ExtensionCount* property. *Extensions* lets you code open-ended support; if a new version of ImageMan supports more image formats, you can switch out controls, but may not need to rewrite your code.

**Printing Images**  You print an image by setting the *DoPrint* property to 1. Before doing this, however, you need to define the area of the printed page on which the image will appear. The *DstLeft, DstTop, DstRight,* and *DstBottom* properties define the target area on the printed page. Additionally, you need to set the ImageMan control's *PrnhDC* property to the device context of the printer, *Printer.hDC.*

If only a portion of the image is to be printed, you can use the *SrcLeft, SrcTop, SrcRight,* and *SrcBottom* properties to select some rectangular area of the image. The image defined by these four properties is then mapped to the destination area defined by the four *Dst* properties.

**Saving Images**  You can save an image to disk by assigning a file name to the *SaveAs* property. The format of the image is determined by the file's extension. If *SaveAs* is assigned an empty string, a Save As file dialog box is displayed, allowing the user to enter or select a file name. A string property, *SaveOptions,* lets you set a variety of compression and multipage document options.

# Example

The example program, shown in Figure 8-5, provides the framework for a document imaging application. It uses the ImageMan image control to display digitized documents, which are stored within an Access database. ImageMan is a bound control, so no code was required to load the image from the database and display it.

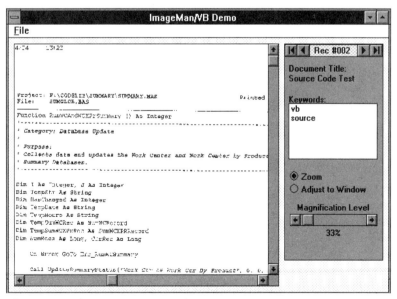

**Figure 8-5** The ImageMan example program

The application lets the user add new records, assigning an image file when the record is created. The image is then stored as a binary field within the Access database. The data control is used to move from record to record.

The user can print the image in the current record using the Print option on the File menu. The printing subroutine sets margins on the destination page, and maintains the aspect ratio of the image while scaling the image to the width of the page.

The option buttons and magnification scroll bar let the user control the display of the image itself. The magnification ability is especially necessary when attempting to read digitized documents, whose legibility can vary greatly.

## Steps

1. Create a new project called IMAGEMAN.MAK. Add the ImageMan image control, IMVB3.VBX, and the Microsoft Common Dialog control, CMDIALOG.VBX, to the project. Create a new form with the objects and properties described in Table 8-7. Save this form as IMAGEMAN.FRM.

**Table 8-7** Objects and properties of IMAGEMAN.FRM

| OBJECT | PROPERTY | SETTING |
| --- | --- | --- |
| Form | FormName | frmImageMan |
| | BackColor | &H00E0FFFF& |
| | Caption | "ImageMan/VB Demo" |
| ImageMan | Name | ImageMan1 |
| | AutoDraw | 0 'False |
| | AutoScale | 0 'None |
| | BackColor | &H00FFFFFF& |
| | DataField | "DocImage" |
| | DataSource | "Data1" |
| | Ext | " " |
| | Picture | " " |
| | ScaleLeft | 0 |
| | ScaleTop | 0 |
| | Scrollbars | -1 'True |
| | Select | 0 'False |
| PictureBox | Name | picContainer |
| | BackColor | &H00C0C0C0& |

2. Place the controls listed in Table 8-8 inside the picContainer PictureBox control. Make sure to select the picContainer control on the form before placing these controls inside it.

**Table 8-8** Controls contained within the picContainer PictureBox control

| OBJECT | PROPERTY | SETTING |
| --- | --- | --- |
| Label | Name | Label1 |
| | BackStyle | 0 'Transparent |
| | Caption | "Document Title:" |
| Label | Name | lblDocTitle |
| | BackStyle | 0 'Transparent |
| | DataField | "DocName" |
| | DataSource | "Data1" |
| | ForeColor | &H00800000& |
| Label | Name | Label2 |
| | BackStyle | 0 'Transparent |
| | Caption | "Keywords:" |
| Label | Name | Label3 |
| | Alignment | 2 'Center |
| | BackStyle | 0 'Transparent |
| | Caption | "Magnification Level" |
| Label | Name | lblMagLevel |
| | Alignment | 2 'Center |
| | BackStyle | 0 'Transparent |
| | ForeColor | &H00800000& |
| Data | Name | Data1 |
| | BackColor | &H0080FFFF& |
| | Connect | " " |
| | DatabaseName | "DOCUMENT.MDB" |
| | Exclusive | 0 'False |
| | Options | 0 |
| | ReadOnly | 0 'False |
| | RecordSource | "Documents" |
| ListBox | Name | lstKeywords |
| OptionButton | Name | optSize |
| | BackColor | &H00C0C0C0& |
| | Caption | "Zoom" |
| | Index | 0 |
| OptionButton | Name | optSize |
| | BackColor | &H00C0C0C0& |
| | Caption | "Adjust to Window" |
| | Index | 1 |
| | Value | -1 'True |

*(continued on next page)*

8 ◄

| OBJECT | PROPERTY | SETTING |
|--------|----------|---------|
| *(continued from previous page)* | | |
| HScrollBar | Name | hscrMaglevel |
| | LargeChange | 25 |
| | Max | 200 |
| | Min | 25 |
| | SmallChange | 25 |
| | Value | 100 |

3. Add a menu to IMAGEMAN.FRM using the Visual Basic Menu Design window, setting the captions and names as shown in Table 8-9.

**Table 8-9** Menu definition for IMAGEMAN.FRM

| CAPTION | NAME |
|---------|------|
| &File | mnuFile |
| ————&Add Document | mnuFileAdd |
| ————&Print Document | mnuFilePrint |
| ————- | mnuFileSep1 |
| ————E&xit | mnuFileExit |

4. After creating the IMAGEMAN.FRM, add the following code to its declarations section.

```
Option Explicit
'------------------------------------------------
' Constants, variables, and declarations used in
' IMAGEMAN.FRM.
'------------------------------------------------

Const MINIMIZED = 1

Dim MinFormWidth As Integer
Dim MinFormHeight As Integer

Declare Sub SetMapMode Lib "gdi.exe" (ByVal hDC As Integer, ByVal Mode As Integer)
```

5. Add the following subroutines to the IMAGEMAN.FRM form.

```
Sub BuildKeywordList (AList As ListBox, ByVal KeyWords As String)
'------------------------------------------------
' Parse individual words out of the keyword string,
' and load into the list box.
'------------------------------------------------
Dim pos As Integer

    On Error GoTo BuildKeywordList_Error

    ' Clear the current list contents.
    AList.Clear
```

```
    ' Move through the string, parsing contents.
    While Len(KeyWords) > 0
        pos = InStr(KeyWords, ";")
        If pos = 0 Then pos = Len(KeyWords) + 1
        AList.AddItem Left$(KeyWords, pos - 1)
        KeyWords = Mid$(KeyWords, pos + 1)
    Wend
Exit Sub
BuildKeywordList_Error:
    KeyWords = ""
    Resume Next
End Sub

Sub Data1_Reposition ()
'--------------------------------------------------
' Parse a new keyword string and update the
' ImageMan control when we move to a new record.
'--------------------------------------------------

    If Not IsNull(Data1.Recordset!DocKeywords) Then
        BuildKeywordList lstKeywords, Data1.Recordset!DocKeywords
    End If
    Data1.Caption = " Rec #" & Format$(Data1.Recordset!DocNumber, "00#")
    ImageMan1.Refresh
End Sub

Sub Form_Load ()
'--------------------------------------------------
' Position and initialize the main form.
'--------------------------------------------------

    ' Center the form on the screen.
    Me.Move (Screen.Width - Me.Width) \ 2, (Screen.Height - Me.Height) \ 2

    ' Remember the form's original dimensions.
    MinFormWidth = Me.Width
    MinFormHeight = Me.Height

    Me.Show

    ' Set the image display defaults.
    hscrMagLevel_Change
    optSize_Click 1
End Sub

Sub Form_Resize ()
'--------------------------------------------------
' Adjust the size of the ImageMan control when
' the form is resized.
'--------------------------------------------------
Dim margin As Integer

    If WindowState = MINIMIZED Then Exit Sub

    ' Don't let the window get too small.
    If Me.Width < MinFormWidth Then Me.Width = MinFormWidth
    If Me.Height < MinFormHeight Then Me.Height = MinFormHeight

    margin = ImageMan1.Left
```

(continued on next page)

8 ◀

*(continued from previous page)*

```
    ImageMan1.Top = margin
    picContainer.Top = margin

    ' Left align controls.
    ImageMan1.Width = Me.ScaleWidth - picContainer.Width - (margin * 3)
    picContainer.Left = Me.ScaleWidth - picContainer.Width - margin

    ' Top align controls.
    ImageMan1.Height = Me.ScaleHeight - (margin * 2)
End Sub

Sub hscrMagLevel_Change ()
'----------------------------------------------------
' Adjust the magnification level of the image.
'----------------------------------------------------

    ' Update the label.
    lblMagLevel = Format$(hscrMagLevel) & "%"
    If hscrMagLevel = 100 Then lblMagLevel = "Actual Size (" & lblMagLevel & ")"

    ' Change the ImageMan control magnification.
    ImageMan1.Magnification = hscrMagLevel
    ImageMan1.Refresh
End Sub

Sub mnuFileAdd_Click ()
'----------------------------------------------------
' Load the "Add Record" form modally.
'----------------------------------------------------
    frmAddRecord.Show 1
End Sub

Sub mnuFileExit_Click ()
'----------------------------------------------------
' Exit the program.
'----------------------------------------------------
    Unload Me
End Sub

Sub mnuFilePrint_Click ()
'----------------------------------------------------
' Print the current record's image to the default
' printer.
'----------------------------------------------------
Dim PageCenterX As Integer, PageCenterY As Integer
Dim iWidth As Integer, iHeight As Integer
Dim nWidth As Integer, nHeight As Integer
Dim Res As Integer
Dim margin As Integer

    ' Determine the image's dots-per-inch resolution.
    Res = ImageMan1.ImageXRes
    If Res = 0 Then Res = 300

    ' Calculate the center of the page.
    PageCenterX = Printer.ScaleWidth / 2
    PageCenterY = (Printer.ScaleHeight / 2) * -1
```

```
    ' Set an arbitrary margin value.
    margin = Printer.ScaleWidth / 10

    ' Calculate the image size in Twips.
    iWidth = ImageMan1.ImageWidth * 1440 / Res
    iHeight = ImageMan1.ImageHeight * 1440 / Res

    ' Set the printer image's dimensions.
    nWidth = iWidth * ((Printer.ScaleWidth - margin) / iWidth)
    nHeight = iHeight * ((Printer.ScaleWidth - margin) / iWidth)

    ' Set the print position for the image.
    ImageMan1.DstLeft = PageCenterX - nWidth / 2
    ImageMan1.DstTop = PageCenterY + nHeight / 2
    ImageMan1.DstRight = PageCenterX + nWidth / 2
    ImageMan1.DstBottom = PageCenterY - nHeight / 2

    Printer.Print ""
    ImageMan1.PrnHdc = Printer.hDC

    ' Set printer to MM_TWIPS (declared from windows GDI).
    SetMapMode Printer.hDC, 6

    Me.MousePointer = CSR_HOURGLASS

    ImageMan1.DoPrint = 1
    Printer.EndDoc

    MousePointer = CSR_NORMAL
End Sub

Sub optSize_Click (index As Integer)
'----------------------------------------------------
' Toggle between magnification sizing and window-fit
' sizing.
'----------------------------------------------------
    ImageMan1.AutoScale = index
    If index = 1 Then
        hscrMagLevel.Enabled = False
    Else
        hscrMagLevel.Enabled = True
        ImageMan1.Magnification = hscrMagLevel
    End If
    ImageMan1.Refresh
End Sub
```

6. Create a second form with the objects and properties described in Table 8-10. Save this form as ADDREC.FRM.

**Table 8-10** Objects and properties of ADDREC.FRM

| OBJECT | PROPERTY | SETTING |
|--------|----------|---------|
| Form | FormName | frmAddRecord |
| | BackColor | &H00C0C0C0& |
| | BorderStyle | 3 'Fixed Double |
| | Caption | "Add Image Record" |

*(continued on next page)*

| OBJECT | PROPERTY | SETTING |
|---|---|---|
| *(continued from previous page)* | | |
| | MaxButton | 0 'False |
| | MinButton | 0 'False |
| Label | Name | Label1 |
| | BackStyle | 0 'Transparent |
| | Caption | "Document Title:" |
| | ForeColor | &H00800000& |
| Label | Name | Label2 |
| | BackStyle | 0 'Transparent |
| | Caption | "Keywords:" |
| | ForeColor | &H00800000& |
| Label | Name | Label3 |
| | BackStyle | 0 'Transparent |
| | Caption | "Image File Name:" |
| | ForeColor | &H00800000& |
| Label | Name | lblImageName |
| | BackColor | &H00E0FFFF& |
| | BorderStyle | 1 'Fixed Single |
| TextBox | Name | txtDocName |
| | MaxLength | 30 |
| TextBox | Name | txtDocKeywords |
| | MaxLength | 40 |
| CommandButton | Name0 | btnSelectImage |
| | Caption | "&Select Image" |
| CommandButton | Name | btnAddRecord |
| | Caption | "&Add Record" |
| CommandButton | Name | btnCancel |
| | Cancel | -1 'True |
| | Caption | "&Cancel" |
| CommonDialog | Name | CMDialog1 |

7. After creating IMAGEMAN.FRM, add the following subroutines.

```
Sub btnAddRecord_Click ()
'-------------------------------------------------
' Add a new record to the image database.
'-------------------------------------------------
Dim NewRecNum As Integer
Dim retcode As Integer

    On Error GoTo btnAddRecord_Error

    ' Don't add the record if they haven't selected an image.
```

```
    If lblImageName = "" Then
        MsgBox "You must select an image before adding a new record.", MB_OK Or
MB_ICONINFORMATION, "Adding Document Record"
        Exit Sub
    End If

    retcode = 0
    frmImageMan.Data1.Recordset.MoveLast

    ' Determine the next document number.
    If retcode  0 Then
        NewRecNum = 1
    Else
        NewRecNum = frmImageMan.Data1.Recordset!DocNumber + 1
    End If

    retcode = 0

    ' Add a new record, and assign new field values.
    frmImageMan.Data1.Recordset.AddNew

    frmImageMan.Data1.Recordset!DocNumber = NewRecNum
    frmImageMan.Data1.Recordset!DocName = txtDocName
    frmImageMan.Data1.Recordset!DocKeywords = txtDocKeywords
    frmImageMan.ImageMan1.Picture = lblImageName
    frmImageMan.Data1.Recordset.Update

    ' Move to the new record, assign the image file to the image field,
    ' and update the database.
    frmImageMan.Data1.Recordset.MoveLast
    frmImageMan.Data1.Recordset.Edit
    frmImageMan.ImageMan1.Picture = lblImageName
    frmImageMan.Data1.Recordset.Update

    Unload Me
Exit Sub
btnAddRecord_Error:
    retcode = Err
    Resume Next
End Sub

Sub btnCancel_Click ()
'----------------------------------------------------
' Unload the "Add Record" form.
'----------------------------------------------------
    Unload Me
End Sub

Sub btnSelectImage_Click ()
'----------------------------------------------------
' Display the standard file dialog to get an
' image file name.
'----------------------------------------------------
Dim fnum As Integer
Dim i As Integer, f As Integer, b As Integer
Dim Astr As String, ext As String
Dim Canceled As Integer

    On Error GoTo btnSelectImage_Error
```

*(continued on next page)*

8 ◀

*(continued from previous page)*

```
    Canceled = False
    cmDialog1.Flags = OFN_HIDEREADONLY
    cmDialog1.CancelError = True
    cmDialog1.Filter = "Image Files|*.pcx;*.dcx;*.tif;*.bmp;*.gif"
    cmDialog1.DialogTitle = "Select a Document Image File"

    ' Display the standard dialog.
    cmDialog1.Action = 1

    ' If no file was selected, then exit.
    If (Canceled) Or (cmDialog1.Filename = "") Then Exit Sub

    ' Assign the file name the label control.
    lblImageName = LCase$(cmDialog1.Filename)

Exit Sub

btnSelectImage_Error:
    Canceled = True
    Resume Next
End Sub

Sub Form_Load ()
'-------------------------------------------------
' Center the form on the screen.
'-------------------------------------------------
    Me.Move (Screen.Width - Me.Width) \ 2, (Screen.Height - Me.Height) \ 2
End Sub
```

8. Using the Visual Basic Data Manager, or another Access database tool, build the database described in Table 8-11. This database should be called DOCUMENT.MDB, and saved in the same directory as the application.

**Table 8-11** Database definition for DOCUMENT.MDB

| FIELD NAME | TYPE | SIZE | INDEX INFORMATION |
|------------|------|------|-------------------|
| DocNumber | Integer | 2 | Unique Primary Index |
| DocName | String | 30 | |
| DocImage | Binary | 0 | |
| Dockeywords | String | 40 | |

# Tips and Comments

The wide variety of supported image formats and image processing options make the ImageMan control useful for many imaging and multimedia applications. The scanning and multipage document support, coupled with ImageMan's bound data control capabilities, make this package especially well-suited for document imaging applications. The remaining hurdle is still the huge amount of disk real estate that images, even compressed ones, take up.

# ImageStream - VB (ISVB.VBX)

| USAGE: | Image Processing |
|---|---|
| MANUFACTURER: | Visual Tools |
| COST: | $295 |

The ImageStream image control can display and manipulate a wide variety of bitmapped and vector images. Supported image formats include Adobe Illustrator (.AI), Windows Bitmap (.BMP), CorelDRAW (.CDR), Harvard Graphics (.CHT and .CH3), Micrographx Drawings (.DRW), AutoCAD (.DXF), and Kodak Photo CD (.PCD), as well as numerous other formats. The ImageStream control can be used as a bound data control, which means that images can be stored and retrieved as fields in databases. The ImageStream control also features a wide variety of built-in dialog boxes for reading in, saving, and manipulating images.

## Syntax

Since the ImageStream control supports the numerous image file formats, it is an appropriate tool for image display and conversion, especially if your application needs to process some of the less common file formats that other image controls don't support. The ImageStream control's nonstandard properties and event are listed in Table 8-12.

**Table 8-12** Nonstandard properties and event of the ImageStream control

### PROPERTIES

| | | |
|---|---|---|
| bBox_bottom | bBox_left | bBox_right |
| bBox_top | Brightness | ClipboardOpt |
| Contrast | Copy | CopyMF |
| Cut | Display | ErrorCode |
| ErrorPrmt | ErrorString | ExportFileHandle |
| ExportFileSpec | ExportFileType | FileOffset |
| Gamma | Height_Inches | hMF |
| ImportFileHandle | ImportFileSpec | ImportFileType |
| Inch | Left_DClk | Left_ShiftDClk |
| MarginBottom | MarginLeft | MarginRight |
| MarginTop | Open | PaletteMode |
| Paste | Preferences | PrintImage |
| PrintSetup | PrintSize | Right_CClk |
| Right_ShiftDClk | SaveAs | ViewMode |
| Width_Inches | Zoom | |

### EVENT

Change

8 ◀

**Loading an Image into the ImageStream Control**   There are two ways to load an image from a file. Using the *ImportFileSpec* property, you can simply assign a file name and the image is loaded and displayed. The second method is to use ImageStream's built-in File Open dialog box, which looks much like the standard File dialog, but sports a Preview Picture area. You can highlight the name of a file and then press a Preview button to see the image. Once you've found the image you want, just press the OK button and the picture is loaded and displayed. The File Open dialog is displayed using the *Open* property, as shown here:

```
' Display the File Open dialog and load an image.
ISVB1.Open = True
```

Since ImageStream can also serve as a bound data control, you can load images that have been stored in databases. To do this, you set the *DataSource* and *DataField* properties to point to a particular database table and field. After that, images are automatically loaded and displayed from that table.

You can also load images from the Windows Clipboard using the *Paste* property. When set to *True,* this property copies the current contents of the Clipboard (which might be a bitmap, device-independent bitmap (.DIB), or metafile) into the specified control. The complements of the *Paste* property are the *Cut* and *Copy* properties. These, too, are Boolean properties that, when set to *True,* copy the contents of an ImageStream control to the Clipboard. Since pictures can be stored in the Windows Clipboard in several different formats, the *ClipboardOpt* property specifies what format should be used when executing cuts and copies. The valid values for this property are listed in Table 8-13.

**Table 8-13** Values for the ClipboardOpt property

| VALUE | MEANING |
| --- | --- |
| 0 | Metafile format |
| 1 | Bitmap format |
| 2 | DIB (Device Independent Bitmap) format |
| 3 | All formats |

**Image Processing**   Several properties let you alter the color values of an image. *Contrast, Brightness,* and *Gamma* are all integer properties within the range −100 to +100. By default, these values are 0 for a newly loaded image. Setting them to positive or negative values alters the appearance of the image. For example, setting a positive *Contrast* value increases the image's contrast, while a negative value decreases it. When the *Brightness* property is set to positive values, the RGB values of the image are moved toward white; negative values move the RGB values toward black. With *Gamma* settings, the middle RGB values are moved toward white when positive values are assigned.

**Built-In Dialogs**   In addition to the File Open dialog, the ImageStream control provides a number of other built-in dialogs. The preference dialog lets the user change certain image preprocessing values before a new image file is loaded or saved. Images can be color reduced and their image sizes changed, among other things, via the preference dialogs. Different image formats allow different sets of preferences, so the dialogs contain different settings depending upon the file format. The user accesses the preference dialog by marking a check box in the File Open or Save As dialog box. This check box is only displayed if the image's *Preference* property is set to *True*. Figure 8-6 show an example preference dialog.

Once an image is loaded, the user can change several image properties—including the contrast, brightness, and gamma values—using the View Options dialog. The dialog also lets the user set the scaling option of the image. The user can either display the image actual size, "best fit" (which fills as much of the window as possible while retaining the aspect ratio), or "stretch to fit" (which fills the entire window, ignoring the aspect ratio).

To let the user display the View Options dialog, you must tie it to a special mouse double-click event. There are four special properties called *Left_DClk, Left_ShiftDClk, Right_DClk,* and *Right_ShiftDClk.* These four properties tell the ImageStream control what action to take when the user double-clicks the left or right mouse button, either with or without the keyboard (SHIFT) key pressed. By default, nothing occurs during these mouse events; Table 8-14 lists the events that you can assign to them.

**Table 8-14** Values for the _DClk properties

| VALUE | MEANING |
| --- | --- |
| 0 | No action is taken |
| 1 | Zoom in |
| 2 | Zoom out |
| 3 | Display the View Options dialog |

**Printing an Image**  To print an image, simply set its Boolean *PrintImage* property to *True*. By default, the image prints at its actual size. If you want more control over how the image is placed on the printed page, you can take advantage of several properties. The *MarginBottom, MarginLeft, MarginRight,* and *MarginTop* properties set the margins (in inches) for the printed page. The *PrintSize* property determines the scale at which the image is printed; its values are listed in Table 8-15.

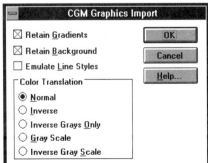

**Figure 8-6** An example preference dialog

**Table 8-15** Values for the PrintSize property

| VALUE | MEANING |
|---|---|
| 0 | Actual size |
| 1 | Best fit (maintain aspect ratio) |
| 2 | Stretch to fit (doesn't maintain aspect ratio) |

The *PrintSetup* property, when set to *True,* displays the standard printer setup dialog, allowing the user to change print settings such as page orientation and print quality.

**Saving an Image**   As with loading an image, you have two choices when saving an image. You can either supply a file name to the *ExportFileSpec* property, which then initiates the saving of the file, or you can set the *SaveAs* property to *True,* providing the user with a built-in Save As dialog box.

**Palette Adjustment**   When displaying multiple images, particularly images that include numerous colors, one problem that can crop up is *palette shifting.* For example, a 256-color Windows driver can display only 256 colors at one time, although the total number of different colors that can be displayed is considerably larger. If only one 256-color image is displayed—say a photograph of red roses—the palette can be optimized for that image, which will consist mostly of shades of red. If you then attempt to display a second image alongside the first—this time perhaps a photograph of earth from space— you may have a problem. The second picture is mostly shades of blue, but the current (rose) palette may have few, if any blues available. Windows will automatically shift palettes to accommodate this, and display the earth colors correctly. As a result, however, the palette has few if any reds available for the roses image, and the roses will suffer. If you return focus to the roses image by clicking on it, or by some other means, Windows will again shift palettes and restore the roses to their former glory. As you would now suspect, the earth suffers.

You may have seen this bizarre palette shifting before when running multiple applications that display images or use nonstandard colors. ImageStream provides a property, *PaletteMode,* that is quite useful for handling situations like this. The *PaletteMode* property has three settings. The first setting (0) simply uses the default palette when displaying an image. The second setting (1) displays the image with a palette optimized just for that image. This can have adverse effects on other images displayed simultaneously. Finally, there is a setting (2) to optimize the palette for all ImageStream controls on the screen. This setting is often the best trade-off. While each image will be altered somewhat, unless the colors in the pictures are radically different, the images should still remain relatively clear and recognizable.

# Example

Palette shifting is at the heart of the example program. This program, shown in Figure 8-7, lets you load an image from a file into the main ImageStream control. The main image can then be copied to one of the three thumbnail ImageStream controls. Because the main

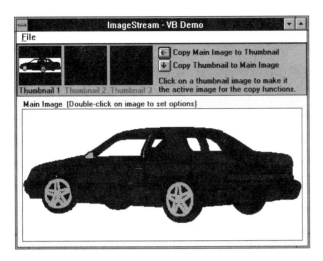

**Figure 8-7** The ImageStream example program

image's *PaletteMode* property is set to 2, global palette optimization is performed. This means that all four possible images (the main image and three thumbnails) will share an average palette. If you load several 256-color images, you will see subtle, and sometimes not-so-subtle, shifts in the appearance of each picture.

The example program tries to make good use of the built-in dialogs, to show these features can reduce the amount of code required. For example, double-clicking within the main image control triggers the View Options dialog box, which lets the user change the scaling and color values of the main image.

## Steps

1. Create a new project called IMAGSTRM.MAK. Add the ImageStream image control, ISVB.VBX, to the project. Create a new form with the objects and properties described in Table 8-16. Save this form as IMAGSTRM.FRM.

**Table 8-16** Objects and properties of IMAGSTRM.FRM

| OBJECT | PROPERTY | SETTING |
|--------|----------|---------|
| Form | FormName | frmImageStream |
|  | BackColor | &H00E0FFFF& |
|  | Caption | "ImageStream - VB Demo" |
| Label | Name | Label1 |
|  | BackStyle | 0 'Transparent |
|  | Caption | "Main Image" |
| Label | Name | Label4 |
|  | BackStyle | 0 'Transparent |
|  | Caption | "(Double-click on image to set options)" |

(continued on next page)

| OBJECT | PROPERTY | SETTING |
|---|---|---|
| *(continued from previous page)* | | |
| | ForeColor | &H00000080& |
| ISVB | Name | ISVB1 |
| | BackColor | &H00FFFFFF& |
| | ClipboardOpt | 0 'MetaFile |
| | Display | -1 'True |
| | PaletteMode | 2 'Global |
| | Preferences | 0 'False |
| | PrintSize | 0 'Actual Size |
| PictureBox | Name | Picture1 |
| | Align | 1 'Align Top |
| | BackColor | &H00C0C0C0& |

2. Place the contols shown in Table 8-17 inside the Picture1 PictureBox control. Make sure to select the Picture1 control on the form before adding these controls.

**Table 8-17** Controls contained inside the Picture1 PictureBox control

| OBJECT | PROPERTY | SETTING |
|---|---|---|
| Label | Name | lblImages |
| | Alignment | 2 'Center |
| | BackStyle | 0 'Transparent |
| | Caption | "Thumbnail 1" |
| | Index | 0 |
| Label | Name | lblImages |
| | Alignment | 2 'Center |
| | BackStyle | 0 'Transparent |
| | Caption | "Thumbnail 2" |
| | Index | 1 |
| Label | Name | lblImages |
| | Alignment | 2 'Center |
| | BackStyle | 0 'Transparent |
| | Caption | "Thumbnail 3" |
| | Index | 2 |
| Label | Name | Label2 |
| | BackStyle | 0 'Transparent |
| | Caption | "Copy Main Image to Thumbnail" |
| Label | Name | Label3 |
| | BackStyle | 0 'Transparent |
| | Caption | "Copy Thumbnail to Main Image" |
| Label | Name | Label5 |

| OBJECT | PROPERTY | SETTING |
|---|---|---|
| | BackStyle | 0 'Transparent |
| | Caption | "Click on a thumbnail image to make it the active image for the copy functions." |
| | ForeColor | &H00800000& |
| ISVB | Name | ISVBThumbNail |
| | BackColor | &H00000000& |
| | Index | 0 |
| | PaletteMode | 1 'Local |
| | ViewMode | 1 'Best Fit |
| ISVB | Name | ISVBThumbNail |
| | BackColor | &H00000000& |
| | Index | 1 |
| | PaletteMode | 1 'Local |
| | ViewMode | 1 'Best Fit |
| ISVB | Name | ISVBThumbNail |
| | BackColor | &H00000000& |
| | Index | 2 |
| | PaletteMode | 1 'Local |
| | ViewMode | 1 'Best Fit |
| CommandButton | Name | btnCopyFromMain |
| | Caption | "ß" |
| | FontName | "Wingdings" |
| CommandButton | Name | btnCopyToMain |
| | Caption | "â" |
| | FontName | "Wingdings" |

3. Add a menu to IMAGSTRM.FRM using the Visual Basic Menu Design window, setting the captions and names shown in Table 8-18.

**Table 8-18** Menu definition for IMAGSTRM.FRM

| CAPTION | NAME |
|---|---|
| &File | mnuFile |
| ----&Open | mnuFileOpen |
| ----&Clear | mnuFileClear |
| ----Save &As | mnuFileSaveAs |
| ----- | mnuFileSep1 |
| ----&Print | mnuFilePrint |
| ----P&rint Setup | mnuFilePrintSetup |
| ----- | mnuFileSep2 |
| ----E&xit | mnuFileExit |

**8**

4. Add the following code to the declarations section of the IMAGSTRM.FRM form.

```
Option Explicit
'-----------------------------------------------------
' Constants and variables used in the ImageStream
' example program.
'-----------------------------------------------------

' Color constants used for thumbnail labels.
Const RED = &H80&
Const DK_GRAY = &H808080

' WindowState constant.
Const MINIMIZED = 1

' Constant used to set main image double-click action.
Const VIEW_OPTIONS_DLG = 3

' The number of thumbnail images.
Const NumImages = 3

' The minimum form dimensions.
Dim MinFormWidth As Integer
Dim MinFormHeight As Integer

' The index of the currently active thumbnail image.
Dim ActiveThumbnail As Integer
```

5. Add the following subroutines to the IMAGSTRM.FRM form. This example program is very short, even though it seems to be doing quite a bit. This is mainly due to the large set of built-in dialogs that ImageStream provides, making it possible to include many extra functions automatically.

```
Sub btnCopyFromMain_Click ()
'-----------------------------------------------------
' Copy the main image to the currently selected
' thumbnail image via the Clipboard.
'-----------------------------------------------------

    ISVB1.Copy = True
    ISVBThumbNail(ActiveThumbnail).Paste = True
End Sub

Sub btnCopyToMain_Click ()
'-----------------------------------------------------
' Copy the currently selected thumbnail image to
' the main image via the Clipboard.
'-----------------------------------------------------

    ISVB1.ImportFileSpec = ""
    ISVBThumbNail(ActiveThumbnail).Copy = True
    ISVB1.Paste = True
End Sub

Sub Form_Load ()
'-----------------------------------------------------
' Set initial options and form position.
'-----------------------------------------------------
```

```
    ' Center the form on the screen.
    Me.Move (Screen.Width - Me.Width) \ 2, (Screen.Height - Me.Height) \ 2

    ' The initial size of the form is the smallest size allowed.
    MinFormWidth = Me.Width
    MinFormHeight = Me.Height

    Me.Show

    ' The first thumbnail image is initially active.
    ISVBThumbNail_Click 0

    ' Show the View Options dialog when user double-clicks
    ' on the main image.
    ISVB1.Left_DClk = VIEW_OPTIONS_DLG
End Sub

Sub Form_Resize ()
'---------------------------------------------------
' Resize the main form.
'---------------------------------------------------

    ' Don't resize if they minimized.
    If WindowState = MINIMIZED Then Exit Sub

    ' Don't let form get too small.
    If Me.Width < MinFormWidth Then Me.Width = MinFormWidth
    If Me.Height < MinFormHeight Then Me.Height = MinFormHeight

    ' Adjust the main image control to the new window size.
    ISVB1.Width = Me.ScaleWidth - (ISVB1.Left * 2)
    ISVB1.Height = Me.ScaleHeight - ISVB1.Top - ISVB1.Left
End Sub

Sub ISVBThumbNail_Click (index As Integer)
'---------------------------------------------------
' Set a new active thumbnail when the user clicks
' on a thumbnail image.
'---------------------------------------------------
Dim i As Integer

    For i = 0 To NumImages - 1
        If i = index Then
            lblImages(i).ForeColor = RED
            ActiveThumbnail = i
        Else
            lblImages(i).ForeColor = DK_GRAY
        End If
    Next
End Sub

Sub mnuFileClear_Click ()
'---------------------------------------------------
' Clear the current picture from the main image
' control.
'---------------------------------------------------
    ISVB1.ImportFileSpec = ""
End Sub

Sub mnuFileExit_Click ()
```

8

*(continued on next page)*

*(continued from previous page)*

```
'----------------------------------------------------------------
' Exit the program.
'----------------------------------------------------------------
    Unload Me
End Sub

Sub mnuFileOpen_Click ()
'----------------------------------------------------------------
' Use the built-in File Open dialog to select an
' image file.
'----------------------------------------------------------------

    ' Display the Preferences check box in the File dialog.
    ISVB1.Preferences = True

    ' Show the File dialog.
    ISVB1.Open = True
End Sub

Sub mnuFilePrint_Click ()
'----------------------------------------------------------------
' Print the main image.
'----------------------------------------------------------------
    ISVB1.PrintImage = True
End Sub

Sub mnuFilePrintSetup_Click ()
'----------------------------------------------------------------
' Display the default printer setup dialog box.
'----------------------------------------------------------------
    ISVB1.PrintSetup = True
End Sub

Sub mnuFileSaveAs_Click ()
'----------------------------------------------------------------
' Save the main image using the built-in Save As
' dialog box.
'----------------------------------------------------------------
    ISVB1.SaveAs = True
End Sub
```

## Tips and Comments

The diversity of the image formats supported by ImageStream is enough to recommend it for projects where something other than just TIF, GIF, and BMP formats need to be supported (although those formats are supported as well). Support for these file formats is through *import* and *export filters*. These filters are Windows executable files with a special .FLT extension. For each image file format you want to support, you must also distribute its associated filters, which can run from 30 to 140K per filter.

**JPEG Image Compressor VBX (VSIMAGE.VBX)**

| USAGE: | Manipulation and Compression of Bitmapped Images |
|---|---|
| MANUFACTURER: | Crisp Technology Inc. |
| COST: | $199 |

The JPEG Image Compressor control can display, print, and compress images. It supports many of the popular image file formats, including TIFF, Targa, GIF, BMP, PCX, and DIB, as well as JPEG compressed images. JPEG is an acronym for Joint Photographic Experts Group, the originators of the file format. JPEG is a *lossy* compression method, meaning that some image data may be lost or modified during the compression process. JPEG compression can be "tuned" to provide greater compression but lower picture quality.

## Syntax

On the surface, the JPEG control works very much like a standard picture box control. You place the JPEG control on a form as you would place an ordinary picture box, and use it to display bitmaps. The JPEG control goes considerably farther, however, allowing you to import images from a variety of different formats. You can compress these images into JPEG format, or convert and save them to other image formats. You can control the amount of JPEG compression you want, to either optimize picture quality or minimize file size.

The JPEG control has a number of nonstandard properties, mostly for returning information about an image or image file (such as its dimensions or format) or for setting up the image to print. Table 8-19 lists the control's nonstandard properties.

**8** ◀

**Table 8-19** Nonstandard properties for the JPEG Image Compressor control

| | | |
|---|---|---|
| Action | AutoRedraw | AutoSize |
| DibCopy | DibHandle | DispBitsPerPixel |
| EraseBackgnd | FileName | InfoDibBitCount |
| InfoDibSize | InfoFileBitCount | InfoFileCompress |
| InfoFileFormat | InfoFileSize | InfoHeight |
| InfoStatus | InfoWidth | JpgQuality |
| NewColorNum | OptimalView | OriginX |
| OriginY | Picture | PrnDstHeight |
| PrnDstWidth | PrnDstX | PrnDstY |
| PrnSrcHeight | PrnSrcWidth | PrnSrcX |
| PrnSrcY | SaveFileFormat | ScaleHeight |
| ScaleMode | ScaleWidth | |

**Reading Images**  Many of the functions of the JPEG control are accomplished through the *Action* property. For example, you can retrieve information about an image file on disk without actually loading the image. Simply assign the file's name to the JPEG control's *FileName* property, and then assign the AC_QUERYPICT constant value to the control's *Action* property:

```
vsPix1.FileName = "c:\windows\marble.bmp"
vsPiz1.Action = AC_QUERYPICT
```

The AC_QUERYPICT constant, as well as other constants referenced in this section, are provided in a constants file that is included with the JPEG control. After the query action has been performed, you can inspect one of several *Info* properties. These properties return information about the specified bitmap.

The *InfoFileBitCount* property indicates the number of colors in the current bitmap. This is expressed in terms of bits-per-pixel. Table 8-20 shows the possible return values and the number of colors to which they correspond.

**Table 8-20** Bits-per-pixel values for the InfoFileBitCount property

| VALUE | MEANING |
|---|---|
| 1 | Black and White (1 color) |
| 4 | 16 colors |
| 8 | 256 colors |
| 15 | 32,768 colors |
| 24 | 16 million colors |

The integer *InfoFileCompress* property indicates the type of compression method used on the picture. The integer *InfoFileFormat* property returns the type of image format the file is stored in. *InfoFileSize* returns the number of bytes in the file. The *InfoHeight* and *InfoWidth* properties return the dimensions of the image in pixels.

You can load an image into the JPEG control by using the *Action* property with AC_LOADPICT, or by assigning an image's file name to the *Picture* property.

**Displaying an Image**  A loaded image is automatically displayed within the JPEG control. You can use the *AutoSize* property to resize the picture to fit your needs. By default, the image is displayed with no size adjustment. If the image is larger than the control, a portion of the image will be clipped. With the *AutoSize* option, you can also resize the image to fit the picture (with or without retention of aspect ratio) or resize the control to fit the image size.

You use the *OriginX* and *OriginY* properties to specify the upper-left corner of the image. For example, setting the *OriginY* property to 20 clips the top 20 pixels of the image. These properties allow you to easily construct scrollable views onto large images, as you will do shortly in the example.

**Adjusting the Image**  Several properties let you make changes to a loaded image. The first and most obvious change is to apply JPEG compression to the image. With JPEG compression, you select a quality value between 1 and 100. The higher the value, the better the quality of the resulting image. Lower values can distort the image, but provide better compression. To compress an image, you first set the *JpgQuality* property to your desired quality value, and then set the *Action* property to AC_JPEG_COMPRESS_AND_REFRESH. If you don't specify a *JpgQuality* value, the quality is set to 93 by default.

You can also reduce the number of colors in an image—for example, reducing a 24-bit (16-million color) picture to 256 colors. You do this by setting the *NewColorNum* property to an integer value representing the number of colors, and then setting the associated *Action* property as shown here:

```
vsPix1.NewColorNum = 256
vsPix1.Action = AC_COLOR_REDUCTION
```

Dithering is accomplished in the same way, by setting a new value for *NewColorNum*. But here you set the *Action* property to AC_DITHERING.

Finally, you can apply image smoothing to the picture. Smoothing tends to blur the image, but unlike the previous two processes, it causes no reduction in the number of colors. All that's required for smoothing is to set the *Action* property to AC_SMOOTHING.

**Printing an Image**  By setting the *Action* property to AC_PRINT, you can easily dump the current image to the default printer, using that printer's page orientation. If you need more control over the placement of the image, you can use the eight properties provided for defining the placement of the image on the page. The first four— *PrnSrcHeight, PrnSrcWidth, PrnSrcX,* and *PrnSrcY*—specify what part of the source image is printed. This allows you to crop the image and print just the section you want. The other four properties—*PrnDstHeight, PrnDstWidth, PrnDstX,* and *PrnDstY*—define where on the output page to print the image. These properties permit you to change the aspect ratio of the printed image, and to specify exactly where on the page the image will appear.

**Saving Images**  By default, images are saved to their original formats. However, you can save files to other formats as well. You can use the *SaveFileFormat* property in conjunction with the *FileName* and *Action* properties to convert a file to a new format, as shown here:

```
vsPix1.SaveFileFormat = SF_PCX
vsPix1.FileName = "c:\windows\marble.pcx"
vsPix1.Action = AC_SAVEPICT
```

You only need to use the last line of code if you don't want to change the file. The support SaveFileFormat values are listed in Table 8-21.

**Table 8-21** Values for the SaveFileFormat property

| VALUE | MEANING |
|---|---|
| SF_JPEG | JPEG compressed format |
| SF_TIFLZW | TIFF with LZW compression |
| SF_TIFNOLZW | TIFF without LZW compression |
| SF_PCX | PCX format |
| SF_BMP | BMP format |
| SF_TGA | Targa format |

# Example

The example program illustrates most of the features and capabilities of the JPEG control. Images can be loaded from files, manipulated, printed, and saved back to disk in the same or a different image format. The example program is shown in Figure 8-8.

The example program has a main image area to the left of the main form, with an information and command button area on the upper right. When the user resizes the form, the JPEG control and scroll bars resize, and the information area moves accordingly. The code is contained in the *Form_Resize* event routine. This routine also adjusts the range of the scrollers.

The scrollers to the right and bottom of the JPEG control are not part of the control, but are separate standard scroll bars. They are always "connected" to the picture box. If the image is larger than the control, the *Max* property of the scroller is adjusted so that it's "in sync" with the picture. When the user moves the scrollers, the JPEG control's *OriginX* and *OriginY* properties are adjusted accordingly, effectively scrolling the image.

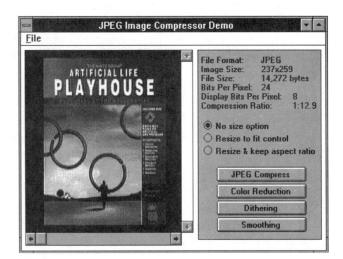

**Figure 8-8** The JPEG Image Compressor example program

The command buttons allow you to JPEG compress, color reduce, dither, and smooth images. The information area describes the properties of the image that was loaded from disk.

## Steps

1. Create a new project called JPEG.MAK. Add the JPEG Image Compressor control, VSIMAGE.VBX, and the Visual Basic Common Dialog control, CMDIALOG.VBX, to the project. Create a new form with the objects and properties described in Table 8-22. Save this form as JPEG.FRM.

**Table 8-22** Objects and properties of JPEG.FRM

| OBJECT | PROPERTY | SETTING |
|---|---|---|
| Form | FormName | frmJPEG |
| | Caption | "JPEG Image Compressor Demo" |
| | ForeColor | &H00000000& |
| PictureBox | Name | picContainer |
| | AutoRedraw | -1 'True |
| | BackColor | &H00C0C0C0& |
| VScrollBar | Name | vscrImage |
| | LargeChange | 25 |
| | SmallChange | 10 |
| HScrollBar | Name | hscrImage |
| | LargeChange | 25 |
| | SmallChange | 10 |
| CommonDialog | Name | CMDialog1 |
| VisionSoft | Name | Picture |
| | AutoRedraw | -1 'True |
| | BackColor | &H00FFFFFF& |
| | OptimalView | -1 'True |

2. Place the controls shown in Table 8-23 inside the picContainer PictureBox control. Make sure to select the picContainer control on the form before adding these controls.

**Table 8-23** Controls contained inside the picContainer PictureBox control

| OBJECT | PROPERTY | SETTING |
|---|---|---|
| CommandButton | Name | btnCompress |
| | Caption | "JPEG Compress" |
| CommandButton | Name | btnReduce |
| | Caption | "Color Reduction" |
| CommandButton | Name | btnDither |
| | Caption | "Dithering" |

*(continued on next page)*

479

| OBJECT | PROPERTY | SETTING |
|---|---|---|
| *(continued from previous page)* | | |
| CommandButton | Name | btnSmooth |
| | Caption | "Smoothing" |
| OptionButton | Name | optAutoSize |
| | BackColor | &H00C0C0C0& |
| | Caption | "No size option" |
| | ForeColor | &H00000000& |
| | Index | 0 |
| | Value | -1 'True |
| OptionButton | Name | optAutoSize |
| | BackColor | &H00C0C0C0& |
| | Caption | "Resize to fit control" |
| | ForeColor | &H00000000& |
| | Index | 1 |
| OptionButton | Name | optAutoSize |
| | BackColor | &H00C0C0C0& |
| | Caption | "Resize && keep aspect ratio" |
| | ForeColor | &H00000000& |
| | Index | 2 |

3. Add a menu to JPEG.FRM using the Visual Basic Menu Design window, setting the captions and names shown in Table 8-24.

**Table 8-24** Menu definition for JPEG.FRM

| CAPTION | NAME |
|---|---|
| &File | mnuFile |
| ————&Open | mnuFileOpen |
| ————&Close | mnuFileClose |
| ————— | mnuFileSep1 |
| ————&Print | mnuFilePrint |
| ————— | mnuFileSep2 |
| ————E&xit | mnuFileExit |

4. Add the constants file, VSPIXVB.TXT, to the project. This file, which comes with the JPEG Image Compressor control, contains the constants used throughout the example program.

5. After creating the form JPEG.FRM as explained in steps 1 through 3, add the following code to its declarations section.

```
Option Explicit
'-------------------------------------------------
' Constants and variables used in the JPEG image
' compressor example program.
'-------------------------------------------------


' Used to space text info in picture box.
Dim LineHeight As Integer
Dim LeftMargin As Integer

' Stores the JPEG image's dimensions to assist in scrolling.
Dim vsPicWidth As Integer
Dim vsPicHeight As Integer

' These are the smallest dimensions to which the form can be sized.
Dim MinFormWidth As Integer
Dim MinFormHeight As Integer

' Cursor (mouse pointer) constants.
Const CSR_NORMAL = 0
Const CSR_HOURGLASS = 11

' WindowState constant.
Const MINIMIZED = 1

' Colors used to write text on picture box.
Const BLUE = &H800000
Const RED = &H80&

' Message box constants.
Const MB_OK = &H0
Const MB_ICONEXCLAMATION = &H30
```

6. Add the following subroutines to the JPEG.FRM form. The *Form_Resize* code shows how to adjust controls to a new form size at run time. While this can require several lines of code, the result is more flexible than a fixed-border form.

```
Sub btnCompress_Click ()
'-------------------------------------------------
' JPEG compress the current image, given a compression
' quality value.
'-------------------------------------------------
Dim answer As String

    answer = InputBox$("Enter the JPEG Compression quality. This value must be in the range 1 ⇒
to 100.", "JPEG Compression")
    If answer = "" Then Exit Sub

    If IsNumeric(answer) Then
        If (Val(answer) >= 1) And (Val(answer) <= 100) Then
            vsPix1.JpgQuality = Val(answer)
            Screen.MousePointer = CSR_HOURGLASS
            vsPix1.Action = AC_JPEG_COMPRESS_AND_REFRESH
            Screen.MousePointer = CSR_NORMAL
            UpdateInfo
        Else
            MsgBox "JPEG Compression quality value is not within the valid range.", MB_OK Or ⇒
MB_ICONEXCLAMATION, "JPEG Compression"
        End If
```

*(continued on next page)*

8 ◀

481

*(continued from previous page)*

```
    Else
      MsgBox "Invalid JPEG Compression value.", MB_OK Or MB_ICONEXCLAMATION, "JPEG Compression"
    End If

End Sub

Sub btnDither_Click ()
'---------------------------------------------------
' Dither the current image, using the number of
' colors specified.
'---------------------------------------------------
Dim answer As String

    answer = InputBox$("Enter the new number of colors", "Image Dithering")
    If answer = "" Then Exit Sub

    If IsNumeric(answer) Then
        vsPix1.NewColorNum = Val(answer)
        Screen.MousePointer = CSR_HOURGLASS
        vsPix1.Action = AC_DITHERING
        Screen.MousePointer = CSR_NORMAL
        UpdateInfo
    Else
        MsgBox "Invalid new color value.", MB_OK Or MB_ICONEXCLAMATION, "Image Dithering"
    End If

End Sub

Sub btnReduce_Click ()
'---------------------------------------------------
' Color reduce the image, using the number of
' colors entered by the user.
'---------------------------------------------------
Dim answer As String

    answer = InputBox$("Enter the new number of colors", "Image Color Reduction")
    If answer = "" Then Exit Sub

    If IsNumeric(answer) Then
        vsPix1.NewColorNum = Val(answer)
        Screen.MousePointer = CSR_HOURGLASS
        vsPix1.Action = AC_COLOR_REDUCTION
        Screen.MousePointer = CSR_NORMAL
        UpdateInfo
    Else
        MsgBox "Invalid new color value.", MB_OK Or MB_ICONEXCLAMATION, "Image Color Reduction Error"
    End If
End Sub

Sub btnSmooth_Click ()
'---------------------------------------------------
' Smooth the current image.
'---------------------------------------------------

    Screen.MousePointer = CSR_HOURGLASS
    vsPix1.Action = AC_SMOOTHING
    Screen.MousePointer = CSR_NORMAL
    UpdateInfo
```

```
End Sub

Sub Form_Load ()
'--------------------------------------------------
' Center the form on the screen, and remember the
' form's current width and height.
'--------------------------------------------------
    Me.Move (Screen.Width - Me.Width) \ 2, (Screen.Height - Me.Height) \ 2

    MinFormWidth = Me.Width
    MinFormHeight = Me.Height
End Sub

Sub Form_Resize ()
'--------------------------------------------------
' Adjust the JPEG image control, scroll bars, and
' other form elements to the new window size.
'--------------------------------------------------
Dim Margin As Integer

    If WindowState = MINIMIZED Then Exit Sub

    ' Don't let the window get too small.
    If Me.Width < MinFormWidth Then Me.Width = MinFormWidth
    If Me.Height < MinFormHeight Then Me.Height = MinFormHeight

    Margin = vsPix1.Left
    vsPix1.Top = Margin
    picContainer.Top = Margin

    ' Left align controls.
    vsPix1.Width = Me.ScaleWidth - picContainer.Width - vscrImage.Width - (Margin * 3)
    hscrImage.Width = vsPix1.Width
    picContainer.Left = Me.ScaleWidth - picContainer.Width - Margin

    ' Top align controls.
    vsPix1.Height = Me.ScaleHeight - hscrImage.Height - (Margin * 2)
    vscrImage.Height = vsPix1.Height

    ' Adjust vertical and horizontal scrollers to the right and bottom
    ' of the JPEG control.
    vscrImage.Top = vsPix1.Top
    vscrImage.Left = vsPix1.Left + vsPix1.Width - 15

    hscrImage.Left = vsPix1.Left
    hscrImage.Top = vsPix1.Top + vsPix1.Height - 15

    vsPicWidth = vsPix1.ScaleWidth
    vsPicHeight = vsPix1.ScaleHeight

    ' Set the horizontal scroller's range value based on the
    ' width of the image.
    If vsPicWidth < vsPix1.InfoWidth Then
        hscrImage.Enabled = True
        hscrImage.Max = vsPix1.InfoWidth - vsPicWidth
    Else
        hscrImage.Enabled = False
    End If
```

8 ◄

*(continued on next page)*

*(continued from previous page)*

```
    ' Set the vertical scroller's range based on the
    ' height of the image.
    If vsPicHeight < vsPix1.InfoHeight Then
        vscrImage.Enabled = True
        vscrImage.Max = vsPix1.InfoHeight - vsPicHeight
    Else
        vscrImage.Enabled = False
    End If

    ' Reset scrollers to show top left corner of image.
    vscrImage = 0
    hscrImage = 0
End Sub

Function GetFileFormat (ByVal FileFormat As Integer) As String
'-------------------------------------------------------
' Return a string describing the file format based
' on the JPEG InfoFileFormat constants.
'-------------------------------------------------------
    Select Case FileFormat
        Case IF_UNKNOWN: GetFileFormat = "Unknown"
        Case IF_BMP_DIB: GetFileFormat = "BMP or DIB"
        Case IF_PCX: GetFileFormat = "PCX"
        Case IF_TIF: GetFileFormat = "TIFF"
        Case IF_TGA: GetFileFormat = "TARGA"
        Case IF_GIF: GetFileFormat = "GIF"
        Case IF_JPG: GetFileFormat = "JPEG"
    End Select
End Function

Sub hscrImage_Change ()
'-------------------------------------------------------
' Clip the left side of the image when the horizontal
' scroller is moved.
'-------------------------------------------------------
    vsPix1.OriginX = hscrImage
End Sub

Sub mnuFileClose_Click ()
'-------------------------------------------------------
' Clear the picture and disable all buttons.
'-------------------------------------------------------
    vsPix1.Clear
    picContainer.Cls
    btnReduce.Enabled = False
    btnSmooth.Enabled = False
    btnDither.Enabled = False
End Sub

Sub mnuFileExit_Click ()
'-------------------------------------------------------
' Exit the program.
'-------------------------------------------------------
    Unload Me
End Sub

Sub mnuFileOpen_Click ()
'-------------------------------------------------------
' Open and load a picture file.
'-------------------------------------------------------
```

```
Dim Canceled As Integer

    Canceled = False
    On Error GoTo mnuFileOpen_Error

    CMDialog1.Filter = "Image Files|*.jpg;*.tif;*.tga;*.gif;*.bmp;*.pcx;*.dib"
    CMDialog1.DialogTitle = "Open Image File"
    CMDialog1.CancelError = True
    CMDialog1.Action = 1

    If Not Canceled Then
        If CMDialog1.Filename = "" Then Exit Sub
        vsPix1.FileName = CMDialog1.Filename
        Screen.MousePointer = CSR_HOURGLASS
        vsPix1.Action = AC_LOADPICT
        Screen.MousePointer = CSR_NORMAL
        Form_Resize
        UpdateInfo
    End If
Exit Sub
mnuFileOpen_Error:
    Canceled = True
    Screen.MousePointer = CSR_NORMAL
    Resume Next
End Sub

Sub mnuFilePrint_Click ()
'----------------------------------------------------
' Print the currently loaded image.
'----------------------------------------------------
Dim Pmargin As Integer

    ' Define a margin that is 1/10th the width of the paper.
    Pmargin = (Printer.ScaleWidth / Printer.TwipsPerPixelX) / 10

    vsPix1.PrnDstX = Pmargin
    vsPix1.PrnDstY = Pmargin

    vsPix1.PrnDstWidth = (Printer.ScaleWidth / Printer.TwipsPerPixelX) - (Pmargin * 2)

    ' Scale the destination height to the width.
    vsPix1.PrnDstHeight = vsPix1.PrnDstWidth * (vsPix1.InfoHeight / vsPix1.InfoWidth)

    ' Print the image.
    vsPix1.Action = AC_PRINT
End Sub

Sub mnuFileSaveAs_Click ()
'----------------------------------------------------
' Save the current image, using the file extension
' to determine the format to save as.
'----------------------------------------------------
Dim Canceled As Integer
Dim ext As String

    Canceled = False
    On Error GoTo mnuFileSaveAs_Error

    CMDialog1.Filter = "Image Files|*.jpg;*.tif;*.tga;*.gif;*.bmp;*.pcx;*.dib"
```

*(continued on next page)*

8 ◄

485

*(continued from previous page)*

```vb
    CMDialog1.DialogTitle = "Save Image File As"
    CMDialog1.CancelError = True
    CMDialog1.Action = 1

    If Not Canceled Then
        If CMDialog1.Filename = "" Then Exit Sub

        If Len(CMDialog1.Filename) >= 5 Then
            ext = Right$(CMDialog1.Filename, 4)
        Else
            Exit Sub
        End If

        ' Set the file format based on the file extension.
        Select Case ext
            Case ".JPG": vsPix1.SaveFileFormat = SF_JPEG
            Case ".TIF": vsPix1.SaveFileFormat = SF_TIFLZW
            Case ".PCX": vsPix1.SaveFileFormat = SF_PCX
            Case ".BMP": vsPix1.SaveFileFormat = SF_BMP
            Case ".TGA": vsPix1.SaveFileFormat = SF_TGA
        End Select

        vsPix1.FileName = CMDialog1.Filename
        Screen.MousePointer = CSR_HOURGLASS

        ' Save the image.
        vsPix1.Action = AC_SAVEPICT

        Screen.MousePointer = CSR_NORMAL

    End If
Exit Sub
mnuFileSaveAs_Error:
    Canceled = True
    Screen.MousePointer = CSR_NORMAL
    Resume Next

End Sub

Sub optAutoSize_Click (Index As Integer)
'----------------------------------------------------
' Set the AutoSize property.
'----------------------------------------------------
    Select Case Index
        Case 0: vsPix1.AutoSize = AS_NONE
        Case 1: vsPix1.AutoSize = AS_ZOOM_PICTURE_TO_FIT
        Case 2: vsPix1.AutoSize = AS_ZOOM_PICTURE_TO_FIT_AR
    End Select
End Sub

Sub PrintUpdateLine (pic As PictureBox, ByVal LabelStr As String, ByVal DataStr As String)
'----------------------------------------------------
' Print a single information line to the picture
' box.
'----------------------------------------------------
Dim ATab As String

    ATab = Chr$(9)
```

```
        ' Print the label, followed by a tab character.
        pic.ForeColor = BLUE
        pic.Print LabelStr & ATab;
        ' Print the data after the label
        pic.ForeColor = RED
        pic.Print DataStr;

        ' Skip to a new line.
        pic.CurrentX = LeftMargin
        pic.CurrentY = pic.CurrentY + LineHeight
    End Sub

    Sub UpdateInfo ()
    '-------------------------------------------------------
    ' Update the Information area of the window.
    '-------------------------------------------------------
    Dim ATab As String

        ATab = Chr$(9)

        picContainer.Cls
        LineHeight = picContainer.TextHeight("Aj")
        LeftMargin = picContainer.TextWidth("l")

        picContainer.CurrentX = LeftMargin
        picContainer.CurrentY = LineHeight / 2

        PrintUpdateLine picContainer, "File Format:", GetFileFormat(vsPix1.InfoFileFormat)
        If vsPix1.InfoFileFormat  IF_UNKNOWN Then
        PrintUpdateLine picContainer, "Image Size:", Format$(vsPix1.InfoWidth) & "x" & ⇒
Format$(vsPix1.InfoHeight)
        PrintUpdateLine picContainer, "File Size:", Format$(vsPix1.InfoFileSize, "###,###,###") & " bytes"
        PrintUpdateLine picContainer, "Bits Per Pixel:", Format$(vsPix1.InfoDibBitCount)
        PrintUpdateLine picContainer, "Display Bits Per Pixel:", Format$(vsPix1.DispBitsPixel)
        If vsPix1.InfoFileSize > 0 Then
            PrintUpdateLine picContainer, "Compression Ratio:", "1:" & Format$(vsPix1.InfoDibSize / ⇒
vsPix1.InfoFileSize, "###.0")
            End If
    End If

    ' Enable or disable the command buttons
    If vsPix1.InfoDibBitCount = 24 Then
        btnDither.Enabled = True
        btnSmooth.Enabled = True
        btnReduce.Enabled = True
    Else
        btnDither.Enabled = False
        btnSmooth.Enabled = False
        btnReduce.Enabled = False
    End If
End Sub

Sub vscrImage_Change ()
'-------------------------------------------------------
' Clip the top of the image when the vertical
' scroller is moved.
'-------------------------------------------------------
    vsPix1.OriginY = vscrImage
End Sub
```

8 ◄

## Tips and Comments

Considering the large space savings that you can achieve using image compression, the JPEG Image Compressor control can be quite useful in applications that must display a large number of images. You must balance the price for this space savings against the amount of time required to display compressed images, which can be significantly longer than the display time for other formats when standard hardware is used. Crisp Technology also offers a compression/decompression hardware accelerator, which can overcome this problem, although this option will not be cost-effective in all cases. On fast machines, software JPEG decompression may prove to be sufficient for many applications.

# Picture Clip (PICCLIP.VBX)

| USAGE: | Bitmap Animation |
| --- | --- |
| MANUFACTURER: | Microsoft |
| COST: | Provided with Visual Basic 3.0 Professional Edition |

The Picture Clip control (PicClip), which comes with the professional edition of Visual Basic 3.0, allows you to store a large bitmap on a form and access it in smaller "chunks." This is useful when performing bitmap animation and smooth bitmap scrolling.

## Syntax

You can think of PicClip as a container for bitmaps. You don't use it to display bitmaps, but instead use it to store bitmaps that will be displayed either on a form or in a Picture control. This may not seem particularly useful until you realize that PicClip lets you select just a part of the bitmap it stores. This feature makes PicClip ideal for bitmap animation.

In cartoon animation, artists draw frames or "cels." When these cels are photographed onto motion picture film, the illusion of movement is achieved. PicClip allows you to achieve similar effects on a smaller scale. First you'll see how PicClip is used to create frame animation, and then you'll discover how it can be used to provide smooth bitmap scrolling.

**Table 8-25** Nonstandard properties of the Picture Clip control

| Clip | ClipHeight | ClipWidth |
| --- | --- | --- |
| ClipX | ClipY | Cols |
| GraphicCell | Height | Picture |
| Rows | StretchX | StretchY |
| Width | | |

First let's cover some of the nonstandard properties of the PicClip control, which are listed in Table 8-25. Foremost is the *Picture* property, which you use to assign a bitmap that the control will store. This bitmap can be any BMP format bitmap. You can create and edit such files with bitmap editors such as Paintbrush.

*Height* and *Width* return the dimensions of the control, and these are always returned in pixels. This is important to remember, as the Picture control and forms by default return dimension values in twips. For this reason, when using a Picture control or form as a target for a PicClip bitmap, make sure the *ScaleMode* property is set to *pixels*.

To do frame animation, you've got to create a sequence of cels. Look at the bitmap shown in Figure 8-9. This bitmap contains four pictures of a "space rover" that will be used in the example program later. Each picture is slightly different. If all the pictures were displayed in rapid succession, the results would look like a single rover that was moving. PicClip gives you an easy way to access each of the frames in this bitmap. The *Rows* and *Cols* properties tell PicClip how to break a large bitmap into smaller ones. In the bitmap shown in Figure 8-9, we want two rows and two columns. These properties can be set at run time or design time.

To assign a particular frame to a Picture control, use the *GraphicCell()* array property. When the *Rows* and *Cols* properties are set, their values are used to determine the size of the one-dimensional *GraphicCell()* array. The example in Figure 8-9 has four frames, so you would have four array elements, numbered 0 through 3. The following code shows how to set a Picture control to contain the second cel (the upper-right one in the bitmap) of Figure 8-9.

```
PicClip1.Rows = 2
PicClip2.Cols = 2
Picture1.Picture = PicClip1.GraphicCell(1)
```

The next example animates the rover by changing the bitmap displayed in the Picture control. Assume that the Boolean value *Moving* can be set to *False* by some event such as a button click.

```
CurrentCell = 0
Moving = True
While Moving
    Picture1.Picture = PicClip1.GraphicCell(CurrentCell)
    CurrentCell = (CurrentCell + 1) Mod 4
Wend
```

8 ◄

**Figure 8-9** A bitmap of four frames to be used in animation

The second use of the PicClip control is for smooth bitmap scrolling. This also has an analogy in cartoon animation, in this case the Saturday morning TV variety. This type of animation uses a "wraparound" background. As characters move to the left or right, the background scrolls past them. Eventually, the characters loop back around to the beginning of the background.

Look at the bitmap in Figure 8-10, which shows the landscape of some alien planet. Notice that parts of the bitmap are identical. Imagine cutting a rectangular hole out of a piece of paper, the height of the picture but only about a third as wide. If you placed this piece of paper over the picture, you could create a "viewport" into the picture. If you slide this viewport from left to right, the landscape would appear to move. If you moved the viewport from left to right, and immediately moved the viewport back to the matching landscape area on the left when you reached the right edge, the image would appear to be scrolling continuously.

You can achieve this effect with the PicClip control. Using the *ClipX, ClipY, ClipWidth,* and *ClipHeight* properties, you can define a specific rectangular area with the PicClip bitmap. You can assign this area to a form or Picture control through the *Clip* property. The following code assigns the left quarter of the bitmap shown in Figure 8-10 to a Picture control.

```
PicClip1.ClipX = 0
PicClip1.ClipY = 0
PicClip1.ClipWidth = PicClip1.Width / 4
PicClip1.ClipHeight = PicClip1.Height
Picture1.Picture = PicClip1.Clip
```

Continuing this example, to scroll 2 pixels to the right, simply change the *ClipX* value and reassign the Picture.

```
PicClip1.ClipX = PicClip1.ClipX + 2
Picture1.Picture = PicClip1.Clip
```

With the addition of a little code to handle wrapping around when the edges of the bitmap are reached you can easily achieve a smooth scrolling effect.

# Example

The example puts together the two techniques, frame editing and smooth scrolling, described earlier to produce an interactive animation of the Space Rover moving across an alien terrain. The program is shown in Figure 8-11.

By pressing and holding down the mouse button over the arrows, you can move the Rover to the left and right. The scroller adjusts the speed of the Rover simply by changing the number of pixels it moves during each iteration.

### Steps

1. Create a new project called PICCLIP.MAK. Add the Picture Clip control, PICCLIP.VBX, to the project. Create a new form with the objects and properties described in Table 8-26. Save this form as PICCLIP.FRM.

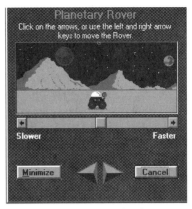

**Figure 8-10** Bitmap of an alien landscape

**Figure 8-11** The PicClip demo program

**Table 8-26** Objects and properties of PICCLIP.FRM

| OBJECT | PROPERTY | SETTING |
|--------|----------|---------|
| Form | FormName | frmPicClip |
| | BackColor | &H00404040& |
| | BorderStyle | 0 'None |
| | Caption | "PicClip Demo" |
| | KeyPreview | -1 'True |
| Image | Name | imgLeftArrow |
| | Picture | (set at design time in Properties window) |
| Image | Name | imgRightArrow |
| | Picture | (set at design time in Properties window) |
| Label | Name | Label1 |
| | BackStyle | 0 'Transparent |
| | Caption | "Slower" |
| | ForeColor | &H00FFFFFF& |
| Label | Name | Label2 |
| | Alignment | 1 'Right Justify |
| | BackStyle | 0 'Transparent |
| | Caption | "Faster" |
| | ForeColor | &H00FFFFFF& |
| Label | Name | Label3 |
| | Alignment | 2 'Center |
| | BackStyle | 0 'Transparent |
| | Caption | "SPEED" |

*(continued on next page)*

8 ◄

491

| OBJECT | PROPERTY | SETTING |
|---|---|---|
| *(continued from previous page)* | | |
| | ForeColor | &H000000FF& |
| Label | Name | Label4 |
| | Alignment | 2 'Center |
| | BackStyle | 0 'Transparent |
| | Caption | "Click on the arrows, or use the left and right arrow keys to move the Rover." |
| | FontBold | 0 'False |
| | ForeColor | &H00FFFFFF& |
| Label | Name | Label5 |
| | Alignment | 2 'Center |
| | BackStyle | 0 'Transparent |
| | Caption | "Planetary Rover" |
| | FontSize | 12 |
| | ForeColor | &H00FFFF00& |
| PictureBox | Name | picBackground |
| | BackColor | &H00FFFFFF& |
| | ScaleMode | 3 'Pixel |
| CommandButton | Name | btnCancel |
| | Caption | "&Cancel" |
| Timer | Name | Timer1 |
| | Enabled | 0 'False |
| | Interval | 2 |
| PictureClip | Name | PicClip1 |
| | Picture | (set at design time in Properties window) |
| PictureClip | Name | PicClip2 |
| | Cols | 2 |
| | Picture | (set at design time in Properties window) |
| | Rows | 2 |
| HScrollBar | Name | hscrSpeed |
| | Max | 20 |
| | Min | 1 |
| | Value | 11 |
| CommandButton | Name | btnMinimize |
| | Caption | "&Minimize" |

2. Place the controls shown in Table 8-27 inside the picBackground PictureBox control. Make sure to select the picBackground control on the form before adding these controls.

**Table 8-27** Controls contained inside the picBackground PictureBox control

| OBJECT | PROPERTY | SETTING |
|---|---|---|
| PictureBox | Name | picRover |
| | AutoSize | -1 'True |
| | BackColor | &H00C0C0C0& |
| | BorderStyle | 0 'None |

3. The PicClip images are assigned to the form at design time, and can be created with a bitmap editor such as Windows Paintbrush. Use Figures 8-9 and 8-10 as a guide to create these pictures. You can create left and right arrow images in the same way, using Figure 8-11 as a guide.

4. Add the following code to the declarations section of the PICCLIP.FRM form that you created in steps 1 and 2.

```
Option Explicit
'------------------------------------------------
' Variables and constants used by the PicClip form.
'------------------------------------------------

Const PAN_DEFAULT = 2

Dim PicWidth As Integer
Dim PanAmount As Integer
Dim RoverIdx As Integer

' Used for keyboard operation of panning.
Const KEY_LEFT = &H25
Const KEY_RIGHT = &H27

' WindowState constant.
Const MINIMIZE = 1

' Color constants.
Const DARK_GRAY = &H808080
Const WHITE = &HFFFFFF
Const BLACK = &H0
```

5. Add the following subroutines to the PICCLIP.FRM form.

```
Sub btnCancel_Click ()
'------------------------------------------------
' Exit the program.
'------------------------------------------------
    Unload Me
End Sub

Sub btnMinimize_Click ()
'------------------------------------------------
' Since we have no control menu, allow them to
' minimize using this button.
'------------------------------------------------
    WindowState = MINIMIZE
End Sub
```

(continued on next page)

*(continued from previous page)*

```
Sub Form_KeyDown (KeyCode As Integer, Shift As Integer)
'-----------------------------------------------------
' If they press a right or left arrow, then pan
' accordingly. Eat the KeyCode to avoid having
' the scroller use it to adjust the speed.
'-----------------------------------------------------
    If KeyCode = KEY_LEFT Then
        KeyCode = 0
        PanLandscape -hscrSpeed.Value
    ElseIf KeyCode = KEY_RIGHT Then
        KeyCode = 0
        PanLandscape hscrSpeed.Value
    End If
End Sub

Sub Form_Load ()
'-----------------------------------------------------
' Set up the initial pictures.
'-----------------------------------------------------

    Me.Move (Screen.Width - Me.Width) \ 2, (Screen.Height - Me.Height) \ 2

    ' Set up the initial image for the background.
    PicWidth = picBackground.ScaleWidth
    PicClip1.ClipHeight = PicClip1.Height
    PicClip1.ClipWidth = PicWidth
    PicClip1.ClipY = 0
    PicClip1.ClipX = 0
    picBackground.Picture = PicClip1.Clip

    ' Set the initial image for the Rover.
    RoverIdx = 0
    picRover.Picture = PicClip2.GraphicCell(RoverIdx)
End Sub

Sub Form_Paint ()
'-----------------------------------------------------
' Repaint our 3D effects.
'-----------------------------------------------------
    Make3D frmPicClip, picBackground
    Form3D 2
End Sub

Sub Form3D (ByVal BorderWidth As Integer)
'-----------------------------------------------------
' Put a 3D border around the outside of this form.
'-----------------------------------------------------
Dim AdjustX As Integer, AdjustY As Integer
Dim i As Integer

    AdjustX = Screen.TwipsPerPixelX
    AdjustY = Screen.TwipsPerPixelY

    ' Set the top shading line.
    Me.Line (0, 0)-(Me.ScaleWidth - AdjustX, 0), BLACK
    Me.Line -(Me.ScaleWidth - AdjustX, Me.ScaleHeight - AdjustY), BLACK
    Me.Line -(0, Me.ScaleHeight - AdjustY), BLACK
    Me.Line -(0, 0), BLACK
```

```
      ' Set the top shading line.
      For i = 1 To BorderWidth
          Me.Line (AdjustX * i, AdjustY * i)-(Me.ScaleWidth - (AdjustX * (i + 1)), AdjustY * i), WHITE
          Me.Line -(Me.ScaleWidth - (AdjustX * (i + 1)), Me.ScaleHeight - (AdjustY * (i + 1))), DARK_GRAY
          Me.Line -(AdjustX * i, Me.ScaleHeight - (AdjustY * (i + 1))), DARK_GRAY
          Me.Line -(AdjustX * i, AdjustY * i), WHITE
      Next
End Sub

Sub imgLeftArrow_MouseDown (Button As Integer, Shift As Integer, X As Single, Y As Single)
'------------------------------------------------
' If they've clicked over the arrow, start
' panning (via timer) until they let up on button.
'------------------------------------------------
      PanAmount = -hscrSpeed.Value
      Timer1.Enabled = True
End Sub

Sub imgLeftArrow_MouseUp (Button As Integer, Shift As Integer, X As Single, Y As Single)
'------------------------------------------------
' Stop panning.
'------------------------------------------------
      Timer1.Enabled = False
End Sub

Sub imgRightArrow_MouseDown (Button As Integer, Shift As Integer, X As Single, Y As Single)
'------------------------------------------------
' If they've clicked over the arrow, start
' panning (via timer) until they let up on button.
'------------------------------------------------
      PanAmount = hscrSpeed
      Timer1.Enabled = True
End Sub

Sub imgRightArrow_MouseUp (Button As Integer, Shift As Integer, X As Single, Y As Single)
'------------------------------------------------
' Stop panning.
'------------------------------------------------
      Timer1.Enabled = False
End Sub

Sub Make3D (pic As Form, ctl As Control)
'------------------------------------------------
' Wrap a 3D effect around a control on a form.
'------------------------------------------------
Dim AdjustX As Integer, AdjustY As Integer

      AdjustX = Screen.TwipsPerPixelX
      AdjustY = Screen.TwipsPerPixelY

      ' Set the top shading line.
      pic.Line (ctl.Left - AdjustX, ctl.Top - AdjustY)-(ctl.Left + ctl.Width, ctl.Top - AdjustY), DARK_GRAY
      pic.Line -(ctl.Left + ctl.Width, ctl.Top + ctl.Height), WHITE
      pic.Line -(ctl.Left - AdjustX, ctl.Top + ctl.Height), WHITE
      pic.Line -(ctl.Left - AdjustX, ctl.Top - AdjustY), DARK_GRAY
End Sub

Sub PanLandscape (ByVal PanAmount As Integer)
```

*(continued on next page)*

8 ◀

*(continued from previous page)*

```
'----------------------------------------------------
' Pan the landscape by PanAmount. Positive values
' pan right; negative values pan left. Check and
' handle if we go off either edge.
'----------------------------------------------------
Dim NewX As Integer

    NewX = PicClip1.ClipX + PanAmount
    If NewX <= 0 Then
        NewX = PicClip1.Width - picBackground.ScaleWidth
    ElseIf (NewX + picBackground.ScaleWidth) >= PicClip1.Width Then
        NewX = 0
    End If

    PicClip1.ClipX = NewX
    picBackground.Picture = PicClip1.Clip

    RoverIdx = (RoverIdx + 1) Mod 4
    picRover = PicClip2.GraphicCell(RoverIdx)
End Sub

Sub Timer1_Timer ()
'----------------------------------------------------
' Pan the landscape until the timer is disabled.
'----------------------------------------------------
    PanLandscape PanAmount
End Sub
```

## Tips and Comments

With a little artistic ingenuity, and the PicClip control, you can produce some very nice animations. You can use these as the basis for games or animated presentation graphics. Animations also make eye-catching "moving logos" for About dialog boxes.

# VBX Artist and PicScroll (ARTIST.VBX and PICSCRLL.VBX)

| USAGE: | Graphics Creation and Display |
|---|---|
| MANUFACTURER: | Bennet-Tec |
| COST: | $50 (PicScroll alone)  $250 (Artist and PicScroll together |

Artist (ARTIST.VBX) is a graphics control that gives you all the power of MSPaint or MSDraw and then some for the creation and modification of .BMPs and .WMF files. It also lets you copy screen images from other windows, or draw on other windows, if you have the need. In addition, you can control Artist programmatically or let your user do his or her own drawing. Artist provides several custom events and properties that make drawing easier and give you more flexibility and extendibility.

PicScroll (PICSCRLL.VBX) is an enhanced picture control that gives you scroll bars that allow you to display pictures that are larger than the visible portion of the control.

You can access the visible portion of the control via custom properties if you need to or you can access the entire picture. PicScroll handles both .WMFs and .BMPs, and it has special properties dealing specifically with .WMF files. It can also accept file drops from File Manager. Finally, PicScroll can act as a container control and resize any children controls as it changes size.

# Syntax

VBX Artist and PicScroll complement each other. Artist provides the drawing ability and PicScroll provides the canvas for storing the drawing. A detailed explanation of each follows.

**VBX Artist**   VBX Artist (ARTIST.VBX) can draw on the entire desktop, but generally you'll want to draw on something that lets you save the artwork that you've generated, such as a VB Picture control or a PicScroll control.

Table 8-28 lists VBX Artist's custom properties and events.

**Table 8-28** VBX Artist's nonstandard properties and events

**PROPERTIES**

| | | |
|---|---|---|
| Active | AutoEnable | AutoRelease |
| Clip | Filter | hBrush |
| hFont | hPen | hWndDest |
| LastX | LastY | Mode |
| PicHeight | PicLeft | PicTop |
| PicWidth | StartX | StartY |
| Stretch | | |

**EVENTS**

| | | |
|---|---|---|
| BeginPaint | EndPaint | EnterArea |
| ExitArea | NextPaint | |

Artist knows where it's allowed to draw based on the *Filter* property. *Filter* is set either to the *hWnd* of a specific window or control, or to a list of values that tell Artist how far it can stray to do its job. You can select the drawing tool to use via the *Mode* property. See Table 8-29 for a list of the valid drawing tools.

**Table 8-29** Values for the Mode property

| VALUE | MEANING |
|---|---|
| 0 | Marker - used for cutting or pasting |
| 1 | Pencil - freehand drawing |
| 2 | Line |
| 3 | Brush - based on the BrushShape property |
| 4 | Airbrush - shape based on the BrushShape property |

*(continued on next page)*

8 ◀

| VALUE | MEANING |
|---|---|
| *(continued from previous page)* | |
| 5 | FloodFill |
| 6 | Text |
| 7 | Eraser - draws BrushShape in BackColor |
| 8 | Rectangle |
| 9 | Circle |
| 10 | RoundRect |
| 11 | Rectangle filled with BackColor |
| 12 | Circle filled with BackColor |
| 13 | RoundRect filled with BackColor |

Table 8-30 lists valid brush shapes for Artist.

**Table 8-30** Values for the BrushShape property

| VALUE | MEANING |
|---|---|
| 0 | Circle |
| 1 | Square |
| 2 | Line slanted (/) |
| 3 | Line slanted (\) |

The *AutoEnable* property tells Artist at what kind of keystroke or mouse click to start drawing. *AutoRelease* tells Artist when to stop drawing. You can also start Artist drawing programmatically by setting the *Active* property to *True*.

You control Artist's brush using the *Brush* and *LineStyle* properties. These properties control the shape and fill style of the brush. You can load a custom brush using the *BrushMask* or *BrushPattern* properties. *BrushPattern* replaces the selected color with the 8x8-pixel pattern from the bitmap. *BrushMask* uses a 32x32-pixel black-and-white bitmap as a mask for paint and spray painting in the chosen foreground color. You can also assign an icon to *BrushMask*, but then the icon itself is used as a brush, and all other brush-related properties are ignored.

Artist does screen capture using the *Marker* mode, mode 0. You set *Mode* and initiate a drag event, which highlights the selected area. In the resulting *EndPaint* event of Artist, *Clip* property can capture the highlighted area.

**PicScroll**   PicScroll (PICSCRLL.VBX) lets you display pictures that are larger than the visible area of the control. The user can scroll the picture by using scroll bars or optionally clicking on the picture and dragging it around. PicScroll can also accept Drop messages from File Manager. PicScroll can display Bitmap (.BMP) files or Windows Metafiles (.WMF).

Table 8-31 lists PicScroll's nonstandard properties and events.

**Table 8-31** PicScroll's nonstandard properties and events

**PROPERTIES**

| | | |
|---|---|---|
| BackPattern | Clip | DropMode |
| Hpic | HView | MetaCount |
| MetaEnumerate | MetaSelected | MouseScroll |
| PicHeight | PicLeft | PicScaling |
| PicTop | PictureCopy | PictureSize |
| PictureType | PicWidth | ScrollBars |
| ScrollChildren | Stretch | WPic |
| Wview | X0 | Y0 |

**EVENTS**

| | | |
|---|---|---|
| DropFile | MetaEnum | Scrolled |

PicScroll also has some unique capabilities. PicScroll can scale files automatically, or it can display a window into a bigger picture and use scroll bars or mouse "grabbing" capability to move the picture around. The appearance of the scroll bars is controlled appropriately by the *ScrollBars* property. The *MouseScroll* property controls whether you can scroll PicScroll using the mouse.

*MouseScroll* values are listed in Table 8-32.

**Table 8-32** Values for the MouseScroll property

| VALUE | MEANING |
|---|---|
| 0 | No mouse scroll |
| 1 | Drag with the left mouse |
| 2 | Drag with the right mouse |
| 4 | When Or'd with 1 or 2, requires a (SHIFT) + mouse button |
| 8 | When Or'd with 1 or 2, requires (CTRL) + mouse button |

When you load a picture, you control or return the size of the image using the *PicLeft*, *PicTop*, *PicWidth*, and *PicHeight* properties. You control the scale mode of the picture with the *PicScaling* property. You can only change these properties when there is no picture in the control. *HPic* and *WPic* are the area of the visible picture, and *HView* and *WView* are the dimensions of the "viewport" into the picture. These properties get their scale mode from the parent form/control's *ScaleMode* property.

PicScroll has special abilities for Windows metafiles. PicScroll lets you play back portions of the metafile. You can also add records or remove records from the metafile record and change the logical units of the metafile.

PicScroll can also act as a parent control. The chief benefit of placing controls within a PicScroll is that you can scroll the child controls just as you'd scroll a picture. PicScroll also optionally resizes the child controls as PicScroll resizes.

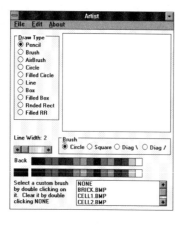

**Figure 8-12** The Artist example program

# Example

This example program shows how to construct a simple bitmap painter using ARTIST.VBX to do the drawing and PICSCRLL.VBX to act as a drawing board. It also demonstrates how to do screen grabbing from anywhere on the Windows desktop, and it handles drag and drop from File Manager. Figure 8-12 illustrates the example program.

## Steps

1. Create a new project called ARTIST.MAK and add ARTIST.VBX and PICSCROLL.VBX. Create a new form with the objects and properties shown in Table 8-33. Save this form as ARTIST1.FRM.

**Table 8-33** Objects and properties of the ARTIST1 form

| OBJECT | PROPERTY | SETTING |
|--------|----------|---------|
| Label | Name | lblForeColor |
| | BorderStyle | 1 'Fixed Single |
| | Index | 0 |
| Label | Name | lblBackColor |
| | BorderStyle | 1 'Fixed Single |
| | Index | 0 |
| Label | Name | lblForeColor |
| | BorderStyle | 1 'Fixed Single |
| | Index | 1 |
| Label | Name | lblBackColor |
| | BorderStyle | 1 'Fixed Single |
| | Index | 1 |
| Label | Name | lblForeColor |
| | BorderStyle | 1 'Fixed Single |

| OBJECT | PROPERTY | SETTING |
|--------|----------|---------|
| | Index | 2 |
| Label | Name | lblBackColor |
| | BorderStyle | 1 'Fixed Single |
| | Index | 2 |
| Label | Name | lblForeColor |
| | BorderStyle | 1 'Fixed Single |
| | Index | 3 |
| Label | Name | lblBackColor |
| | BorderStyle | 1 'Fixed Single |
| | Index | 3 |
| Label | Name | lblForeColor |
| | BorderStyle | 1 'Fixed Single |
| | Index | 4 |
| Label | Name | lblBackColor |
| | BorderStyle | 1 'Fixed Single |
| | Index | 4 |
| Label | Name | lblForeColor |
| | BorderStyle | 1 'Fixed Single |
| | Index | 5 |
| Label | Name | lblBackColor |
| | BorderStyle | 1 'Fixed Single |
| | Index | 5 |
| Label | Name | lblFore |
| | Alignment | 2 'Center |
| | Caption | "Fore" |
| Label | Name | lblBack |
| | Alignment | 2 'Center |
| | Caption | "Back" |
| Label | Name | lblBackColor |
| | BorderStyle | 1 'Fixed Single |
| | Index | 6 |
| Label | Name | lblForeColor |
| | BorderStyle | 1 'Fixed Single |
| | Index | 6 |
| Label | Name | lblBackColor |
| | BorderStyle | 1 'Fixed Single |
| | Index | 7 |
| Label | Name | lblForeColor |
| | BorderStyle | 1 'Fixed Single |

*(continued on next page)*

8

| OBJECT | PROPERTY | SETTING |
|--------|----------|---------|
| *(continued from previous page)* | | |
| | Index | 7 |
| Label | Name | lblBackColor |
| | BorderStyle | 1 'Fixed Single |
| | Index | 8 |
| Label | Name | lblForeColor |
| | BorderStyle | 1 'Fixed Single |
| | Index | 8 |
| Label | Name | lblBackColor |
| | BorderStyle | 1 'Fixed Single |
| | Index | 9 |
| Label | Name | lblBackColor |
| | BorderStyle | 1 'Fixed Single |
| | Index | 10 |
| Label | Name | lblBackColor |
| | BorderStyle | 1 'Fixed Single |
| | Index | 11 |
| Label | Name | lblBackColor |
| | BorderStyle | 1 'Fixed Single |
| | Index | 12 |
| Label | Name | lblBackColor |
| | BorderStyle | 1 'Fixed Single |
| | Index | 13 |
| Label | Name | lblBackColor |
| | BorderStyle | 1 'Fixed Single |
| | Index | 14 |
| Label | Name | lblBackColor |
| | BorderStyle | 1 'Fixed Single |
| | Index | 15 |
| Label | Name | lblForeColor |
| | BorderStyle | 1 'Fixed Single |
| | Index | 9 |
| Label | Name | lblForeColor |
| | BorderStyle | 1 'Fixed Single |
| | Index | 10 |
| Label | Name | lblForeColor |
| | BorderStyle | 1 'Fixed Single |
| | Index | 11 |
| Label | Name | lblForeColor |
| | BorderStyle | 1 'Fixed Single |

| OBJECT | PROPERTY | SETTING |
|---|---|---|
| | Index | 12 |
| Label | Name | lblForeColor |
| | BorderStyle | 1 'Fixed Single |
| | Index | 13 |
| Label | Name | lblForeColor |
| | BorderStyle | 1 'Fixed Single |
| | Index | 14 |
| Label | Name | lblForeColor |
| | BorderStyle | 1 'Fixed Single |
| | Index | 15 |
| Label | Name | lblLineSize |
| | BackStyle | 0 'Transparent |
| | Caption | "Line Width:" |
| Label | Name | Label1 |
| | BackStyle | 0 'Transparent |
| | Caption | "Select a custom brush by double-clicking on it. Clear it by double-clicking NONE." |
| Frame | Name | Frame1 |
| | BackColor | &H00E0FFFF& |
| | Caption | "&Draw Type" |
| Artist | Name | Art1 |
| | BrushHatch | 6 'Solid fill |
| | FillColor | &H00000000& |
| | Filter | 0 |
| | Mode | 8 'Boxes |
| | Transparent | 0 'False |
| Frame | Name | Frame2 |
| | BackColor | &H00E0FFFF& |
| | Caption | "&Brush" |
| HScrollBar | Name | hScrLineWidth |
| | LargeChange | 10 |
| | Max | 50 |
| | Min | 1 |
| | Value | 1 |
| PicScroll | Name | picScroll1 |
| | BackColor | &H00FFFFFF& |
| | HPic | 1500 |
| | MouseScroll | 2 'Right button pressed |
| | PicHeight | 100 |

8

*(continued on next page)*

| OBJECT | PROPERTY | SETTING |
|---|---|---|
| *(continued from previous page)* | | |
| | PicLeft | 0 |
| | PicScaling | 4 'User |
| | PicTop | 0 |
| | PicWidth | 300 |
| | Stretch | 0 'Leave picture size as is |
| | TabStop | 0 'False |
| | WPic | 3000 |
| | X0 | 0 |
| | Y0 | 0 |
| PictureBox | Name | picInitial |
| | AutoRedraw | -1 'True |
| | Visible | 0 'False |
| Artist | Name | artCopy |
| | BrushHatch | 6 'Solid fill |
| | FillColor | &H00000000& |
| | Filter | 0 |
| | Mode | 0 'Mark area |
| ListBox | Name | lstCustomBrushes |
| Form | FormName | Artist1 |
| | BackColor | &H00E0FFFF& |
| | BorderStyle | 3 'Fixed Double |
| | Caption | "Artist" |
| | MaxButton | 0 'False |

2. Select Frame1 and add the objects and properties listed in Table 8-34.

**Table 8-34** Objects and properties of the Frame1 frame

| OBJECT | PROPERTY | SETTING |
|---|---|---|
| OptionButton | Name | optDrawTools |
| | BackColor | &H00E0FFFF& |
| | Caption | "Box" |
| | Index | 8 |
| OptionButton | Name | optDrawTools |
| | BackColor | &H00E0FFFF& |
| | Caption | "Circle" |
| | Index | 9 |
| OptionButton | Name | optDrawTools |
| | BackColor | &H00E0FFFF& |

| OBJECT | PROPERTY | SETTING |
|---|---|---|
| | Caption | "Line" |
| | Index | 2 |
| OptionButton | Name | optDrawTools |
| | BackColor | &H00E0FFFF& |
| | Caption | "Pencil" |
| | Index | 1 |
| OptionButton | Name | optDrawTools |
| | BackColor | &H00E0FFFF& |
| | Caption | "Filled Box" |
| | Index | 11 |
| OptionButton | Name | optDrawTools |
| | BackColor | &H00E0FFFF& |
| | Caption | "Rnded Rect" |
| | Index | 10 |
| OptionButton | Name | optDrawTools |
| | BackColor | &H00E0FFFF& |
| | Caption | "Filled RR" |
| | Index | 13 |
| OptionButton | Name | optDrawTools |
| | BackColor | &H00E0FFFF& |
| | Caption | "Filled Circle" |
| | Index | 12 |
| OptionButton | Name | optDrawTools |
| | BackColor | &H00E0FFFF& |
| | Caption | "AirBrush" |
| | Index | 4 |
| OptionButton | Name | optDrawTools |
| | BackColor | &H00E0FFFF& |
| | Caption | "Brush" |
| | Index | 3 |

3. Select Frame2 and add the objects and properties listed in Table 8-35.

**Table 8-35** Objects and properties of the Frame2 frame

| OBJECT | PROPERTY | SETTING |
|---|---|---|
| OptionButton | Name | optBrush |
| | BackColor | &H00E0FFFF& |
| | Caption | "Circle" |
| | Index | 0 |

*(continued on next page)*

| OBJECT | PROPERTY | SETTING |
|---|---|---|
| *(continued from previous page)* | | |
| OptionButton | Name | optBrush |
| | BackColor | &H00E0FFFF& |
| | Caption | "Square" |
| | Index | 1 |
| OptionButton | Name | optBrush |
| | BackColor | &H00E0FFFF& |
| | Caption | "Diag /" |
| | Index | 2 |
| OptionButton | Name | optBrush |
| | BackColor | &H00E0FFFF& |
| | Caption | "Diag \" |
| | Index | 3 |

4. Add the following code to the declarations section of the ARTIST1 form. This code sets up any declarations needed in the ARTIST1 form.

```
Option Explicit
    '-----------------------------
    ' Define global variables and constants used in Artist1.
    '-----------------------------

    Dim picdirty As Integer

    Const CHECKED = 1
    Const MB_OK = 1
    Const MB_ICONQUESTION = 32
    Const IDOK = 1
    Const CF_BITMAP = 2

    Const MOUSE_LEFT = 1

    Dim ArtSaveMode ' Used to restore the drawing mode after a paste.
```

5. Add the following code to the ARTIST1 form. The code in this form binds the Art1 Artist control to the picScroll1 object so the user can draw on it. There is also code to initiate painting in several places and code to either load or clear a custom paintbrush from Art1. In addition, ArtCopy is set up so it can cut from anywhere on the desktop and place the cut bitmap on the Clipboard.

```
Sub Art1_EndPaint (hdcDest As Integer, X As Integer, Y As Integer, hdcTemp As Integer)
    '-----------------------------
    ' Paste from the Clipboard.
    '-----------------------------

    If art1.Mode = PM_MARKER Then
        art1.Clip = clipboard.GetData(CF_BITMAP)
        art1.Mode = ArtSaveMode
    End If
    picdirty = True
```

```
End Sub

Sub Art1_MouseDown (Button As Integer, Shift As Integer, X As Integer, Y As Integer)
    '-----------------------------
    ' Start drawing (dragging).
    '-----------------------------

    If Button And 2 Then
        art1.Drag 0
    End If

End Sub

Sub Art1_MouseUp (Button As Integer, Shift As Integer, X As Integer, Y As Integer)
    '-----------------------------
    ' Stop drawing.
    '-----------------------------
    If Button And 2 Then
        art1.Drag 2
    End If
End Sub

Sub artCopy_EndPaint (hdcDest As Integer, X As Integer, Y As Integer, hdcTemp As Integer)
    '-----------------------------
    ' Stop drawing.
    '-----------------------------
    clipboard.SetData artCopy.Clip, CF_BITMAP
    artCopy.Drag 2
End Sub

Sub Form_Load ()
    '-----------------------------
    ' Set up the form.
    '-----------------------------

    Me.Move (Screen.Width - Me.Width) \ 2, (Screen.Height - Me.Height) \ 2

    Dim I As Integer
    Dim HoldBmp As String

    ' Set the color selections.
    For I = 0 To 15
        lblForeColor(I).BackColor = QBColor(I)
        lblBackColor(I).BackColor = QBColor(I)
    Next I

    Me.Show

    '-----------------------------
    ' Set up the color selection.
    '-----------------------------
    lblFore.BackColor = QBColor(0)
    lblback.BackColor = QBColor(15)
    art1.ForeColor = QBColor(0)
    art1.BackColor = QBColor(15)

    '-----------------------------
    ' Initialize the display controls and Art1 via
    ' control events.
    '-----------------------------
```

8 ◄

*(continued on next page)*

*(continued from previous page)*

```
    picInitial.Cls
    picScroll1.Picture = picInitial.Image
    hScrLineWidth.Value = 2
    optDrawTools(PM_PENCIL) = True
    optBrush(SHAPE_CIRCLE) = True

    art1.Filter = picScroll1.hWnd
    artCopy.Mode = PM_MARKER
    artCopy.Filter = CANDRAW_SCREEN

    '-----------------------------
    ' "Handle" any errors in line for the next chunk
    ' of code.
    '-----------------------------
    On Error Resume Next

    HoldBmp = Dir$(app.Path & "\" & "*.bmp")

    If Err > 0 Or HoldBmp = "" Then Exit Sub

    lstCustomBrushes.AddItem "NONE"

    Do While HoldBmp  "" And Err = 0
        lstCustomBrushes.AddItem HoldBmp
        HoldBmp = Dir$
    Loop

    On Error GoTo 0
    ' Clear the error handler.

End Sub

Sub Form_QueryUnload (Cancel As Integer, UnloadMode As Integer)
    '-----------------------------
    ' Verify the user wants to abandon the picture.
    '-----------------------------
    Dim res%

    If picdirty% = True Then
        '32+1
        res% = MsgBox("You've changed your picture. Are you sure you want to unload?",
MB_OKCANCEL + MB_ICONQUESTION, "Picture Changed")
        If res% = IDOK Then ' OK
            Exit Sub
        Else
            Cancel = 1 ' Any value will do.
        End If
    End If
End Sub

Sub hScrLineWidth_Change ()
    lblLineSize = "Line Width: " & Format$(hScrLineWidth.Value)
    art1.Thickness = hScrLineWidth.Value
    picScroll1.SetFocus
End Sub

Sub lblBackColor_Click (index As Integer)
    lblback.BackColor = lblBackColor(index).BackColor
```

```
    art1.FillColor = lblback.BackColor
    picScroll1.SetFocus
End Sub

Sub lblForeColor_Click (index As Integer)
    lblFore.BackColor = lblForeColor(index).BackColor
    art1.ForeColor = lblFore.BackColor
    picScroll1.SetFocus
End Sub

Sub lstCustomBrushes_DblClick ()
    '-----------------------------
    ' Custom brushes loaded and unloaded here.
    '-----------------------------
    If lstCustomBrushes.List(lstCustomBrushes.ListIndex) = "NONE" Then
        ' Clear the brush.
        art1.BrushPattern = LoadPicture()
    Else
        art1.BrushPattern = LoadPicture(app.Path + "\" + lstCustomBrushes.List(lstCustomBrushes.ListIndex))
    End If
End Sub

Sub mnuAbout_Click ()
    frmabout.Show
End Sub

Sub mnuCopy_Click ()
    '-----------------------------
    ' Start marking a copy. Note that this uses
    ' a separate "Artist" control.
    '-----------------------------
    artCopy.Drag 1
End Sub

Sub mnuExit_Click ()
    Unload frmabout
    Unload Me
End Sub

Sub mnuLoad_Click ()
    '-----------------------------
    ' Load a new picture.
    '-----------------------------
    Dim inputfile As String
    Dim workstring As String
    Dim HoldErr As Integer
    Dim res As Integer


    '-----------------------------
    ' Verify that user wants to lose his or her masterpiece.
    '-----------------------------
    If picdirty = True Then
        res = MsgBox("You've changed the picture. Do you want to save?", MB_YESNO +
MB_ICONQUESTION, "Picture Changed")
        If res = IDYES Then
            mnuSave_click ' Save the picture.
        End If
    End If
```

*(continued on next page)*

*(continued from previous page)*

```
    inputfile = InputBox$("Enter a file to load", "Enter a file")

    If inputfile = "" Then Exit Sub

    On Error Resume Next

    workstring = Dir$(inputfile)

    '-----------------------------
    ' Stash the error message so we can check it.
    '-----------------------------
    HoldErr = Err

    On Error GoTo 0

    If HoldErr  0 Or workstring = "" Then Exit Sub

    artist1.Caption = "Artist - " & inputfile
    picScroll1.Tag = inputfile
    picScroll1.Picture = LoadPicture(inputfile)
    mnuSave.Enabled = True
    picdirty% = False
End Sub

Sub mnuNew_Click ()
    '-----------------------------
    ' Clear PicScroll using the blank picture control.
    '-----------------------------
    picScroll1.Picture = LoadPicture()
    picScroll1.Picture = picInitial.Image
    picdirty% = False
    picScroll1.Tag = ""
    artist1.Caption = "Artist"
    mnuSave.Enabled = False
End Sub

Sub mnuPaste_Click ()
    '-----------------------------
    ' Handle pasting into the PicClip.
    '-----------------------------

    If Not clipboard.GetFormat(CF_BITMAP) Then Exit Sub

    ArtSaveMode = art1.Mode

    art1.Mode = PM_MARKER
    ArtMoveTo art1, 0, 0
    art1.Drag 1

End Sub

Sub mnuSave_click ()
    Dim FileName As String

    If picScroll1.Tag = "" Then
        mnuSaveAs_Click
        Exit Sub
    End If
```

```
    FileName = picScroll1.Tag
    SavePicture picScroll1.Picture, FileName
End Sub

Sub mnuSaveAs_Click ()
    '----------------------------
    ' Save As code.
    '----------------------------
    Dim inputfile As String
    Dim workstring As String
    Dim HoldErr As Integer
    Dim res As Integer

    inputfile = InputBox$("Enter a file to Save", "Enter a file")

    If inputfile = "" Then Exit Sub

    On Error Resume Next

    workstring = Dir$(inputfile)

    '----------------------------
    ' Stash the error message so we can check it.
    '----------------------------
    HoldErr = Err

    On Error GoTo 0

    If HoldErr  0 Then Exit Sub

    '----------------------------
    ' Verify that the user wants to
    ' overwrite an existing file.
    '----------------------------
    If workstring  "" Then
        res = MsgBox("File " & inputfile & " exists. Do you want to overwrite?", MB_YESNO +
MB_ICONQUESTION, "File Exists")
        If res = IDNO Then
            Exit Sub
        End If
    End If

    artist1.Caption = "Artist - " & inputfile
    picScroll1.Tag = inputfile
    SavePicture picScroll1.Picture, inputfile
    mnuSave.Enabled = True
    picdirty% = False
End Sub

Sub optBrush_Click (index As Integer)
    art1.BrushShape = index
End Sub

Sub optDrawTools_Click (index As Integer)
    art1.Mode = index
    picScroll1.SetFocus
End Sub

Sub PicScroll1_DropFile (X As Long, Y As Long, fname As String, FIndex As Integer)
```

*(continued on next page)*

8 ◄

511

*(continued from previous page)*

```
'-----------------------------
' Handle drop messages.
'-----------------------------
Dim suffix As String

suffix = Right$(fname, 3)

If suffix = "BMP" Or suffix = "WMF" Then
    picScroll1.Picture = LoadPicture(fname)
End If
End Sub

Sub PicScroll1_MouseDown (Button As Integer, Shift As Integer, X As Single, Y As Single)
    picScroll1.SetFocus
End Sub

Sub PicScroll1_MouseMove (Button As Integer, Shift As Integer, X As Single, Y As Single)

    If Button  0 Or art1.Mode < 0 Then Exit Sub
    art1.Drag 1
    picScroll1.SetFocus

End Sub
```

## Tips and Comments

ARTIST.VBX lets you "drop" a BMP or WMF drawing package or screen capture package into your VB program. Combined with PICSCRLL.VBX, this control enables you to easily edit and update large or small drawings.

PicScroll also lets you select specific records from the metafile and play them back or add your own metafile records using Windows API calls. Once you've got the right set of records, you can control what's being displayed based on whatever criteria you need. This gives you flexibility in what you display and when. Being able to add metafile records lets you annotate drawings right in the metafile itself, which is very useful.

# SYSTEM TOOLS

Visual Basic makes Windows programming accessible because it does a good job of hiding the complexity of the Windows API. This API is a collection of hundreds of function calls, event messages, and assorted arcana that can make trivial tasks horribly complex to implement.

Visual Basic was not the first tool designed to make Windows programming easier, but it is arguably the most successful. In VB, you can solve a wide range of problems without knowing about the Windows API.

Eventually, you will run into a task that Visual Basic cannot handle. You often know that Windows can perform the task, but can't quite figure out how to convince VB to do it. You can overcome many obstacles by learning to use the API functions you can call from Visual Basic. For example, to play a wave audio (.WAV) file, you just need to declare the API *sndPlaySound* function and some constants in the declarations section of your Visual Basic application like this:

```
Const SND_SYNC = &H0
Const SND_ASYNC = &H1
Declare Function sndPlaySound Lib "MMSystem" (ByVal lpsound As String, ByVal flag As Integer)
As Integer
```

To use the function in your program, you simply call it like any other VB function:

```
Result = sndPlaySound ("C:\WINDOWS\CHIMES.WAV", SND_ASYNC)
```

In this example, the first parameter is the wave file name, and the second parameter is a flag that tells Windows to play the sound file asynchronously.

While the Windows API can greatly extend Visual Basic, some problems require "outside" assistance because not all API functions can be called directly from Visual Basic. The Windows API was designed originally for C programmers, and many of the parameters used aren't easily accessible to VB.

For example, suppose you want status line help for menu options. This type of help updates the status line with a short message when the user moves the cursor over a menu option. Because Visual Basic only alerts the program when a menu item is clicked, this type of menu help seems impossible in VB.

This is where specialized controls can help. Since these controls are actually Windows dynamic link libraries (DLLs), they can bypass Visual Basic's limitations and do things such as processing Windows messages that Visual Basic never lets you see.

This chapter explores some controls that let you do just that. Some are highly specialized, performing a single function, while others are designed to serve as general-purpose tools. All of them let you perform tasks or access Windows features that would be difficult or downright impossible using Visual Basic alone.

▲ **Alarm** This control is a specialized timer control that you can use to set multiple "time of day" alarms. You'll use it to build a functional analog alarm clock that you can set to any time of day.

▲ **App-Link** This control provides an easy way for your separate Visual Basic apps to communicate with each other. You'll use it to build a small e-mail application.

▲ **FMDrop** This control lets you write programs that accept files dragged from the Windows File Manager and dropped on a Visual Basic form.

▲ **IniCon** This control encapsulates Windows .INI file functions. You'll build an .INI file viewer that can browse through the different sections of WIN.INI.

▲ **Key Status**  This control lets you determine the status of special keys. You'll learn how to use the "multistate" features of keys like (SCROLL LOCK) and (INS) to build a simple text editor with overtype and read-only capabilities.

▲ **MenuEv**  This control provides status line "help" for menu options as the user highlights them.

▲ **Message Hook**  This control gives you access to Windows messages not normally available to Visual Basic. You'll see how to "lock down" a Visual Basic form, preventing it from being moved.

▲ **OLE 2.0 Control**  This control lets you link to or embed OLE objects in your applications. You'll build a simple object viewer to see how it works.

▲ **SpyWorks-VB**  You'll use this powerful message handler to lock a form as an icon and create owner draw controls.

▲ **VB Messenger**  You'll use this control to add a Free System Memory button to a form's title bar, and also retrieve internal information about Visual Basic controls on a form.

# Alarm (ALARM.VBX)

| USAGE: | Event Scheduling |
|---|---|
| MANUFACTURER: | Mabry Software |
| COST: | $10 ($5 if registered on CompuServe) |

The Alarm control provides a way to set multiple "time of day" alarms, and triggers an event when an alarm time is reached.

## Syntax

This control is a variation on the standard Visual Basic timer control. Like the timer control, this control fires an alarm when some timing condition is met. But the timer control fires at a constant interval and has a maximum resolution of a little more than a minute. In contrast, the Alarm control functions more like a traditional alarm clock. Events are triggered based on alarm times that you have set explicitly. And since you can set multiple alarms, you can use this control to easily write scheduling programs and Personal Information Managers (PIMs). Table 9-1 lists the nonstandard properties and events of the Alarm control.

**Table 9-1** Nonstandard properties and events of the Alarm control

| PROPERTIES | |
|---|---|
| AlarmTime | DateFormat |
| **EVENTS** | |
| Alarm | NewDate |

9 ◄

The Alarm control is extremely simple to use. Like the timer control, it has no visual element at run time. At design time, only its ToolBox bitmap appears in a form.

You set an alarm using the *AlarmTime* property, a string array that can store multiple alarm values. The format for this string is "HH:MM:SS", where "HH" is the hour, "MM" is the minute, and "SS" is the second. You can use question marks as wildcards in any of these positions. The following section of code sets several alarms:

```
' Set Alarm to go off every hour.
Alarm1.AlarmTime(1) = "??:00:??"
' Set Alarm to go off every second.
Alarm1.AlarmTime(2) = "??:??:??"
' Set Alarm to go off at 3:37 PM.
Alarm1.AlarmTime(3) = "15:37:00"
```

When a previously set alarm time occurs, the *Alarm* event is triggered. It has the form

```
Sub CntlName_Alarm (AlarmIndex as long, TimeNow as string)
```

*AlarmIndex* corresponds to the *AlarmTime* array index used to set the alarm.

*TimeNow* is the actual time that the *Alarm* event was fired. The Alarm control provides one other event, *NewDate* which has the form

```
Sub CntlName_NewDate (DateNow as string)
```

This event is fired when the date changes. The *DateNew* parameter uses the date formatting specified in the [Intl] section of the Windows WIN.INI file, and so this value may vary greatly depending on the user's Windows configuration. To avoid this problem, the Alarm control provides a *DateFormat* property. You can set this property to a string that follows the date formatting conventions of the Visual Basic *Formats* function. A valid *DateFormat* property will override the default international settings.

The Alarm control provides a single method, *Clear* that removes all alarms defined with *AlarmTime.* You can remove individual alarms by setting the *AlarmTime* property for that particular alarm index to an empty string ("").

# Example

The example program implements an old-fashioned analog alarm clock, complete with a ringing bell on top. The program's main form is shown in Figure 9-1. The user can set a new alarm value by clicking on the values in the Alarm Time fields. Notice that this also moves the alarm "hand" on the clock.

This program uses two alarms. The first is set to go off every second, and is used to update the clock hands. The second alarm sets the actual "alarm clock" alarm, and this value is reset each time the user changes the "Alarm Time" values. The alarm sound is provided by playing a WAV file on the Alarm event procedure.

## Steps

1. Create a new project called ALARM.MAK. Add the Alarm control, ALARM.VBX, to the project. Create a new form with the objects and properties described in Table 9-2. Save this form as ALARM.FRM.

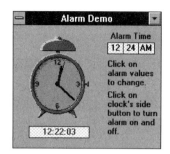

**Figure 9-1** Example program for the Alarm control

**Table 9-2** Objects and properties of ALARM.FRM

| OBJECT | PROPERTY | SETTING |
|---|---|---|
| Form | FormName | frmAlarm |
| | BackColor | &H00C0C0C0& |
| | BorderStyle | 1 'Fixed Single |
| | Caption | "Alarm Demo" |
| | MaxButton | 0 'False |
| Image | Name | picClock |
| | Picture | (set at design time in Properties window) |
| Line | Name | linSeconds |
| | BorderColor | &H00000000& |
| | X1 | 1020 |
| | X2 | 1500 |
| | Y1 | 1200 |
| | Y2 | 1200 |
| Label | Name | lblDigitalTime |
| | Alignment | 2 'Center |
| | BackColor | &H0080FFFF& |
| | BorderStyle | 1 'Fixed Single |
| | ForeColor | &H000000FF& |
| Line | Name | linMinutes |
| | BorderColor | &H00800000& |
| | BorderWidth | 2 |
| | X1 | 1020 |
| | X2 | 1560 |
| | Y1 | 1320 |
| | Y2 | 1320 |
| Line | Name | linHours |
| | BorderColor | &H00800000& |
| | BorderWidth | 3 |
| | X1 | 1020 |

*(continued on next page)*

| OBJECT | PROPERTY | SETTING |
|---|---|---|
| *(continued from previous page)* | | |
| | X2 | 1440 |
| | Y1 | 1440 |
| | Y2 | 1440 |
| Label | Name | lblAlarmHour |
| | Alignment | 2 'Center |
| | BackColor | &H0080FFFF& |
| | BorderStyle | 1 'Fixed Single |
| | Caption | "12" |
| Label | Name | lblAlarmMinute |
| | Alignment | 2 'Center |
| | BackColor | &H0080FFFF& |
| | BorderStyle | 1 'Fixed Single |
| | Caption | "01" |
| Label | Name | Label2 |
| | Alignment | 2 'Center |
| | BackStyle | 0 'Transparent |
| | Caption | "Alarm Time" |
| | ForeColor | &H00000080& |
| Label | Name | Label3 |
| | BackStyle | 0 'Transparent |
| | Caption | "Click on alarm values to change." |
| | ForeColor | &H00800000& |
| Label | Name | lblAlarmAMPM |
| | Alignment | 2 'Center |
| | BackColor | &H0080FFFF& |
| | BorderStyle | 1 'Fixed Single |
| | Caption | "AM" |
| Label | Name | Label4 |
| | BackStyle | 0 'Transparent |
| | Caption | "Click on clock's side button to turn alarm on and off." |
| | ForeColor | &H00800000& |
| Line | Name | linAlarm |
| | BorderColor | &H000000FF& |
| | X1 | 1020 |
| | X2 | 1200 |
| | Y1 | 1560 |
| | Y2 | 1560 |
| PictureBox | Name | picBell |
| | AutoSize | -1 'True |

| OBJECT | PROPERTY | SETTING |
|---|---|---|
| | BorderStyle | 0 'None |
| | Picture | (set at design time in Properties window) |
| PictureBox | Name | picButton |
| | AutoSize | -1 'True |
| | BorderStyle | 0 'None |
| | Picture | (set at design time in Properties window) |
| MabryAlarm | Name | Alarm1 |
| | DateFormat | " " |

2. Add the following code to the declarations section of the ALARM.FRM form.

```
Option Explicit
'----------------------------------------------------
' Constants, variables, and function declarations
' used throughout the form.
'----------------------------------------------------

Dim ButtonInPos As Integer
Dim ButtonOutPos As Integer

Dim BellUpPos As Integer
Dim BellDownPos As Integer

Dim HandLen As Integer

Dim PiOver180 As Single

Const UPDATE_CLOCK = 1
Const SOUND_ALARM = 2

Dim AM_PM_Value As Integer

' Functions and constants used to play sounds.
Declare Function sndPlaySound Lib "MMSystem" (ByVal lpsound As String, ByVal flag As Integer)⇒
As Integer

Const SND_SYNC = &H0        ' Return when sound ends (the default)
Const SND_ASYNC = &H1       ' Return as soon as sound starts
Const SND_NODEFAULT = &H2   ' Don't play default sound if not found
Const SND_MEMORY = &H4      ' lpszSoundName -> memory image of file
Const SND_LOOP = &H8        ' Loop continuously; needs SND_ASYNC
Const SND_NOSTOP = &H10     ' Don't interrupt sound to play new one

' Global string used for by NoiseGet() and NoisePlay() to play .WAV files in memory.
Dim SoundBuffer As String
```

3. Add the following subroutines to the ALARM.FRM form.

```
Sub Alarm1_Alarm (AlarmIndex As Long, TimeNow As String)
'----------------------------------------------------
' Update the clock hands, or ring the alarm,
' depending on the value of AlarmIndex.
'----------------------------------------------------
```

9 ◀

(continued on next page)

*(continued from previous page)*

```vb
Dim degrees As Single
Dim radians As Single

    Select Case AlarmIndex
        Case UPDATE_CLOCK
            lblDigitalTime = TimeNow

            ' Set seconds hand.
            degrees = 180 - (Val(Mid$(TimeNow, 7, 2)) * 6)
            radians = degrees * PiOver180
            linSeconds.X1 = HandLen * Sin(radians) + linSeconds.X2
            linSeconds.Y1 = HandLen * Cos(radians) + linSeconds.Y2

            ' Set minutes hand.
            degrees = 180 - (Val(Mid$(TimeNow, 4, 2)) * 6)
            radians = degrees * PiOver180
            linMinutes.X1 = HandLen * Sin(radians) + linMinutes.X2
            linMinutes.Y1 = HandLen * Cos(radians) + linMinutes.Y2

            ' Set hours hand.
            degrees = (180 - (Val(Mid$(TimeNow, 1, 2)) * 30) - (Val(Mid$(TimeNow, 4, 2)) * .5))
            radians = degrees * PiOver180
            linHours.X1 = (HandLen * .75) * Sin(radians) + linHours.X2
            linHours.Y1 = (HandLen * .75) * Cos(radians) + linHours.Y2

        Case SOUND_ALARM
            While picButton.Left = ButtonOutPos
                If picBell.Top = BellUpPos Then
                    picBell.Top = BellDownPos
                Else
                    picBell.Top = BellUpPos
                End If
                DoEvents
                NoisePlay
            Wend
    End Select
End Sub

Sub Form_Load ()
'-------------------------------------------------
' Set up Alarm Clock.
'-------------------------------------------------
Dim OK As Integer
Dim CenterX As Integer, CenterY As Integer

    ' Set Alarm button and bell positions.
    ButtonOutPos = picButton.Left
    ButtonInPos = ButtonOutPos - 65
    picButton.Left = ButtonInPos

    BellUpPos = picBell.Top
    BellDownPos = BellUpPos + 40

    ' Initialize values global to form.
    PiOver180 = (4 * Atn(1)) / 180
    AM_PM_Value = 0

    ' Set clock hand length and center position.
    HandLen = (picClock.Width / 2) * .7
```

```vb
    CenterX = (picClock.Width / 2) + picClock.Left - 1
    CenterY = (picClock.Height / 2) + picClock.Top - 1

    linSeconds.X2 = CenterX
    linSeconds.Y2 = CenterY

    linMinutes.X2 = CenterX
    linMinutes.Y2 = CenterY

    linHours.X2 = CenterX
    linHours.Y2 = CenterY

    linAlarm.X2 = CenterX
    linAlarm.Y2 = CenterY

    ' This alarm just updates the clock hands.
    Alarm1.AlarmTime(UPDATE_CLOCK) = "??:??:??"

    ' Set the initial alarm.
    SetAlarm lblAlarmHour + AM_PM_Value, lblAlarmMinute

    ' Load the alarm noise into memory for later.
    OK = NoiseGet(App.Path & "\ALARM.WAV")

    ' Center the form on the screen.
    Me.Move (Screen.Width - Me.Width) \ 2, (Screen.Height - Me.Height) \ 2
End Sub

Sub Form_Unload (Cancel As Integer)
'---------------------------------------------------
' In case the alarm is still ringing, force the
' program to end.
'---------------------------------------------------
    End
End Sub

Sub lblAlarmAMPM_Click ()
'---------------------------------------------------
' Change the alarm label's AM/PM value, and reset
' alarm.
'---------------------------------------------------
    If lblAlarmAMPM = "AM" Then
        lblAlarmAMPM = "PM"
        AM_PM_Value = 12
    Else
        lblAlarmAMPM = "AM"
        AM_PM_Value = 0
    End If

    SetAlarm lblAlarmHour + AM_PM_Value, lblAlarmMinute
End Sub

Sub lblAlarmHour_Click ()
'---------------------------------------------------
' Change the alarm label's Hour value, and reset
' alarm.
'---------------------------------------------------
Dim NewHour As Integer

    NewHour = Val(lblAlarmHour) + 1
```

9 ◀

*(continued on next page)*

(continued from previous page)

```
    If NewHour >= 13 Then NewHour = 1
    lblAlarmHour = Format$(NewHour, "00")

    SetAlarm lblAlarmHour + AM_PM_Value, lblAlarmMinute
End Sub

Sub lblAlarmMinute_Click ()
'----------------------------------------------------
' Change the alarm label's Minute value, and reset
' alarm.
'----------------------------------------------------
Dim newmin As Integer

    newmin = Val(lblAlarmMinute) + 1
    If newmin >= 60 Then newmin = 0
    lblAlarmMinute = Format$(newmin, "00")

    SetAlarm lblAlarmHour + AM_PM_Value, lblAlarmMinute
End Sub

Sub lblAlarmMinute_DblClick ()
'----------------------------------------------------
' Change the alarm label's Minute value, and reset
' alarm.
'----------------------------------------------------
Dim newmin As Integer

    newmin = Val(lblAlarmMinute) + 9
    If newmin >= 60 Then newmin = 0
    lblAlarmMinute = Format$(newmin, "00")

    SetAlarm lblAlarmHour + AM_PM_Value, lblAlarmMinute
End Sub

Function NoiseGet (ByVal FileName) As Integer
'----------------------------------------------------
' Load a sound file into the global string variable
' SoundBuffer. This must be called before NoisePlay
'----------------------------------------------------
Dim buffer As String
Dim f As Integer

    On Error GoTo NoiseGet_Error

    buffer = Space$(1024)
    SoundBuffer = ""
    f = FreeFile
    Open FileName For Binary As f
    Do While Not EOF(f)
        Get #f, , buffer      ' Load in 1K chunks.
        SoundBuffer = SoundBuffer & buffer
    Loop
    Close f
    SoundBuffer = Trim$(SoundBuffer)
    NoiseGet = True
Exit Function

NoiseGet_Error:
```

```
        NoiseGet = False
        SoundBuffer = ""
        Exit Function
End Function

Sub NoisePlay ()
'-------------------------------------------------
' Plays a sound previously loaded into memory with
' function NoiseGet().
'-------------------------------------------------
Dim r As Integer

        If SoundBuffer = "" Then Exit Sub
        r = sndPlaySound(ByVal SoundBuffer, SND_SYNC Or SND_MEMORY)
End Sub

Sub picButton_Click ()
'-------------------------------------------------
' Set the alarm.
'-------------------------------------------------
        If picButton.Left = ButtonInPos Then
            picButton.Left = ButtonOutPos
        Else
            picButton.Left = ButtonInPos
            picBell.Top = BellUpPos
        End If
End Sub

Sub SetAlarm (ByVal NewHour As Integer, ByVal NewMinute As Integer)
'-------------------------------------------------
' Update the value for the clock's alarm.
'-------------------------------------------------
Dim degrees As Single
Dim radians As Single

        If NewHour >= 24 Then NewHour = 0
        Alarm1.AlarmTime(SOUND_ALARM) = Format$(NewHour, "00") & ":" & Format$(NewMinute, "00") & ":01"

        ' Set alarm hand.
        degrees = (180 - (NewHour * 30) - (NewMinute * .5))
        radians = degrees * PiOver180
        linAlarm.X1 = (HandLen * .45) * Sin(radians) + linAlarm.X2
        linAlarm.Y1 = (HandLen * .45) * Cos(radians) + linAlarm.Y2
End Sub
```

# Tips and Comments

The Alarm control provides a straightforward means of implementing alarms that previously required use of the Timer control and a fair amount of Visual Basic code. Although the example program is fairly basic, this control can greatly simplify more complex applications that require some form of "time of day" scheduling.

# App-Link (APPLINK.VBX)

| USAGE: | Inter-App and Intra-App Messaging |
|---|---|
| MANUFACTURER: | Synergy Technologies |
| COST: | $69.95 |

App-Link is a unique control that lets you to send data not only between multiple forms in a VB application, but also between separate VB applications. Rather than building a single, monolithic .EXE, many VB developers take advantage of Windows' ability to run multiple applications simultaneously by splitting their apps into many small cooperative .EXEs. App-Link lets you send data back and forth between those .EXEs, increasing the practicality of that approach. While it's possible to use DDE directly to accomplish the same task, App-Link makes it easy.

## Syntax

An App-Link control is called a Socket and can be both a sender and receiver of messages. You can have as many Sockets as you want but usually you can get by with just one per form or application. Table 9-3 lists the nonstandard properties, event, and functions for the App-Link Socket control.

**Table 9-3** App-Link nonstandard properties, event, and functions

**PROPERTIES**

| Command | Dest | Flags |
|---|---|---|
| Msg | MsgLen | Priority |
| Protocol | SocketName | Timeout |

**EVENT**

ReceiveMessage

**FUNCTIONS**

AplkVBTypeToString    AplkStringToVBType

App-Link uses the Microsoft DDE Management Library (DDEML) as its messaging infrastructure so you can send messages directly (synchronous) or post them to the recipient's message queue (asynchronous). You can send messages to Sockets on other nodes (that is, workstations) across a network as well, just as if the messages were on the same machine as the source Socket.

A Socket is identified by its *SocketName* property, which is not the same as the standard *Name* property that every control has. To send a message to a Socket, you need to know its *SocketName*. The *SocketName* is set at design time but may be changed at run time. The *SocketName* must be unique within a given node.

Setting the *Command* property to 1 (Send) causes the Socket to send the message in its *Msg* property to the Socket identified by its *Dest* property. When *Command* is set to 2 (Receive) the Socket retrieves the next message from its message queue (Table 9-4).

**Table 9-4** Command property values

| VALUE | MEANING |
| --- | --- |
| 1 | Send |
| 2 | Receive |

The *Flags* property (see Table 9-5 for values) determines how the message is sent to the receiver.

**Table 9-5** Flags property values

| VALUE | MEANING |
| --- | --- |
| 0 | Default |
| 1 | Queue message |
| 2 | Start destination app |
| 4 | No wait - send message asynchronously |

A 0 (default) means that the message will be sent directly to the receiver's *ReceiveMessage* event, and the sending app will not continue until the receiver acknowledges receipt of the message or a timeout occurs. A value of 1 (queue message) posts the message to the receiver's message queue. Control returns to the sender immediately and the receiver must explicitly retrieve the message from its message queue. No *ReceiveMessage* event is fired. A value of 2 (start destination app) instructs App-Link to start the destination app if it isn't already running. For this to work, the design time *SocketName* of the receiver must be the same as the file name of the receiver's .EXE file minus the .EXE extension. A value of 4 (no wait) is like the default (0) except that it doesn't wait for the receiver to acknowledge receipt of the message. A *ReceiveMessage* event is fired on the receiving Socket. The *Dest* property contains the *SocketName* of the intended receiver, including the name of the node if the Socket is located on a remote node.

Each message sent to a Socket's message queue has a priority assigned to it, based on the *Priority* property of the sender when the message was sent. Messages sent directly to a Socket don't have a priority because they are processed immediately upon receipt. *Protocol* determines what communications server to use when sending messages to Sockets on remote computers; currently only NetBIOS is available. If a message is sent with *Flags* set to 0 (default), the sender will wait until the receiver acknowledges that it received the message. How long it will wait is determined by the *Timeout* property, set in milliseconds. Setting *Timeout* to -1 causes the sender to wait indefinitely.

The *Msg* property contains the actual message being sent to the receiver. It is a standard VB string that may be up to 64K in size and may contain embedded nulls. Two functions allow you to pass user-defined type variables between Sockets by converting

9

them to VB Strings. *AplkVBTypeToString* takes a type variable and converts it to a string, and *AplkStringToVBType* takes the generated string and converts it back to a type variable. The only limitation is that all the elements in the type definition must be fixed length; no variable length strings may be used. Another tool, FieldPack from Software Source (42808 Christy Street, Ste. 222, Fremont, California 94538 USA Tel. (510) 623-7854), overcomes this limitation and is a good complement to App-Link if you plan to pass user-defined type variables as messages. *MgsLen* is simply the length of the message being sent and can be easily derived using VB's *Len* function.

Whenever a message is received, the *ReceiveMessage* event fires. This occurs when a message is sent directly to a Socket and when a Socket sets its *Command* property to 2 (receive) to retrieve a message from its message queue. *ReceiveMessage* contains four parameters: the name of the sender, the size of the message, the message itself, and the return code to send back to the sender. The return code appears to the sender as an error code that can be retrieved with the *Err* statement just like any other trappable error. This allows you to define your own internal error codes—just make sure they don't conflict with the values reserved by VB or App-Link. Since the *SocketName* of the sender is included, it's quite easy to perform callback messaging, where the receiver would "call back" the sender, perhaps to acknowledge the receipt of a message that was sent asynchronously.

# Example

The sample application (Figure 9-2) is a small e-mail demonstration program. There is no persistent storage involved so all messages from each session are discarded when the application ends. The program demonstrates how to change the *SocketName* of a Socket dynamically, handle possible errors, determine where a message originated, and find out if a message was sent successfully. It also provides a number of functions that you can easily extract and reuse in other applications.

**Figure 9-2** App-Link MiniMail sample application

## Steps

1. Create a new project called APPLNK.MAK. Create a new form with the objects and properties shown in Table 9-6. Save this form as APPLNK.FRM.

**Table 9-6** App-Link main form's objects and properties

| OBJECT | PROPERTY | SETTING |
|--------|----------|---------|
| Form | FormName | frmMain |
| | BorderStyle | 1 'Fixed Single |
| | Caption | "MiniMail" |
| | ClipControls | 0 'False |
| | MaxButton | 0 'False |
| Label | Name | lblMessageOut |
| | BackStyle | 0 'Transparent |
| | Caption | "&Outgoing Message:" |
| Label | Name | lblTo |
| | BackStyle | 0 'Transparent |
| | Caption | "&To:" |
| Label | Name | lblNode |
| | BackStyle | 0 'Transparent |
| | Caption | "&Node:" |
| Label | Name | lblNodeNote |
| | Alignment | 1 'Right Justify |
| | BackStyle | 0 'Transparent |
| | Caption | "(leave blank if local)" |
| | FontBold | 0 'False |
| Label | Name | lblStatusBar |
| | BackStyle | 0 'Transparent |
| | BorderStyle | 1 'Fixed Single |
| | FontBold | 0 'False |
| | FontSize | 9.75 |
| Label | Name | lblMessagesReceived |
| | BackStyle | 0 'Transparent |
| | Caption | "Messages Received:" |
| Label | Name | Label1 |
| | Caption | "Date From Message" |
| Label | Name | lblViewMessage |
| | Caption | "Double-click list item to view entire message" |
| | FontBold | 0 'False |

*(continued on next page)*

9

| OBJECT | PROPERTY | SETTING |
|---|---|---|
| *(continued from previous page)* | | |
| Socket | Name | sktMain |
| | Dest | " " |
| | Priority | 100 |
| | Protocol | 0 'NetBIOS |
| | SocketName | "MINIMAIL" |
| | Timeout | 10000 |
| CommandButton | Name | cmdSendMessage |
| | Caption | "&Send" |
| CheckBox | Name | chkClearOnSend |
| | Caption | "Clear on Send" |
| | TabStop | 0 'False |
| | Value | 1 'Checked |
| TextBox | Name | txtMessageOut |
| | FontBold | 0 'False |
| | FontName | "Fixedsys" |
| | FontSize | 9 |
| | MaxLength | 256 |
| | MultiLine | -1 'True |
| | ScrollBars | 2 'Vertical |
| TextBox | Name | txtSocket |
| | MaxLength | 40 |
| TextBox | Name | txtNode |
| | MaxLength | 16 |
| ListBox | Name | lstMessagesReceived |

2. Add the following code to APPLNK.FRM.

```
Option Explicit
DefInt A-Z

Sub cmdSendMessage_Click ()

    Call SendAppLinkMessage

End Sub

Sub Form_Load ()
    Dim rtn&
    ReDim arrTabStops%(1)

    '-- Center the form on the screen.
    Me.Move (Screen.Width - Width) \ 2, (Screen.Height - Height) \ 2

    arrTabStops%(0) = 40
    arrTabStops%(1) = 80
```

```
    rtn& = SendMessage(lstMessagesReceived.hWnd, LB_SETTABSTOPS, 2, arrTabStops%(0))

End Sub

Sub Form_Resize ()

    lblStatusBar.Width = frmMain.ScaleWidth + 30
    lblStatusBar.Top = frmMain.ScaleHeight - (lblStatusBar.Height - 15)

End Sub

Sub lstMessagesReceived_DblClick ()
    Dim Cap$
    Dim Msg$
    Dim tMsg As T_MESSAGE

    tMsg = gtarrMsg(lstMessagesReceived.ListIndex)
    Cap$ = "Sent: " & Format$(tMsg.Sent, "Short Date") & "  From: " & tMsg.Source
    Msg$ = tMsg.Msg
    MsgBox Msg$, 0, Cap$

End Sub

Sub mnuFile_Click (Index As Integer)

    Select Case Index%
        Case 0 'EXIT
            Unload Me
    End Select

End Sub

Sub mnuHelp_Click (Index As Integer)

    Select Case Index%
        Case 0 'ABOUT
            frmAbout.Show MODAL
    End Select

End Sub

Sub sktMain_ReceiveMessage (Orig As String, MsgLen As Long, Msg As String, RetCode As Long)
    Dim tMsg As T_MESSAGE

    tMsg.Source = Orig$
    tMsg.Dest = gCurUser$
    tMsg.Sent = Now
    tMsg.Msg = Msg$
    Call AddMsgToInBox(tMsg)

End Sub
```

3. Create a new module called APPLNK.BAS and add the following code to it. These are declarations and procedures used by the sample program.

```
Option Explicit
DefInt A-Z

Global Const SENDMSG = 1              '-- App-Link command
```

9 ◄

*(continued on next page)*

*(continued from previous page)*

```
Global Const ALERR_NO_ERROR = 0&      '-- App-Link return code

Declare Function SendMessage Lib "User" (ByVal hWnd As Integer, ByVal wMsg As Integer, ByVal
wParam As Integer, lParam As Any) As Long
Global Const WM_USER = &H400
Global Const LB_SETTABSTOPS = (WM_USER + 19)

Global Const MODAL = 1

' MsgBox parameters
Global Const MB_OK = 0
Global Const MB_ICONSTOP = 16

' MsgBox return values
Global Const IDOK = 1

' Colors
Global Const BLACK = &H0&
Global Const RED = &HFF&


Type T_MESSAGE
    Source  As String
    Dest    As String
    Sent    As Double
    Msg     As String
End Type
Global gtarrMsg() As T_MESSAGE

Global gCurUser$

Sub AddMsgToInBox (tMsg As T_MESSAGE)
    Dim ListItem$

    '-- Increase the size of our global message
    '   array by one. This isn't super-efficient,
    '   but should be fine for demonstration
    '   purposes.
    On Error GoTo AddMsgToInBoxErr
        ReDim Preserve gtarrMsg(UBound(gtarrMsg) + 1)
    On Error GoTo 0

    '-- Assign the new message to the last element
    '   in the array (the one we just added).
    gtarrMsg(UBound(gtarrMsg)) = tMsg

    ListItem$ = Format$(tMsg.Sent, "short date") & Chr$(9) & tMsg.Source & Chr$(9) & tMsg.Msg
    frmMain!lstMessagesReceived.AddItem ListItem$

    Exit Sub

AddMsgToInBoxErr:
    ReDim gtarrMsg(0)
    Resume Next

End Sub

Function aplkChangeSocketName% (Skt As Socket, NewSocketName$)
```

```
    Dim RtnCode%

    On Error GoTo aplkChangeSocketNameErr
        Skt.SocketName = NewSocketName$
    On Error GoTo 0

aplkChangeSocketNameExit:
    On Error GoTo 0
    aplkChangeSocketName% = RtnCode%
    Exit Function

aplkChangeSocketNameErr:
    RtnCode% = Err
    Resume aplkChangeSocketNameExit

End Function

Function aplkError$ (ErrorCode%)
    Dim Desc$

    '-- Error Codes 20000-20999 are Reserved by
    '   the AppLink Developers.
    Select Case ErrorCode%
        Case 20000
            Desc$ = "System Error"
        Case 20001
            Desc$ = "Unable to allocate memory"
        Case 20002
            Desc$ = "Unable to load application"
        Case 20500
            Desc$ = "Unable to query node name"
        Case 20501
            Desc$ = "Request aborted"
        Case 20502
            Desc$ = "Transaction Failure"
        Case 20503
            Desc$ = "Unable to locate net instance"
        Case 20504
            Desc$ = "Duplicate socket name"
        Case 20505
            Desc$ = "Unable to locate socket"
        Case 20506
            Desc$ = "Unable to locate conversation"
        Case 20507
            Desc$ = "Message queue is empty"
        Case 20509
            Desc$ = "Unable to register object class"
        Case 20510
            Desc$ = "Timeout occurred"
        Case 20511
            Desc$ = "Unable to establish connection"
        Case 20512
            Desc$ = "Invalid message priority"
        Case 20513
            Desc$ = "Invalid timeout value"
        Case 20514
            Desc$ = "Invalid message length. Broadcast message lengths must be in the range 1
to 256 inclusive."
        Case 20515
            Desc$ = "Null message pointer"
```

*(continued on next page)*

9

*(continued from previous page)*

```
        Case 20516
            Desc$ = "Invalid local session number"
        Case 20517
            Desc$ = "No remote resources available"
        Case 20518
            Desc$ = "Network session was closed"
        Case 20519
            Desc$ = "Network command canceled"
        Case 20523
            Desc$ = "No answer from partner"
        Case 20524
            Desc$ = "Unable to find network name"
        Case 20525
            Desc$ = "Too many network commands"
        Case 20526
            Desc$ = "Network adapter malfunction"
        Case 20528
            Desc$ = "Synchronus transaction pending"
        Case 20529
            Desc$ = "PostMessage failed"
        Case 20535
            Desc$ = "Connection was dropped"
        Case 20536
            Desc$ = "Destination is missing"
        Case 20537
            Desc$ = "Destination contains blanks"
        Case 20538
            Desc$ = "Destination missing separators"
        Case 20539
            Desc$ = "Invalid node name length. The length must be 1 - 16 bytes inclusive.
NetBIOS node names cannot exceed 14 bytes in length."
        Case 20540
            Desc$ = "Socket name is missing"
        Case 20541
            Desc$ = "Invalid socket name length"
        Case 20542
            Desc$ = "Invalid separator in socket name"
        Case 20543
            Desc$ = "Socket name contains blanks"
        Case 20544
            Desc$ = "Application terminated"
        Case 30000
            Desc$ = "Unknown method specified"
    End Select

    aplkError$ = Desc$

End Function

Function aplkSendMessage% (sktSource As Socket, DestNode$, DestSocket$, Msg$)
'-------------------------------------------------------
'-- This is a wrapper function used to hide all the
'   socket property accesses from the calling app
'   and provide error handling.
'
'-- Returns: 0 if successful
'            AppLink Error code if an error occurs
'-------------------------------------------------------
```

```
        Dim Dest$
        Dim RtnCode%

        Dest$ = ""
        If Len(DestNode$) Then
            Dest$ = "\\" & DestNode$ & "\"
        End If
        Dest$ = Dest$ & DestSocket$

        On Error GoTo aplkSendMessageErr
            sktSource.Dest = Dest$
            sktSource.Msg = Msg$
            sktSource.MsgLen = Len(Msg$)
            sktSource.Command = SENDMSG
        On Error GoTo 0

aplkSendMessageExit:
        On Error GoTo 0
        aplkSendMessage% = RtnCode%
        Exit Function

aplkSendMessageErr:
        RtnCode% = Err
        Resume aplkSendMessageExit

End Function

Sub Main ()
        Dim rtnOK%
        Dim UserName$

        Load frmMain

        UserName$ = InputBox$("Please enter your name", "MiniMail Logon")
        If Len(UserName$) Then
            '-- Change the socket name so we can spawn
            '   multiple instances via START_DEST_APP.
            rtnOK% = aplkChangeSocketName%(frmMain!sktMain, UserName$)
            While rtnOK%   ALERR_NO_ERROR
                UserName$ = InputBox$("Please try again.", aplkError$(rtnOK%))
                If UserName$ = "" Then
                    Unload frmMain
                    End
                End If
                rtnOK% = aplkChangeSocketName%(frmMain!sktMain, UserName$)
            Wend
            frmMain.Caption = "MiniMail - " & UserName$
            frmMain.Show
        Else
            Unload frmMain
            End
        End If

End Sub

Sub SendAppLinkMessage ()
        Dim alRtn%
        Dim DestNode$
        Dim DestSocket$
        Dim Msg$
```

9 ◀

*(continued on next page)*

*(continued from previous page)*

```
    DestNode$ = frmMain!txtNode.Text
    DestSocket$ = frmMain!txtSocket.Text
    Msg$ = frmMain!txtMessageOut.Text
    alRtn% = aplkSendMessage(frmMain!sktMain, DestNode$, DestSocket$, Msg$)
    '-- See if it went out OK.
    If alRtn% = ALERR_NO_ERROR Then
        frmMain.ForeColor = BLACK
        Call UpdateStatus("Message Sent Successfully")
        If frmMain!chkClearOnSend.Value Then
            frmMain!txtMessageOut.Text = ""
        End If
    Else
        '-- An error occurred while sending the message.
        frmMain.ForeColor = RED
        Call UpdateStatus(aplkError$(alRtn%))
    End If

End Sub

Sub UpdateStatus (NewStatus$)

    frmMain!lblStatusBar.Caption = "   " & NewStatus$

End Sub
```

4. Create a new form with the objects and properties shown in Table 9-7. Save this form as FRMABOUT.FRM.

**Table 9-7** Objects and properties for FRMABOUT.FRM

| OBJECT | PROPERTY | SETTING |
|---|---|---|
| Form | FormName | frmAbout |
| | BackColor | &H00C0C0C0& |
| | BorderStyle | 3 'Fixed Double |
| | Caption | " " |
| | MaxButton | 0 'False |
| | MinButton | 0 'False |
| CommandButton | Name | btnOK |
| | Cancel | -1 'True |
| | Caption | "&OK" |
| | Default | -1 'True |
| TextBox | Name | txtAbout |
| | FontBold | 0 'False |
| | ForeColor | &H00800000& |
| | MultiLine | -1 'True |
| | ScrollBars | 2 'Vertical |
| | Text | " " |

5. Add the following code to FRMABOUT.BAS.

```
Option Explicit

' Color constants
Const DARK_GRAY = &H808080
Const WHITE = &HFFFFFF
Const BLACK = &H0

' Maximum allowable title string length
Const MAX_TITLE_LEN = 80

Sub btnOK_Click ()
'-----------------------------------------------------
' Close the About window.
'-----------------------------------------------------
    Unload Me
End Sub

Sub Form_Load ()
'-----------------------------------------------------
' Try to read the text file FRMABOUT.TXT in the
' application's subdirectory and display its contents
' in the About box. Use the first line as the
' About window caption.
'-----------------------------------------------------
Dim FileName As String
Dim fnum As Integer
Dim InText As String
Dim pos As Integer

    On Error Resume Next

    ' Build the file name.
    FileName = App.Path
    If Right$(FileName, 1)  "\" Then FileName = FileName & "\"
    FileName = FileName & "frmabout.txt"

    ' Read in the file.
    fnum = FreeFile
    Open FileName For Input As fnum
    InText = Input$(FileLen(FileName), fnum)

    ' Load the text into the caption and text control.
    pos = InStr(InText, Chr$(13) & Chr$(10))
    If (pos < MAX_TITLE_LEN) And (pos > 0) Then
        Me.Caption = Left$(InText, pos - 1)
        txtAbout.Text = Mid$(InText, pos + 2)
    ElseIf pos > 0 Then
        Me.Caption = "About the " & App.Title & " Demo"
        txtAbout.Text = InText
    End If

    ' Center the form.
    Me.Move (Screen.Width - Me.Width) \ 2, (Screen.Height - Me.Height) \ 2
End Sub

Sub Form_Paint ()
```

(continued on next page)

9 ◄

*(continued from previous page)*

```
'---------------------------------------------------
' Paint the 3D effect around the text box.
'---------------------------------------------------
    Make3D Me, txtAbout
End Sub

Sub Make3D (pic As Form, ctl As Control)
'---------------------------------------------------
' Wrap a 3D effect around a control on a form.
'---------------------------------------------------
Dim AdjustX As Integer, AdjustY As Integer
Dim RightSide As Single

    AdjustX = Screen.TwipsPerPixelX
    AdjustY = Screen.TwipsPerPixelY

    ' Set the top shading line.
    pic.Line (ctl.Left - AdjustX, ctl.Top - AdjustY)-(ctl.Left + ctl.Width, ctl.Top - ⇒
AdjustY), DARK_GRAY
    pic.Line -(ctl.Left + ctl.Width, ctl.Top + ctl.Height), WHITE
    pic.Line -(ctl.Left - AdjustX, ctl.Top + ctl.Height), WHITE
    pic.Line -(ctl.Left - AdjustX, ctl.Top - AdjustY), DARK_GRAY
End Sub

Sub txtAbout_KeyPress (KeyAscii As Integer)
'---------------------------------------------------
' Prevent accidental editing of help text.
'---------------------------------------------------
    KeyAscii = 0
End Sub
```

6. Create a new text file and add the following text to it. Save the file as FRMABOUT.TXT.

```
About - AppLink Demo
The Mini-Mail app can be used to send messages to users on other machines (by using the node
name in the Node text box) but it can also be tested on a single machine. Here's how:
Start one instance of Mini-Mail and log on with your name.
Start a second instance of Mini-Mail and log on with a different name.
Now you can send messages back and forth between the two instances of Mini-Mail.
```

## Tips and Comments

App-Link is not limited to sending data in messages. If you provide it with a suitable function, an application can send commands as well, much like DDE LinkExecute commands, which allow separate applications to control one another. App-Link also supports broadcast messages—that is, messages that are sent to multiple Sockets simultaneously. To specify that a message should be a broadcast message, use an asterisk (*) for the node name (in the *Dest* property) and include the *SocketName* as you normally would. For example, if the *Dest* property contains "\\*\MailBox", App-Link knows to broadcast the message to the Socket named MailBox on every node that has an App-Link communications server loaded.

In addition to the VB version, Synergy has developed a version of App-Link for C programmers that will allow C and VB apps to send and receive messages transparently.

# FMDrop (FMDROP1.VBX)

| USAGE: | Drag Target for Windows File Manager |
|---|---|
| MANUFACTURER: | Mabry Software |
| COST: | $15 ($10 if registered on CompuServe) |

The FMDrop control allows a Visual Basic program to receive the names of files that have been "dragged" from the Windows File Manager.

## Syntax

When you place the FMDrop control on a Visual Basic form, the entire form is made a "target" for files that have been dragged over from the File Manager. The *DropFiles* event is triggered when files are dropped on a form. Table 9-8 lists FMDrop's nonstandard properties and event.

**Table 9-8** Nonstandard properties and event of the FMDrop control

| PROPERTIES | | |
|---|---|---|
| FileCount | FileName() | InClient |
| X | Y | |

| EVENT |
|---|
| DropFiles |

After a *DropFiles* event has been fired, you can retrieve the names of the dropped files by inspecting FMDrop's *FileName()* property array. This array contains the full file name, including drive and path information, for each file dropped from File Manager. The *FileCount* property indicates how many files are in the array.

To put each file name dragged from File Manager into a list box, you just need the following code:

```
For i=0 to FMDrop1.FileCount - 1
    List1.AddItem FMDrop1.FileName(i)
Next
```

FMDrop provides properties for determining where in the Visual Basic form the drop took place. *InClient* is a Boolean property that indicates whether the drop occurred in the form's client or nonclient area. The client area of a window is the region that you can "paint"; this excludes the area taken up by the title bar and borders. The $X$ and $Y$ properties provide the coordinates, in pixels, where the file drop took place. These coordinates are relative to the upper-left corner of the client area.

9

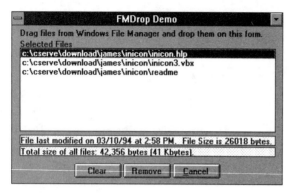

**Figure 9-3** The FMDrop example program

## Example

The example program, shown in Figure 9-3, accepts files dragged from the Windows File Manager and displays them in a list box. The program also provides information on when each file was last modified, the file size, and the total size of all the files in the list.

To use this program, run the program and then start File Manager. Select one or more files and drag them to the example program, releasing the mouse button anywhere over the form. The file names appear in the program's list box. Dragging subsequent files from File Manager adds them to the list box as well.

### Steps

1. Create a new project called FMDROP.MAK. Add the FMDrop control, FMDROP1.VBX, to the project. Create a new Visual Basic module and add the following code to it. Save this module as FMDROP.BAS. This module contains the data structure used within the main form.

```
Option Explicit
' Include this type in a .BAS module.
Type tFileInfo
    Size As Long
    DateTime As Variant
End Type
```

2. Create a new form with the objects and properties described in Table 9-9. Save this form as FMDROP.FRM.

**Table 9-9** Objects and properties for FMDROP.FRM

| OBJECT | PROPERTY | SETTING |
|--------|----------|---------|
| Form | FormName | Form1 |
| | BackColor | &H00C0C0C0& |
| | BorderStyle | 1 'Fixed Single |
| | Caption | "FMDrop Demo" |
| | MaxButton | 0 'False |

| OBJECT | PROPERTY | SETTING |
|---|---|---|
| Label | Name | Label1 |
| | BackStyle | 0 'Transparent |
| | Caption | "Selected Files" |
| | ForeColor | &H00000080& |
| Label | Name | lblFileInfo |
| | BackColor | &H00E0FFFF& |
| | BorderStyle | 1 'Fixed Single |
| | ForeColor | &H00800000& |
| Label | Name | lblTotalSize |
| | BackColor | &H00E0FFFF& |
| | BorderStyle | 1 'Fixed Single |
| Label | Name | Label2 |
| | ForeColor | &H00800000& |
| | BackStyle | 0 'Transparent |
| | Caption | "Drag files from Windows File Manager and drop them on this form." |
| | ForeColor | &H00800000& |
| FMDrop | Name | FMDrop1 |
| ListBox | Name | lstFiles |
| | Sorted | -1 'True |
| CommandButton | Name | btnClear |
| | Caption | "Clear" |
| CommandButton | Name | btnCancel |
| | Caption | "&Cancel" |
| CommandButton | Name | btnRemove |
| | Caption | "Remove" |

3. Add the following code to the declarations section of the FMDROP.FRM form.

```
Option Explicit
'-----------------------------------------------------
' Variables used in this form.
'-----------------------------------------------------

Dim FileArr() As tFileInfo
Dim NumFiles As Integer
Dim TotalSize As Long
```

4. Add the following subroutines to the FMDROP.FRM form.

```
Sub btnCancel_Click ()
'-----------------------------------------------------
' Exit program when the Cancel button is clicked.
'-----------------------------------------------------
```

(continued on next page)

9 ◀

*(continued from previous page)*

```
    Unload Me
End Sub

Sub btnClear_Click ()
'------------------------------------------------------
' Reinitialize all data structures when the Clear
' button is clicked.
'------------------------------------------------------
    lstFiles.Clear
    ReDim FileArr(1)
    NumFiles = 0
    TotalSize = 0
    lblFileInfo = ""
    lblTotalSize = ""
End Sub

Sub btnRemove_Click ()
'------------------------------------------------------
' Remove the currently selected item from the
' list box.
'------------------------------------------------------
    If lstFiles.ListIndex >= 0 Then
      TotalSize = TotalSize - FileArr(lstFiles.ItemData(lstFiles.ListIndex)).Size
      lstFiles.RemoveItem lstFiles.ListIndex
      lblTotalSize = "Total size of all files: " & Format$(TotalSize, "#,###,###,###") & " bytes
"
      lblTotalSize = lblTotalSize & "(" & Format$(TotalSize / 1024, "#,###,###") & " Kbytes)."
      lblFileInfo = ""
    End If
End Sub

Sub FMDrop1_DropFiles ()
'------------------------------------------------------
' Add the items selected from File Manager to the
' current contents of the list box.
'------------------------------------------------------
Dim i As Integer
Dim TimeStamp As String

    For i = 0 To FMDrop1.FileCount - 1
        lstFiles.AddItem LCase$(FMDrop1.FileName(i))

        NumFiles = NumFiles + 1
        ReDim Preserve FileArr(NumFiles)

        FileArr(NumFiles).DateTime = FileDateTime(FMDrop1.FileName(i))
        FileArr(NumFiles).Size = FileLen(FMDrop1.FileName(i))
        TotalSize = TotalSize + FileLen(FMDrop1.FileName(i))

        lstFiles.ItemData(lstFiles.NewIndex) = NumFiles
    Next
    lblTotalSize = "Total size of all files: " & Format$(TotalSize, "#,###,###,###") & " bytes "
    lblTotalSize = lblTotalSize & "(" & Format$(TotalSize / 1024, "#,###,###") & " Kbytes)."

    ' Select the first item.
    If lstFiles.ListCount > 0 Then lstFiles.ListIndex = 0
End Sub
```

```
Sub Form_Load ()
'------------------------------------------------
' Position the form and press the Clear button.
'------------------------------------------------
    Me.Move 10, 10

    btnClear.Value = 1 ' Simulate "clicking" the Clear button.
End Sub

Sub lstFiles_Click ()
'------------------------------------------------
' Update file statistics when a new file is
' clicked in the list box.
'------------------------------------------------
Dim idx As Integer
    If lstFiles.ListCount > 0 Then
      idx = lstFiles.ItemData(lstFiles.ListIndex)
      lblFileInfo = "File last modified on " & Format$(FileArr(idx).DateTime, "MM/DD/YY") & " at "
      lblFileInfo = lblFileInfo & Format$(FileArr(idx).DateTime, "h:mm AM/PM") & ". File Size is "
      lblFileInfo = lblFileInfo & FileArr(idx).Size & " bytes."
    End If
End Sub
```

## Tips and Comments

The FMDrop control makes it trivial to receive files dragged from the File Manager. You can use the example program as the starting point for a diskette-building utility that checks for sufficient disk space before copying files, a "trash-can"-style file deletion utility, or any number of other add-ons that can complement File Manager.

# IniCon (INICON3.VBX)

| USAGE: | Accessing Windows Initialization (.INI) Files |
|---|---|
| MANUFACTURER: | Mabry Software |
| COST: | $5 ($3 if registered on CompuServe) |

The IniCon control allows easy access to Windows initialization (.INI) files, without resorting to the Windows API. With this control, you can easily read or write to .INI files.

## Syntax

Use the IniCon control to replace calls to Windows API functions such as *GetPrivateProfileString* and *WritePrivateProfileString*. You can do this by reading or setting the values of four properties: *FileName, Application, Parameter,* and *Value.* Table 9-10 lists IniCon's nonstandard properties. The IniCon control handles no events and methods.

**Table 9-10** Nonstandard properties of the IniCon control

| Application | DeleteApp | DeleteParm |
|---|---|---|
| FileName | Parameter | Value |

To better understand how to access Windows initialization (.INI) files, you first must understand the layout of an .INI file. An .INI file is just a simple text file, which means that you can view and edit it with applications such as Windows Notepad. Windows uses two special .INI files, WIN.INI and SYSTEM.INI, to store information on the way Microsoft Windows and some of its applications are configured. Other applications can create their own .INI files, called *private* .INI files, to store information related specifically to them. They may also choose to store this information in WIN.INI.

All .INI files have the same basic format. The following example shows two sections from a typical WIN.INI file.

```
[Desktop]
Pattern=(None)
Wallpaper=(None)
TileWallPaper=1
GridGranularity=0
IconSpacing=67


[TrueType]
TTEnable=1
TTOnly=0
```

The heading enclosed in square brackets ([ ]) is called the *application name*. This is used to separate sections of an .INI file into logical groupings. The "section header" can be any string value; it is not limited to the name of the application as the name implies. Individual entries for each application always have two parts. The *parameter*, found to the left of the equal sign, can be thought of as a "key" for a particular piece of data. The data itself is stored to the right of the equal sign.

In the IniCon control, the *FileName* property is a string that specifies the initialization file to be accessed. If a path is not included as part of the file name, the Windows directory is assumed, and IniCon looks there for the file. If the *FileName* is not set, or is set to an empty string (""), IniCon uses the Windows WIN.INI file.

The *Application* property corresponds to the application name described earlier. This string is the name found in brackets at the beginning of each section of an .INI file.

The *Parameter* property corresponds to the "key" string found to the left of the equal sign.

When the *FileName, Application,* and *Parameter* properties are set, IniCon retrieves the matching value (the string to the right of the equal sign) from the .INI file and assigns it to the *Value* property. Any time the *FileName, Application,* and *Parameter* property is changed, a new *Value* is automatically retrieved.

You save data in the .INI file by assigning a new string to *Value.* IniCon saves the data to the section and parameter specified by the current values of the *Application* and *Parameter* properties.

IniCon provides two Boolean properties for deleting data from an .INI file. Use the first, *DeleteApp* to delete an entire application section from an .INI file. Set this property to *True* and IniCon deletes the section indicated by the *Application* property from the

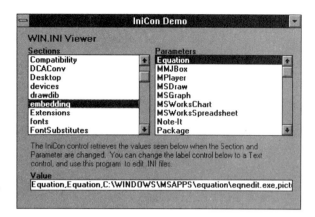

**Figure 9-4** The IniCon example program

.INI file specified by the current *FileName* property. The *DeleteParam* property is similar, but deletes only a single entry that matches the current *Parameter* value.

# Example

The example program implements a WIN.INI viewer, shown in Figure 9-4. Two list boxes display all the application sections and the parameters for the currently selected application. A label control at the bottom of the form displays the value of the selected parameter.

This program starts out by scanning the entire WIN.INI file, using standard Visual Basic data input commands, to extract the application and parameter information. The IniCon control can only do its job when it knows the specific names of the applications and parameters. The program stores this information in an array, and uses it to fill the list boxes. When the user selects a new parameter from the Parameters list box, the program sets IniCon's *Application* and *Parameter* properties and reads IniCon's *Value* property. The program then assigns this information to the Value label.

## Steps

1. Create a new form called INICON.MAK. Add the IniCon control, INICON3.VBX, to the project. Create a new form with the objects and properties described in Table 9-11. Save this form as INICON.FRM.

**Table 9-11** Objects and properties for INICON.FRM

| OBJECT | PROPERTY | SETTING |
|--------|----------|---------|
| Form | FormName | frmIniCon |
| | BackColor | &H00C0C0C0& |
| | BorderStyle | 1 'Fixed Single |
| | Caption | "IniCon Demo" |
| | MaxButton | 0 'False |

*(continued on next page)*

9

| OBJECT | PROPERTY | SETTING |
|---|---|---|
| *(continued from previous page)* | | |
| Label | Name | lblValue |
| | BorderStyle | 1 'Fixed Single |
| | Caption | "Label1" |
| Label | Name | Label1 |
| | BackStyle | 0 'Transparent |
| | Caption | "Sections" |
| | ForeColor | &H00800000& |
| Label | Name | Label2 |
| | BackStyle | 0 'Transparent |
| | Caption | "Parameters" |
| | ForeColor | &H00800000& |
| Label | Name | Label3 |
| | BackStyle | 0 'Transparent |
| | Caption | "Value" |
| | ForeColor | &H00800000& |
| Label | Name | Label4 |
| | BackStyle | 0 'Transparent |
| | Caption | "WIN.INI Viewer" |
| | FontSize | 9.75 |
| | ForeColor | &H00000080& |
| Label | Name | Label5 |
| | BackStyle | 0 'Transparent |
| | Caption | "The IniCon control retrieves the values seen below when the Section and Parameter are changed. You can change the label control below to a Text control, and use this program  to edit .INI files." |
| | FontBold | 0 'False |
| | ForeColor | &H00000080& |
| Init | Name | Init1 |
| | Application | " " |
| | Filename | " " |
| | Parameter | " " |
| | Value | " " |
| ListBox | Name | lstParms |
| | Sorted | -1 'True |
| ListBox | Name | lstSections |
| | Sorted | -1 'True |

2. Add the following code to the declarations section of the INICON.FRM form.

```
Option Explicit
'----------------------------------------------------
' Declare variables and functions used in this form.
'----------------------------------------------------

Dim WinIni() As String

Const CSR_NORMAL = 0
Const CSR_HOURGLASS = 11

Declare Function GetWindowsDirectory Lib "Kernel" (ByVal lpBuffer As String, ByVal nSize As ⇒
Integer) As Integer
```

3. Add the following subroutines to the INICON.FRM form.

```
Sub Form_Load ()
'----------------------------------------------------
' Center the form on the screen.
'----------------------------------------------------
Dim WinDir As String
Dim WinDirLen As Integer
Dim retcode As Integer

    Me.Move (Screen.Width - Me.Width) \ 2, (Screen.Height - Me.Height) \ 2

    WinDir = Space$(255)
    WinDirLen = 255
      retcode = GetWindowsDirectory(WinDir, WinDirLen)
      If retcode > 0 Then
        WinDir = Left$(WinDir, retcode)
      Else
        MsgBox "Could not find the WINDOWS directory.", , "Error in IniCon Demo Program"
        End
    End If
    retcode = ReadINI(WinDir & "\WIN.INI")
    LoadSections
    If lstSections.ListCount > 0 Then
      lstSections.ListIndex = 0
    End If
End Sub

Function GetLine (Fnum As Integer) As String
'----------------------------------------------------
' We use this routine to read a line from the file
' with all characters intact.
'----------------------------------------------------
Dim char As String
Dim ALine As String

    ' Build the string until we reach a line feed character.
    Do While (char <> Chr$(10)) And (Not EOF(Fnum))
    char = Input(1, Fnum)
    If (char <> Chr$(13)) And (char <> Chr$(10)) Then
        ALine = ALine & char
    End If
    Loop
    GetLine = ALine
End Function
```

(continued on next page)

*(continued from previous page)*

```
Sub LoadParms (ByVal IndexValue As Integer)
'---------------------------------------------------
' Load WIN.INI parameters for a particular app.
' These values have previously been stored in the
' array WinIni.
'---------------------------------------------------
Dim AParm As String
Dim AStr As String

    AStr = WinIni(IndexValue)
    lstParms.Clear

    ' Strip off section name.
    AStr = Mid$(AStr, InStr(AStr, "=") + 1)
    While AStr <> ""
        AParm = Left$(AStr, InStr(AStr, "=") - 1)
        lstParms.AddItem AParm
        AStr = Mid$(AStr, InStr(AStr, "=") + 1)
    Wend

End Sub

Sub LoadSections ()
'---------------------------------------------------
' Load WIN.INI sections that were previously read
' from the file into the WinIni array.
'---------------------------------------------------
Dim i As Integer

    For i = 1 To UBound(WinIni)
        lstSections.AddItem Left$(WinIni(i), InStr(WinIni(i), "=") - 1)
        lstSections.ItemData(lstSections.NewIndex) = i
    Next

End Sub

Sub lstParms_Click ()
'---------------------------------------------------
' Retrieve the value of an .INI parameter, given
' the application (section) name and parameter.
'---------------------------------------------------
    If (lstParms.ListIndex >= 0) And (lstSections.ListIndex >= 0) Then
        Screen.MousePointer = CSR_HOURGLASS
        Init1.Application = lstSections.List(lstSections.ListIndex)
        Init1.Parameter = lstParms.List(lstParms.ListIndex)
        lblValue = Init1.Value
        Screen.MousePointer = CSR_NORMAL
    End If
End Sub

Sub lstSections_Click ()
'---------------------------------------------------
' Load a new set of parameters when a new section
' is selected.
'---------------------------------------------------
    If lstSections.ListIndex >= 0 Then
        LoadParms lstSections.ItemData(lstSections.ListIndex)
        If lstParms.ListCount > 0 Then
```

```
            lstParms.ListIndex = 0
        End If
    End If
End Sub

Function ReadINI (ByVal INIFile As String) As Integer
'-------------------------------------------------
' Read through an .INI file and store its information
' into an array, WinIni. Each section and its
' parameters is stored as an element of the array
' in the form "SectionName=Parm1=Parm2=...=ParmN".
'-------------------------------------------------
Dim Fnum As Integer
Dim CurSection As Integer
Dim ALine As String

    CurSection = 0

    Fnum = FreeFile
    Open INIFile For Input As Fnum

    Do While Not EOF(Fnum)
        ALine = GetLine(Fnum)
        ALine = Trim$(ALine)
        If Left$(ALine, 1) = "[" Then
            CurSection = CurSection + 1
            ReDim Preserve WinIni(CurSection)
            WinIni(CurSection) = Mid$(ALine, 2, Len(ALine) - 2) & "="
        ElseIf (Left$(ALine, 1)  ";") And (Len(ALine) > 3) And (InStr(ALine, "=")) Then
            WinIni(CurSection) = WinIni(CurSection) & Left$(ALine, InStr(ALine, "="))
        End If
    Loop

    Close Fnum

End Function
```

## Tips and Comments

By changing the Value label control in the example program to a text edit control, you could easily turn the program into an .INI file editor.

While some functions of this control could be accomplished by calls to the Windows API, this control clearly simplifies the process of reading and writing initialization files.

# Key Status (KEYSTAT.VBX)

| USAGE: | Graphical Display of Data |
|---|---|
| MANUFACTURER: | MicroHelp, Inc. |
| COST: | Provided with Visual Basic 3.0 Professional Edition |

The Key Status control provides feedback on the status of the (INS), (CAPS LOCK), (SCROLL LOCK), and (NUM LOCK) keys. Since all these keys are "dual state," it is sometimes useful in a program to know when their state has changed. For example, word processors often use the state of the (INS) key to determine when to insert typed text and when to overtype text.

# Syntax

Table 9-12 shows the nonstandard properties and event of the Key Status control. You set the property to determine which of the four keys the control will monitor. Table 9-13 shows the integer values associated with each key.

**Table 9-12** Nonstandard properties and event of the Key Status control

**PROPERTIES**

| | | |
|---|---|---|
| Height | Style | TimeInterval |
| Value | Width | |

**EVENT**

Change

**Table 9-13** Values for the property

| VALUE | MEANING |
|---|---|
| 0 | Monitor the (CAPS LOCK) key. |
| 1 | Monitor the (NUM LOCK) key. |
| 2 | Monitor the (INS) key. |
| 3 | Monitor the (SCROLL LOCK) key. |

To use the Key Status control, you simply place the control on a Visual Basic form and set its *Style* property. By default, the control's *AutoSize* property is set to *True* preventing the user from resizing the control. The control appears as a small, square button with text on the button face to indicate the name of the key being monitored and its current state, either on or off.

If you just want to give the user visual feedback on the state of a key, you don't have to proceed further. The Key Status control updates itself automatically when the state of the key changes. In addition, by clicking on the Key Status button, the user can set the state of a key without pressing it on the keyboard. This feature can be useful if you need to create a "virtual keyboard" on the screen, where all input comes from the mouse or other pointing devices.

The Key Status control provides one event, *Change,* that is fired every time the state of the key changes, either when the actual key on the keyboard is pressed, or the Key Status button on the screen is pressed.

Actually, the control's *TimeInterval* property determines how frequently the keyboard is checked for status changes. By default, this value is set to 1,000 milliseconds, or every second. One second can create a quite perceptible delay, so you may find that a smaller interval looks better. Using smaller intervals may cause performance problems, as the keyboard must be checked more frequently. If you use multiple Key Status controls in your application, changing the interval for one control automatically changes it for the others as well.

Note that *TimeInterval* controls how soon after a key is pressed the *Change* event is fired. A 5,000-millisecond interval causes a 5-second delay between the time the button is pressed on the keyboard and the program is notified. However, the *TimeInterval* property causes no delay between the pressing of the Key Status button and the firing of the *Change* event. This happens immediately, and the keyboard's status is updated immediately.

The *Value* property of the control is a Boolean value that, when set to *True* indicates the key is on, and, when set to *False* indicates the key is off. *Value* lets you change the status of a key through your program code.

# Example

The example program, shown in Figure 9-5, illustrates some of the uses of Key Status. It's a simple multiline editor created with the standard Visual Basic text box control. One of the frequent complaints about the text box is that it doesn't provide an "overtype" mode that allows you to type over existing text, rather than inserting it. Another complaint is that the text box provides no good "read-only" or browsing capabilities, where input is not allowed. (While you can prevent input by setting the *Enabled* property to *False*, this unfortunately also disables the scroller, making the text box unusable as a method for providing a multiline text browser.)

The example program uses a couple of common tricks to provide these two features using the Key Status controls and the text box's *KeyPress* event.

To provide an overtype mode, the *KeyPress* event checks each key as it's pressed. The state of the (INS) key is checked, and if it's off the program simulates overtype mode by

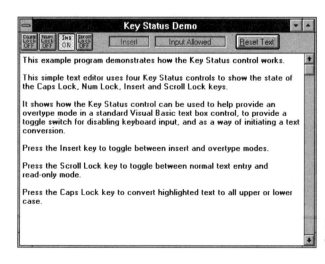

**Figure 9-5** The Key Status example program

9 ◀

"selecting" the character in the text box to the right of our current position. Since any selected text is replaced by the next key typed, the program essentially replaces one character in the text box for each new one that is typed.

It's even simpler to provide a read-only mode. The (SCROLL LOCK) key serves as the toggle between text-entry and read-only mode. When (SCROLL LOCK) is on, we simply discard any key sent to the *KeyPress* event by changing the event's *KeyAscii* value to 0. This prevents any key typed into the text box from being added to the *Text* property.

Finally, you'll see how to use the Key Status control to add features, such as upper- and lowercase conversions, to a program. Highlight a section of text in the text box, and then press the (CAPS LOCK) key. The selected text will be converted to either all upper- or all lowercase text, based on the current value of the Key Status button.

## Steps

1. Create a new project called KEYSTAT1.MAK. Add the Key Status control, KEYSTAT.VBX, to the project. Create a new form with the objects and properties described in Table 9-14. Save this form as KEYSTAT1.FRM.

**Table 9-14** Objects and properties for KEYSTAT1.FRM

| OBJECT | PROPERTY | SETTING |
|--------|----------|---------|
| Form | FormName | frmKeyStatus |
| | BackColor | &H00C0C0C0& |
| | Caption | "Key Status Demo" |
| | FontBold | 0 'False |
| | FontSize | 9.75 |
| | ForeColor | &H00C0C0C0& |
| Label | Name | lblInsertMode |
| | Alignment | 2 'Center |
| | BackColor | &H00FFFFFF& |
| | BackStyle | 0 'Transparent |
| | BorderStyle | 1 'Fixed Single |
| | FontBold | 0 'False |
| | ForeColor | &H00000080& |
| Label | Name | lblReadOnly |
| | Alignment | 2 'Center |
| | BackColor | &H00FFFFFF& |
| | BackStyle | 0 'Transparent |
| | BorderStyle | 1 'Fixed Single |
| | FontBold | 0 'False |
| | ForeColor | &H00000080& |
| MhState | Name | keyCapsLock |
| | Autosize | -1 'True |

| OBJECT | PROPERTY | SETTING |
|---|---|---|
| | BackColor | &H00C0C0C0& |
| | TimerInterval | 300 |
| | Value | 0 'False |
| MhState | Name | keyNumLock |
| | Autosize | -1 'True |
| | BackColor | &H00C0C0C0& |
| | Style | 1 'Num Lock |
| | TimerInterval | 300 |
| | Value | 0 'False |
| MhState | Name | keyInsert |
| | Autosize | -1 'True |
| | BackColor | &H00C0C0C0& |
| | Style | 2 'Insert State |
| | TimerInterval | 300 |
| | Value | 0 'False |
| TextBox | Name | txtEditor |
| | MultiLine | -1 'True |
| | ScrollBars | 2 'Vertical |
| MhState | Name | keyScrollLock |
| | Autosize | -1 'True |
| | BackColor | &H00C0C0C0& |
| | Style | 3 'Scroll Lock |
| | TimerInterval | 300 |
| | Value | 0 'False |
| CommandButton | Name | btnReset |
| | Caption | "&Reset Text" |
| | FontBold | 0 'False |

2. Add the following code to the declarations section of the KEYSTAT1.FRM form.

```
Option Explicit
'---------------------------------------------------
' Constants and variables used by the Key Status
' example program.
'---------------------------------------------------

' Used by the Reset Text button.
Dim OriginalText As String

' Color constants
Const DARK_GRAY = &H808080
Const WHITE = &HFFFFFF
Const BLACK = &H0
Const RED = &H80&
Const GREEN = &H8000&
```

*(continued on next page)*

*(continued from previous page)*

```
' 3D border styles
Const BORDER_INSET = 0
Const BORDER_RAISED = 1
```

3. Add the following subroutines to the KEYSTAT1.FRM form.

```
Sub btnReset_Click ()
'--------------------------------------------------
' Restore the original text in the editor.
'--------------------------------------------------
    txtEditor = OriginalText
End Sub

Sub Form_Load ()
'--------------------------------------------------
' Initialize the original editor text and save it.
'--------------------------------------------------
Dim CRLF As String

    CRLF = Chr$(13) & Chr$(10)

    ' Center the form on the screen.
    Me.Move (Screen.Width - Me.Width) \ 2, (Screen.Height - Me.Height) \ 2
    Me.Show

    ' Set initial button values.
    keyInsert.Value = True
    keyScrollLock.Value = True
    keyScrollLock.Value = False

    ' Set the original text.
    txtEditor = "This example program demonstrates how the "
    txtEditor = txtEditor & "Key Status control works." & CRLF & CRLF
    txtEditor = txtEditor & "This simple text editor uses four Key Status "
    txtEditor = txtEditor & "controls to show the state of the "
    txtEditor = txtEditor & "Caps Lock, Num Lock, Insert and Scroll Lock keys." & CRLF & CRLF
    txtEditor = txtEditor & "It shows how the Key Status "
    txtEditor = txtEditor & "control can be used to help provide "
    txtEditor = txtEditor & "an overtype mode in a standard "
    txtEditor = txtEditor & "Visual Basic text box control, to provide "
    txtEditor = txtEditor & "a toggle switch for disabling keyboard "
    txtEditor = txtEditor & "input, and as a way of initiating a text conversion." & CRLF & CRLF
    txtEditor = txtEditor & "Press the Insert key to toggle "
    txtEditor = txtEditor & "between insert and Overtype modes." & CRLF & CRLF
    txtEditor = txtEditor & "Press the Scroll Lock key to toggle "
    txtEditor = txtEditor & "between normal text entry and read-only mode." & CRLF & CRLF
    txtEditor = txtEditor & "Press the Caps Lock key to "
    txtEditor = txtEditor & "convert highlighted text to all upper- or lowercase." & CRLF & CRLF

    ' Save the original text so it can be restored later if necessary.
    OriginalText = txtEditor
End Sub

Sub Form_Paint ()
'--------------------------------------------------
' Redraw the 3D effects around labels.
'--------------------------------------------------
    Make3D Me, lblInsertMode, 1, BORDER_INSET
```

```
    Make3D Me, lblReadOnly, 1, BORDER_INSET
End Sub

Sub Form_Resize ()
'--------------------------------------------------
' Adjust the text box to fit the new form size.
'--------------------------------------------------
Dim Border As Integer

    On Error Resume Next
    Border = Screen.TwipsPerPixelX
    txtEditor.Move -Border, txtEditor.Top, Me.ScaleWidth + (Border * 2), Me.ScaleHeight -
txtEditor.Top + Border
End Sub

Sub keyCapsLock_Change ()
'--------------------------------------------------
' If text is selected, shift it to upper-or lower-
' case.
'--------------------------------------------------
Dim SelStart As Long
Dim SelLength As Long

    If txtEditor.SelLength > 0 Then
      SelStart = txtEditor.SelStart
      SelLength = txtEditor.SelLength

      If keyCapsLock Then
          txtEditor.SelText = UCase$(txtEditor.SelText)
      Else
          txtEditor.SelText = LCase$(txtEditor.SelText)
      End If

      txtEditor.SelStart = SelStart
        txtEditor.SelLength = SelLength
        DoEvents
    End If
    txtEditor.SetFocus
End Sub

Sub keyInsert_Change ()
'--------------------------------------------------
' When the Insert key shifts, set a new mode.
'--------------------------------------------------
    txtEditor.SetFocus
    If keyInsert.Value = True Then
        lblInsertMode.ForeColor = GREEN
        lblInsertMode = "Insert"
      Else
        lblInsertMode.ForeColor = RED
        lblInsertMode = "Overstrike"
    End If
End Sub

Sub keyNumLock_Change ()
'--------------------------------------------------
' Revert focus back to the text editor.
'--------------------------------------------------
    txtEditor.SetFocus
End Sub
```

9 ◀

(continued on next page)

*(continued from previous page)*

```
Sub keyScrollLock_Change ()
'----------------------------------------------------
' Change to or from read-only mode.
'----------------------------------------------------
    txtEditor.SetFocus
    If keyScrollLock.Value = True Then
        lblReadOnly.ForeColor = GREEN
        lblReadOnly = "Read Only"
    Else
        lblReadOnly.ForeColor = RED
        lblReadOnly = "Input Allowed"
    End If

End Sub

Sub Make3D (pic As Form, ctl As Control, ByVal BorderWidth As Integer, ByVal BorderStyle As
Integer)
'----------------------------------------------------
' Wrap a 3D effect around a control on a form.
'----------------------------------------------------
Dim AdjustX As Integer, AdjustY As Integer
Dim RightSide As Single
Dim BW As Integer', BorderWidth As Integer, BorderStyle As Integer
Dim LeftTopColor As Long, RightBottomColor As Long
Dim i As Integer

    If Not ctl.Visible Then Exit Sub

    AdjustX = Screen.TwipsPerPixelX
    AdjustY = Screen.TwipsPerPixelY

    Select Case BorderStyle
      Case 0: ' Inset
          LeftTopColor = DARK_GRAY
          RightBottomColor = WHITE
      Case 1: ' Raised
          LeftTopColor = WHITE
          RightBottomColor = DARK_GRAY
    End Select


    ' Set the top shading line.
    For BW = 1 To BorderWidth
    ' Top
    pic.CurrentX = ctl.Left - (AdjustX * BW)
    pic.CurrentY = ctl.Top - (AdjustY * BW)
    pic.Line -(ctl.Left + ctl.Width + (AdjustX * (BW - 1)), ctl.Top - (AdjustY * BW)),
LeftTopColor
    ' Right
    pic.Line -(ctl.Left + ctl.Width + (AdjustX * (BW - 1)), ctl.Top + ctl.Height + (AdjustY *
(BW - 1))), RightBottomColor
    ' Bottom
    pic.Line -(ctl.Left - (AdjustX * BW), ctl.Top + ctl.Height + (AdjustY * (BW - 1))),
RightBottomColor
    ' Left
    pic.Line -(ctl.Left - (AdjustX * BW), ctl.Top - (AdjustY * BW)), LeftTopColor
    Next
End Sub

Sub txtEditor_KeyPress (KeyAscii As Integer)
```

```
'-------------------------------------------------
' If Scroll Lock is on, input is discarded
' (read-only mode). If we're not in insert mode,
' we fake overstrike mode by 'eating' characters
' to the right of where we're typing.
'-------------------------------------------------
    If keyScrollLock Then
        KeyAscii = 0
    ElseIf (Not keyInsert) And (txtEditor.SelLength = 0) Then
        txtEditor.SelLength = 1
    End If
End Sub
```

## Tips and Comments

If you simply need to monitor the status of a key to provide some type of internal "toggle switch" and don't want to display the state of the key to the user, just set the Key Status' *Visible* property to *False*.

The Key Status control tends to be overlooked in the midst of the other controls that ship with Visual Basic Professional 3.0. However, it can provide a needed service when you're developing applications that include word processing features or that require an onscreen keyboard.

# MenuEv (MENUEV3.VBX)

| USAGE: | Capturing Menu Information |
|---|---|
| MANUFACTURER: | Mabry Software |
| COST: | $10 ($5 if registered on CompuServe) |

The MenuEv control retrieves information on the current menu option, firing an event each time a new menu item is highlighted. This gives the programmer an easy way to add to an application features such as status line menu help information. Information on how the option was selected, the attributes of the menu option itself, tag information, and help context information are also provided.

## Syntax

Table 9-15 shows the MenuEv control's two events. The second event, MenuExit, is similar in concept to a standard LostFocus event. It is triggered when the user presses the Y key, clicks somewhere outside the menu, or selects a menu option.

**Table 9-15** Nonstandard events of the MenuEv control

| MenuEvent | MenuExit |
|---|---|

The *MenuEvent* event is triggered when a new menu option has been selected. It has the following form:

```
CtrlName_MenuEvent (MenuText As String, Flags As Integer, Tag As String, HelpContextID As Long)
```

*MenuText* is a string containing the actual text displayed on the menu, including any ampersands (&) used to embed underlines. The second parameter, *Flags,* indicates the state of the menu option. Several pieces of information are packed into this integer value. Table 9-16 shows the different bit values and their significance.

**Table 9-16** The bit values for the  parameter.

| BIT VALUE | DESCRIPTION |
|-----------|-------------|
| &H0001 | The menu option is grayed. |
| &H0002 | The menu option is disabled. |
| &H0004 | The menu option is a bitmap. |
| &H0008 | The menu option is checked. |
| &H0010 | The menu option is part of a pop-up menu. |
| &H0100 | This is an OwnerDraw menu option. |
| &H2000 | This option is part of the system menu. |
| &H4000 | This option was selected using the mouse. |

To determine whether a bit value is set, use the bit-wise *And* operator, as in the following example, which tests whether the current menu option is disabled:

```
Const MF_DISABLED = &H2

If (Flags And MF_DISABLED) = MF_DISABLED Then
    Label1 = "This option is disabled"
Else
    Label = "This option is not disabled"
End_If
```

The *Tag* parameter corresponds to the value set in the selected menu option's *Tag* property. Since this field is a string, it is a handy place to store status line help information about the current menu option. Likewise, the *HelpContextID* parameter corresponds to the menu option property of the same name.

# Example

The example program demonstrates how to implement a simple status help line that is updated whenever a new menu item is selected. This program, shown in Figure 9-6,  also checks the flags and tells the user the state of the current menu option. The menu's *Tag* property, passed to the *MainEvent* event, is used to set the status line information.

## Steps

1. Create a new project called MENUEV.MAK. Add the MenuEv control, MENUEV3.VBX, to the project. Create a new form with the objects and properties described in Table 9-17. Save this form as MENUEV.FRM.

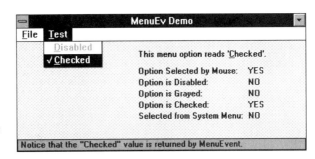

**Figure 9-6** The MenuEv example program

**Table 9-17** Objects and properties for MENUEV.FRM

| OBJECT | PROPERTY | SETTING |
|--------|----------|---------|
| Form | FormName | frmMenuEv |
| | BackColor | &H0080FFFF& |
| | BorderStyle | 1 'Fixed Single |
| | Caption | "MenuEv Demo" |
| | MaxButton | 0 'False |
| Label | Name | lblMenuText |
| | BackStyle | 0 'Transparent |
| | Caption | "Menu not currently selected." |
| | ForeColor | &H00800000& |
| Label | Name | lblMouseSelect |
| | BackStyle | 0 'Transparent |
| | ForeColor | &H00000080& |
| Label | Name | lblDisabled |
| | BackStyle | 0 'Transparent |
| | ForeColor | &H00000080& |
| Label | Name | lblGrayed |
| | BackStyle | 0 'Transparent |
| | ForeColor | &H00000080& |
| Label | Name | lblChecked |
| | BackStyle | 0 'Transparent |
| | ForeColor | &H00000080& |
| Label | Name | lblSysMenu |
| | BackStyle | 0 'Transparent |
| | ForeColor | &H00000080& |
| Label | Name | Label1 |
| | BackStyle | 0 'Transparent |
| | Caption | "Option Selected by Mouse:" |
| | ForeColor | &H00800000& |
| | Index | 0 |

*(continued on next page)*

| OBJECT | PROPERTY | SETTING |
|---|---|---|
| *(continued from previous page)* | | |
| Label | Name | Label2 |
| | BackStyle | 0 'Transparent |
| | Caption | "Option is Disabled:" |
| | ForeColor | &H00800000& |
| Label | Name | Label3 |
| | BackStyle | 0 'Transparent |
| | Caption | "Option is Grayed:" |
| | ForeColor | &H00800000& |
| Label | Name | Label4 |
| | BackStyle | 0 'Transparent |
| | Caption | "Option is Checked:" |
| | ForeColor | &H00800000& |
| Label | Name | Label1 |
| | BackStyle | 0 'Transparent |
| | Caption | "Selected from System Menu:" |
| | ForeColor | &H00800000& |
| | Index | 1 |
| MenuEvent | Name | MenuEv1 |
| PictureBox | Name | picStatusLine |
| | Align | 2 'Align Bottom |
| | BackColor | &H00C0C0C0& |
| | ForeColor | &H00000080& |

2. Add the menu described in Table 9-18 to the MENUEV.FRM form.

**Table 9-18** Menu definition for MENUEV.FRM

| CAPTION | NAME | STATUS |
|---|---|---|
| &File | File | |
| ----E&xit | FileExit | |
| &Test | Test | |
| ----&Checked | TestChecked | Checked |
| ----&Disabled | TestDisabled | Disabled |

3. Add the following code to the declarations section of the MENUEV.FRM form.

```
Option Explicit
'------------------------------------------------
' Constants used to check Flags parameter of
' MenuEvent event.
'------------------------------------------------
```

```
Const MF_GRAYED = &H1
Const MF_DISABLED = &H2
Const MF_BITMAP = &H4
Const MF_CHECKED = &H8
Const MF_POPUP = &H10
Const MF_OWNERDRAW = &H100
Const MF_SYSMENU = &H2000
Const MF_MOUSESELECT = &H8000
```

4. Add the following subroutines and functions to the MENUEV.FRM form.

```
Function BitSet (ByVal FlagValue As Integer, ByVal BitValue As Integer) As String
'--------------------------------------------------
' Return the string "YES" if the bit is set in the
' flag, "NO" otherwise.
'--------------------------------------------------
    If (FlagValue And BitValue) = BitValue Then
        BitSet = "YES"
    Else
        BitSet = "NO "
    End If
End Function

Sub FileExit_Click ()
'--------------------------------------------------
' Exit the program when this menu option is picked.
'--------------------------------------------------
    Unload Me
End Sub

Sub Form_Load ()
'--------------------------------------------------
' Center the form on the screen.
'--------------------------------------------------

    Me.Move (Screen.Width - Me.Width) \ 2, (Screen.Height - Me.Height) \ 2
End Sub

Sub MenuEv1_MenuEvent (MenuText As String, Flags As Integer, Tag As String, HelpContextID As Long)
'--------------------------------------------------
' Let the user know what's been picked, set the
' status "help" line, and show the flag values.
'--------------------------------------------------
    picStatusLine.Cls
    picStatusLine.Print " " & Tag

    lblMenuText = "This menu option reads '" & MenuText & "'."
    lblMouseSelect = BitSet(Flags, MF_MOUSESELECT)
    lblDisabled = BitSet(Flags, MF_DISABLED)
    lblGrayed = BitSet(Flags, MF_GRAYED)
    lblChecked = BitSet(Flags, MF_CHECKED)
    lblSysMenu = BitSet(Flags, MF_SYSMENU)
    If lblSysMenu = "YES" Then
      picStatusLine.Cls
      picStatusLine.Print " " & "The '" & MenuText & "' option is on the System Menu."
    End If
End Sub

Sub MenuEv1_MenuExit ()
```

(continued on next page)

9 ◄

*(continued from previous page)*

```
'---------------------------------------------------
' If we're leaving the menu, set some defaults.
'---------------------------------------------------
    lblMenuText = "Menu not currently selected."
    lblMouseSelect = "N/A"
    lblDisabled = "N/A"
    lblGrayed = "N/A"
    lblChecked = "N/A"
    lblSysMenu = "N/A"
    picStatusLine.Cls
End Sub

Sub TestChecked_Click ()
'---------------------------------------------------
' Toggle the test menu Checked option.
'---------------------------------------------------
    TestChecked.Checked = Not TestChecked.Checked
End Sub
```

## Tips and Comments

MenuEv is a simple, complete control for adding menu information to your Visual Basic application. It is especially well suited for providing professional-looking menu help information as user moves through menu items.

# Message Hook (MSGHOOK.VBX)

| USAGE: | Capturing Windows System Messages |
|---|---|
| MANUFACTURER: | The Waite Group |
| COST: | Included with *Visual Basic How-To, Second Edition* |

The Message Hook control gives you access to Windows messages that are not directly available through Visual Basic. This lets you exploit features of Windows that Visual Basic hides.

## Syntax

Part of the appeal of Visual Basic is that it makes Windows programming much simpler than it is with languages such as C, C++, or Pascal. A fairly large amount of the "guts" of Windows is hidden from the Visual Basic programmer.

Much low-level Windows programming involves handling Windows "messages." These messages are sent to windows and controls that then must either react to or ignore them. The Visual Basic programmer can react to some of these messages through *events*. For example, when a form is resized, the VB programmer knows about it through the *Resize* event. The C programmer would know about it when the form window received a WM_WINDOWPOSCHANGED message. These messages are actually integer constants. Both the C and the Visual Basic programmer can write code that reacts to the resizing of a form window.

Unfortunately, there are many Windows messages for which Visual Basic provides no corresponding event. This limits what Visual Basic can do, and that is the problem that the Message Hook (MsgHook) control solves. Table 9-19 shows this control's nonstandard properties and event.

**Table 9-19** Nonstandard properties and event of the Message Hook control

| PROPERTIES | |
| --- | --- |
| hwndHook | Message |

| EVENT |
| --- |
| Message |

MsgHook lets you trap messages for a particular window handle. This window handle is the value stored in the *hWnd* property of many forms and controls. This means that you can intercept messages for an entire window or just, for example, a text control. You associate window handles with a MsgHook control through the *hWndHook* property.

The *Message ()* property array provides the mechanism for trapping specific Windows messages. As mentioned, these messages are nothing more than integer constants. These message constants, which are defined in the WIN31API.HLP help file that comes with Visual Basic 3.0, serve as indexes into the *Message ()* array. The following code tells MsgHook to trap WM_MOVE messages for form Form1. WM_MOVE messages are sent to a window any time the window's position has changed on the screen.

```
Const WM_MOVE = &H3
MsgHook1.hWndHook = Form1.hWnd
MsgHook1.Message(WM_MOVE) = True
```

Setting the WM_MOVE element of the *Message* array to *True* tells MsgHook to begin trapping the WM_MOVE messages that are sent to Form1. You can trap other messages simply by setting their associated *Message* elements to *True* as well.

The *Message* event is fired every time a trapped message occurs. It has the form

```
MsgHook1_Message (msg As Integer, wParam as Integer, lParam As Long, action As Integer, ⇒
result As Long)
```

The *Msg* parameter is the value of the message constant (such as WM_MOVE) that triggered the event. Messages pass additional information in the *wParam* and *lParam* parameters. The *Action* parameter can be set within the *Message* event to indicate how the message is passed on to Windows. When *Action* is set to 1, the message is not passed on to its destination and Windows is passed back the value in the *result* parameter. If *Action* is set to 0, the message is passed on to the form or control for which it was intended.

MsgHook provides two functions, *MsgHookGetData* and *MsgHookSetData* for processing data provided by a message.

```
Declare Sub MsgHookGetData Lib "MSGHOOK.VBX" (ByVal lParam as Long, DestSize as Integer,
DestType As Any)
Declare Sub MsgHookSetData Lib "MSGHOOK.VBX" (ByVal lParam as Long, SrcSize as Integer, SrcType As Any)
```

9 ◄

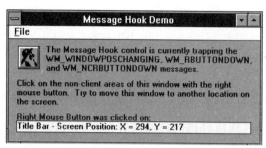

**Figure 9-7** The Message Hook example program

In some Windows messages, the *lParam* parameter holds a pointer to a memory location where some information is stored. This information is often stored in data structures similar to those defined with the basic *Type* statement. Visual Basic can't get to this information directly, so MsgHook provides functions for accessing these data structures.

# Example

The example program, shown in Figure 9-7, traps three Windows messages, WM_RBUTTONDOWN, WM_NCRBUTTONDOWN, and WM_WINDOWPOSCHANGING. The first message is sent any time the right mouse button is pressed in the *client area* of the form. The client area of a window is the area inside the window, excluding any border, title bar, minimize and maximize buttons, and system menu. These areas make up what is called the *nonclient area* of the window. While Visual Basic provides an event, *MouseDown,* for mouse clicks to the client area of the form, it excludes mouse clicks that occur over controls on the form (these are captured by the individual control's *MouseDown* event). The WM_RBUTTONDOWN message is triggered anywhere in the client area.

WM_NCRBUTTONDOWN is sent any time the right mouse button is clicked on the nonclient areas of the form. There are no Visual Basic events that correspond to this message.

While Visual Basic tells you, by way of a *Resize* event, when the size of a window has changed, it doesn't tell you when a window has been moved. The WM_WINDOWPOSCHANGING message not only tells you when the window is about to move, it lets you prevent the window from moving as well. By changing the flags in the tWindowPos structure, you can tell Windows not to allow the form to move. You retrieve and alter the data structure using MsgHook's *MsgHookGet Data* and *MsgHookSetData* functions.

## Steps

1. Create a new project called MSGHOOK.MAK. Add the Message Hook control, MSGHOOK.VBX, to the project. Create a new Visual Basic module called MSGHOOK.BAS, and add the following code to its declarations section.

```
Option Explicit
'-------------------------------------------------------
' Globals, types, and declarations used in the
' MsgHook demo program.
'-------------------------------------------------------

' Structure returned while handling WM_WINDOWPOSCHANGING.
Type tWindowPos
    Hwnd As Integer
    HWndInsertAfter As Integer
    x As Integer
    y As Integer
    cx As Integer
    cy As Integer
    flags As Integer
End Type

' Constants for messages handled by MsgHook.
Global Const WM_WINDOWPOSCHANGING = &H46
Global Const WM_NCRBUTTONDOWN = &HA4
Global Const WM_RBUTTONDOWN = &H204

' Constants for flags returned in WM_NCRBUTTONDOWN.
Global Const HTNOWHERE = 0
Global Const HTCAPTION = 2
Global Const HTSYSMENU = 3
Global Const HTMENU = 5
Global Const HTMINBUTTON = 8
Global Const HTMAXBUTTON = 9
Global Const HTLEFT = 10
Global Const HTRIGHT = 11
Global Const HTTOP = 12
Global Const HTTOPLEFT = 13
Global Const HTTOPRIGHT = 14
Global Const HTBOTTOM = 15
Global Const HTBOTTOMLEFT = 16
Global Const HTBOTTOMRIGHT = 17

' Const used to prevent window move.
Global Const SWP_NOMOVE = &H2

' Functions imported from MSGHOOK.VBX.
Declare Sub MsgHookGetData Lib "MSGHOOK.VBX" (ByVal lParam As Long, ByVal SrcSize As ⇒
Integer, SrcType As Any)
Declare Sub MsgHookSetData Lib "MSGHOOK.VBX" (ByVal lParam As Long, ByVal DestSize As ⇒
Integer, DestType As Any)
```

2. Add the following two functions to MSGHOOK.BAS.

```
Function HiWord (ByVal LongValue As Long) As Integer
'-------------------------------------------------------
' Returns the upper 16 bits of a word (long integer).
'-------------------------------------------------------
    HiWord = (LongValue \ (2 ^ 16)) And &HFFFF&
End Function

Function LoWord (ByVal LongValue As Long) As Integer
```

*(continued on next page)*

**9**

*(continued from previous page)*

```
'----------------------------------------------------
' Returns the lower 16 bits of a word (long integer).
'----------------------------------------------------
    LoWord = LongValue And &HFFFF&
End Function
```

3. Create a new form with the objects and properties described in Table 9-20. Save this form as MSGHOOK.FRM.

**Table 9-20** Objects and properties for MSGHOOK.FRM

| OBJECT | PROPERTY | SETTING |
|---|---|---|
| Form | FormName | frmMsgHook |
| | BackColor | &H00C0C0C0& |
| | Caption | "Message Hook Demo" |
| Label | Name | lblInfo |
| | BackColor | &H00E0FFFF& |
| | BorderStyle | 1 'Fixed Single |
| Label | Name | lblRightMouse |
| | BackStyle | 0 'Transparent |
| | Caption | "Right Mouse Button was clicked on:" |
| | ForeColor | &H00000080& |
| Label | Name | lblMessage |
| | BackStyle | 0 'Transparent |
| | Caption | "Click on the nonclient areas of this window with the right mouse button. Try to move this window to another location on the screen." |
| | ForeColor | &H00800000& |
| Label | Name | Label1 |
| | BackStyle | 0 'Transparent |
| | Caption | "The Message Hook control is currently trapping the WM_WINDOWPOSCHANGING, WM_RBUTTONDOWN, and WM_NCRBUTTONDOWN messages." |
| | ForeColor | &H00800000& |
| Image | Name | Image1 |
| | Picture | (set at design time in Properties window) |
| | Stretch | -1 'True |
| MsgHook | Name | MsgHook1 |

4. Add the following code to the declarations section of the MSGHOOK.FRM form.

```
Option Explicit

'-----------------------------------------------------
' Variable used by WM_WINDOWPOSCHANGING.
'-----------------------------------------------------

Dim WinPos As tWindowPos
```

5. Add the following subroutines to the MSGHOOK.FRM form.

```
Sub FileExit_Click ()
'-----------------------------------------------------
' Exit the program.
'-----------------------------------------------------
    Unload Me
End Sub

Sub Form_Load ()
'-----------------------------------------------------
' Position the window on the screen and hook the
' messages we want to handle.
'-----------------------------------------------------
    On Error GoTo Main_Error

    Me.Move (Screen.Width - Me.Width) \ 2, (Screen.Height - Me.Height) \ 2
    Me.Show

    ' Tell MsgHook that we want to capture the main window.
    MsgHook1.HwndHook = Me.hWnd

    ' Hook these messages.
    MsgHook1.Message(WM_RBUTTONDOWN) = True
    MsgHook1.Message(WM_NCRBUTTONDOWN) = True
    MsgHook1.Message(WM_WINDOWPOSCHANGING) = True
Exit Sub
Main_Error:
    MsgBox "Error " & Err & " occurred in the MsgHook Demo: " & Error$
End Sub

Sub MsgHook1_Message (msg As Integer, wParam As Integer, lParam As Long, Action As Integer,⇒
result As Long)
'-----------------------------------------------------
' Handle hooked messages and ignore anything else.
'-----------------------------------------------------
Dim Where As String

    Select Case msg
        Case WM_RBUTTONDOWN:
            lblInfo = "Client Area of Window: X = " & Format$(LoWord(lParam)) & ", Y = " &
Format$(HiWord(lParam))
            Action = 0
        Case WM_NCRBUTTONDOWN:
            Select Case wParam
                Case HTBOTTOM: Where = "Bottom Border"
                Case HTBOTTOMLEFT: Where = "Bottom Left Border"
                Case HTBOTTOMRIGHT: Where = "Bottom Right Border"
                Case HTCAPTION: Where = "Title Bar"
                Case HTLEFT: Where = "Left Border"
```

*(continued on next page)*

*(continued from previous page)*

```
            Case HTRIGHT: Where = "Right Border"
            Case HTMAXBUTTON: Where = "Maximize Button"
            Case HTMENU: Where = "Menu"
            Case HTMINBUTTON: Where = "Minimize Button"
            Case HTSYSMENU: Where = "System Menu"
            Case HTTOP: Where = "Top Border"
            Case HTTOPLEFT: Where = "Top Left Border"
            Case HTTOPRIGHT: Where = "Top Right Border"
        End Select
        lblInfo = Where & " - Screen Position: X = " & Format$(LoWord(lParam)) & ", Y = " &
Format$(HiWord(lParam))
        Action = 0
    Case WM_WINDOWPOSCHANGING:
        ' Retrieve the data structure pointed to by lParam.
        MsgHookGetData lParam, Len(WinPos), WinPos
        ' Set the flags in the data structure so that the
        ' window is not moved, but preserve any other flags set.
        WinPos.Flags = WinPos.Flags Or SWP_NOMOVE
        ' Copy the data structure back to location lParam.
        MsgHookSetData lParam, Len(WinPos), WinPos

        Action = 0
    Case Else
        Action = 0
    End Select
End Sub
```

## Tips and Comments

Visual Basic does an excellent job of hiding the complexities of Windows from the programmer. This makes it a very productive development environment for solving a huge set of problems. Occasionally, you'll run into a problem that Visual Basic just can't handle, and that's where a message handling control comes in.

It's impossible to cover every Windows message that Windows processes, but the number is quite large. If you want more information on messages and what they do, the first place to look is in the WINAPI directory installed with Visual Basic. This directory includes help files that provide a good overview of the lower level workings of Windows.

#  OLE 2.0 Control (MSOLE2.VBX)

| USAGE: | Object Linking and Embedding |
|---|---|
| MANUFACTURER: | Microsoft |
| COST: | Included with Visual Basic 3.0 |

Support for Object Linking and Embedding Version 2.0, or OLE2, was included with Version 3.0 of Visual Basic. Along with support for OLE Automation in the Visual Basic language, Microsoft included an OLE control to help programmers build OLE client applications. OLE client applications can serve as front ends to OLE server applications. OLE server applications usually provide one or more objects that can be linked or

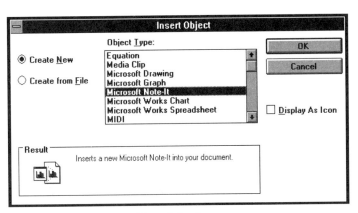

**Figure 9-8** The Insert Object dialog box

embedded into an OLE client. The OLE control lets developers use Visual Basic as the glue to bond applications such as Microsoft Project, Visio, and Microsoft Excel together into enterprise-wide custom solutions.

## Syntax

While the subject of OLE can be quite daunting, learning to use the OLE control is actually fairly simple. You place the OLE control on a form and size it much as you would size a picture box. Figure 9-8 shows the Insert Object dialog box that is displayed when an OLE control is first placed on a form. You can select an object to link or embed at this point, and the object will be displayed within the OLE control's frame when the program is run.

Table 9-21 lists the nonstandard properties and event of the OLE. As you will learn, most of the power of this control is accessed by setting the Action property. But before you delve too deeply into the control itself, you'll take a brief tour of OLE itself.

**Table 9-21** Nonstandard properties and event of the OLE control

**PROPERTIES**

| | | |
|---|---|---|
| Action | AppIsRunning | AutoActivate |
| AutoVerbMenu | Class | Data |
| DataText | DisplayType | FileNumber |
| Format | HostName | lpOLEObject |
| ObjectAcceptFormatsCount | ObjectAcceptFormats | ObjectGetFormatsCount |
| ObjectGetFormats | Object | ObjectVerbFlags |
| ObjectVerbCount | ObjectVerbs | OLETypeAllowed |
| OLEType | PasteOK | SizeMode |
| SourceDoc | SourceItem | UpdateOptions |
| Verb | | |

(continued on next page)

9

(continued from previous page)

**EVENT**

Updated

**Linking and Embedding**  Your Visual Basic program is an OLE *client* program. The client puts a box on the screen and tells another application, called the OLE *server*, that it should display some of the client's data inside the box. The client program trusts the server to display its data in some meaningful way.

The client program's OLE control can hold either linked or embedded objects. The difference between the two is in how the object's data is managed. A *linked* object merely displays a copy of the object's data. The OLE server application actually maintains the data. Linking is useful for displaying data from objects that may be updated from another source. For example, suppose you wanted to develop an Executive Information System (EIS) that would display a range of spreadsheet cells from Excel. The Excel spreadsheet is stored on a network and updated frequently. The EIS, written in Visual Basic, contains an OLE control that is linked to the spreadsheet. When the user changes data on the spreadsheet, OLE updates the data displayed in the EIS application's OLE control as well.

With object *embedding*, the object's data is controlled by the OLE client application and can be stored in a special OLE file format. For example, you could create an application that stored information about your family. You could have one OLE control that stored a bitmapped picture of a family member as a Paintbrush object, and another control that stored the person's biography as a Word document. Both these objects could be saved and accessed through the client application only.

**Using the OLE Control**  The easiest way to learn how to use the OLE control is to walk through a simple example. Let's say you want to link to a Paintbrush file. You create a new Visual Basic project and add the OLE control (MSOLE2.VBX) to the project. Then you drag an instance of the OLE control from the Visual Basic toolbox onto a new Visual Basic form.

The first time you place an OLE control on a form, the Insert Object dialog box appears. This lets you select an object to link or embed at design time. Suppose that you prefer to load the object from your Visual Basic code, so you press the dialog's Cancel button, closing the dialog. To link to the Paintbrush object, you can add the following code to the form's event.

```
OLE1.Class = "Pbrush"
OLE1.SourceDoc = "c:\windows\marble.bmp"
OLE1.Action = OLE_CREATE_FROM_FILE
```

That's about it. The *Class* property tells the control what kind of OLE object it will be working with; you can view a list of the class names available on your computer by double-clicking the *Class* entry in the Visual Basic properties list for the OLE control. Each OLE server application usually has at least one object class. The *SourceDoc* property tells the OLE control the name of the file it will link to. Finally, you set the *Action* property of the control, telling it that you want to create an OLE object from the file specified in *SourceDoc*.

What the user sees is the bitmap displayed within the OLE control. While the Visual Basic OLE client app cannot control the content of the OLE control (its general appearance is dictated by the OLE server application), you do have a little control over how the contents are displayed. You can use the *SetMode* property to clip, stretch, or autosize the control, as shown in Table 9-22.

**Table 9-22** Values for the SizeMode property

| VALUE | MEANING |
|---|---|
| 0 | Clip the OLE contents to the size of the control (the default) |
| 1 | Stretch the OLE contents to the size of the control |
| 2 | Resize the control to the size of the OLE contents |

You're linked to a Paintbrush object, so now what? If the user double-clicks the mouse anywhere on the OLE control, she activates an instance of the object's associated OLE server application, in this case Paintbrush. The bitmap is loaded for you, and you can now edit the image. If you situate Paintbrush and your Visual Basic client app on the screen so that you can see the bitmap in both applications, you can observe how linking works. When the user draws a line on the bitmap in Paintbrush, the line also appears on the image in the OLE control of the client app.

If you want to prevent the user from activating the OLE server application, you can set the *AutoActive* property to 0. By default, this property is set to 2, which allows activation by double-click, as just explained. A value of 1 causes the OLE server to be activated whenever the OLE control gains the focus.

**Finding Out About an Object** While the preceding example shows how to link a specific object of a predetermined type, some applications need to receive objects without knowing what they are beforehand. Several properties can tell you what kind of object you're dealing with.

The *OLEType* property returns an integer value that indicates whether the current object is linked or embedded. The Boolean *AppIsRunning* property returns *True* if the object's associated OLE server application is currently running.

Each OLE object supports a set of *verbs*. These verbs are commands to which the object will respond. For example, many objects support an *Edit* verb, which allows the user to edit the object via its OLE server. The *ObjectVerbs* property array returns the names of all verbs the current object supports. The *ObjectVerbsCount* property returns the total number of verbs in the array. Another way to view this list at run time is to click the right mouse button over the OLE control. This displays a pop-up menu containing the verb list. When a verb, such as *Edit,* is selected from the menu, that action is initiated. Selecting *Edit* would activate the object's server application, for example. You can disable this pop-up menu by setting the *AutoVerbMenu* property to *False*.

# Example

The example program, shown in Figure 9-9, implements a simple object viewer. The intent was to present a single object, along with all the associated information that the OLE control allows you to retrieve. The example is as simple as possible so that the basics are easy to follow.

The New option on the File menu displays the Insert Object dialog, which lets the user create a new embedded object or link an existing file to the application. The default behavior of *AutoActivate* and *AutoVerbMenu* are unchanged so the user can activate a server application by double-clicking on the OLE control, and display the verb menu by clicking the right mouse button over it.

The programmer implements several of the OLE control actions in the Action menu. These include copy and paste functions, server activation and closing, and object updating. With this example program, the user can create an OLE object, copy it to the Clipboard, and then paste the object into another OLE client application. For example, the user could create an embedded bitmap using Paintbrush, copy it to the Clipboard using the example program's OLE_COPY option (under the Action menu), and then paste the object into Windows Write using the Edit menu's Paste Special option. A copy of the image would then appear within the Write document, and the user could edit it by double-clicking the image within Write.

Alternately, the user can paste data from other sources. To experiment, create a document in Microsoft Word. Copy some text from the document to the Clipboard using the Edit menu's Copy option. Now run the Visual Basic example program and select the OLE_PASTE option from the Action menu. The Word object will be embedded in the example application.

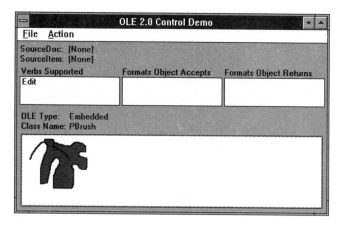

**Figure 9-9** The OLE control example program

## Steps

1. Create a new project called OLE.MAK. Add the OLE control, MSOLE2.VBX, to the project. Create a new module called OLECONST.BAS that will contain the OLE constants used by the example program. Add the constant declarations shown in this listing:

```
'-------------------------------------------------------
' Constants for OLE 2.0 client control
'-------------------------------------------------------

' Action property values.
Global Const OLE_CREATE_EMBED = 0
Global Const OLE_CREATE_NEW = 0
Global Const OLE_CREATE_LINK = 1
Global Const OLE_CREATE_FROM_FILE = 1
Global Const OLE_COPY = 4
Global Const OLE_PASTE = 5
Global Const OLE_UPDATE = 6
Global Const OLE_ACTIVATE = 7
Global Const OLE_CLOSE = 9
Global Const OLE_DELETE = 10
Global Const OLE_SAVE_TO_FILE = 11
Global Const OLE_READ_FROM_FILE = 12
Global Const OLE_INSERT_OBJ_DLG = 14
Global Const OLE_PASTE_SPECIAL_DLG = 15
Global Const OLE_FETCH_VERBS = 17
Global Const OLE_SAVE_TO_OLE1FILE = 18

' OLEType property values.
Global Const OLE_LINKED = 0
Global Const OLE_EMBEDDED = 1
Global Const OLE_NONE = 3

' AutoActivate property values.
Global Const OLE_ACTIVATE_MANUAL = 0
Global Const OLE_ACTIVATE_GETFOCUS = 1
Global Const OLE_ACTIVATE_DOUBLECLICK = 2

' SizeMode property values.
Global Const OLE_SIZE_CLIP = 0
Global Const OLE_SIZE_STRETCH = 1
Global Const OLE_SIZE_AUTOSIZE = 2

' Verb property values.
Global Const VERB_PRIMARY = 0
Global Const VERB_SHOW = -1
Global Const VERB_OPEN = -2
Global Const VERB_HIDE = -3
```

2. Create a new form with the objects and properties described in Table 9-23. Save this form as OLE.FRM.

**Table 9-23** Objects and properties for OLE.FRM

| OBJECT | PROPERTY | SETTING |
|--------|----------|---------|
| Form | FormName | Form1 |
| | BackColor | &H00C0C0C0& |

(continued on next page)

9 ◀

| OBJECT | PROPERTY | SETTING |
|---|---|---|
| *(continued from previous page)* | | |
| | Caption | "OLE 2.0 Control Demo" |
| Label | Name | lblSourceDoc |
| | BackStyle | 0 'Transparent |
| | Caption | "[none]" |
| | ForeColor | &H00000080& |
| Label | Name | Label1 |
| | BackStyle | 0 'Transparent |
| | Caption | "SourceDoc:" |
| | ForeColor | &H00800000& |
| Label | Name | Label2 |
| | BackStyle | 0 'Transparent |
| | Caption | "Verbs Supported" |
| | ForeColor | &H00800000& |
| Label | Name | Label3 |
| | BackStyle | 0 'Transparent |
| | Caption | "Formats Object Accepts" |
| | ForeColor | &H00800000& |
| Label | Name | Label4 |
| | BackStyle | 0 'Transparent |
| | Caption | "Formats Object Returns" |
| | ForeColor | &H00800000& |
| Label | Name | Label5 |
| | BackStyle | 0 'Transparent |
| | Caption | "OLE Type:" |
| | ForeColor | &H00800000& |
| Label | Name | lblOLEType |
| | BackStyle | 0 'Transparent |
| | Caption | "[none]" |
| | ForeColor | &H00000080& |
| Label | Name | Label6 |
| | BackStyle | 0 'Transparent |
| | Caption | "SourceItem:" |
| | ForeColor | &H00800000& |
| Label | Name | lblSourceItem |
| | BackStyle | 0 'Transparent |
| | Caption | "[none]" |
| | ForeColor | &H00000080& |
| Label | Name | Label7 |

| OBJECT | PROPERTY | SETTING |
|--------|----------|---------|
|  | BackStyle | 0 'Transparent |
|  | Caption | "Class Name: " |
|  | ForeColor | &H00800000& |
| Label | Name | lblClassName |
|  | BackStyle | 0 'Transparent |
|  | Caption | "[none]" |
|  | ForeColor | &H00000080& |
| OLE | Name | OLE1 |
| ListBox | Name | lstObjectVerbs |
| ListBox | Name | lstObjectAcceptFormats |
| ListBox | Name | lstObjectGetFormats |

3. Add a menu to OLE.FRM using the Visual Basic Menu Design window, setting the captions and names as shown in Table 9-24.

**Table 9-24** Menu definition for OLE.FRM

| CAPTION | NAME |
|---------|------|
| &File | mnuFile |
| ––––&New | mnuFileNew |
| –––––– | mnuFileSep1 |
| ––––E&xit | mnuFileExit |
| &Action | mnuAction |
| ––––OLE_COPY | mnuOLECopy |
| ––––OLE_PASTE | mnuOLEPaste |
| ––––OLE_UPDATE | mnuOLEUpdate |
| ––––OLE_ACTIVATE | mnuOLEActivate |
| ––––OLE_CLOSE | mnuOLEClose |

4. After creating OLE.FRM, add the following code to its declarations section.

```
Option Explicit
'-----------------------------------------------
' Variables and constants used in OLE.FRM.
'-----------------------------------------------

' Track the minimum form dimensions.
Dim MinFormWidth As Integer
Dim MinFormHeight As Integer

' WindowState constant.
Const MINIMIZED = 1

Const MB_OK = &H0
Const MB_ICONQUESTION = &H20
```

*(continued on next page)*

*(continued from previous page)*

```
Const MB_ICONEXCLAMATION = &H30
Const MB_ICONINFORMATION = &H40
Const MB_ICONSTOP = &H10
```

5. Add the following subroutines to the OLE.FRM form.

```
Sub Form_Load ()
'------------------------------------------------------
' Position the main form and initialize variables.
'------------------------------------------------------

    ' Center the form on the screen.
    Me.Move (Screen.Width - Me.Width) \ 2, (Screen.Height - Me.Height) \ 2

    ' The current size of the form is the smallest allowable.
    MinFormWidth = Me.Width
    MinFormHeight = Me.Height

    ' Set the OLE control's host name, which usually appears in the
    ' title of an OLE application during editing.
    OLE1.HostName = "[" & Me.Caption & "]"

End Sub

Sub Form_Resize ()
'------------------------------------------------------
' Resize controls when the form is resized.
'------------------------------------------------------
Dim Margin As Integer

    ' Do nothing if the form was minimized.
    If WindowState = MINIMIZED Then Exit Sub

    ' Make sure the form isn't too small.
    If Me.Width < MinFormWidth Then Me.Width = MinFormWidth
    If Me.Height < MinFormHeight Then Me.Height = MinFormHeight

    ' Resize the OLE control.
    Margin = OLE1.Left
    OLE1.Width = Me.ScaleWidth - (Margin * 2)
    OLE1.Height = Me.ScaleHeight - OLE1.Top - Margin
End Sub

Sub mnuFileExit_Click ()
'------------------------------------------------------
' Exit the program.
'------------------------------------------------------
    Unload Me
End Sub

Sub mnuFileNew_Click ()
'------------------------------------------------------
' Try to insert a new object into the OLE control.
'------------------------------------------------------

    On Error GoTo mnuFileNew_Error

    ' Display the standard Insert Object dialog.
```

```
    OLE1.Action = OLE_INSERT_OBJ_DLG

    ' Check if we want to activate the OLE application now.
    If OLE1.OLEType <> OLE_NONE Then
      If OLE1.SourceDoc = "" Then
          OLE1.Action = OLE_ACTIVATE
      End If
    End If

    ' Update the information about this object.
    UpdateOLEInfo
Exit Sub
mnuFileNew_Error:
    MsgBox "Error " & Format$(Err) & ": " & Error$, MB_OK And MB_ICONEXCLAMATION, "OLE Error"
    Resume Next
End Sub

Sub mnuOLEActivate_Click ()
'----------------------------------------------------
' Activate the OLE application.
'----------------------------------------------------
    On Error Resume Next

    OLE1.Action = OLE_ACTIVATE
End Sub

Sub mnuOLEClose_Click ()
'----------------------------------------------------
' Close the OLE application.
'----------------------------------------------------
    On Error Resume Next

    OLE1.Action = OLE_CLOSE
End Sub

Sub mnuOLECopy_Click ()
'----------------------------------------------------
' Copy the current object to the Clipboard.
'----------------------------------------------------
Dim AppRunning As Integer

    AppRunning = OLE1.AppIsRunning
    ' See if we need to activate a hidden copy of the
    ' OLE application.
    If Not AppRunning Then
        OLE1.Verb = VERB_HIDE
        OLE1.Action = OLE_ACTIVATE
    End If

    ' Copy object to the Clipboard.
    OLE1.Action = OLE_COPY

    If Not AppRunning Then
        OLE1.Verb = VERB_PRIMARY
        OLE1.Action = OLE_CLOSE
    End If
End Sub

Sub mnuOLEPaste_Click ()
```

9 ◄

(continued on next page)

*(continued from previous page)*

```
'-----------------------------------------------
' Paste an object in the Clipboard into the OLE
' control.
'-----------------------------------------------

    On Error Resume Next

    ' Paste from the Clipboard.
    If OLE1.PasteOK Then OLE1.Action = OLE_PASTE

    ' Update the object information fields.
    UpdateOLEInfo
End Sub

Sub mnuOLEUpdate_Click ()
'-----------------------------------------------
' Update the OLE control.
'-----------------------------------------------

    ' Update the contents of the OLE control.
    OLE1.Action = OLE_UPDATE

    ' Update the information about the object.
    UpdateOLEInfo
End Sub

Sub UpdateOLEInfo ()
'-----------------------------------------------
' Update the labels and list boxes containing
' information about the current object.
'-----------------------------------------------
Dim i As Integer

    On Error GoTo UpdateOLEInfo_Error

    ' Show all the supported verbs.
    lstObjectVerbs.Clear
    For i = 1 To OLE1.ObjectVerbsCount - 1
        lstObjectVerbs.AddItem OLE1.ObjectVerbs(i)
    Next

    ' Show all the formats that this object can accept.
    lstObjectAcceptFormats.Clear
    For i = 0 To OLE1.ObjectAcceptFormatsCount - 1
        lstObjectAcceptFormats.AddItem OLE1.ObjectAcceptFormats(i)
    Next

    ' Show all the formats that this object can return.
    lstObjectGetFormats.Clear
    For i = 0 To OLE1.ObjectGetFormatsCount - 1
        lstObjectGetFormats.AddItem OLE1.ObjectGetFormats(i)
    Next

    ' What type of object is this?
    Select Case OLE1.OLEType
        Case 0: lblOLEType = "Linked"
        Case 1: lblOLEType = "Embedded"
        Case 3: lblOLEType = "[None]"
    End Select
```

```
' From what source document did this originate?
If OLE1.SourceDoc = "" Then
    lblSourceDoc = "[None]"
Else
    lblSourceDoc = OLE1.SourceDoc
End If

' What source item does this object refer to?
If OLE1.SourceItem = "" Then
    lblSourceItem = "[None]"
Else
    lblSourceItem = OLE1.SourceItem
End If

' What class of object is this?
If OLE1.Class = "" Then
    lblClassName = "[None]"
Else
    lblClassName = OLE1.Class
End If

Exit Sub
UpdateOLEInfo_Error:
    Resume Next
End Sub
```

## Tips and Comments

While this section can only scratch the surface of OLE, the subject is becoming of pivotal importance to Windows developers in general, and Visual Basic programmers in particular. Visual Basic has especially strong and accessible support for both OLE automation, which wasn't covered here, and linking and embedding. Microsoft has indicated that OLE will play an increasing role in their future operating system offerings. The advent of OLE controls, and their impact on Visual Basic developers, is still another reason for programmers to delve deeper into this subject.

## SpyWorks-VB

| USAGE: | VB Extension and Debugging Tools That Let VB Apps Use Subclassing, Callback Functions, and Hooks |
|---|---|
| MANUFACTURER: | Desaware |
| COST: | $ 129 |

SpyWorks-VB isn't designed to perform one, specific task. It's a set of extension tools designed to let you perform any task you need with Visual Basic: subclassing, intercepting Windows messages (including messages sent to graphical controls), callback functions (program functions called by the API which are necessary for use with certain API functions), and hooks (both keyboard and Windows hooks). Debugging tools are also provided to make life easier when working with the Windows API and the SpyWorks extension tools. One control (SBCEASY) offers partially prepackaged solutions for some common tasks that require subclassing, such as creating tiny caption bars, or tracking highlighted menu selections.

# Syntax

SpyWorks extension tools are five custom controls that extend VB in a variety of ways: subclassing, system hooks, callback functions, and keyboard hooks. All of the controls work behind the scenes (that is they are visible only at design time).

**SBC.VBX**   SBC.VBX is a generic subclassing control that can intercept Windows messages sent to any form or control in the system. You can detect messages before or after Windows default processing has occurred by setting the *Type* property. When a message is detected, a *WndMessage* event fires, which is where you process the message. If messages are detected before default processing occurs, the message or its parameters may be changed or the message can be ignored. If you don't act on a message and you don't pass it on to Windows for default processing, it's as if the message never existed. In addition to detecting Windows messages, the SBC *Detect* property can be set to detect messages sent from Visual Basic. When a VB message is sent to a control, even a graphical control, a *CtlMessage* event fires. Table 9-25 lists the nonstandard properties and events for SBC.

**Table 9-25** SBC.VBX nonstandard properties and events

| PROPERTIES | | |
|---|---|---|
| About | AddHctl | AddHwnd |
| ClearMessage | CtlParam | Detect |
| HctlArray | HctlParam | HookCount |
| HwndArray | HwndParam | MessageArray |
| MessageCount | Messages | PostEvent |
| PostMsgBoxMax | PostOnMsgBox | RegMessage1 |
| RegMessage2 | RegMessage3 | RegMessage4 |
| RegMessage5 | RemoveHctl | RemoveHwnd |
| Type | | |

| EVENTS | | |
|---|---|---|
| CtlMessage | DelayedEvent | WndMessage |

SBC provides a design time Message Selection dialog box (Figure 9-10) for you to specify which messages to detect. The dialog provides a list of message groups (such as mouse, a nonclient) and a list of available messages for each of them. Simply select the message(s) desired and press the Add button to include a message in a list. You can also alter the list of messages SBC will detect, and which windows (or controls) are monitored, at run time.

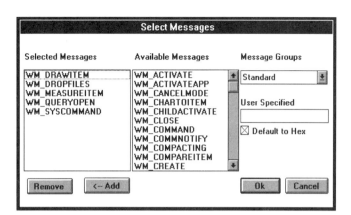

**Figure 9-10** Design time Message Selection dialog for SBC.VBX

**CBK.VBX**   Certain API functions require the use of callback functions. A callback function is a function in your application that the API calls in response to your calling certain API functions. To call a function, the API needs that function's address. The problem is that VB doesn't support function pointers (that is, addresses) because it doesn't compile to machine code. That's where SpyWorks comes in. A callback function must meet two requirements: the parameter list and return type must both match the function the API is expecting to call or you will likely cause a GPF (General Protection Fault).

Using CBK is straightforward. First, set the *Type* property to correspond with the API function you are using. Many standard API callback definitions (for example, *EnumWindows* and *DdeCallback*) are provided, as well as a number of generic ones. Next, set the *Convention* and *EventTrigger* properties. *Convention* tells CBK whether to use Pascal or C calling conventions. Most Windows API functions use the Pascal calling convention but some third-party DLLs may use the C calling convention, so it is a useful property. *EventTrigger* determines whether the callback event takes place immediately or is deferred via a posted event. When a callback function is required, simply pass the *ProcAddress* property of the CBK control and wait for the appropriate callback event to fire. Table 9-26 lists the nonstandard properties and events for CBK.

**Table 9-26**. CBK.VBX nonstandard properties and events

**PROPERTIES**

| | | |
|---|---|---|
| About | Convention | EventTrigger |
| hWnd | PostedReturn | ProcAddress |
| TriggerTask | Type | |

**EVENTS**

| | | |
|---|---|---|
| AbortProc | cbxLI | cbxLLFFFL |
| cbxLLFFFFL | cbxLLLILL | cbxILL |

(continued on next page)

## EVENTS

*(continued from previous page)*

| | | |
|---|---|---|
| cbxLL | cbxLLL | cbxLLLL |
| cbxllLLLL | CommEvent | DdeCallback |
| EnumFonts | EnumMetaFile | EnumObjects |
| EnumProps | EnumWindows | GrayString |
| HookFunc | IntParam | LineDDA |
| mciYieldProc | mmioProc | NoParam |
| WinHook | WndProc | |

CBK provides over 100 function addresses to be used as callback functions, and those functions offer more than a dozen standard parameter sequences that cover all normal situations. If you need a callback function that isn't listed, Desaware will add it for you and send you an upgraded version of the control.

**SBCKBD.VBX** VB applications only see the keystrokes meant for them, not those meant for other apps in the system. This makes it impossible to perform certain tasks, such as having a hot key pop up an application. You also can't intercept some key combinations because they're processed before they get to your app. SBCKBD uses keyboard hooks to detect keystrokes before they're sent to an application. Table 9-27 lists the nonstandard properties and event for SBCKBD.

**Table 9-27** SBCKBD.VBX nonstandard properties and event

### PROPERTIES

| | | |
|---|---|---|
| About | ClearKey | Enabled |
| KeyArray | KeyCount | Keys |
| Monitor | Notify | |

### EVENT

KbdHook

SBCKBD can detect keystrokes on a system-wide basis, or just for the task that contains the control, based on the value of the *Monitor* property. To keep overhead low SBCKBD lets you specify what key combinations to detect, much as SBC lets you specify which messages to detect. The *Keys* property determines what key combinations are detected. You can set *Keys* at design time with the Select Keys dialog provided by SBCKBD (Figure 9-11) or at run time by assigning a key value to *Keys*. Setting a key value to the *ClearKey* property removes that key from the filter list of keys that will be detected. A key value is a long integer. The low 16 bits determine the virtual key code of the key; the high 16 bits determine the state of the (CTRL), (ALT), and (SHIFT) keys.

When a keystroke event occurs a *KbdHook* event fires, telling you which key combination was detected. The *discard* parameter in the *KbdHook* event lets you discard the keystroke before it is processed.

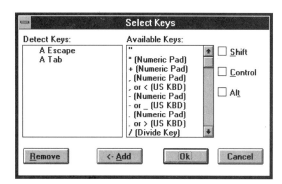

**Figure 9-11** Design time Select Keys dialog for SBCKBD.VBX

**SBCHOOK.VBX**   Unlike SBC, which subclasses specific windows and controls, SBCHOOK uses Windows hooks that monitor operations on a global level. If you need to monitor specific windows and controls, you should use SBC; but if you need to monitor all messages sent to your application or anywhere in the system, you should use SBCHOOK. Table 9-28 lists the nonstandard properties and events for SBCHOOK.

**Table 9-28** SBCHOOK.VBX nonstandard properties and events

**PROPERTIES**

| | | |
|---|---|---|
| About | HookType | HwndParam |
| Monitor | Notify | TaskParam |

**EVENTS**

| | | |
|---|---|---|
| DelayedEvent | MessageProc | MouseProc |
| WndMessage | | |

Five different types of Windows hooks are available through SBCHOOK (Table 9-29). The *HookType* property determines which hook is used. Each hook detects a different subset of messages.

**Table 9-29** SBCHOOK property settings

| VALUE | MEANING |
|---|---|
| 0 | GetMessage |
| 1 | Mouse |
| 2 | MessageProc |
| 3 | SysMessageProc |
| 4 | WindowProc |

If *HookType* is set to 2 (MessageProc) or 3 (SysMessageProc), a *MessageProc* event fires when messages are detected. For a *HookType* setting of 1 (Mouse), a *MouseProc* event is fired; and for *HookType* settings of 0 (GetMessage) or 4 (WindowProc), a *WndMessage* event is fired.

Windows hooks are designed to detect messages on a global basis. You can limit the scope of the hook with the *Monitor* property (Table 9-30).

**Table 9-30** SBCHOOK property settings

| VALUE | MEANING |
| --- | --- |
| 0 | Form containing SBCHOOK control |
| 1 | Children of Form containing SBCHOOK control |
| 2 | Form whose handle is in HwndParam property |
| 3 | Children of Form whose handle is in HwndParam property |
| 4 | Task that owns SBCHOOK control |
| 5 | Windows whose task ID is in the TaskParam property |
| 6 | All Tasks, system-wide |

**SBCEASY.VBX** SBCEASY performs more specific tasks than the other SpyWorks controls. It provides solutions to common problems (like adding scroll bars to forms and controls, or tracking the mouse status bar information) without forcing you to learn much about the API. Table 9-31 lists the nonstandard properties and events for SBCEASY.

**Table 9-31** SBCEASY.VBX nonstandard properties and events

| PROPERTIES | | |
| --- | --- | --- |
| CaptionHeight | CaptionStyle | ForceActive |
| ForceCtlBox | ForceOutline | ForceTitle |
| HLargeChange | HMax | HMin |
| HSmallChange | HValue | MouseTransit |
| ScrollBars | ScrollUpdate | ScrollViewport |
| ScrollWindow | VLargeChange | VMax |
| VMin | VSmallChange | VValue |

| EVENTS | | |
| --- | --- | --- |
| DrawCaption | HChange | HScroll |
| MenuSelect | MouseEnter | MouseExit |
| StateButton | SystemCommand | SysMenuRequest |
| VChange | VScroll | |

SBCEASY fires *MouseEnter* and *MouseExit* events for forms and controls, even graphical controls, so you can easily provide status line help. The *MenuSelect* event provides the same capability for menus. You can create mini title bars (like the one on VB's toolbox) and roll-up windows by changing the *CaptionStyle* property. The *ScrollBars* property adds scroll bars to forms and most container controls (picture boxes, for example). You can add custom system menus to VB applications by processing the *SystemCommand* event, which fires when a system menu command is selected.

**DWSPYDLL.DLL**   All the SpyWorks VBXs use functions provided by DWSPYDLL, which you need to distribute with your app. In addition, DWSPYDLL provides almost 100 functions that can be called directly from an application. These functions provide VB API functions, API rectangle functions, port I/O functions, printer driver function access, type conversions, and functions for indirect property access and control analysis. Table 9-32 lists the functions exported from DWSPYDLL.DLL.

**Table 9-32**  DWSPYDLL.DLL exported functions

### VISUAL BASIC API FUNCTIONS

| | | |
|---|---|---|
| dwGetAppTitle | dwGetControlHwnd | dwGetControlHwndByID |
| dwGetControlID | dwGetControlIDByHwnd | dwGetControlName |
| dwGetControlNameByID | dwGetHwndControl | dwGetInstance |
| dwGetModelInfo | dwVBClientToScreen | dwVBGetControl |
| dwVBGetControlByID | dwVBGetVersion | dwVBIsControlEnabled |
| dwVBIsControlVisible | dwVBPaletteChanged | dwVBRecreateControlHwnd |
| dwVBScreenToClient | dwVBSendControlMsg | dwVBSetControlFlags |
| dwXCapture | dwXControlOp | dwXConvertCoord |
| dwXGetControl | dwXGetControlHwnd | dwXGetControlInfo |
| dwXGetControlName | dwXGetFullControlName | dwXGetFullControlNamebuf |
| dwXGetHwndControl | dwXGetVBInfo | dwXPixelsToTwips |
| dwXTwipsToPixels | dwYPixelsToTwips | dwYTwipsToPixels |

### RECTANGLE FUNCTIONS

| | | |
|---|---|---|
| dwVBGetClientRect | dwVBGetControlRect | dwVBGetRectInContainer |
| dwXGetRect | | |

### MISCELLANEOUS FUNCTIONS

| | |
|---|---|
| dwFindFile | GetSpyWorksVersion |

### PORT I/O FUNCTIONS

| | | |
|---|---|---|
| dwInp | dwInpw | dwOutp |
| dwOutpw | | |

### PRINTER DRIVER FUNCTIONS

| | | |
|---|---|---|
| dwDeviceCapabilities | dwDeviceMode | dwExtDeviceMode |

*(continued on next page)*

9

*(continued from previous page)*

## DATA AND MEMORY ACCESS FUNCTIONS

| | | |
|---|---|---|
| dw2IntegersToDWORD | dw4BytesToDWORD | dwCopyData |
| dwDWORDto2Integers | dwDWORDto4Bytes | dwGetAddressForInteger |
| dwGetAddressForLong | dwGetAddressForLPSTR | dwGetAddressForObject |
| dwGetAddressForVBString | dwGetStringFromLPSTR | dwHugeOffset |
| dwPOINTAPItoLong | | |

## INDIRECT PROPERTY FUNCTIONS

| | | |
|---|---|---|
| dwGetPropertyPic | dwGetPropertyValue | dwSetPropertyPic |
| dwSetPropertyValue | | |

## CONTROL ANALYSIS FUNCTIONS

| | | |
|---|---|---|
| dwGetEventCount | dwGetEventName | dwGetEventParamName |
| dwGetEventParamType | dwGetEventPointer | dwGetModelFromVBX |
| dwGetModelInfo2 | dwGetModelPointer | dwGetPropCount |
| dwGetPropEnumList | dwGetPropName | dwGetPropPointer |
| dwGetStandardBufAddr | | |

## Example

The example program seen in Figure 9-12 shows some of the things you can do with SpyWorks. (It would be impossible to illustrate everything you can do because the only limits are those of the Windows API itself.) The program demonstrates some common tasks, including locking a form as an icon, accepting dropped files from File Manager,

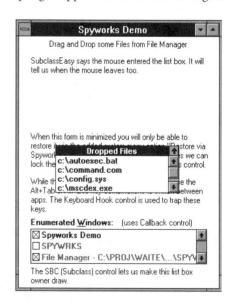

**Figure 9-12** SpyWorks demo program

tracking the mouse, intercepting system keystrokes, creating owner draw controls, and enumerating active windows in the system.

## Steps

1. Create a new project called SPYWRKS.MAK. Create a new form with the objects and properties shown in Table 9-33. Save this form as SPYWRKS.FRM.

**Table 9-33** SpyWorks main form's objects and properties

| OBJECT | PROPERTY | SETTING |
|---|---|---|
| Label | Name | lblKybdHookNote |
| | Caption | "While this app is running you won't be able to use the Alt+Tab or Alt+Esc key combinations to switch between apps. The Keyboard Hook control is used to trap these keys." |
| | FontBold | 0 'False |
| Label | Name | lblEnumeratedWindows |
| | BackStyle | 0 'Transparent |
| | Caption | "Enumerated &Windows:" |
| | Index | 0 |
| Label | Name | lblWhatsRunning |
| | Alignment | 1 'Right Justify |
| | BackStyle | 0 'Transparent |
| | Caption | "(uses Callback control)" |
| | FontBold | 0 'False |
| | Index | 1 |
| Label | Name | lblDropFiles |
| | BackStyle | 0 'Transparent |
| | Caption | "Mini Title bar and drop-down effect courtesy of SubclassEasy control. You can move the list as well." |
| | FontBold | 0 'False |
| | Index | 1 |
| Label | Name | lblResizeInfo |
| | BackStyle | 0 'Transparent |
| | Caption | "The resizing of the lists is done with plain VB code; no subclassing is involved. " |
| | FontBold | 0 'False |
| Label | Name | Label1 |
| | Caption | "The SBC (Subclass) control lets us make this list box owner draw." |

*(continued on next page)*

9 ◄

| OBJECT | PROPERTY | SETTING |
|---|---|---|
| *(continued from previous page)* | | |
| | FontBold | 0 'False |
| PictureBox | Name | picDroppedFiles |
| ListBox | Name | lstEnumeratedWindows |
| | BackColor | &H00FFFFFF& |
| | MultiSelect | 2 'Extended |
| ccHookKbd | Name | HookKbd1 |
| | Keys | (set at design time in Properties window) |
| | Monitor | 1 'All Tasks |
| ccCallback | Name | Callback1 |
| | IntVersion | 5 |
| | Type | 6 'EnumWindows |
| ccSubClass | Name | sbcMain |
| | Messages | (set at design time in Properties window) |
| Form | FormName | frmMain |
| | Caption | "SpyWorks Demo" |

2. Inside the form's picDroppedFiles Picture Box control, add the controls shown in Table 9-34.

**Table 9-34** Objects inside the picDroppedFiles Picture Box control

| OBJECT | PROPERTY | SETTING |
|---|---|---|
| ccSbcEasy | Name | sbcezDroppedFiles |
| | CaptionHeight | 75 |
| | CaptionStyle | 2 'Rollup |
| | ForceActive | -1 'True |
| | ForceCtlBox | 0 'False |
| | ForceTitle | "Dropped Files" |
| | HMax | 0 |
| | MouseTransit | 1 'Track windows only |
| | VLargeChange | 10 |
| | VMax | 0 |
| ListBox | Name | lstDroppedFiles |

3. Add the following code to SPYWRKS.FRM. As you see, dealing with the API can involve a lot of work. Much of the code related to the owner draw list box was appropriated from a sample that comes with SpyWorks.

```
Option Explicit
DefInt A-Z
```

```
Dim mOldCaption$

Sub Callback1_EnumWindows (hWnd As Integer, lpData As Long, retval As Integer)
    Dim Buffer$
    Dim BytesCopied%

    '-- We add 1 to the text length to allow for the NULL terminator.
    Buffer$ = Space$(GetWindowTextLength(hWnd%) + 1)
    BytesCopied% = GetWindowText(hWnd%, Buffer$, Len(Buffer$))
    If Len(Buffer$) > 1 Then
        frmMain!lstEnumeratedWindows.AddItem Buffer$
    End If

End Sub

Sub DrawList (ds As DRAWITEMSTRUCT, retval&)
'------------------------------------------------
'-- This is our drawing code for the owner draw
'   list box.
'------------------------------------------------
    Dim rc       As RECT
    Dim rctext   As RECT
    Dim listentry%
    Dim ItemText$
    Dim Colr%
    Dim OldBkMode%
    Dim BkBrush%
    Dim OldBrush%
    Dim OldPen%
    Dim RtnCode%
    Dim dc%
    Dim dl&

    '-- It's a draw item command.
    listentry% = ds.itemID
    ItemText$ = lstEnumeratedWindows.List(listentry%)

    OldBkMode% = SetBkMode(ds.hDC, TRANSPARENT)
    BkBrush% = CreateSolidBrush(lstEnumeratedWindows.BackColor)

    '-- Cycle through colors based on position in list.
    Colr% = listentry% Mod 16
    If QBColor(Colr%) = lstEnumeratedWindows.BackColor Then
        Colr% = Colr% + 1
        If Colr% = 16 Then Colr% = 0
    End If
    dl& = SetTextColor(ds.hDC, QBColor(Colr%))
    '-- Clear the background of this entry.
    RtnCode% = FillRect(ds.hDC%, ds.rcItem, BkBrush%)

    LSet rctext = ds.rcItem
    rctext.Left = rctext.Left + 16   ' Allow extra 16 pixels for our checkbox
    RtnCode% = DrawText(ds.hDC%, ItemText$, Len(ItemText$), rctext, DT_SINGLELINE Or DT_VCENTER)

    OldBkMode% = SetBkMode(dc%, OldBkMode%)
    If BkBrush%  <>0 Then
        RtnCode% = DeleteObject(BkBrush%)
    End If

    '-- Draw a box in the leading space.
```

(continued on next page)

9 ◄

*(continued from previous page)*

```
    OldPen% = SelectObject(ds.hDC, GetStockObject(BLACK_PEN))
    dl& = MoveTo(ds.hDC, 2, ds.rcItem.top + 2)
    RtnCode% = LineTo(ds.hDC, 2, ds.rcItem.bottom - 4)
    RtnCode% = LineTo(ds.hDC, 12, ds.rcItem.bottom - 4)
    RtnCode% = LineTo(ds.hDC, 12, ds.rcItem.top + 2)
    RtnCode% = LineTo(ds.hDC, 2, ds.rcItem.top + 2)
    '-- Draw an X if it's selected.
    If ds.itemState And ODS_SELECTED Then
        dl& = MoveTo(ds.hDC, 2, ds.rcItem.top + 2)
        RtnCode% = LineTo(ds.hDC, 12, ds.rcItem.bottom - 4)
        dl& = MoveTo(ds.hDC, 12, ds.rcItem.top + 2)
        RtnCode% = LineTo(ds.hDC, 2, ds.rcItem.bottom - 4)
    End If
    RtnCode% = SelectObject(ds.hDC, OldPen%)


End Sub

Sub Form_Load ()
    Dim EnumOK%
    Dim di%

    ' Changing the list box to owner draw is trickier.
    ' We need to recreate the window itself.
    ' First we set the model style for list boxes to
    ' owner draw.
    Call SetModelOwnerDraw(lstEnumeratedWindows, True)
    di% = dwVBRecreateControlHwnd(dwGetControlID(lstEnumeratedWindows))
    ' And be sure to change the model back to the original
    ' style to prevent screwing up future list boxes.
    Call SetModelOwnerDraw(lstEnumeratedWindows, False)
    lstEnumeratedWindows.Visible = True

    EnumOK% = EnumWindows(Callback1.ProcAddress, 0)

End Sub

Sub Form_Resize ()
    Dim NewWidth%

    Select Case WindowState
        Case 1       ' MINMIZED
            Me.Caption = "Locked as Icon"
        Case Else    ' NORMAL, MAXIMIZED
            Me.Caption = "SpyWorks Demo"
            '-- Resize the List Boxes.
            NewWidth% = Me.ScaleWidth - picDroppedFiles.Left - lstEnumeratedWindows.Left
            lstDroppedFiles.Width = NewWidth%
            picDroppedFiles.Width = NewWidth%
            lstEnumeratedWindows.Width = Me.ScaleWidth - (lstEnumeratedWindows.Left * 2)
    End Select

End Sub

Sub HookKbd1_KbdHook (keycode As Integer, keystate As Long, shiftstate As Integer, discard As
Integer)
```

```
'-------------------------------------------------------
'-- All we're doing here is causing Windows to ignore
'    the Alt+Tab and Alt+Esc key combinations. This
'    technique is useful if you want to prevent users
'    from switching to other apps if, say, your app is
'    maximized.
'-------------------------------------------------------

    '-- Discard the key so Windows won't process it.
    discard% = True

    '-- We could act on each key we trap if we wanted to.
    '    The keys to trap were designated at design time
    '    and the Keyboard Hook control stores them for us.
    Select Case keycode%
        Case KEY_TAB     '-- Alt+Tab
        Case KEY_ESCAPE '-- Alt+Esc
    End Select

End Sub

Sub MeasureList (lp As Long, retval As Long)
'-------------------------------------------------
'-- This is a support function for the owner
'    draw list box.
'-------------------------------------------------

    Dim ms As MEASUREITEMSTRUCT
    Dim rc As RECT

    '-- Get a copy of the structure.
    Call dwCopyData(ByVal lp, ms, 14)
    Call GetClientRect(lstEnumeratedWindows.hWnd, rc)
    ms.itemWidth = rc.right

    '-- We're basing this now on the standard height of
    '    the default screen font. A more sophisticated
    '    application would need to recalculate the font.
    ms.itemHeight = (TextHeight("M") \ Screen.TwipsPerPixelY) + 1

    '-- And set the data.
    Call dwCopyData(ms, ByVal lp&, 14)

    retval& = 1

End Sub

Sub sbcezDroppedFiles_MouseEnter (FormDesc As String, ControlDesc As String)

    Select Case ControlDesc$
        Case "lstDroppedFiles"
            mOldCaption$ = lblDropFiles(1).Caption
            lblDropFiles(1).Caption = "SubclassEasy says the mouse entered the list box. It
will tell us when the mouse leaves too."
    End Select

End Sub

Sub sbcezDroppedFiles_MouseExit (FormDesc As String, ControlDesc As String)
```

9 ◄

*(continued on next page)*

*(continued from previous page)*

```
        Select Case ControlDesc$
            Case "lstDroppedFiles"
                lblDropFiles(1).Caption = mOldCaption$
        End Select

End Sub

Sub sbcMain_DelayedEvent (lvalue As Long)

    Select Case lvalue&
        '-- System menu items
        Case FS_SYSMENUID_RESTORE
            gbOKToRestore% = True
            frmMain.WindowState = 0
        Case FS_SYSMENUID_ABOUT
            MsgBox "This is where our About box would go"
    End Select

End Sub

Sub sbcMain_WndMessage (wnd As Integer, msg As Integer, wp As Integer, lp As Long, retval As
Long, nodef As Integer)
    Dim hDrop%
    Dim di As DRAWITEMSTRUCT

    Select Case msg%
        Case WM_DROPFILES
            hDrop% = wp%
            Call ParseDroppedFiles(hDrop%)
            Call DragFinish(hDrop%)
            Call DisplayDroppedFiles
        Case WM_QUERYOPEN
            If gbOKToRestore% = False Then
                nodef% = True
                retval& = 0
                gbOKToRestore% = False
            End If
        Case WM_SYSCOMMAND
            Select Case wp%
                Case FS_SYSMENUID_RESTORE, FS_SYSMENUID_ABOUT
                    '-- If it's one of our menu items, kill
                    '    default processing and pass the ID
                    '    along to trigger a DelayedEvent.
                    nodef% = True
                    retval& = 0
                    sbcMain.PostEvent = wp%
                Case Else
                    '-- Do nothing.
                    gbOKToRestore% = False
            End Select
        '-- Owner draw list box messages
        Case WM_DRAWITEM
            Call dwCopyData(ByVal lp, di, 26)
            Call DrawList(di, retval)
        Case WM_MEASUREITEM
            ' Have to inform Windows of the list's measurements.
            Call MeasureList(lp, retval)
    End Select
```

```
End Sub

Sub SetModelOwnerDraw (lstTarget As ListBox, bSetStyle%)
'------------------------------------------------
'-- Sets the style of lstTarget to be owner draw
'   if bSetStyle is True. If bSetStyle is False
'   the owner draw style is removed.
'------------------------------------------------
    Dim lpModel&
    Dim NewStyle&
    Static OldStyle&

    '-- Get a pointer to the Lists Model structure.
    lpModel& = dwGetModelPointer(dwGetControlID(lstTarget))
    If lpModel& Then
        '-- Window class is offset by 12 - see CDK for MODEL structure.
        lpModel& = lpModel& + 12
        If (bSetStyle% = True) Then '-- Set new style.
            Call dwCopyData(ByVal lpModel&, OldStyle&, 4)
            NewStyle& = OldStyle& Or LBS_OWNERDRAWFIXED Or LBS_HASSTRINGS
            Call dwCopyData(NewStyle&, ByVal lpModel&, 4)
        Else '-- Restore previous style.
            Call dwCopyData(OldStyle&, ByVal lpModel&, 4)
        End If
    Else
        '-- lpModel& = 0 so we can't do anything.
    End If

End Sub
```

4. Create a new module called SPYWRKS.BAS. Place the following code in the declarations section of that module. These are the Type and Function declarations used by the example program organized by topic.

```
Option Explicit
DefInt A-Z

'-- API Type declarations
Type RECT
    left As Integer
    top As Integer
    right As Integer
    bottom As Integer
End Type

Type DRAWITEMSTRUCT      ' 26 bytes
    CtlType As Integer
    CtlID As Integer
    itemID As Integer
    itemAction As Integer
    itemState As Integer
    hwndItem As Integer
    hDC As Integer
    rcItem As RECT
    itemData As Long
End Type

Type MEASUREITEMSTRUCT  ' 14 bytes
```

*(continued on next page)*

*(continued from previous page)*

```
    CtlType As Integer
    CtlID As Integer
    itemID As Integer
    itemWidth As Integer
    itemHeight As Integer
    itemData As Long
End Type

'-- DWSPYDLL declarations
Declare Sub dwCopyData Lib "dwspydll.dll" (source As Any, dest As Any, ByVal nCount%)
Declare Function dwGetControlID& Lib "dwspydll.dll" (hctl As Control)
Declare Function dwVBRecreateControlHwnd% Lib "dwspydll.dll" (ByVal hctl&)
Declare Function dwGetModelPointer& Lib "dwspydll.dll" (ByVal hctl&)

'-- EnumWindows declarations
Declare Function EnumWindows% Lib "User" (ByVal lpEnumFunc&, ByVal lParam&)
Declare Function GetWindowText% Lib "User" (ByVal hWnd%, ByVal lpszBuffer$, ByVal⇒
cbBufferSize%)
Declare Function GetWindowTextLength% Lib "User" (ByVal hWnd%)

'-- OwnerDraw list box declarations
Global Const ODS_SELECTED = &H1

Global Const DT_VCENTER = &H4
Global Const DT_SINGLELINE = &H20

Global Const LBS_OWNERDRAWFIXED = &H10&
Global Const LBS_HASSTRINGS = &H40&

Global Const WM_DRAWITEM = &H2B
Global Const WM_MEASUREITEM = &H2C

Global Const BLACK_PEN = 7
Global Const TRANSPARENT = 1

Declare Function CreateSolidBrush% Lib "GDI" (ByVal crColor&)
Declare Sub GetClientRect Lib "User" (ByVal hWnd%, lpRect As RECT)
Declare Function GetStockObject% Lib "GDI" (ByVal nIndex%)
Declare Function DeleteObject% Lib "GDI" (ByVal hObject%)
Declare Function DrawText% Lib "User" (ByVal hDC%, ByVal lpStr$, ByVal nCount%, lpRect ⇒
As RECT, ByVal wFormat%)
Declare Function FillRect% Lib "User" (ByVal hDC%, lpRect As RECT, ByVal hBrush%)
Declare Function LineTo% Lib "GDI" (ByVal hDC%, ByVal x%, ByVal y%)
Declare Function MoveTo& Lib "GDI" (ByVal hDC%, ByVal x%, ByVal y%)
Declare Function SelectObject% Lib "GDI" (ByVal hDC%, ByVal hObject%)
Declare Function SetBkMode% Lib "GDI" (ByVal hDC%, ByVal nBkMode%)
Declare Function SetTextColor& Lib "GDI" (ByVal hDC%, ByVal crColor&)

'-- System menu related declarations
Declare Function AppendMenuByString% Lib "User" Alias "AppendMenu" (ByVal hMenu%, ByVal⇒
wFlags%, ByVal wIDNewItem%, ByVal lpNewItem$)
Declare Function GetSystemMenu% Lib "User" (ByVal hWnd%, ByVal bRevert%)

Global Const MF_BYPOSITION = &H400
Global Const MF_SEPARATOR = &H800
Global Const MF_STRING = &H0
Global Const WM_SYSCOMMAND = &H112
Global Const WM_QUERYOPEN = &H13
```

```
'-- FileMan Drop related declarations
Declare Sub DragAcceptFiles Lib "shell.dll" (ByVal hWnd%, ByVal fAccept%)
Declare Sub DragFinish Lib "shell.dll" (ByVal hDrop%)
Declare Function DragQueryFile% Lib "shell.dll" (ByVal hDrop%, ByVal iFile%, ByVal lpszFile$,⇒
ByVal cb%)
Declare Function QueryDroppedFileSize% Lib "shell.dll" Alias "DragQueryFile" (ByVal hDrop%, ⇒
ByVal iFile%, ByVal lpszFile&, ByVal cb%)

Global Const WM_DROPFILES = &H233

'-- Keyboard Hook declarations
Global Const KEY_TAB = &H9
Global Const KEY_ESCAPE = &H1B

'-- Our system menu item IDs (use numbers less than &HF000)
Global Const FS_SYSMENUID_RESTORE = &H100
Global Const FS_SYSMENUID_ABOUT = &H101

'-- App variables
Dim marrDroppedFile$()   '-- Array of Filenames dropped by File Manager
Global gbOKToRestore%    '-- Used to keep Form locked as Icon
```

5. Place the following procedures in SPYWRKS.BAS as well. Most of the procedures support the dropping of files from File Manager. They have been designed so they can be extracted easily for use in other applications.

```
Private Sub AddSysMenuItems (F As Form)
'-------------------------------------------------
'-- Adds custom items to the system menu.
'-------------------------------------------------
    Dim hSysMenu%
    Dim rtn%

    hSysMenu% = GetSystemMenu(F.hWnd, 0)
    rtn% = AppendMenuByString(hSysMenu%, MF_SEPARATOR, 0, "")
    rtn% = AppendMenuByString(hSysMenu%, MF_STRING, FS_SYSMENUID_RESTORE, "Restore via⇒
Spyworks...")
    rtn% = AppendMenuByString(hSysMenu%, MF_STRING, FS_SYSMENUID_ABOUT, "About Spyworks Demo...")

End Sub

Sub DisplayDroppedFiles ()
'-------------------------------------------------
'-- Fills the roll-up list with the file names
'   dropped by File Manager.
'-------------------------------------------------
    Dim i%

    frmMain!lstDroppedFiles.Clear
    For i% = 0 To UBound(marrDroppedFile)
      frmMain!lstDroppedFiles.AddItem marrDroppedFile(i%)
    Next i%

End Sub

Sub Main ()
    Dim hWnd%

    If App.PrevInstance = 0 Then
```

**9** ◀

*(continued on next page)*

*(continued from previous page)*

```
        Load frmMain
            Call AddSysMenuItems(frmMain)
            hWnd% = frmMain.hWnd
            Call DragAcceptFiles(hWnd%, True)
            frmMain!sbcMain.HwndParam = hWnd%
        frmMain.Show
        End If

End Sub

Sub ParseDroppedFiles (ByVal hDrop%)
'------------------------------------------------
'-- Load the names of the files dropped by File
'   Manager into our module level array for
'   storage and display.
'------------------------------------------------
    Dim NumFiles%
    Dim i%

    NumFiles% = QueryNumFilesDropped(hDrop%)
    ReDim marrDroppedFile(NumFiles% - 1)
    For i% = 0 To NumFiles% - 1
        marrDroppedFile(i%) = QueryDroppedFile(hDrop%, i%)
    Next i%

End Sub

Private Function QueryDroppedFile$ (ByVal hDrop%, ByVal Index%)
'------------------------------------------------
'-- Retrieve the name of a file dropped by File
'   Manager.
'------------------------------------------------
    Dim SizeOfFilename%
    Dim Buffer$
    Dim BytesCopied%

    SizeOfFilename% = QueryDroppedFileSize(hDrop%, Index%, 0&, 0) + 1
    Buffer$ = Space$(SizeOfFilename%)
    BytesCopied% = DragQueryFile(hDrop%, Index%, Buffer$, SizeOfFilename%)
    QueryDroppedFile$ = Left$(Buffer$, BytesCopied%)

End Function

Private Function QueryNumFilesDropped% (ByVal hDrop%)
'------------------------------------------------
'-- Find out how many files were dropped by File
'   Manager.
'------------------------------------------------

    QueryNumFilesDropped% = DragQueryFile(hDrop%, -1, "", 0)

End Function
```

6. Set the Start up Form for the project to be Sub Main by selecting Project from the VB Options menu and changing the Start up Form setting.

## Tips and Comments

To take full advantage of SpyWorks, you need to be familiar with how Windows works and you can't be afraid to crash your computer. Be sure to save files in other applications and set VB to save updated project files before running an app that uses SpyWorks tools. The sample programs that come with SpyWorks show you how to use SpyWorks properly and are enormously valuable when you're in unfamiliar API territory.

SBCEASY provides simple solutions to common problems like mouse and menu tracking, and DWSPYDLL is full of handy functions that fill some gaps in VB. Using callback functions is straightforward if you understand the concept. Windows hooks and keyboard hooks are also very easy to use, although you can certainly cause problems with them if you're not careful. Making use of full-blown subclassing requires care, a deeper knowledge of how Windows works, and a good pair of hip-waders. It can be dangerous but the rewards are enormous.

# VB Messenger (VBMSG.VBX)

| USAGE: | Capturing Windows System Messages |
|---|---|
| MANUFACTURER: | JOSWare, Inc. |
| COST: | $29.95 |

The VB Messenger control intercepts Windows messages that Visual Basic normally hides. This control allows you to get around the built-in limitations of Visual Basic and exploit more of the low-level power of the Microsoft Windows environment. For a basic explanation of what messages are and how Windows processes them, see the earlier section on the Message Hook control.

## Syntax

The VB Messenger control is similar to some of the other message handling controls covered in this chapter, but it has some unique features as well. Table 9-35 lists the nonstandard properties and events of the VB Messenger control.

**Table 9-35** Nonstandard properties and events of the VB Messenger control

**PROPERTIES**

| | | |
|---|---|---|
| AddMessage | ClearMessages | HiWord |
| LoWord | lParam | lParam2String |
| MessageCount | MessageList | MessageSelector |
| MessageText | MessageTypes | PostMessage |
| PostDefault | RemoveMessage | SendMessage |
| ReturnValue | String | SubclasshWnd |
| wParam | | |

**EVENTS**

| | |
|---|---|
| WindowMessage | WindowDestroyed |

Windows provides well over 200 possible messages, and your application will probably only want to process a few of these. Messages that aren't handled by Visual Basic can be intercepted and processed by VB Messenger. This act of intercepting and processing messages sent to a control or form is called *Subclassing*.

All messages trapped by VB Messenger are passed to the *WindowMessage* event, which has the form:

```
Sub VB_Msg1_WindowMessage (hWindow As Integer, Msg As Integer, wParam As Integer, lParam As ⇒
Long, RetVal As Long, CallDefProc As Integer)
```

The *hWindow* parameter indicates the handle of the window to which the message was sent. You specify this handle in your program by assigning a form's *hWnd* to VB Messenger's *SubclasshWnd* property.

The actual message number processed by *WindowMessage* is passed in the *Msg* parameter. The *lParam* and *wParam* parameters contain extra information sent along with the message. The Boolean *CalDefProc* parameter is set inside the subroutine to tell VB Messenger whether to call the default Windows procedure to process the message. If this parameter is set to *False,* the default Windows procedure is not called and VB Messenger returns the value specified by *RetVal* parameter. If *CallDefProc* is set to *True*, the default Windows procedure is called after VB Messenger's *WindowMessage* event finishes.

At design time, VB Messenger provides a simple and flexible way to specify which messages will be trapped. The *MessageSelector* property, which appears only in the Properties window at design time, displays a dialog box (see Figure 9-13) that lists virtually every Windows message by its mnemonic. This is a great time saver, especially if you know what messages you want to trap but can't remember their exact name. Specifying multiple messages is simple; the dialog lets you move messages into a Selected Messages list box, and you can add and remove them until the list box includes just those messages you need.

At run time, you can tell VB Messenger how to handle the list of messages through the *MessageType* property. Table 9-36 shows the different ways that VB Messenger can interpret the message list.

**Table 9-36** Values for the MessageType property

| VALUE | MEANING |
|---|---|
| 0 | Trap only those messages specified in the message list |
| 1 | Trap all messages, ignoring the message list |
| 2 | Trap no messages |
| 3 | Trap all messages  specified in the message list |

At run time, you can access the list of messages through the *MessageList ()* property array. This integer array contains all the currently selected messages, and the *MessageCount* property contains the number of messages in the array.

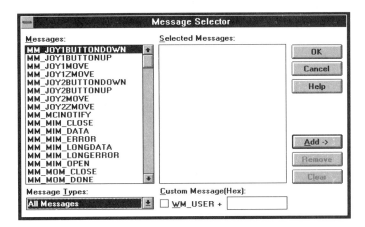

**Figure 9-13** The MessageSelector dialog

You can add and remove messages from the list with the *AddMessage* and *RemoveMessage* properties. You can assign a message value to these properties, adding or removing that message from the message list. This code

```
VBMsg1.AddMessage = WM_MOVE
VBMsg1.RemoveMessage = WM_FONTCHANGE
```

adds the message WM_MOVE to the message list, and removes WM_FONTCHANGE. To easily remove all items from the message list, set the Boolean property *ClearMessages* to *True*.

By default, VB Messenger intercepts messages in the *WindowMessage* event before calling the default Windows procedure. At times you might prefer for Windows to handle its default processing first, and then call the *WindowMessage* event. To do this set the Boolean *PostDefault* property to *True*.

VB Messenger provides ways not only to intercept but also to send Windows messages. Two properties, *PostMessage* and *SendMessage* allow you to send messages directly to the form or control you have subclassed. The control provides two properties for setting the parameters of the message you're sending, *lParam* and *wParam*. The following code tells VB Messenger to post a message to repaint the nonclient area of the subclassed form.

```
VBMsg1.lParam = 0
VBMsg1.wParam = 0
VBMsg1.PostMessage = WM_NCPAINT
```

The difference between the two events is that *PostMessage* places messages into the Windows message queue, while *SendMessage* sends them directly to the subclassed form or control. Use the *RetVal* property to inspect the return values from these two events.

In addition to the properties and events available through the VB Messenger control, dynamic link library calls provide several other functions. Most of these functions assist in converting to and from the data types used by the Windows API for message handling.

9

A few, however, give you access to internal control information that Visual Basic doesn't provide.

The *ptGetControlName* function returns the name of a Visual Basic control that it's passed at run time. You can retrieve even more information about a control with the *ptGetControlModel* function, which returns a model data record containing information on the Class Name and other data not readily accessible through Visual Basic. The *ptSetControlModel* function does the reverse, allowing you to change information in this model data structure.

The VB Messenger control provides an event to help clean up any loose ends when a subclassed form or control is unloaded. The *WindowDestroyed* event is called whenever a window (or control) is sent a WM_DESTROY message. This usually corresponds to a form being unloaded.

# Example

The example program uses the subclassing abilities of VB Messenger to create a form with an extra "button" on its title bar. The user presses this button to display the amount of system free memory. The program also demonstrates the VB Messenger API by listing the names of each control, along with their class names, in a list box. Figure 9-14 shows the example program.

You create the extra button by capturing the form's WM_NCPAINT messages, which are called whenever the nonclient area of the form needs to be redrawn. (The nonclient area of the form includes the window's title bar; minimize, maximize, and system menu buttons; and the window's border.) When the nonclient area is painted, an extra "button" bitmap is drawn to the left of the system menu, over the title bar. The WM_NCLBUTTONDOWN and WM_NCLBUTTONUP messages are also intercepted so that when the mouse is clicked in the nonclient area, you can determine if it was clicked over the new "button." When the button is clicked, its appearance is changed and the system memory information is displayed.

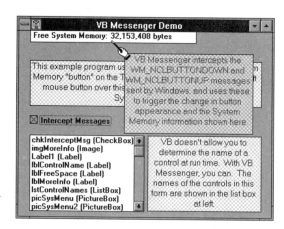

**Figure 9-14** The VB Messenger example program

The calls to the VB Messenger API are accomplished when the form is loaded. The program calls the *ptGetControlName* and *ptGetControlModel* functions once for each control in Visual Basic's *Controls* collection, allowing you to fill a list box with the name of every control on the form, as well as the control's class name.

## Steps

1. Create a new project called VBMSG1.MAK. Add the VB Messenger control, VBMSG.VBX to the project. Create a new Visual Basic module, adding the code listed next. Save this module as VBMSG1.BAS.

```
Option Explicit
'-----------------------------------------------------
' Constants, data types, and declarations used by
' the VB Messenger example program.
'-----------------------------------------------------


' Windows messages trapped by VB Messenger.
Global Const WM_NCPAINT = &H85
Global Const WM_NCACTIVATE = &H86
Global Const WM_NCLBUTTONDOWN = &HA1
Global Const WM_NCLBUTTONUP = &HA2
Global Const WM_PAINT = &HF

' System Metrics codes.
Global Const SM_CYCAPTION = 4
Global Const SM_CXFRAME = 32
Global Const SM_CYFRAME = 33

Global Const SRCCOPY = &HCC0020

' MessageType Property constants.
Global Const SELECTED_MESSAGES = 0
Global Const NO_MESSAGES = 2

' WM_NCHITTEST return code.
Global Const HTCAPTION = 2

' Window field offset for GetWindowLong() and GetWindowWord().
Global Const GWW_HINSTANCE = (-6)

Type tBitmap
    bmType As Integer
    bmWidth As Integer
    bmHeight As Integer
    bmWidthBytes As Integer
    bmPlanes As String * 1
    bmBitsPixel As String * 1
    bmBits As Long
End Type

Type tModel
    usVersion       As Integer    ' VB version used by control
    fl              As Long       ' Bitfield structure
    pctlproc        As Long       ' The control procedure
    fsClassStyle    As Integer    ' Window class style
    flWndStyle      As Long       ' Default window style
    cbCtlExtra      As Integer    ' Numbers of bytes allocated for HCTL structure
```

*(continued on next page)*

*(continued from previous page)*

```
    idBmpPalette        As Integer      ' Bitmap ID for tool palette
    npszDefCtlName      As Integer      ' Default control name prefix (near ptr)
    npszClassName       As Integer      ' Visual Basic class name (near ptr)
    npszParentClassName As Integer      ' Parent window class if subclassed (near ptr)
    npproplist          As Integer      ' Property list (near ptr)
    npeventlist         As Integer      ' Event list (near ptr)
    nDefProp            As String * 1   ' Index of default property
    nDefEvent           As String * 1   ' Index of default event
    nValueProp          As String * 1   ' Index of control value property
End Type

' Windows API function calls.
Declare Function DefWindowProc Lib "User" (ByVal hWnd As Integer, ByVal wMsg As Integer, ⇒
ByVal wParam As Integer, lParam As Any) As Long
Declare Function CreateCompatibleDC Lib "GDI" (ByVal hDC As Integer) As Integer
Declare Function GetWindowDC Lib "User" (ByVal hWnd As Integer) As Integer
Declare Function DeleteDC Lib "GDI" (ByVal hDC As Integer) As Integer
Declare Function ReleaseDC Lib "User" (ByVal hWnd As Integer, ByVal hDC As Integer) As Integer
Declare Function BitBlt Lib "GDI" (ByVal hDestDC As Integer, ByVal X As Integer, ByVal Y As ⇒
Integer, ByVal nWidth As Integer, ByVal nHeight As Integer, ByVal hSrcDC As Integer, ByVal ⇒
XSrc As Integer, ByVal YSrc As Integer, ByVal dwRop As Long) As Integer
Declare Function APIGetObject Lib "GDI" Alias "GetObject" (ByVal hObject As Integer, ByVal ⇒
nCount As Integer, lpObject As Any) As Integer
Declare Function SelectObject Lib "GDI" (ByVal hDC As Integer, ByVal hObject As Integer) As ⇒
Integer
Declare Function GetSystemMetrics Lib "User" (ByVal nIndex As Integer) As Integer
Declare Function GetWindowWord Lib "User" (ByVal hWnd As Integer, ByVal nIndex As Integer) ⇒
As Integer
Declare Function GetFreeSpace Lib "kernel" (ByVal flag As Integer) As Long

' VB Messenger API calls.
Declare Function ptLoWord Lib "VBMSG.VBX" (ByVal lParam As Long) As Integer
Declare Function ptGetControlName Lib "VBMSG.VBX" (ctl As Control) As String
Declare Function ptGetControlModel Lib "VBMSG.VBX" (ctl As Control, lpmodel As tModel) As Long
Declare Function ptGetStringFromAddress Lib "VBMSG.VBX" (ByVal lAddress As Long, ByVal ⇒
cbBytes As Integer) As String
Declare Function ptConvertUShort Lib "VBMSG.VBX" (ByVal ushortVal As Integer) As Long
```

2. Create a new form with the objects and properties listed in Table 9-37. Save this form as
   VBMSG1.FRM.

**Table 9-37** Objects and properties for VBMSG1.FRM

| OBJECT | PROPERTY | SETTING |
| --- | --- | --- |
| Form | FormName | frmVBMsg |
| | BackColor | &H00C0C0C0& |
| | Caption | "VB Messenger Demo" |
| Label | Name | lblFreeSpace |
| | BorderStyle | 1 'Fixed Single |
| | Visible | 0 'False |
| Label | Name | lblMoreInfo |
| | Alignment | 2 'Center |

| OBJECT | PROPERTY | SETTING |
|---|---|---|
| | BackColor | &H00FFFF80& |
| | BorderStyle | 1 'Fixed Single |
| | Caption | "VB Messenger intercepts the WM_NCLBUTTONDOWN and WM_NCLBUTTONUP messages sent by windows, and uses these to trigger the change in button appearance and the System Memory information shown here." |
| | FontBold | 0 'False |
| | FontSize | 9.75 |
| | ForeColor | &H000000FF& |
| | Visible | 0 'False |
| Image | Name | imgMoreInfo |
| | Picture | (set at design time in Properties window) |
| | Visible | 0 'False |
| VBMsg | Name | VBMsg1 |
| | MessageCount | (set at design time in Properties window) |
| | MessageList | (set at design time in Properties window) |
| | MessageTypes | 0 'Selected Messages |
| | PostDefault | 0 'False |
| PictureBox | Name | picSysMenu2 |
| | AutoSize | -1 'True |
| | Picture | (set at design time in Properties window) |
| | Visible | 0 'False |
| PictureBox | Name | picSysMenu |
| | AutoSize | -1 'True |
| | Picture | (set at design time in Properties window) |
| | Visible | 0 'False |
| CheckBox | Name | chkInterceptMsg |
| | BackColor | &H00C0C0C0& |
| | Caption | "Intercept Messages" |
| | Value | 1 'Checked |
| ListBox | Name | lstControlNames |
| | ForeColor | &H00800000& |
| | Sorted | -1 'True |

3. Add the following code to the VBMSG1.FRM form's declarations section.

```
Option Explicit
'--------------------------------------------------
```

4. Add the following subroutines to the VBMSG1.FRM form.

```
Sub chkInterceptMsg_Click ()
'----------------------------------------------------
' Change the message type when the check box is
' clicked.
'----------------------------------------------------
    If chkInterceptMsg = 1 Then
        VBMsg1.MessageTypes = SELECTED_MESSAGES
    Else
        VBMsg1.MessageTypes = NO_MESSAGES
    End If

    ' Force a repaint to either draw or "undraw" the button.
    VBMsg1.lParam = 0
    VBMsg1.wParam = 0
    VBMsg1.PostMessage = WM_NCPAINT
    Me.Caption = Me.Caption
End Sub


Sub DrawBitmapNCArea (hWindow As Integer, hbmp As Integer, cxLeft As Integer, cyTop As Integer)
'----------------------------------------------------
' This routine was adapted from a subroutine in a
' VB Messenger example program distributed with
' the shareware distribution files on CompuServe.
'----------------------------------------------------
Dim hdc As Integer
Dim hdcMem As Integer
Dim bmp As tBitmap
Dim hbmpOld As Integer
Dim hinst As Integer
Dim retcode As Long

    hinst = GetWindowWord(hWindow, GWW_HINSTANCE)
    hdc = GetWindowDC(hWindow)
    hdcMem = CreateCompatibleDC(hdc)

    retcode = APIGetObject(hbmp, Len(bmp), bmp)
    hbmpOld = SelectObject(hdcMem, hbmp)
    retcode = BitBlt(hdc, cxLeft + bmp.bmWidth + 1, cyTop, bmp.bmWidth, bmp.bmHeight, hdcMem,
0, 0, SRCCOPY)
    retcode = SelectObject(hdcMem, hbmpOld)

    retcode = DeleteDC(hdcMem)
    retcode = ReleaseDC(hWnd, hdc)

End Sub


Sub Form_Load ()
'----------------------------------------------------
' Set the form to subclass, and extract control
' information into a list box.
'----------------------------------------------------
Dim i As Integer
Dim lptr As Long
Dim Model As tModel
Dim ClassName As String
Dim AnAddress As Long
Dim cbBytes As Integer
```

```
    ' Tell VB Messenger to subclass the form.
    VBMsg1.SubClasshWnd = frmVBMsg.hWnd

    ' Use VB Messenger API calls to extract control information
    cbBytes = 80
    For i = 0 To Me.Controls.Count - 1
        lptr = ptGetControlModel(Me.Controls(i), Model)
        ' Take the segment from lptr and add the offset from the structure.
        AnAddress = (lptr And &HFFFF0000) + (Model.npszClassName)
        ClassName = ptGetStringFromAddress(AnAddress, cbBytes)
        If InStr(ClassName, Chr$(0)) Then ClassName = Left$(ClassName, InStr(ClassName, ⇒
Chr$(0)) - 1)
        lstControlNames.AddItem ptGetControlName(Me.Controls(i)) & " (" & ClassName & ")"
    Next
End Sub

Function FreeSpace () As Long
'---------------------------------------------------
' Get the amount of free system memory.
'---------------------------------------------------
Dim FreeMemory As Long

    FreeMemory = GetFreeSpace(0)
    ' Take care if high bit is set (two's complement).
    If Sgn(FreeMemory) = -1 Then
        FreeMemory = CLng(FreeMemory + 1&) Xor &HFFFFFFFF
    End If
    FreeSpace = FreeMemory
End Function

Sub VBMsg1_WindowMessage (hWindow As Integer, Msg As Integer, wParam As Integer, lParam As ⇒
Long, RetVal As Long, CallDefProc As Integer)
'---------------------------------------------------
' This is the message-handling routine for VB
' Messenger.
'---------------------------------------------------
Dim InsideLeft As Integer

    Select Case Msg
        ' Non-client area paint messages.
        Case WM_NCPAINT:
            RetVal = DefWindowProc(hWindow, Msg, wParam, lParam)
            DrawBitmapNCArea hWindow, (picSysMenu.Picture), GetSystemMetrics(SM_CXFRAME), ⇒
GetSystemMetrics(SM_CYFRAME)
            CallDefProc = False
        ' Non-client area activate messages.
        Case WM_NCACTIVATE:
            If wParam = False Then
                RetVal = True
            Else
                RetVal = DefWindowProc(hWindow, Msg, wParam, lParam)
            End If
            DrawBitmapNCArea hWindow, (picSysMenu.Picture), GetSystemMetrics(SM_CXFRAME), ⇒
GetSystemMetrics(SM_CYFRAME)
            CallDefProc = False
        ' Non-client area left mouse button down messages.
        Case WM_NCLBUTTONDOWN:
            If wParam = HTCAPTION Then
                InsideLeft = (Me.Left / Screen.TwipsPerPixelX)
                ' Are we inside the button area?
```

*(continued on next page)*

9 ◀

*(continued from previous page)*

```
                 If (ptLoWord(lParam) - InsideLeft) < (GetSystemMetrics(SM_CYCAPTION) * 2) Then
                     DrawBitmapNCArea hWindow, (picSysMenu2.Picture), ⇒
GetSystemMetrics(SM_CXFRAME), GetSystemMetrics(SM_CYFRAME)
                     lblFreeSpace.Visible = True
                     lblMoreInfo.Visible = True
                     imgMoreInfo.Visible = True
                     lblFreeSpace = " Free System Memory: " & Format$(FreeSpace(), ⇒
"###,###,##0") & " bytes"
                     CallDefProc = False
                 Else
                     CallDefProc = True
                 End If
                 Exit Sub
             End If
         ' Non-client area left mouse button down messages.
         Case WM_NCLBUTTONUP:
                 DrawBitmapNCArea hWindow, (picSysMenu.Picture), GetSystemMetrics(SM_CXFRAME), ⇒
GetSystemMetrics(SM_CYFRAME)
                 lblFreeSpace.Visible = False
                 lblMoreInfo.Visible = False
                 imgMoreInfo.Visible = False
                 CallDefProc = True
     End Select
End Sub
```

## Tips and Comments

If you look at the declarations section of VBMSG1.BAS in the example program listing, you'll see that, for a relatively small program, it uses a fairly large number of API calls. This should help you appreciate the complexity that Visual Basic hides from programmers. When you need to peel away the veneer of Visual Basic and look underneath the surface, a control of this type can be invaluable.

# TEXT AND DATA MANIPULATION

The controls and libraries covered in this chapter are all designed to manipulate data in some way. They include two spell checkers, a library of data compression routines, and a text parsing control similar to the awk programming language.

The two spell checkers are an excellent illustration of how the same concept can be realized in different ways.

The awk text processing language was originally available on UNIX systems, but has since been ported to other platforms as well. The VSAwk control, while not a complete implementation of the VSAwk language, still manages to include many of the features that make awk so useful. It breaks text lines into sets of individual words for fast and easy processing. If you need to sift through large amounts of text data, this control can be a lifesaver.

The Compression Plus library is compatible with the .ZIP file compression standard used by the DOS utility, PKZIP. The Compression Plus library lets you create and access .ZIP archive files, as well as perform other compression and decompression tasks.

All these controls provide functions that you almost certainly would not want to build from scratch. Most of the example programs in this chapter are utilities.

▲ **Compression Plus**  Using this data compression library, you build a Windows utility similar to PKUNZIP. This utility lets you view the statistics of files within .ZIP archives, and selectively decompress those files.

▲ **SpellPro**  You'll use SpellPro to build a Notepad clone with spell checking capabilities.

▲ **VSAwk**  You build a utility to view and print subroutines from Visual Basic forms and modules. This utility even provides some rudimentary syntax-highlighted printing, by printing single-line comments in italics. You can easily find and copy code from one Visual Basic project and paste it into your current Visual Basic project.

▲ **VT-Speller**  You'll use this control to make a Windows Clipboard spell checker. You can copy text from an application to the Clipboard, and then use the utility to spell check the text. The utility automatically places corrected text back in the Windows Clipboard.

# Compression Plus

| USAGE: | Compression of Data and Files |
|---|---|
| MANUFACTURER: | EllTech |
| COST: | $249 |

Compression Plus is a dynamic link library and a set of Visual Basic routines that provide data and file compression services. These services range from emulation of PKZIP and PKUNZIP to low-level DOS file-handling functions.

## Syntax

The Compression Plus functions are divided into three groups: user, high-level, and low-level. The user functions are the most abstract and the simplest to use. Depending on the type of application you're developing, these may be the only routines you need to use. The high-level and low-level routines are used less frequently, and provide lower-level services. Table 10-1 lists the user functions.

**Table 10-1** User functions in the Compression Plus library

| EtArcType | EtArjCnt | EtArjDir |
|---|---|---|
| EtArjDirLong | EtCPrint | EtCPrintIsOn |
| EtCPrintOff | EtCPrintOn | EtFileDate |
| EtLhaCnt | EtLhaDir | EtLhaDirLong |
| EtUnZip | EtUnZipMem | EtUnZipMultiVolume |
| EtUnZipString | EtViewZip | EtZip |
| EtZipClose | EtZipCnt | EtZipComment |
| EtZipDir | EtZipDirLong | EtZipDirLonger |
| EtZipMem | EtZipMultiVolume | EtZipNewComment |
| EtZipNewFileComments | EtZipOpen | EtZipString |

The user and high-level routines are actually Visual Basic routines stored in the module COMPRESS.BAS, which must be added to your project. The low-level routines are stored in the .DLL, COMPRESS.DLL. This three-tiered approach to the design library works fairly well. You can develop a complete application using only the user functions, but there are several treasures among the other routines as well.

**Zipping and Unzipping**  First, let's look at the user functions. Accessing and creating PKZIP-compatible files is easy. You just need three functions to either add files to or extract files from a .ZIP archive. The following example extracts the file README.TXT from the existing .ZIP archive, TEST1.ZIP, and places the extracted file in the root directory.

```
AccessMode = 0 'Exclusive Access
ZipFileName = "TEST1.ZIP"

' Open the .ZIP file.
retcode = EtZipOpen(ZipFileName, AccessMode, ZipHandle)
If retcode <> 0 Then
    MsgBox "Unable to open .zip file", MB_OK, "Error Opening .ZIP File"
    Exit Sub
End If

' Unzip selected files.
AFileName = "README.TXT"
DestDir = "C:\"

' Unzip a file.
retcode = EtUnZip(ZipHandle, DestDir, AFileName, "")
If retcode <> 0 Then
    MsgBox "Unable to unzip file" & AFileName & ".", MB_OK, "Error Unzipping File"
    Exit For
End If

' Close the .ZIP file.
EtZipClose ZipHandle
```

The first function, *EtZipOpen,* must be called before any other operation that will affect a .ZIP file. The *EtZipOpen* function provides a DOS file handle that other

**10◀**

functions will use to reference the .ZIP archive. The *AccessMode* parameter sets the access rights other users will have while your program has the file open. Several different read/write options are available, but the example uses the most stringent, and safest. An *AccessMode* of 0 gives your application exclusive rights to the file, and prevents other users from either reading or writing the file. Table 10-2 shows the other values for this parameter.

**Table 10-2** Values for EtZipOpen's AccessMode parameter

| VALUE | MEANING |
| --- | --- |
| 0 | Exclusive access; no one else can use the file. |
| 16 | Deny all access; this is the same as 0. |
| 32 | Deny write access. |
| 48 | Deny read access. |
| 64 | Allow others to access file at the same time. |

The next function call, *EtUnZip,* actually extracts the selected file, decompresses it, and places it in the specified destination directory. The function accepts four parameters: the file handle previously attained by *EtZipOpen,* the destination directory, the name of the file in the archive, and a string that can optionally contain "feature" switches. These switches are similar to the command-line switches used by PKZIP and PKUNZIP, and are simply appended together.

The final function call is to *EtZipClose,* which closes the opened .ZIP archive. You add a file to a .ZIP archive in the same manner, but you use the *EtZip* function instead of *EtUnZip.* The *EtZip* function accepts three parameters: the file handle to the opened .ZIP archive file, an array of strings containing the file specifications (which can include wildcards), and a string containing feature switches.

### Getting Information About a .ZIP Archive
If you only need to extract information about the contents of a .ZIP archive, there are several functions from which to choose. *EtZipDir* fills a string array with the names of all the files in an archive, as illustrated in the following code fragment:

```
ReDim DirArr(0) as string
AccessMode = 0 ' Exclusive Access

' Try to open the .ZIP file.
retcode = EtZipOpen(AFileName, AccessMode, ZipHandle)
If retcode <> 0 Then
    MsgBox "Unable to open .zip file", MB_OK, "Error Opening .ZIP File"
    Exit Sub
End If

' Load the .ZIP file directory information array.
retcode = EtZipDir(ZipHandle, DirArr())
If retcode <> 0 Then
    MsgBox "Unable to read .ZIP file directory", MB_OK, "Error Reading .ZIP File Directory"
    Exit Sub
End If
```

```
' Transfer the directory info into a formatted list box.
AList.Clear
For i = LBound(DirArr) To UBound(DirArr)
    AList.AddItem DirArr(i)
Next

' Close the .ZIP file.
EtZipClose ZipHandle
```

Two related functions provide more directory information. *EtZipDirLong* returns an array of data structures in addition to the file name array. This data structure contains the CRC value, compressed and uncompressed sizes, file attributes, and date/time stamps for each file in the archive. *EtZipDirLonger* returns everything that *EtZipDirLong* returns, as well as any file comments that were stored for each file.

**Using the High- and Low-Level Functions**  While you can easily avoid using the high- and low-level functions, you may find several of them quite useful. For example, the high-level function *EtCreatePath* creates any directories required to complete the path string passed to it. If you pass it the path "C:\MYDIR\DIR1\DIR2\MYFILE.TXT", and only the MYDIR directory currently exists, *StCreatePath* creates DIR1 and DIR2 for you. In this example, the function would not try to create a MYFILE.TXT directory because the string does not end in a backslash character.

The *EtPathName* function takes a full path string and breaks it into three resulting strings: the drive, the path, and the file name. Given the path in the previous example, this function would return the strings "C:", "\MYDIR\DIR1\DIR2\", and "MYFILE.TXT".

Several of the low-level functions provide useful DOS-related information. *EtDriveStatus* tells you if a specified drive is local, removable, or network. *EtFileExist* and *EtDirExist* tell you if a file or directory path actually exists.

# Example

The example program, shown in Figure 10-1, demonstrates how to use the Compression Plus library to build a Windows replacement for PKUNZIP. You pick a .ZIP archive by selecting the Open option on the File menu and choosing a .ZIP file from the common File Open dialog. The contents of the .ZIP file are displayed in a list box, along with each file's uncompressed size and its internal time and date stamps. The list box allows multiple selection, so the user can simply click on the files to be unzipped. The directory and drive list boxes, along with the text box at the bottom of the form, let the user pick the destination directory in which to place the unzipped files.

If the destination directory doesn't exist, the program attempts to create it for you using the high-level *EtCreatePath* function.

10◄

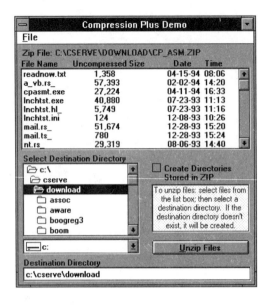

**Figure 10-1** The Compression Plus example program

## Steps

1. Create a new project called COMPRESS.MAK. Add to the project three forms from the Compression Plus library: ETCPRNT1.FRM and ETCPRNT1.BAS, used to provide a status dialog during decompression, and COMPRESS.BAS, which includes the declarations for the low-level functions and the Visual Basic source code for the user and high-level functions.

2. Create a new form with the objects and properties described in Table 10-3. Save this form as COMPRESS.FRM.

**Table 10-3** Objects and properties for COMPRESS.FRM

| OBJECT | PROPERTY | SETTING |
|--------|----------|---------|
| Form | FormName | frmCompress |
| | BackColor | &H00C0C0C0& |
| | Caption | "Compression Plus Demo" |
| | MaxButton | 0 'False |
| Label | Name | Label1 |
| | BackStyle | 0 'Transparent |
| | Caption | "File Name    Uncompressed Size Date    Time" |
| | ForeColor | &H00800000& |
| Label | Name | Label2 |
| | BackStyle | 0 'Transparent |
| | Caption | "Select Destination Directory" |
| | ForeColor | &H00800000& |

| OBJECT | PROPERTY | SETTING |
|---|---|---|
| Label | Name | Label3 |
| | BackColor | &H00FFFFFF& |
| | BackStyle | 0 'Transparent |
| | Caption | "Zip File:" |
| | ForeColor | &H00800000& |
| Label | Name | lblZipFileName |
| | BackStyle | 0 'Transparent |
| | Caption | "[none]" |
| | ForeColor | &H00000080& |
| Label | Name | Label4 |
| | BackStyle | 0 'Transparent |
| | Caption | "Destination Directory" |
| | ForeColor | &H00800000& |
| Label | Name | Label5 |
| | BackStyle | 0 'Transparent |
| | Caption | "Stored in ZIP" |
| Label | Name | Label6 |
| | Alignment | 2 'Center |
| | BackColor | &H00E0FFFF& |
| | BorderStyle | 1 'Fixed Single |
| | Caption | "To unzip files: select files from the list box; then select a destination directory. If the destination directory doesn't exist, it will be created." |
| | FontBold | 0 'False |
| | ForeColor | &H00800000& |
| | Tag | "/3D/" |
| ListBox | Name | lstZipDir |
| | MultiSelect | 1 'Simple |
| | Tag | "/3D/" |
| CommonDialog | Name | CMDialog1 |
| CommandButton | Name | btnUnZip |
| | Caption | "&Unzip Files" |
| DriveListBox | Name | Drive1 |
| | Tag | "/3D/" |
| DirListBox | Name | Dir1 |
| | Tag | "/3D/" |
| CheckBox | Name | chkCreateDirs |
| | BackColor | &H00C0C0C0& |
| | Caption | "Create Directories " |
| TextBox | Name | txtDestDir |
| | Tag | "/3D/" |

10◀

3. Add a menu to COMPRESS.FRM using the Visual Basic Menu Design window, setting the captions and names as shown in Table 10-4.

**Table 10-4** Menu definition for COMPRESS.FRM

| CAPTION | NAME |
|---|---|
| &File | mnuFile |
| − − − − &Open ZIP File | mnuFileOpen |
| − − − − − | mnuFileSep1 |
| − − − − E&xit | mnuFileExit |

4. After creating COMPRESS.FRM, add the following code to the declarations section of the form.

```
Option Explicit
'------------------------------------------------
' Variables and constants used in the Compression
' Plus example program.
'------------------------------------------------

' Minimum dimensions for the main window.
Dim MinFormWidth As Integer
Dim MinFormHeight As Integer

' Color constants.
Const DARK_GRAY = &H808080
Const WHITE = &HFFFFFF
Const BLACK = &H0

' 3D effect constants.
Const BORDER_INSET = 0
Const BORDER_RAISED = 1

' WindowState constant.
Const MINIMIZED = 1

' MsgBox constants.
Const MB_OK = 0
Const MB_YESNO = 4
Const MB_ICONINFORMATION = 64
Const MB_ICONQUESTION = &H20
Const MB_ICONEXCLAMATION = &H30

' MsgBox responses.
Const IDOK = 1
Const IDYES = 6

' File Open/Save dialog flags.
Const OFN_READONLY = &H1&
Const OFN_HIDEREADONLY = &H4&
```

5. Add the following subroutines to the COMPRESS.FRM form. The *Make3D* subroutine gives some of the controls a 3D appearance. These controls all have a *Tag* property set to "/3D/". The form's *Paint* event checks for any control with this tag and puts a 3D border around it by drawing lines on the underlying form.

```
Sub btnUnZip_Click ()
'------------------------------------------------
' Unzip selected files and place them in a specified
' directory.
'------------------------------------------------
Dim AFileName As String
Dim DestDir As String
Dim AccessMode As Integer
Dim ZipHandle As Integer
Dim retcode As Integer
Dim i As Integer
Dim SomethingSelected As Integer
Dim Switches As String

    ' Check to see if any items were selected.
    SomethingSelected = False
    For i = 0 To lstZipDir.ListCount - 1
      If lstZipDir.Selected(i) Then
          SomethingSelected = True
          Exit For
      End If
    Next

    ' If no items were selected, don't continue.
    If Not SomethingSelected Then
          MsgBox "No files were selected to unzip.", MB_OK And MB_ICONEXCLAMATION, "No Files
Selected"
          Exit Sub
    End If

    ' Fix the destination directory string.
    DestDir = txtDestDir
    If Right$(DestDir, 1) <> "\" Then DestDir = DestDir & "\"

    ' Create the destination directory if necessary.
    If EtCreatePath(DestDir)  0 Then
          MsgBox "Unable to create destination directory: " & DestDir & ".", MB_OK And
MB_ICONEXCLAMATION, "Error Creating Destination Directory"
          Exit Sub
    End If

    AccessMode = 0 'Exclusive Access

    ' Open the .ZIP file.
    retcode = EtZipOpen((lblZipFileName), AccessMode, ZipHandle)
    If retcode <> 0 Then
          MsgBox "Unable to open .zip file: " & AFileName & ".", MB_OK And MB_ICONEXCLAMATION,
"Error Opening .ZIP File"
          Exit Sub
    End If

    ' Set any unzipping switches required.
    Switches = ""
    If chkCreateDirs.Value = 1 Then
          Switches = Switches & " -d "
    End If

    ' Unzip selected files.
    For i = 0 To lstZipDir.ListCount - 1
      If lstZipDir.Selected(i) Then
```

(continued on next page)

**10◄**

*(continued from previous page)*

```
            ' Extract the file name from the list box.
            AFileName = Trim$(Left$(lstZipDir.List(i), InStr(lstZipDir.List(i), " ") - 1))

            ' Unzip a file.
            retcode = EtUnZip(ZipHandle, DestDir, AFileName, "")
            If retcode <> 0 Then
                    MsgBox "Unable to unzip file: " & AFileName & ".", MB_OK And
MB_ICONEXCLAMATION, "Error Unzipping File"
                    Exit For
            End If

            lstZipDir.Selected(i) = False
        End If
    Next

    ' Close the .ZIP file.
    EtZipClose ZipHandle
End Sub

Sub Dir1_Change ()
'-------------------------------------------------
' Change the "Destination Directory" text box when
' the directory box changes.
'-------------------------------------------------
    txtDestDir = Dir1.Path
End Sub

Sub Drive1_Change ()
'-------------------------------------------------
' Update the directory list when the current drive
' changes.
'-------------------------------------------------
    Dir1.Path = Drive1.Drive
End Sub

Sub Form_Load ()
'-------------------------------------------------
' Position the form and initialize variables.
'-------------------------------------------------

    ' Center the form on the screen.
    Me.Move (Screen.Width - Me.Width) \ 2, (Screen.Height - Me.Height) \ 2

    ' Set the destination directory to the current directory.
    txtDestDir = Dir1.Path

    ' Save the current form dimensions.
    MinFormWidth = Me.Width
    MinFormHeight = Me.Height
End Sub

Sub Form_Paint ()
Dim i As Integer

    For i = 0 To Me.Controls.Count - 1
        If InStr(UCase$(Me.Controls(i).Tag), "/3D/") Then
                Make3D Me, Me.Controls(i), BORDER_INSET
        End If
    Next
```

```
End Sub

Sub Form_Resize ()
'-------------------------------------------------
' Keep the window at its original dimensions.
'-------------------------------------------------

    ' If the window has been minimized, do nothing.
    If WindowState = MINIMIZED Then Exit Sub

    ' Don't let the window be resized.
    If Me.Width  MinFormWidth Then Me.Width = MinFormWidth
    If Me.Height  MinFormHeight Then Me.Height = MinFormHeight
End Sub

Sub GetZipFileDir (ByVal AFileName As String, AList As ListBox)
'-------------------------------------------------
' Retrieve directory information for the .ZIP file,
' AFileName, and place it into list box AList.
'-------------------------------------------------
Dim AccessMode As Integer
Dim ZipHandle As Integer
Dim retcode As Integer
Dim i As Integer
Dim ATab As String
Dim ALine As String
ReDim DirArr(0) As String
ReDim DirInfo(0) As CentralDirRec

    ' Tab character used for spacing data fields in list box.
    ATab = Chr$(9)

    AccessMode = 0 'Exclusive Access

    ' Try to open the .ZIP file.
    retcode = EtZipOpen(AFileName, AccessMode, ZipHandle)
    If retcode <> 0 Then
        MsgBox "Unable to open .zip file: " & AFileName & ".", MB_OK And MB_ICONEXCLAMATION,
"Error Opening .ZIP File"
        Exit Sub
    End If

    ' Load the .ZIP file directory information into arrays.
    retcode = EtZipDirLong(ZipHandle, DirInfo(), DirArr())
    If retcode <> 0 Then
        MsgBox "Unable to read ZIP file directory: " & AFileName & ".", MB_OK And
MB_ICONEXCLAMATION, "Error Reading ZIP File Directory"
        Exit Sub
    End If

    ' Transfer the directory info into a formatted list box.
    AList.Clear
    For i = LBound(DirArr) To UBound(DirArr)
        ALine = RPad(LCase$(DirArr(i)) & " ", 6) & ATab
        ALine = ALine & RPad(Format$(DirInfo(i).UnCompSize, "#,###,##0"), 8) & ATab
        ALine = ALine & RPad(EtFileDate(DirInfo(i).FDate), 6) & ATab
        ALine = ALine & RPad(EtFileTime(DirInfo(i).FTime), 6)
        AList.AddItem ALine
    Next
```

10◄

*(continued on next page)*

*(continued from previous page)*

```
    ' Close the .ZIP file.
    EtZipClose ZipHandle
End Sub

Function LPad (ByVal AStr As String, ByVal ALen As Integer) As String
'----------------------------------------------------
' Left pad a proportional font to a specified length.
'----------------------------------------------------
Dim TxtWidth As Integer

    TxtWidth = Me.TextWidth("A") * ALen

    While Me.TextWidth(AStr) < TxtWidth
        AStr = " " & AStr
    Wend
    LPad = AStr
End Function

Sub Make3D (pic As Form, ctl As Control, ByVal BorderStyle As Integer)
'----------------------------------------------------
' Wrap a 3D effect around a control on a form.
'----------------------------------------------------
Dim AdjustX As Integer, AdjustY As Integer
Dim RightSide As Single
Dim BW As Integer, BorderWidth As Integer
Dim LeftTopColor As Long, RightBottomColor As Long
Dim i As Integer

    If Not ctl.Visible Then Exit Sub

    AdjustX = Screen.TwipsPerPixelX
    AdjustY = Screen.TwipsPerPixelY

    BorderWidth = 1

    Select Case BorderStyle
    Case 0: ' Inset
    LeftTopColor = DARK_GRAY
    RightBottomColor = WHITE
    Case 1: ' Raised
    LeftTopColor = WHITE
    RightBottomColor = DARK_GRAY
    End Select


    ' Set the top shading line.
    For BW = 1 To BorderWidth
    ' Top
    pic.CurrentX = ctl.Left - (AdjustX * BW)
    pic.CurrentY = ctl.Top - (AdjustY * BW)
    pic.Line -(ctl.Left + ctl.Width + (AdjustX * (BW - 1)), ctl.Top - (AdjustY * BW)),
LeftTopColor
    ' Right
    pic.Line -(ctl.Left + ctl.Width + (AdjustX * (BW - 1)), ctl.Top + ctl.Height + (AdjustY *
(BW - 1))), RightBottomColor
    ' Bottom
    pic.Line -(ctl.Left - (AdjustX * BW), ctl.Top + ctl.Height + (AdjustY * (BW - 1))),
RightBottomColor
```

```
    ' Left
    pic.Line -(ctl.Left - (AdjustX * BW), ctl.Top - (AdjustY * BW)), LeftTopColor
    Next
End Sub

Sub mnuFileExit_Click ()
'------------------------------------------------------
' Exit the program.
'------------------------------------------------------
    Unload Me
End Sub

Sub mnuFileOpen_Click ()
'------------------------------------------------------
' Open a .ZIP file and display its contents.
'------------------------------------------------------
Dim Canceled As Integer

    On Error GoTo mnuFileOpen_Error
    Canceled = False

    ' Set up and display the File Open dialog box.
    CMDialog1.Flags = OFN_HIDEREADONLY
    CMDialog1.CancelError = True
    CMDialog1.Filter = "ZIP Files|*.zip"
    CMDialog1.DialogTitle = "Open a ZIP File"
    CMDialog1.Action = 1

    If Canceled Or (CMDialog1.Filename = "") Then Exit Sub

    lblZipFileName = CMDialog1.Filename

    ' Extract information from the .ZIP file.
    GetZipFileDir lblZipFileName, lstZipDir
Exit Sub

mnuFileOpen_Error:
    Canceled = True
    Resume Next
End Sub

Function RPad (ByVal AStr As String, ByVal ALen As Integer) As String
'------------------------------------------------------
' Right pad a proportional font to a specified length.
'------------------------------------------------------
Dim TxtWidth As Integer

    TxtWidth = Me.TextWidth("A") * ALen

    While Me.TextWidth(AStr) < TxtWidth
        AStr = AStr & " "
    Wend
    RPad = AStr
End Function
```

10◄

## Tips and Comments

In addition to supporting access to .ZIP file archives, this library can be used as a general compression tool for data within your programs. For example, the *EtZipString* function will compress a variable-length Visual Basic string and store it in a file. Several other routines, in particular *EtZipMem* and *EtUnZipMem,* allow you to store your data in compressed form in memory and access it when you need it.

# SpellPro (MHSPELL.VBX)

| USAGE: | Spell Checking |
| --- | --- |
| MANUFACTURER: | MicroHelp, Inc |
| COST: | $129 |

The SpellPro control allows you to integrate spell checking into your applications. SpellPro can spell check any text that can be stored in a Visual Basic string variable. This control can add words to custom dictionaries, ignore words that are all uppercase or contain numbers, and suggest replacements for misspelled words.

SpellPro includes a main dictionary of over 50,000 American English words, and MicroHelp currently offers medical and legal dictionaries, as well as dictionaries for some foreign languages.

## Syntax

The SpellPro control provides spell checking services similar to those found in Microsoft Word. A built-in "Bad Word" dialog box, shown in Figure 10-2, can be displayed automatically when a word that is not in the dictionary is discoverd.

The SpellPro control checks text provided to it, and allows you to take appropriate actions when misspelled words are encountered. Table 10-5 lists the nonstandard properties, events, and methods of the SpellPro control.

**Figure 10-2** The "Bad Word" built-in dialog box

**Table 10-5** Nonstandard properties, events, and methods of the SpellPro control

### PROPERTIES

| | | |
|---|---|---|
| AddCustomWord | BadWordDialog | ChangeAll |
| ChangeAllCount | ChangeAllToWord | ChangeWord |
| CheckWord | ClearChangeAll | ClearIgnoreAll |
| CommonWordCache | CustomDictFile | DialogLeft |
| DialogTitle | DialogTop | IgnoreAll |
| IgnoreAllCount | IgnoreAllWord | IgnoreInUppercase |
| IgnoreWithNumbers | MainDictFile | OptionBtnCaption |
| OptionBtnVisible | SelLength | SelStart |
| Start | StillChecking | Suggest |
| Suggestion | SuggestionCount | Text |

### EVENTS

| | | |
|---|---|---|
| BadWord | Changed | Complete |
| OptionBtnClick | Suggestion | |

### METHODS

| | |
|---|---|
| Clear | AddItem |

**A Simple Example** To spell check a document, assign the text, as a string, to the SpellPro Text property. For controls like the standard text control, this is a simple matter. The following example presents the simplest way to spell check text in a text control.

```
' Load the text control into SpellPro.
MhSpellPro1.Text = Text1.Text

' Use the English bad word dialog.
MhSpellPro1.BadWordDialog = 1

' Start spell checking.
MhSpellPro1.Start = True

' Assign the spell checked text back to the text control.
Text1.Text = MhSpellPro1.Text

MsgBox "Spell Checking is Complete.", MB_OK Or MB_ICONINFORMATION, "Spell Check"
```

First, you assign the text in the text control, Text1, to the SpellPro control's *Text* property. Next, you set *BadWordDialog* to 1, which tells SpellPro that you want to use the built-in English dialog box. You could also have chosen dialog boxes in Spanish, German, or French, or no dialog box at all. Don't confuse these foreign language dialog boxes with foreign language dictionaries. Only the labels and buttons in the dialog are presented in the foreign language; spell checking operations are still performed using the American English dictionary.

To initiate the spell checking, set the *Start* property to *True*. Every time a misspelled word is encountered, the "Bad Word" dialog box appears automatically.

The "Bad Word" dialog displays the misspelled word, along with an optional list of suggested replacement words. The user can choose to ignore the word, ignore all further occurrences of the word, change the word to the word suggested in the Change To box, change all occurrences of the word, or add the word to the custom dictionary.

Finally, when the spell check is completed, you reassign the SpellPro *Text* property, which contains any corrections, back to the text control.

**Custom Dictionaries**   The custom dictionary is a file whose name you have previously specified, either at design or run time, by setting the *CustomDictFile* property. The custom dictionary is simply an unsorted text file containing one word per line, with each line separated by a carriage return and a line feed character. You can create this file and edit using a simple text editor such as Windows Notepad; the file cannot exceed 64K in length. Words are added to the file automatically when the "Bad Word" dialog's Add button is pressed. You can also add words by assigning them to the *AddCustomWord* property or by using the custom *AddItem* method.

**Spell Checking Options**   You can fine-tune the spell checking process by setting any of several properties. When you set the *IgnoreInUppercase* property to *True,* the spell check ignores any words that appear entirely in uppercase. This can be very useful if you are checking a document that's filled with acronyms not likely to be found in your dictionary. Similarly, when you set the *IgnoreWithNumbers* Boolean property to *True,* no words that contain numbers are displayed during the spell checking process.

The Boolean *Suggest* property is set to *True* by default, which causes SpellPro to present a list of suggested replacement words in the "Bad Word" dialog whenever a misspelled word is encountered.

The Common Word Cache is a list of common words that are stored within the SpellPro control. This cache speeds the spell checking process by reducing the need to access the main dictionary file. The *CommonWordCache* property is normally set to a value of 1, telling SpellPro to use the American English cache by default. You can disable the Common Word Cache by setting this property to 0.

**Customizing the "Bad Word" Dialog**   You can customize the built-in "Bad Word" dialog box. By default, the dialog appears centered on the screen, but you can specify its position in twips using the *DialogLeft* and *DialogTop* properties. You can set the title of the dialog  with the *DialogTitle* property. If this property is blank (an empty string), the dialog displays with the title "Spelling Check."

The *OptionBtnVisible* Boolean property determines if a special Options button appears in the dialog box. Pressing this button fires an *OptionBtnClick* event. You can use this event to display your own Options dialog or to take any other necessary action during the spell checking process. You can change the caption on the Options button using the *OptionBtnCaption* property.

Similarly, the *AddBtnVisible* property determines whether the Add button is displayed in the dialog to let the user add words to a custom dictionary.

**Handling Spell Checking Yourself**  While the built-in "Bad Word" dialog makes it quite simple to perform the more traditional spell checking operations, at times you may need better control over the process. For example, you may want to build an application that spell checks an entire document without requiring any feedback from a user. If you set the *BadWordDialog* property to *False,* the built-in dialog is disabled.

With the dialog disabled, you now must program actions that occur when a misspelled word is encountered. You still invoke spell checking in the same way, by setting the *Start* property to *True,* but now you must respond appropriately to events that SpellPro generates during the process.

The *Suggestion* event is fired if the *Suggest* property is *True,* and SpellPro finds suggested words in the dictionaries or Common Word Cache. It is fired once for each suggested word that SpellPro finds. After the last *Suggestion* event, the *BadWord* event is fired. In this event, you can display a custom dialog box or take other actions required to process the misspelled word. The misspelled word is automatically assigned to the *CheckWord* property. The *Change* event is fired when the SpellPro text is changed. This can occur when either the *ChangeWord* or *ChangeAllToWord* property is changed.

# Example

The example program, shown in Figure 10-3, is a simple Notepad-style text editor built using the standard multiline text control. The spell checking in this text editor uses the built-in "Bad Word" dialog. The user can set spell checking options through a dialog form that's tied to a menu option. The user also starts spell checking through a menu option. The text editor can read and write text files that are small enough to fit into a standard text control.

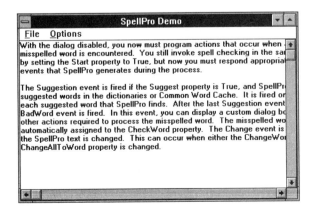

**Figure 10-3** The SpellPro example program

10◄

## Steps

1. Create a new project called SPELLPRO.MAK. Add the SpellPro control, MHSPELL.VBX, and the common dialog control, CMDIALOG.VBX, to the project. Create a new form with the objects and properties described in Table 10-6. Save this form as SPELLPRO.FRM.

**Table 10-6** Objects and properties of SPELLPRO.FRM

| OBJECT | PROPERTY | SETTING |
|---|---|---|
| Form | FormName | frmSpellPro |
| | Caption | "SpellPro Demo" |
| TextBox | Name | txtDoc |
| | BorderStyle | 0 'None |
| | MultiLine | -1 'True |
| | ScrollBars | 3 'Both |
| CommonDialog | Name | CMDialog1 |
| MhSpellPro | Name | MhSpellPro1 |
| | AddBtnVisible | -1 'True |
| | BadWordDialog | 1 'English Dialog |
| | CommonWordCache | 1 'American English |
| | Suggest | -1 'True |

2. Add a menu to SPELLPRO.FRM using the Visual Basic Menu Design window, setting the captions and names as shown in Table 10-7.

**Table 10-7** Menu definition for SPELLPRO.FRM

| CAPTION | NAME |
|---|---|
| &File | mnuFile |
| – – – – &Open | mnuFileOpen |
| – – – – – | mnuFileSep1 |
| – – – – E&xit | mnuFileExit |
| &Options | mnuOptions |
| – – – – &Spell Check | mnuOptionsSpellCheck |
| – – – – Spell Checking &Options | mnuOptionsSCOptions |

3. After creating SPELLPRO.FRM, add the following code to the form's declarations section.

```
Option Explicit
'--------------------------------------------------
' Variables and constants used by the SpellPro
' example program.
'--------------------------------------------------
```

```
' Store the original form dimensions.
Dim MinFormWidth As Integer
Dim MinFormHeight As Integer

' The currently loaded text file.
Dim TextFileName As String

' Current status of spell checking operation.
Dim SpellCheckCompleted As Integer

' Used for updating the caption in the title bar.
Dim DefaultCaption As String
Dim WholeCaption As String

' WindowState constant.
Const MINIMIZED = 1

' Form.Show constants.
Const SHOW_MODAL = 1
Const SHOW_NONMODAL = 0

' MsgBox constants.
Const MB_OK = &H0
Const MB_YESNOCANCEL = &H3
Const MB_YESNO = &H4

Const MB_ICONQUESTION = &H20
Const MB_ICONEXCLAMATION = &H30
Const MB_ICONINFORMATION = &H40
Const MB_ICONSTOP = &H10

' File Open/Save dialog flags.
Const OFN_READONLY = &H1&
Const OFN_HIDEREADONLY = &H4&
```

4. Add the following subroutines to the SPELLPRO.FRM form. We've included a subroutine called *AdjustCaption,* which you might find useful in other programs. This routine will truncate and add ellipses (...) to a title bar caption if the caption's text is too wide.

```
Sub AdjustCaption (ByVal ACaption As String)
'-------------------------------------------------
' Adjust the caption, ACaption, so that it fits
' in within the current title bar area. If the
' caption is too wide, it's shortened and ellipses
' (...) are appended.
'-------------------------------------------------
Dim TitleWidth As Integer
Dim BordersWidth As Integer
Dim CaptionBarHeight As Integer
Dim HasMenu As Integer

Dim OldFont As String
Dim OldSize As Single
Dim OldBold As Integer
Dim OldItalic As Integer

    ' Do we need to account for height of menu?
```

*(continued on next page)*

10◄

*(continued from previous page)*

```vb
    HasMenu = True

    ' Get the combined width of the left and right borders.
    BordersWidth = Me.Width - Me.ScaleWidth

    ' Get the height of the title bar.
    CaptionBarHeight = Me.Height - Me.ScaleHeight - BordersWidth
    If HasMenu Then CaptionBarHeight = CaptionBarHeight / 2

    ' CaptionBarHeight * 3 roughly removes the width of the min/max/system buttons.
    TitleWidth = Me.ScaleWidth - (CaptionBarHeight * 3)

    ' Save original font settings.
    OldFont = Me.FontName
    OldSize = Me.FontSize
    OldBold = Me.FontBold
    OldItalic = Me.FontItalic

    ' Change the form's font to the system font, which is (usually)
    ' the font used on the title bar.
    Me.FontName = "System"
    Me.FontBold = True
    Me.FontItalic = False
    Me.FontSize = 9.75

    ' Check if we need to shorten the caption.
    If Me.TextWidth(ACaption) > TitleWidth Then
        ' Shorten the caption and add elipses.
        While (Me.TextWidth(ACaption & "...") > TitleWidth) And (Len(ACaption) > 1)
            ACaption = Left$(ACaption, Len(ACaption) - 1)
        Wend
        ACaption = ACaption & "..."
    End If

    ' Update the caption.
    Me.Caption = ACaption

    ' Reset original font settings.
    Me.FontName = OldFont
    Me.FontSize = OldSize
    Me.FontBold = OldBold
    Me.FontItalic = OldItalic
End Sub

Sub Form_Load ()
'-------------------------------------------------
' Position the form on the screen and initialize
' variables.
'-------------------------------------------------

    ' Center the form on the screen.
    Me.Move (Screen.Width - Me.Width) \ 2, (Screen.Height - Me.Height) \ 2

    ' Save the original form dimensions.
    MinFormWidth = Me.Width
    MinFormHeight = Me.Height

    ' Save the original caption.
    DefaultCaption = Me.Caption
```

```
    ' WholeCaption is used when caption width adjustments are required.
    WholeCaption = DefaultCaption

    ' Specify a custom dictionary file.
    MhSpellPro1.CustomDictFile = App.Path & "\CUSTOM1.TXT"
End Sub

Sub Form_Resize ()
'-------------------------------------------------
' Resize the text control and adjust the caption
' when the window is resized.
'-------------------------------------------------

    ' If the form is minimized, do nothing.
    If WindowState = MINIMIZED Then Exit Sub

    ' Don't let the form get smaller than 1/2 its original width and height.
    If Me.Width < (MinFormWidth / 2) Then Me.Width = MinFormWidth / 2
    If Me.Height < (MinFormHeight / 2) Then Me.Height = MinFormHeight / 2

    ' Resize the text control.
    txtDoc.Move 0, 0, Me.ScaleWidth, Me.ScaleHeight

    ' Adjust the caption if the title bar is too narrow.
    AdjustCaption WholeCaption
End Sub

Sub LoadTextFile (ByVal AFile As String)
'-----------------------------------------------------
' Load the text file, AFile, into the text control.
'-----------------------------------------------------
Const ByteLimit = (32& * 1024&)

Dim fnum As Integer
Dim FileSize As Integer

    FileSize = FileLen(AFile)

    ' Don't bother loading files greater than 32K.
    If FileSize > ByteLimit Then
        MsgBox "File larger than size limit.", MB_OK Or MB_ICONEXCLAMATION, "File Too Large"
        TextFileName = ""
        Exit Sub
    End If

    fnum = FreeFile
    Open AFile For Input As fnum

    ' Read the file as one big chunk.
    txtDoc = Input$(FileSize, fnum)

    ' If we didn't get the whole file, we've failed.
    If Len(txtDoc) < FileLen(AFile) Then
        MsgBox "File was too large to load.", MB_OK Or MB_ICONEXCLAMATION, "File Too Large"
        txtDoc = ""
        TextFileName = ""
        Exit Sub
    End If

    ' Set the new caption.
```

(continued on next page)

*(continued from previous page)*

```vb
    WholeCaption = DefaultCaption & " - [" & LCase$(AFile) & "]"
    AdjustCaption WholeCaption

    Close fnum
End Sub

Sub MhSpellPro1_BadWord (Problem As Integer)
'----------------------------------------------------
' Highlight the bad word in the text control.
'----------------------------------------------------

    txtDoc.SelStart = MhSpellPro1.SelStart
    txtDoc.SelLength = MhSpellPro1.SelLength
End Sub

Sub MhSpellPro1_Changed ()
'----------------------------------------------------
' Update the text in the text control when a
' word is changed by SpellPro.
'----------------------------------------------------

    txtDoc.Text = MhSpellPro1.Text
End Sub

Sub MhSpellPro1_Complete (Cancelled As Integer)
'----------------------------------------------------
' Set the flag that indicates that checking is over.
'----------------------------------------------------

    If Not Cancelled Then SpellCheckCompleted = True
End Sub

Sub mnuFileExit_Click ()
'----------------------------------------------------
' Exit the program.
'----------------------------------------------------

    Unload Me
End Sub

Sub mnuFileOpen_Click ()
'----------------------------------------------------
' Display the common File Open dialog and load
' the selected text file into the text control.
'----------------------------------------------------
Dim Canceled As Integer
Dim i As Integer

    On Error GoTo mnuFileOpen_Error
    Canceled = False

    ' Set up and display the File Open dialog box.
    CMDialog1.Flags = OFN_HIDEREADONLY
    CMDialog1.CancelError = True
    CMDialog1.Filter = "Text Files|*.txt"
    CMDialog1.DialogTitle = "Open a Text File"
    CMDialog1.Action = 1

    If Canceled Or (CMDialog1.Filename = "") Then Exit Sub
```

```
    ' Save the new text file's name.
    TextFileName = CMDialog1.Filename

    ' Load the text file into text control.
    LoadTextFile TextFileName
Exit Sub

mnuFileOpen_Error:
    Canceled = True
    Resume Next
End Sub

Sub mnuFileSaveAs_Click ()
'----------------------------------------------------
' Display the common File Save As dialog and save
' the contents of the text control into the
' selected file.
'----------------------------------------------------
Dim Canceled As Integer
Dim i As Integer

    On Error GoTo mnuFileSaveAs_Error
    Canceled = False

    ' Set up and display the File Save As dialog box.
    CMDialog1.Flags = OFN_HIDEREADONLY
    CMDialog1.CancelError = True
    CMDialog1.Filter = "Text Files|*.txt"
    CMDialog1.DialogTitle = "Save Text File As"
    CMDialog1.Action = 1

    If Canceled Or (CMDialog1.Filename = "") Then Exit Sub

    ' Save the contents of the text control to the
    ' selected file.
    SaveTextFile CMDialog1.Filename
Exit Sub

mnuFileSaveAs_Error:
    Canceled = True
    Resume Next
End Sub

Sub mnuOptionsSCOptions_Click ()
'----------------------------------------------------
' Show the Spell Checking Options dialog form.
'----------------------------------------------------

    frmSpellOptions.Show SHOW_MODAL
End Sub

Sub mnuOptionsSpell Check_Click ()
'----------------------------------------------------
' Perform spell checking.
'----------------------------------------------------
Dim retcode As Integer

    ' Disable the Spell Check menu option.
    mnuOptionsSpell Check.Enabled = False
```

10◄

(continued on next page)

*(continued from previous page)*

```vb
    ' Load the text control into SpellPro.
    MhSpellPro1.Text = txtDoc.Text

    ' Spell checking has not yet completed.
    Spell CheckCompleted = False

    ' Start spell checking.
    MhSpellPro1.Start = True

    ' Make sure that spell checking is completed
    ' before proceeding.
    Do Until MhSpellPro1.Start = 0
        retcode = DoEvents()
    Loop

    ' Let users know when spell checking is over,
    ' unless they canceled the operation.
    If Spell CheckCompleted Then
        MsgBox "Spell Checking is Complete.", MB_OK Or MB_ICONINFORMATION, "Spell Check"
    End If

    ' Enable the Spell Check menu option.
    mnuOptionsSpell Check.Enabled = True

    ' Assign the spell checked text back to the text control.
    txtDoc.Text = MhSpellPro1.Text

    ' Make sure no text is selected.
    txtDoc.SelLength = 0

    ' Set focus back to text control.
    txtDoc.SetFocus
End Sub

Sub SaveTextFile (ByVal AFile As String)
'-----------------------------------------------------
' Save the contents of the text control to the
' file AFile.
'-----------------------------------------------------
Dim fnum As Integer

    fnum = FreeFile
    Open AFile For Output As fnum

    ' Save the whole file as one big chunk.
    Print #fnum, txtDoc;

    Close fnum

    ' Update the caption to reflect the new file name.
    TextFileName = AFile
    WholeCaption = DefaultCaption & " - [" & LCase$(AFile) & "]"
    AdjustCaption WholeCaption

Exit Sub
SaveTextFile_Error:
    MsgBox "Error " & Format$(Err) & ": " & Error$, MB_OK Or MB_ICONEXCLAMATION, "Error Saving File"
    Exit Sub
End Sub
```

5. Create another form, with the objects and properties described in Table 10-8. Save this form as SPELLOPT.FRM.

**Table 10-8** Objects and properties of SPELLOPT.FRM

| OBJECT | PROPERTY | SETTING |
|---|---|---|
| Form | FormName | frmSpellOptions |
| | BackColor | &H00C0C0C0& |
| | BorderStyle | 3 'Fixed Double |
| | Caption | "Spell Checking Options" |
| | MaxButton | 0 'False |
| | MinButton | 0 'False |
| CheckBox | Name | chkIgnoreInUpperCase |
| | BackColor | &H00C0C0C0& |
| | Caption | "Ignore words in all uppercase" |
| CheckBox | Name | chkIgnoreWithNumbers |
| | BackColor | &H00C0C0C0& |
| | Caption | "Ignore words containing numbers" |
| CheckBox | Name | chkSuggest |
| | BackColor | &H00C0C0C0& |
| | Caption | "Suggest Words" |
| CommandButton | Name | btnOK |
| | Caption | "&OK" |
| | Default | -1 'True |
| CommandButton | Name | btnCancel |
| | Cancel | -1 'True |
| | Caption | "&Cancel" |

6. After creating the SPELLOPT.FRM form, add the following code to its declarations section.

```
Option Explicit
'-------------------------------------------------
' The Options dialog box for the SpellPro example.
'-------------------------------------------------
```

7. Add the following subroutines to the SPELLOPT.FRM form. This is the Spell Checking Options form, which allows the user to specify what types of words should be included in the spell check, and whether replacement words should be suggested.

```
Sub btnCancel_Click ()
'-------------------------------------------------
' Unload the form when the user presses "Cancel."
'-------------------------------------------------

    Unload Me
```

10◄

(continued on next page)

*(continued from previous page)*

```
End Sub

Sub btnOK_Click ()
'----------------------------------------------------
' Update the SpellPro options and unload the form.
'----------------------------------------------------

    frmSpellPro.MhSpellPro1.IgnoreInUppercase = (chkIgnoreInUpperCase = 1)
    frmSpellPro.MhSpellPro1.IgnoreWithNumbers = (chkIgnoreWithNumbers = 1)
    frmSpellPro.MhSpellPro1.Suggest = (chkSuggest = 1)

    Unload Me
End Sub

Sub Form_Load ()
'----------------------------------------------------
' Center the form and set the check boxes based
' on the current values of the SpellPro properties.
'----------------------------------------------------

    Me.Move (Screen.Width - Me.Width) \ 2, (Screen.Height - Me.Height) \ 3

    chkIgnoreInUpperCase = Abs(frmSpellPro.MhSpellPro1.IgnoreInUppercase)
    chkIgnoreWithNumbers = Abs(frmSpellPro.MhSpellPro1.IgnoreWithNumbers)
    chkSuggest = Abs(frmSpellPro.MhSpellPro1.Suggest)
End Sub
```

## Tips and Comments

You can approach the SpellPro control from two levels. You can use the default values, including the built-in "Bad Word" dialog box, and very quickly integrate spell checking into an application. Or, you can opt to control the spell checking operation, and code the process yourself.

The ease with which you can incorporate custom dictionaries opens all sorts of possibilities, and you can even use multiple custom dictionaries and switch between them on the fly simply by changing the file name in the *CustomDictFile* property. As an example, you could have one dictionary of technical terms, another that contained business terms, and so on.

# VSAwk (VSVBX.VBX)

| USAGE: | Text and File Processing |
|---|---|
| MANUFACTURER: | VideoSoft |
| COST: | $45 |

VSAwk is one of three controls that comes with VideoSoft's VSVBX.VBX (the other two controls are described in Chapter 1). VSAwk implements text processing similar to what you can perform with the UNIX language awk. Using this control you can automatically parse text files and text strings, simplifying the task of manipulating text and data files.

For example, VSAwk can easily break text in a file into individual words, or extract fields from a comma-delimited file.

# Syntax

If you're familiar with the original UNIX awk language, you'll immediately see both the similarities and differences between awk and VSAwk. The most obvious difference is that awk is a stand-alone programming language with its own syntax and control constructs, whereas VSAwk is a Visual Basic control that provides several of the text parsing and processing features of awk within the framework of Visual Basic properties and events. The nonstandard properties and events of VSAwk are shown in Table 10-9.

**Table 10-9** Nonstandard properties and events of the VSAwk control

**PROPERTIES**

| | | |
|---|---|---|
| Action | Case | CurrPos |
| Error | F | FieldAt |
| FileName | FileType | FilterQuotes |
| FS | L | MatchQuotes |
| NF | PercentDone | PosAt |
| RN | Val | |

**EVENTS**

| | | |
|---|---|---|
| Begin | End | Error |
| Scan | Variable | |

VSAwk is geared toward handling entire files of text. In most text file processing problems, you write code to initialize variables, open the text file and process it line by line, and then close the file and do some cleanup and postprocessing. These three basic steps are contained in the three VSAwk events *Begin, Scan,* and *End.*

To understand how these events work, we'll first look at the *Action* property. The values for this property are given in Table 10-10.

**Table 10-10** Values for the Action property

| VALUE | MEANING |
|---|---|
| 0 | Begin scanning the file. |
| 1 | Move to the next line. |
| 2 | Close the file. |

Setting the *Action* property to 0 tells VSAwk to start processing the file specified by the *FileName* property. This causes a sequence of events, beginning with the opening of the file. Second, the *Begin* event is fired. Next, the Scan event is called once for each line read from the text file. Finally, when all the lines have been read, the file is closed and VSAwk fires the *End* event.

Typically, the *Scan* event handles most of the file processing. VSAwk provides several properties to assist in parsing a line in the *Scan* event.

The *FS* (for "field separator") property is a string of characters that tells VSAwk how to break a text line into parts. The default value is a string containing the space character, the comma character, and the tab character, but this property can be set to any sequence of characters. If you change *FS* in a *Scan* event, the current line is immediately reparsed using the new field separators.

To illustrate how VSAwk processes a line, let's look at an example string:

```
This is a line text,, and it's separated by spaces    and commas.
```

If this line appeared in a text file, VSAwk would break it into 13 fields. These fields are stored in the *F()* property array. In this case, the value of *F(5)* is "text", the value of *F(6)* is "", and the value of *F(13)* is "commas." Notice that the separator characters are not included in the field text. Also notice that multiple spaces are treated as a single space. This is only true of spaces as a field separator. The 0 element of the *F()* array contains the entire text line, unparsed. This same string can be accessed with the *L* (for "line") property.

You can tell how many fields are in the current line with the *NF* ("number of fields") property. In the example, *NF* would be equal to 13. To determine the byte offset into the file, use the *CurrPos* property. You can quickly return to a line by setting the *CurrPos* property to a position value saved earlier in a file scan.

The *FieldAt()* property returns the field number of a character at a specified location in the string. In the example, *FieldAt(14)* would return the value of 4, because the fourteenth character is in the word "line," which is the fourth field. The reverse of this function is the *PosAt()* property, which returns the starting character position of a specified field number. In the example, *PosAt(9)* would return the value 32 because the ninth field, "separated," starts at position 32.

VSAwk considers each line of a text file to be a single record. The *RN* property returns the record number of the current text line being processed. You can also use the integer *PercentDone* property to determine how much of the file has been scanned.

VSAwk provides the Boolean *MatchQuotes* property to help parse lines that contain quoted strings. By default this property is set to *False;* when set to *True* it treats strings contained within double or single quotes as a single field. This is very useful for parsing comma-delimited file formats. For example, look at the following record from a text file:

```
1,"Smith, John","1600 Pine Street"
```

In this line, "Smith, John" and "1600 Pine Street" are considered the second and third fields when *MatchQuotes* is set to *True.*

VSAwk handles file-processing errors with a special *Error* event and an *Error* property. Because VSAwk does not generate a Visual Basic run-time error, errors are ignored by default. Each time a file-processing error occurs, VSAwk fires the *Error* event. The *Error* property contains the last error encountered by VSAwk, and can be evaluated either in the *Error* event, or while processing the file. The valid *Error* property values are given in Table 10-11.

**Table 10-11** Values for the Error property

| VALUE | MEANING |
|-------|---------|
| 0 | No error. |
| 1 | VSAwk cannot open the file. |
| 2 | The line is too long (more than 64K characters). |
| 3 | The field is too long (more than 64K characters). |
| 4 | Tried to set a field value for a field that doesn't exist. |
| 5 | Tried to get a field value for a field that doesn't exist. |

# Example

The example program, shown in Figure 10-4, uses VSAwk to parse Visual Basic .FRM and .BAS files, list their functions and subroutines in a list box, and selectively view and print those routines.

The example program uses two VSAwk controls. The first reads a file, finds the routines, adds their names to a list box, and saves the routine's starting position (the *CurrPos* property) in the list box's *ItemData* field. The second VSAwk control uses the information in the list box to seek to the exact position of the routine, and extracts the text of the routine for viewing and printing.

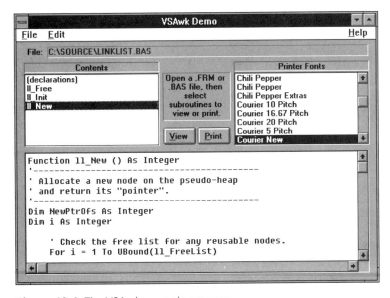

**Figure 10-4** The VSAwk example program

## Steps

1. Create a new project called VSAWK.MAK. Add the Videosoft control, VSVBX.VBX, and the common dialog control, CMDIALOG.VBX, to the project. Create a new form with the objects and properties described in Table 10-12. Save this form as VSAWK.FRM.

**Table 10-12** Objects and properties for the VSAWK.FRM form

| OBJECT | PROPERTY | SETTING |
|---|---|---|
| Form | FormName | frmVSAwk |
| | BackColor | &H00C0C0C0& |
| | Caption | "VSAwk Demo" |
| Label | Name | Label1 |
| | Alignment | 1 'Right Justify |
| | BackColor | &H00C0C0C0& |
| | Caption | "File:" |
| | ForeColor | &H00000000& |
| Label | Name | lblFileName |
| | BackColor | &H00C0C0C0& |
| | Caption | "[none]" |
| | ForeColor | &H00000080& |
| Label | Name | lblContents |
| | Alignment | 2 'Center |
| | BackStyle | 0 'Transparent |
| | Caption | "Contents" |
| | ForeColor | &H00000000& |
| Label | Name | lblFonts |
| | Alignment | 2 'Center |
| | BackStyle | 0 'Transparent |
| | Caption | "Printer Fonts" |
| | ForeColor | &H00000000& |
| Label | Name | lblInfo |
| | Alignment | 2 'Center |
| | BackStyle | 0 'Transparent |
| | Caption | "Open a .FRM or .BAS file; then select subroutines to view or print." |
| CommonDialog | Name | CMDialog1 |
| ListBox | Name | lstFileParts |
| | Sorted | -1 'True |
| TextBox | Name | txtCode |

| OBJECT | PROPERTY | SETTING |
|---|---|---|
| | FontBold | 0 'False |
| | FontName | "Fixedsys" |
| | FontSize | 9 |
| | MultiLine | -1 'True |
| | ScrollBars | 3 'Both |
| VideoSoftAwk | Name | VSAwk1 |
| | FS | " , " |
| CommandButton | Name | btnView |
| | Caption | "&View" |
| CommandButton | Name | btnPrint |
| | Caption | "&Print" |
| VideoSoftAwk | Name | VSAwk2 |
| | FS | " , " |
| ListBox | Name | lstFonts |
| | Sorted | -1 'True |

2. Add a menu to the VSAWK.FRM form using the Visual Basic Menu Design window, setting the captions and names as shown in Table 10-13.

**Table 10-13** Menu definition for VSAWK.FRM

| CAPTION | NAME |
|---|---|
| &File | mnuFile |
| − − − −&Open | mnuFileOpen |
| − − − − − | mnuFileSep1 |
| − − − −E&xit | mnuFileExit |
| &Edit | mnuEdit |
| − − − −&Copy | mnuCopy |
| − − − −Copy &All | mnuCopyAll |

3. After creating VSAWK.FRM, add the following code to the form's declarations section.

```
Option Explicit
'------------------------------------------------
' Constants and variables used in VSAwk demo.
'------------------------------------------------

' Color constants.
Const DARK_GRAY = &H808080
Const WHITE = &HFFFFFF
Const BLACK = &H0

' Awk Action constants.
Const AWK_SCANFILE = 0
```

(continued on next page)

10◄

*(continued from previous page)*

```
Const AWK_NEXTLINE = 1
Const AWK_CLOSEFILE = 2

' Holds the section of basic code.
Dim CodeString As String

' Boolean used while looking for [declarations] section.
Dim FoundDecl As Integer

' Are we printing or just viewing?
Dim ActionType As Integer

' Used to indicate declarations section of code.
Const DECLARE_STRING = "(declarations)"

' WindowState constant.
Const MINIMIZED = 1

' Cursor shape constants.
Const CSR_NORMAL = 0
Const CSR_HOURGLASS = 11

' ActionType constants.
Const GO_VIEW = 0
Const GO_PRINT = 1

' Default margin constants.
Const LR_MARGIN = 5
Const TOP_MARGIN = 3

Const MB_OK = 0                   ' OK button only
Const MB_ICONEXCLAMATION = 48     ' Warning message
```

4. Add the following functions and subroutines to the VSAWK.FRM form.

```
Sub btnPrint_Click ()
'-------------------------------------------------
' Print the routine selected in the list box.
'-------------------------------------------------

    If lstFileParts.ListIndex < 0 Then Exit Sub

    Screen.MousePointer = CSR_HOURGLASS

    VSAwk2.FileName = CMDialog1.Filename
    ActionType = GO_PRINT
    VSAwk2.Action = AWK_SCANFILE

    Screen.MousePointer = CSR_NORMAL
End Sub

Sub btnView_Click ()
'-------------------------------------------------
' View the routine selected in the list box.
'-------------------------------------------------

    If lstFileParts.ListIndex < 0 Then Exit Sub

    Screen.MousePointer = CSR_HOURGLASS

    VSAwk2.FileName = CMDialog1.Filename
    ActionType = GO_VIEW
```

```
        VSAwk2.Action = AWK_SCANFILE

        Screen.MousePointer = CSR_NORMAL
    End Sub

    Sub ClearForm ()
    '----------------------------------------------------
    ' Get rid of any old data in the controls.
    '----------------------------------------------------
        lstFileParts.Clear
        txtCode.Text = ""
    End Sub

    Sub Form_Load ()
    '----------------------------------------------------
    ' Position the form and load Printer Font list box.
    '----------------------------------------------------
    Dim i As Integer

        For i = 0 To Printer.FontCount - 1
            lstFonts.AddItem Printer.Fonts(i)
        Next
        For i = 0 To lstFonts.ListCount - 1
            If i = 0 Then lstFonts.ListIndex = i
            If lstFonts.List(i) = "Courier New" Then lstFonts.ListIndex = i
        Next

        Me.Move (Screen.Width - Me.Width) \ 2, (Screen.Height - Me.Height) \ 2
        Me.Show
    End Sub

    Sub Form_Paint ()
    '----------------------------------------------------
    ' Repaint 3D effect where necessary.
    '----------------------------------------------------
        Set3DControls
    End Sub

    Sub Form_Resize ()
    '----------------------------------------------------
    ' Adjust the size of the text control and the
    ' File Name label when window size changes.
    '----------------------------------------------------
    Dim NewWidth As Integer, NewHeight As Integer
    Dim Margin As Integer

        On Error Resume Next

        If WindowState = MINIMIZED Then Exit Sub
        Me.Cls
        Margin = lstFileParts.Left
        NewWidth = (Me.ScaleWidth - txtCode.Left - Margin)
        NewHeight = (Me.ScaleHeight - txtCode.Top - Margin)
        txtCode.Move txtCode.Left, txtCode.Top, NewWidth, NewHeight

        lblFilename.Width = Me.ScaleWidth - lblFilename.Left - Margin

        ' Draw 3D effect around selected controls.
        Set3DControls
```

10◀

(continued on next page)

*(continued from previous page)*

```
End Sub

Function IsTextFile (ByVal AFileName As String) As Integer
'------------------------------------------------------
' A quick little check to see if this is a text
' file or not. Not 100% accurate, but better
' than nothing.
'------------------------------------------------------
Dim fnum As Integer
Dim i As Integer
Dim ch As String

    On Error GoTo IsTextFile_Error

    IsTextFile = True
    fnum = FreeFile
    Open AFileName For Input As fnum
    For i = 1 To 25
        ch = Input$(1, fnum)
        ' If it's not lower ASCII then it's probably
        ' not a text file.
        If Asc(ch) > 127 Then
            IsTextFile = False
            Exit For
        End If
        If EOF(fnum) Then Exit For
    Next

Exit Function
IsTextFile_Error:
    IsTextFile = False
    Exit Function
End Function

Sub lstFileParts_DblClick ()
'------------------------------------------------------
' Double-clicking on list box is the same as
' pressing the View button.
'------------------------------------------------------
    btnView.Value = 1
End Sub

Sub Make3D (pic As Form, ctl As Control)
'------------------------------------------------------
' Wrap a 3D effect around a control on a form.
'------------------------------------------------------
Dim AdjustX As Integer, AdjustY As Integer
Dim RightSide As Single

    AdjustX = Screen.TwipsPerPixelX
    AdjustY = Screen.TwipsPerPixelY

    ' Set the top shading line.
    pic.Line (ctl.Left - AdjustX, ctl.Top - AdjustY)-(ctl.Left + ctl.Width, ctl.Top - AdjustY),
DARK_GRAY
    pic.Line -(ctl.Left + ctl.Width, ctl.Top + ctl.Height), WHITE
    pic.Line -(ctl.Left - AdjustX, ctl.Top + ctl.Height), WHITE
    pic.Line -(ctl.Left - AdjustX, ctl.Top - AdjustY), DARK_GRAY
End Sub
```

```
Sub mnuFileExit_Click ()
'-----------------------------------------------------
' End the program.
'-----------------------------------------------------
    Unload Me
End Sub

Sub mnuFileOpen_Click ()
'-----------------------------------------------------
' Open a Visual Basic source code file.
'-----------------------------------------------------
    CMDialog1.DialogTitle = "Open a Visual Basic Source File"
    CMDialog1.Filter = "VB Source Code (.FRM,.BAS)|*.frm;*.bas"
    CMDialog1.Action = 1

    If CMDialog1.Filename = "" Then Exit Sub
    If Not IsTextFile(CMDialog1.Filename) Then
        MsgBox "Source files must be saved as text.", MB_OK Or MB_ICONEXCLAMATION
        Exit Sub
    End If

    ClearForm

    lblFilename = CMDialog1.Filename
    VSAwk1.FileName = CMDialog1.Filename

    Screen.MousePointer = CSR_HOURGLASS
    VSAwk1.Action = AWK_SCANFILE
    Screen.MousePointer = CSR_NORMAL
End Sub

Sub PrintHeading ()
'-----------------------------------------------------
' Print heading at top of a printer page.
'-----------------------------------------------------
Dim i As Integer

    On Error Resume Next

    Printer.CurrentY = 0
    Printer.CurrentX = 0
    For i = 1 To TOP_MARGIN
        Printer.Print
    Next

    Printer.FontBold = True

    Printer.Print Space$(LR_MARGIN) & "File:    "; CMDialog1.Filename;
    PrintRightAlign "Page " & Format$(Printer.Page)
    Printer.Print
    Printer.Print Space$(LR_MARGIN) & "Printed: " & Format$(Now, "MM/DD/YYYY")

    Printer.CurrentX = Printer.TextWidth(Space$(LR_MARGIN))
    Printer.CurrentY = Printer.CurrentY + (Printer.TextHeight("W") \ 2)
    Printer.DrawWidth = 3
    Printer.Line -(Printer.ScaleWidth - Printer.TextWidth(Space$(LR_MARGIN)),
Printer.CurrentY), RGB(0, 0, 0)
    Printer.CurrentY = Printer.CurrentY + (Printer.TextHeight("W") \ 2)

    Printer.CurrentX = 0
```

*(continued on next page)*

**10**

**639**

*(continued from previous page)*

```
      Printer.FontBold = False
End Sub

Sub PrintLine (ByVal ALine As String)
'------------------------------------------------------
' Print a single line to the printer. Break up
' long lines and pass them to PrintLine recursively.
'------------------------------------------------------
Dim indent As Integer
Dim i As Integer, j As Integer
Dim LeftMargin As String
Dim ATab As String

    On Error Resume Next

    ATab = Chr$(9)
    ALine = RTrim$(ALine)

    indent = 0
    For i = 1 To Len(ALine)
        If Mid$(ALine, i, 1) = " " Then
            indent = indent + 1
        ' This converts tabs to spaces.
        ElseIf Mid$(ALine, i, 1) = ATab Then
            indent = indent + 8
        Else
            Exit For
        End If
    Next
    ALine = Space$(indent) & Mid$(ALine, i)

    LeftMargin = Space$(LR_MARGIN)

    ' Check if we're at the end of the page.
    If (Printer.CurrentY + Printer.TextHeight(ALine)) >= Printer.ScaleHeight Then
        Printer.NewPage
        PrintHeading
    End If

    ' Check if we can fit Aline on a single line.
    If Printer.TextWidth(LeftMargin & ALine & LeftMargin) <= Printer.ScaleWidth Then
        If Left$(Trim$(ALine), 1) = "'" Then Printer.FontItalic = True
        Printer.Print LeftMargin & ALine
        Printer.FontItalic = False
    Else
        For i = 1 To Len(ALine)
            If Printer.TextWidth(LeftMargin & Left$(ALine, i) & LeftMargin) >
Printer.ScaleWidth Then
                Exit For
            End If
        Next
        ' Try to adjust for a word break nearby.
        For j = i To (j - 12) Step -1
            If InStr(" :()", Mid$(ALine, j, 1)) > 0 Then
                i = j + 1
                Exit For
            End If
        Next
        Printer.Print LeftMargin & Left$(ALine, i - 1)
```

```vb
        PrintLine Space$(indent) & ">> " & Mid$(ALine, i)
    End If
End Sub

Sub PrintRightAlign (ByVal Astr As String)
'--------------------------------------------------
' Print a string at the far right side of the page.
'--------------------------------------------------
    On Error Resume Next

    Printer.CurrentX = Printer.ScaleWidth - Printer.TextWidth(Astr) -
Printer.TextWidth(Space$(LR_MARGIN))
    Printer.Print Astr;
End Sub

Sub Set3DControls ()
'--------------------------------------------------
' Draw 3D effect around selected controls.
'--------------------------------------------------
    Make3D frmVSAwk, lstFileParts
    Make3D frmVSAwk, txtCode
    Make3D frmVSAwk, lblFilename
    Make3D frmVSAwk, lblContents
    Make3D frmVSAwk, lblFonts
    Make3D frmVSAwk, lstFonts
    Make3D frmVSAwk, lblInfo
End Sub

Sub VSAwk1_Begin ()
'--------------------------------------------------
' Check whether we need to skip the "form definition"
' stuff at the beginning of a .FRM file.
'--------------------------------------------------
    If Right$(CMDialog1.Filename, 4) <> ".FRM" Then
        lstFileParts.AddItem DECLARE_STRING
        lstFileParts.ItemData(lstFileParts.NewIndex) = VSAwk1.CurrPos
    Else
        FoundDecl = False
    End If
End Sub

Sub VSAwk1_Scan ()
'--------------------------------------------------
' Build the list box with sub, function, and
' declaration names.
'--------------------------------------------------
    If VSAwk1.NF = 0 Then Exit Sub
    If (Right$(CMDialog1.Filename, 4) = ".FRM") And (Not FoundDecl) And (VSAwk1.L = "End") Then
        FoundDecl = True
        lstFileParts.AddItem DECLARE_STRING
        lstFileParts.ItemData(lstFileParts.NewIndex) = VSAwk1.CurrPos + Len(VSAwk1.L) + 2
    End If
    If (VSAwk1.F(1) = "Sub") Or (VSAwk1.F(1) = "Function") Then
        lstFileParts.AddItem Trim$(VSAwk1.F(2))
        lstFileParts.ItemData(lstFileParts.NewIndex) = VSAwk1.CurrPos
    End If
End Sub

Sub VSAwk2_Begin ()
```

**10**

*(continued on next page)*

*(continued from previous page)*

```
'-----------------------------------------------------
' Prepare to view (and optionally print) a sub,
' function, or declaration section.
'-----------------------------------------------------
    VSAwk2.CurrPos = lstFileParts.ItemData(lstFileParts.ListIndex)
    CodeString = ""

    ' Define printer font and print first page header.
    If ActionType = GO_PRINT Then
        If lstFonts.ListIndex >= 0 Then
            Printer.FontName = lstFonts.List(lstFonts.ListIndex)
        End If
        Printer.FontSize = 8.25
        Printer.FontBold = False
        Printer.FontItalic = False
        Printer.FontUnderline = False
        PrintHeading
    End If
End Sub

Sub VSAwk2_End ()
'-----------------------------------------------------
' Load VB code into text control and, if necessary,
' end the print job.
'-----------------------------------------------------
    txtCode = CodeString
    If ActionType = GO_PRINT Then Printer.EndDoc
End Sub

Sub VSAwk2_Scan ()
'-----------------------------------------------------
' Process a source code line.
'-----------------------------------------------------
Dim ShutDown As Integer

    ' Parsing [Declarations] section
    If lstFileParts.List(lstFileParts.ListIndex) = DECLARE_STRING Then
        If ((VSAwk2.F(1) = "Sub") Or (VSAwk2.F(1) = "Function")) Then
            VSAwk2.Action = AWK_CLOSEFILE
            Exit Sub
        End If
    ' Parsing sub or function
    Else
        If ((VSAwk2.L = "End Sub") Or (VSAwk2.L = "End Function")) Then
            ShutDown = True
        End If
    End If

    CodeString = CodeString & VSAwk2.L & Chr$(13) & Chr$(10)
    If ActionType = GO_PRINT Then
        PrintLine VSAwk2.L
    End If

    If ShutDown Then VSAwk2.Action = AWK_CLOSEFILE
End Sub
```

## Tips and Comments

VSAwk is similar to awk in its preprocessing and postprocessing abilities, and in the parallels between several VSAwk properties and some of awk's built-in variables. Noticeably missing is awk's strong regular expression abilities. As Videosoft points out in the documentation, much of the power of regular expressions is available through Visual Basic's *Like* operator.

Text file processing is often tedious and cumbersome, but it is essential in many applications. With the VSAwk control, you could write an interpreter to add scripting capabilities to your application. You can use VSAwk to aid in importing comma-delimited files into a database. Combined with native Visual Basic features such as the *Like* operator, this control can provide quick, efficient, and powerful parsing capabilities to your programs.

# VT-Speller (VTSPELL.VBX)

| USAGE: | Spell Checking |
|---|---|
| MANUFACTURER: | Visual Tools |
| COST: | $149 |

The VT-Speller control is designed as a general-purpose spell checker, and in that respect it's similar to MicroHelp's SpellPro, which you learned about earlier in this chapter. While VT-Speller and SpellPro have several similarities, they approach the problem of spell checking with slightly different goals. SpellPro appears to be designed for compatibility in appearance and function with Microsoft Word's spell checking function. VT-Speller is more oriented to customization.

## Syntax

VT-Speller comes with a standard dictionary of American English words, and can also support user-defined custom dictionaries, which are stored as ASCII text files. You can use multiple standard and custom dictionaries during spell checking. VT-Speller supports ignore/replace lists, single word or block text checking, and automatic suggestion generation. It also lets you optimize the spell checking process for either memory conservation or spell checking speed. Table 10-14 lists the nonstandard properties and events of VT-Speller.

**Table 10-14** Nonstandard properties and events of the VT-Speller control

**PROPERTIES**

| | | |
|---|---|---|
| AddIREntry | AddSuggestion | AddToCustom |
| AddToIRList | AllowJoinedWords | AutoPopUp |
| AutoReplace | AutoSuggest | BeginCheck |

*(continued on next page)*

10◄

## PROPERTIES

(continued from previous page)

| | | |
|---|---|---|
| BreakWordCount | CacheSize | CheckText |
| CheckWord | ClearCounts | ClearIREntries |
| ClearOffsets | ClearSuggestions | CloseDictionary |
| CompleteEvent | CreateCustomOnOpen | CurrentLine |
| CustomCount | DialogBgColor | DialogLeft |
| DialogLeftActual | DialogTop | DialogTopActual |
| DictionaryLanguage | DictionaryName | DictionaryStatus |
| DLLHandle | Enabled | EnableOnOpen |
| ErrorEvent | ErrorOffset | EventAction |
| EventOptions | FindSuggestions | FoundEvent |
| FullDictionaryName | GetEntry | Hyphenation |
| IgnoreFullCaps | IgnorePartialNumbers | IgnoreReplaceAction |
| IRListEnabled | IRWhereFound | LineBreak |
| LineOffset | Loaded | LoadOnOpen |
| MaxSuggestions | MisspelledWord | MisspellEvent |
| MultiLine | OpenCustom | OpenStandard |
| PerformanceLevel | PopUp | PopUpEvent |
| RemoveIREntry | ReplaceCount | ReplaceEvent |
| ReplaceLastWord | ReplacementWord | ReplaceOccurred |
| ReplaceRecheck | ResultCode | ResumeCheck |
| ResumeOffset | SearchOnOpen | SearchOrder |
| SpellOptions | StandardCount | StatusEventSuggestion |
| SuggestionCount | SuggestionsLimit | SuggestionsMade |
| SuggestOptions | Text | Updateable |
| Version | WhereFound | WordCount |
| WordOffset | | |

## EVENTS

| | | |
|---|---|---|
| AfterPopUp | AfterReplace | BeforeReplace |
| CheckError | CheckStatus | Complete |
| Found | Misspelled | |

VT-Speller also comes with a program that lets you create and maintain your own standard dictionaries. Since these dictionaries are stored as binary files, their performance should be better than that of the text-based custom dictionaries, especially when a large number of words are involved.

### Implementing Simple Spell Checking with VT-Speller

The VT-Speller spell checking process normally takes place in a Visual Basic While loop. Just before entering the loop, the *CheckText* property is assigned a text string to spell check.

This initiates the spell checking process. A typical spell checking code segment is shown here.

```
' Reset the ReplaceCount and WordCount properties to 0.
VTSpell1.ClearCounts = True

' Start spell checking.
VTSpell1.CheckText = OurText
retcode = VTSpell1.ResultCode

' Loop until we've finished spell checking.
Do While retcode <= 0
    Select Case retcode
        ' Spell checking is completed.
        Case 0:
            Exit Do
        ' Handle misspelled word or ignore/replace condition.
        Case VTST_WORD_MISSPELLED, VTST_IGNORE_REPLACE:

            ' Invoke pop-up.
            VTSpell1.PopUp = VTPOP_MISSPELL
            retcode = VTSpell1.ResultCode

            ' Exit on error or if the user pushed the cancel button.
            If (retcode > 0) Or (retcode = VTST_CHECK_CANCELED) Then
                Exit Do
            End If
    End Select

    ' Resume spell checking the text.
    VTSpell1.ResumeCheck = VTRC_NOCHECK
    retcode = VTSpell1.ResultCode
Loop
OurText = VTSpell1.CheckText
```

Before starting the spell check, you'll notice that we set the *ClearCounts* property to *True*. VT-Speller keeps track of the total number of words that have been spell checked, as well as the number of words that have been replaced, in the *WordCount* and *ReplaceCount* properties. These properties retain their values between spell checking sessions, so you can reset them to zero simply by setting *ClearCounts* to any value.

The spell checking process begins when you set the *CheckText* string. The process is interrupted either when a misspelled word is encountered or VT-Speller has finished checking the text. To determine what has interrupted the process, you check the *ResultCode* property. The example assigns the *ResultCode* to a variable called *retcode* whose value is checked for the While loop condition.

Inside the loop, you evaluate *retcode* to see what action you should take. If the *retcode* is 0, then spell checking has completed and you can exit the loop. If VT-Speller has encountered a misspelled word or ignore/replace condition, you want to display the built-in Word Not Found dialog, which is shown in Figure 10-5. You show the dialog by setting the *PopUp* property to the constant VTPOP_MISSPELL. You can also use the *PopUp* property to display the built-in Spelling Options and Error dialog boxes.

The Word Not Found dialog shows the user the misspelled word and lets him or her select a replacement or ignore the word. The dialog provides options for ignoring or

**10◀**

replacing all subsequent occurrences of the word, and for adding the word to a custom dictionary. The user can also set spell checking options from here, or abandon the entire spell checking process.

Once the user has selected an option from the dialog, control is returned to the Visual Basic program. In the example, the next step is to check the return code set after the dialog was displayed. If an error occurred or the user selected the Cancel Spellcheck option, then we want to exit the spell checking loop.

At the end of the loop, you set the *ResumeCheck* property, which tells VT-Speller to continue spell checking the current text string. The value passed to *ResumeCheck* indicates whether the replacement word (the word the user told VT-Speller to use as a replacement for the last misspelling) should be rechecked. At this point the program jumps to the beginning of the loop and begins the process again.

**Setting Spell Checking Options**  VT-Speller gives you considerable control over the spell checking process, so you don't have to use the built-in dialogs. You can, in fact, completely automate the spell checking process so that no user feedback is required.

Several VT-Speller options affect the performance of the spell checking process. The easiest way to set these options is to use the built-in Spell Options dialog mentioned earlier, and shown in Figure 10-6. You can display this dialog by setting the *PopUp* property to the integer constant VTPOP_OPTIONS at run time.

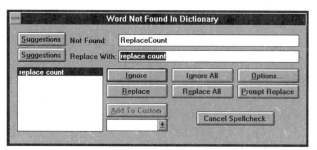

**Figure 10-5** The built-in Word Not Found dialog box

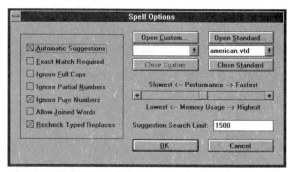

**Figure 10-6** The built-in Spell Options dialog box

The check boxes on the left of the dialog show several of the word checking criteria. Most of these options are self-explanatory. The Allow Joined Words check box determines whether hyphenated words should be considered "correct" if both parts of the word are spelled correctly. Otherwise, the entire hyphenated word must be found in the dictionary for it to be considered correct.

The Performance scroll bar lets the user determine the trade-off between spell checking speed and memory conservation. The dictionary drop-down lists let the user change dictionaries on the fly.

You can also set all of the options presented in the dialog by setting properties in your Visual Basic code. You set most of these options using the *SpellOptions* property, which forms a bit-mask that determines the current options. VT-Speller defines constants that are combined using the logical Or operator. For example, this statement:

```
VTSpell1.SpellOptions = VTSP_AUTO_REPLACE Or VTSP_AUTO_SUGGEST
```

is the same as setting the *AutoReplace* and *AutoSuggest* properties to *True*.

# Example

While many high-end applications such as word processors come equipped with built-in spell checking features, there is still a wide range of applications that handle text but don't provide this feature. One of the great things about Windows is its ability to exchange data between different programs using Dynamic Data Exchange (DDE). The simplest form of DDE is the ability to cut, copy, and paste data, including text data, through the Windows Clipboard.

The example program is a Clipboard spell checker. It extracts unformatted text from the Windows Clipboard, spell checks it, and then returns the corrected text to the Clipboard. This lets you add spell checking abilities to a wide range of applications that don't currently support it. The example program works with programs that deal in formatted text, such as Windows Write, but with these applications you may lose some of the text formatting, including boldfaced and italicized text, after spell checking.

Figure 10-7 shows the example program. Spell checking an application's text is a three-step process. As an example, suppose you want to spell check a README file you've written using the Windows Notepad. First, you load the file into Notepad, choose Select All from the Edit menu to select and highlight all the text in the file, and then select Copy from the Edit menu to copy the text to the Windows Clipboard. Second,

**Figure 10-7** The VT-Speller example program

you run the example program and press the Spell Check button. This initiates the spell checking process, which continues until the entire Clipboard has been checked or you elect to cancel. During the spell checking process, the built-in Word Not Found dialog displays any misspelled words, and the phrase, with the misspelled word highlighted, appears in a text box in the example program. This allows you to see the misspelled word in context. The example program copies the corrected text back to the Clipboard. The third and final step is to return to Notepad and replace the highlighted text with the corrected text using the Paste option on the Edit menu. You can spell check individual paragraphs and sections of text in a similar manner.

## Steps

1. Create a new project called VTSPELLR.MAK. Add the VT-Speller control, VTSPELL.VBX, and the VT-Speller constants file, VTSPELL.BAS, to the project.

2. Create a new form with the objects and properties described in Table 10-15. Save this form as VTSPELLR.FRM.

**Table 10-15** Objects and properties of VTSPELLR.FRM

| OBJECT | PROPERTY | SETTING |
|--------|----------|---------|
| Form | FormName | frmVTSpeller |
| | BackColor | &H00C0C0C0& |
| | BorderStyle | 1 'Fixed Single |
| | Caption | "VT-Speller Demo" |
| | MaxButton | 0 'False |
| Label | Name | Label1 |
| | BackStyle | 0 'Transparent |
| | Caption | "Context:" |
| | ForeColor | &H00000080& |
| Label | Name | Label2 |
| | BackStyle | 0 'Transparent |
| | Caption | "Select text from another application and Copy it to the Clipboard. After spell checking, you can paste the corrected text back into the application from the Clipboard." |
| | FontBold | 0 'False |
| | ForeColor | &H00800000& |
| Label | Name | Label3 |
| | BackStyle | 0 'Transparent |
| | Caption | "Clipboard Spell Checker" |
| | FontSize | 9.75 |
| | ForeColor | &H00000080& |

| OBJECT | PROPERTY | SETTING |
| --- | --- | --- |
| CommandButton | Name | btnCheck |
|  | Caption | "Spell &Check" |
| TextBox | Name | txtFromClip |
|  | HideSelection | 0 'False |
|  | MultiLine | -1 'True |
|  | Visible | 0 'False |
| VTSPELL | Name | VTSpell1 |
| TextBox | Name | txtDisplay |
|  | BackColor | &H00808080& |
|  | ForeColor | &H00FFFFFF& |
|  | HideSelection | 0 'False |
|  | MultiLine | -1 'True |
| CommandButton | Name | btnCancel |
|  | Caption | "E&xit" |

3. Add the following code to the declarations section of the VTSPELLR.FRM form.

```
Option Explicit
'-------------------------------------------------------
' Constants used by the VT-Speller example program.
'-------------------------------------------------------

' Clipboard constant used by SetText/GetText.
Const CF_TEXT = 1

' MsgBox constants.
Const MB_OK = &H0
Const MB_YESNO = &H4

Const MB_ICONQUESTION = &H20
Const MB_ICONEXCLAMATION = &H30
Const MB_ICONINFORMATION = &H40
Const MB_ICONSTOP = &H10

Const IDYES = 6
```

4. Add the following subroutines to the VTSPELLR.FRM form. Most of the work in this program is handled in the Spell Check button's click event, which contains the main spell checking loop.

```
Sub btnCancel_Click ()
'-------------------------------------------------------
' Exit the program.
'-------------------------------------------------------

    Unload Me
End Sub

Sub btnCheck_Click ()
```

*(continued on next page)*

**10**

*(continued from previous page)*

```
'---------------------------------------------------
' Extract the text contents of the clipboard,
' spell check the text, and then replace the corrected
' text back into the Clipboard.
'---------------------------------------------------
Dim retcode As Integer
Dim i As Integer
Dim LF As String
Dim answer As Integer
Dim ChangesMade As Integer

    On Error GoTo btnCheck_Error

    ' LineFeed character
    LF = Chr$(&HA)

    ' Extract text from the clipboard.
    txtFromClip = Clipboard.GetText(CF_TEXT)

    ' Reset the ReplaceCount and WordCount properties to 0.
    VTSpell1.ClearCounts = True

    ' We don't want pop-up to remain onscreen all the time
    ' this would prevent us from highlighting the text in the text control.
    VTSpell1.AutoPopUp = False

    ' Determine which events are enabled (none).
    VTSpell1.EventOptions = 0

    ' Handle global replace conditions automatically.
    VTSpell1.AutoReplace = True

    ' We've made no changes to the data.
    ChangesMade = False

    ' Start spell checking.
    VTSpell1.CheckText = txtFromClip
    retcode = VTSpell1.ResultCode

    ' Loop until we've finished spell checking
    Do While retcode <= 0
        Select Case retcode
            ' Spell checking is completed.
            Case 0:
                Exit Do
            ' Handle misspelled word or ignore/replace condition.
            Case VTST_WORD_MISSPELLED, VTST_IGNORE_REPLACE:

                ' Detected a misspelled word.
                If (VTSpell1.ReplaceOccurred = True) Then
                    txtFromClip = VTSpell1.Text
                End If

                ' Highlight the word in the text "buffer" control
                txtFromClip.SelStart = VTSpell1.WordOffset
                txtFromClip.SelLength = Len(VTSpell1.MisspelledWord)

                ' Display just a substring of the text, including the
                ' misspelled word, to let the user see the word in context.
```

```
                    For i = txtFromClip.SelStart To (txtFromClip.SelStart - 50) Step -1
                        If (i = 0) Then
                            Exit For
                        ElseIf (Mid$(txtFromClip, i, 1) = LF) Then
                            Exit For
                        End If
                    Next
                    txtDisplay = Mid$(txtFromClip, i + 1, (txtFromClip.SelStart - i +
            txtFromClip.SelLength + 140))
                    txtDisplay.SelStart = txtFromClip.SelStart - i
                    txtDisplay.SelLength = txtFromClip.SelLength

                    ' Invoke pop-up.
                    VTSpell1.PopUp = VTPOP_MISSPELL
                    retcode = VTSpell1.ResultCode

                    ' Exit if an error occurred.
                    If (retcode > 0) Then Exit Do

                    ' Exit if the user pushed the Cancel button.
                    If (retcode = VTST_CHECK_CANCELED) Then
                        Exit Do
                    End If

                    ' If the word was replaced, update the text.
                    If (VTSpell1.ReplaceOccurred = True) Then
                        txtFromClip = VTSpell1.Text
                        ChangesMade = True
                    End If
            End Select

            ' Allow other events during spell checking.
            DoEvents

            ' Resume spell checking the text.
            VTSpell1.ResumeCheck = VTRC_NOCHECK
            retcode = VTSpell1.ResultCode
        Loop

        ' Replace the changed text.
        If (VTSpell1.ReplaceOccurred = True) Or ChangesMade Then
            answer = MsgBox("Do you want to update the Clipboard with the corrected text?",
    MB_YESNO Or MB_ICONQUESTION, "Update Clipboard")
            If answer = IDYES Then
                txtFromClip = VTSpell1.CheckText
                Clipboard.Clear
                Clipboard.SetText txtFromClip, CF_TEXT
            End If
        End If
        txtDisplay = ""
    Exit Sub
    btnCheck_Error:
        MsgBox "Error " & Format$(Err) & ": " & Error$(Err), MB_OK Or MB_ICONEXCLAMATION, "Error
    During Spell Check"
        Resume Next
    End Sub

    Sub Form_Load ()
```

10◄

*(continued on next page)*

*(continued from previous page)*

```
'-------------------------------------------------
' Position the form in the upper-left corner of
' the screen.
'-------------------------------------------------

    Me.Move 0, 0
End Sub
```

## Tips and Comments

Visual Tools' VT-Speller and MicroHelp's SpellPro are both good, solid products that can meet most any spell checking needs. Like any set of similar products, their differences arise from slightly different design goals. You'll have to decide which product's features and design best meet your application's needs.

# 11

# DATABASE CONTROLS
# AND LIBRARIES

At the core of almost every business or personal productivity application is some form of database. There is a staggering number of PC database file formats. XBase, Paradox, Access, SQL Server, Oracle, and many others are available to developers. Which product is best for a particular task? This question can easily lead to heated debates among developers. What is safe to say is that databases, together with the user interface, represent the bulk of the effort required to deploy most modern business (and many nonbusiness) applications.

With Visual Basic 3.0, Microsoft provided a built-in method for getting to much of this data. The database control and ODBC-compatible database objects included in that version of Visual Basic pointed to the power of Visual Basic as a tool for Windows database development. ODBC, or Open Database Connectivity, is Microsoft's standard interface for connecting to heterogeneous database systems.

The concept of data-aware, or bound, controls also changed the way many programmers thought about database development. Data-aware controls saved developers from having to extract data from a database and populate the fields of a form through tedious coding. They could now simply bind a field to a data-aware control at design time, and let the data control handle retrieving and saving data.

While some of the products covered in this chapter are designed to work with Microsoft's Data control, others take a more traditional approach. Several of the products are not .VBX controls at all; some are dynamic link libraries (DLL) and one is a Visual Basic source code library.

▲ **Crystal Reports** Crystal Reports can produce printed reports of data gathered from a wide variety of sources. Its report designer gives you complete control over the size and placement of fields at design time, and gives you control of the run time report via formulas that you build.

▲ **Data Widgets** Data Widgets builds on the strength of the data control. Data Widgets provides a set of bound controls that extend the data control's power.

▲ **VB/ISAM** VB/ISAM is a robust and powerful ISAM data manager packed into a small (less than 50K) dynamic link library (DLL). VB/ISAM can easily handle large (up to 512 MB) data files.

▲ **Visual/db** Visual/db isn't a control at all, but rather a library of dBASE file access routines. It's completely procedural, and is written entirely in Visual Basic. It illustrates Visual Basic's power as a general-purpose application development tool.

▲ **Data Control** Microsoft's Data Control created the concept of bound, data-aware controls. This control can automatically perform many of the simple database-navigation functions, such as stepping back and forth through records.

# Crystal Reports (CRYSTAL.VBX)

| USAGE: | Database Report Writer |
|---|---|
| MANUFACTURER: | Crystal Reports |
| COST: | $495, Upgrade from VB3 available |

One thing Visual Basic does not do well is print and generate reports. One thing Crystal Reports does *very* well is generate and print reports from an amazing number of data sources. It can read and print reports from Access 1.1/2.0, Paradox, Oracle, FoxPro, dBASE, SyBase, and any number of other data formats. Crystal Reports is also shipped with a large number of applications as the "report writer of choice," which makes it a very popular package.

Crystal Reports combines a powerful stand-alone report designer and data dictionary with a report engine that you can access directly through calls to a CRPE.DLL or by using the properties and events of CRYSTAL.VBX. The Crystal Reports report designer gives you full design time control over the size and placement of fields and allows you to control the run time report via formulas that you build. Using formulas gives you total control over a report's data and appearance. The report designer comes with "wizards" that make it easier to design reports; and it understands Cross Tab reports, mailing labels, and the standard report formats.

The Data Dictionary is a very effective addition to the Crystal Reports package. It allows you to give meaningful names to the "interesting" columns in a table, and to build in formulas and table joins so the end users don't need to know the dirty details of SQL and table design. In other words, you can hide the difficult-to-implement details of table manipulation and at the same time enforce the correct use of data. The Data Dictonary can also store graphic images used to make a report look more professional, such as a bitmap of a company logo. Once you've set up the Data Dictonary with all the necessary information, the end user can build any reports using the Crystal Reports report designer, and you can devote your precious time to developing more useful software (or playing Solitaire).

As mentioned, you can access the Crystal Reports engine directly or via the CRYSTAL.VBX custom control. Both approaches have their advantages. CRPE.DLL gives you direct access to much of the functionality of Crystal Reports. It enables you to control the printer; control the report formatting; change the records selected for the report; change the grouping criteria; and determine whether the report should go to a preview window, a formatted output file, or directly to the printer. When you save your report as a file, you can format it for most of the major word processing packages or as a CSV or fixed-length text file. You can change the default location of your database using CRPE.DLL. CRPE.DLL handles logging on to a remote SQL server.

While CRYSTAL.VBX doesn't have all the features available by direct calls to CRPE.DLL, it does have most of them. You can direct the report to a file, a window, or directly to the printer, although you don't have all the file extraction capabilities. You can update formulas and selection criteria, but you can't add any new formulas. You can control the location of any data files, but logging on to remote servers is handled via ODBC and not CRPE. You can control the selection of records for a report, but your selection criteria is "Anded" to the section criteria in a report, and doesn't replace it as it does in CRPE. One thing that the custom control does that CRPE doesn't do is allow you to print a report from custom controls bound to a data control. CRYSTAL.VBX also ties in with the TrueGrid grid control from Apex software, which gives you a bit more control than just a bound control. One problem with printing a report from bound data controls is that you have no control over the format of the report that's generated. If your report line extends past the edge of the paper you lose that information. Both approaches will print report files generated by the Crystal Reports report designer, so if your customer designs a report you can easily add it to your VB program.

11◄

The example program for Crystal Reports shows how to print from controls bound to a database selected at run time. It also demonstrates how to print a report built and saved in the Crystal Reports report designer.

# Syntax

The Crystal Reports VBX allows you to set its basic functionality at design time so that at run time you only need to use the *PrintReport* or *Action* property to print the report to the chosen destination. The most useful properties are listed in Table 11-1 and explained in detail below.

**Table 11-1** Nonstandard properties of the Crystal Reports control

| | | |
|---|---|---|
| AutoDesign | DataFiles | DataSource |
| Destination | PrintFileName | PrintFileType |
| ReportSource | SelectionFormula | SortFields |

The *Destination* property controls where the report is sent. Table 11-2 lists its possible values.

**Table 11-2** Values for the Destination property

| VALUE | MEANING |
|---|---|
| 0 | Window |
| 1 | Printer |
| 2 | File |
| 3 | All data control fields |

You control the source of the data and report layout for the Crystal control using the *DataSource* property. Table 11-3 shows the different settings for this property.

**Table 11-3** Values for the DataSource property

| VALUE | MEANING |
|---|---|
| 0 | Report files built by Crystal Reports |
| 1 | Bound TrueGrid control |
| 2 | Other bound controls |
| 3 | All data control fields |

The *AutoDesign* property lets you generate a .RPT file from the bound controls at design time. Once you've generated the report, you can use the Cystal Reports report designer to customize the layout.

The *SelectionFormula* and *GroupSelectionFormula* properties allow you to customize the data selected and summed by Crystal Reports. This is a Crystal Reports formula you enter at run time rather than design time. If you're using CRYSTAL.VBX, anything you put in this property is Anded to any criteria you've already entered at report design time.

You can also use SQL in the *RecordSource* property of the data control if you're using bound controls or TrueGrid to generate the report.

You use the *PrintFileType* and *PrintFileName* properties when *Destination* is a file and not a window or printer. Using the Crystal control, you have the options for *PrintFileType* listed in Table 11-4. The output file name itself goes into *PrintFileName*.

**Table 11-4** Values for PrintFileType

| VALUE | MEANING |
| --- | --- |
| 0 | Fixed width record |
| 1 | Tab delimited table, text in quotes |
| 2 | Print the report to a text file |
| 3 | DIF |
| 4 | Comma-separated file |
| 6 | Tab-separated ASCII file |

Crystal Reports also lets you exert some control over the appearance of the print preview window by using the *Window...* properties. These properties mirror the same properties for a form, letting you control the size and position of the print preview window; the type of border; the max, min, and system menu; and the window's title.

# Example

The program shown in Figure 11-1 builds a form using control arrays to display data from a database, table, and columns selected at run time.

This example program uses the ability to print "ad hoc" reports from a data control and bound controls at run time. The user tells the example program what database to print a report from. By exploiting the TableDefs and Fields object arrays of the data control, the combo box presents the user with a list of tables, and then the list box presents a list of fields to display on the form and print on the report. By selecting a table and clicking on the Process button, and then choosing fields and clicking the Load button, you load the controls and display data. The DB Options frame controls whether the database is updateable, and whether the database is opened exclusively or is a shared resource.

After choosing the table and fields to be displayed, you select one of the print options from the File menu. Print to Window brings up the Crystal Reports print preview screen shown in Figure 11-2.

From the print preview window, you can choose to print the report, save the report to a file, mail the report via MAPI or VIM, or close the window.

If you choose the Print to File option, a dialog box prompts you for a file to save the report output to and the format for the report. This dialog box is shown in Figure 11-3.

The File menu has one other option, Print .RPT file. This option brings up the dialog box shown in Figure 11-4. If you enter a .RPT file name or take the default one, you'll be given the option to print the report or do a print preview.

11◀

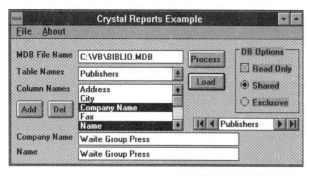

**Figure 11-1** Crystal
Reports example program

**Figure 11-2** The Crystal
Reports print preview window

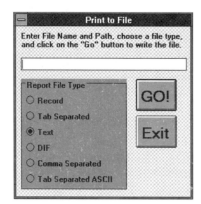

**Figure 11-3** File Save dialog box

**Figure 11-4** Print Report
File dialog box

## Steps

1. Create a new project called DBFORM.MAK. Add CRYSTAL.VBX and CMDIALOG.VBX. Create a new form with the objects and properties shown in Table 11-5. Save this form as DBFORM.FRM.

**Table 11-5** DBFORM main form's objects and properties

| OBJECT | PROPERTY | SETTING |
|---|---|---|
| Label | Name | Label1 |
| | BackStyle | 0 'Transparent |
| | Caption | "MDB File Name" |
| Label | Name | Label2 |
| | BackStyle | 0 'Transparent |
| | Caption | "Table Names" |
| Label | Name | Label3 |
| | BackStyle | 0 'Transparent |
| | Caption | "Column Names" |
| Label | Name | lblMDBField |
| | AutoSize | -1 'True |
| | BackStyle | 0 'Transparent |
| | Caption | "Label4" |
| | Index | 0 |
| | Visible | 0 'False |
| Data | Name | Data1 |
| | Connect | " " |
| | DatabaseName | " " |
| | Exclusive | 0 'False |
| | Options | 0 |
| | ReadOnly | -1 'True |
| | RecordSource | " " |
| TextBox | Name | txtMDBField |
| | DataSource | "Data1" |
| | Index | 0 |
| | Visible | 0 'False |
| TextBox | Name | txtMDBFileName |
| ComboBox | Name | cmbTableNames |
| | Style | 2 'Dropdown List |
| CommandButton | Name | cmdProcess |
| | Caption | "Process" |
| Frame | Name | fraDBOptions |
| | BackColor | &H0080FF80& |
| | Caption | "DB Options" |

*(continued on next page)*

**11◄**

| OBJECT | PROPERTY | SETTING |
|---|---|---|
| *(continued from previous page)* | | |
| CommandButton | Name | cmdLoad |
| | Caption | "Load" |
| ListBox | Name | lstColumnNames |
| | MultiSelect | 2 'Extended |
| | Sorted | -1 'True |
| CommonDialog | Name | CMDialog1 |
| | DefaultExt | "mdb" |
| | DialogTitle | "Locate MDB Files" |
| | Filename | "*.mdb" |
| | Filter | "*.mdb" |
| CrystalReport | Name | Report1 |
| | BoundReportFooter= | 'False |
| | Connect | " " |
| | CopiesToPrinter | 1 |
| | DataSource | "Data1" |
| | Destination | 0 'Window |
| | PrintFileName | " " |
| | PrintFileType | 2 'Text |
| | ReportFileName | " " |
| | ReportSource | 3 'All Data Control Fields |
| | SessionHandle | 0 |
| | UserName | " " |
| | WindowBorderStyle= | 'Sizable |
| | WindowControlBox= | 'True |
| | WindowHeight | 300 |
| | WindowLeft | 100 |
| | WindowMaxButton | -1 'True |
| | WindowMinButton | -1 'True |
| | WindowTitle | " " |
| | WindowTop | 100 |
| | WindowWidth | 480 |
| CommandButton | Name | cmdAdd |
| | Caption | "Add" |
| CommandButton | Name | cmdDel |
| | Caption | "Del" |
| Form | FormName | DBForm |
| | BackColor | &H0080FF80& |
| | Caption | "Crystal Reports Example" |

2. Select fraDBOptions and add objects and properties shown in Table 11-6.

**Table 11-6** fraDBOptions' objects and properties

| OBJECT | PROPERTY | SETTING |
|---|---|---|
| OptionButton | Name | optDBopts |
| | BackColor | &H0080FF80& |
| | Caption | "Shared" |
| | Index | 1 |
| | Value | -1 'True |
| OptionButton | Name | optDBopts |
| | BackColor | &H0080FF80& |
| | Caption | "Exclusive" |
| | Index | 2 |
| CheckBox | Name | chkReadOnly |
| | BackColor | &H0080FF80& |
| | Caption | "Read Only" |
| | Value | 1 'Checked |

3. Add the menu shown in Table 11-7 to DBFORM.

**Table 11-7** DBForm main form's menu

| CAPTION | NAME |
|---|---|
| &File | mnuFile |
| – – – – S&earch | mnuSearch |
| – – – – – | mnuDash1 |
| – – – – Print To &Window | mnuPrint(1) |
| – – – – Print To &Printer | mnuPrint(2) |
| – – – – Print To &File | mnuPrint(3) |
| – – – – – | mnuDash2 |
| – – – – Print .&RPT File | mnuPrintRPTFile |
| – – – – – | mnuDash3 |
| – – – – E&xit | mnuExit |
| &About | mnuAbout |

4. Add the following code to the declarations section of the DBFORM form. These declarations set up the constants and shared variables used by DBFORM.

```
Option Explicit

    Const CM_OPEN = 1
    Const CHECKED = 1
```

**11**◄

*(continued on next page)*

*(continued from previous page)*

```
      Const OPT_SHARED = 1 ' Which option button is which.

      Dim TopOff As Integer ' where the first text box should go.
      Dim FieldSep As Integer ' DIstance between 2 columns.
      Dim StartHeight As Integer ' Offset due to menu.
      Dim textBoxHeight As Integer ' How tall is my text box.

      Dim MDBTextTable() As textbox

      Const DB_BOOLEAN = 1 '  True/False Integer (0 or 1)      c
      Const DB_BYTE = 2'  Byte Integer (0  255)
      Const DB_INTEGER = 3 ' Integer Integer
      Const DB_LONG = 4'   Long Long
      Const DB_CURRENCY = 5 '   Currency Double
      Const DB_SINGLE = 6 '   Single Single
      Const DB_DOUBLE = 7 '   Double Double
      Const DB_DATE = 8'  Date/Time Variant
      Const DB_TEXT = 10'  Text String
      Const DB_LONGBINARY = 11 ' Long Binary String
      Const DB_MEMO = 12'  Memo String
```

5. Add the following constants to the PRNTFILE form.

```
      Option Explicit
      Const REPORTTOFILE = 2

      Const MB_OKCANCEL = 1
      Const MB_ICONQUESTION = 32
      Const IDOK = 1

      Dim printing As Integer
```

6. Add the following code to the DBFORM form. This code gets the table from the text box and loads it into the data control. Once the data control is loaded, it uses the TableDefs collection to list all the tables. Notice that the system tables are filtered out in a very sophisticated fashion. When a table is chosen using the Process button the fields from the Fields collection are loaded into the list box. After the program fills in the list box the user selects the columns to view and clicks on the load button. The program loads text on label controls to display the selected columns. The text controls are also loaded into a table of text box objects so it's simple to clear them when the time comes.

```
Sub chkReadOnly_Click ()
    If chkReadOnly = CHECKED Then
          data1.ReadOnly = True
    Else
          data1.ReadOnly = False
    End If

    data1.Refresh

End Sub

Sub clearcols ()
    Dim TopofTable As Integer
    Dim i As Integer
```

```
        ' TopofTable = UBound(txtMDBField)
        If TopofTable > 1 Then
          ' I don't care if there's an error here because
          ' it's possible there are holes in the control array.
          On Error Resume Next
          For i = 1 To TopofTable - 1
              Unload txtMDBField(i)
          Next i
          ' Reset error handling.
          On Error GoTo 0
        End If

End Sub

Sub cmbTableNames_Click ()

    Dim numcols As Integer
    Dim i As Integer

    lstColumnNames.Clear

    numcols = data1.Database.TableDefs(cmbTableNames.Text).Fields.Count

    data1.Caption = cmbTableNames.Text

    If numcols = 0 Then Exit Sub

    For i = 0 To numcols - 1
          ' Can't easily handle LONGBINARY or MEMO, so skip'm.
          If data1.Database.TableDefs(cmbTableNames.Text).Fields(i).Type <> DB_LONGBINARY Then
          If data1.Database.TableDefs(cmbTableNames.Text).Fields(i).Type <> DB_MEMO Then
            lstColumnNames.AddItem data1.Database.TableDefs(cmbTableNames.Text).Fields(i).Name
          End If
      End If
    Next i

End Sub

Sub cmdAdd_Click ()
    If data1.RecordSource  "" And Not (MDBTextTable(1) Is Nothing) And chkReadOnly <> CHECKED Then
          data1.Recordset.AddNew
    End If
End Sub

Sub cmdDel_Click ()
    If data1.RecordSource  "" And Not (MDBTextTable(1) Is Nothing) And chkReadOnly <> CHECKED Then
      data1.Recordset.Delete
      data1.Recordset.MoveFirst
    End If
End Sub

Sub cmdLoad_Click ()

    Static ProcessingMDB As Integer

    If cmbTableNames.Text = "" Or ProcessingMDB = True Then
          Exit Sub
    End If
```

*(continued on next page)*

11◀

*(continued from previous page)*

```
    data1.RecordSource = cmbTableNames.Text
    ProcessingMDB = True

    Dim i As Integer
    Dim j As Integer
    Dim cntl_ss As Integer
    Dim ColumnName As String

    i = lstColumnNames.ListIndex

    'Unload any existing controls.
    UnloadControls

    data1.Refresh

    DoEvents

    cntl_ss = 0

    For i = 0 To lstColumnNames.ListCount - 1
        If lstColumnNames.Selected(i) = True Then
            j = i + 1
            ColumnName = lstColumnNames.List(i)
            Load txtMDBField(j)
            Load lblMDBField(j)
            ' Doing this preserves resources at the expense of
            'speed.
            cntl_ss = cntl_ss + 1
            ReDim Preserve MDBTextTable(1 To cntl_ss)
            txtMDBField(j).Top = TopOff + ((cntl_ss - 1) * (textBoxHeight + FieldSep))
            lblMDBField(j).Top = txtMDBField(j).Top
            txtMDBField(j).DataField = ColumnName
            lblMDBField(j) = ColumnName
            txtMDBField(j).Tag = Format$(j, "000") & ColumnName
            lblMDBField(j).Tag = ColumnName
            ' These are just rough approximations of file sizes
            'for a text column; you should probably use the size
            ' property.
            Select Case
data1.Database.TableDefs(cmbTableNames.Text).Fields(ColumnName).Type
            'Case DB_BOOLEAN    ' True/False  Integer (0 or 1)
            Case DB_BYTE       ' Byte     Integer (0  255)
                txtMDBField(j).Width = Me.TextWidth("999")
            Case DB_INTEGER    ' Integer Integer
                txtMDBField(j).Width = Me.TextWidth("999999")
            Case DB_LONG       ' Long     Long
                txtMDBField(j).Width = Me.TextWidth("99999999999")
            Case DB_CURRENCY   ' Currency    Double
                txtMDBField(j).Width = Me.TextWidth("9999999.9999")
            Case DB_SINGLE     ' Single Single
                txtMDBField(j).Width = Me.TextWidth("99999999.999")
            Case DB_DOUBLE     ' Double Double
                txtMDBField(j).Width = Me.TextWidth("9999999999999.99999")
            Case DB_DATE       ' Date/Time   Variant
                txtMDBField(j).Width = Me.TextWidth("M") * 20
            Case DB_TEXT       ' Text    String
                txtMDBField(j).Width = Me.TextWidth("M") *
data1.Database.TableDefs(cmbTableNames.Text).Fields(ColumnName).Size
            'Case DB_LONGBINARY ' Long Binary String
```

```
                    'Case DB_MEMO           '  Memo     String
            End Select
                If txtMDBField(j).Width > Me.Width Then
                        txtMDBField(j).Width = Me.Width - (txtMDBField(j).Left * 2)
                End If
                txtMDBField(j).Visible = True
                lblMDBField(j).Visible = True
                Set MDBTextTable(cntl_ss) = txtMDBField(j)
            End If
    Next i

    DoEvents

    Me.Height = StartHeight + (textBoxHeight + FieldSep) * cntl_ss

    data1.Refresh
    ProcessingMDB = False

End Sub

Sub cmdProcess_Click ()

    Dim i As Integer
    Dim tempDBName As String

    If txtMDBFileName = "" Then Exit Sub

    ' Restore form height
    Me.Height = StartHeight

    ' Clear any loaded controls
    UnloadControls

    data1.DatabaseName = txtMDBFileName
    data1.RecordSource = ""' Clear out the old table name.
    data1.Caption = ""
    setDBOpts
    data1.Refresh

    cmbTableNames.Clear ' Clear the combo and list box.
    lstColumnNames.Clear

    For i = 0 To data1.Database.TableDefs.Count - 1
      tempDBName = data1.Database.TableDefs(i)
      If Left(UCase(tempDBName), 4) <> "MSYS" Then
          cmbTableNames.AddItem tempDBName
      End If
    Next i

End Sub

Sub Form_Load ()
    Me.Move (Screen.Width - Me.Width) \ 2, (Screen.Height - Me.Height) \ 2

    'Separate the fields by 1/10 the field height.
    FieldSep = txtMDBField(0).Height \ 10

    ReDim MDBTextTable(1 To 1)

    StartHeight = Me.Height
```

**11**

*(continued on next page)*

*(continued from previous page)*

```vb
        TopOff = TopOff + lstColumnNames.Top + lstColumnNames.Height + FieldSep
        textBoxHeight = txtMDBField(0).Height

End Sub

Sub mnuAbout_Click ()
        frmAbout.Show
End Sub

Sub mnuExit_Click ()
        ' Unload all the forms used in this demo.
        Unload frmAbout
        Unload PrintReport
        Unload PrinttoFile
        Unload Me
End Sub

Sub mnuPrint_Click (index As Integer)

        Const GETFILEINFO = 2

        Dim res As Integer

        If index = GETFILEINFO Then
                report1.PrintFileName = ""
                PrinttoFile.Show 1 ' show the form modally
                If report1.PrintFileName = "" Then Exit Sub
        Else
                report1.Destination = index
        End If
        res = (report1.PrintReport)

        If res <> 0 Then MsgBox "Crystal Reports Error" & " " & Format$(res) & " " &
report1.LastErrorString

End Sub

Sub mnuPrintRPTFile_Click ()
        PrintReport.Show
End Sub

Sub mnuSearch_Click ()
        CMDialog1.Action = CM_OPEN

        If CMDialog1.Filename  "" Then
          txtMDBFileName = CMDialog1.Filename
        End If
End Sub

Sub optDBopts_Click (index As Integer)
        If index = 1 Then
                data1.Exclusive = False
        Else
                data1.Exclusive = True
        End If
                data1.Refresh
End Sub

Sub setDBOpts ()
        If optDBopts(OPT_SHARED) = True Then
```

```
        data1.Exclusive = False
    Else
        data1.Exclusive = True
    End If

    If chkReadOnly = CHECKED Then
        data1.ReadOnly = True
    Else
        data1.ReadOnly = False
    End If
End Sub

Sub UnloadControls ()
    Dim i As Integer
    Dim j As Integer
    Dim cntl_ss As Integer

    j = UBound(MDBTextTable)

    For i = 1 To j
        ' test for nothing to verify we have actually loaded
        ' a control in the array.  This will only happen
        ' first time into this program.
        If Not (MDBTextTable(i) Is Nothing) Then
            cntl_ss = Val(Left$(MDBTextTable(i).Tag, 3))
            Set MDBTextTable(i) = Nothing
            Unload txtMDBField(cntl_ss)
            Unload lblMDBField(cntl_ss)
        End If
    Next i

End Sub
```

7. Create a new form with the objects and properties shown in Table 11-8. Save this form as PRNTFILE.FRM.

**Table 11-8** PRNTFILE form's objects and properties

| OBJECT | PROPERTY | SETTING |
|---|---|---|
| TextBox | Name | txtPrintFileName |
| CommandButton | Name | cmdGo |
| | Caption | "GO!" |
| | Default | -1 'True |
| | FontSize | 24 |
| CommandButton | Name | cmdExit |
| | Cancel | -1 'True |
| | Caption | "Exit" |
| | FontSize | 24 |
| Frame | Name | fraReportFileType |
| | BackColor | &H00FFFF00& |
| | Caption | "Report File Type" |

11◀

*(continued on next page)*

| OBJECT | PROPERTY | SETTING |
|---|---|---|
| *(continued from previous page)* | | |
| Form | FormName | PrinttoFile |
| | BackColor | &H0080FFFF& |
| | Caption | "Print to File" |
| | MaxButton | 0 'False |
| | MinButton | 0 'False |

8. Select the fraReportFileType control and add the objects and properties shown in Table 11-9.

**Table 11-9** fraReportFileType's objects and properties

| OBJECT | PROPERTY | SETTING |
|---|---|---|
| OptionButton | Name | optReportType |
| | BackColor | &H00FFFF00& |
| | Caption | "Record" |
| | Index | 0 |
| OptionButton | Name | optReportType |
| | BackColor | &H00FFFF00& |
| | Caption | "Tab Separated" |
| | Index | 1 |
| OptionButton | Name | optReportType |
| | BackColor | &H00FFFF00& |
| | Caption | "Text" |
| | Index | 2 |
| | Value | -1 'True |
| OptionButton | Name | optReportType |
| | BackColor | &H00FFFF00& |
| | Caption | "DIF" |
| | Index | 3 |
| OptionButton | Name | optReportType |
| | BackColor | &H00FFFF00& |
| | Caption | "Comma Separated" |
| | Index | 4 |
| OptionButton | Name | optReportType |
| | BackColor | &H00FFFF00& |
| | Caption | "Tab Separated" |
| | Index | 6 |

9. Add the following code to the PRNTFILE form. This code gets the data set from the text box and loads it into the Crystal control. Before the Crystal control is loaded, the hard drive is searched to see if the requested output file exists. If it does, the app prompts you to verify whether you really want to overwrite the output file.

```
Sub cmdExit_Click ()
    If printing = True Then Exit Sub
    Unload Me
End Sub

Sub cmdGo_Click ()

    Dim holdname As String
    Dim res As Integer

    On Error Resume Next

    holdname = ""

    If txtPrintFileName = "" Then Exit Sub ' No file entered:  just get out.

    holdname = Dir$(txtPrintFileName)

    If Err Then
        MsgBox "File name was invalid or other error occurred."
        Exit Sub
    End If

    If holdname <> "" Then
        res = MsgBox("File " & txtPrintFileName & " exists, overwrite?", MB_OKCANCEL +
MB_ICONQUESTION, "Overwrite File?")
        If res <> IDOK Then Exit Sub
    End If

    printing = True
    dbForm!Report1.PrintFileName = txtPrintFileName
    dbForm!Report1.Destination = REPORTTOFILE
    printing = False
    Unload Me
End Sub

Sub Form_Load ()
    Me.Move (Screen.Width - Me.Width) \ 2, (Screen.Height - Me.Height) \ 2
End Sub

Sub Form_QueryUnload (cancel As Integer, UnloadMode As Integer)
    If printing = True Then cancel = True
End Sub

Sub optReportType_Click (index As Integer)
    dbForm!Report1.PrintFileType = index
End Sub
```

10. Create a new form with the objects and properties shown in Table 11-10. Save this form as PRINTRPT.FRM.

**Table 11-10** PRINTRPT form's objects and properties

| OBJECT | PROPERTY | SETTING |
|---|---|---|
| CrystalReport | Name | rptReportFile |
| | BoundReportFooter= | 'False |
| | Connect | " " |
| | CopiesToPrinter | 1 |
| | Destination | 0 'Window |
| | PrintFileName | " " |
| | PrintFileType | 2 'Text |
| | ReportFileName | " " |
| | ReportSource | 0 'Report File |
| | SessionHandle | 0 |
| | UserName | " " |
| | WindowBorderStyle= | 'Sizable |
| | WindowControlBox= | 'True |
| | WindowHeight | 300 |
| | WindowLeft | 100 |
| | WindowMaxButton | -1 'True |
| | WindowMinButton | -1 'True |
| | WindowTitle | " " |
| | WindowTop | 100 |
| | WindowWidth | 480 |
| CommandButton | Name | Command1 |
| | Caption | "Print" |
| Frame | Name | fraDestination |
| | Caption | "Destination" |
| TextBox | Name | txtReportFileName |
| Form | FormName | PrintReport |
| | Caption | "Print Report File" |

11. Select fraDestination and add the objects and properties shown in Table 11-11.

**Table 11-11** fraDestination's objects and properties

| OBJECT | PROPERTY | SETTING |
|---|---|---|
| OptionButton | Name | optReportDestination |
| | Caption | "Printer" |
| | Index | 1 |
| OptionButton | Name | optReportDestination |
| | Caption | "Window" |
| | Index | 0 |
| | Value | -1 'True |

12. Add the menu shown in Table 11-12 to PRINTRPT.

**Table 11-12** PRINTRPT form's menu

| CAPTION | NAME |
| --- | --- |
| &Exit | mnuExit |

13. Finally, add the following code to the PRINTRPT form. This form deals with .RPT files generated from Crystal Reports.

```
Option Explicit

Sub Command1_Click ()

    Dim res As Integer

    rptReportFile.ReportFileName = txtReportFileName
    res = (rptReportFile.PrintReport)

    If res  0 Then MsgBox "Crystal Reports Error" & " " & Format$(res) & " " &
rptReportFile.LastErrorString


End Sub

Sub Form_Load ()
    ' Load the report file name with the "default report."
    txtReportFileName = app.Path & "\" & "wggbcrwt.rpt"

    Me.Move (Screen.Width - Me.Width) \ 2, (Screen.Height - Me.Height) \ 2

End Sub

Sub mnuExit_Click ()
Unload Me
End Sub

Sub optReportDestination_Click (index As Integer)
    rptReportFile.Destination = index
End Sub
```

# Tips and Comments

Crystal Reports is a powerful add-on for Visual Basic. It lets you print reports designed by you or your customers from a database or data dictionary, or lets you print ad hoc reports from controls built at run time. Crystal Reports provides many ways of approaching report management. Crystal Reports has some clumsy portions and its documentation can be rough going. At the same time, it's a very flexible and easy-to-use tool. Its biggest shortcoming is its inability to control the format of a report built at run time (see Figure 11-2), but if you stick to designing your reports in the Crystal Report editor that won't be a problem.

11

# Data Control

| USAGE: | Database Access |
|---|---|
| MANUFACTURER: | Microsoft |
| COST: | Included with Visual Basic 3.0 Professional Editor |

The Data control, which comes with Visual Basic 3.0, can be used to establish a connection to several database formats, including Microsoft Access. The Data control has VCR-style buttons that you can use to automatically move between records in a database table.

## Syntax

You can use the Data control as the glue that binds other controls, such as labels, images, and check boxes, to fields in a database. Table 11-13 lists the nonstandard properties, events, and methods of the Data control.

**Table 11-13** Nonstandard properties, events, and methods for the Data control

### PROPERTIES

| | | |
|---|---|---|
| Connect | Database | DatabaseName |
| EditMode | Exclusive | Options |
| ReadOnly | RecordSet | RecordSource |

### EVENTS

| | | |
|---|---|---|
| Error | Reposition | Validate |

### METHODS

| | |
|---|---|
| UpdateControls | UpdateRecords |

The Data control makes it easy to connect to a simple database table and display its contents. Let's say you've built a simple Access database with just two fields: your friends' names (called *Name*) and their phone numbers (called *Phone*). You've saved the table as *PhoneNumbers* in a database file called FRIENDS.MDB. Now you want to write a little Visual Basic program to display your table.

The first step is to create a form and place three controls on it: the Data control and two label controls. You should change the *Name* property of the labels to *lblName* and *lblPhone* to help tell them apart. You can leave the Data control with its default name, *Data1*.

Next, you set the *DatabaseName* property of the Data control so that it points to FRIENDS.MDB. Double-clicking on this property in the Visual Basic Properties window displays a common File Open dialog box, making it easy to set the property. Now you can set the *RecordSource* property, where you tell the Data control which table you want to connect to. If you click on the *RecordSource* property, a list of available tables is displayed. In this case, there's only one, *PhoneNumbers,* so you select it. You are done with the Data control.

Now you need to bind the two labels to the database. Click on the label *lblName* and press the (F4) key to pop up the Visual Basic Properties window. Double-click on the *DataSource* property and the property's value changes to *Data1*, the name of the Data control. If you were using multiple data controls on the same form, you could have selected from a list of the available data controls. Next, select the *DataField* property and click on the drop-down list button near the top of the Properties window. You should see a list of the fields available in the *PhoneNumber* table. Select the *Name* field from the list. Repeat this process for the *lblPhone* label, this time selecting the *Phone* field.

That's it. Now you should be able to run the program, which will automatically display the first record in the *PhoneNumbers* table. Using the VCR buttons on the Data control, you can move back and forth through the records.

**Data Control Events and Methods** When you are using the Data control to let your program's user edit data, perhaps by using bound text controls, you may want to check that the contents of the controls are valid before allowing them to be saved to the database. You can use the *Validate* event for this purpose. When the user clicks on one of the Data control's VCR buttons to move to a new record, a *Validate* event is fired before the new record is loaded. This gives you the chance to check data in any bound controls, or to explicitly save any data in unbound controls. The *Validate* event receives two parameters. The integer *Action* parameter indicates what action initiated the event; you can also change this *Action* parameter to abort the action. The integer *Save* event indicates whether any data in bound controls has changed.

The *Reposition* event occurs immediately after the control moves to a new record. You can use this event to perform any necessary operations, such as explicitly loading data into unbound controls, each time the control retrieves a new record.

The *UpdateRecord* method allows you to update the contents of bound controls within a *Validate* event without triggering yet another *Validate* event.

The *UpdateControls* method retrieves the current record again, and updates all bound controls with their original values. You can connect this method to a "cancel edits" option, allowing the user to easily undo changes made to bound controls such as text boxes.

# Example

The example program is a front end to a Microsoft Access database. The program's main form is shown in Figure 11-5. You build the database using tools supplied with Visual Basic 3.0 Professional Edition; Microsoft Access itself is not required. To build the program, you need Visual Basic Professional Edition. Even though the Data control comes with the standard edition, the program creates dynasets and snapshots, and views into the data, which require the Professional Edition.

If you want to build anything fairly complex using the database tools that come with Visual Basic, you should certainly expect to write some code. You can tie a data table or query to the Data control without coding, but other things, such as showing the results of a one-to-many relationship in a list box, will require some programming.

11◄

**Figure 11-5** The Data control example program

The example database consists of four data tables that together provide information about the controls in this book. The *Products* table contains information about individual controls, such as a description and the cost. The *Keywords* table contains zero or more keywords related to each product. The *Vendors* table contains information about the vendors who created the controls, including addresses and phone numbers. Finally, the *Categories* table relates each product to a primary category, such as "Word Processing" or "Communications."

The last three tables are all related to the Products table by a common key. For example, each product is related to a vendor by the common key field *VendorId*. In other words, for each product there is one and only one vendor. This forms a one-to-one relationship between the two tables. Similarly, the Keywords table is related to Products by a common *ProductID* field. This case is different from the vendors example, though, as there can be several keywords for each product. This creates a one-to-many relationship between the Products and Keywords tables.

The tables can be *joined* to create a single view of the data. You do this by defining an SQL (Structured Query Language) query that combines selected data from several of the tables. The example program joins three of the four tables using the SQL statement shown here:

```
SELECT
  a.ProductID, a.ProductName, a.Cost, c.CategoryName, a.Description,
  b.VendorName, b.VendorAddr, b.VendorPhone, b.VendorTechPhone, b.VendorFaxPhone
FROM
  ((Products AS a LEFT JOIN Vendors AS b ON a.VendorID = b.VendorID)
  LEFT JOIN Categories AS c ON a.CategoryID = c.CategoryID)
ORDER BY
  a.ProductName
```

It's beyond the scope of this book to explain SQL syntax in any detail. Basically, the fields that will be included in the resulting SQL view (which can be treated like a table) are listed after the SELECT keyword. The join itself is defined after the FROM keyword, which forms a join between Products and the Vendors and Categories tables. Finally, the ORDER statement tells SQL to sort the resulting view by the *ProductName* field.

## Steps

1. Using the VisData sample application that comes with Visual Basic 3.0 Professional, build a database called CONTROLS.MDB, containing the four data tables listed in Tables 11-14, 11-15, 11-16, and 11-17. You can build them with the Visual Basic Data Manager, but you will need an application like VisData to build the SQL QueryDefs described in subsequent steps.

**Table 11-14** Products table definition

| FIELD NAME | TYPE | SIZE | INDEX |
|---|---|---|---|
| ProductID | Integer | | Primary;Unique |
| ProductName | String | 50 | |
| VendorID | Integer | | |
| Cost | Currency | | |
| CategoryID | Integer | | |
| Description | Memo | | |

**Table 11-15** Vendors table definition

| FIELD NAME | TYPE | SIZE | INDEX |
|---|---|---|---|
| VendorID | Integer | | Primary;Unique |
| VendorName | String | 50 | |
| VendorAddr | String | 255 | |
| VendorPhone | String | 25 | |
| VendorTechPhone | String | 25 | |
| VendorFaxPhone | String | 25 | |
| Comments | Memo | | |

**Table 11-16** Categories table definition

| FIELD NAME | TYPE | SIZE | INDEX |
|---|---|---|---|
| CategoryID | Integer | | Primary;Unique |
| CategoryName | String | 75 | |

**Table 11-17** Keywords table definition

| FIELD NAME | TYPE | SIZE | INDEX |
|---|---|---|---|
| ProductID | Integer | | Primary |
| Keyword | String | 25 | |

2. With VisData, create a QueryDef called QueryByName, using the following SQL statement.

```
SELECT
  a.ProductID, a.ProductName, a.Cost, c.CategoryName, a.Description,
  b.VendorName, b.VendorAddr, b.VendorPhone, b.VendorTechPhone, b.VendorFaxPhone
FROM
  ((Products AS a LEFT JOIN Vendors AS b ON a.VendorID = b.VendorID)
  LEFT JOIN Categories AS c ON a.CategoryID = c.CategoryID)
ORDER BY
  a.ProductName
```

3. With VisData, create another QueryDef called QueryByCategory, using the following SQL statement. This statement is identical to the first, except that it has a different ORDER clause. You will use these two QueryDefs to alternate between data sorted by product name and data sorted by categories.

```
SELECT
  a.ProductID, a.ProductName, a.Cost, c.CategoryName, a.Description,
  b.VendorName, b.VendorAddr, b.VendorPhone, b.VendorTechPhone, b.VendorFaxPhone
FROM
  ((Products AS a LEFT JOIN Vendors AS b ON a.VendorID = b.VendorID)
  LEFT JOIN Categories AS c ON a.CategoryID = c.CategoryID)
ORDER BY
  c.CategoryName, a.ProductName
```

4. Create a new project called MSDATA.MAK. Copy the database file created in the preceding steps into the directory where MSDATA.MAK resides. Create a new form with the objects and properties described in Table 11-18. Save this form as MSDATA.FRM. This is the main form for the example program, which will display the data from the four tables.

**Table 11-18** Objects and properties of MSDATA.FRM

| OBJECT | PROPERTY | SETTING |
|---|---|---|
| Form | FormName | frmMSData |
| | BackColor | &H00C0C0C0& |
| | Caption | "MS Data Control Demo" |
| | MaxButton | 0 'False |
| Label | Name | Label5 |
| | BackColor | &H00E0FFFF& |
| | BackStyle | 0 'Transparent |
| | BorderStyle | 1 'Fixed Single |

| OBJECT | PROPERTY | SETTING |
|---|---|---|
| | Caption | " Sort By:" |
| | Tag | "/3d/" |
| Label | Name | lblProductName |
| | BackColor | &H00E0FFFF& |
| | BorderStyle | 1 'Fixed Single |
| | Caption | "Label1" |
| | DataField | "ProductName" |
| | DataSource | "Data1" |
| | FontSize | 9.75 |
| | ForeColor | &H00000080& |
| | Tag | "/3dup/" |
| Label | Name | lblVendorName |
| | BackColor | &H00E0FFFF& |
| | BorderStyle | 1 'Fixed Single |
| | Caption | "Label2" |
| | DataField | "VendorName" |
| | DataSource | "Data1" |
| | ForeColor | &H00000080& |
| | Tag | "/3dup/" |
| Label | Name | Label1 |
| | Alignment | 1 'Right Justify |
| | BackStyle | 0 'Transparent |
| | Caption | "Control Name" |
| | ForeColor | &H00800000& |
| Label | Name | Label2 |
| | Alignment | 1 'Right Justify |
| | BackStyle | 0 'Transparent |
| | Caption | "Vendor" |
| | ForeColor | &H00800000& |
| Label | Name | lblCategoryName |
| | BackColor | &H00E0FFFF& |
| | BorderStyle | 1 'Fixed Single |
| | Caption | "Label2" |
| | DataField | "CategoryName" |
| | DataSource | "Data1" |
| | ForeColor | &H00000080& |
| | Tag | "/3dup/" |
| Label | Name | Label4 |
| | Alignment | 1 'Right Justify |

*(continued on next page)*

11

| OBJECT | PROPERTY | SETTING |
|--------|----------|---------|
| *(continued from previous page)* | | |
| | BackStyle | 0 'Transparent |
| | Caption | "Category" |
| | ForeColor | &H00800000& |
| Label | Name | lblShadow |
| | BackStyle | 0 'Transparent |
| | Caption | "VB Controls Desk Reference" |
| | FontItalic | -1 'True |
| | FontSize | 12 |
| | ForeColor | &H00000000& |
| Label | Name | lblTitle |
| | BackStyle | 0 'Transparent |
| | Caption | "VB Controls Desk Reference" |
| | FontItalic | -1 'True |
| | FontSize | 12 |
| | ForeColor | &H00FF0000& |
| Label | Name | Label3 |
| | Alignment | 1 'Right Justify |
| | BackStyle | 0 'Transparent |
| | Caption | "Description" |
| | ForeColor | &H00800000& |
| Label | Name | lblCost |
| | BackColor | &H00E0FFFF& |
| | BorderStyle | 1 'Fixed Single |
| | Caption | "Label2" |
| | DataField | "Cost" |
| | DataSource | "Data1" |
| | ForeColor | &H00000080& |
| | Tag | "/3dup/" |
| Label | Name | Label6 |
| | Alignment | 1 'Right Justify |
| | BackStyle | 0 'Transparent |
| | Caption | "Cost" |
| | ForeColor | &H00800000& |
| Label | Name | lblVendorAddr |
| | BackColor | &H00E0FFFF& |
| | BorderStyle | 1 'Fixed Single |
| | Caption | "Label2" |
| | DataField | "VendorAddr" |

| OBJECT | PROPERTY | SETTING |
|--------|----------|---------|
|  | DataSource | "Data1" |
|  | ForeColor | &H00000080& |
|  | Tag | "/3dup/" |
| Label | Name | Label7 |
|  | BackColor | &H00E0FFFF& |
|  | BorderStyle | 1 'Fixed Single |
|  | Caption | "Label2" |
|  | DataField | "VendorPhone" |
|  | DataSource | "Data1" |
|  | ForeColor | &H00000080& |
|  | Tag | "/3dup/" |
| Label | Name | Label8 |
|  | BackColor | &H00E0FFFF& |
|  | BorderStyle | 1 'Fixed Single |
|  | Caption | "Label2" |
|  | DataField | "VendorFaxPhone" |
|  | DataSource | "Data1" |
|  | ForeColor | &H00000080& |
|  | Tag | "/3dup/" |
| Label | Name | Label9 |
|  | Alignment | 1 'Right Justify |
|  | BackStyle | 0 'Transparent |
|  | Caption | "Address" |
|  | ForeColor | &H00800000& |
| Label | Name | Label10 |
|  | Alignment | 1 'Right Justify |
|  | BackStyle | 0 'Transparent |
|  | Caption | "Sales Phone" |
|  | ForeColor | &H00800000& |
| Label | Name | Label11 |
|  | Alignment | 1 'Right Justify |
|  | BackStyle | 0 'Transparent |
|  | Caption | "Fax" |
|  | ForeColor | &H00800000& |
| Label | Name | Label12 |
|  | BackStyle | 0 'Transparent |
|  | Caption | "Keywords" |
|  | ForeColor | &H00000000& |
| Data | Name | Data1 |

*(continued on next page)*

11◄

| OBJECT | PROPERTY | SETTING |
|---|---|---|
| *(continued from previous page)* | | |
| | Connect | " " |
| | DatabaseName | "CONTROLS.MDB" |
| | Exclusive | 0 'False |
| | Options | 0 |
| | ReadOnly | 0 'False |
| | RecordSource | "QueryByName" |
| | Tag | "/3dup/" |
| ListBox | Name | lstKeywords |
| | Tag | "/3d/" |
| CommandButton | Name | btnAddKeyword |
| | Caption | "&Add Keyword" |
| CommandButton | Name | btnDeleteKeyword |
| | Caption | "Delete Keyword" |
| TextBox | Name | txtDescription |
| | BackColor | &H00E0FFFF& |
| | DataField | "Description" |
| | DataSource | "Data1" |
| | FontBold | 0 'False |
| | ForeColor | &H00000000& |
| | MultiLine | -1 'True |
| | Tag | "/3d/" |
| OptionButton | Name | optByControlName |
| | BackColor | &H00C0C0C0& |
| | Caption | "Control Name" |
| | Value | -1 'True |
| OptionButton | Name | optByCategory |
| | BackColor | &H00C0C0C0& |
| | Caption | "Category" |
| CommandButton | Name | btnSearch |
| | Caption | "&Search..." |
| CommandButton | Name | btnCancel |
| | Caption | "E&xit" |

5. Add the following constants and form-level global variables to the MSDATA.FRM form.

```
Option Explicit
'-------------------------------------------------
' Constants and variables used in MSDATA.FRM.
'-------------------------------------------------

' Form.Show constant
Const SHOW_MODAL = 1
```

```
' The dimension of the main form.
Dim FormWidth As Integer
Dim FormHeight As Integer
```

6. Add the following code to the MSDATA.FRM form. While three of the tables are joined using a QueryDef and are bound to label or text controls, the Keywords table has to be handled differently. Since there can be several keywords for each Product record, you retrieve those records and place them in a list box each time the data control's *Reposition* event is fired. The *GetKeywords* subroutine does the actual work, building a SQL query and creating a data snapshot of just the records for the current product, and then dumping that information into the list box.

```
Sub btnAddKeyword_Click ()
'----------------------------------------------------
' Show the Add Keyword dialog.
'----------------------------------------------------

    frmAddKeyword.Show SHOW_MODAL
End Sub

Sub btnCancel_Click ()
'----------------------------------------------------
' Exit the program.
'----------------------------------------------------

    Unload Me
End Sub

Sub btnDeleteKeyword_Click ()
'----------------------------------------------------
' Delete a keyword selected in the list box.
'----------------------------------------------------
Dim db As DataBase
Dim ds As DynaSet
Dim criteria As String

    ' If nothing is selected, exit.
    If lstKeywords.ListIndex < 0 Then Exit Sub

    ' Open the same database used by main form's data control.
    Set db = OpenDatabase(frmMSData.Data1.DatabaseName)

    ' Create a dynaset on the Keywords table.
    Set ds = db.CreateDynaset("Keywords")

    ' Build the criteria string for the record we want to delete.
    criteria = "(ProductID = " & Format$(Data1.Recordset!ProductID)
    criteria = criteria & ") AND (Keyword = '" & lstKeywords.List(lstKeywords.ListIndex) & "')"

    ' Find and delete it.
    ds.FindFirst criteria
    ds.Delete

    ' Close the dynaset and database.
    ds.Close
    db.Close
```

*(continued on next page)*

*(continued from previous page)*

```
        ' Remove the item from the list.
        lstKeywords.RemoveItem lstKeywords.ListIndex
Exit Sub
btnAddKeyWord_Error:
        MsgBox "Error " & Format$(Err) & ": " & Error$
        Exit Sub
End Sub

Sub btnSearch_Click ()
'------------------------------------------------------
' Show the Search for Control dialog.
'------------------------------------------------------

        frmSearch.Show SHOW_MODAL
End Sub

Sub Data1_Error (DataErr As Integer, Response As Integer)
'------------------------------------------------------
' Display a message if a data error occurs.
'------------------------------------------------------

        MsgBox "Data Error " & Format(DataErr) & "."
End Sub

Sub Data1_Reposition ()
'------------------------------------------------------
' Get keyword list when a new record is moved to.
'------------------------------------------------------

        On Error GoTo Data1_Validate_Error

        ' Build new keyword list for this product.
        GetKeyWords Data1.Recordset!ProductID

Exit Sub
Data1_Validate_Error:
        MsgBox "Error " & Format$(Err) & ": " & Error$
        Resume Next
End Sub

Sub Form_Load ()
'------------------------------------------------------
' Adjust controls and form, and initialize variables.
'------------------------------------------------------

        ' Center the form on the screen.
        Me.Move (Screen.Width - Me.Width) \ 2, (Screen.Height - Me.Height) \ 2

        ' Adjust the shadow label beneath the title label.
        lblShadow.Move lblTitle.Left + Screen.TwipsPerPixelX, lblTitle.Top + Screen.TwipsPerPixelY

        ' Remember the current form dimensions.
        FormWidth = Me.Width
        FormHeight = Me.Height

        Data1.DatabaseName = App.Path & "\CONTROLS.MDB"
End Sub

Sub Form_Paint ()
```

```
'----------------------------------------------------
' Draw 3D effect around selected controls on form.
'----------------------------------------------------
Dim i As Integer

    ' Look at the tag fields of all controls.
    For i = 0 To Me.Controls.Count - 1
        If InStr(UCase$(Me.Controls(i).Tag), "/3D/") Then
            Make3D Me, Me.Controls(i), BORDER_INSET
        ElseIf InStr(UCase$(Me.Controls(i).Tag), "/3DUP/") Then
            Make3D Me, Me.Controls(i), BORDER_RAISED
        End If
    Next
End Sub

Sub Form_Resize ()
'----------------------------------------------------
' Keep the form at its original dimensions.
'----------------------------------------------------

    ' If the form is minimized, do nothing.
    If WindowState = MINIMIZED Then Exit Sub

    ' Resize form to original size.
    Me.Width = FormWidth
    Me.Height = FormHeight
End Sub

Sub GetKeyWords (ByVal ProductID As Integer)
'----------------------------------------------------
' Given a ProductID, load all of the matching
' records from Keywords table into the list box.
'----------------------------------------------------
Dim db As DataBase
Dim snap As SnapShot
Dim SQLStr As String

    On Error Resume Next

    ' Open the database used by the data control.
    Set db = OpenDatabase(Data1.DatabaseName)

    ' Create a snapshot with just the data we need.
    SQLStr = "SELECT KeyWord from KeyWords WHERE ProductID = " & Format$(ProductID)
    Set snap = db.CreateSnapshot(SQLStr)

    ' Empty the current list.
    lstKeywords.Clear

    ' Add all snapshot records to the list box.
    snap.MoveFirst
    While Not snap.EOF
        lstKeywords.AddItem snap!KeyWord
        snap.MoveNext
    Wend

    ' Clean up.
    snap.Close
    db.Close
End Sub
```

11◀

(continued on next page)

*(continued from previous page)*

```
Sub optByCategory_Click ()
'------------------------------------------------
' Switch the record source to a different query.
' Then refresh the data control.
'------------------------------------------------

    Data1.RecordSource = "QueryByCategory"
    Data1.Refresh
End Sub

Sub optByControlName_Click ()
'------------------------------------------------
' Switch the record source to a different query.
' then refresh the data control.
'------------------------------------------------

    Data1.RecordSource = "QueryByName"
    Data1.Refresh
End Sub
```

7. Create another form with the objects and properties described in Table 11-19. Save this form as ADDKEY.FRM.

**Table 11-19** Objects and properties of ADDKEY.FRM

| OBJECT | PROPERTY | SETTING |
|---|---|---|
| Form | FormName | frmAddKeyword |
| | BackColor | &H00C0C0C0& |
| | BorderStyle | 3 'Fixed Double |
| | Caption | "Add Keyword" |
| | MaxButton | 0 'False |
| | MinButton | 0 'False |
| Label | Name | Label1 |
| | BackStyle | 0 'Transparent |
| | Caption | "New Keyword" |
| Label | Name | lblMessage |
| | Alignment | 2 'Center |
| | BackStyle | 0 'Transparent |
| | ForeColor | &H00000080& |
| TextBox | Name | txtNewKeyword |
| | Tag | "/3d/" |
| CommandButton | Name | btnAddKeyword |
| | Caption | "&Add Keyword" |
| | Default | -1 'True |
| CommandButton | Name | btnCancel |
| | Cancel | -1 'True |
| | Caption | "&Cancel" |

8. Add the following lines to the declarations section of ADDKEY.FRM. *Option Explicit* ensures that all variables must be explicitly defined, using the *Dim* statement, before they are used.

```
Option Explicit
'------------------------------------------------
' ADDKEY.FRM
'------------------------------------------------
```

9. Add the following code to the ADDKEY.FRM form. This form is used to add new keywords to the keyword list.

```
Sub btnAddKeyword_Click ()
'------------------------------------------------
' When user presses the Add button, add the new
' keyword to the Keyword table for the current
' ProductID.
'------------------------------------------------
Dim i As Integer
Dim exists As Integer
Dim db As DataBase
Dim ds As Dynaset

    On Error GoTo btnAddKeyword_Error

    ' Check if keyword already exists.
    exists = False
    For i = 0 To frmMSData.lstKeywords.ListCount - 1
        If Trim$(LCase$(frmMSData.lstKeywords.List(i))) = Trim$(LCase$(txtNewKeyword)) Then
            exists = True
            Exit For
        End If
    Next

    ' If the keyword is new, add it to Keywords table.
    If Not exists Then
        ' Use the same database as main form's data control.
        Set db = OpenDatabase(frmMSData.Data1.DatabaseName)

        ' Build a dynaset on Keywords table.
        Set ds = db.CreateDynaset("Keywords")

        ' Add the record.
        ds.AddNew
        ds!ProductID = frmMSData.Data1.Recordset!ProductID
        ds!KeyWord = Trim$(txtNewKeyword)
        ds.Update

        ' Clean up.
        ds.Close
        db.Close

        ' Add keyword to list box in main form.
        frmMSData.lstKeywords.AddItem Trim$(txtNewKeyword)
        txtNewKeyword = ""
        lblMessage = "Keyword Added"
    Else
        lblMessage = "Keyword already exists"
        Beep
```

*(continued on next page)*

11◄

685

*(continued from previous page)*

```
      End If
Exit Sub
btnAddKeyword_Error:
      MsgBox "Error " & Format$(Err) & ": " & Error$
      Exit Sub
End Sub

Sub btnCancel_Click ()
'-----------------------------------------------------
' Close the Add Key dialog.
'-----------------------------------------------------
      Unload Me
End Sub

Sub Form_Load ()
'-----------------------------------------------------
' Center the dialog on the screen.
'-----------------------------------------------------

      Me.Move (Screen.Width - Me.Width) \ 2, (Screen.Height - Me.Height) \ 2
End Sub

Sub Form_Paint ()
'-----------------------------------------------------
' Draw 3D effect around selected controls.
'-----------------------------------------------------
Dim i As Integer

      ' Look for controls tagged as "3D."
      For i = 0 To Me.Controls.Count - 1
          If InStr(UCase$(Me.Controls(i).Tag), "/3D/") Then
              Make3D Me, Me.Controls(i), BORDER_INSET
          End If
      Next
End Sub
```

10. Create another new form with the objects and properties described in Table 11-20. Save this form as SEARCH.FRM.

**Table 11-20** Objects and properties of SEARCH.FRM

| OBJECT | PROPERTY | SETTING |
|--------|----------|---------|
| Form | FormName | frmSearch |
| | BackColor | &H00C0C0C0& |
| | BorderStyle | 3 'Fixed Double |
| | Caption | "Search for Control" |
| | MaxButton | 0 'False |
| | MinButton | 0 'False |
| Label | Name | Label1 |
| | BackStyle | 0 'Transparent |
| | Caption | "Enter Control Name:" |
| | ForeColor | &H00800000& |
| Label | Name | Label2 |

| OBJECT | PROPERTY | SETTING |
|---|---|---|
| | BackStyle | 0 'Transparent |
| | Caption | "Matches:" |
| | ForeColor | &H00800000& |
| TextBox | Name | txtSearchName |
| | Tag | "/3d/" |
| ListBox | Name | lstMatches |
| | Tag | "/3d/" |
| CommandButton | Name | btnGoto |
| | Caption | "&Goto" |
| | Default | -1 'True |
| CommandButton | Name | btnCancel |
| | Cancel | -1 'True |
| | Caption | "&Cancel" |

11. Add the following lines to the declarations section of the SEARCH.FRM form.

```
Option Explicit
'---------------------------------------------------
' SEARCH.FRM
'---------------------------------------------------
```

12. Add the following code to the SEARCH.FRM form. This form searches for product names that match what the user types into a text box. A query is issued each time the text changes. This means that as each letter is typed, the database is searched for any *ProductName* field that begins with the same sequence of letters. The results of the query are loaded into a list box. With a relatively small database and a relatively fast disk drive, this technique can be quite effective. When a desired record is found, the user can highlight it and press the Goto buttons to have the main form jump to that record.

```
Sub btnCancel_Click ()
'---------------------------------------------------
' Close the Search for Control dialog.
'---------------------------------------------------

    Unload Me
End Sub

Sub btnGoto_Click ()
'---------------------------------------------------
' If a record is selected, jump to that record
' in the data control's RecordSet.
'---------------------------------------------------
Dim Criteria As String

    ' If nothing is selected, exit.
    If lstMatches.ListCount < 0 Then Exit Sub

    ' Find the selected record.
```

(continued on next page)

**11◄**

*(continued from previous page)*

```
    Criteria = "ProductName = '" & lstMatches.List(lstMatches.ListIndex) & "'"
    frmMSData.Data1.Recordset.FindFirst Criteria

    Unload Me
End Sub

Sub Form_Paint ()
'----------------------------------------------------
' Draw 3D effect around selected controls.
'----------------------------------------------------
Dim i As Integer

    ' Look for controls tagged as "3D."
    For i = 0 To Me.Controls.Count - 1
            If InStr(UCase$(Me.Controls(i).Tag), "/3D/") Then
                Make3D Me, Me.Controls(i), BORDER_INSET
            End If
    Next
End Sub

Sub txtSearchName_Change ()
'----------------------------------------------------
' Perform a query on the current txtSearchName
' string and display results in list box.
'----------------------------------------------------
Dim db As DataBase
Dim snap As SnapShot
Dim SQLStr As String

    On Error Resume Next

    ' Clear the old contents of list box.
    lstMatches.Clear

    ' If we have an empty string, exit.
        If Trim$(txtSearchName) = "" Then
            Exit Sub
    End If

    ' Use the database used by the main form's data control.
    Set db = OpenDatabase(frmMSData.Data1.DatabaseName)

    ' Build a query for the snapshot.
    SQLStr = "SELECT ProductName from Products WHERE ProductName LIKE '" & Trim$(txtSearchName) & "*'"

    ' Create a snapshot of just those products that start with same string as txtSearchName.
    Set snap = db.CreateSnapshot(SQLStr)

    ' Build list from contents of snapshot.
    snap.MoveFirst
    While Not snap.EOF
            lstMatches.AddItem snap!ProductName
            snap.MoveNext
    Wend

    ' Close the snapshot and database.
    snap.Close
    db.Close
End Sub
```

## Tips and Comments

The Data control can significantly cut down the amount of code needed to display the contents of data tables and the results of queries. Many programmers seem to have an aversion to the Data control, and prefer to handle data access entirely in their source code.

The Data control lends itself well to prototyping. You can quickly build databases and use the Data control to create forms during the design process, getting feedback from your users, who can manipulate "real" data and get a feel for how well the screens flow. Also, you don't have to use the Data control for movement between records. You can hide the Data control by setting its *Visible* property to *False.* Then you can create your own code and controls for navigating the database, but still benefit from having other controls easily bound to the Data control.

When using the Data control, always be careful about the *DatabaseName* property. If you plan on distributing your application to other machines where it may reside in a directory other than the one in which it was designed, you cannot rely on the *DatabaseName* path set in the Properties window at design time. You'll need to devise some other strategy for determining the true location of the database at run time, and set the *DatabaseName* property in your code when the form containing the control first loads.

 # Data Widgets

| USAGE: | Display of Data Using Bound Controls |
| --- | --- |
| MANUFACTURER: | Sheridan Software Systems |
| COST: | $129 |

With the advent of the Data control in Visual Basic 3.0, the data-aware or bound control was born. When you place a data control on a form and associate it with a database table, you can bind the field of the table to data-aware controls. In Version 3.0, several of the standard controls were modified so that you could automatically connect them to database fields in this way. Connecting to a data field using these controls is as simple as setting two properties, one to indicate the data control and another to indicate the data field.

Control developers can create their own data-aware controls, and Data Widgets is a collection of six bound data controls from Sheridan. The controls include an enhanced data control, a grid control, a combo box, a drop-down list control that you can integrate into the grid, an option button, and a data button that can automatically perform selected data positioning functions.

## Syntax

The first step in using any of these controls is to create a data table, and then associate a standard data control with that table. Once you've done this, you're ready to take

**11◀**

advantage of these controls. This section describes each control, and concentrates on quickly putting them to use with the minimum amount of program code.

**The DataGrid Control** The DataGrid control is similar to the standard Grid control that comes with Visual Basic, but differs in several important ways. The obvious one is that it is data-aware, which means that it will automatically display the data from the table with which it is associated. The second difference is that you can edit the data in the DataGrid directly. This makes the control an extremely powerful tool for editing tables.

The DataGrid control also differs from the standard bound data controls, which are usually bound to a single field of a single record. The DataGrid control actually displays an entire data table in spreadsheet format, allowing you to scroll through and view the entire table. Table 11-21 lists the nonstandard properties and events of the DataGrid control.

**Table 11-21** Nonstandard properties and events of the DataGrid control

### PROPERTIES

| | | |
|---|---|---|
| AllowAdditions | AllowDeletions | AllowUpdates |
| BookMark | CaptionType | Col |
| ColAllowEnterKey | ColAllowNulls | ColAllowInput |
| ColBackColor | ColBtn | ColBtnPicture |
| ColCase | ColChanged | ColDropDownHwnd |
| ColFieldLen | ColFieldName | ColFieldNum |
| ColFieldType | ColForeColor | ColFormat |
| ColHeading | ColHeadingAlignment | ColHeadingLines |
| ColPtX | Cols | ColText |
| ColUpdateable | ColVisible | ColWidth |
| ColumnAlignment | ColumnLayout | DataSourceHwnd |
| DefBtnPicture | DefColWidth | DividerStyle |
| DividerType | DropDownPtX | DropDownPtY |
| DroppedDown | EvalRowBookmark | EvalRowIsSelected |
| EvalRowNumber | Font3D | HdgForeColor |
| HwndEdit | LeftCol | MaxRowsEachScroll |
| ListStyle | Redraw | Row |
| RowHeight | RowLabels | Rows |
| ScrollBars | SelBookmark | SelCount |
| SelectByCell | SelectionTypeCol | SelectionTypeRow |
| SelEndBookmark | SelEndCol | SelEndRow |
| SelRow | SelStartBookmark | SelStartCol |
| SelStartRow | ShadowColor | TopRow |
| VariableColWidth | VariableRowHeight | UseExactRowCount |
| VisibleRows | | |

**EVENTS**

| | | |
|---|---|---|
| BtnClicked | CellUpdated | Change |
| CloseUp | ColResize | DeleteBegin |
| DeleteEnd | FirstRowAdd | InitColumnProps |
| LeftColChange | RowColChange | RowLoaded |
| RowsResized | SelChange | TopRowChange |
| UpdateBegin | UpdateEnd | UpdateError |

To bind a DataGrid, you simply set its *DataSource* property to the name of the data control whose data table you wish to view. That's all there is to it. When the program is run, the data from that table is displayed in the grid.

The DataGrid allows *in-place* editing of data fields: You just click on a cell of the grid, and that cell's row becomes the current record. You can then edit the field just as if it were a simple text box. You can abandon changes to a field by pressing the (ESC) key.

The DataGrid even allows you to display and modify the data returned from *joined views*, tables that result from a relational joining of multiple data table.

Once you've associated a DataGrid with a Data control, you can use the special *ColumnLayout* property to set the individual attributes of fields in the data table. Double-clicking on the *ColumnLayout* property in the Visual Basic Properties window displays the Column Layout Editor, which is shown in Figure 11-6. This tool lets you determine the order in which columns will be displayed, and select visual attributes such as colors and column widths. You can also prevent the editing of selected columns, and even hide columns from the view.

**The DataDropDown Control**   You use the DataDropDown control with the DataGrid control to give the user a simple way to select data for a field. For example, if a column of the DataGrid displays state abbreviations, you can use the DataDropDown to present a list of all state abbreviations, along with a separate column containing the full

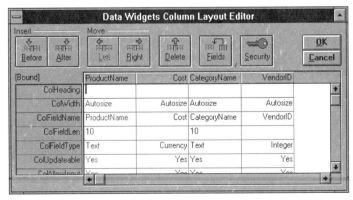

**Figure 11-6** The Data Widgets Column Layout Editor

state name. This can simplify data entry and prevent data errors. Table 11-22 lists the nonstandard properties and events of the DataDropDown control.

**Table 11-22** Nonstandard properties and events of the DataDropDown control

### PROPERTIES

| | | |
|---|---|---|
| ColumnLayout | AllowNulls | AllowInput |
| BevelInner | BevelOuter | BevelWidth |
| BorderWidth | Case | Col |
| ColAlignment | ColBackColor | ColFieldLen |
| ColFieldName | ColFieldNum | ColFieldType |
| ColForeColor | ColFormat | ColHeading |
| ColHeadingAlignment | ColHeadingLines | Cols |
| ColPtX | ColText | ColVisible |
| ColWidth | DataSourceHwnd | DefColWidth |
| DividerStyle | DividerType | DroppedDown |
| Font3D | HdgForeColor | LeftCol |
| ListAutoPosition | ListAutoValidate | ListLinkedCol |
| ListSequence | ListStyle | ListWidth |
| ListWidthAutoSize | MaxDropDownItems | MaxRowsEachScroll |
| MinDropDownItems | Redraw | Row |
| RowHeight | Rows | ScrollBars |
| ShadowColor | TopRow | UseExactRowCount |
| VisibleRows | | |

### EVENTS

| | | |
|---|---|---|
| Click | InitColumnProps | LeftColChange |
| PositionList | RowLoaded | TopRowChange |
| ValidateList | | |

The DataDropDown control is actually associated with two data tables: the table associated with the grid, and a second table containing the data that will be displayed in the drop-down list. To build on the state abbreviation example, suppose the DataGrid contained a list of addresses, including one field for the two-character state abbreviation, which happens to be the fourth column of the grid. The second table might be a simple two-field look-up table containing only state abbreviations and full state names. Associating the column in the DataGrid with the look-up table is a three-step process. First, set the *DataSource* property of the DataDropDown control to point to the data control associated with the look-up table. Then set the *ListLinkedCol* property of the DataDropDown control to point to the column of the look-up table that contains the abbreviations. Finally, in the DataGrid control's *InitColumnProps* event, add a line of code something like this:

```
SSDataGrid1.ColDropDownHwnd(3) = SSDropDown1.hWnd
```

This associates the fourth column (column numbering starts with 0) of the DataGrid with the window handle of the DataDropDown control.

Now, when the DataGrid control is displayed and the user selects a cell in the state abbreviation column, a small drop-down button appears on the right side of the cell. When the user pushes this button, the look-up table is displayed over the DataGrid. The user can now select a new record, thereby updating the state abbreviation in the DataGrid.

**The DataCombo Control**   The DataCombo control is similar to the DataDropDown control, but it is not associated with a DataGrid, and the user can edit the data displayed in its drop-down list. Table 11-23 lists the DataCombo control's nonstandard properties and events. The DataCombo control is associated with two data tables: one for the edit section of the control, and the other for the drop-down section of the control. No code is required to bind the control to the two tables.

**Table 11-23** Nonstandard properties and events of the DataCombo control

### PROPERTIES

| | | |
|---|---|---|
| ColumnLayout | AllowNulls | AllowInput |
| BevelInner | BevelOuter | BevelWidth |
| BorderWidth | Case | Col |
| ColAlignment | ColBackColor | ColFieldLen |
| ColFieldName | ColFieldNum | ColFieldType |
| ColForeColor | ColFormat | ColHeading |
| ColHeadingAlignment | ColHeadingLines | Cols |
| ColPtX | ColText | ColVisible |
| ColWidth | DataSourceHwnd | DataSourceList |
| DataSourceListHwnd | DefColWidth | DividerStyle |
| DividerType | DroppedDown | Font3D |
| Format | HdgForeColor | HwndEdit |
| LeftCol | ListAutoPosition | ListAutoValidate |
| ListLinkedCol | ListSequence | ListStyle |
| ListWidth | ListWidthAutoSize | MaxDropDownItems |
| MaxRowsEachScroll | MinDropDownItems | Redraw |
| Row | RowHeight | Rows |
| ScrollBars | ShadowColor | TopRow |
| UseExactRowCount | VisibleRows | |

### EVENTS

| | | |
|---|---|---|
| Click | DblClick | InitColumnProps |
| LeftColChange | PositionList | RowLoaded |
| TopRowChange | ValidateList | |

**11**◀

Let's say you're creating an order entry application and you have a table that stores valid order information, including a shipping code. A second table contains a list of all possible valid shipping codes. You have two data controls, Orders and ShipCodes, and you want to connect these two control's data tables to a DataCombo control, SSDataCombo1. First, you would set the *DataSource* property of SSDataCombo1 to point to the Orders table, and the *DataField* property to point to the Shipping Code field in the Orders table. Setting these two properties associates the edit section of the control with the Orders table. Next, you would set the *DataSourceList* property to point to the ShipCodes table, and set the *ListLinkedCol* property to point to the Shipping Code column within the ShipCodes table. The linked column will be the one that "fills in" the edit section of DataCombo when the user selects a row from the drop-down list. The user will be able to select from a list of all valid Shipping Codes, reducing the chance of a data-entry error.

**The Enhanced Data Control**  The Enhanced Data control is exactly what its name implies: an extension or enhancement to the standard Visual Basic Data control. The standard Data control has four VCR-style buttons that let you move to the first, last, previous, or next record. Figure 11-7 shows the Enhanced Data control, which includes four additional buttons that let you set a bookmark, return to the bookmark, or jump back and forth between multiple records. Table 11-24 lists this control's nonstandard properties.

**Table 11-24** Nonstandard properties of the Enhanced Data control

**PROPERTIES**

| | | |
|---|---|---|
| Alignment | BevelInner | BevelOuter |
| BevelWidth | BookmarkCurrent | BorderWidth |
| ButtonSize | CaptionAlignment | DataSourceHwnd |
| DelayInitial | DelaySubsequent | Font3D |
| Outline | PageValue | PictureButtons |
| PictureCaption | PictureCaptionAlign | RoundedCorners |
| ShadowColor | ShowBookmarkButton | ShowFirstLastButton |
| ShowPageButton | ShowPrevNextButton | |

The Enhanced Data control does not *replace* the Data control. In fact, it is very much dependent on it, as are the other Data Widget controls. You associate the Enhanced Data control with a standard Data control by setting its *DataSource* property to the name of the standard Data control. In general, you'll want to set the standard Data control's *Visible* property to *False* or move it off the visible area of the form.

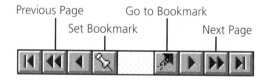

**Figure 11-9**  The Enhanced Data control

The Enhanced Data control looks and works much like the standard one, except for its four additional buttons. When moving through a record set using this control, the user can press the bookmark button (which displays a pushpin) at any time, saving the position of that record. Later the user can push another button to automatically jump back to the marked record.

The *PageValue* property determines by how many records the control jumps when the user presses the Page Forward or Page Backward buttons. On the Enhanced Data control, unlike the standard Data control, when the user presses and holds down these buttons, or the next and previous buttons, he or she will continue to move. The standard buttons instead move only once per mouse click. This lets the user easily move through the record set. The *DelayInitial* and *DelaySubsequent* properties set the amount of time, in milliseconds, between record jumps.

The Enhanced Data control is actually two separate controls: one that's horizontally oriented, like the traditional Data control, and another that's vertically oriented.

**The DataCommand Button**  The DataCommand button is similar to the 3D command button that comes with Visual Basic Professional 3.0, except that it can automatically perform data table positioning functions. Its nonstandard properties are listed in Table 11-25. This control basically provides the same functions as one of the buttons in the Enhanced Data control. You can set the DataCommand button's *DataSource* property to the name of a Data control, and then set the *DatabaseAction* property to associate the button with a positioning action value, as shown in Table 11-26.

**Table 11-25**  Nonstandard properties of the DataCommand button

| | | |
|---|---|---|
| AutoSize | BevelWidth | BookmarkCurrent |
| DatabaseAction | DataSourceHwnd | DelayInitial |
| DelaySubsequent | Font3D | RoundedCorners |
| SavedBookmark | | |

**Table 11-26**  Values for the DatabaseAction property

| VALUE | MEANING |
|---|---|
| 0 | Jump to first row. |
| 1 | Jump to previous page. |
| 2 | Jump to previous row. |
| 3 | Jump to next row. |
| 4 | Jump to next page. |
| 5 | Jump to last row. |
| 6 | Save bookmark for current row. |
| 7 | Jump to bookmarked record. |
| 8 | Refresh data control's RecordSet. |

11◄

**The DataOption Button** The DataOption button is a 3D data-aware version of the standard option button. Table 11-27 lists its nonstandard properties. You set this button's *DataSource* and *DataField* properties to a Data control and table field. You then set the *OptionValue* property to a value that will be compared against the bound field. When the user selects a DataOption button, the DataOption button assigns the *OptionValue* value to the bound field.

**Table 11-27** Nonstandard properties of the DataOption button

| PROPERTIES | | |
| --- | --- | --- |
| DataSourceHwnd | Font3D | OptionValue |

# Example

The example program displays data from the Controls database created in this chapter's section on the Data control. You will use the DataGrid, DataDropDown, and Enhanced Data controls, as well as some standard controls, to present the data in a different way. The example program is shown in Figure 11-8.

## Steps

1. If you haven't done so already, create the Controls database by following steps 1 through 3 of the example in the "Data Control" section of this chapter.

2. Create a new project called DATWIDGT.MAK. Add two of the Data Widgets controls, SSDATA1.VBX and SSDATA2.VBX, to the project. Also add the constants file, SSDATA.BAS, which comes with Data Widgets, to the project.

**Figure 11-8** The Data Widgets example program

3. Create a new form with the objects and properties described in Table 11-28. Save this form as DATWIDGT.FRM.

**Table 11-28** Objects and properties for DATWIDGT.FRM

| OBJECT | PROPERTY | SETTING |
|---|---|---|
| Form | FormName | frmDataWidgets |
| | BackColor | &H00C0C0C0& |
| | Caption | "Data Widgets Demo" |
| Label | Name | lblKeywords |
| | BackStyle | 0 'Transparent |
| | Caption | "Label1" |
| | FontBold | 0 'False |
| | ForeColor | &H00800000& |
| Label | Name | lblVendorName |
| | BackStyle | 0 'Transparent |
| | Caption | "Label1" |
| | FontBold | 0 'False |
| | ForeColor | &H00000080& |
| Label | Name | lblVendorAddr |
| | BackStyle | 0 'Transparent |
| | Caption | "Label1" |
| | FontBold | 0 'False |
| | ForeColor | &H00800000& |
| Label | Name | Label1 |
| | Alignment | 1 'Right Justify |
| | BackStyle | 0 'Transparent |
| | Caption | "Vendor:" |
| | FontBold | 0 'False |
| | ForeColor | &H00800000& |
| Data | Name | Data1 |
| | Caption | "Data1" |
| | Connect | "" |
| | DatabaseName | "CONTROLS.MDB" |
| | Exclusive | 0 'False |
| | Options | 16 |
| | ReadOnly | 0 'False |
| | RecordSource | "QueryByNameVID" |
| | Visible | 0 'False |
| SSDataGrid | Name | SSDataGrid1 |
| | AllowAdditions | 0 'False |

*(continued on next page)*

11◄

| OBJECT | PROPERTY | SETTING |
|---|---|---|
| *(continued from previous page)* | | |
| | AllowDeletions | 0 'False |
| | Caption | "Controls Database for VB Controls Desk Reference" |
| | DataSource | "Data1" |
| | FontBold | 0 'False |
| | RowHeight | 405 |
| Data | Name | Data2 |
| | Caption | "Data2" |
| | Connect | " " |
| | DatabaseName | "CONTROLS.MDB" |
| | Exclusive | 0 'False |
| | Options | 0 |
| | ReadOnly | 0 'False |
| | RecordSource | "KeyWords" |
| | Visible | 0 'False |
| ListBox | Name | lstKeywords |
| | BackColor | &H00E0FFFF& |
| | FontBold | 0 'False |
| Data | Name | Data3 |
| | Caption | "Data3" |
| | Connect | " " |
| | DatabaseName | "CONTROLS.MDB" |
| | Exclusive | 0 'False |
| | Options | 0 |
| | ReadOnly | 0 'False |
| | RecordSource | "Vendors" |
| | Visible | 0 'False |
| SSDropDown | Name | SSDropDown1 |
| | DataSource | "Data3" |
| | RowHeight | 150 |
| SSHData | Name | SSHData1 |
| | Alignment | 2 'Center |
| | BackColor | &H00E0FFFF& |
| | BevelOuter | 1 'Inset |
| | DataSource | "Data1" |
| | FontBold | 0 'False |
| | ForeColor | &H00800000& |

4. Add the following constants and form-level global variables to the declarations section of the DATWIDGT.FRM form.

```
Option Explicit
'--------------------------------------------------
' Constants and variables used in the Data Widgets
' example program.
'--------------------------------------------------

' Store the dimensions of the main form.
Dim MinFormWidth As Integer
Dim MinFormHeight As Integer

' The default caption for the form.
Dim MainCaption As String

' WindowState constant.
Const MINIMIZED = 1

' MsgBox constants.
Const MB_OK = &H0
Const MB_OKCANCEL = &H1
Const MB_YESNOCANCEL = &H3
Const MB_YESNO = &H4

Const MB_ICONQUESTION = &H20
Const MB_ICONEXCLAMATION = &H30
Const MB_ICONINFORMATION = &H40
Const MB_ICONSTOP = &H10
```

5. Add the following code to the DATWIDGT.FRM form. This is a fairly short program, with most of the code used to either load data into the unbound controls, or to resize the form.

```
Sub Data1_Reposition ()
'--------------------------------------------------
' Update the "unbound" data controls when the
' Primary Data record is repositioned.
'--------------------------------------------------

    On Error GoTo Data1_Reposition_Error

    ' Update the keywords label with the new product name.
    lblKeywords = "Keywords for " & Data1.Recordset!ProductName

    ' Tell the Data2 control to get all the keywords for this product ID.
    Data2.RecordSource = "SELECT KeyWord FROM Keywords WHERE ProductID = " &
Format$(Data1.Recordset!ProductID)
    Data2.Refresh

    ' Dump all the keywords into a list box.
    lstKeyWords.Clear
    Data2.Recordset.MoveFirst
    While Not Data2.Recordset.EOF
        lstKeyWords.AddItem Data2.Recordset!KeyWord
        Data2.Recordset.MoveNext
    Wend
```

*(continued on next page)*

**11◄**

*(continued from previous page)*

```
    ' Tell the Data2 control to get the vendor name and address for this vendor ID.
    Data2.RecordSource = "Select VendorName, VendorAddr FROM Vendors WHERE VendorID = " &
Format$(Data1.Recordset!VendorID)
    Data2.Refresh

    ' Dump the name and address to label controls.
    Data2.Recordset.MoveFirst
    If Not Data2.Recordset.EOF Then
        lblVendorName = Data2.Recordset!VendorName
        lblVendorAddr = Data2.Recordset!VendorAddr
    End If

    ' Update the caption with the new product name.
    Me.Caption = MainCaption & " - [" & Data1.Recordset!ProductName & "]"
    SSHData1.Caption = "Product ID: " & Format$(Data1.Recordset!ProductID, "00000")
Exit Sub
Data1_Reposition_Error:
    Resume Next
End Sub

Sub Form_Load ()
'---------------------------------------------------
' Position the form and save initial values.
'---------------------------------------------------

    ' Center the form on the screen.
    Me.Move (Screen.Width - Me.Width) \ 2, (Screen.Height - Me.Height) \ 2

    ' Save the current form dimensions.
    MinFormWidth = Me.Width
    MinFormHeight = Me.Height

    ' Save the inital caption.
    MainCaption = Me.Caption
End Sub

Sub Form_Resize ()
'---------------------------------------------------
' Resize the grid and the center enhanced
' data control.
'---------------------------------------------------

    ' If the user minimized the form, exit.
    If WindowState = MINIMIZED Then Exit Sub

    ' Don't allow form to be resized smaller than original size.
    If Me.Width < MinFormWidth Then Me.Width = MinFormWidth
    If Me.Height < MinFormHeight Then Me.Height = MinFormHeight

    ' Adjust the grid to the form size.
    SSDataGrid1.Move SSDataGrid1.Left, SSDataGrid1.Top, Me.ScaleWidth - SSDataGrid1.Left,
Me.ScaleHeight - SSDataGrid1.Top - SSHData1.Height

    ' Center the enhanced data control at the bottom of the form.
    SSHData1.Move (Me.ScaleWidth - SSHData1.Width) / 2, Me.ScaleHeight - SSHData1.Height
End Sub

Sub SSDataGrid1_InitColumnProps ()
```

```
'---------------------------------------------------
' Associate the special DropDown data control with
' (zero-based) column 3 of the grid control.
'---------------------------------------------------
    SSDataGrid1.ColDropDownHwnd(3) = SSDropDown1.hWnd
End Sub
```

## Tips and Comments

The Data Widget controls are a set of well-designed controls that extend the capabilities of the Visual Basic Data control, and require little or no coding to use. The DataGrid control is especially powerful and useful when you are displaying and editing large amounts of data, and you can use it to automatically update, insert, and delete records. These controls are data-aware, and they also sport customizable 3D effects such as inset and raised borders.

# VB/ISAM (VBIS23DM.DLL)

| | |
|---|---|
| USAGE: | Data Management |
| MANUFACTURER: | Software Source |
| COST: | $129.95 Single User/$199.95 Multiuser |

VB/ISAM is a small, robust, high-performance ISAM data manager. How small? The .DLL is less than 50K yet VB/ISAM can handle files of up to 512 MB without flinching. ISAM stands for "Indexed Sequential Access Method." What this means is that you find records through indexes, and the index keys are automatically kept in sorted sequence so you can step forward or backward from any point. If you know your A B Cs, you should be able to use VB/ISAM without any trouble. VB/ISAM is so easy to use that the manual is just under 80 pages even though it covers the product completely, and is extremely entertaining to boot! Although, VB/ISAM is extremely easy to use, it is also quite powerful.

## Syntax

One of VB/ISAM's greatest strengths is its simplicity. It includes only 16 functions (Table 11-29) and, of those, only about half are regularly used. The functions are designed to emulate VB's file access statements (Open, Close, Get, Put, and so on) so they seem immediately familiar. As a single concession to the bells-and-whistles temptation, the developers added two functions to read, write, and delete "file notes," an optional mini-database of about 1,000 bytes within each file. VB/ISAM files are referred to as "datasets" in the documentation. You are never required to use the *vmxEncode* and *vmxDecode* functions, but they enable you to store multiple record types in a single VB/ISAM dataset.

11◄

**Table 11-29** VB/ISAM function summary

| FUNCTION | PURPOSE |
|---|---|
| vmxCreate | Create a new, empty dataset |
| vmxKill | Delete an entire dataset |
| vmxOpen | Open an existing dataset |
| vmxClose | Close an open dataset |
| vmxBOF | Move to the beginning of an index |
| vmxEOF | Move to the end of an index |
| vmxGet | Retrieve a record from a dataset |
| vmxPut | Write a record to a dataset |
| vmxDelete | Delete a record from a dataset |
| vmxEncode | Convert a type variable into a variable-length string |
| vmxDecode | Convert a variable-length string into a type variable |
| vmxReadNote | Read a file note from a dataset |
| vmxWriteNote | Write a file note to a dataset |
| vmxFlush | Flush changes to disk |
| vmxInfo | Retrieve dataset statistics |
| vmxReturnCode | Returns descriptive error message of VB/ISAM error code |

The format of a dataset is determined by the *StandardFormat$* parameter passed to *vmxCreate*. The format is based on a type structure you have defined (each record in the dataset is a variable of that type). Each element in the type is represented, in the *StandardFormat$* string, by its corresponding VB data type identifier (%, &, !, #, @, $, or $*size). Table 11-30 shows a sample type definition and its corresponding VB/ISAM format string.

**Table 11-30** Sample type definition and VB/ISAM format string

| TYPE DEFINITION | | FORMAT STRING ELEMENT |
|---|---|---|
| Type T_Person | | |
| FirstName | As String | $ |
| LastName | As String | X15$ (Indexed, 15 chars max) |
| Address | As String * 50 | $*50 |
| NumAccounts | As Integer | % |
| TotalValue | As Currency | @ |
| HighRoller | As String * 1 | X$*1 (Indexed) |
| Notes | As String | $ |
| End Type | | |
| | | |
| T_Person FormatString: | | "$ X15$ $*50 % @ X$*1 $" |

In VB/ISAM, only string fields may be indexed. If the field is a fixed-length string, just add an X to the beginning to define it as an index (as in X$*size). If the field is a variable-length string, you must also tell VB/ISAM the maximum allowable length of the index key for that field (for example, X*nn*$). The string is still variable length, but VB/ISAM will return an error code if you try to add a record to the dataset that has more than *nn* characters in that index field. Each index field in the type is a secondary index, which means the contents don't have to be unique. The primary key (index) for each record *must* be unique and is not part of the type definition; it is simply a string variable used with the *vmxGet*, *vmxPut*, and *vmxDelete* functions. When you add a record to a dataset the record must have a nonnull primary key, which is that record's identifier.

Once a dataset has been created, you use *vmxOpen* and *vmxClose* just as you would use VB's Open and Close statements. *vmxOpen* returns a file handle to use with other VB/ISAM functions. All VB/ISAM functions return an integer code, which will tell you if the function call was successful or if there was an error. If a dataset is opened successfully, you can add, delete, and retrieve records from it. You add records with *vmxPut,* which takes four parameters: a dataset handle (returned by *vmxOpen),* a primary key for the record (must be unique), the record itself (a variable of the type you defined), and the desired *UpdateMode* (Table 11-31). For example, if a record with the same primary key exists in the dataset, and you specified an *UpdateMode* of ADD_ONLY, VB/ISAM returns a VIS_UPDATE_VIOLATION error code to warn you and doesn't add the record to the dataset.

**Table 11-31** vmxPut UpdateMode parameter values and their meanings

| UPDATEMODE | MEANING |
| --- | --- |
| 0-ADD_OR_REPLACE | Doesn't care whether primary key exists |
| 1-ADD_ONLY | Primary key must be new |
| 2-REPLACE_ONLY | Primary key must exist in file |

*vmxDelete* is even simpler than *vmxPut.* It takes only two parameters: a dataset handle and the primary key of the record you want to delete. That's it.

*vmxGet* is, by far, the most complex of the VB/ISAM functions, taking seven parameters and serving two purposes. The first purpose is to search an index for a record in a dataset, and the second is to move forward or backward by one record in the current index. The first mode (search/look-up) is like VB's Data Access *Seek* method, and the second is similar to VB's Data Access *MoveNext/MovePrevious* methods. On a related note, the *vmxBOF* and *vmxEOF* functions are analogous to VB's Data Access *MoveFirst* and *MoveLast* methods. When using Next/Previous mode, you can specify comparison options (=, <>, <, >, <=, >=, begins with) to find groups of matching records quickly and easily. The sample program demonstrates how to do this.

**11**

# Example

You can use the VB/ISAM sample program to generate a dataset containing the name of every file on your system and search that dataset for a specific file. This program is great for finding duplicate files. It demonstrates the speed of VB/ISAM when searching and updating datasets and shows how to find groups of records in a dataset. The VB/ISAM sample program is shown in Figure 11-9.

## Steps

1. Create a new project called VBISAM.MAK. Create a new form with the objects and properties shown in Table 11-32. Save this form as VBISAM.FRM.

**Table 11-32** VB/ISAM main form's objects and properties

| OBJECT | PROPERTY | SETTING |
|---|---|---|
| Label | Name | lblStatus |
| | BackColor | &H00FFFFFF& |
| | BorderStyle | 1 'Fixed Single |
| | ForeColor | &H00FF0000& |
| Label | Name | lblFileToFind |
| | Caption | "File to Fi&nd:" |
| Label | Name | lblFilesFound |
| | Caption | "Files Found:" |
| Label | Name | lblWildcardNote |
| | Caption | "NOTE: If a wildcard (*) is used in the File to Find box, everything to the right of it is ignored." |
| | FontBold | 0 'False |
| | ForeColor | &H000000FF& |
| Frame | Name | fmeDrivesToIndex |
| | Caption | "Select Drives to Index" |
| TextBox | Name | txtFileSpec |
| CommandButton | Name | cmdFindFile |
| | Caption | "&Find" |
| CommandButton | Name | cmdExit |
| | Caption | "Exit" |
| ListBox | Name | lstFilesFound |
| | FontBold | 0 'False |
| Form | FormName | frmMain |
| | Caption | "VB/ISAM Demo" |
| | ScaleMode | 3 'Pixel |

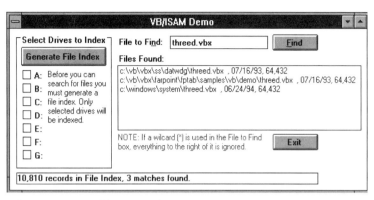

**Figure 11-9** VB/ISAM sample program

2. Inside the form's fmeDrivesToIndex Frame control, add the controls shown in Table 11-33.

**Table 11-33** Objects inside the fmeDrivesToIndex Frame control

| OBJECT | PROPERTY | SETTING |
|---|---|---|
| Label | Name | lblFileGenNote |
| | Caption | "Before you can search for files you must generate a file index. Only selected drives will be indexed." |
| | FontBold | 0 'False |
| CheckBox | Name | chkDrive |
| | Caption | "A:" |
| | Index | 0 |
| CommandButton | Name | cmdGenerateFileIndex |
| | Caption | "Generate File Index" |
| DriveListBox | Name | drvList |
| | Visible | 0 'False |

3. Add the following code to the VBISAM form.

```
Sub chkDrive_Click (Index As Integer)

    gbarrDriveSelected%(Index%) = Not (gbarrDriveSelected%(Index%))

End Sub

Sub cmdExit_Click ()

    Unload Me

End Sub
```

11◄

*(continued on next page)*

*(continued from previous page)*

```
Sub cmdFindFile_Click ()
    Dim FileSpec$

    FileSpec$ = Trim$(txtFileSpec.Text)
    FindFile (FileSpec$)

End Sub

Sub cmdGenerateFileIndex_Click ()

    cmdGenerateFileIndex.Enabled = False
        Call GenerateFileIndex
    cmdGenerateFileIndex.Enabled = True

End Sub

Sub Form_Resize ()

    lblStatus.Top = frmMain.ScaleHeight - 25
    lstFilesFound.Width = frmMain.ScaleWidth - lstFilesFound.Left - 8

End Sub

Sub Form_Unload (Cancel As Integer)

    End

End Sub

Sub txtFileSpec_KeyPress (KeyAscii As Integer)
    Dim FileSpec$

    If KeyAscii% = KEY_ENTER Then
        KeyAscii% = 0
        FileSpec$ = Trim$(txtFileSpec.Text)
        FindFile (FileSpec$)
    End If

End Sub
```

4. Create a new module called VBISAM.BAS and add the following code to the declarations section.

```
Option Explicit
DefInt A-Z

'------------------------------------
'-- VB/ISAM declarations.
'------------------------------------
Global Const VIS_OK = 0

Global Const ADD_ONLY = 1

Global Const XLOOKUP = 1
Global Const XNEXT = 2

Global Const XEQ = 32
Global Const XBEGINS = 64
```

```
Type VBISAMInfo
    RecordsInFile          As Long
    GroupsUsed             As Integer
    AllocatedGpsAvail      As Integer
    MaxPrimaryKeyLen       As Integer
    GroupSize              As Long
    InitialAllocation      As Integer
    IncrementalAllocation  As Integer
    FreeFileNoteSpace      As Integer
    StandardFormat         As String
    Reserved               As String
End Type


Declare Function VmxCreate Lib "VBIS23DM.DLL" (DatasetName$, MaxPrimaryKeyLength%,
StandardFormat$) As Integer
Declare Function VmxKill Lib "VBIS23DM.DLL" (DatasetName$) As Integer

Declare Function VmxOpen Lib "VBIS23DM.DLL" (DatasetName$, RDatasetNumber%) As Integer
Declare Function VmxClose Lib "VBIS23DM.DLL" (DatasetNumber%) As Integer

Declare Function VmxGet Lib "VBIS23DM.DLL" (DatasetNumber%, SecIndexField%, Options%,
SelectorKey$, RIndexEntry$, RPrimaryKey$, RRecordVariable As Any) As Integer
Declare Function VmxPut Lib "VBIS23DM.DLL" (DatasetNumber%, PrimaryKey$, RecordVariable As Any,
UpdateMode%) As Integer


'----------------------------------
'-- App specific declarations.
'----------------------------------


'-- SetParent is used to place dynamically loaded
'   check boxes into a Frame control at run time.
Declare Function SetParent% Lib "User" (ByVal hwndChild%, ByVal hwndNewParent%)


Global Const KEY_ENTER = &HD

' MsgBox parameters.
Global Const MB_OK = 0                    ' OK button only
Global Const MB_ABORTRETRYIGNORE = 2      ' Abort, Retry, and Ignore buttons
Global Const MB_YESNO = 4                 ' Yes and No buttons

Global Const MB_ICONSTOP = 16             ' Critical message
Global Const MB_ICONQUESTION = 32         ' Warning query

' MsgBox return values.
Global Const IDABORT = 3                  ' Abort button pressed
Global Const IDRETRY = 4                  ' Retry button pressed
Global Const IDIGNORE = 5                 ' Ignore button pressed
Global Const IDYES = 6                    ' Yes button pressed
Global Const IDNO = 7                     ' No button pressed

' SetAttr, Dir, GetAttr functions.
Global Const ATTR_NORMAL = 0
Global Const ATTR_HIDDEN = 2
Global Const ATTR_SYSTEM = 4
Global Const ATTR_DIRECTORY = 16


Type T_File
```

11◄

*(continued on next page)*

*(continued from previous page)*

```
        Drive       As String * 1
        Path        As String
        Name        As String * 12
        TimeStamp   As Double
        Size        As Long
End Type
Global Const FMT_FILE_INDEX = "$*1 $ X$*12 # &"
Global Const IDX_PRIMARY = 0
Global Const IDX_FILENAME = 3

Global Const IGNORE_RTN_KEY = ""

Global Const APP_FILENAME = "FILEINDX.ISD"

Global garrDrives() As String * 1   ' A, B, etc. 1 for each available drive.
Global gbarrDriveSelected%()         ' Boolean flag if drive check box is selected.
```

5. Add the following code to the VBISAM.BAS module.

```
Sub EnumDirectories (Drive$, arrDirs$())
'--------------------------------------------------
'-- We have to work around the fact that the VB
'    Dir$ function can't be called recursively.
'    We do this with (gasp) a GOTO. This procedure
'    will load arrDirs$() with all the directories
'    found on the specified drive.
'--------------------------------------------------
    Dim FileFound$  '-- File Found
    Dim CurPath$    '-- Directory being searched
    Dim DirCount%   '-- Number of actual directories found
    Dim EnumMarker% '-- Tracks where in the array to start the next enumeration

    ReDim arrDirs$(100)

    CurPath$ = Drive$ & ":\"
    arrDirs$(0) = CurPath$
    EnumMarker% = 0

EnumStart:
    FileFound$ = Dir$(CurPath$, ATTR_DIRECTORY)
    While Len(FileFound$)

        '-- Make sure to ignore the parent directories
        If (InStr(FileFound$, ".") = 0) Or (InStr(FileFound$, ".") > 1) Then

            '-- We found a file, so we'll see if it's a directory
            If GetAttr(CurPath$ & FileFound$) And ATTR_DIRECTORY Then
                DirCount% = DirCount% + 1

                '-- If we run out of space, we need to bump up
                '    the size of our array.
                If DirCount% > UBound(arrDirs$) Then
                    ReDim Preserve arrDirs$(UBound(arrDirs$) + 100)
                End If

                '-- Add the newly found directory to our array.
                arrDirs$(DirCount%) = CurPath$ & FileFound$ & "\"
            End If
        End If
    End If
```

```
            '-- Look for another one.
            FileFound$ = Dir$
            DoEvents
        Wend

        '-- At this point we've enumerated all the subdirs in CurPath,
        '   so now we bump our EnumMarker, set the new path, and do it
        '   all again.
        EnumMarker% = EnumMarker% + 1
        If EnumMarker% <= DirCount% Then
            CurPath$ = arrDirs$(EnumMarker%)
            GoTo EnumStart
        End If

        '-- Trim unused elements from array.
        ReDim Preserve arrDirs$(DirCount% - 1)

End Sub

Sub FindFile (FileSpec$)
    Dim Msg$          '-- MsgBox Message
    Dim vmxRtn%       '-- VB/ISAM return code
    Dim hFile%        '-- VB/ISAM dataset handle
    Dim WildcardPos%  '-- Wildcard position in FileSpec$
    Dim Op%           '-- Find Operation (equal or BeginsWith)
    Dim FileCount&    '-- Number of Files found
    Dim RecsInFile$   '-- Number of Records in File Index
    Dim tFile As T_File      '-- File Record in VB/ISAM file
    Dim tInfo As VBISAMInfo '-- VB/ISAM file info

    '-- Make sure they only gave us a file name.
    If InStr(FileSpec$, "\") Then
        MsgBox "Enter the file name only, no path information.", MB_OK
        Exit Sub
    End If

    '-- Clear any previous entries from the list.
    frmMain!lstFilesFound.Clear

    '-- Check to make sure they generated a file for us to search.
    If Len(Dir$(App.Path & "\" & APP_FILENAME)) = 0 Then
        MsgBox "You need to generate a File Index before searching for files", MB_OK +
MB_ICONSTOP, "File Index not Found"
        Exit Sub
    End If

    '-- First we have to open the file (bail out on failure).
    vmxRtn% = VmxOpen(App.Path & "\" & APP_FILENAME, hFile%)
    If vmxRtn% <> VIS_OK Then
        Msg$ = "Error Opening File Index Dataset. Aborting File Find Operation"
        MsgBox Msg$, MB_OK + MB_ICONSTOP, VmxReturnCode$(vmxRtn%)
        Exit Sub
    End If

    '-- Check for a wildcard (*).
    WildcardPos% = InStr(FileSpec$, "*")
    Select Case WildcardPos%
        Case 0
            Op% = XEQ
        Case 1
```

**11**

*(continued on next page)*

*(continued from previous page)*

```
                MsgBox "There must be something to the left of the wildcard in order to do a
partial match search", MB_OK
                Exit Sub
        Case Else
                FileSpec$ = Left$(FileSpec$, WildcardPos% - 1)
                Op% = XBEGINS
    End Select

    '-- Find the first matching record using XLOOKUP. An extra step is required
    '   if a wildcard was used because our XLOOKUP will *probably*
    '   fail due to the fact that our FileSpec$ is only a partial match.
    vmxRtn% = VmxGet(hFile%, IDX_FILENAME, XLOOKUP, FileSpec$, IGNORE_RTN_KEY, ⇒
IGNORE_RTN_KEY, tFile)
    If vmxRtn% <> VIS_OK Then
            '-- This XBEGINS clause is inside the IF block because the XLOOKUP
            '   *might* have worked, in which case we wouldn't want to move to
            '   the next record.
            If Op% = XBEGINS Then
                vmxRtn% = VmxGet(hFile%, IDX_FILENAME, XNEXT + Op%, FileSpec$, IGNORE_RTN_KEY,
IGNORE_RTN_KEY, tFile)
            End If
            If vmxRtn% <> VIS_OK Then
                frmMain!lstFilesFound.AddItem "No Matches Found"
                Beep
                Exit Sub
            End If
    End If

    '-- Find the rest of the matches using XNEXT + Op% (Op% = XEQ or XBEGINS).
    While vmxRtn% = VIS_OK
            FileCount& = FileCount& + 1
            frmMain!lstFilesFound.AddItem LCase$(tFile.Path & tFile.Name & ", " &
Format$(tFile.TimeStamp, "mm/dd/yy") & ", " & Format$(tFile.Size, "#,##0"))
            vmxRtn% = VmxGet(hFile%, IDX_FILENAME, XNEXT + Op%, FileSpec$, IGNORE_RTN_KEY,
IGNORE_RTN_KEY, tFile)
    Wend

    '-- Tell them how many we found and give them some file info.
    vmxRtn% = VMXInfo(hFile%, tInfo)
    If vmxRtn% = VIS_OK Then
        RecsInFile$ = Format$(tInfo.RecordsInFile, "#,##0")
    Else
        RecsInFile$ = "Unable to retrieve "
    End If
    Call UpdateStatus(RecsInFile$ & " records in File Index, " & Format$(FileCount&, "0") & "
matches found.")

    '-- We have to close the file when we're done.
    vmxRtn% = VmxClose(hFile%)
    If vmxRtn% <> VIS_OK Then
        Msg$ = "Error Closing File Index Dataset."
        MsgBox Msg$, MB_OK + MB_ICONSTOP, VmxReturnCode$(vmxRtn%)
    End If


End Sub

Sub GenerateFileIndex ()
    Dim FileName$    '-- File Index Filename
    Dim Msg$         '-- MsgBox Message
```

```
    Dim mbRtn%        '-- MsgBox return code
    Dim vmxRtn%       '-- VB/ISAM return code
    Dim hFile%        '-- VB/ISAM dataset handle
    Dim nDrive%       '-- Drive Loop counter
    Dim nDir%         '-- Dir Loop Counter
    Dim Attr%         '-- File Attributes
    Dim DirFound$     '-- Directory being indexed
    Dim FileFound$    '-- File being indexed
    Dim FileCount&    '-- Number of Files indexed
    Dim RecID$        '-- Record ID in VB/ISAM file
    Dim tFile As T_File '-- File Record in VB/ISAM file
    ReDim arrDirs$(0)    '-- All directories enumerated on drive

    FileName$ = App.Path & "\" & APP_FILENAME

    '-- See if the file already exists.
    If Len(Dir$(FileName$)) Then
        Msg$ = "A File Index currently exists. Do you want to overwrite it?"
        mbRtn% = MsgBox(Msg$, MB_YESNO + MB_ICONQUESTION, "File Exists")
        If mbRtn% = IDNO Then
            Exit Sub
        Else
            vmxRtn% = VmxKill(FileName$)
            If vmxRtn% <> VIS_OK Then
                Msg$ = "Error deleting existing File Index Dataset. Aborting File Index
Generation"
                MsgBox Msg$, MB_OK + MB_ICONSTOP, VmxReturnCode$(vmxRtn%)
                Exit Sub
            End If
        End If
    End If

    '-- Warn them that this is a lengthy operation
    '   and give them a chance to bail out.
    Msg$ = "This will index every file on the selected drives so it could"
    Msg$ = Msg$ & " take a while. Are you sure you want to do it now?"
    mbRtn% = MsgBox(Msg$, MB_YESNO + MB_ICONQUESTION, "Confirm Operation")
    If mbRtn% = IDNO Then
        Exit Sub
    End If

    '-- First we have to create the file (bail out on failure).
    vmxRtn% = VmxCreate(FileName$, 6, FMT_FILE_INDEX)
    If vmxRtn% <> VIS_OK Then
        Msg$ = "Error Creating File Index Dataset. Aborting File Index Generation"
        MsgBox Msg$, MB_OK + MB_ICONSTOP, VmxReturnCode$(vmxRtn%)
        Exit Sub
    End If

    '-- Next we have to open it (bail out on failure).
    vmxRtn% = VmxOpen(FileName$, hFile%)
    If vmxRtn% <> VIS_OK Then
        Msg$ = "Error Opening File Index Dataset. Aborting File Index Generation"
        MsgBox Msg$, MB_OK + MB_ICONSTOP, VmxReturnCode$(vmxRtn%)
        Exit Sub
    End If


    For nDrive% = 0 To UBound(garrDrives$)
```

*(continued on next page)*

**11**

*(continued from previous page)*

```
            '-- First see if the drive box is checked.
            If gbarrDriveSelected%(nDrive%) Then
                On Error GoTo GenerateFileIndexErr

                '-- We need to find all the directories on the drive.
                Call UpdateStatus("Enumerating Directory Information for drive " &
garrDrives(nDrive%))
                Call EnumDirectories(garrDrives(nDrive%), arrDirs$())

                '-- Now we loop through all the directories we found.
                For nDir% = 0 To UBound(arrDirs$)
                    Call UpdateStatus(" Files Indexed: " & Format$(FileCount&, "#,##0") & "
Currently indexing: " & arrDirs$(nDir%))

                    '-- First get all the files in the directory.
                    Attr% = ATTR_NORMAL Or ATTR_HIDDEN Or ATTR_SYSTEM
                    FileFound$ = Dir$(arrDirs$(nDir%), Attr%)
                    While Len(FileFound$)

                        '-- Increment our file counter and assign a record ID.
                        FileCount& = FileCount& + 1
                        RecID$ = Hex$(FileCount&)

                        '-- Build our record.
                        tFile.Drive = garrDrives(nDrive%)
                        tFile.Path = arrDirs$(nDir%)
                        tFile.Name = FileFound$
                        tFile.TimeStamp = TimeValue(FileDateTime(tFile.Path & FileFound$))
                        tFile.Size = FileLen(tFile.Path & FileFound$)

                        vmxRtn% = VmxPut(hFile%, RecID$, tFile, ADD_ONLY)
                        If vmxRtn% <> VIS_OK Then
                            Msg$ = "Error adding record to File Index Dataset. Do you want to
continue?"
                            mbRtn% = MsgBox(Msg$, MB_YESNO + MB_ICONSTOP,
VmxReturnCode$(vmxRtn%))

                            If mbRtn% = IDNO Then
                                GoTo GenerateFileIndexExit
                            End If
                        End If

                        '-- Get the next file.
                        FileFound$ = Dir$
                        DoEvents
                    Wend
                Next nDir%
                On Error GoTo 0
            End If
        Next nDrive%

        Call UpdateStatus("Index complete!")

GenerateFileIndexExit:
    '-- We have to close the file when we're done.
    vmxRtn% = VmxClose(hFile%)
    If vmxRtn% <> VIS_OK Then
        Msg$ = "Error Closing File Index Dataset."
        MsgBox Msg$, MB_OK + MB_ICONSTOP, VmxReturnCode$(vmxRtn%)
    End If
```

```
    Exit Sub

GenerateFileIndexErr:
    Beep
    Msg$ = "Target Drive: " & garrDrives(nDrive%) & Chr$(13) & Chr$(10)
    Msg$ = Msg$ & "Target Path: " & arrDirs$(nDir%) & Chr$(13) & Chr$(10)
    mbRtn% = MsgBox(Msg$, MB_ABORTRETRYIGNORE, Error$(Err))
    Select Case mbRtn%
        Case IDABORT
            Resume GenerateFileIndexExit
        Case IDRETRY
            Resume
        Case IDIGNORE
            Resume Next
    End Select

End Sub

Sub GetAvailableDrives (Drv As DriveListBox, arrDrives() As String * 1)
    Dim i%

    ReDim arrDrives$(Drv.ListCount - 1)
    For i% = 0 To Drv.ListCount - 1
        arrDrives$(i%) = UCase$(Left$(Drv.List(i%), 1))
    Next i%

End Sub

Sub LoadDriveCheckBoxes (arrDrives() As String * 1)
    Dim NumDrives%
    Dim DriveIndex%
    Dim xPos&, yPos&
    Dim hwndOldParent%
    Dim DriveCount%
    Dim BottomOfLastCheckBox&

    NumDrives% = UBound(arrDrives$) - LBound(arrDrives$) + 1
    ReDim gbarrDriveSelected%(NumDrives% - 1)

    frmMain!chkDrive(0).Caption = arrDrives$(0) & ":"
    If NumDrives% > 0 Then
        For DriveIndex% = 1 To (NumDrives% - 1)
            DriveCount% = DriveCount% + 1

            '-- Load the new check box.
            Load frmMain!chkDrive(DriveIndex%)

            '-- Set its caption.
            frmMain!chkDrive(DriveIndex%).Caption = arrDrives$(DriveIndex%) & ":"

            '-- Put it inside the frame (so the frame is its parent control).
            hwndOldParent% = SetParent((frmMain!chkDrive(DriveIndex%).hWnd),
(frmMain!fmeDrivesToIndex.hWnd))

            '-- Position it in the frame.
            xPos& = frmMain!chkDrive(0).Left
            yPos& = frmMain!chkDrive(0).Top + (DriveIndex% * frmMain!chkDrive(0).Height)
            frmMain!chkDrive(DriveIndex%).Move xPos&, yPos&

            '-- Make sure it shows up.
```

11

*(continued on next page)*

*(continued from previous page)*

```
            frmMain!chkDrive(DriveIndex%).Visible = True
        Next DriveIndex%

        '----------------------------------------------------
        '-- Size the Frame to accommodate all the check
        '   boxes. We have to do some unit conversions
        '   because the form's ScaleMode is pixels not
        '   twips.
        '----------------------------------------------------
        BottomOfLastCheckBox& = frmMain!chkDrive(NumDrives% - 1).Top +
    frmMain!chkDrive(NumDrives% - 1).Height
        frmMain!fmeDrivesToIndex.Height = (BottomOfLastCheckBox& + 150) \ Screen.TwipsPerPixelY

    End If

End Sub

Sub Main ()

    Load frmMain
        Call GetAvailableDrives(frmMain!drvList, garrDrives())
        Call LoadDriveCheckBoxes(garrDrives())
    frmMain.Show

End Sub

Sub UpdateStatus (NewStatus$)

    frmMain!lblStatus.Caption = NewStatus$

End Sub
```

## Tips and Comments

There's no doubt that VB/ISAM is up to the task of handling large datasets. In addition, you can use it for error logs, configuration files, or almost any time you would use an ASCII file for simplicity's sake. Keep in mind that VB/ISAM is about as rock-solid as a product can be—a breath of fresh air in this age where "maintenance" releases are the norm, rather than the exception.

## Visual/db

| USAGE: | Access to XBase Database Files |
|---|---|
| MANUFACTURER: | AJS Publishing, Inc. |
| COST: | $149 (Single User Version), $299 (Network Version) |

Visual/db is not a control but is instead a library of Visual Basic routines that let you access XBase-format database files. To use this library, you only need to add a single Visual Basic source code (.BAS) file to your project, and then make the appropriate procedure calls. There are no dynamic link libraries or custom controls required. The main advantage of this approach is that no extra executable files (except the Visual Basic runtime .DLL) need to be distributed with your application. Visual/db also comes with a utility program, COP, (Code Optimization Program), that extracts unused Visual/db code from a project before it's compiled, thereby reducing the size of the resulting .EXE file.

# Syntax

Every operation in Visual/db is handled through subroutine calls. These include calls for basic database functions such as opening and closing .DBF files; reading, writing and appending records; and retrieving and setting database field values. You can also retrieve information about the database itself, its record length, the number of records in the file, and so forth. Visual/db also provides functions for accessing indexes and memo fields, as well as saving and retrieving bitmaps and sounds into database fields. Table 11-34 lists the 44 Visual/db subroutines.

**Table 11-34** The Visual/db subroutines

| AddKey | ASCIICONV | Cipher |
|---|---|---|
| CloseDBF | CloseDBT | CloseNDX |
| CommitSTR | CompEXP | ConfigLIB |
| CreateDBF | Decipher | DefineSTR |
| DeleteKEY | Encipher | EvalEXP |
| Exist | FlushDBF | FlushDBT |
| FlushNDX | GetERROR | GetFLD |
| GetFLDS | GetKEY | GetMEMO |
| GetPIC | GetREC | GetSND |
| LockNDX | LockREC | OpenDBF |
| OpenDBT | OpenNDX | PutFLD |
| PutFLDS | PutMEMO | PutPIC |
| PutREC | PutSND | ReturnSTR |
| SizeDBF | StatusDBF | StatusLIB |
| UnlockNDX | UnlockREC | |

**The Framework of a Visual/db Database Program**  The easiest way to learn about Visual/db is to start with a simple example. Suppose you have a list of cities where your company has branch offices. This list is stored in a .DBF file named BRANCHES.DBF. You're writing a database program, and one of the fields is the branch office. To make data entry more reliable, you want to load all of the branch office city names into a combo box named cmbBranch. Look at the following code:

```
' Open the Branches database.
DBFfile = "BRANCHES.DBF"
OpenMode = READWRITE And SHARE
OpenDBF dbHandle, Status, DBFfile, DBFtype, OpenMode
```

11

(continued on next page)

*(continued from previous page)*

```
If Status <> 0 Then
    MsgBox "Unable to open database.", MB_OK Or MB_ICONSTOP, "Error Opening Database"
    End
End If

' Find out how many records are in the database.
StatusDBF dbHandle, Status, DBFtype, DBFptr, NumRecs, NumFields, RecLength, Updated

' Make sure the combo box is empty.
cmbBranch.Clear

' Load all data (there's only 1 field) into the combo box.
FieldNum = 1
For CurRec = 1 To NumRecs
    GetRec dbHandle, Status, CurRec, RecData
    FieldName = ""
    GetFld dbHandle, Status, FieldNum, FieldName, FieldData, RecData

    If Status = 0 Then
        cmbBranch.AddItem FieldData
    End If
Next

' Close the database.
CloseMode = CLOSEFLUSH
CloseDBF dbHandle, Status, CLOSEFLUSH
```

The example first opens the database file using the *OpenDBF* subroutine call. This routine returns an integer database handle, *dbHandle,* that is used to uniquely identify the file in later Visual/db function calls. *OpenDBF* also returns an integer, *Status,* that indicates whether the function was successful. This is Visual/db's preferred method of error handling: you inspect the *Status* variable after a subroutine call, and take the appropriate action in the event of a problem. The example checks *Status,* displays an error message to the user, and then terminates the program.

After opening the database, the program uses the *StatusDBF* procedure to return the number of records in the Branches database. This call returns several other useful pieces of information: the type of database (dBASE III, FoxPro 1.0/2.0, dBASE IV, and so on), the length of records, the number of fields in each record, the date the database was last updated, and a pointer to a memo field, if one exists.

Given the number of records, the program now simply sets up a for loop to extract each one and add its data to the combo box. The *GetRec* subroutine extracts a database record. Given a record number, it retrieves the record data into a string. You extract individual database fields from the record using the *GetFld* subroutine. All fields are returned as strings, so you will need to convert fields to their proper types. For example, you may need to use the Visual Basic *Val()* function to convert string data to numeric data.

Finally, the database is closed using the *CloseDBF* procedure. This updates the file header and releases any system resources that were held to manage the file.

# Example

Figure 11-10 shows the example program, a trouble call log application used to log technical support phone calls. The user of the program simply presses the Add button whenever he or she receives a technical support call. The program automatically assigns a new call number, a unique number used to identify the call. The new record is saved after the call number is generated. The user can then enter information about the call.

Four buttons, First, Last, Previous, and Next, allow the user to browse the records in the database. Before a new record is displayed, the current record is automatically updated, saving any changes. You can also explicitly save the current record by pressing the Update button.

You can automatically enter the start and stop time of the call using the Start Time and Stop Time buttons. The user can also enter this information by typing it in the From and To fields.

The program uses two databases, CATEGORY and CALL_LOG. The CATEGORY database is simply a look-up table of valid categories that will be used for data entry into CALL_LOG, the main database table.

## Steps

1. Create two .DBF format data files. You can create these using a number of tools, including the sample program, CREATE, that comes with Visual/db. The first file, which you should save as CATEGORY.DBF, is defined in Table 11-35. The second file, which you should save as CALL_LOG.DBF, is defined in Table 11-36.

**Table 11-35** CATEGORY.DBF database definition

| FIELD NAME | TYPE | SIZE |
|------------|------|------|
| CATEGORY | Character | 50 |

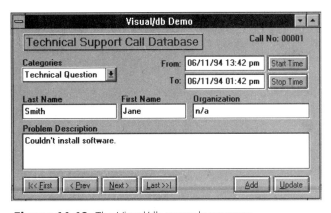

**Figure 11-10** The Visual/db example program

**Table 11-36** CALL_LOG.DBF database definition

| FIELD NAME | TYPE | SIZE |
|---|---|---|
| CALL_NO | Numeric | 2 |
| CATEGORY | Character | 50 |
| START_TIME | Character | 20 |
| STOP_TIME | Character | 20 |
| LAST_NAME | Character | 25 |
| FIRST_NAME | Character | 15 |
| ORG_NAME | Character | 50 |
| PROBLEM | Character | 254 |

2. Create a new project called VISUALDB.MAK. Copy the databases created in step 1 into the same directory as this new project. Add the Visual/db file, DBVB.BAS, to the project. Create a new form with the objects and properties described in Table 11-37. Save this form as VISUALDB.FRM.

**Table 11-37** Objects and properties of VISUALDB.FRM

| OBJECT | PROPERTY | SETTING |
|---|---|---|
| Form | FormName | frmVisualDB |
| | BackColor | &H00C0C0C0& |
| | Caption | "Visual/db Demo" |
| Label | Name | Label1 |
| | BackStyle | 0 'Transparent |
| | Caption | "Categories" |
| | ForeColor | &H00800000& |
| Label | Name | Label3 |
| | BackStyle | 0 'Transparent |
| | Caption | "Last Name" |
| | ForeColor | &H00800000& |
| Label | Name | Label4 |
| | BackStyle | 0 'Transparent |
| | Caption | "First Name" |
| | ForeColor | &H00800000& |
| Label | Name | Label5 |
| | BackStyle | 0 'Transparent |
| | Caption | "Problem Description" |
| | ForeColor | &H00800000& |
| Label | Name | Label6 |
| | Alignment | 1 'Right Justify |
| | BackStyle | 0 'Transparent |

| OBJECT | PROPERTY | SETTING |
|---|---|---|
| | Caption | "From:" |
| | ForeColor | &H00800000& |
| Label | Name | Label7 |
| | Alignment | 1  'Right Justify |
| | BackStyle | 0  'Transparent |
| | Caption | "To:" |
| | ForeColor | &H00800000& |
| Label | Name | Label8 |
| | BackStyle | 0  'Transparent |
| | Caption | "Organization" |
| | ForeColor | &H00800000& |
| Label | Name | lblCallNo |
| | BackStyle | 0  'Transparent |
| | Caption | "[none]" |
| | ForeColor | &H00000080& |
| Label | Name | Label2 |
| | BackStyle | 0  'Transparent |
| | Caption | "Call No:" |
| | ForeColor | &H00800000& |
| Label | Name | Label9 |
| | Alignment | 2  'Center |
| | BackStyle | 0  'Transparent |
| | BorderStyle | 1  'Fixed Single |
| | Caption | "Technical Support Call Database" |
| | FontSize | 12 |
| | ForeColor | &H00000080& |
| | Tag | "/3dup/" |
| ComboBox | Name | cmbCategories |
| | ForeColor | &H00000000& |
| | Style | 2  'Dropdown List |
| | Tag | "/3dup/" |
| TextBox | Name | txtLastName |
| | ForeColor | &H00000000& |
| | Tag | "/3d/" |
| TextBox | Name | txtFirstName |
| | ForeColor | &H00000000& |
| | Tag | "/3d/" |
| TextBox | Name | txtProblem |

*(continued on next page)*

**11**◀

| OBJECT | PROPERTY | SETTING |
|---|---|---|
| *(continued from previous page)* | | |
| | ForeColor | &H00000000& |
| | Tag | "/3d/" |
| TextBox | Name | txtTimeStart |
| | ForeColor | &H00000000& |
| | Tag | "/3d/" |
| TextBox | Name | txtTimeEnd |
| | ForeColor | &H00000000& |
| | Tag | "/3d/" |
| CommandButton | Name | btnTimeStart |
| | Caption | "Start Time" |
| | FontBold | 0 'False |
| | Tag | "/3d/" |
| CommandButton | Name | btnTimeEnd |
| | Caption | "Stop Time" |
| | FontBold | 0 'False |
| | Tag | "/3d/" |
| TextBox | Name | txtOrganization |
| | ForeColor | &H00000000& |
| | Tag | "/3d/" |
| CommandButton | Name | btnFirst |
| | Caption | "I<< &First" |
| | FontBold | 0 'False |
| | Tag | "/3d/" |
| CommandButton | Name | btnPrevious |
| | Caption | "< &Prev" |
| | FontBold | 0 'False |
| | Tag | "/3d/" |
| CommandButton | Name | btnNext |
| | Caption | "&Next >" |
| | FontBold | 0 'False |
| | Tag | "/3d/" |
| CommandButton | Name | btnLast |
| | Caption | "&Last >>I" |
| | FontBold | 0 'False |
| | Tag | "/3d/" |
| CommandButton | Name | btnAdd |
| | Caption | "&Add" |
| | FontBold | 0 'False |
| | Tag | "/3d/" |

| OBJECT | PROPERTY | SETTING |
|---|---|---|
| CommandButton | Name | btnUpdate |
| | Caption | "&Update" |
| | FontBold | 0 'False |
| | Tag | "/3d/" |

3. Add the following lines to the declarations section of VISUALDB.FRM. These are the constants and form-level global variable used by the form.

```
Option Explicit
'-----------------------------------------------------
' Constants and variables used By the Visual/db
' example program.
'-----------------------------------------------------

' Global variables used for database operations.
Dim CallLogFile As String
Dim globRecData As String
Dim globHandle As Integer
Dim globCurRec As Long

' Color constants.
Const DARK_GRAY = &H808080
Const WHITE = &HFFFFFF
Const BLACK = &H0

' 3D effect constants.
Const BORDER_INSET = 0
Const BORDER_RAISED = 1

' WindowState constant.
Const MINIMIZED = 1

' StatusDBF constants used in GetRecordInfo routine.
Const INFO_STATUS = 1
Const INFO_DBFTYPE = 2
Const INFO_DBFPTR = 3
Const INFO_NUMRECS = 4
Const INFO_NUMFIELDS = 5
Const INFO_RECLEN = 6
Const INFO_UPDATED = 7

' MsgBox constants.
Const MB_OK = &H0
Const MB_YESNOCANCEL = &H3
Const MB_YESNO = &H4

Const MB_ICONQUESTION = &H20
Const MB_ICONEXCLAMATION = &H30
Const MB_ICONINFORMATION = &H40
Const MB_ICONSTOP = &H10
```

4. Add the following code to the VISUALDB.FRM. It includes several generic subroutines to encapsulate some of the Visual/db functions. For example, the *LoadRecord* function reads a record and places its fields into the appropriate controls on the main form. The

**11◀**

*RecordMove* subroutine calls *LoadRecord* any time a new record is to be displayed. *LoadRecord* is in turn called by the *Click* event routines of the four record navigation buttons. Building these higher-level routines that can be called from several places within the program reduces the amount of redundant code.

```
Sub btnAdd_Click ()
'----------------------------------------------------
' Add a new record to the CALL_LOG database.
' Automatically generate the next CALL_NO value.
'----------------------------------------------------
Dim Status As Integer
Dim RecNum As Long

    ' Clear all fields.
    txtTimeStart = ""
    txtTimeEnd = ""
    txtLastName = ""
    txtFirstName = ""
    txtOrganization = ""
    txtProblem = ""
    cmbCategories.ListIndex = -1

    ' Determine next CALL_NO
    lblCallNo = Format$(GetLastCallNo() + 1, "00000")

    ' Append as a new record to end of CALL_LOG.
    RecNum = 0
    PutField 1, Format$(Val(lblCallNo))
    PutRec globHandle, Status, RecNum, globRecData

    ' Make this the new current record.
    globCurRec = RecNum
End Sub

Sub btnFirst_Click ()
'----------------------------------------------------
' Move to the first record in the database.
'----------------------------------------------------

    RecordMove globCurRec, 1
End Sub

Sub btnLast_Click ()
'----------------------------------------------------
' Move to the last record in the database.
'----------------------------------------------------

    RecordMove globCurRec, GetRecordInfo(globHandle, INFO_NUMRECS)
End Sub

Sub btnNext_Click ()
'----------------------------------------------------
' Move to the next record in the database.
'----------------------------------------------------

    RecordMove globCurRec, globCurRec + 1
End Sub

Sub btnPrevious_Click ()
```

```
'-----------------------------------------------------
' Move to the previous record in the database.
'-----------------------------------------------------

    RecordMove globCurRec, globCurRec - 1
End Sub

Sub btnTimeEnd_Click ()
'-----------------------------------------------------
' Update the Stop Time field with the current time.
'-----------------------------------------------------

    txtTimeEnd = Format$(Now, "MM/DD/YY HH:MM am/pm")
End Sub

Sub btnTimeStart_Click ()
'-----------------------------------------------------
' Update the Start Time field with the current time.
'-----------------------------------------------------

    txtTimeStart = Format$(Now, "MM/DD/YY HH:MM am/pm")
End Sub

Sub btnUpdate_Click ()
'-----------------------------------------------------
' Save the current record.
'-----------------------------------------------------

    If Not SaveRecord(globCurRec) Then
        MsgBox "Unable to save record.", MB_OK Or MB_ICONSTOP, "Error Saving Record"
    End If
End Sub

Sub Form_Load ()
'-----------------------------------------------------
' Position the form, load categories into the
' combo box, and open the Call Log database.
'-----------------------------------------------------
Dim retcode As Integer
Dim Status As Integer
Dim DBFtype As Integer
Dim OpenMode As Integer

    ' Center the form.
    Me.Move (Screen.Width - Me.Width) \ 2, (Screen.Height - Me.Height) \ 2

    ' Load Category data into the combo box.
    If Not LoadCategories(App.Path & "\CATEGORY.DBF") Then
        MsgBox "The program cannot continue because a database could not be loaded.", MB_OK Or
MB_ICONEXCLAMATION, "Program Ending"
    End If

    ' Open the CALL_LOG database.
    CallLogFile = App.Path & "\CALL_LOG.DBF"
    OpenMode = READWRITE And SHARE
    OpenDBF globHandle, Status, CallLogFile, DBFtype, OpenMode
    If Status <> 0 Then
        MsgBox "Unable to open Call Log database.", MB_OK Or MB_ICONSTOP, "Error Opening
Database"
        End
```

*(continued on next page)*

**11◀**

**723▶**

*(continued from previous page)*

```vb
        End If

        ' Load the first record into the form's fields.
        retcode = LoadRecord(1)
End Sub

Sub Form_Paint ()
'----------------------------------------------------
' Draw 3D effect around selected controls on form.
'----------------------------------------------------
Dim i As Integer

        ' Look at the tag fields of all controls.
        For i = 0 To Me.Controls.Count - 1
            If InStr(UCase$(Me.Controls(i).Tag), "/3D/") Then
                Make3D Me, Me.Controls(i), BORDER_INSET
            ElseIf InStr(UCase$(Me.Controls(i).Tag), "/3DUP/") Then
                Make3D Me, Me.Controls(i), BORDER_RAISED
            End If
        Next
End Sub

Sub Form_Unload (Cancel As Integer)
'----------------------------------------------------
' Save the current record and close the Call Log
' database.
'----------------------------------------------------
Dim Status As Integer
Dim OpenMode As Integer

        ' Save the current record.
        If Not SaveRecord(globCurRec) Then
            MsgBox "Unable to save record.", MB_OK Or MB_ICONSTOP, "Error Saving Record"
        End If

        OpenMode = READWRITE And SHARE
        CloseDBF globHandle, Status, OpenMode
End Sub

Function GetField (ByVal AFieldNum As Integer) As String
'----------------------------------------------------
' Given the field number, return the value stored
' in a record field.
'----------------------------------------------------
Dim Status As Integer
Dim FieldName As String
Dim FieldVal As String

        GetFld globHandle, Status, AFieldNum, FieldName, FieldVal, globRecData
        GetField = FieldVal
End Function

Function GetLastCallNo () As Integer
'----------------------------------------------------
' Get the value of the last CALL_NO field in the
' database.
'----------------------------------------------------
Dim NumRecs As Integer
Dim Status As Integer
```

```
Dim RecData As String
Dim FieldNum As Integer
Dim FieldName As String
Dim FieldData As String

    ' Get the number of records in the database.
    NumRecs = GetRecordInfo(globHandle, INFO_NUMRECS)

    ' Get the last record in the database.
    GetRec globHandle, Status, NumRecs, RecData

    FieldNum = 1
    ' Get the CALL_NO field from that record.
    GetFld globHandle, Status, FieldNum, FieldName, FieldData, RecData

    ' Return the last CALL_NO.
    GetLastCallNo = Val(FieldData)
End Function

Function GetRecordInfo (ByVal dbHandle As Integer, ByVal InfoConst As Integer) As Variant
'-------------------------------------------------
' Get selected .DBF information based on a user-
' supplied constant.
'-------------------------------------------------
Dim Status As Integer
Dim DBFtype As Integer
Dim DBFptr As Integer
Dim NumRecs As Long
Dim NumFields As Integer
Dim RecLength As Integer
Dim Updated As String

    ' Extract all the .DBF information for the open database
    ' specified by dbHandle.
    StatusDBF dbHandle, Status, DBFtype, DBFptr, NumRecs, NumFields, RecLength, Updated

    ' Return just the requested information.
    Select Case InfoConst
        Case INFO_STATUS: GetRecordInfo = Status
        Case INFO_DBFTYPE: GetRecordInfo = DBFtype
        Case INFO_DBFPTR: GetRecordInfo = DBFptr
        Case INFO_NUMRECS: GetRecordInfo = NumRecs
        Case INFO_NUMFIELDS: GetRecordInfo = NumFields
        Case INFO_RECLEN: GetRecordInfo = RecLength
        Case INFO_UPDATED: GetRecordInfo = Updated
    End Select
End Function

Function LoadCategories (ByVal DBFfile As String) As Integer
'-------------------------------------------------
' Load all data from the Categories database into
' the combo box.
'-------------------------------------------------
Dim dbHandle As Integer
Dim NumRecs As Integer
Dim Status As Integer
Dim OpenMode As Integer
Dim DBFtype As Integer
Dim CurRec As Integer
Dim RecData As String
```

11◄

(continued on next page)

*(continued from previous page)*

```vb
Dim FieldNum As Integer
Dim FieldName As String
Dim FieldData As String

    LoadCategories = False

    ' Open the Categories database.
    OpenMode = READWRITE And SHARE
    OpenDBF dbHandle, Status, DBFfile, DBFtype, OpenMode
    If Status <> 0 Then
        MsgBox "Unable to open Categories database.", MB_OK Or MB_ICONSTOP, "Error Opening
Database"
        Exit Function
    End If

    ' Find out how many records are in the database.
    NumRecs = GetRecordInfo(dbHandle, INFO_NUMRECS)

    ' Make sure the combo box is empty.
    cmbCategories.Clear

    ' Load all Category data (there's only 1 field) into combo box.
    FieldNum = 1
    For CurRec = 1 To NumRecs
        GetRec dbHandle, Status, CurRec, RecData
        FieldName = ""
        GetFld dbHandle, Status, FieldNum, FieldName, FieldData, RecData

        If Status = 0 Then
            cmbCategories.AddItem FieldData
        End If
    Next

    ' Close the database.
    CloseDBF dbHandle, Status, OpenMode

    ' Set return code (successful).
    LoadCategories = True
End Function

Function LoadRecord (ByVal RecNum As Integer) As Integer
'------------------------------------------------------
' Load the record indicated by RecNum into the
' form's data fields.
'------------------------------------------------------
Dim Status As Integer
Dim OpenMode As Integer
Dim DBFtype As Integer
Dim Category As String
Dim i As Integer

    LoadRecord = True

    ' Get the specified record.
    GetRec globHandle, Status, RecNum, globRecData
    If Status <> 0 Then
        LoadRecord = False
        Exit Function
    End If
    globCurRec = RecNum
```

```
    ' Load the data into form's controls.
    lblCallNo = Format$(Val(GetField(1)), "00000")

    ' Set the combo box if there's a match.
    Category = GetField(2)
    For i = 0 To cmbCategories.ListCount - 1
        If Trim$(Category) = Trim$(cmbCategories.List(i)) Then
            cmbCategories.ListIndex = i
            Exit For
        End If
    Next

    ' Set all the text controls.
    txtTimeStart = GetField(3)
    txtTimeEnd = GetField(4)
    txtLastName = GetField(5)
    txtFirstName = GetField(6)
    txtOrganization = GetField(7)
    txtProblem = GetField(8)
End Function

Sub Make3D (pic As Form, ctl As Control, ByVal BorderStyle As Integer)
'----------------------------------------------------
' Wrap a 3D effect around a control on a form.
'----------------------------------------------------
Dim AdjustX As Integer, AdjustY As Integer
Dim RightSide As Single
Dim BW As Integer, BorderWidth As Integer
Dim LeftTopColor As Long, RightBottomColor As Long
Dim i As Integer

    If Not ctl.Visible Then Exit Sub

    AdjustX = Screen.TwipsPerPixelX
    AdjustY = Screen.TwipsPerPixelY

    BorderWidth = 1

    Select Case BorderStyle
    Case 0: ' Inset
    LeftTopColor = DARK_GRAY
    RightBottomColor = WHITE
    Case 1: ' Raised
    LeftTopColor = WHITE
    RightBottomColor = DARK_GRAY
    End Select


    ' Set the top shading line.
    For BW = 1 To BorderWidth
    ' Top
    pic.CurrentX = ctl.Left - (AdjustX * BW)
    pic.CurrentY = ctl.Top - (AdjustY * BW)
    pic.Line -(ctl.Left + ctl.Width + (AdjustX * (BW - 1)), ctl.Top - (AdjustY * BW)),
LeftTopColor
    ' Right
    pic.Line -(ctl.Left + ctl.Width + (AdjustX * (BW - 1)), ctl.Top + ctl.Height + (AdjustY *
(BW - 1))), RightBottomColor
    ' Bottom
    pic.Line -(ctl.Left - (AdjustX * BW), ctl.Top + ctl.Height + (AdjustY * (BW - 1))),
```

(continued on next page)

**11**

*(continued from previous page)*

```
RightBottomColor
    ' Left
    pic.Line -(ctl.Left - (AdjustX * BW), ctl.Top - (AdjustY * BW)), LeftTopColor
    Next
End Sub


Sub PutField (ByVal AFieldNum As Integer, ByVal AFieldVal As String)
'---------------------------------------------------
' Given a field number and a field value, insert
' that data into the Record Data string.
'---------------------------------------------------
Dim Status As Integer
Dim FieldName As String

    PutFld globHandle, Status, AFieldNum, FieldName, AFieldVal, globRecData
End Sub


Sub RecordMove (ByVal FromRec As Long, ByVal ToRec As Long)
'---------------------------------------------------
' Save the record FromRec, and then load the record
' ToRec into the form's controls, making ToRec
' the current record.
'---------------------------------------------------

    If Not SaveRecord(FromRec) Then
        MsgBox "Unable to save record.", MB_OK Or MB_ICONSTOP, "Error Saving Record"
    Else
        If Not LoadRecord(ToRec) Then
            Beep
        End If
    End If
End Sub


Function SaveRecord (ByVal RecNum As Long) As Integer
'---------------------------------------------------
' Save the current contents of the form's controls
' to the database as record RecNum.
'---------------------------------------------------
Dim Status As Integer

    PutField 1, Format$(Val(lblCallNo))
    PutField 2, cmbCategories.Text
    PutField 3, txtTimeStart
    PutField 4, txtTimeEnd
    PutField 5, txtLastName
    PutField 6, txtFirstName
    PutField 7, txtOrganization
    PutField 8, txtProblem

    PutRec globHandle, Status, RecNum, globRecData
    If Status  0 Then
        SaveRecord = False
    Else
        SaveRecord = True
    End If
End Function
```

## Tips and Comments

Visual/db serves as an interesting counterpoint to many of the other tools discussed in this book. Most of those tools are in the form of .VBX controls—specialized .DLLs that are tightly bound to the event-driven model of Visual Basic. Visual/db, while designed entirely as a function library, shows that you can develop a solid and full-featured programming tool using nothing but Visual Basic. One advantage to this approach is that you don't need to distribute additional .VBX or .DLL files with your applications. You can create database programs that are single executables, minimizing the number of files you need to distribute with your app.

11◄

# OTHER INTERESTING CONTROLS

$S$ ome controls are easy to categorize, falling neatly into areas such as word processing or spreadsheets. Others are more general, but can still be put into a broader category, such as widgets or image processing. Then there are controls that just don't fit into any broad category. The controls in this chapter are good examples.

▲ **Assoc** The Assoc control creates a new data structure through a Visual Basic control, which seems to be a fairly unique but nonetheless very useful idea.

▲ **JoyStk** JoyStk gives you a way to use joysticks inside your VB applications.

▲ **M.4** M.4 gives you access to an entire expert system language through Visual Basic.

▲ **VersionStamper-VB** VersionStamper-VB helps you avoid file version problems that have become much more prevalent with the advent of common, shared dynamic link libraries.

▲ **ZipInf** ZipInf can view the contents of .ZIP archive files, including uncompressed file sizes, and file time and date stamps.

#  Assoc (ASSOC.VBX)

| USAGE: | Associative Array Implementation |
|---|---|
| MANUFACTURER: | Axiomatic Software Limited |
| COST: | Free |

The Assoc control implements a new data structure in Visual Basic: associative arrays. This new data structure allows easy look-up of text information using a text "key." Assoc is unusual in that it doesn't provide a Visual Basic program with any visual element, such as a label or a button, but rather extends the language by providing a new data structure.

## Syntax

Table 12-1 lists the nonstandard properties and event of the Assoc control.

**Table 12-1** Nonstandard properties and event of the Assoc control

| PROPERTIES | | |
|---|---|---|
| Action | Defined | Delimiter |
| Key | KeyValue | NextKey |
| Value | | |
| **EVENT** | | |
| Enumerate | | |

### Associative Arrays Defined
Associative arrays are arrays whose index subscripts are strings instead of integers. To better illustrate this, consider an example where you would normally use pairs of strings. Suppose you are tracking names and addresses in a program, and want to store them all internally in a data structure. The obvious way is to define two arrays such as these:

```
Dim Names() As String
Dim Addresses() As String
```

You then assign values to the arrays in tandem, so that each entry in *Addresses* is associated with the entry in *Names* that has the same array index. This method generally works well for storing the data, but requires some programming effort to find an individual item. Assuming the names aren't sorted, a linear search would be required to find the desired entry:

```
Function FindName (ByVal TargetName As String) As Integer
Dim i As Integer

    FindName = 0
    For i=1 to UBound(Names)
        If Names(i) = TargetName then
            Findname = i
            Exit For
        End If
    Next
End Function
```

With Assoc, you can create arrays where the array index is meaningful. For example, let's say you wanted to associate telephone area codes to the state that uses them. With a normal array, you could define a 999 element array of strings and assign values this way:

```
AreaCodeStates(804) = "Virginia"
```

and search for values like this:

```
i = 201
AState = AreaCodeStates (i)
```

This works because the array index is meaningful, that is, the value it contains has meaning beyond just being an offset into an array. Unfortunately, with normal arrays you can only do this with integer index values. Also, if your array is sparse, this method is extremely wasteful of system memory.

Associative arrays simplify the task of building and searching through paired data such as this, when both parts of the pairing are strings. While this data structure is found in such text-processing languages such as UNIX's awk, it is not generally found in third-generation languages such as BASIC. In awk, an array's subscript can be a string, so a search for "Smith, Jim" might look as simple as this:

```
AnAddress = PeopleArray ("Smith, Jim")
```

where PeopleArray is an associative array containing addresses, and "Smith, Jim" is an index into the array.

The Assoc control implements this kind of array, but because of the constraints of the custom control interface, the syntax is different. When the Assoc control is placed on a form, its button bitmap is displayed. Like other "nonvisual" controls such as the Timer, however, this button is invisible at run time. Once on the form, data can be assigned to this control in the program. Data is stored using two properties: *Key* and *Value*. These properties correspond to an array index and the array's data. To assign data, first assign the *Key* property, and then assign the *Value* property.

```
Assoc1.Key = "Smith, Jim"
Assoc1.Value = "1206 North Main Street"
```

Once it's assigned, a value can be retrieved by first assigning the *Key* value, and then reading the *Value* property.

```
Assoc1.Key = "Johnson, Fred"
AnAddress = Assoc1.Value
```

If no entry exists for a *Key* value, an empty string ("") is returned. This could cause some confusion, as an empty string can be a valid *Value*. To avoid this problem, the Assoc control provides the Boolean *Defined* property, which returns *True* if the current *Key* value is a defined array element.

**Using the Action Property** The *Action* property provides several useful functions, which are initiated based on the value assigned to *Action*. Table 12-2 describes the basic actions.

**Table 12-2** Values used by the Action property

| VALUE | MEANING |
| --- | --- |
| 0 | Enumerate through entire array. |
| 1 | Remove (clear) all data from the array. |
| 2 | Delete the current item (based on Key) from the array. |

Setting the *Action* value to 0 triggers the control's *Enumerate* event once for each element in the associative array. You can only trigger the *Enumerate* event by setting the *Action* property. This event was designed to let you quickly scan through the entire array. The *Enumerate* event receives two parameters: the current *Key* and *Value*.

An *Action* value of 1 removes any existing data from the control. A value of 2 removes just the current item, based on the value in the *Key* property. For example,

```
Assoc1.Key = "Smith, Jim"
Assoc1.Action = 2
```

would delete the entry for Jim Smith from the array.

The Assoc control automatically sorts array entries by their *Key* values as they are added to the control. To step through the entire array in order you can use the *NextKey* property. This property returns the next key value. To find the first key in an Assoc array, set the *Key* to "", and then read the value of *NextKey*. When *NextKey* encounters the end of an array, it returns an empty string. The following piece of code would dump all the *Key* values in a control into a list box using *NextKey*.

```
Sub DumpAssoc (Assoc1 As ASSOC, AList As ListBox)

    Assoc1.Key = ""
    Do
        Assoc1.Key = Assoc1.NextKey
        If Assoc1.Key = "" Then Exit Do
        AList.AddItem Assoc1.Key
    Loop
End Sub
```

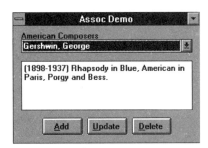

**Figure 12-1** The Assoc example program

The Assoc control also provides the *KeyValue* property, which allows you to set and retrieve array data in one statement. The earlier example, which added an array entry for John Smith, could be replaced with this:

```
Assoc1.KeyValue = "Smith, Jim=1206 North Main Street"
```

Likewise, *KeyValue* will retrieve data in the same format, based on the current value of the *Key* property. The equal sign delimiter used to separate the data in the string is merely a default; you can change this character by setting the *Delimiter* property at either design or run time.

# Example

This example, shown in Figure 12-1, uses a single Assoc control to implement a simple database. Data for this database is stored in a simple text file and read into the associative array when the program is loaded. The database contains a list of American classical composers, with brief information on each. The composer's name forms the *Key* value for the associative array, while the information is stored in the *Value* property.

The *Key* values are loaded into a combo box, and when the user clicks a new name, the program displays data from that entry's associated *Value* property in a text control. Buttons allow the user to add new entries, update information, and delete entries.

## Steps

1. Create a new project called ASSOC.MAK. Add the Assoc control, ASSOC.VBX, to the project. Create a new form with the objects and properties described in Table 12-3. Save this form as ASSOC.FRM.

**Table 12-3** Objects and properties for the ASSOC.FRM form

| OBJECT | PROPERTY | SETTING |
|--------|----------|---------|
| Form | FormName | frmAssoc |
| | BackColor | &H00C0C0C0& |
| | BorderStyle | 1 'Fixed Single |
| | Caption | "Assoc Demo" |

*(continued on next page)*

**12◄**

**735**

| OBJECT | PROPERTY | SETTING |
|---|---|---|
| *(continued from previous page)* | | |
| | MaxButton | 0 'False |
| Label | Name | lblComposerPrompt |
| | BackStyle | 0 'Transparent |
| | Caption | "American Composers" |
| | ForeColor | &H00FF0000& |
| ASSOC | Name | Assoc1 |
| | Delimiter | "=" |
| ComboBox | Name | cmbCompList |
| | Sorted | -1 'True |
| | Style | 2 'Dropdown List |
| TextBox | Name | txtCompInfo |
| | MultiLine | -1 'True |
| CommandButton | Name | btnAdd |
| | Caption | "&Add" |
| CommandButton | Name | btnUpdate |
| | Caption | "&Update" |
| CommandButton | Name | btnDelete |
| | Caption | "&Delete" |
| TextBox | Name | txtNewComposer |
| | Visible | 0 'False |

2. Add the following code to the ASSOC.FRM form's declarations section.

```
Option Explicit

'--------------------------------------------------
' Constants used by the Assoc control's Action
' property.
'--------------------------------------------------
Const ASSOC_ENUMERATE = 0
Const ASSOC_CLEAR_ALL = 1
Const ASSOC_DELETE_KEY = 2

Sub Assoc1_Enumerate (Key As String, Value As String)
'--------------------------------------------------
' This Enumerate event is fired once for each
' element of the Assoc array. It is started when
' the Assoc''s Action property is assigned 0. In
' this case it is used to initially load the combo
' box.
'--------------------------------------------------
    cmbCompList.AddItem Key
End Sub
```

3. Add the following functions and subroutines to the ASSOC.FRM form.

```
Sub btnAdd_Click ()
```

```
'------------------------------------------------
' Enable the "new composer" text entry field, and
' hide the combo box. Also hide the Add and
' Delete buttons.
'------------------------------------------------
    cmbCompList.Visible = False
    btnAdd.Visible = False
    btnDelete.Visible = False

    txtNewComposer.Move cmbCompList.Left, cmbCompList.Top, cmbCompList.Width,
cmbCompList.Height
    txtNewComposer.Visible = True
    txtCompInfo = ""
    txtNewComposer.SetFocus
End Sub

Sub btnDelete_Click ()
'------------------------------------------------
' Delete the current selection in the combo box,
' and remove it from the ASSOC array by setting the
' Action property to the value 2.
'------------------------------------------------
    If cmbCompList.ListIndex >= 0 Then
        Assoc1.Key = cmbCompList.List(cmbCompList.ListIndex)
        Assoc1.Action = ASSOC_DELETE_KEY
        cmbCompList.RemoveItem cmbCompList.ListIndex
        If cmbCompList.ListCount > 0 Then cmbCompList.ListIndex = 0
    End If
End Sub

Sub btnUpdate_Click ()
'------------------------------------------------
' This button could have been pressed during the
' process of adding a new record, or when merely
' updating an existing record. We check to see
' if the "new composer" text box is visible to
' figure out which condition we have.
'------------------------------------------------
    If txtNewComposer.Visible Then
        Assoc1.Key = Trim$(txtNewComposer.Text)
        cmbCompList.AddItem Assoc1.Key
    Else
        Assoc1.Key = Trim$(cmbCompList.List(cmbCompList.ListIndex))
    End If
    Assoc1.Value = Trim$(txtCompInfo.Text)

    txtNewComposer.Visible = False
    cmbCompList.Visible = True
    btnAdd.Visible = True
    btnDelete.Visible = True
End Sub

Sub cmbCompList_Click ()
'------------------------------------------------
' This routine shows how easily an associated
' string can be found. Set the Assoc key field
' with the current combo box value, then simply
' inspect the Assoc's Value property to get the
' associated text.
'------------------------------------------------
```

12◄

*(continued on next page)*

*(continued from previous page)*

```vb
    If cmbCompList.ListIndex >= 0 Then
        Assoc1.Key = cmbCompList.List(cmbCompList.ListIndex)
        txtCompInfo.Text = Assoc1.Value
    End If
End Sub


Sub Form_Load ()
'-----------------------------------------------------
' Center the form on the screen, and load data from
' the text file into the associative array and
' combo box.
'-----------------------------------------------------
Dim retcode As Integer

    Me.Move (Screen.Width - Me.Width) \ 2, (Screen.Height - Me.Height) \ 2

    retcode = LoadAssoc(Assoc1, App.Path & "\AMERCOMP.DAT")
    Assoc1.Action = ASSOC_ENUMERATE
    cmbCompList.ListIndex = 0
End Sub


Function LoadAssoc (AnAssoc As ASSOC, ByVal AFileName As String) As Integer
'-----------------------------------------------------
' Given an Assoc control and a file name, this
' function will load information from the text file
' into the Assoc control. Information is formatted
' as double-quoted strings: alternating lines
' contain people's names and a brief biography.
'-----------------------------------------------------
Dim Fnum As Integer
Dim AName As String
Dim ABio As String

    LoadAssoc = False
    On Error GoTo LoadAssoc_Error

    Fnum = FreeFile
    Open AFileName For Input As Fnum
    Do While Not EOF(Fnum)
        Input #Fnum, AName
        If EOF(Fnum) Then Exit Do

        Input #Fnum, ABio

        AnAssoc.Key = Trim$(AName)
        AnAssoc.Value = Trim$(ABio)
    Loop
    Close Fnum
    LoadAssoc = True
Exit Function

LoadAssoc_Error:
    Exit Function
End Function
```

## Tips and Comments

The Assoc control illustrates that custom controls are not restricted just to the visual elements of an application; they can be an effective way to extend its data structures as well. It seems quite possible that similar controls could be developed to allow linked lists, queues, or tree structures.

#  JoyStk (JOYSTK1.VBX)

| USAGE: | Joystick Control |
| --- | --- |
| MANUFACTURER: | Mabry Software |
| COST: | $15 Shareware ($10 if registered on CompuServe) |

The JoyStk control allows you to integrate a Microsoft-compatible joystick into your Visual Basic programs. For this control to work properly, a Windows joystick driver must be installed (through the Drivers applet in the Control Panel).

## Syntax

While most Visual Basic programmers are used to dealing with the mouse as a pointing device, relatively few are practiced in the art of using a joystick in Windows programs. There are many cases where a joystick is a superior method for handling interaction between the user and the program. This is most obvious in arcade-style computer games.

A conventional joystick can generally be moved in two directions on an x-y plane, although some "three-dimensional" joysticks support movement in the z direction as well. Joysticks also have one or more "fire" buttons. The JoyStk control provides feedback on the current position and button states of a joystick. Table 12-4 lists the nonstandard properties and events of the JoyStk control.

**Table 12-4** Nonstandard properties and events of the JoyStk control

**PROPERTIES**

| | | |
| --- | --- | --- |
| Button1 | Button2 | Button3 |
| Button4 | Buttons | Devices |
| Manufacturer | Period | PeriodMax |
| PeriodMin | Port | Product |
| ProductName | Threshold | XMax |
| XMin | XPos | YMax |
| YMin | YPos | ZMax |
| ZMin | ZPos | |

**EVENTS**

| | | |
| --- | --- | --- |
| ButtonDown | ButtonUp | Move |

12◄

**What Kind of Joystick Is This?**   Since there are so many joysticks available, the JoyStk control provides several properties for determining what type of device Windows thinks you have attached to your joystick port. *Manufacturer* is an integer property that indicates the manufacturer of the joystick driver software. The only valid value is 1, which indicates a Microsoft driver.

The *Product* property is an integer that gives the product ID for the joystick device. Table 12-5 supplies the valid values for this property. *ProductName* is a string that indicates the name of the device. *Manufacturer, Product,* and *ProductName* are only valid after the JoyStk control has been enabled. This is also true for most of the other properties.

**Table 12-5**  Values for the Product property

| VALUE | MEANING |
|-------|---------|
| 1 | Microsoft MIDI mapper |
| 2 | Microsoft wave mapper |
| 3 | Sound Blaster MIDI output port |
| 4 | Sound Blaster MIDI input port |
| 5 | Sound Blaster internal synthesizer |
| 6 | Sound Blaster waveform output port |
| 7 | Sound Blaster waveform input port |
| 9 | AdLib-compatible synthesizer |
| 10 | MPU401 MIDI output port |
| 11 | MPU401 MIDI input port |
| 12 | IBM game control adapter |

The *Devices* property is an integer that indicates how many joysticks can be handled by the current joystick driver. The *Buttons* property returns the number of buttons on the current joystick. The JoyStk control can support joysticks with up to four distinct buttons.

By setting the *Port* property, you can choose which joystick port the control returns information about. The valid values are 1 and 2, for the first and second joystick ports.

*Polling rate*   refers to how often the joystick driver checks the joystick for new information. There are three properties related to this process: *Period, PeriodMin,* and *PeriodMax. PeriodMin* and *PeriodMax* are read-only values that return the minimum and maximum interval (in milliseconds) that the joystick driver supports. The *Period* property allows you to set the polling rate to a value between the minimum and maximum.

**Getting Feedback from the Joystick**   The *XMin, XMax, YMin, YMax, ZMin,* and *ZMax* properties return the integer lower and upper bounds of the X, Y, and Z coordinates returned by the joystick. These run time properties are read-only and are only available after you have enabled the joystick by setting the *Enabled*  property to *True.*

The JoyStk control provides three events, *ButtonDown, ButtonUp,* and *Move,* that are fired when the joystick's state changes. These events can only occur once per polling interval, which as mentioned is set with the *Period* property. *ButtonUp* and *ButtonDown* are fired whenever a joystick button is pressed or released. These events both have an integer *Button* argument that indicates which of the (up to) four joystick buttons was pressed.

The *Move* event is fired whenever the joystick's position changes. This could generate a huge number of event calls, so a *Threshold* property gives you some control over how much stick movement is required before a *Move* event is fired. You can change *Threshold* at run time, but you must disable the JoyStk control before changing the value, and then reenable it afterward, as shown here:

```
JoyStick1.Enabled = False
JoyStick1.Threshold = 500
JoyStick1.Enabled = True
```

The *Move* event receives three parameters, *X, Y,* and *Z.* These integers indicate the coordinates of the stick when it was last polled.

Outside the *Move* event, you can inspect the current coordinates of the stick using the *XPos, YPos,* and *ZPos* properties. These properties return the position of the stick when it was last polled. Likewise, the *Button1, Button2, Button3,* and *Button4* properties are *True/False* values that indicate whether these buttons were pressed during the last polling.

# Example

Since joysticks are most commonly associated with games, the example program is a game that demonstrates how to use the JoyStk control. In this game, PotHoles, you use the joystick to steer a car down an uncommonly bad road. By moving the joystick from left to right, you can move the car in either direction. You can also use the ⬅ and ➡ keys to accomplish the same thing. The game is shown in Figure 12-2.

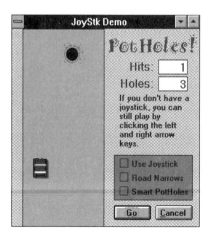

**Figure 12-2** The JoyStk demo program

12◀

Notice that the program doesn't handle the joystick car movement with the *Move* event, but instead inspects the *XPos* property in the *Timer* event. Since the *Timer* event handles the movement of PotHoles anyway, it makes sense to adjust the position of the car in the same event. Also, the *Move* event doesn't get called when the joystick isn't moving.

## Steps

1. Create a new project called JOYSTK.MAK. Add the JoyStk control, JOYSTK1.VBX, to the project. Create a new form with the objects and properties described in Table 12-6. Save this form as JOYSTK.FRM.

**Table 12-6** Objects and properties of the JOYSTK.FRM form

| OBJECT | PROPERTY | SETTING |
|---|---|---|
| Form | FormName | frmJoyStk |
| | BackColor | &H0080FF80& |
| | BorderStyle | 1 'Fixed Single |
| | Caption | "JoyStk Demo" |
| | KeyPreview | -1 'True |
| Image | Name | Image1 |
| | Picture | (set at design time in Properties window) |
| Label | Name | Label1 |
| | Alignment | 1 'Right Justify |
| | BackStyle | 0 'Transparent |
| | Caption | "Hits:" |
| | FontSize | 12 |
| | ForeColor | &H00000080& |
| Label | Name | Label2 |
| | Alignment | 1 'Right Justify |
| | BackStyle | 0 'Transparent |
| | Caption | "Holes:" |
| | FontSize | 12 |
| | ForeColor | &H00000080& |
| Label | Name | lblHits |
| | Alignment | 1 'Right Justify |
| | BorderStyle | 1 'Fixed Single |
| | Caption | "0" |
| | FontSize | 12 |
| | ForeColor | &H00800000& |
| Label | Name | lblHoles |
| | Alignment | 1 'Right Justify |
| | BorderStyle | 1 'Fixed Single |

| OBJECT | PROPERTY | SETTING |
|---|---|---|
| | Caption | "0" |
| | FontSize | 12 |
| | ForeColor | &H00800000& |
| Label | Name | Label3 |
| | BackStyle | 0 'Transparent |
| | Caption | "If you don't have a joystick, you can still play by clicking the left and right arrow keys." |
| | ForeColor | &H00000080& |
| PictureBox | Name | picRoad |
| | BackColor | &H00C0C0C0& |
| CommandButton | Name | btnGo |
| | Caption | "&Go" |
| Timer | Name | Timer1 |
| | Enabled | 0 'False |
| | Interval | 5 |
| CommandButton | Name | btnCancel |
| | Caption | "&Cancel" |
| PictureBox | Name | Picture1 |
| | BackColor | &H0000FF00& |
| Joystick | Name | Joystick1 |
| | Enabled | 0 'False |

2. Place the controls shown in Table 12-7 inside the picRoad PictureBox control. Make sure to select the picRoad control on the form before adding these controls.

**Table 12-7** Controls contained inside the picRoad PictureBox control

| OBJECT | PROPERTY | SETTING |
|---|---|---|
| PictureBox | Name | picHole |
| | AutoSize | -1 'True |
| | BackColor | &H00C0C0C0& |
| | BorderStyle | 0 'None |
| PictureBox | Name | picPotHoles |
| | AutoSize | -1 'True |
| | BackColor | &H00C0C0C0& |
| | BorderStyle | 0 'None |
| | Index | 0 |
| | Picture | (set at design time in Properties window) |
| | Visible | 0 'False |

(continued on next page)

12◄

| OBJECT | PROPERTY | SETTING |
|---|---|---|
| *(continued from previous page)* | | |
| PictureBox | Name | picPotHoles |
| | AutoSize | -1 'True |
| | BackColor | &H00C0C0C0& |
| | BorderStyle | 0 'None |
| | Index | 1 |
| | Picture | (set at design time in Properties window) |
| | Visible | 0 'False |
| PictureBox | Name | picCar |
| | AutoSize | -1 'True |
| | BackColor | &H00C0C0C0& |
| | BorderStyle | 0 'None |
| PictureBox | Name | picCars |
| | AutoSize | -1 'True |
| | BackColor | &H00C0C0C0& |
| | BorderStyle | 0 'None |
| | Index | 0 |
| | Picture | (set at design time in Properties window) |
| | Visible | 0 'False |
| PictureBox | Name | picCars |
| | AutoSize | -1 'True |
| | BackColor | &H00C0C0C0& |
| | BorderStyle | 0 'None |
| | Index | 1 |
| | Picture | (set at design time in Properties window) |
| | Visible | 0 'False |
| PictureBox | Name | picCars |
| | AutoSize | -1 'True |
| | BackColor | &H00C0C0C0& |
| | BorderStyle | 0 'None |
| | Index | 2 |
| | Picture | (set at design time in Properties window) |
| | Visible | 0 'False |
| PictureBox | Name | picCars |
| | AutoSize | -1 'True |
| | BackColor | &H00C0C0C0& |
| | BorderStyle | 0 'None |
| | Index | 3 |
| | Picture | (set at design time in Properties window) |
| | Visible | 0 'False |

| OBJECT | PROPERTY | SETTING |
|---|---|---|
| PictureBox | Name | picCars |
| | AutoSize | -1 'True |
| | BackColor | &H00C0C0C0& |
| | BorderStyle | 0 'None |
| | Index | 4 |
| | Picture | (set at design time in Properties window) |
| | Visible | 0 'False |
| PictureBox | Name | picCarHit |
| | AutoSize | -1 'True |
| | BackColor | &H00C0C0C0& |
| | BorderStyle | 0 'None |
| | Picture | (set at design time in Properties window) |
| | Visible | 0 'False |
| PictureBox | Name | picPotHoles |
| | AutoSize | -1 'True |
| | BackColor | &H00C0C0C0& |
| | BorderStyle | 0 'None |
| | Index | 2 |
| | Picture | (set at design time in Properties window) |
| | Visible | 0 'False |
| PictureBox | Name | picPotHoles |
| | AutoSize | -1 'True |
| | BackColor | &H00C0C0C0& |
| | BorderStyle | 0 'None |
| | Index | 3 |
| | Picture | (set at design time in Properties window) |
| | Visible | 0 'False |

3. Place the controls listed in Table 12-8 inside the Picture1 PictureBox control. Make sure to select the Picture1 control on the form before adding these controls.

**Table 12-8**  Controls contained inside the Picture1 PictureBox control

| OBJECT | PROPERTY | SETTING |
|---|---|---|
| CheckBox | Name | chkJoystick |
| | BackColor | &H0000FF00& |
| | Caption | "Use Joystick" |
| | ForeColor | &H00000080& |
| CheckBox | Name | chkRoadNarrows |
| | BackColor | &H0000FF00& |

*(continued on next page)*

12◄

| OBJECT | PROPERTY | SETTING |
|---|---|---|
| *(continued from previous page)* | | |
| | Caption | "Road Narrows" |
| | ForeColor | &H00000080& |
| CheckBox | Name | chkSmartPotHoles |
| | BackColor | &H0000FF00& |
| | Caption | "Smart PotHoles" |
| | ForeColor | &H00000080& |

4. You'll need to use a bitmap editor (such as Windows Paintbrush) to create the bitmaps used by the program. You'll need a series of bitmaps showing the car in increasing states of damage, as well as an "impact" bitmap that's used when the car collides. You'll also need to create a series of pothole bitmaps that serve as obstacles.

5. After creating the JOYSTK.FRM form, add the following code to its declarations section.

```
Option Explicit

'----------------------------------------------------
' Variables, constants, and declarations needed for
' the JoyStk control demo.
'----------------------------------------------------

Dim Speed As Integer       ' Current Speed of the car per interval.
Dim Steering As Integer    ' How much car moves left/right in one interval.

Dim CarIndex As Integer    ' Current bitmap array index.
Dim CarY As Integer        ' Car's position from end (top) of road.

Dim StartRoadWidth As Integer

Const START_SPEED = 50
Const START_STEERING = 50

' Used for keyboard operation of the game.
Const KEY_LEFT = &H25
Const KEY_RIGHT = &H27

' Functions and constants used to play sounds.
Declare Function sndPlaySound Lib "MMSystem" (lpsound As Any, ByVal flag As Integer) As Integer

Const SND_SYNC = &H0         ' Return when sound ends (the default).
Const SND_ASYNC = &H1        ' Return as soon as sound starts.
Const SND_NODEFAULT = &H2    ' Don't play default sound if not found.
Const SND_MEMORY = &H4       ' lpszSoundName -> memory image of file.
Const SND_LOOP = &H8         ' Loop continuously; needs SND_ASYNC.
Const SND_NOSTOP = &H10      ' Don't interrupt sound to play new one.

' Global string used for by NoiseGet() and NoisePlay() to play .WAV files in memory.
Dim SoundBuffer As String
```

6. Add the following functions and subroutines to the ASSOC.FRM form.

```
Sub btnCancel_Click ()
```

```
'-------------------------------------------------
' Unload the main form, ending the program.
'-------------------------------------------------

    Unload Me
End Sub

Sub btnGo_Click ()
'-------------------------------------------------
' If the game is playing, stop it. If the game is
' not playing, initialize everything and start game.
'-------------------------------------------------
    Timer1.Enabled = Not Timer1.Enabled
    If Timer1.Enabled Then
        lblHits = 0
        lblHoles = -1
        SetupCar
        Randomize
        picHole.Top = picRoad.Height
        Speed = START_SPEED
        Steering = START_STEERING
        btnGo.Caption = "&Stop"
    Else
        btnGo.Caption = "&Go"
    End If
End Sub

Sub chkJoystick_Click ()
    btnGo.SetFocus
End Sub

Sub chkRoadNarrows_Click ()
    btnGo.SetFocus
End Sub

Sub chkSmartPotHoles_Click ()
    btnGo.SetFocus
End Sub

Sub Form_KeyDown (KeyCode As Integer, Shift As Integer)
'-------------------------------------------------
' Keyboard handling for car movement.
'-------------------------------------------------
    If KeyCode = KEY_LEFT Then
        MoveCar -Steering
    ElseIf KeyCode = KEY_RIGHT Then
        MoveCar Steering
    End If
End Sub

Sub Form_Load ()
'-------------------------------------------------
' Set up the game.
'-------------------------------------------------
Dim OK As Integer

    StartRoadWidth = picRoad.Width
    Joystick1.Enabled = False
    SetupCar
    OK = NoiseGet(App.Path & "\" & "IM_HIT!.WAV")
```

12◄

(continued on next page)

*(continued from previous page)*

```vb
    Me.Move (Screen.Width - Me.Width) \ 2, (Screen.Height - Me.Height) \ 2
End Sub

Sub JoystickMoveCar (ByVal X As Long)
'----------------------------------------------------
' Move car based on new Joystick X value.
'----------------------------------------------------
Dim NewX As Long
Dim XMin As Long, XMax As Long, XCenter As Long
Dim Slop As Long

    Slop = 1000

    ' Adjust for integer overflow.
    If Joystick1.XMax < 0 Then
        XMax = 65536 + Joystick1.XMax
    Else
        XMax = Joystick1.XMax
    End If

    XMin = Joystick1.XMin
    XCenter = (XMax - XMin) / 2

    NewX = X
    ' Adjust for integer overflow.
    If NewX < 0 Then NewX = 65536 + NewX

    ' Move the car.
    If NewX > (XCenter + Slop) Then
        MoveCar Steering
    ElseIf NewX < (XCenter - Slop) Then
        MoveCar -Steering
    End If
End Sub

Sub MoveCar (ByVal SteerValue As Integer)
'----------------------------------------------------
' Change position of car by SteerValue twips.
'----------------------------------------------------
    picCar.Left = picCar.Left + SteerValue
    If (picCar.Left + picCar.Width) > picRoad.Width Then
        picCar.Left = picRoad.Width - picCar.Width
    ElseIf picCar.Left < 0 Then
        picCar.Left = 0
    End If
End Sub

Function NoiseGet (ByVal FileName) As Integer
'----------------------------------------------------
' Load a sound file into the global string variable
' SoundBuffer. This must be called before NoisePlay.
'----------------------------------------------------
Dim buffer As String
Dim f As Integer

    On Error GoTo NoiseGet_Error

    buffer = Space$(1024)
    SoundBuffer = ""
```

```
    f = FreeFile
    Open FileName For Binary As f
    Do While Not EOF(f)
        Get #f, , buffer        ' Load in 1K chunks.
        SoundBuffer = SoundBuffer & buffer
    Loop
    Close f
    SoundBuffer = Trim$(SoundBuffer)
    NoiseGet = True
Exit Function

NoiseGet_Error:
    NoiseGet = False
    SoundBuffer = ""
    Exit Function
End Function

Sub NoisePlay ()
'--------------------------------------------------
' Plays a sound previously loaded into memory with
' function NoiseGet().
'--------------------------------------------------
Dim r As Integer

    If SoundBuffer = "" Then Exit Sub
    r = sndPlaySound(ByVal SoundBuffer, SND_ASYNC Or SND_MEMORY)
End Sub

Sub SetupCar ()
'--------------------------------------------------
' Set initial position and picture for car.
'--------------------------------------------------
    picRoad.Width = StartRoadWidth

    CarIndex = 0
    picCar.Picture = picCars(0).Picture
    CarY = picRoad.Height * .75
    picCar.Top = CarY
    picCar.Left = (picRoad.Width - picCar.Width) \ 2
End Sub

Sub Timer1_Timer ()
'--------------------------------------------------
'  This routine handles the game dynamics.
'--------------------------------------------------
Static Y As Integer
Static idx As Integer
Static CarHit As Integer
Dim HolePos As Integer

    If chkJoystick.Value = 1 Then JoystickMoveCar Joystick1.XPos

    ' Select a new pothole and increase difficulty.
    If picHole.Top >= picRoad.Height Then
        ' Heat things up a bit.
        Speed = Speed + 1
        If picCar.Top > (picRoad.Height / 6) Then
            picCar.Top = picCar.Top - (picCar.Height / 4)
        End If
        If chkRoadNarrows = 1 Then picRoad.Width = picRoad.Width * .99
```

(continued on next page)

12◄

*(continued from previous page)*

```
            ' Get next pothole.
            idx = (idx + 1) Mod 4
            picHole.Picture = picPotHoles(idx)
            picHole.Left = Rnd * (picRoad.Width - picHole.Width)
            Y = -picHole.Height
            lblHoles = lblHoles + 1
    ' Check for collision.
    Else
            ' New pothole position.
            Y = Y + Speed

            HolePos = picHole.Top + picHole.Height
            If ((HolePos - picCar.Top) > 0) And ((HolePos - picCar.Top) <= Speed) Then
                If Abs(picCar.Left - picHole.Left) < (picCar.Width * .75) Then
                    NoisePlay
                    ' Did it do any damage?
                    If (Int(Rnd * 2) = 1) Then CarIndex = CarIndex + 1
                    CarHit = 1
                    picCar.Picture = picCarHit.Picture
                    lblHits = lblHits + 1
                    If CarIndex = 4 Then
                        lblHoles = lblHoles + 1
                        picCar.Picture = picCars(CarIndex).Picture
                        btnGo.Value = 1
                    End If
                End If
            End If
    End If

    ' Move pothole.
    If chkSmartPotHoles = 1 Then
        If picHole.Left > picCar.Left Then
            picHole.Left = picHole.Left - 10
        ElseIf picHole.Left < picCar.Left Then
            picHole.Left = picHole.Left + 10
        End If

    End If
    picHole.Top = Y

    If CarHit = 5 Then
        picCar.Picture = picCars(CarIndex).Picture
        CarHit = 0
    ElseIf CarHit > 0 Then
        CarHit = CarHit + 1
    End If
End Sub
```

# Tips and Comments

You can use the JoyStk control to easily integrate joystick processing into your Visual Basic program. Even so, it can be a daunting task to deal with the values returned by the control. You usually need to experiment to get the joystick to react the way you want. Also, as with any game program, you should test PotHoles on several different machines, particularly machines with different processor speeds.

#  M.4 (M4CTRL.VBX)

| | |
|---|---|
| USAGE: | Development of Embedded Expert Systems |
| MANUFACTURER: | Cimflex Teknowledge |
| COST: | $995 |

M.4 is a complete expert system language, coupled with a custom control that allows you to embed an expert system in a Visual Basic application. Expert systems can be used to capture knowledge from many areas of expertise, from automobile repair to medical diagnosis.

## Syntax

There are two distinct halves to M.4 from the perspective of a Visual Basic programmer. The first and most familiar half is the M.4 control, which allows you to integrate an M.4 knowledge base into your Visual Basic program. The M.4 control is fairly simple, consisting of only a few properties and events, and some necessary function calls, as listed in Table 12-9.

**Table 12-9** Nonstandard property, events, and functions of the M.4 control

| PROPERTY | | |
|---|---|---|
| API_exec | | |
| **EVENTS** | | |
| call | get | put |
| **FUNCTIONS** | | |
| M4_init | M4_exec | |

The second half of the product consists of the M.4 kernel. The kernel processes a *knowledge base*, an expert system language program designed to solve a problem within some narrow area of expertise. In general, expert systems solve problems that an expert could solve if given the needed information and a reasonable amount of time.

**Building Knowledge Systems**   M.4 has its own expert system language, and if you intend to develop your own expert systems from scratch, you'll need to learn both the basics of creating knowledge systems, and the M.4 language.

M.4's documentation provides a good introduction to the basics of designing knowledge systems. The first step is to determine the problem that you want the knowledge system to solve. Some problems are simply not appropriate or feasible for knowledge engineering. For your first knowledge system, you'll probably want to pick a problem that is both small and familiar to you. In this way, you can serve as the expert. Otherwise, you'll have to work with an expert in that particular problem domain.

12◀

The M.4 system comes with a number of sample knowledge bases, and these are invaluable for learning the structure and syntax of the M.4 language. To get the general "feel" of the language, you look at some sections from the Wine knowledge base included with M.4. This knowledge base is designed to solve a clear, discrete problem: what type of wine would go well with a particular meal.

Knowledge bases are stored as simple text files, usually with a .KB file extension, so you can use any text editor to work with them. The first line of the Wine knowledge base, WINE.KB, is

```
goal = wine.
```

This says that the goal is to acquire one or more values, for the expression "wine". In the knowledge base, what follows is a collection of rules. These rules are usually in the form of *IF...THEN* statements. For example, if the meal consists of a red meat but the meat is not veal, the following rule is applied:

```
rule-6: if main-component = meat and
           has-veal = no
        then best-color = red cf 90.
```

What this rule says is that for red meats other than veal, the best color of wine is red. The *cf*, or certainty factor, for this rule is 90. Certainty factors indicate the strength in belief that the fact is true. The range for certainty factors is from -100 to 100, where 100 indicates complete certainty that the fact is true, and -100 indicates complete certainty that the fact is false. A value of 0 indicates that there's no evidence for or against the fact. In the example, you can be fairly certain that a red wine is the best choice. Certainty factors are not required for facts, but if they're omitted the certainty is assumed to be 100.

In actual practice, the user interacts with the knowledge system through a *consultation*, a series of questions asked by the knowledge system in order to gather enough facts to reach a conclusion. To do this, the M.4 language has a question construct. Here's an example from the Wine knowledge base:

```
question(has-sauce) =
        ' Does the meal have a sauce on it?'.
legalvals(has-sauce) =
        [yes, no].
```

The first statement poses the question, while the second indicates the legal values for that question. It is through these questions that M.4 builds facts from which it can reach a conclusion.

While the job of building a knowledge system is far from trivial, it is by no means insurmountable either. M.4 comes with programs that help you design and debug knowledge systems.

## Integrating a Knowledge System into a Visual Basic Program

Once you've completed a working knowledge base, you'll probably want to build a custom end user application. M.4 comes with some Visual Basic example programs that provide general-purpose consultation sessions. For specific applications, however, you may want to tailor the presentation to the needs of your user, and perhaps integrate the knowledge base into a larger application. To do this, you can use the M.4 control, which lets you communicate with the M.4 kernel during a consultation session.

M.4 has initialization and exit routines that you must call before using the kernel and before exiting your program. These routines, *M4_init* and *M4_exit,* are functions that your program must declare. Usually, M.4 will be initialized in your main form's *Load* event, and exited in the same form's *Unload* event.

You use the *API_exec* property to send commands to the M.4 kernel. These commands are in the form of simple text strings. For example, to load the Wine knowledge base and begin a consultation, you would assign the *API_exec* property as shown here:

```
quote = chr$(34)
M4Control1.API_exec = "load " & quote & "WINE.KB" & quote
M4Control1.API_exec = "go"
```

Once a consultation has started, you communicate with the kernel through the *get* and *put* events. The *get* routine passes information from the user back to the kernel. Usually, this event spins a *DoEvents()* loop while waiting for some input to pass back to the control.

The *put* event receives information passed back from the kernel. This information might be the text of a question, a list of possible responses, the text of an error message, or some other information. This event is generally where Visual Basic takes M.4 information and places it in the appropriate controls. For example, if the incoming text is a question, the program can display the question text in a label or text control.

# Example

The example program, shown in Figure 12-3, allows the user to interact with the Wine knowledge base. A question is displayed in the upper text box, and possible responses are displayed in a list box. The user can select an answer, and then press the Process Reply

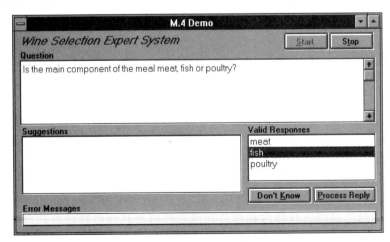

**Figure 12-3** The M.4 Expert System example program

12◄

button. If the user is not sure how to answer, he or she can optionally press the Don't Know button. In either case, the knowledge base uses the response to formulate its next question. Once the knowledge base has gathered enough facts to reach a conclusion, the names of one or more wines are listed in the Suggestions list box. Next to each suggestion is the percentage of certainty for that choice. For example, M.4 might suggest that the best wines for your particular meal are a Riesling or a Chardonnay, with a certainty of 64 percent for each.

## Steps

1. Create a new project called M4EXPERT.MAK. Copy the Wine knowledge base, WINE.KB, into the directory where this new project resides. Add the M.4 control, M4CTRL.VBX, and the M.4 constants module, M4.BAS, to the project.

2. Create a new form with the objects and properties described in Table 12-10. Save this form as M4EXPERT.FRM.

**Table 12-10** Objects and properties for the M4EXPERT.FRM form

| OBJECT | PROPERTY | SETTING |
| --- | --- | --- |
| Form | FormName | lstSuggestions |
| | BackColor | &H00C0C0C0& |
| | Caption | "M.4 Demo" |
| Label | Name | lblStatLine |
| | Alignment | 2 'Center |
| | BackColor | &H00E0FFFF& |
| | BorderStyle | 1 'Fixed Single |
| | ForeColor | &H000000FF& |
| | Tag | "/3dup/" |
| Label | Name | Label1 |
| | BackStyle | 0 'Transparent |
| | Caption | "Question" |
| | ForeColor | &H00800000& |
| Label | Name | Label2 |
| | BackStyle | 0 'Transparent |
| | Caption | "Suggestions" |
| | ForeColor | &H00800000& |
| Label | Name | Label3 |
| | BackStyle | 0 'Transparent |
| | Caption | "Valid Responses" |
| | ForeColor | &H00800000& |
| Label | Name | Label4 |
| | BackStyle | 0 'Transparent |
| | Caption | "Error Messages" |

| OBJECT | PROPERTY | SETTING |
|---|---|---|
| | ForeColor | &H00800000& |
| Label | Name | Label5 |
| | BackStyle | 0 'Transparent |
| | Caption | "Wine Selection Expert System" |
| | FontItalic | -1 'True |
| | FontSize | 12 |
| | ForeColor | &H00000080& |
| M4Class | Name | M4Ctrl1 |
| | API_exec | " " |
| | Visible | 0 'False |
| TextBox | Name | txtMain |
| | FontBold | 0 'False |
| | FontSize | 9.75 |
| | ForeColor | &H00000000& |
| | MultiLine | -1 'True |
| | ScrollBars | 2 'Vertical |
| | Tag | "/3d/" |
| CommandButton | Name | btnStart |
| | Caption | "&Start" |
| | Tag | "/3d/" |
| CommandButton | Name | btnProcess |
| | Caption | "&Process Reply" |
| | Tag | "/3d/" |
| CommandButton | Name | btnStop |
| | Caption | "S&top" |
| | Tag | "/3d/" |
| ListBox | Name | lstOptions |
| | FontBold | 0 'False |
| | FontSize | 9.75 |
| | ForeColor | &H00000000& |
| | Tag | "/3d/" |
| ListBox | Name | lstSuggestions |
| | FontBold | 0 'False |
| | FontSize | 9.75 |
| | ForeColor | &H00000080& |
| | Tag | "/3d/" |
| CommandButton | Name | btnUnknown |
| | Caption | "Don't &Know" |
| | Tag | "/3d/" |

12◄

3. Add the following code to the M4EXPERT.FRM form. This is a minimal interface to the M.4 kernel, although it does some processing in the *put* event to place the question responses into a list box, and the question itself into a text control. Errors are displayed in a status line label, and the final suggestions are listed in a list box.

The knowledge base is loaded and the session started when the user presses the Start button. Likewise, the user can abandon the session at any time by pressing the Stop button. Double-clicking on one of the Valid Responses list items has the same effect as highlighting the response and pressing the Process Reply button.

```
Option Explicit
'----------------------------------------------------
' Variables, constants, and declarations used in
' the M.4 example program.
'----------------------------------------------------

' M.4 function declarations.
Declare Function M4_init Lib "M4CTRL.VBX" Alias "_M4_init" () As Integer
Declare Sub M4_Exit Lib "M4CTRL.VBX" Alias "_M4_exit" ()
Declare Function IO_get_Stuffer Lib "M4CTRL.VBX" (ByVal expr As String, ByVal flag As Integer)
As Long

' Globals used during a consultation.
Dim Buffer As String
Dim ActiveConsult As Integer
Dim FirstSuggestion As Integer

' Color constants.
Const DARK_GRAY = &H808080
Const WHITE = &HFFFFFF
Const BLACK = &H0

' 3D effect constants.
Const BORDER_INSET = 0
Const BORDER_RAISED = 1

' WindowState constant
Const MINIMIZED = 1

' MsgBox constants.
Const MB_OK = 0
Const MB_YESNO = 4
Const MB_ICONINFORMATION = 64
Const MB_ICONQUESTION = &H20
Const MB_ICONEXCLAMATION = &H30
Const MB_ICONSTOP = &H10

' MsgBox responses.
Const IDOK = 1
Const IDYES = 6

Sub btnProcess_Click ()
'----------------------------------------------------
' Put the user's reply into the global buffer. The
' M4Ctrl1_get event will process it.
'----------------------------------------------------

    If lstOptions.ListIndex >= 0 Then
        Buffer = lstOptions.List(lstOptions.ListIndex)
```

```
      End If
End Sub

Sub btnStart_Click ()
'------------------------------------------------------
' Start a consultation session.
'------------------------------------------------------
Dim Quote As String

    ' Initialize Boolean flags.
    ActiveConsult = True
    FirstSuggestion = True

    ' Clear list boxes.
    lstSuggestions.Clear
    lstOptions.Clear

    ' Allow user to abort the consultation.
    btnStop.Enabled = True
    btnStart.Enabled = False

    Quote = Chr$(34)

    ' Load the Wine Knowledge Base file.
    M4Ctrl1.API_exec = "load " & Quote & app.Path & "\wine.kb" & Quote

    ' Begin the consultation.
    M4Ctrl1.API_exec = "go"
End Sub

Sub btnStop_Click ()
'------------------------------------------------------
' Terminate the consultation.
'------------------------------------------------------

    ' Tell M.4 to stop this session. Buffer will
    ' be processed in the M4Ctrl1_get event routine.
    Buffer = "abort"

    ' We no longer have an active consultation session.
    ActiveConsult = False

    ' Reset controls to prepare for another consultation.
    txtMain = ""
    lstOptions.Clear

    ' Allow user to start another consultation.
    btnStop.Enabled = False
    btnStart.Enabled = True
End Sub

Sub btnUnknown_Click ()
'------------------------------------------------------
' Tell M.4 that the answer to the current question
' is unknown.
'------------------------------------------------------

    ' Buffer is processed in the M4Ctrl1_get event routine.
    Buffer = "unknown"
End Sub

Sub Form_Load ()
```

(continued on next page)

12◄

*(continued from previous page)*

```vb
'----------------------------------------------------
' Position the form and initialize M.4.
'----------------------------------------------------

    ' Center the form on the screen.
    Me.Move (Screen.Width - Me.Width) \ 2, (Screen.Height - Me.Height) \ 2

    ' Try to initialize M.4.
    If (M4_init() = 0) Then
        MsgBox "Unable to initialize M4 System", MB_OK Or MB_ICONSTOP, "Error"
        End
    End If

    ' We do not yet have an active consultation session.
    ActiveConsult = False
End Sub

Sub Form_Paint ()
'----------------------------------------------------
' Draw 3D effect around selected controls on form.
'----------------------------------------------------
Dim i As Integer

    On Error Resume Next
    ' Look at the tag fields of all controls.
    For i = 0 To Me.Controls.Count - 1
        If InStr(UCase$(Me.Controls(i).Tag), "/3D/") Then
            Make3D Me, Me.Controls(i), BORDER_INSET
        ElseIf InStr(UCase$(Me.Controls(i).Tag), "/3DUP/") Then
            Make3D Me, Me.Controls(i), BORDER_RAISED
        End If
    Next
End Sub

Sub Form_QueryUnload (Cancel As Integer, UnloadMode As Integer)
'----------------------------------------------------
' Don't let the user exit if an active Consultation
' is in progress.
'----------------------------------------------------

    If ActiveConsult Then
        MsgBox "You must stop or complete the current consultation before exiting.", MB_OK Or
MB_ICONINFORMATION, "Consultation in Progress"
        Cancel = True
    End If
End Sub

Sub Form_Unload (Cancel As Integer)
'----------------------------------------------------
' Shut down M.4 and exit the program.
'----------------------------------------------------

    M4_Exit
End Sub

Sub lstOptions_DblClick ()
'----------------------------------------------------
' If the user double-clicks on a selection, process
' that response.
'----------------------------------------------------
```

```
    ' Simulate pressing the Process Reply button.
    btnProcess_Click
End Sub

Sub M4Ctrl1_call (chnl As Integer, cmd As Integer, p1 As Integer, p2 As Long)
'------------------------------------------------------
' Clear the main text control if M.4 instructs us to.
'------------------------------------------------------

    If cmd = IO_CLEAR_WINDOW And chnl = O_CONSULT Then
        txtMain = ""
    End If
End Sub

Sub M4Ctrl1_get (chnl As Integer)
'------------------------------------------------------
' Wait for something new to enter the Buffer: then
' send the data on to M.4. This data will almost
' always be the reply to a question.
'------------------------------------------------------
Dim retcode As Integer

    ' Clear out the buffer.
    Buffer = ""

    ' Wait for new data to enter the buffer.
    Do While Buffer = ""
        retcode = DoEvents()
    Loop

    ' Send buffer to M.4.
    retcode = IO_get_Stuffer(Buffer & Chr$(0), 1)
End Sub

Sub M4Ctrl1_put (chnl As Integer, pText As String)
'------------------------------------------------------
' Process data received from M.4. Look at the
' channel ID of the incoming text and decide how
' to process it.
'------------------------------------------------------
Dim pos As Integer
Dim LF As String
Dim CR As String

Static Text As String

    lblStatLine = ""

    ' Carriage return and line feed characters.
    CR = Chr$(13)
    LF = Chr$(10)

    ' The incoming text contains only line feed characters.
    ' This inserts carriage returns into the text as well.
    pos = InStr(1, pText, LF)
    Do While pos > 0
        pText = Left$(pText, pos - 1) & CR & Mid$(pText, pos)
        pos = pos + 2
        pos = InStr(pos, pText, LF)
    Loop
```

**12**

*(continued on next page)*

*(continued from previous page)*

```vb
    Text = Text & pText

    If Right$(Text, 1) = LF Then
        Text = Left$(Text, Len(Text) - 1) & CR & LF

        ' Process the text based on the Output channel.
        Select Case chnl
            ' For this Knowledge Base, we'll assume that any O_CONSULT
            ' is a final list of suggested wines.
            Case O_CONSULT:
                If FirstSuggestion Then
                    lstSuggestions.Clear
                    FirstSuggestion = False
                End If

                Text = Mid$(Text, InStr(Text, "=") + 2)

                ' Add item to list of suggestions.
                lstSuggestions.AddItem Left$(Text, InStr(Text, CR) - 1)

                ' End the current consultation.
                btnStop_Click

            ' If we have a question, display it in the main text control.
            Case O_QUESTION:
                txtMain = Text

                ' Clear the options (Responses) list.
                lstOptions.Clear

            ' Display any error in the status line label.
            Case O_ERROR:
                lblStatLine = Text

            ' Display the valid responses to the question.
            Case O_OPTION:
                lstOptions.AddItem Left$(Text, InStr(Text, CR) - 1)
        End Select
        Text = ""
    End If
End Sub

Sub Make3D (pic As Form, ctl As Control, ByVal BorderStyle As Integer)
'--------------------------------------------------
' Wrap a 3D effect around a control on a form.
'--------------------------------------------------
Dim AdjustX As Integer, AdjustY As Integer
Dim RightSide As Single
Dim BW As Integer, BorderWidth As Integer
Dim LeftTopColor As Long, RightBottomColor As Long
Dim i As Integer

    If Not ctl.Visible Then Exit Sub

    AdjustX = Screen.TwipsPerPixelX
    AdjustY = Screen.TwipsPerPixelY

    BorderWidth = 1

    Select Case BorderStyle
```

```
    Case 0: ' Inset
    LeftTopColor = DARK_GRAY
    RightBottomColor = WHITE
    Case 1: ' Raised
    LeftTopColor = WHITE
    RightBottomColor = DARK_GRAY
    End Select


    ' Set the top shading line.
    For BW = 1 To BorderWidth
    ' Top
    pic.CurrentX = ctl.Left - (AdjustX * BW)
    pic.CurrentY = ctl.Top - (AdjustY * BW)
    pic.Line -(ctl.Left + ctl.Width + (AdjustX * (BW - 1)), ctl.Top - (AdjustY * BW)),
LeftTopColor
    ' Right
    pic.Line -(ctl.Left + ctl.Width + (AdjustX * (BW - 1)), ctl.Top + ctl.Height + (AdjustY *
(BW - 1))), RightBottomColor
    ' Bottom
    pic.Line -(ctl.Left - (AdjustX * BW), ctl.Top + ctl.Height + (AdjustY * (BW - 1))),
RightBottomColor
    ' Left
    pic.Line -(ctl.Left - (AdjustX * BW), ctl.Top - (AdjustY * BW)), LeftTopColor
    Next
End Sub
```

## Tips and Comments

Don't imagine that M.4 will turn you into a knowledge engineer in a day. While the M.4 expert system language is easy enough to understand, the concepts of expert systems themselves will require some study. But if you have a problem that can be solved by a knowledge base system, M.4 is an approachable and economical solution. The M.4 documentation explains the basics of knowledge systems well, and provides beginners with in-depth guidance on the development of these systems.

#  VersionStamper-VB (DWVSTAMP.VBX)

| USAGE: | Version Control |
| --- | --- |
| MANUFACTURER: | Desaware |
| COST: | $129 |

Although custom controls are one of the most powerful and exciting ideas ever in the world of software development, they have their drawbacks. Custom controls (VBXs) are actually DLLs with a little something extra. The problem with these wonderful tools is also one of their prime benefits: reuse. Multiple applications can use a DLL or VBX simultaneously while only requiring that a single copy exist on the system. The problem comes when two applications use the same VBX but not necessarily the same version of that VBX. Since only one copy of the VBX is loaded into memory, it's first come first served. If application A loads first, application B may not run properly or at all, because A got there first and loaded its version of the DLL that they both use.

12◄

Windows applications let you embed version information in an EXE or DLL to avoid the problem, but developers are responsible for checking and honoring that information, which doesn't always happen. Another problem is that VB doesn't provide any way to embed version information into the EXEs it generates. VersionStamper-VB addresses these issues and, under certain circumstances, may lower your blood pressure in the process.

## Syntax

There are three sections in a version resource: Fixed File Information, Language/Code Page Translation Tables, and String File Information. Fixed File Information contains numeric version information and flags that define the file type. Language Translation Tables list all of the languages in the version resource. String File Information contains descriptive information about the file, such as the company name and copyright notice. Each language table in the version resource has its own set of strings. Table 12-11 lists the nonstandard properties, events, and functions for the DWVSTAMP control.

**Table 12-11** DWVSTAMP nonstandard properties, events, and functions

### VERSION RESOURCE PROPERTIES

| | | |
|---|---|---|
| exeComments | exeCompanyName | exeFileDescription |
| exeFileVersion | exeInternalName | exeLanguage |
| exeLegalCopyright | exeLegalTrademarks | exeOriginalFilename |
| exePrivateBuild | exeProductName | exeProductVersion |
| exeSpecialBuild | FileVersion | FlagDebug |
| FlagPatched | FlagPreRelease | FlagPrivate |
| FlagSpecial | LanguageStrings | ProductVersion |

### COMPONENT INFORMATION PROPERTIES

| | | |
|---|---|---|
| FileCurrentDir | FoundDate | FoundDateString |
| FoundFlags | FoundVersion | FoundVersionBuffer |
| OtherCount | OtherDate | OtherDateString |
| OtherFile | OtherFlags | OtherSource |
| OtherVersion | ReadPropError | RefDate |
| RefDateString | RefFlags | RefVersion |
| ScanFile | SelectFiles | VerifyFile |
| VerifyMode | | |

### OTHER PROPERTIES

| | | |
|---|---|---|
| About | Index | Slave |

### EVENTS

| | | |
|---|---|---|
| EnumComplete | FileConflict | FileScan |

### FUNCTIONS

| | | |
|---|---|---|
| vsCopyData | vsDWORDto2Integers | vsGetStringFromLPSTR |
| vsGetAddressForObject | vsGetAddressForVBString | |

**Embedded Version Information** VersionStamper-VB makes it easy to add version information to VB applications. Simply set some DWVSTAMP properties and it automatically creates a standard Windows version resource in the compiled EXE. A copy of the original EXE, without the version resource, is created automatically as a precaution.

The *FileVersion* and *ProductVersion* properties define the numeric version information for the file. There are five *Flag* properties (*FlagDebug, FlagPatched, FlagPreRelease, FlagPrivate*, and *FlagSpecial*), which define the contents of the FileFlags field in the version resource.

The String properties all have an *exe* prefix to denote that they are related. *exeLanguage* determines the language and character set for the String properties. The *LanguageStrings* property allows you to define up to 16 sets of String information to be used in the version resource via the Language Strings dialog box. To follow the Microsoft specification for version resources, you should always set the following DWVSTAMP properties: *exeCompanyName, exeFileVersion, exeInternalName, exeOriginalFileName*, and *exeProductVersion*. Do not confuse *exeFileVersion* and *exeProductVersion* with their numeric counterparts, *FileVersion* and *ProductVersion*. If the *FlagPrivate* or *FlagSpecial* properties are set to *True, exePrivateBuild* and *exeSpecialBuild* should be set as well, respectively.

If a project includes multiple DWVSTAMP controls, the *Slave* property determines which one is used to generate the version resource. Only one control should have the *Slave* property set to *False;* this is the control that will be used to generate the version resource. All other controls should have *Slave* set to *True*. This is a small but important point, since you will rarely use more than one control in a project.

**Embedded Component Information** VersionStamper-VB permits you to embed component information into an application via the *SelectFiles* property and the *SelectFiles* dialog (Figure 12-4). This information consists of a list of files. For each file,

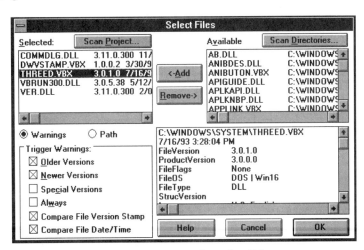

**Figure 12-4** VersionStamper-VB Select Files dialog

12

you specify a version or file date. You also specify warning conditions. The warning conditions determine when VersionStamper will fire its *FileConflict* event. Not only can you scan the current project for file dependencies, you can scan *any* VB project, which lets VersionStamper-VB create "rescue" programs. For example, suppose a large application has been released and it isn't feasible to rebuild it with VersionStamper. Simply create a small rescue program using VersionStamper-VB and scan the project file for the main program instead of the current project (the rescue program). Now you can run the rescue program to check for incompatible files that will affect the main program. You could also accomplish the same thing by using the *VerifyFile* property, which enables you to perform component verification on other EXEs.

**Verification**   Once a component list exists, VersionStamper-VB can verify that the proper components exist on the target system and warns you if it discovers any incompatibilities. The verification can be performed automatically or manually, based on the value of the *VerifyMode* property (Table 12-12). Only values 0 and 1 are valid at design time; you use values 2 and 3 at run time to trigger verification manually.

**Table 12-12**  DWVSTAMP VerifyMode values

| VALUE | MEANING |
| --- | --- |
| 0 | None - automatic verification does not occur. |
| 1 | On Load - automatic verification occurs when the form containing the DWVSTAMP control is loaded. |
| 2 | Manual Verify - triggers immediate component verification. |
| 3 | Manual Scan - triggers *FileScan* event for each component. |

When VersionStamper-VB performs its verification magic, it enumerates the list of embedded components in a file and fires a *FileConflict* event if any incompatibilities are found, based on the warning conditions specified in the component list. If a conflict occurs, a number of properties are loaded with information about the *ReferenceFile* (the file it expected to find) and the *FoundFile* (the file VersionStamper-VB actually found that triggered the *FileConflict* event). The related properties contain the location, timestamp, and version information for both files. The *FileConflict* event also contains a *Flags* parameter to tell you exactly why the event was fired (Table 12-13). *Flags* is a bit field that may contain multiple values.

**Table 12-13**  FileConflict event Flags parameter values

| VALUE | MEANING |
| --- | --- |
| Bit 0 | Older file was found (date compare). |
| Bit 1 | Newer file was found (date compare). |
| Bit 2 | Older version was found (version compare). |
| Bit 3 | Newer version was found (version compare). |
| Bit 4 | Special version was found. |

| VALUE | MEANING |
| --- | --- |
| Bit 5 | Always warn was set. |
| Bit 6 | File was found in memory. |
| Bit 7 | No matching file was found. |
| Bit 8 | No version information was found in the FoundFile. |

You can also scan the component list for a file without performing any actual verification. When the *ScanFile* property is set to a valid file name, VersionStamper-VB scans that file for a list of embedded components and, for each component found in the list, fires a *FileScan* event. The *FileScan* event is comparable to the *FileConflict* event but doesn't perform any verification. You can use it to obtain information for files other than the EXE containing the DWVSTAMP control.

When the scanning, or verification, process is complete, an *EnumComplete* event is fired.

# Example

The sample program (Figure 12-5) makes use of VersionStamper-VB's verification capabilities and also demonstrates how you can use version information in a more general way. When the program starts, the DWVSTAMP control performs automatic verification (*VerifyMode* = 1). For each incompatibility found a message box is displayed and, upon completion of the verification process, another message box displays the total number of conflicts found.

When an item is selected from the combo box, the specified files in the system directory (.VBX, .DLL, or .EXE) are examined and their version information, timestamp, and file size are displayed. You can display detailed version information by pressing the Detail command button or double-clicking on a file name in the list. The code behind the detail form demonstrates how the API version information functions are used.

**Figure 12-5** VersionStamper sample program

## Steps

1. Create a new project called VERSTAMP.MAK. Create a new form with the objects and properties shown in Table 12-14. Save this form as VERSTAMP.FRM.

**Table 12-14** VersionStamper main form's objects and properties.

| OBJECT | PROPERTY | SETTING |
|---|---|---|
| Form | FormName | frmMain |
| | BackColor | &H00C0C0C0& |
| | BorderStyle | 3 'Fixed Double |
| | Caption | "VersionStamper Demo" |
| | ClipControls | 0 'False |
| | MaxButton | 0 'False |
| | MinButton | 0 'False |
| | ScaleMode | 3 'Pixel |
| VersionStamp | Name | verstampMain |
| | exeComments | (set at design time in Properties window) |
| | FileVersion | (set at design time in Properties window) |
| | SelectFiles | (set at design time in Properties window) |
| | VerifyMode | 1 'On Load |
| Label | Name | lblList |
| | BackStyle | 0 'Transparent |
| | Caption | "List:" |
| Label | Name | lblSelectAnItem |
| | BackStyle | 0 'Transparent |
| | Caption | "<-- Select an Item" |
| | FontBold | 0 'False |
| | ForeColor | &H00FF0000& |
| CommandButton | Name | cmdClose |
| | Caption | "&Close" |
| CommandButton | Name | cmdDetail |
| | Caption | "&Detail..." |
| SSPanel | Name | pnlCombo |
| | AutoSize | 3 'AutoSize Child To Panel |
| | BevelOuter | 1 'Inset |
| SSPanel | Name | pnlList |
| | AutoSize | 3 'AutoSize Child To Panel |
| | BevelOuter | 1 'Inset |

2. Place the controls listed in Table 12-15 within the pnlCombo SSPanel control.

**Table 12-15** PnlCombo child controls

| OBJECT | PROPERTY | SETTING |
|---|---|---|
| ComboBox | Name | cboFileSpec |
| | Style | 2 'Dropdown List |

3. Place the controls listed in Table 12-16 within the pnlList SSPanel control.

**Table 12-16** PnlList child controls

| OBJECT | PROPERTY | SETTING |
|---|---|---|
| ListBox | Name | lstItems |
| | FontBold | 0 'False |

4. Add the following code to VERSTAMP form.

```
Option Explicit
DefInt A-Z

Sub cboFileSpec_Click ()

    Select Case cboFileSpec.ListIndex
        Case LIST_SYSTEM_DLLS
            Call LoadListWithFiles(lstItems, "*.DLL")
        Case LIST_SYSTEM_VBXS
            Call LoadListWithFiles(lstItems, "*.VBX")
        Case LIST_SYSTEM_EXES
            Call LoadListWithFiles(lstItems, "*.EXE")
    End Select

End Sub

Sub cmdClose_Click ()

    Unload frmMain

End Sub

Sub cmdDetail_Click ()

    Call lstItems_DblClick

End Sub

Sub Form_Load ()

    cboFileSpec.AddItem "System VBX's"
    cboFileSpec.AddItem "System DLL's"
    cboFileSpec.AddItem "System EXE's"

End Sub

Sub lstItems_Click ()
```

**12**◄

*(continued on next page)*

*(continued from previous page)*

```vb
    '--Something must be selected in the list or details can be viewed.
    If lstItems.ListIndex > 1 Then
        cmdDetail.Enabled = True
    Else
        cmdDetail.Enabled = False
    End If

End Sub

Sub lstItems_DblClick ()
    Dim Filename$
    '--Make the double-click act like a click on the Detail button.
    If lstItems.ListIndex > 1 Then
        Filename$ = Left$(lstItems.Text, InStr(lstItems.Text, gTab$) - 1)
        Call DisplayFileDetails(Filename$)
    End If

End Sub

Sub verstampMain_EnumComplete ()
    Dim Msg$
    Beep
    Msg$ = "VersionStamper-VB Verification Complete."
    Msg$ = Msg$ & gCRLF$ & gCRLF$
    Msg$ = Msg$ & CStr(gNumConflicts%) & " File Conflicts Found."
    MsgBox Msg$

End Sub

Sub verstampMain_FileConflict (ReferenceFile As String, FoundFile As String, Flags As Long,
StopVerify As Integer)
'----------------------------------------------------------
'-- A file conflict was discovered during the verification
'   process. Let the user know what happened.
'----------------------------------------------------------
    Dim Msg$     '-- MsgBox Message
    Dim Con$     '-- List of conflicts that file triggered.
    Dim Bit%     '-- Current flag Bit under test
    Dim BitVal&  '-- Value of flag Bit under test

    gNumConflicts% = gNumConflicts% + 1

    '-- Build our list of conflicts.
    For Bit% = 0 To 8
        BitVal& = (2 ^ Bit%)
        If (Flags& And BitVal&) Then
            Select Case Bit%
                Case 0:
                    Con$ - Con$ & "Older file was found" & gCRLF$
                Case 1:
                    Con$ = Con$ & "Newer file was found" & gCRLF$
                Case 2:
                    Con$ = Con$ & "Older version was found" & gCRLF$
                Case 3:
                    Con$ = Con$ & "Newer file was found" & gCRLF$
                Case 4:
                    Con$ = Con$ & "Special version was found" & gCRLF$
                Case 5:
                    Con$ = Con$ & "Always warn was set" & gCRLF$
                Case 6:
```

```
                    Con$ = Con$ & "File was found in memory" & gCRLF$
            Case 7:
                    Con$ = Con$ & "No matching file was found" & gCRLF$
            Case 8:
                    Con$ = Con$ & "No version information in file" & gCRLF$
        End Select
    End If
Next Bit%

Msg$ = "File Expected: " & ReferenceFile$ & gCRLF$
Msg$ = Msg$ & "File Found:     " & FoundFile$ & gCRLF$
Msg$ = Msg$ & gCRLF$ & Con$

MsgBox Msg$, MB_OK + MB_ICONSTOP, "File Conflict!"

End Sub
```

5. Create a new form with the objects and properties shown in Table 12-17. Save this form as DETAIL.FRM.

**Table 12-17** VersionStamper Detail form's objects and properties

| OBJECT | PROPERTY | SETTING |
|---|---|---|
| Form | FormName | frmFileDetails |
| | BackColor | &H00C0C0C0& |
| | BorderStyle | 3 'Fixed Double |
| | Caption | "File Details" |
| | ClipControls | 0 'False |
| | MaxButton | 0 'False |
| | MinButton | 0 'False |
| | ScaleMode | 3 'Pixel |
| CommandButton | Name | cmdOK |
| | Caption | "OK" |
| | Default | -1 'True |
| SSPanel | Name | pnlSelectedItem |
| | AutoSize | 3 'AutoSize Child To Panel |
| | BevelOuter | 1 'Inset |
| SSPanel | Name | pnlList |
| | AutoSize | 3 'AutoSize Child To Panel |
| | BevelOuter | 1 'Inset |

6. Place the controls shown in Table 12-18 within the pnlSelectedItem SSPanel control.

**Table 12-18** VersionStamper pnlSelectedItem SSPanel control

| | | |
|---|---|---|
| TextBox | Name | txtSelectedItem |
| | BackColor | &H00FFFFFF& |
| | MultiLine | -1 'True |
| | ScrollBars | 2 'Vertical |

**12**◄

769▶

7. Place the controls shown in Table 12-19 within the pnlList SSPanel control.

**Table 12-19** VersionStamper pnlLst SSPanel control

| ListBox | Name | lstItems |
|---------|------|----------|
| | FontBold | .0 'False |

8. Add the following code to the DETAIL form.

```
Option Explicit
DefInt A-Z

Sub cmdOK_Click ()

    Unload Me

End Sub

Sub lstItems_Click ()
    Dim ListItem$
    Dim TabPos%
    Dim Item$

    ListItem$ = lstItems.Text
    TabPos% = InStr(ListItem$, gTab$)
    Item$ = Right$(ListItem$, Len(ListItem$) - TabPos%)
    txtSelectedItem.Text = Item$

End Sub
```

9. Create a new module. Save this form as VERSTAMP.BAS. Add the following code to the module. Much of the version information related code was derived from the high-quality samples that come with VersionStamper-VB.

```
Option Explicit
DefInt A-Z

Type FIXEDFILEINFO      ' 52 Bytes
    dwSignature         As Long
    dwStrucVersion      As Long
    dwFileVersionMS     As Long
    dwFileVersionLS     As Long
    dwProductVersionMS  As Long
    dwProductVersionLS  As Long
    dwFileFlagsMask     As Long
    dwFileFlags         As Long
    dwFileOS            As Long
    dwFileType          As Long
    dwFileSubType       As Long
    dwFileDateMS        As Long
    dwFileDateLS        As Long
End Type

' Version info functions.
Declare Function GetFileVersionInfoSize% Lib "ver.dll" (ByVal lpszFileName$, lpdwHandle&)
Declare Function GetFileVersionInfo% Lib "ver.dll" (ByVal lpszFileName$, ByVal Handle&, ByVal
cbBuf&, ByVal lpvData&)
Declare Function VerQueryValue% Lib "ver.dll" (ByVal lpvBlock&, ByVal SubBlock$, lpBuffer&, lpcb%)
```

```
' The following utility functions are present in DWVSTAMP.VBX.
Declare Sub vsCopyDataBynum Lib "dwvstamp.vbx" Alias "vsCopyData" (ByVal source&, ByVal dest&,
ByVal nCount%)
Declare Function vsGetAddressForObject& Lib "dwvstamp.vbx" (object As Any)
Declare Function vsGetAddressForVBString& Lib "dwvstamp.vbx" (vbstring$)


Declare Function GetSystemDirectory% Lib "Kernel" (ByVal lpBuffer$, ByVal nSize%)

'-- Used by SetListTabStops.
Declare Function SendMessage Lib "User" (ByVal hWnd As Integer, ByVal wMsg As Integer, ByVal
wParam As Integer, lParam As Any) As Long
Const WM_USER = &H400
Const LB_SETTABSTOPS = WM_USER + 19


Global Const MODAL = 1

Global Const MB_OK = 0
Global Const MB_ICONSTOP = 16

Global Const DEFAULT = 0
Global Const HOURGLASS = 11

Global Const LIST_SYSTEM_VBXS = 0
Global Const LIST_SYSTEM_DLLS = 1
Global Const LIST_SYSTEM_EXES = 2


'-- The following should be set in Sub Main
'   and not altered after that.
Global gCRLF$    '-- (Can't use Chr$() to define global const)
Global gTab$     '-- (Can't use Chr$() to define global const)

Global gNumConflicts%   '-- Number of file conflicts found.

Private Sub CenterFormOnForm (theForm As Form, frmParent As Form)
    Dim NewLeft%
    Dim NewTop%

    NewLeft% = frmParent.Left + ((frmParent.Width - theForm.Width) \ 2)
    NewTop% = frmParent.Top + ((frmParent.Height - theForm.Height) \ 2)

    theForm.Move NewLeft%, NewTop%

End Sub

Sub DisplayFileDetails (Filename$)

    Load frmFileDetails
        Call LoadListWithDetails(frmFileDetails!lstItems, Filename$)
        frmFileDetails.Caption = "File Details - " & Filename$
        Call CenterFormOnForm(frmFileDetails, frmMain)
    frmFileDetails.Show MODAL

End Sub

Function FileVerFromFFI$ (FFI As FIXEDFILEINFO)
'-----------------------------------------------------
'-- This function receives a FixedFileInfo structure
'   and returns the file version as a string.
'-----------------------------------------------------
```

**12**

(continued on next page)

*(continued from previous page)*

```
    Dim LeastSig$
    Dim MostSig$

    LeastSig$ = VerStrFromVerNum(FFI.dwFileVersionLS)
    MostSig$ = VerStrFromVerNum(FFI.dwFileVersionMS)
    FileVerFromFFI$ = MostSig$ & "." & LeastSig$

End Function

Function GetSystemDir$ ()
    Dim RtnBuffer$
    Dim RtnLen%

    RtnBuffer$ = Space$(255)
    RtnLen% = GetSystemDirectory(RtnBuffer$, Len(RtnBuffer$))
    GetSystemDir$ = Left$(RtnBuffer$, RtnLen%)

End Function

Function GetVerBufferAddr& (Filename$, Buffer$)
'---------------------------------------------------
'-- This function uses both GetFileVersion functions
'   of the API to set Buffer$ to version info and
'   returns the address of Buffer$.
'---------------------------------------------------
    Dim bOK%
    Dim VerInfoHandle&
    Dim VerInfoSize%

    VerInfoSize% = GetFileVersionInfoSize(Filename$, VerInfoHandle&)
    If VerInfoSize% > 0 Then
        '-- Pre-initialize our buffer.
        Buffer$ = String$(VerInfoSize% + 1, Chr$(0))
        bOK% = GetFileVersionInfo(Filename$, VerInfoHandle&, VerInfoSize%,
vsGetAddressForVBString&(Buffer$))
        If bOK% Then
            GetVerBufferAddr& = vsGetAddressForVBString(Buffer$)
        End If
    End If

End Function

Sub LoadListWithDetails (Lst As ListBox, Filename$)
    Dim VerInfoAddr&
    Dim Buffer$
    ReDim arrTabStops(0)

    arrTabStops(0) = 18
    Call SetListTabStops(Lst, arrTabStops%())

    Lst.Clear

    '-- Get the version info.
    VerInfoAddr& = GetVerBufferAddr(Filename$, Buffer$)
    If VerInfoAddr& <> 0 Then
        Lst.AddItem "Comments" & gTab$ & QueryVerString$(VerInfoAddr&, "Comments")
        Lst.AddItem "Company Name" & gTab$ & QueryVerString$(VerInfoAddr&, "CompanyName")
        Lst.AddItem "File Description" & gTab$ & QueryVerString$(VerInfoAddr&,
"FileDescription")
        Lst.AddItem "File Version" & gTab$ & QueryVerString$(VerInfoAddr&, "FileVersion")
```

```
            Lst.AddItem "Internal Name" & gTab$ & QueryVerString$(VerInfoAddr&, "InternalName")
            Lst.AddItem "Legal Copyright" & gTab$ & QueryVerString$(VerInfoAddr&, "LegalCopyright")
            Lst.AddItem "Legal Trademarks" & gTab$ & QueryVerString$(VerInfoAddr&,
"LegalTrademarks")
            Lst.AddItem "Original Filename" & gTab$ & QueryVerString$(VerInfoAddr&,
"OriginalFilename")
            Lst.AddItem "Private Build" & gTab$ & QueryVerString$(VerInfoAddr&, "PrivateBuild")
            Lst.AddItem "Product Name" & gTab$ & QueryVerString$(VerInfoAddr&, "ProductName")
            Lst.AddItem "Product Version" & gTab$ & QueryVerString$(VerInfoAddr&, "ProductVersion")
            Lst.AddItem "Special Build" & gTab$ & QueryVerString$(VerInfoAddr&, "SpecialBuild")
        Else
            Lst.AddItem "No Version Details Available"
        End If

End Sub

Sub LoadListWithFiles (Lst As ListBox, FileSpec$)
        Dim Header$
        Dim OrigDir$
        Dim FileFound$
        Dim FileVer$
        Dim FileDate$
        Dim FileSize$
        Dim VerInfoAddr&
        Dim ffiAddr&
        Dim ffiLen%
        Dim Buffer$
        Dim bOK%
        Dim FFI As FIXEDFILEINFO
        ReDim arrTabStops(2)

        Screen.MousePointer = HOURGLASS

        '-----------------------------
        '-- Set up the list.
        '-----------------------------
        arrTabStops(0) = 16
        arrTabStops(1) = 28
        arrTabStops(2) = 38
        Call SetListTabStops(frmMain!lstItems, arrTabStops%())

        Lst.Clear

        Header$ = " File" & gTab$ & "Version" & gTab$ & "Date" & gTab$ & "Size"
        Lst.AddItem Header$
        Lst.AddItem String$(100, "-")

        OrigDir$ = CurDir
        ChDir GetSystemDir$()

        '--------------------------------------------------
        '-- Load the list with files and file information.
        '--------------------------------------------------
        FileFound$ = Dir$(FileSpec$)
        While Len(FileFound$)
            VerInfoAddr& = GetVerBufferAddr(FileFound$, Buffer$)
            If VerInfoAddr& <> 0 Then
                '-- Get the address of the FixedFileInfo (ffiAddr&).
                bOK% = VerQueryValue(VerInfoAddr&, "\", ffiAddr&, ffiLen%)
                If bOK% Then
```

*(continued on next page)*

**12◀**

*(continued from previous page)*

```
                    '-- Here the ffiAddr&() is used to fill the FFI structure.
                    Call vsCopyDataBynum(ffiAddr&, vsGetAddressForObject&(FFI), Len(FFI))
                    FileVer$ = FileVerFromFFI$(FFI)
                End If
            Else
                FileVer$ = ""
            End If
            FileDate$ = Format$(FileDateTime(FileFound$), "Short Date")
            FileSize$ = Format$(FileLen(FileFound$), "#,##0")
            Lst.AddItem FileFound$ & gTab$ & FileVer$ & gTab$ & FileDate$ & gTab$ & FileSize$

            '-- Look for another matching file.
            FileFound$ = Dir$
    Wend

    '-- Reset the original directory.
    ChDir OrigDir$

    Screen.MousePointer = DEFAULT

End Sub

Sub Main ()

    If App.PrevInstance = False Then
        gCRLF$ = Chr$(13) & Chr$(10)
        gTab$ = Chr$(9)
        frmMain.Show
    End If

End Sub

Function QueryVerString$ (VerInfoAddr&, QueryString$)
    Dim Addr&
    Dim BufSize%
    Dim Buffer$
    Dim NullPos%
    Dim bOK%

    bOK% = VerQueryValue(VerInfoAddr&, "\StringFileInfo\040904E4\" & QueryString$, Addr&,
BufSize%)
    If bOK% Then
        '-- Pre-initialize our buffer.
        Buffer$ = String$(BufSize% + 1, Chr$(0))
        '-- Copy version data into our Buffer$.
        Call vsCopyDataBynum(Addr&, vsGetAddressForVBString&(Buffer$), BufSize%)
        NullPos% = InStr(Buffer$, Chr$(0))
        If NullPos% > 1 Then
            QueryVerString$ = Left$(Buffer$, NullPos% - 1)
        End If
    End If

End Function

Sub SetListTabStops (Lst As Control, arrTabStops%())
'----------------------------------------------------
'-- arrTabStops%() Tab stops should be specified
'   in *characters*; this procedure will convert
'   them to DialogUnits for you. If the list uses
'   a font other than the system font, it won't be
'   spot-on but it'll be close.
'----------------------------------------------------
```

```
    Dim hWnd%
    Dim bOK&
    Dim i%

    hWnd% = Lst.hWnd

    '-- Convert character-based tab stops to DialogUnit-based tab stops.
    For i% = 0 To UBound(arrTabStops)
        arrTabStops(i%) = arrTabStops(i%) * 4
    Next i%

    bOK& = SendMessage(hWnd%, LB_SETTABSTOPS, UBound(arrTabStops) + 1, arrTabStops(0))
    If bOK& = False Then
        MsgBox "Error setting TabStops in SetListTabStops", MB_OK + MB_ICONSTOP, "Error!"
    End If

End Sub

Function VerStrFromVerNum$ (VerNum&)
'------------------------------------------------------
'-- Takes a 32-bit version number and returns it
'   as a formatted string.
'------------------------------------------------------
    Dim MajorVer$
    Dim MinorVer$

    MajorVer$ = Format$(VerNum& \ &H10000, "0")
    MinorVer$ = Format$(VerNum& And &HFFFF&, "0")
    VerStrFromVerNum$ = MajorVer$ & "." & MinorVer$

End Function
```

## Tips and Comments

Desaware has done all the hard work and provided you with the tools you need to customize VersionStamper-VB's operation to suit your needs. The sample applications provided with VersionStamper-VB are top notch and should answer any questions that might arise. You can also use their source code in your own applications. A thorough explanation of how version resources work, or should work, is included in the documentation as well.

With the popularity of .VBXs has come a great deal of responsibility for both vendors and developers. Vendors must act responsibly by embedding version information into their controls and developers must use that information for its intended purpose. VersionStamper-VB makes it easy to use version resource information and automatically reduces the risk of file conflicts that can afflict your applications.

##  ZipInf (ZIPINF1.VBX)

| USAGE: | Read Information in Compressed .ZIP Files |
|---|---|
| MANUFACTURER: | Mabry Software |
| COST: | $10 ($5 if registered on CompuServe) |

**12**

The ZipInf control retrieves directory information contained in files compressed in the .ZIP format used by the popular PKZIP utility. ZipInf provides you with access to file names, comments, compression methods, and other internal information.

## Syntax

The ZipInf control makes it extremely easy to gain access to the directory contents of a .ZIP file. It doesn't allow you to extract or compress files, but it can give you information on the files that are stored in an existing .ZIP archive. Table 12-20 lists the nonstandard properties and method of ZipInf.

**Table 12-20** Nonstandard properties and method of the ZipInf control

| PROPERTIES | | |
|---|---|---|
| DateFormat | FileComment | FileName |
| ItemCompressed | ItemCRC | ItemDate |
| ItemFileComment | ItemFileName | ItemMethod |
| ItemTime | ItemUncompressed | ListCount |

| METHOD |
|---|
| Clear |

If you Set a new value for ZipInf's *FileName* property, the control attempts to extract directory information for that file. If ZipInf cannot extract the information, an error condition is set. Table 12-21 describes the most common errors.

**Table 12-21** Common error codes when setting the FileName property

| ERROR CODE | DESCRIPTION |
|---|---|
| 7 | File not found. |
| 29998 | .ZIP file is corrupt. |
| 29999 | File is not a .ZIP file. |

When ZipInf successfully extracts directory information from a .ZIP file, it stores this information in several read-only property arrays. The *ListCount* property indicates how many elements are in these arrays. Each element of these property arrays relates to an individual compressed file within the .ZIP archive file. Each of these property arrays begins with "Item," indicating that it refers to an item in the archive.

*ItemFileName(FileIndex)* gives the name of the file stored in the .ZIP archive, where *FileIndex* is an integer between 0 and *ListCount-1*. The following example would place the names of all the files in TEST.ZIP into a list box control.

```
ZipInfo1.FileName = "TEST.ZIP"
For i=0 To ZipInfo1.ListCount-1
   List1.AddItem ZipInfo.ItemFileName(i)
Next
```

All the other *Item* properties are accessed in the same manner. Table 12-22 briefly explains each *Item* property.

**Table 12-22** The Item properties

| PROPERTY NAME | DESCRIPTION |
|---|---|
| ItemCompressed | Size in bytes of this file, after compression |
| ItemCRC | 32-bit Cyclic Redundancy Check value for this file |
| ItemDate | Date stamp of this file |
| ItemFileComment | Comment associated with this file |
| ItemFileName | Name of this file |
| ItemTime | Timestamp for this file |
| ItemUncompressed | Size in bytes of this file, before compression |

ZipInf provides no events and only one method. The *Clear* method is used to remove all data retrieved when the *FileName* property was last set.

# Example

The example program is a fully functional .ZIP file navigator. It uses the standard Visual Basic File, Directory, and Drive controls to provide access to available files. When a .ZIP file is selected, information about the individual files within the archive are stored in the list box at the top of the form. The example program is shown in Figure 12-6.

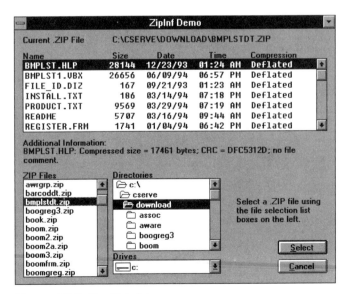

**Figure 12-6** The ZipInf demo program

## Steps

1. Create a new project called ZIPINF.MAK. Add the ZipInf control, ZIPINF1.VBX, to the project. Create a new form with the objects and properties described in Table 12-23. Save this form as ZIPINF.FRM.

**Table 12-23** Objects and properties of the ZIPINF.FRM form

| OBJECT | PROPERTY | SETTING |
|--------|----------|---------|
| Form | FormName | Form1 |
| | BackColor | &H00C0C0C0& |
| | BorderStyle | 1 'Fixed Single |
| | Caption | "ZipInf Demo" |
| | MaxButton | 0 'False |
| Label | Name | Label1 |
| | BackStyle | 0 'Transparent |
| | Caption | ".ZIP Files" |
| | ForeColor | &H00800000& |
| Label | Name | Label2 |
| | BackStyle | 0 'Transparent |
| | Caption | "Directories" |
| | ForeColor | &H00800000& |
| Label | Name | Label3 |
| | BackStyle | 0 'Transparent |
| | Caption | "Drives" |
| | ForeColor | &H00800000& |
| Label | Name | Label4 |
| | BackStyle | 0 'Transparent |
| | Caption | "Name    Size    Date    Time    Compression" |
| | ForeColor | &H00800000& |
| Label | Name | Label6 |
| | BackStyle | 0 'Transparent |
| | Caption | "Current .Zip File Name:" |
| | ForeColor | &H00800000& |
| Label | Name | lblZipFileName |
| | BackStyle | 0 'Transparent |
| | Caption | "[none]" |
| | ForeColor | &H00000080& |
| Label | Name | lblMoreInfo |
| | BackStyle | 0 'Transparent |
| | Caption | "[none]" |
| | ForeColor | &H00000080& |

| OBJECT | PROPERTY | SETTING |
|---|---|---|
| Label | Name | Label7 |
| | BackStyle | 0 'Transparent |
| | Caption | "Additional Information:" |
| | ForeColor | &H00800000& |
| Label | Name | Label5 |
| | BackStyle | 0 'Transparent |
| | Caption | "Select a .ZIP file using the file selection list boxes on the left." |
| | ForeColor | &H00800000& |
| DriveListBox | Name | Drive1 |
| DirListBox | Name | Dir1 |
| FileListBox | Name | File1 |
| | Pattern | "*.zip" |
| CommandButton | Name | btnSelect |
| | Caption | "&Select" |
| | Default | -1 'True |
| ListBox | Name | lstZipInfo |
| | FontBold | 0 'False |
| | FontName | "Fixedsys" |
| | FontSize | 9 |
| | Sorted | -1 'True |
| MabryZipInfo | Name | ZipInfo1 |
| | DateFormat | "" |
| CommandButton | Name | btnCancel |
| | Caption | "&Cancel" |

2. Add the following code to the ZIPINF.FRM form's declarations section.

```
Option Explicit
'------------------------------------------------
' ZipInf demo program.
'------------------------------------------------
```

3. Add the following subroutines to the ZIPINF.FRM.

```
Sub btnCancel_Click ()
'------------------------------------------------
' Unload the main form when Cancel button is clicked.
'------------------------------------------------
    Unload Me
End Sub

Sub btnSelect_Click ()
```

**12**

*(continued on next page)*

*(continued from previous page)*

```
'-----------------------------------------------------
' When a new .ZIP file is selected, cycle through
' all its file information and display it in a
' list box.
'-----------------------------------------------------
Dim i As Integer
Dim FileInfo As String
Dim ItemMethod As String
Dim ErrorMsg As String

    On Error GoTo btnSelect_Error

    ' Set the FileName property to get new information.
    ZipInfo1.FileName = Dir1.Path & "\" & File1.FileName
    lblZipFileName = UCase$(ZipInfo1.FileName)

    lstZipInfo.Clear
    For i = 0 To ZipInfo1.ListCount - 1
        FileInfo = Left$(ZipInfo1.ItemFileName(i) & Space$(13), 13)
        FileInfo = FileInfo & Right$(Space$(8) & Format$(ZipInfo1.ItemUncompressed(i)), 8) & "
"
        FileInfo = FileInfo & Format$(ZipInfo1.ItemDate(i), "MM/DD/YY") & "  "
        FileInfo = FileInfo & Format$(ZipInfo1.ItemTime(i), "hh:mm AM/PM") & "   "
        Select Case ZipInfo1.ItemMethod(i)
            Case 0: ItemMethod = "None"
            Case 1: ItemMethod = "Shrunk"
            Case 2 - 5: ItemMethod = "Reduced"
            Case 6: ItemMethod = "Imploded"
            Case 7: ItemMethod = "Tokenized"
            Case 8: ItemMethod = "Deflated"
            Case Else: ItemMethod = "Unknown"
        End Select
        FileInfo = FileInfo & ItemMethod
        lstZipInfo.AddItem FileInfo
        lstZipInfo.ItemData(lstZipInfo.NewIndex) = i
    Next

    ' Select the first item in the list.
    If lstZipInfo.ListCount > 0 Then
        lstZipInfo.ListIndex = 0
    End If
Exit Sub
btnSelect_Error:

    Select Case Err
        Case 7: ErrorMsg = "File '" & File1.FileName & "' could not be found."
        Case 29998: ErrorMsg = "File '" & File1.FileName & "' is corrupt."
        Case 29999: ErrorMsg = "File '" & File1.FileName & "' is not a ZIP file."
        Case Else: ErrorMsg = "Error " & Format$(Err) & ": " & Error$
    End Select

    MsgBox ErrorMsg, , "Error"

    Exit Sub
End Sub

Sub Dir1_Change ()
```

```
'--------------------------------------------------
' Reset the File control when new directory picked.
'--------------------------------------------------
    File1.Path = Dir1.Path
End Sub

Sub Drive1_Change ()
'--------------------------------------------------
' Reset the Directory control when new drive picked.
'--------------------------------------------------
    Dir1.Path = Drive1.Drive
End Sub

Sub File1_DblClick ()
'--------------------------------------------------
' If user double-clicks on file name, treat it as
' if the Select button were pressed.
'--------------------------------------------------
    btnSelect.Value = 1 ' Click the "Select" button.
End Sub

Sub Form_Load ()
'--------------------------------------------------
' Center the form on the screen.
'--------------------------------------------------

    Me.Move (Screen.Width - Me.Width) \ 2, (Screen.Height - Me.Height) \ 2
End Sub

Sub lstZipInfo_Click ()
'--------------------------------------------------
' When a new file is selected, build its
' Additional Information.
'--------------------------------------------------
Dim i As Integer

    If lstZipInfo.ListIndex >= 0 Then
        i = lstZipInfo.ItemData(lstZipInfo.ListIndex)
        lblMoreInfo = ZipInfo1.ItemFileName(i) & ": "
        lblMoreInfo = lblMoreInfo & "Compressed size = " & Format$(ZipInfo1.ItemCompressed(i))
& " bytes; "
        lblMoreInfo = lblMoreInfo & "CRC = " & Hex$(ZipInfo1.ItemCRC(i)) & "; "
        If ZipInfo1.ItemFileComment(i) = "" Then
            lblMoreInfo = lblMoreInfo & "no file comment."
        Else
            lblMoreInfo = lblMoreInfo & "File Comment = '" & ZipInfo1.ItemFileComment(i) & "'."
        End If
    End If
End Sub
```

# Tips and Comments

With the proliferation of .ZIP files on many users' systems, the ZipInf control can provide an easy way to extend conventional file searching capabilities to include the contents of .ZIP archives.

12◀

# INDEX

## INDEX

## T

## U

## V ▲

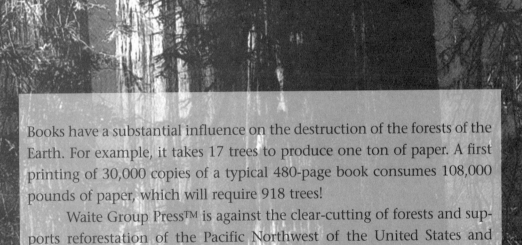

Books have a substantial influence on the destruction of the forests of the Earth. For example, it takes 17 trees to produce one ton of paper. A first printing of 30,000 copies of a typical 480-page book consumes 108,000 pounds of paper, which will require 918 trees!

Waite Group Press™ is against the clear-cutting of forests and supports reforestation of the Pacific Northwest of the United States and Canada, where most of this paper comes from. As a publisher with several hundred thousand books sold each year, we feel an obligation to give back to the planet. We will therefore support organizations which seek to preserve the forests of planet Earth.

This is a legal agreement between you, the end user and purchaser, and The Waite Group®, Inc., and the authors of the programs contained in the disk. By opening the sealed disk package, you are agreeing to be bound by the terms of this Agreement. If you do not agree with the terms of this Agreement, promptly return the unopened disk package and the accompanying items (including the related book and other written material) to the place you obtained them for a refund.

## SOFTWARE LICENSE

1.   The Waite Group, Inc. grants you the right to use one copy of the enclosed software programs (the programs) on a single computer system (whether a single CPU, part of a licensed network, or a terminal connected to a single CPU). Each concurrent user of the program must have exclusive use of the related Waite Group, Inc. written materials.

2.   The program, including the copyrights in each program, is owned by the respective author and the copyright in the entire work is owned by The Waite Group, Inc. and they are therefore protected under the copyright laws of the United States and other nations, under international treaties. You may make only one copy of the disk containing the programs exclusively for backup or archival purposes, or you may transfer the programs to one hard disk drive, using the original for backup or archival purposes. You may make no other copies of the programs, and you may make no copies of all or any part of the related Waite Group, Inc. written materials.

3.   You may not rent or lease the programs, but you may transfer ownership of the programs and related written materials (including any and all updates and earlier versions) if you keep no copies of either, and if you make sure the transferee agrees to the terms of this license.

4.   You may not decompile, reverse engineer, disassemble, copy, create a derivative work, or otherwise use the programs except as stated in this Agreement.

## GOVERNING LAW

This Agreement is governed by the laws of the State of California.

# SATISFACTION REPORT CARD

Please fill out this card if you wish to know of future updates to
*Visual Basic Controls Desk Reference CD*, or to receive our catalog.

Company Name: _____

Division/Department: _____ Mail Stop: _____

Last Name: _____ First Name: _____ Middle Initial: _____

Street Address: _____

City: _____ State: _____ Zip: _____

Daytime telephone: (        ) _____

Date product was acquired: Month _____ Day _____ Year _____ Your Occupation: _____

**Overall, how would you rate *Visual Basic Controls Desk Reference CD*?**

☐ Excellent      ☐ Very Good      ☐ Good
☐ Fair           ☐ Below Average  ☐ Poor

**What did you like MOST about this book?** _____
_____

**What did you like LEAST about this book?** _____
_____
_____

**Please describe any problems you may have encountered with installing or using the disk:** _____
_____

**How did you use this book (problem-solver, tutorial, reference...)?**
_____

**What is your level of computer expertise?**
☐ New          ☐ Dabbler      ☐ Hacker
☐ Power User   ☐ Programmer   ☐ Experienced Professional

**What computer languages are you familiar with?** _____
_____

**Please describe your computer hardware:**
Computer _____ Hard disk _____
5.25" disk drives _____ 3.5" disk drives _____
Video card _____ Monitor _____
Printer _____ Peripherals _____
Sound board _____ CD-ROM _____

**Where did you buy this book?**
☐ Bookstore (name): _____
☐ Discount store (name): _____
☐ Computer store (name): _____
☐ Catalog (name): _____
☐ Direct from WGP          ☐ Other _____

**What price did you pay for this book?** _____

**What influenced your purchase of this book?**
☐ Recommendation              ☐ Advertisement
☐ Magazine review             ☐ Store display
☐ Mailing                     ☐ Book's format
☐ Reputation of Waite Group Press   ☐ Other

**How many computer books do you buy each year?** _____

**How many other Waite Group books do you own?** _____

**What is your favorite Waite Group book?** _____
_____

**Is there any program or subject you would like to see Waite Group Press cover in a similar approach?** _____
_____

**Additional comments?** _____
_____

Please send to:   **Waite Group Press**
                  **Attn: *Visual Basic Controls Desk Reference CD***
                  **200 Tamal Plaza**
                  **Corte Madera, CA 94925**

☐ **Check here for a free Waite Group catalog**

# Dear Visual Basic™ Developer,

Have you ever tried to find a VB add-on for a particular need but couldn't find one, or wanted to buy a particular product for VB but couldn't get a decent price? If so, then you are not alone! As a VB developer myself, I had the same problems. My solution to these problems was to create VBxtras, the Ultimate Visual Basic Tools Catalog.

In my VBxtras catalog, you will find the best Visual Basic add-ons complete with product descriptions in a conversational tone that are both informative and entertaining. To get your free copy of my VBxtras catalog, call or fax your address and phone number today; you might even find that perfect product you didn't even know existed!

Sincerely,

Mike Schinkel, President

P.S. If you find a better price or want something we don't have, let me know and I'll take care of it for you. Thanks for your interest!

P.P.S. Be sure to call us for descriptions of products or download them from Compuserve. To download, search for VBX*.* in the libraries of the 3rd party section of the MSBASIC forum, and look for "VBxtras" in the description.

# Call For Your FREE Catalog!
# 1-800-788-4794
### 404-952-6356 / Fax: 404-952-6388

## STOP!

**BEFORE YOU OPEN THE DISK OR CD-ROM PACKAGE ON THE FACING PAGE, CAREFULLY READ THE LICENSE AGREEMENT.**

Opening this package indicates that you agree to abide by the license agreement found in the back of this book. If you do not agree with it, promptly return the unopened disk package (including the related book) to the place you obtained them for a refund.